JEAN SIMPSON'S

Numbers Diet™

Also by Jean Simpson

Hot Numbers™

Hot Lotto Numbers™

JEAN SIMPSON'S

Numbers Diet™

The Diet That Works–Based on Your Personal Numbers

Crown Publishers, Inc., New York

DEDICATION

For my three friends who have been by my side since day number 1:

Libby Walker, my capable and dedicated assistant, who makes invaluable contributions to all of my projects and helps me accomplish all that I do.

Michael Wallach, my personal manager, who helps me set priorities and uses his incredible business intuition to shape my career.

Barbara Grossman, my editor, who has trained me well and used her genius to turn my ideas into book form.

Published by Crown Publishers, Inc., 201 East 50th Street,
New York, New York 10022

CROWN is a trademark of Crown Publishers, Inc.

THE NUMBERS DIET is a trademark of Jean Simpson.

Manufactured in the United States of America

Gerri French, M.S., R.D., nutritional consultant for *Jean Simpson's Numbers Diet*

Library of Congress Cataloging-in-Publication Data
Simpson, Jean
Jean Simpson's numbers diet / by Jean Simpson.
1. Symbolism of numbers. 2. Reducing diets—Miscellanea.
I. Title.

BF1623.P9S547 1990 89-9895
133.3'35—dc19 CIP

ISBN 0-517-57500-0

1 3 5 7 9 10 8 6 4 2

First Edition

CONTENTS

FOREWORD

Jean Simpson's Numbers Diet is a unique springboard to good health. The guidelines set forth in the following pages can be used over a lifetime to achieve and maintain ideal weight. Furthermore, the joy of practicing optimum nutrition and possessing physical, mental, and emotional togetherness is within reach of anyone who chooses to follow this diet.

Based on the latest medical, physiological, and dietetic research, *Jean Simpson's Numbers Diet* reflects the positive attitude of the author, who is a veteran of the diet wars and a motivational marvel. Jean Simpson's commonsense regimen is easy to follow and almost anyone can lose weight safely on these 1,000-1,200-calorie daily menus, which were analyzed by a registered dietitian.

As a psychiatrist, I am fully aware of the average person's healthy need for oral gratification. In my practice, I help basically healthy people deal more effectively with various problems of everyday living, such as weight management. Many of us suffer from bad habits, impaired attitudes, improper training, lack of formal knowledge, low self-confidence, or poor self-discipline. We are often victims of myth, misunderstanding, faltering motivation, and last, a shortage of perserverance and determination. *Jean Simpson's Numbers Diet* provides a wonderfully varied diet and the inspiration we need to overcome the many challenges we face as dieters. I anticipate that readers will benefit from self-discovery in regard to their personalities, and they will learn about what factors direct their behavior, both positively and negatively.

The principles of my Hippocratic Oath prevent me from endorsing the *numerological* aspect of the author's presentation. Nevertheless, I hasten to add that the numerological aspect of the Numbers Diet can be used effectively as a motivational tool in order to alleviate the boredom that so often sabotages the dieter. Jean Simpson's system of numerology, in conjunction with these scientifically accepted nutritional principles, is an extremely effective catalyst to acquire the discipline needed to lose weight.

It is a personal privilege to be associated with Jean Simpson, whose creative zeal combines with a high level of physical and psychic energy to chart new paths of self-understanding and self-growth. I have watched her conquer her own diet struggles. She knows firsthand how hard it is to lose the first pound, and how to stay motivated. A dynamic and dedicated teacher, Jean affords each one of us who struggles for better control over mind and body the opportunity to profit from her own experiences. As you begin to digest her wisdom, as well as the delicious meals in the next nine chapters, remember that the journey of a thousand miles starts with just a single step. For me, that first step was adopting the Numbers Diet as a way of life.

Thank you, Jean Simpson, for walking beside me toward a better approach to eating, exercising, living, and loving.

Julius Griffin, M.D.
Diplomate, American Board of Psychiatry & Neurology, 1960
Encino, California

If you are interested in having Jean Simpson personally analyze your full name as it appears on your birth certificate and tell you what kind of dieter, lover, friend, parent, and co-worker you are, please send a self-addressed, stamped business-size envelope to:

Jean Simpson
c/o Teletel, Inc.
100 Wilshire Blvd.
Suite #420
Santa Monica, CA 90401

INTRODUCTION

After years of starving myself and failing to control my weight, I was disgusted with "doing diets." Every time I went "on" a diet all I did was dream of the foods I could eat when I went "off" the diet. Imagine my surprise when finally, after twenty-four years, I discovered that the answer to my diet dilemma was right under my own nose.

But first a little history. To begin at the beginning, an early bout with rheumatic fever turned me into a skinny, sickly child and prompted my family to ply me with food to keep up my strength and improve my health. Along with the message to eat came the warning not to stress my presumably weakened heart with exercise. Excluded from P.E. from grade school through college, I capitalized on my "condition" and was a confirmed couch potato by my early teens. Not only did I miss out on establishing exercise as a habit, I also passed up the opportunity to develop the athletic skills most people use to make exercise an enjoyable part of a healthy lifestyle.

In my early twenties, my life changed. I began a teaching career, which has taken me from the kindergarten classroom to the university level. During this period I married and had three babies in thirty-two months. It seemed as if, almost overnight, I changed from a skinny weakling to a healthy heifer, sometimes tipping the scale at as much as 167 pounds, even when I wasn't pregnant.

Between babies and teaching assignments, I became fascinated with the ancient science of numerology. I started "doing numbers" for fun. With uncanny accuracy and regularity, the messages in the numbers helped me to understand myself and others better. By adding the numeric values of the letters in peoples' names and reducing them to a single digit from 1 to 9, I discovered what really makes people tick. From the numbers in their birth dates, I could tell them what had happened in their lives in any given day, month, or year in the past and help them to take advantage of events in the future. After doing numbers for thousands of people, I developed my own system of numerology, and to my amazement, the numbers were always right.

The success of my system led me to describe it in my first book about numerology, *Hot Numbers*. Later, in response to requests from my readers, I shared my system for lucky numbers based on playing cards, astrology, and numerology in my book *Hot Lotto Numbers*.

Throughout this period, my personal battle of the bulge continued, and I fought it on all fronts, gaining and losing the same seven to forty pounds at least sixteen times. I spent over twenty thousand dollars on diet pills and powders, books and tapes, seminars, hypnosis, behavior modification classes, diet centers with *daily* weigh-ins, diet clinics with *weekly* weigh-ins and packaged food, laboratory tests, fat farms, injections, expensive fasting programs, and phony flab-buster exercise equipment. At one point, after I had lost fifteen pounds on a program, I even worked for them as a diet counselor, with great success. After all, I had *seen it all* and *done it all* myself. Yet even after I had *heard it all,* my weight crept up again. The diet foods I ate didn't satisfy me, and I began to eat my old favorites.

You name it, I've tried it. I used to drive my doctor nuts asking him to check my thyroid every few months, hoping a change in medication would solve my weighty problem. Even though I had enough credentials to consider myself a professional dieter, in my heart I knew I was just a first-class diet drop-out.

Meanwhile, my love of numerology grew, as did my clients and bookings as an entertainer. One year I spent thirteen weeks out of fifty-two on cruise ships, doing numbers for passengers and eating my way from port to port. When the public relations people billed me as "a party waiting to happen," they politely neglected to say that I had obviously enjoyed the food as much as the party.

Dieting became an uphill battle. The more I tried to lose, the more I gained. Starvation rations no longer produced the results I wanted, and I was at the end of my rope, not to mention my belt. I theorized that if my numerology system could help my clients and me turn our lives around, plus win thousands of dollars on lotto, my numbers could certainly help me win my battle of the bulge.

The turning point came when I began to keep a food diary. I wrote down every morsel I put into my mouth, the date, the time, the place, and my feelings when I ate it. When I analyzed my entries, I was amazed to see a pattern linking the foods I craved to my Personal Day Number. On a Personal Day #5 I was always racing around and needed to eat on the run. With no time to prepare the spicy foods I craved that day, I fell off my diet wagon with predictable regularity in front of my favorite chili hot dog stand. My yen for exotic flavors did my diet in on a Personal Day #9. Unable to resist Mexican, Chinese, or Italian food, I would

OD on these high-calorie dishes and blow my diet *again!* On a Personal Day #3 I was tempted by my favorites from childhood, etc, etc.

Convinced by the evidence in my diary, I decided to think of my Personal Day Number as my Diet Day Number. I duplicated the flavors I longed for with low-calorie recipes, and prepared them on the days my numbers indicated I would crave them. Since I've never been willing, or able, to stay on a diet that left me unsatisfied and hungry, I devised balanced menus using low-calorie recipes that are satisfying and downright delicious. Once I did a number on myself, I lost thirty pounds in five months—and that was two years ago. For the first time in my life, I've kept the weight off and haven't felt hungry or deprived. In addition, after forty-six years of inactivity, I even discovered the fun of exercise and how to vary it according to my Diet Day Number so I wouldn't get bored. Necessity was the mother of my invention: the Numbers Diet was born.

Because I've heard the cries of downtrodden dieters and walked in your shoes, I understand the diet dilemmas we all face on certain diet days. Best of all, I can predict the kinds of diet downfalls that are most likely to occur on each Diet Day, #1 to #9, and show you how to deal with them.

Whether you are a new-age thinker who huffed and puffed up the nearest hill to witness the last harmonic convergence, or are sick and tired of feeling sick and tired, the Numbers Diet *will* work for you. Finally, there's a personalized diet that's got *your* number! At long last, you'll be a loser and love it!

JEAN SIMPSON'S

Numbers Diet™

HOW TO USE THIS BOOK

Caution: You should never undertake a new diet or exercise program without consulting your personal physician.

HOW NUMEROLOGY RELATES TO DIET

The Numbers Diet combines the latest information in sound nutrition, exercise, and metabolism with the age-old science of numerology to give you a weight control program that works.

Numerology is based on mathematics. A Greek named Pythagoras, the father of mathematics, theorized that every number has a vibration. For centuries numerologists have used his system and the messages in the numbers to help people better understand themselves and their lives.

Based on a system I developed over twenty-three years, this book will tell you what your Diet Day Number is. Your Diet Day Number tells what kind of foods you're in the mood to eat, and what thoughts, feelings, and activities you are likely to experience on *each day* of a nine-day cycle. Feelings often affect *what* you eat and *why*. Activities influence *where* you eat and *what* you eat. Your schedule dictates *how much* or *how little time* you have for meal planning and preparation.

I am living proof that if you don't take into account your Diet Day Number and the way it affects your feelings and your schedule, you are sure to fail in trying to lose weight. Since I began to practice what I preach about the numbers in all other areas of my life, I have lost thirty pounds and kept them off.

HOW TO FIND YOUR DIET DAY NUMBER

Your Diet Day Number is based upon your birthday. It changes daily over a nine-day cycle. It is calculated using the month, day, and year of your *last* birthday, and the month and date of the day you want to diet. Sounds complicated, doesn't it? It would be if you had to remember the formula and do the calculations yourself. Fortunately, I've done all the work for you, leaving you free to concentrate on the Numbers Diet!

Suppose that today is March 1, 1990, and you want to find your Diet Day Number. Look at the sample Diet Day Number Chart below for March 1. If your birthday is January 6, you will find your Diet Day Number in the square where your birth *month,* January, and your birth *day,* 6, intersect. As you can see on the chart, if your birthday is January 6, your Diet Day Number for March 1, 1990, is 2. If your birthday is April 22, your Diet Day Number for March 1, 1990, is 4.

MARCH 1

	1	2	3	4	5	6	7	8	9	10	11	12	13	14	15	16	17	18	19	20	21	22	23	24	25	26	27	28	29	30	31
Jan	6	7	8	9	1	2	3	4	5	6	7	8	9	1	2	3	4	5	6	7	8	9	1	2	3	4	5	6	7	8	9
Feb	7	8	9	1	2	3	4	5	6	7	8	9	1	2	3	4	5	6	7	8	9	1	2	3	4	5	6	7	8		
Mar	9	1	2	3	4	5	6	7	8	9	1	2	3	4	5	6	7	8	9	1	2	3	4	5	6	7	8	9	1	2	3
Apr	1	2	3	4	5	6	7	8	9	1	2	3	4	5	6	7	8	9	1	2	3	4	5	6	7	8	9	1	2	3	
May	2	3	4	5	6	7	8	9	1	2	3	4	5	6	7	8	9	1	2	3	4	5	6	7	8	9	1	2	3	4	5
Jun	3	4	5	6	7	8	9	1	2	3	4	5	6	7	8	9	1	2	3	4	5	6	7	8	9	1	2	3	4	5	
Jul	4	5	6	7	8	9	1	2	3	4	5	6	7	8	9	1	2	3	4	5	6	7	8	9	1	2	3	4	5	6	7
Aug	5	6	7	8	9	1	2	3	4	5	6	7	8	9	1	2	3	4	5	6	7	8	9	1	2	3	4	5	6	7	8
Sep	6	7	8	9	1	2	3	4	5	6	7	8	9	1	2	3	4	5	6	7	8	9	1	2	3	4	5	6	7	8	
Oct	7	8	9	1	2	3	4	5	6	7	8	9	1	2	3	4	5	6	7	8	9	1	2	3	4	5	6	7	8	9	1
Nov	8	9	1	2	3	4	5	6	7	8	9	1	2	3	4	5	6	7	8	9	1	2	3	4	5	6	7	8	9	1	
Dec	9	1	2	3	4	5	6	7	8	9	1	2	3	4	5	6	7	8	9	1	2	3	4	5	6	7	8	9	1	2	3

For now, that's all you need to know. Beginning on page 268 you'll find 365 daily charts and directions for converting the charts to any year, not just 1990.

Get started by turning to the chart for today's date. Find your Diet Day Number and write it below.

On (today's date) 8 ________ 23 ________ 93 ________

Month Day Year

my Diet Day Number is ~~9~~ ~~4~~ ________. 32

Now turn to the chapter that has the same number as your Diet Day Number, to find the diet that will work best for you on that day. For each Diet Day Number there are four nutritionally sound menus, with recipes giving you the choice of cooking or not cooking, entertaining or eating out without pigging out. You'll find information on managing food and exercise that is geared to each day's activities and emotional climate. In addition, there are strategies for dealing with potential diet downfalls that plague us all on certain days. Finally, I have dished up daily Food for Thought: guaranteed no-calorie pearls of wisdom you can chew on to keep yourself motivated.

If you have had it with fad diets and you want to get a handle on your love handles, read on. I'm going to show you how to focus on the positive side of that four-letter word, *diet*. Get ready to be a loser and love it!

A QUICK COURSE IN DIET DYNAMICS

Half the reason I was overweight can be attributed to the fact that I was a diet dummy. Here, in a nutshell, is a short course in food and how it works in your body.

FOOD AS FUEL

All food contains two kinds of nutrients: organic and inorganic. Organic nutrients include carbohydrates, fats, proteins, and vitamins. Inorganic nutrients are water and minerals.

VITAMINS AND MINERALS

Although the Numbers Diet is nutritionally sound and a well-balanced 1,000 to 1,200 calories daily, it is virtually impossible to get the vitamins and minerals your body needs on a reduced-calorie diet. Take a vitamin and mineral supplement of your choice everyday. To supplement the 500 milligrams of calcium included in the Numbers Diet you may, with your doctor's approval, take an additional 300 to 1,000 milligrams of calcium.

WATER

Approximately seven-tenths of the body is water. The benefits of drinking water are many, but, to your initial delight, you'll notice that your skin is clearer and your tummy seems fuller if you drink at least eight 8-ounce glasses a day. Not only are you going to be slim and satisfied, your skin will glow.

CARBOHYDRATES

Plants convert the sun's energy into carbohydrates, and our bodies convert carbohydrates back into energy. Processed faster than proteins or fats, carbohydrates are a quicker source of energy. Low in calorie but high in bulk, carbohydrates contain half the calories of fats. In addition to giving us energy, complex carbohydrates are an important source of fiber.

It's not the carbohydrates in bread, potatoes, rice, and pasta that make you gain, it's the fat in the butter, sour cream, gravies, and sauces you put on top of them.

FOOD	CALORIES	TOPPING	CALORIES
1 slice bread	65	2 teaspoons butter	90
1 baked potato	90	3 tablespoons sour cream	75
½ cup rice	100	3 tablespoons gravy	180
¾ cup pasta	100	¼ cup Alfredo sauce	190

PROTEIN

Whereas our bodies use carbohydrates and fats primarily for energy, our bodies use proteins as building materials to make and repair muscles, bones, hair, skin, and nails. Proteins are also needed to produce hormones and enzymes.

Complete proteins come from animals, in the form of meat, eggs, and dairy products (milk, yogurt, cream, cheese, and butter). They supply all the essential amino acids needed by the body. Because essential amino acids cannot be produced in the body, we need to eat protein daily.

If you know what you are buying, eating protein doesn't have to break the bank. To get one pound of protein you would have to buy $20 worth of hot dogs, compared to $6 worth of chicken.

Legumes or beans are also an excellent source of protein. Even though they are plant foods and therefore do not provide all the essential amino acids, they can be eaten in combination with complementary plant foods, such as grains (corn, wheat, rice, oats) or seeds (sunflower, sesame), which provide the missing amino acids needed to make a complete protein. For instance, beans eaten with rice, tortillas, or corn bread provide complete protein.

Proteins are very powerful and, contrary to popularly held beliefs, a little goes a long way. Generally, protein amounting to 15 percent of our daily calories is considered nutritionally adequate.

> Protein requirements are usually figured according to body weight, using a formula of .36 gram of protein per pound of ideal weight.

Proteins should always be eaten along with carbohydrates, which supply quick energy and save the proteins for sustaining energy and the building and healing jobs they were intended to do.

It is important to choose protein foods that are low in fat, to avoid the unwanted calories fats provide.

FATS

Face facts. In our society, fat has negative connotations in all forms. Usually associated with overweight and obesity, fat is, however, the source of energy and calories. As such, fat is a vital part of our diet. Of the three major nutrients in food—carbohydrates, proteins, and fats—the last provide the most concentrated form of food energy, at 9 calories per gram, compared to 4 calories per gram in carbohydrates and proteins.

Our bodies use whatever fat they need for energy, and store the excess in fatty tissue in various parts of the body.

> More than the number of calories, the amount of fat we eat plays a key role in how much body fat we develop.

Consuming a reasonable amount of fat, between 20 and 30 percent of daily calories, helps the human body to maintain ideal weight and reduces the risk of heart disease and some forms of cancer. Besides providing food energy, fats account for that satisfied feeling you get after eating, and they prevent hunger pangs. Fats also perform various roles in the body, such as transporting fat-soluble vitamins, insulating organs, and lubricating joints and skin. But no matter what it does, fat is still considered the enemy of the dieter. To outsmart the enemy, you need to know two things

I've discovered. When I cut down on butter and salad dressing and mayonnaise, my former favorite fats, I saw results on the scale. The closer my daily fat intake came to 20 percent instead of 40 percent, the more successful I was at losing and maintaining my weight. In giving up some fats, I liberated calories from my daily allowance that I could spend on twice the volume of carbohydrates and protein, because they have less than half the calories.

> When I am counting calories, I'll take a big plate of the energy-packed complex carbohydrates in pasta primavera, at 250 calories, over the same calories in a measly ⅛ cup of fat-filled mayonnaise any day.

For more information on fats that are saturated, monounsaturated, polyunsaturated, and hydrogenated, and information on cholesterol and triglycerides, see pages 208–210.

FOOD PROCESSING: EXERCISE AND METABOLISM

Short of surgery, I have tried every weight-loss method I could find. None of them resulted in permanent weight loss because I ignored the influence of my Diet Day Numbers. But even with the help of numerology to explain the overtone of each day, I could not have controlled my weight unless I had discovered the key to permanent weight control: eating sensibly and exercising regularly. And that doesn't mean punctuating a week of sedentary living with a game of tennis on Saturday or a round of golf on Sunday. In order for me to lose weight, I discovered, I needed at least thirty minutes of continuous exercise five days per week.

By burning, or oxidizing, food, the body generates energy, measured in calories, to maintain its functions. Calories are needed to digest food and power the heart and lungs. We need to burn some calories just to maintain an average body temperature of 98.6. When other daily activities, like work and play, are added, we must provide the body with more energy by giving it more food or calories. Exercising for fitness helps to burn off still more calories. The process of burning calories is called *metabolism*. It occurs at different rates and can be measured. Someone with a high metabolism burns more calories than someone with a low metabolism. One way we can raise our metabolic rate is exercise.

> The woman who exercises will lose more weight than her sedentary friend who doesn't exercise, even though her friend is the same age, height, and weight and eats the same number of calories.

After all my efforts to eat less, it was a revelation to me that something as simple as increased physical activity would help burn extra calories and stored fat.

Studies have shown that "professional" dieters, like me, who perpetually subject themselves to crash diets of less than 800 to 1,000 calories per day, may cause their bodies to go into starvation mode. The body, triggered by the reduction in calories, automatically reduces its metabolic rate. This lifesaving strategy causes the body to burn calories at a lower rate and actually conserve the stored body fat you are trying so desperately to lose. In other words, the more we diet on super-low-calorie regimens, the slower our metabolism becomes and the harder it is to lose weight.

When I added exercise to my life, and began eating moderately on my Numbers Diet, I discovered the answer to raising my metabolism.

To lose one pound, you must increase your level of activity enough to burn off 3,500 calories, or decrease your food intake by 3,500 calories. A combination of both is best.

> If you decrease your food intake by 500 calories per day, you can lose one pound in a week.

> If you burn 500 calories a day exercising, you can lose one pound in a week.

Besides burning calories, exercise causes the metabolic rate to increase for several hours after exercise. Exercising more than once a day perpetuates this effect, keeping the metabolic rate higher for longer periods of time.

In addition, metabolism is also affected by the number of times you eat during the day. Although the total number of calories you consume in one day is important, the intervals at which they are eaten is crucial in losing weight. If you keep your body busy digesting food by feeding it small meals frequently, you encourage it to burn food as fuel, rather than storing the food as fat.

Subscribing to the diet myth that cutting back to one large meal a day promotes weight loss is a mistake often made by uneducated dieters. The body reacts to one feeding the same way it does to an extremely low-calorie diet. When the starvation-ration alert is sounded, the body immediately goes into starvation mode, storing fat instead of burning it.

Smart dieters begin the day with a good breakfast. They speed up their metabolism by combining frequent exercise with smaller meals eaten often during the day. They keep their bodies moving and digesting food to burn more calories.

In addition to increasing your metabolic rate, exercise causes the body to build muscle while it is losing fat. Even though muscle weighs more than fat, muscle is a demanding tissue, requiring more calories to maintain it than fat does. The more muscle you have, the more calories you will burn.

> Men generally lose weight faster than women, because men's larger bodies and greater muscle mass require more calories. They usually burn up the limited calories on a diet faster than women and start using their stored fat sooner, just to keep going.

Once I got this message, I realized how foolish I had been to sabotage my metabolism on one fad diet after another. Lured by the promise of losing ten pounds in five days, I lost my calorie-burning muscle tissue instead of just fat.

Thanks to the Numbers Diet, I began to lose weight correctly. Eating sensibly and exercising regularly caused inches to disappear faster than pounds. Even though muscle is heavier than fat, muscle takes up less space in your body. As your proportion of body fat is reduced and your proportion of lean body mass, or muscle, increases, you may not see a loss on the scale. However, you will notice that your clothes are suddenly getting too big and you can wear your belt on a tighter notch.

CHECK WITH YOUR DOCTOR

The Numbers Diet, consisting of 1,000 to 1,200 calories daily plus a daily vitamin and mineral supplement, is nutritionally sound and intended for healthy women who have the approval of their doctor. It is not planned to meet the increased nutritional needs of pregnant women.

The Numbers Diet, again with a doctor's approval and an additional 300 to 400 calories per day, is nutritionally adequate for men who want to lose weight. Men should also take a daily vitamin and mineral supplement, as well as one extra serving of protein, two more bread servings, one additional serving of fruit, and one extra serving of vegetables. Men also need one extra fat serving, not to exceed 90 calories, which is equal to a scant tablespoon of salad dressing, margarine, or oil.

GETTING STARTED ON AN EXERCISE PROGRAM

It's important to visit your doctor for an evaluation of your present level of physical fitness before you begin an exercise program. You need to be aware of any health factors that may influence your choice of exercise and the rate at which you should proceed. In setting exercise goals, also consider your age and lifestyle, along with your health status. What benefits do you want from exercise? Do you want to run a marathon or improve your fitness and maintain your ideal weight?

> Jill realized she couldn't hit a moving object, so she gave up tennis lessons. Because she loves music and being outside, she bought a Walkman with earphones and some walking shoes.

Once your long-range goal is established, determine your exercise preferences. Do you prefer exercising alone, or are you looking for a group experience? Do you picture yourself pursuing fitness in the privacy of your own home, indoors or outdoors? How much money are you ready to spend on equipment, clothes, memberships, lessons? How are you going to fit fitness into your schedule? A thirty-minute exercise period can easily stretch into an hour or more if you figure in the travel time to and from the location. And most important of all, what kind of exercise would you like to do? If you don't enjoy an activity, you won't stick with it.

Getting off to a good start means pacing yourself. When I started walking for fitness, I could only stroll the length of my block before I became tired. I remember Jane Fonda's voice coming through my earphones. After three minutes she said, "Good. We are just getting started." How dare she say *just* getting started; I was finished, and I thought I was going to die! The second day I walked three houses farther, the day after that five houses more, until I gradually increased my stamina. It didn't happen overnight, and chances are your progress may not be as rapid as you would like. Before too long I was able to walk ten to fifteen minutes without pooping out. One day I realized that my three- to four-mile jaunts were limited only by my schedule, not my energy.

Keep track of your progress. Use the method introduced on a Diet Day #4, when seeing your results on paper will spur you on to greater heights.

Soon after you begin exercising, you'll notice other benefits besides losing weight. During periods of continuous physical activity, hormones are released that decrease your appetite. In addition to encouraging the development of calorie-burning muscle, exercise strengthens and tones your muscles, giving you a more youthful, vigorous appearance. A proven tension reliever, exercise is nature's best tranquilizer. As a result, your mental outlook will improve, and you will even sleep better. Consistent exercise will increase your energy and improve your ability to concentrate and think more clearly. In addition, exercising the muscles around the weight-bearing bones is credited with increasing their mass, an important step toward the prevention of osteoporosis, a condition associated with brittle bones, common among older women. Finally, exercise improves heart and lung functions and increases HDL, high-density lipoproteins.

Armed with a basic knowledge of nutrition, exercise, and metabolism, you are ready to do a number on yourself. Launch your attack on those unwanted pounds. Watch them disappear as you check off your Diet Day Numbers on your calendar. Now follow me down the road to slimness and health with the Numbers Diet.

DIET DAY #1

READY, SET, GO

This is the gorgeous new beginning you have been waiting for and a perfect day to begin the Numbers Diet. On a Diet Day #1, the slate has been wiped clean. If you have gained weight, or even if you just went off your diet for one day, put the past in the past and begin again. Don't dwell on your mistakes; learn from them. This is the ideal day to see your diet in a new light. Renew your ethusiasm and make a commitment to yourself to take off those unwanted pounds and keep them off. Visualize yourself thin and keep that image in your mind.

Instead of just talking about how you are going to lose weight, do it! A Diet Day #1 is an action day, and you have all the determination you need to reach your goal. Exercise the independence you feel, and don't let others sway you. Capitalize on the assertive mood you are in to make you and your diet a success.

BREAKFAST

On a Diet Day #1 we stress beginnings, so this is a good time to talk about the meal that starts each day, breakfast. To break your fast from the night before, the best thing you can give your body is a well-balanced breakfast of carbohydrates, proteins, and a little fat.

> You *can* have waffles, pancakes, and French toast if you skip the melted butter and don't drown them in syrup. Bits of fresh fruit can be stirred into the batter or mixed with whipped yogurt toppings.

Eating a nutritious breakfast stokes up your metabolism in the morning; it is like shoveling coal into an old furnace that was kept banked all night to run on low. At regular intervals during the day, add more fuel to your body, for consistent energy.

Your energy level during the day depends not only on what you eat but on how much, when, and how often. Skipping a balanced breakfast is the surest way to sabotage a weight reduction and maintenance program. Your blood sugar, already low in the morning, will drop further, causing you to crave a sugary snack at midmorning. If you eat that sweet treat, by lunchtime you are either not ready to eat a balanced lunch or you crave more sugar, setting up a pattern of poor choices for the rest of the day. By the time dinner arrives, you're exhausted and starving.

Giving your body more fuel than it can use late in the day, at a time of relatively low activity, doesn't make any more sense than building a roaring fire in the furnace at night just before you climb into bed under a down comforter. You risk wasting fuel and burning out the firebox in the furnace. In the case of your body, the result is even worse. Excess food or calories that you don't burn up running your body and running around ends up as stored fat.

Unaware of the dynamics of digestion and weight gain, many people collapse on the couch after dinner, where they mindlessly munch more junk food until the wee hours of the morning. Once in bed, they sleep fitfully on full stomachs, only to wake up saying "Breakfast—who needs it? I'm full from last night, and anyway, I'm dieting." Off on another roller-coaster ride, they may spend the day going from one sugar high to the next, trying to "be good" until evening.

To break the vicious circle, you have to start somewhere, and a Diet Day #1 is the *day* and breakfast is the *meal*. If you are drinking juice and coffee and calling it breakfast, forget it! That combination won't keep you going for more than two hours, and caffeine wears off the same way sugar does, trapping you in a cycle of ups and downs.

> Choose fresh fruit over juice. Half a grapefruit has 60 calories less than an 8-ounce glass of grapefruit juice and provides more fiber to keep your blood sugar stable.

For every Diet Day #1 to #9, the Numbers Diet menus and recipes provide traditional breakfasts that are well-balanced and contain carbohydrates, proteins, and small amounts of fat. The menu suggestions for a Diet Day #1 are a good reminder that nontraditional foods are also a good idea for breakfast.

> If you are a toast lover, skip the high-fat, high-calorie butter and cream cheese. Substitute a spread with more protein, such as part-skim ricotta or low-fat cottage cheese.

> Add flavor to bland spreads with sweet additions, such as mashed banana, cinnamon, honey, or raisins. For a different taste, add herbs and crunchy grated vegetables.

If after reading all this you still can't force yourself to eat breakfast at the appointed time, pack a nutritious, well-balanced snack to eat later in the morning when you are hungry. A piece of fresh fruit, some nonfat plain yogurt, and a breadstick will get you a lot farther than a doughnut and a cup of coffee.

Remember, the calories you eat at breakfast will be burned during the day, unlike the excess calories you eat at night. Get every diet day off to a good start, and follow the old maxim: eat like a king in the morning, a prince at noon, and a pauper at night.

> To save 60 calories and 250 milligrams of cholesterol, make a two-egg omelet omitting one egg yolk.

ASSERTIVE BEHAVIOR

Get in touch with the strong, assertive side of your nature, which appears on a Diet Day #1. You'll feel like #1 today, so why not act like it? Be your own advocate in the battle of the bulge.

As an overeater, I experienced a major breakthrough when I discovered that my inability to control food mirrored my inability to control my life. When I got sick and tired as a result of eating the wrong food, allowing other people to run my life by eating what they wanted me to eat, I decided to assert myself by taking control of my eating. Assuming the responsibility for making the correct food choices helped me to make responsible decisions in other areas of my life. When I said "no" to the wrong food I learned I could say "no" to the other things I didn't want to do. It felt so good to stand up and be counted that I became less resentful toward others and happier with myself. Every time a Diet Day #1 appeared on my calendar, I took advantage of my assertive mood to make good things happen for me instead of just for everyone else. Little by little my self-esteem grew as my doormat behavior disappeared.

Believe me, taking that first step to control food on a Diet Day #1 is the beginning of a wonderful journey to self-discovery. Start choosing the correct foods every day with the help of the Numbers Diet. If you are tempted to make poor choices, keep telling yourself that nothing tastes as good as being thin feels. As your self-confidence grows, it will spill over into other areas of your life. You'll discover that people aren't mind readers. You have to assert yourself and speak up for what you want. Otherwise, you aren't going to get it.

Take advantage of a Diet Day #1, when you are feeling more confident. Start out gradually. If you have avoided speaking up in the past for fear of hurting other people's feelings, put yourself first on a Diet Day #1. I think you'll be happily surprised to discover that others are not put off when you express your needs. On the contrary, people will be more comfortable around you; they will appreciate and trust you more because you have let them know where you stand.

If acquiring confidence and a positive attitude seems impossible, here's a little trick I learned to help you get started: by acting as if you are sure of yourself, you activate the behavior that will encourage you to develop an assertive attitude.

By asserting yourself in your own behalf you have nothing to lose but pounds, and everything to gain in control over your life. Think enough of yourself to protect yourself from overeating. Don't let people talk you into eating foods that are not on your diet. If you were a diabetic, you wouldn't let someone talk you into eating sugar. If you are clear about what you need and ask for it nicely, people usually react positively and respect you for sticking to your guns.

ASSERT YOURSELF AT A RESTAURANT

On a Diet Day #1, when you have plenty of drive and creativity, activate those assertive feelings. Make up your mind to solve your old weight problem in new ways.

Dining out is a real challenge because there are so many tempting choices. When other people order just what they want, regardless of the calories, don't go along with the crowd and hate yourself in the morning.

The minute someone suggests a meal out, don't roll over and play dead. Beat everyone to the punch and pick the restaurant yourself. In your Diet Day #1 mood to try something "nouvelle," be careful that you don't end up at a place where there's nothing on the menu you can order. If a new restaurant is on the agenda, take charge and call first to check out the menu. On the phone, ask specific questions. Once you have the answers you need, be sure to get the person's name so you can quote the information later at the restaurant if you have to. Armed with the answers to your questions, decide whether the restaurant satisfies your needs.

Before you set foot in the door, know what you want to order. Once you arrive, stick to your plan in true Diet Day #1 fashion. Even if everyone else has a drink, choose a soft noncaloric drink, because alcohol weakens your resolve. Be the first to order, so you won't be swayed at the last minute by hearing the mouthwatering orders of others. Look your server in the eye and be specific when you order. If the waiter seems reluctant to take a special order, just drop the name of the person who spoke to you on the phone.

When the food arrives, look it over carefully. If it isn't exactly as you ordered it, send it back. You don't have to be obnoxious, just quietly insistent. Put your party at ease by remaining calm, and invite them to eat their food while it's hot. Then change the subject. You can be sure the waiter will hurry with your order so he doesn't jeopardize his tip. Assuming your food comes just as you ordered it, make a point to thank the server and maître d', and tip accordingly.

In case you can't call ahead, use your Diet Day #1 creativity when you order. Items from the appetizer or side order section of the menu and à la carte entrées are less fattening than multicourse dinners with all the trimmings. Don't be embarrassed to consult your server about portion sizes and methods of preparation, or to ask for substitutions.

On a Diet Day #1 you are willing to assert yourself and you aren't afraid to be different. Have confidence in your ability to communicate your needs and expect to have them met. Be positive, not pushy. And remember, there's more to enjoy at a restaurant than food. Don't forget the ambience and the company.

TARGET HEART RATE

During a Diet Day #1 you want to put your individual stamp on everything you do. You can literally march to the beat of your own drum if you learn to figure your personal target heart rate and take your pulse during exercise. Then use your target heart rate to measure your progress as you increase the intensity of your exercise over a period of time. On a Diet Day #1, when you are feeling competitive, it's fun to see if you can beat yourself at your own game by exercising at your target heart rate for longer than the day before.

For the past decade experts have advised a minimum of twenty minutes of rhythmic, continuous exercise three to five times per week, at the target heart rate of 60 to 80 percent of your maximum exercise heart rate, to improve cardiovascular (heart and lung) capacity, increase circulation, and burn fat for fuel. From coast to coast you could see fitness buffs taking their pulses and checking their watches.

New studies indicate that exercising at a target heart rate of 80 percent of your maximum exercise heart rate may not be worth the fatigue or the risk of stressing the heart. Experts are even questioning the necessity of exercising at the 60 percent rate.

We now know that older, more sedentary couch potatoes like myself can develop aerobic capacity while exercising at a target heart rate of only 45 to 60 percent of their maximum exercise heart rate. But there's a catch: in order to control your weight, you have to exercise longer and more frequently at the beginner's target heart rate level of 45 to 60 percent. A minimum of thirty to forty minutes for five days per week is recommended.

You may, with your doctor's approval, choose any exercise you wish; I find that cycling on a stationary bike, swimming laps, or walking briskly for thirty to forty minutes five times a week is ideal for me. I manage to get a great effect by walking and swinging my arms at the same time. As my level of fitness increased, I added hand-held weights to get more benefit from walking.

If you haven't been exercising lately you should take your time to reach your exercise goal of thirty to sixty minutes at a target heart rate of 45 to 60 percent. As your fitness level increases, your exercise goal can be increased to five times a week at a target heart rate of 60 to 75 percent. When you become an elite athlete and are

Beginner's
Target Heart Rate: 45% to 60%

Age	Maximum Heart Rate	Beats per Minute	Beats per 10 Seconds
20	200	90–120	15–21
25	195	88–117	15–20
30	190	85–114	14–19
35	185	83–111	14–19
40	180	81–108	13–18
45	175	79–105	13–18
50	170	76–102	12–17
55	165	74–99	12–17
60	160	72–96	12–16
65	155	70–93	11–16
70	150	67–90	11–15
75	145	65–87	10–15
80	140	63–84	10–14

Intermediate
Target Heart Rate: 60% to 75%

Age	Maximum Heart Rate	Beats per Minute	Beats per 10 Seconds
20	200	120–150	20–25
25	195	117–146	20–24
30	190	114–142	19–24
35	185	111–138	19–23
40	180	108–135	18–23
45	175	105–131	18–22
50	170	102–127	17–21
55	165	99–123	17–20
60	160	96–120	16–20
65	155	93–116	16–19
70	150	90–113	15–19
75	145	87–109	15–18
80	140	84–105	14–17

Advanced
Target Heart Rate: 70% to 85%

Age	Maximum Heart Rate	Beats per Minute	Beats per 10 Seconds
20	200	140–170	23–28
25	195	137–166	23–28
30	190	133–162	22–27
35	185	130–157	22–26
40	180	126–153	21–26
45	175	123–149	21–25
50	170	119–145	20–24
55	165	116–140	19–23
60	160	112–136	19–23
65	155	109–132	18–22
70	150	105–128	18–21
75	145	102–123	17–21
80	140	98–119	16–20

DIET DOWNFALLS AND THEIR SOLUTIONS

A Diet Day #1 finds you feeling rebellious and full of yourself. The declaration of independence you are tempted to make may lead you down the path to a self-styled diet regime that doesn't work. You'll be pleased with the menu choices for a Diet Day #1 because they purposely contain some unusual foods. Take your cue to be assertive when you order at a restaurant. Within the guidelines of the nutrition information given in the Numbers Diet, you can be quite creative to satisfy your urge for the new and different on a Diet Day #1.

There is a tendency today to think you don't need to follow other people's direction. You may feel that you are so different that you can eat a particular food and not gain weight. But remember: calories count every day for everyone. If you catch yourself saying something like "I can eat all the escargots I want and never gain an ounce," realize that today you may want to self-indulge, but that rhymes with *bulge*.

Don't let your one-track mind allow you to be so involved in a creative project that you forget to eat today. If, as a result, you end up eating alone at odd hours, make sure your meals are balanced. Even if you are eating alone, set your place at the table. Be imaginative. Bring out your best china or, if you have one, a bright red plate that says "You are special today." It's easy to eat unconsciously, putting away whole boxes of cookies and crackers while you are preoccupied with something else. On a Diet Day #1 it's also easy to put off eating until the end of the day, when one big meal might overload your system with more food than you can burn off before you go to sleep.

The solution to Diet Day #1 diet downfalls is to get a new attitude about your diet and put yourself and your health first. You are, after all, the most important person in your life. Reaffirm that notion on a Diet Day #1 and look out for #1. You are what you eat. Make it the best.

EXERCISE

A Diet Day #1 is a "watch my dust" kind of day, and you're game for just about any sport, so long as you win. Solo activities are also appealing, so compete against yourself for another set of repetitions, an additional five minutes on the stationary bike, or a longer walk.

If you are contemplating a sport you have never tried before, this is an auspicious day to begin. If you have chosen an old-standby activity for your exercise today, you'll enjoy doing it a little differently or breaking your old record. Give in to your desire to make up some new rules today, and if you exercise with others, take a leadership role.

AEROBICS

On a Diet Day #1 you may want to pursue this activity on your own. You may be feeling a bit too rebellious to follow an instructor in a class setting. If you follow your urge to go right when everyone else goes left, people may not appreciate your independent Diet Day #1 spirit. However, if you are trying aerobics or any other sport for the first time, a Diet Day #1 is the perfect day.

WALKING

Add a new element to your walk by changing your route or driving to an entirely new locale. While you're at it, beat your own record: walk farther, longer, and at a faster pace than last time. Lengthen your stride, and see if you can maintain your target heart rate for an extra five minutes.

PAR COURSE

Many parks provide a par course or path with exercise stations along a jogging route. This kind of independent activity suits you to a T on a Diet Day #1. Proceed at your own pace, following the instructions at each stop, for aerobic benefits as well as exercise for flexibility and strength.

RECIPES FOR DIET DAY #1

The following menus and recipes have been created to satisfy your craving for new and different foods, as well as unusual combinations.

Use the suggestions for eating out to order assertively at a new restaurant.

Food for Thought encourages you to capitalize on the first day of a new nine-day cycle and reminds you to look ahead.

Menu 1

FOOD FOR THOUGHT

Don't let yesterday's mistakes eat up too much of today.

BREAKFAST

(216 calories)

*Peerless Postum**
*Refrigerator Bran Muffin**
1 tablespoon Smucker's apple butter
Decaffeinated coffee

* Recipes follow.

SNACK
(108 calories)

*Celebrity Celery**
Celestial Seasonings Cinnamon Rose herb tea

LUNCH
(196 calories)

*Trailblazer Turkey Sandwich**
*Wishful White Wine**

SNACK
(25 calories)

*Highfalutin Jicama**
Celestial Seasonings Lemon Zinger herb tea

DINNER
(408 calories)

*Personalized Pita Pizza**
*Tossed Leafy Greens**
*Chianti Cup**

DESSERT
(84 calories)

*Unforbidden Fruit**
Celestial Seasonings Emperor's Choice herb tea

TOTAL CALORIES 1,037
PROTEIN 22%
CARBOHYDRATE 55%
FAT 23%

PEERLESS POSTUM

1 cup Postum, prepared according to label directions
¼ cup canned evaporated nonfat skim milk
Apple pie spice

Combine Postum with milk. Dust with spice.

Serves 1

REFRIGERATOR BRAN MUFFINS

1 cup boiling water
1 cup Post Grape Nuts cereal
½ cup safflower oil
6 tablespoons egg substitute
2 cups low-fat buttermilk
1 teaspoon vanilla extract
1 tablespoon fresh lemon juice
½ teaspoon grated lemon rind
2½ cups whole-wheat flour
1 cup sugar
1 teaspoon baking soda
½ teaspoon baking powder
½ teaspoon salt
1 teaspoon nutmeg
2 teaspoons cinnamon
1 cup Quaker Quick Oats
1 cup Quaker Oat Bran cereal

Pour boiling water over the Grape Nuts in a small bowl and set aside. In a large bowl, combine the oil, egg substitute, buttermilk, vanilla, lemon juice, and lemon rind. In another bowl, mix the flour, sugar, baking soda, baking powder, salt, nutmeg, and cinnamon. Add to the oil mixture. Stir in the Grape Nuts, quick oats, and oat bran cereal. Cover and refrigerate.

When ready to bake muffins, spray nonstick muffin pans with Pam. Fill each muffin cup half full. Bake in a 400° oven for 20 minutes, or until a toothpick comes out clean. Covered, the batter will keep for 5 weeks in the refrigerator.

Makes 24 muffins (1 per serving)

CELEBRITY CELERY

1 tablespoon creamy peanut butter
2 stalks celery, washed and trimmed

Spread peanut butter in the groove of the celery stalks.

Serves 1

TRAILBLAZER TURKEY SANDWICH

1 teaspoon Dijon mustard
2 rice cakes
¼ cup unsweetened applesauce
2 ounces thinly sliced turkey breast
2 Boston lettuce leaves

Spread mustard on the rice cakes. Spread the applesauce on the mustard. Place the turkey on top, and finish with lettuce leaves.

Serves 1

WISHFUL WHITE WINE

2 tablespoons apple juice, chilled
6 ounces sparkling water, chilled

Combine in a wineglass.

Serves 1

PERSONALIZED PITA PIZZA

¼ cup Pritikin Spaghetti Sauce with Mushrooms
1 tablespoon chopped onion
3 mushrooms, sliced
¼ green bell pepper, seeded and sliced
¼ medium zucchini, sliced
1 6-inch pita bread
2 tablespoons freshly grated Parmesan cheese
½ ounce Weight Watchers mozzarella cheese, grated

In a nonstick skillet sprayed with Pam, combine the spaghetti sauce, onion, mushrooms, pepper, and zucchini. Cook until the vegetables are partially soft, about 5 minutes. Spread the mixture on pita bread and top with grated cheeses. Bake in 450° oven for 10 minutes, or until the cheese melts.

Serves 1

HIGHFALUTIN JICAMA

½ lime or lemon
½ cup thinly sliced jicama
Cayenne pepper (optional)

Squeeze the lime or lemon over the jicama. If desired, lightly sprinkle on cayenne pepper.

Serves 1

TOSSED LEAFY GREENS

1 cup spinach, torn into bite-size pieces
1 cup red leaf or romaine lettuce, torn into bite-size pieces
2 tablespoons Wish-Bone Lite Classic Dijon Vinaigrette reduced-calorie dressing

Combine and toss.

Serves 1

CHIANTI CUP

2 tablespoons grape juice, chilled
6 ounces sparkling water, chilled

Combine in a wineglass.

Serves 1

UNFORBIDDEN FRUIT

½ cup pineapple chunks, fresh or canned in its own juice and drained
1 small kiwi, peeled and sliced

Thread pineapple and kiwi on a wooden skewer. Chill.

Serves 1

Menu 2

FOOD FOR THOUGHT

Today, look at an old problem in a new way. Make a stepping-stone out of a stumbling block.

BREAKFAST
(336 calories)

*Challenger's Cup**
*Feelin' Your Oats and Raisin' the Roof**
Decaffeinated coffee

LUNCH
(227 calories)

*Discovery Dip**
*Varied Vegetables**
*Tortilla Triangles**
Celestial Seasonings Country Peach Spice herb tea, iced

SNACK
(140 calories)

*Assertive Apple**
Celestial Seasonings Cinnamon Apple Spice herb tea

DINNER
(368 calories)

*Superlative Sweet and Sour Scallops**
*Regal Rice**
*Captain's Cauliflower**
Celestial Seasonings Red Zinger herb tea, iced

TOTAL CALORIES 1,071
PROTEIN 23%
CARBOHYDRATE 68%
FAT 9%

* Recipes follow.

CHALLENGER'S CUP

¼ cup unsweetened pineapple juice
½ banana
½ cup nonfat milk
¼ teaspoon coconut or banana extract
3 ice cubes

Place all ingredients in a blender. Blend until mixed.

Serves 1

FEELIN' YOUR OATS AND RAISIN' THE ROOF

1 cup Ralston Oat Chex cereal
1 tablespoon raisins

Mix and eat dry, bit by bit.

Serves 1

VARIED VEGETABLES

Assorted raw vegetables (jicama, green and red bell pepper, and mushrooms)

Clean and cut into bite-size pieces, about 1 cup per person. Use as a "dipper" for the Discovery Dip.

Serves 1

TORTILLA TRIANGLES

1 corn tortilla
Chili powder

Cut the tortilla into 8 triangles. Spray with a fine mist of water and sprinkle with chili powder to taste. Place the triangles on a nonstick baking sheet and bake at 425° until crisp and dry, approximately 15 minutes. Use as a "dipper" for the Discovery Dip.

Serves 1

DISCOVERY DIP

½ cup chopped onions
1 clove garlic, mashed
2 cups canned pinto beans, drained
1 4-ounce can diced green chilies, drained
¼ cup nonfat plain yogurt
1 tablespoon cider vinegar
1 teaspoon cumin
Paprika

Blend all ingredients except paprika in a food processor or blender. Chill. Garnish with paprika.

Serves 4

ASSERTIVE APPLE

1 medium green or red apple
⅛ teaspoon cinnamon
1½ teaspoons peanut butter
1½ tablespoons nonfat plain yogurt

Wash, core, and slice the apple. Mix the cinnamon, peanut butter, and yogurt. Spread on the apple slices.

Serves 1

REGAL RICE

2 cups cooked brown rice (*not* instant or quick)
4 tablespoons minced fresh parsley

Prepare the rice according to package directions. Garnish with parsley.

Serves 4

SUPERLATIVE SWEET AND SOUR SCALLOPS

Sauce

⅓ cup ketchup
¼ cup cider vinegar
¼ cup apple juice
1 clove garlic, mashed
1 tablespoon sherry
2 tablespoons freshly grated ginger
2 teaspoons soy sauce
1½ tablespoons cornstarch
⅓ cup water

1 cup white wine
½ teaspoon cracked black pepper
1½ pounds bay scallops
½ pound snow peas
2 small red bell peppers, seeded and cut into 1-inch squares
1 8-ounce can sliced water chestnuts, drained

To make the sauce, combine all of the sauce ingredients except cornstarch and water. Bring to a boil. Lower the heat and simmer. Put the cornstarch in a bowl and slowly add the water, stirring constantly. Add the cornstarch mixture slowly to the sauce and cook, stirring constantly, over medium heat for almost 5 minutes, until the sauce is thickened.

In a large nonstick skillet, bring the wine and pepper to a simmer. Add the scallops and cook for 5 minutes. Drain off the wine, leaving the scallops in the skillet.

While the scallops are cooking, fill a 2-quart saucepan half full of water and bring to a boil. Add the snow peas and red peppers and blanch for 2 minutes. Drain.

Add the snow peas, peppers, and water chestnuts to the scallops. Add the sauce and stir over low heat for 5 to 10 minutes, until the vegetables and scallops are coated with sauce and heated through.

Serves 4

CAPTAIN'S CAULIFLOWER

1 small head cauliflower
1 tablespoon Molly McButter

Wash and remove the center stem from the cauliflower. Steam until done. Sprinkle with Molly McButter.

Serves 4

Menu 3

FOOD FOR THOUGHT

Our eyes are placed in front because it's more important to look ahead than back.

BREAKFAST
(277 calories)

*Fearless French Toast**
*Chutney Cream Spread**
Decaffeinated coffee

LUNCH
(241 calories)

*Tiger's Tuna Salad**
5 cocktail round bread slices
Celestial Seasonings Emperor's Choice herb tea, iced

SNACK
(148 calories)

*Ambitious Ambrosia**
Celestial Seasonings Orange Zinger herb tea

DINNER
(287 calories)

*Pasta Primadonna**
*Bogus Burgundy**

* Recipes follow.

DESSERT

(60 calories)

*Papaya Piquante**

Celestial Seasonings Cinnamon Apple Spice herb tea

TOTAL CALORIES 1,013
PROTEIN 29%
CARBOHYDRATE 59%
FAT 12%

* Recipes follow.

FEARLESS FRENCH TOAST

½ cup egg substitute
½ teaspoon grated lemon rind
1 cup nonfat milk
1 teaspoon vanilla extract
½ teaspoon cinnamon
8 thin slices sourdough bread

In a shallow dish or pie plate, whisk together the egg substitute, lemon rind, milk, vanilla, and cinnamon. Dip the bread in the mixture, turning to soak thoroughly. Spray a nonstick skillet with Pam. Heat the skillet and brown the bread on both sides.

Serves 4

CHUTNEY CREAM SPREAD

2 tablespoons chutney
12 tablespoons nonfat plain yogurt

Blend together and use to top Fearless French Toast.

Serves 4

TIGER'S TUNA SALAD

6 ounces water-packed white-meat tuna, drained
¼ cup chopped bell pepper
4 scallions, minced
¼ cup grated carrots

- 1 tablespoon chopped pimiento
- 3 drops Tabasco sauce
- ½ cup nonfat plain yogurt
- 2 teaspoons Dijon mustard
- ½ teaspoon vinegar
- ½ teaspoon soy sauce
- ¼ teaspoon black pepper
- ⅛ teaspoon sesame oil
- 12 ounces tofu, drained and patted dry

Combine all of the ingredients except the tofu. Cube the tofu and gently fold it in. Chill.

Serves 4

AMBITIOUS AMBROSIA

- ½ cup mixed fresh fruit
- 1 tablespoon Post Grape Nuts cereal
- 1 tablespoon nonfat plain yogurt

Combine and chill.

Serves 1

PASTA PRIMADONNA

- 2 cups cooked rotelli pasta
- 1 medium zucchini, shredded
- 2 scallions, minced
- ½ cup fresh or frozen peas
- ½ cup canned artichoke hearts, (not marinated), diced
- 12 ounces cooked chicken breast, sliced
- ½ cup shredded red cabbage
- 1 bell pepper, seeded and diced
- ¼ cup minced fresh parsley
- ½ cup coarsely chopped cherry tomatoes
- 2 tablespoons Parmesan cheese
- ½ cup Wish-Bone Lite Classic Dijon Vinaigrette reduced-calorie dressing

Combine, toss, and chill. To develop the flavor, toss occasionally.

Serves 4

BOGUS BURGUNDY

2 tablespoons cranberry juice, chilled
6 ounces sparkling water, chilled

Combine in a wineglass.

Serves 1

PAPAYA PIQUANTE

1 cup diced fresh papaya
Juice of ½ lime
Dash of chili powder

Sprinkle the papaya with lime juice and chili powder to taste.

Serves 1

Menu 4

EATING OUT

FOOD FOR THOUGHT

You can see today better if you stop looking at yesterday.

BREAKFAST

(294 calories)

¼ cantaloupe or ½ grapefruit
½ cup cottage cheese
1 English muffin, toasted
Decaffeinated coffee

LUNCH

(262 calories)

Chef's Salad made with 3 ounces turkey (no ham or cheese)
1 teaspoon ranch dressing diluted with 1 tablespoon red wine vinegar
1 slice sourdough bread, no butter
iced tea with lemon

SNACK

(90 calories)

Yoplait "Light" yogurt
Perrier

DINNER

(415 calories)

3 ounces veal piccata
½ baked potato with lemon and pepper
Mixed green salad with 1 teaspoon Parmesan cheese and 1 tablespoon red wine vinegar
5 ounces dry white wine or *¾ cup fresh fruit*
Decaffeinated coffee

TOTAL CALORIES 1,061

WITH WINE	WITHOUT WINE
PROTEIN 34%	PROTEIN 34%
CARBOHYDRATE 42%	CARBOHYDRATE 52%
FAT 14%	FAT 14%
ALCOHOL 10%	

DIET DAY #2

DOING YOUR HOMEWORK

On a Diet Day #2 your mind is like a sponge. Cultivate your thirst for knowledge by doing your Numbers Diet homework. You have the patience to compare ingredients, so study the section on reading labels and do some research at your favorite market to raise your diet IQ. This is also a good day to search out the best exercise gyms and equipment.

On a day influenced by the number 2, togetherness and partnership are on your mind. Plan to share a meal or exercise with a friend. If tea for two isn't written on your calendar for today, satisfy your hunger for companionship by talking to a friend on the phone who won't mind your crunching in his or her ear.

A SHORT COURSE IN LABELS AS A SECOND LANGUAGE

Labels often conceal as much as they reveal, because they are loaded with terms that are unintelligible to the average consumer. There are two kinds of labels: one for nutritional information and one for ingredients. An ingredients label is required unless the food is a standard, such as mayonnaise or ketchup. If a food is enriched or fortified, or makes a claim such as "high in Vitamin D" or "low in calories," it must include a nutrition label; otherwise, nutrition labeling is optional, and you may not be able to evaluate a product without contacting the manufacturer.

The Food and Drug Administration does not oversee everything we eat. The Department of Agriculture regulates meat and poultry, and, as fishy as it sounds, no agency provides standards for the condition of the seafood we eat!

PRODUCT NAMES

When the package says "lean" ground beef, it contains a whopping 21 percent fat. "Extra lean" ground beef at 17 percent fat is a better choice, but the round or sirloin steak your butcher grinds fresh to order is the leanest ground beef you can buy. On the Numbers Diet you will be eating lots of white-meat turkey, which is the leanest of all.

> Not all ground turkey is the same. Try to buy Turkey Store or Louis Rich brand, or ask the butcher to grind turkey breast with no skin.

On most labels, the food that has first place in the product's name or description indicates how much of that food you are getting in proportion to other ingredients. For instance, there is more chicken than rice in "chicken and rice," and more rice than chicken in "rice and chicken."

To understand the makeup of flavorings in foods, let's unravel the difference between chocolate pudding, chocolate-flavored pudding, and artificially flavored chocolate pudding. Chocolate pudding contains only natural flavoring; chocolate-flavored pudding contains artificial and natural flavor, which predominates; and artificially flavored chocolate pudding is just that, artificially flavored.

The words *fruit juice* may be used if a product contains 100 percent real fruit juice, whereas you will find 35 to 69 percent real juice in something called *juice drink*. Only 10 to 34 percent real juice qualifies a product as a *fruit drink,* while a mere 10 percent or less real fruit juice is all you can expect to find in something called a *fruit-flavored drink*. The name *chocolate drink* is reserved for products made with partially skimmed milk, while *chocolate milk* adorns the carton containing whole milk.

The word *dietetic* on the label does not mean the product is intended for dieters who want reduced calories. Although *dietetic* may suggest *low-calorie* to you, the word often stands for sugar-free products intended for diabetic diets, or low-sodium foods for people who need to reduce their salt intake. For instance, dietetic ice cream meant for diabetics may not be low in fat calories, just low in sugar.

Be on guard when you see the words *lite* and *light,* because they can be very misleading. If you see them in conjunction with the promise of reduced calories, the product must have a label containing full nutritional information. Read it! However, you may find *lite* or *light* on a product that is merely lighter in color, lighter in weight, more fluffy in texture, lighter-tasting, more thinly sliced, or less salty than similar products. In the case of processed meats, *light* refers to a 25 percent reduction in fat compared to regular processed meats.

Natural is another overworked term. You can be sure of its meaning only when used to describe meat and poultry, in which case *natural* means raised and processed without artificial additives. *Natural* used in the names of foods other than meat and poultry is no guarantee of a superior product unless the products carry nutrition and ingredients labels proving their claims. When you see *natural flavor,* the product must use flavors that come directly from a juice, oil, leaf, herb, or spice. *All natural flavor* doesn't guarantee the absence of artificial colors or preservatives.

Products with the word *imitation* in their names are not necessarily inferior to the original version, just different in nutritional value. In the case of mayonnaise, imitation is better for us on low-fat diets than regular mayonnaise, which is 99 percent fat.

Many foods, like cereals, are "fortified" with added minerals and vitamins to supplement those that were not present in the foods originally or were present in lesser quantities.

"Enriched" foods, like flour, are those in which a select few nutrients, lost in processing, have been replaced.

SERVING SIZE AND SERVINGS PER PACKAGE

The serving size is the next most important item on a label. You and the manufacturer may not agree on the ideal size of a serving. Do you know how much, or how little, a half cup is? Before you begin, check to see how many servings there are in the package. I can easily consume a whole bag of microwave popcorn the manufacturer intended for four people.

CALORIES PER SERVING

The number of calories per specific size serving is always given. When a product is meant to be mixed with other foods, such as pudding mixed with milk, the number of calories per serving with the added ingredients is also given.

Be clear on the number of calories per serving so you won't turn a supposedly low-calorie food into a high-calorie eating episode by consuming too much of it.

FAT

A healthy diet consists of no more than 30 percent fat. To lose weight you should reduce your consumption of fat to 20 to 30 percent of your total calories for the day. In other words, it's acceptable if 200 to 300 calories of a 1,000-calorie diet come from fat.

To analyze a label and determine the percentage of fat calories per serving, multiply each gram of protein and carbohydrate by 4 calories and each gram of fat by 9 calories.

Protein	2 g × 4 =	8 calories
Carbohydrate	5 g × 4 =	20
Fat	3 g × 9 =	27
		55 calories

Since 27 calories out of 55 calories are fat, approximately 50 percent of this food is fat. Before you reject a single food because it contains more than 20 to 30 percent fat, check to see if the number of calories one serving contributes to your total calorie count for the day is within the 20 to 30 percent range. Based on 1,000 calories per day, you can have 200 to 300 calories of fat, so a serving of food that contains 27 fat calories is acceptable.

When reading labels, a safe rule of thumb is to stick with products that have 2 grams of fat or less per 100-calorie serving.

In addition to monitoring the amount of fat in your diet, read labels to determine the kind of fats you are eating. (For more information on fats and cholesterol, see page 208.) *Made with pure vegetable oil* does not tell you what you need to know. It might be palm oil or coconut oil, both of which are highly saturated. The vegetable oil may be hydrogenated, or hardened, thus turned into saturated fat.

Look for margarines whose labels list polyunsaturated oil in liquid form first. Sometimes calorie-reduced margarines list water first, because there is more of that than any other ingredient. In

> Remember that switching from butter to stick margarine to soft margarine means you'll be getting less saturated fat, but it doesn't mean you will be getting less *total* fat. Use any of these products sparingly in a weight-loss program.

that case, the second ingredient should be one of the liquid oils, such as sunflower, corn, or safflower. The best margarine products list the proportion of polyunsaturated to saturated oil. You want one that has twice as much polyunsaturated as saturated oil: 6 grams of polyunsaturated to 3 grams of saturated oil, for example. With the exception of some of the less costly margarines that actually use lard, all other margarines are cholesterol-free. It pays to read labels!

No cholesterol does not indicate the absence of fat in a product, nor does it tell you if the fat is saturated.

Nondairy is no guarantee that saturated fats such as palm oil and coconut oil haven't been used instead of cream and milk.

A product must have less than 2 milligrams of cholesterol per serving to qualify as *cholesterol-free*.

Less than 200 milligrams of cholesterol per serving qualify a product as *low-cholesterol*.

If products have been reformulated to contain 75 percent less cholesterol than the original food, they may be labeled *cholesterol reduced*.

Type of Margarine and Calories per Tablespoon

Stick regular	100	Whipped regular	70
Soft regular	80	Diet	51

Assuming you drink one cup of milk daily, in a year you can save over 23,000 calories by switching from whole milk to skim milk. That translates into a weight loss of almost 7 pounds. If your family protests the change from high-fat homogenized milk to nonfat milk, mix the two in ever decreasing proportions of whole to skim. By the time you are using half whole and half nonfat, you are already saving 36 calories per cup and well on your way to a healthier diet.

SUGAR

Only a sugar sleuth can detect the hidden presence of the sweet stuff in foods. By many aliases sugar delivers empty calories in varying degrees of sweetness and can affect the body adversely. On a label, words that end in *-ose* are sugar in disguise. Watch out for sugar also known as *sucrose, maltose, fructose, lactose, levulose,* and *dextrose*. Other terms used to describe sugar are *modified corn starch, honey, corn syrup, molasses, brown sugar, granulated sugar, powdered sugar, turbinado sugar, invert sugar, caramel syrup, modified tapioca starch, lump sugar, beet sugar, cane sugar, maple sugar, sorghum sugar, brown sugar syrup, malt syrup, sorbitol, mannitol, wheat starch, refiners' syrup,* and *glucose syrup*.

Watch out for the terms *sugarless* and *sugar-free*. According to the Food and Drug Administration, the word *sugar* means sucrose (table sugar). Many products that list other names for sugar are allowed to call themselves *sugar-free* and *sugar-less* but are high in sugar calories.

SODIUM

Sodium is the main regulator of the balance of water in cells. Excess sodium can cause your body to retain excess amounts of water and is linked to hypertension, or high blood pressure. Manufacturers have the option of including sodium information on their labels; if you are salt-sensitive, as I am, it is essential for you to check this ingredient.

Sodium finds its way into food in at least seventy compounds besides what we readily recognize as plain table salt. There is sodium in baking soda, baking powder, celery salt, onion salt, garlic salt, sodium chloride, sodium gluconate, sodium caseinate, sodium nitrite and nitrate, sodium hyroide, salt pork, and brine. In general, the more processed the food, the more sodium it contains.

On a label, sodium is listed in milligrams. Although 1,100 to 3,000 milligrams of sodium is the amount recommended daily for a healthy diet, Americans who tend to eat processed foods may consume as much as 5,000 to 7,000 milligrams every day. Salt, which is 40 percent sodium, contains 2,000 milligrams of sodium per teaspoon. Allowing for the hidden sodium in foods that we do not perceive as salty, most people manage to consume amounts of sodium above the limit considered healthy even before they pick up the saltshaker.

Food containing no more than 140 milligrams of sodium per serving is considered *low-sodium*.

Food containing 35 milligrams or less of sodium per serving is considered *very low sodium*.

If the product has less than 5 milligrams of sodium per serving, it is considered *sodium-free*.

When no salt is added to the product during processing but the food contains significant salt levels naturally or contains sodium from other ingredients, it can still be labeled *salt-free* or *unsalted*.

Food	Mg of Hidden Sodium
1 slice devil's food cake	402
1 slice cheese pizza	600
1 cup canned creamed corn	617
½ cup canned tomato sauce	750
1 cup canned soup	872
1 average TV dinner	1,300
1 fast-food chicken dinner	2,243

LISTING OF INGREDIENTS

Ingredients are listed in descending order by weight, so you will find the main ingredients in a product among the first four ingredients on the list. If flour is the first ingredient, there is more flour than anything else in the product. For a real eye opener, read the labels of popular cold cereals. When sugar is listed as the first ingredient, it's obvious that it is the most plentiful ingredient. What isn't obvious to the uneducated label reader is that sugar can also be the major ingredient even when it is listed on a label by different names, such as dextrose, fructose, corn syrup, etc. Even though all these ingredients are sugar in different forms and together make up the major part of the product, no one of them is used in large enough quantity to warrant first to fourth place in the ingredients list.

Food additives and vitamins and minerals must also be included in the ingredients list.

If preservatives are used, they must be listed and their purpose stated. Beware! Even though preservatives don't affect calories, they may affect your health.

CHOOSING SHOES

If you are just starting to exercise, it's not necessary or cost-effective for you to buy different shoes for various sports. Since walking is the most convenient, least expensive form of exercise and requires no special ability or equipment other than shoes, I recommend walking for everyone.

A Diet Day #2 is an ideal day to select walking shoes. You're in the mood to make a thorough search of the yellow pages for the right store and to shop more than one store to find just what you want. Find the most specialized source available and plan to get an education.

If possible, shop later in the day, when your feet have expanded the way they will when you walk for exercise. When you are trying on shoes, be sure to wear socks that are recommended for walking. They should be made of an absorbent material such as cotton, and fit well enough to conform smoothly to your feet without forming wrinkles or confining your toes.

Shoes should be large enough in the toe area for you to wiggle your toes. There is a fine line between shoes that are big enough and so big that you trip. Walk around on the carpeted area of the store, where you are likely to catch the toe of your shoe if it's too long. The heel of the shoe should hug your foot to prevent slipping. I always look for a shoe with a high counter to accommodate my narrow heels. The sole of a good walking shoe should be flexible and provide proper arch support. Adequate cushioning for the ball and heel of your foot is important to absorb the impact of a hard surface. The upper portion of the shoe should be made of material that breathes, such as canvas, or vented leather or nylon.

A good shoe salesperson should know the stock well enough to suggest the right brand and size to fit your special needs, such as narrow or wide feet, long toes, high or nonexistent arches. If after walking around the store in several pairs you are still not comfortable, ask for the advice of the manager or go to another store for a second opinion.

> Bring your old shoes with you so the salesperson can see where they are worn out and determine how best to fit your foot.

If you have a special problem, such as "pump bumps" or flat arches, that makes fitting a shoe difficult, investigate orthotics. They are supports designed and made especially for your feet by a professional, either an orthopedic doctor or a podiatrist.

Let fit, not fashion or price, be the final determining factor in which shoes you select. On a Diet Day #2 you won't have any trouble gathering all the facts about walking shoes, but you may have trouble saying "no" to a pushy salesperson. Overcome today's urge to please others, and stand up for the welfare of your own feet. If there are many good choices and you're having trouble making a decision, again, stand on your own two feet and let comfort be your guide.

CHOOSING A GYM

A Diet Day #2 is the perfect day to determine whether or not joining a gym fits your needs and to comparison-shop. If you get motivation from being around other people, the group setting of a gym might be your ticket to success. In addition, the variety of activities offered by a fitness club might be added incentive to keep exercising.

The first thing you need to ask yourself is whether the gym is convenient to your home and/or work. Is there adequate parking? What is the fee structure, what does it cover, and can you afford it? Are there a variety of payment plans to suit your budget? Do you pay by the month or year, or sign up for life? Are there any hidden initiation fees? If you have young children, is baby-sitting available; is it free or is there a fee?

Is the gym open during times that fit your schedule? Be sure you visit at a time of day you will be using the facilities. Is it overcrowded? Are there adequate staff members on duty during those hours? Can you attend at least three or four days per week at your convenience?

Is the gym co-ed or do men and women exercise separately?

How long has the establishment been in business? Is there professional staffing? Do the instructors provide adequate instruction on use of the equipment and proper exercise techniques? Exercising the wrong way can do more harm than good. Do the instructors offer individualized programs, or are group activities your only choice? Is there a charge for the individualized instruction, or is it included in the membership fee? Are facilities and classes available for aerobic activity?

Is the place clean and cheerful? Are the employees relaxed and friendly, or are they pushy and trying to sell you more service? Is the equipment well maintained? Are there showers, dressing rooms, and lockers available? Are towels, soap, etc., provided? Are there "frills" such as a pool, Jacuzzi, snack bar, TV?

Can you bring guests?

Is there proper target heart rate monitoring?

Are toning and stretching classes available? Are classes offered at various skill levels or do they expect you to be a triathlete when you begin? Do you want a place that encourages try-athletes?

If you like to exercise outdoors, are classes taught outside or is there equipment outside?

Is the room temperature maintained at 71 to 74 degrees?

If there is a pool, is it attended and staffed?

Is there an indoor or outdoor walking track?

Don't be embarrassed to comparison-shop. Ask about deals such as two-for-one offers—either you and a friend for the price of one, or two years for the price of one.

Ask if you can have a free trial offer or a short-term trial membership.

The gym that passes your test on a Diet Day #2 will bring you years of satisfaction. Take your time with the decision. Bring the contract home and talk it over with someone you trust before you sign it.

DIET DOWNFALLS AND THEIR SOLUTIONS

On a Diet Day #2 it's easy for you to see two sides of every situation. There may be just as many reasons in your mind to eat as not to eat. Remove confusing choices from the picture by sticking strictly to one Numbers Diet menu.

If you're feeling discouraged today because the results of your diet are not apparent on the scale, be patient. Chances are you renewed your efforts only yesterday, and losing weight takes time. You didn't gain weight overnight, and you're not going to lose it overnight. On a Diet Day #2, when you have patience and sensitivity toward others, be as generous and understanding with yourself.

> If you don't see results on the scale, get out the tape measure. Often you lose inches before pounds.

One can be a lonely number, but today you are influenced by 2. Team up with someone or call a friend who will give you moral support. Enlist the help and understanding you need from your friends and family, even if you have to write each one a letter. Tell them you are changing your eating habits and ask for their cooperation. Use phrases like "I'm sure you will understand that I will be eating differently." Tell them they can help you by not questioning or criticizing your food choices.

Sensitive to other's feelings as well as your own, you may be in such a people-pleasing mood on a Diet Day #2 that you can't say "no." To avoid hurting someone's feelings, you may be tempted to eat something you shouldn't, especially if it has been prepared "just for you." Fortunately, you have all the diplomacy you need on a Diet Day #2 to explain why you don't want to consume extra calories. To the offer of a tempting snack, say "The only treat I need is your company." With a little practice, on a Diet Day #2 you can learn to be tactful yet firm on any day.

Replace your urges to eat by listening to positive-thinking tapes or reading inspirational books. Make a list of all of your positive characteristics and accomplishments. Remember to include all the steps you are taking to solve your weight problem. And for a surefire substitute for food, reach for your mate and not your plate.

EXERCISE

On a Diet Day #2, even though you are happiest when exercising with a friend, don't let lack of companionship stop you. Take along your radio or cassette player and earphones, or arrange for other media entertainment.

WALKING

With companionship it seems you can walk twice as far with half the effort. A brisk thirty-minute walk passes in no time. If you are with a loved one, hold hands and swing those arms—it's great for raising your heart rate!

On a Diet Day #2 you may feel as if you are taking two steps forward and one step back. Assuming a high-school track is available and you have a spotter to make sure you don't run into an obstacle, try walking backward for a short while. It's great exercise because you use a different set of muscles.

BICYCLING

Today would be an ideal day to rent a tandem bicycle. Don't think you have to go twice the distance because you are doing only half the work. Be a good sport and pull your weight, especially going uphill.

If a tandem bike isn't available, bicycling is still a fun thing to do with a friend. If you are riding at home on a stationary bike, let the television or a good book keep you company.

On a Diet Day #2 you may find yourself gravitating toward an activity, like tennis, that requires a partner. Playing singles is a better workout than doubles. If you don't have a partner, you can either hit a ball against your garage door or go to the local school and hit a ball against the backboard.

A rousing game of badminton also uses large muscle groups and will get your target heart rate up. Even table tennis will give you a good workout.

RECIPES FOR DIET DAY #2

To satisfy your need for companionship, several dishes have been planned to share. Menus have a "proper tone" and include a high tea for two at noon instead of the usual garden-variety lunch.

Should you choose to eat away from home on a Diet Day #2, the suggestions are geared to fine dining in a traditional sense.

Food for Thought reinforces the overtones of a Diet Day #2, which are patience, diplomacy, and the art of listening.

Menu 1

FOOD FOR THOUGHT

Patience is the ability to count down before blasting off.

BREAKFAST

(245 calories)

Carnation Sugar Free hot cocoa mix
*Bran Muffin à l'Orange**
1 orange, sliced
Decaffeinated coffee

LUNCH

(310 calories)

½ can Campbell's Special Request vegetable soup
*Lemon Parsley Tuna**
4 Wasa Crispbread Savory Sesame Crackers
4 carrot sticks
Celestial Seasonings Lemon Zinger herb tea, iced

SNACK

(105 calories)

2 Fig Newtons
Celestial Seasonings Strawberry Fields herb tea

DINNER

(340 calories)

*Turkey Tenderloin**
*Broiled Parmesan Tomato**
½ cup brown rice
½ cup steamed green beans
*White Sinfindel**

DESSERT

(90 calories)

½ Weight Watchers Double Fudge frozen bar

TOTAL CALORIES 1,090
PROTEIN 27%
CARBOHYDRATE 57%
FAT 16%

* Recipes follow.

BRAN MUFFINS À L'ORANGE

Refrigerator Bran Muffins recipe (page 24)
1 teaspoon grated fresh orange rind

Fill a muffin cup one-quarter full of muffin batter. Sprinkle orange rind on top. Fill the muffin cup half full of batter. Bake according to directions.

Serves 1

LEMON PARSLEY TUNA

1 6½-ounce can water-packed white-meat tuna, drained
4 tablespoons fresh lemon juice
1 teaspoon mayonnaise
1 tablespoon nonfat plain yogurt
½ cup minced fresh parsley
2 scallions, minced

In a bowl, mash the tuna and lemon juice with a fork until flaky. Add the other ingredients and mix well. Spread on 8 Wasa Crispbread Savory sesame crackers (4 per serving).

Serves 2

TURKEY TENDERLOIN

1 8-ounce turkey tenderloin
2 teaspoons Dijon mustard
1 teaspoon white Worcestershire sauce
1 tablespoon white wine
⅛ teaspoon white pepper

Place the turkey tenderloin in a broiling pan. Combine the other ingredients. Spread half of the mustard mixture on the tenderloin and broil for 8 minutes. Turn, spread on the remaining mixture, and broil for another 8 minutes. Slice diagonally.

Serves 2

BROILED PARMESAN TOMATO

1 medium tomato
1 teaspoon grated Parmesan cheese
1 teaspoon minced fresh parsley
Molly McButter

Dip the tomato in boiling water or hold over gas flame to burst the skin. Peel the tomato and cut in half horizontally. Place the tomato halves, cut side up, on a baking sheet. Sprinkle with cheese, parsley, and Molly McButter. Place under a preheated broiler until the cheese is brown and the tomato hot; watch carefully. Serve immediately.

Serves 2

WHITE SINFINDEL

1 tablespoon cranberry juice, chilled
1 tablespoon apple juice, chilled
6 ounces sparkling water, chilled

Combine in a wineglass.

Serves 1

Menu 2

FOOD FOR THOUGHT

The art of diplomacy is letting someone have your way.

BREAKFAST

(305 calories)

*Mutual Muffin**
*Protein-Packed Apple**
Decaffeinated coffee

LUNCH

(270 calories)

*Potato Salad with Leafy Greens**
2 6-inch breadsticks
Celestial Seasonings Mellow Mint herb tea, iced

SNACK
(90 calories)

4 dried apricot halves
4 raw almonds
Celestial Seasonings Almond Sunset herb tea

DINNER
(280 calories)

*Chicken Piccata**
*Steamed Artichoke with Yogurt Dressing**
*Dilly Dash Potatoes**
White Sinfindel (page 50)

DESSERT
(165 calories)

Blue Angel
Celestial Seasonings Wildforest Blackberry herb tea

TOTAL CALORIES 1,110
PROTEIN 20%
CARBOHYDRATE 58%
FAT 22%

* Recipes follow.

MUTUAL MUFFIN

¼ cup nonfat milk
½ cup Quaker Oat Bran cereal
1 egg, lightly beaten
2 carrots, grated
1 tablespoon safflower oil
2 tablespoons molasses
3 tablespoons golden raisins
½ cup whole-wheat flour
2 teaspoons baking powder
½ teaspoon cinnamon
¼ teaspoon nutmeg

Combine the milk and cereal in a bowl and let stand for 5 minutes. Stir in the egg, carrots, oil, molasses, and raisins. Sift the dry

(Continued)

(Continued from page 51)
ingredients: flour, baking powder, cinnamon, and nutmeg. Stir into the egg mixture just until well moistened. Spoon the batter into two 5-inch tart pans that have been sprayed with Pam. Bake in a 350° oven for 20 minutes, or until a toothpick inserted in the center comes out clean. Let cool on a rack. Wrap, label, and freeze one tart pan and share the other.

Serves 4

PROTEIN-PACKED APPLE

1 medium green or red apple
1½ teaspoons peanut butter
1½ tablespoons nonfat plain yogurt

Wash, core, and slice the apple. Mix the peanut butter and yogurt. Spread on the apple slices.

Serves 1

POTATO SALAD ON LEAFY GREENS

¾ pound small red potatoes, unpeeled but scrubbed
2 hard-cooked eggs, sliced
¼ small red onion, finely chopped
¼ cup halved pitted black olives
1 tablespoon chopped pimiento
¼ cup minced fresh parsley
¼ cup sliced water chestnuts
2 stalks celery, sliced

Dressing

6 tablespoons low-fat cottage cheese
6 tablespoons nonfat plain yogurt
1½ tablespoons minced fresh dill or 2 teaspoons dried dill
2 teaspoons fresh lemon juice
1½ teaspoons olive oil
¾ teaspoon Dijon mustard
¼ teaspoon sugar
¼ teaspoon white pepper

½ green bell pepper, seeded and sliced crosswise into rings
8 cups leafy greens (romaine, red leaf lettuce, spinach)

Steam the potatoes until tender when pierced. Do not peel. If they are small, leave them whole; if large, quarter them. Slice the eggs crosswise and place in a bowl with the potatoes. Add the onion, olives, pimiento, parsley, water chestnuts, and celery. Mix carefully.

In a separate bowl, combine the dressing ingredients. Pour the dressing over the salad and toss gently. Surround with green pepper rings. Cover and chill for several hours or overnight. Serve on leafy greens.

Serves 4

CHICKEN PICCATA

16 ounces boneless, skinless chicken breasts
Dash of butter-flavor salt
Juice of 2 lemons
½ cup white wine
2 tablespoons minced fresh parsley

Lightly pound the chicken breasts. Sprinkle with salt. Heat a nonstick skillet sprayed with Pam. Quickly brown the chicken breasts on each side. Add the lemon juice and wine and continue to cook for a few minutes on each side. To serve, sprinkle parsley on top.

Serves 4

DILLY DASH POTATOES

1 pound small red new potatoes
Dried dill
1 tablespoon Molly McButter
2 teaspoons Mrs. Dash

Wash but do not peel the potatoes. Steam and cut into bite-size pieces. Sprinkle with dill, Molly McButter, and Mrs. Dash. Serve immediately.

Serves 4

STEAMED ARTICHOKE WITH YOGURT DRESSING

2 medium artichokes

Dressing

½ cup nonfat plain yogurt
2 teaspoons diet mayonnaise
1 teaspoon Dijon mustard
1 teaspoon dried dill

Wash the artichokes and drain. Using kitchen shears, trim across the end of each leaf to remove the thorn. Cut the stems, leaving a flat surface on the bottom of each artichoke. Place the trimmed artichokes on a rack set over boiling water in a large pan. Cover and steam for 45 minutes. The artichokes are done when a leaf pulls out easily and the flesh at the base of the leaf is tender. Let cool and refrigerate until serving time.

Combine the dressing ingredients thoroughly. Cover and chill for at least 1 hour to allow flavors to blend.

Present the artichokes on salad plates with yogurt dressing. To eat, pull off each leaf and dip the fleshy end in the dressing. Remove the inner thistle and eat the artichoke bottom with the remaining dressing.

Serves 2

BLUE ANGEL

1/12 of an 8-inch uniced angel food cake
½ cup fresh or frozen blueberries

Top the cake with blueberries and serve.

Serves 1

Menu 3

FOOD FOR THOUGHT

A good listener not only is popular everywhere, but after a while knows something.

BREAKFAST

(197 calories)

*Berry Nut Yogurt**
Decaffeinated coffee

"HIGH TEA" LUNCH

(391 calories)

*Cloud Puffs**
*Stuffed Mushrooms**
*Garbanzo Bean Spread**
4 cocktail bread slices
Celestial Seasonings Country Peach Spice herb tea

SNACK

(109 calories)

½ pear, sliced and sprinkled with nutmeg
Alba 77 shake mix

DINNER

(336 calories)

*Caesar Salad**
*Stuffed Pepper**
*Raspberry Refresher**

DESSERT

(42 calories)

*Glacéed Grapes**
Celestial Seasonings Cinnamon Rose herb tea

TOTAL CALORIES 1,075
PROTEIN 24%
CARBOHYDRATE 61%
FAT 15%

* Recipes follow.

BERRY NUT YOGURT

1 cup nonfat plain yogurt
1 tablespoon Post Grape Nuts
1 cup sliced fresh or frozen strawberries

Combine and serve immediately.

Serves 1

CLOUD PUFFS

3 egg whites, at room temperature
⅛ teaspoon cream of tartar
½ teaspoon almond extract
½ cup sugar
2 cups unsweetened oat flakes

Beat the egg whites with cream of tartar and almond extract until soft peaks form. While beating, gradually add the sugar, a little at a time, until glossy peaks form. Fold the egg white mixture into the oat flakes. Spray a nonstick baking sheet with Pam. Drop the batter by teaspoonfuls onto the baking sheet, about 1 inch apart. Bake in a 250° oven for 1 hour, or until the cookies are dry. Remove and let cool on a rack. Store in a tightly covered plastic container.

Makes 24 cookies. (3 per serving)

STUFFED MUSHROOMS

12 large mushrooms, washed and patted dry
2 cloves garlic, minced
2 tablespoons chopped onion
1 tablespoon Italian herbs
2 tablespoons minced fresh parsley
2 slices soft bread, made into crumbs (see note)
½ cup Quaker Old Fashioned Oats

16 ounces tofu, drained and patted dry
1 carrot, grated
2 tablespoons grated Parmesan cheese
¼ teaspoon black pepper
1 teaspoon lemon juice
½ teaspoon Mrs. Dash

Remove the stems from the mushrooms; reserve the caps. Chop the stems fine and combine them with the remaining ingredients. Spoon the mixture into the mushroom caps. Place in a baking pan, cover, and bake in a 400° oven for 10 minutes. Remove the cover and bake for an additional 5 to 10 minutes.

Serves 4

Note: To make bread crumbs in a food processor, place 2 slices of bread, including crust, in the processing bowl and use the steel blade, to process into crumbs. One slice of bread makes approximately ¼ cup bread crumbs.

GARBANZO BEAN SPREAD

2 tablespoons low-fat cottage cheese
1 tablespoon fresh lemon juice
2 teaspoons rice vinegar
½ cup canned garbanzo beans, drained
⅛ teaspoon cumin
¼ teaspoon garlic powder
⅛ teaspoon white pepper
¼ cup finely diced cucumber
1 scallion, finely minced
¼ cup diced tomato
Paprika

Place all of the ingredients except the cucumber, scallion, tomato, and paprika in a food processor or blender. Blend until smooth. In a small bowl, combine the mixture with the cucumber, onion, and tomato. Sprinkle with paprika.

Serves 4

CAESAR SALAD

Dressing

1 clove garlic, mashed
2 tablespoons olive oil
1½ teaspoons anchovy paste
1 egg white
¼ teaspoon black pepper
2 tablespoons fresh lemon juice
1 tablespoon white Worcestershire sauce
2 tablespoons red wine vinegar
2 tablespoons grated Parmesan cheese

8 cups crisp romaine lettuce, torn into bite-size pieces

Blend all of the dressing ingredients. Store in a tightly covered container in the refrigerator for up to a week. To serve, shake the dressing, pour over the lettuce, and toss.

Serves 4

STUFFED PEPPER

1 green bell pepper
6 ounces Turkey Store or Louis Rich ground turkey
1 teaspoon chili powder
1 to 2 cloves garlic, mashed
½ teaspoon fennel seed
¼ teaspoon celery seed
¼ teaspoon coriander
¼ teaspoon black pepper
¼ teaspoon butter-flavor salt
2 tablespoons minced fresh parsley
½ medium onion, chopped
1 stalk celery, chopped
1 cup cooked brown rice (*not* quick or instant)

Cut the green pepper in half vertically. Seed and blanch in hot water for 1 minute. In a nonstick skillet, brown the turkey with chili powder, garlic, fennel, celery seed, coriander, black pepper, salt, parsley, onion, and celery. Add the rice and stuff into the pepper halves.

Place the pepper halves in a shallow baking dish. Add water to fill the dish to a depth of ¼ inch. Cover with foil and bake at 350° for 30 minutes.

Serves 2

RASPBERRY REFRESHER

3 raspberries, fresh or frozen
8 ounces sparkling water, chilled

Combine in a beautiful glass.

Serves 1

GLACÉED GRAPES

12 Thompson seedless or Red Flame grapes

Freeze the grapes. Do not thaw, but serve directly from the freezer.

Serves 1

Menu 4

EATING OUT

FOOD FOR THOUGHT

Nature has given us one tongue and two ears, that we may hear twice as much as we speak.

BREAKFAST
(251 calories)

½ spinach and mushroom omelet
½ blueberry muffin **or**
½ small bran muffin (nonsticky type)
Decaffeinated coffee

LUNCH
(258 calories)

½ turkey sandwich, no mayonnaise
½ tomato, sliced
2 tablespoons cottage cheese
Tossed green salad with 1 tablespoon ranch dressing diluted with red wine vinegar

SNACK
(40 calories)

½ apple

DINNER
(382 calories)

3 ounces filet mignon
½ baked potato with lemon
1 cup steamed fresh vegetables
Perrier with lime

DESSERT
(135 calories)

½ cup sherbet or sorbet
Decaffeinated coffee

TOTAL CALORIES 1,066
PROTEIN 27%
CARBOHYDRATE 46%
FAT 27%

DIET DAY #3

MAKING CHOICES

The child in you wants to come out and play today. You'll have to fight your urge for instant gratification. Food cues from your surroundings, such as radio and TV commercials, ads in magazines, and food other people are eating, will trigger your desire to eat. Sweet treats, especially favorites from your childhood, will be difficult to resist.

A Diet Day #3 tempts you with many choices. Whether it's food or fun, you want to taste it all. Impromptu invitations and your own spontaneity will mean socializing and possibly eating unconsciously. Play up your role as the life of the party; instead of eating, talk your way through a Diet Day #3. To counteract your unpredictable schedule and your impulsive kiddie cravings, rely upon the flexible eating plan in this chapter.

The Numbers Diet won't spoil your fun or ruin your chance to be in the social spotlight. By following a few tips, on a Diet Day #3 you can still shine and dine.

CHILDHOOD CRAVINGS

Eating patterns from childhood influence the way we handle food as adults. Certain foods have powerful influences that begin at the kitchen table and eventually find their way into our vocabulary. *Gravy train* is a synonym for success, and some favorite terms of endearment are *sugar daddy, honey,* and *sweetheart*.

On a Diet Day #3, subliminal messages from childhood will affect the food choices you make. Sugar, the most common craving traced to childhood, is likely to be a problem.

SUGAR

The average American eats 12 teaspoons of sugar per day! That's almost ⅓ cup.

Studies conducted on newborns to document their taste for sweets indicate an early preference for sucrose (sugar) and water over plain water. So from the first sip we are hooked, and it goes downhill from there. When you consider how many cookies are used as bribes or to reward kids' behavior and how many lollipops are handed out by doctors after an "ouchy" shot, it's no wonder so many of us have never outgrown the need for oral gratification that has been reinforced with sugar. As adults we continue to use sweet foods to console ourselves when we are sad, pick us up when we are tired, entertain ourselves when we are bored, and keep our hands busy when we are nervous. Periods of depression lead us to goodies almost as often as celebrations, each one complete with its traditional diet-buster dessert. Buried under a mountain of sugar-induced problems like tooth decay and overweight, we need to be more suspicious of this seductive sweet stuff.

Forgetting calories for a moment, let's examine the negative effect that sugar has on our bodies. Don't be fooled by names like *sucrose* and *glucose:* sugar by any other name is as capable of setting up the "more you have, the more you want" syndrome. When you eat sugar, you get a lift because the level of sugar in your blood rises. At the same time, the high blood sugar triggers your body to produce insulin to regulate the sugar in your blood, moving it into the cells and tissues. When your pancreas overreacts, producing too much insulin, it lowers your blood sugar too much, causing a drastic drop in energy level. If you are out of shape and overweight, experts suspect, insulin doesn't do its job correctly, compounding the problem of fluctuating blood sugar levels. In any event, eating excess sugar creates a vicious circle because you continually crave more sugar to restore the high level of sugar in your blood. When the cycle repeats itself, you find yourself riding the highs and lows of your blood sugar, like a roller coaster, and craving one candy bar after another.

The urge to eat something sweet in the late morning, afternoon, or evening is probably caused by a natural drop in your blood sugar several hours after a meal. For some of us, sugar cravings can be accompanied by uncomfortable side effects, especially if you ate a sweet dessert with your previous meal. When I give in to my passion for cinnamon gummy bears, I always get a headache and feel tired about a half hour later.

It's risky to jump off a moving roller coaster, but in the case of the sugar roller coaster, it's more dangerous for the dieter to stay on it. To slow down the sugar express to the point where you can get off, you need to know exactly what you are dealing with.

White refined sugar. White sugar has 16 calories per teaspoon and no nutrients. Often sugar calories are called "empty calories," because they offer your body no vitamins or minerals.

Raw sugar. Found on the table at many health food restaurants, raw sugar is slightly less refined than white sugar, but contains the same 16 calories per teaspoon, and still has no nutrients.

Brown sugar. White sugar to which a small amount of molasses has been added has the same nutritional value as white sugar (none) and is higher in calories, at 17 calories per teaspoon.

Fructose. This refined sugar contains the same 16 calories as white sugar, and no nutrients. However, fructose does not raise blood sugar levels as much as white sugar, so it's preferred for diabetic and hypoglycemic diets. In foods that are chilled or high in acid, you need half as much fructose as white sugar for the same level of sweetness, for a substantial savings in calories. However, at high temperatures the sweetening powers of fructose are decreased, necessitating the use of additional fructose equal to the amount of white sugar needed to do the same job.

Honey. This contains 22 calories per teaspoon and fractional amounts of nutrients. It raises blood sugar levels more than white sugar. Even though it is more expensive and higher in calories than white sugar, you need less of it because it tastes sweeter.

Sorbitol. At 16 calories per teaspoon, sorbitol is favored for diabetic and hypoglycemic diets because it metabolizes more slowly than sugar, eliminating the roller-coaster effect. However, it is half as sweet as white sugar, so you have to use twice as much for the same taste, at double the calories.

Molasses. This is the only form of sugar that contains substantial amounts of nutrients. One tablespoon of blackstrap molasses accounts for 14 percent of the Recommended Daily Allowance (RDA) for calcium and 28 percent of the iron recommended. Lighter versions of molasses contain one-third the amount of nutrients.

> The next time you add 1 cup of sugar to a recipe, remember that you are adding 770 empty calories.

SUGAR IN OUR FAVORITE FOODS

Now that you know what kinds of sugar are commonly found in foods, let's see how much sugar is hiding in a few of our favorites.

FOOD	TEASPOONS OF SUGAR
1 slice apple pie	12
1 can orange soda	11.8
1 can cola soda	10
12 ounces tonic water	8.4
1 cup fruit yogurt	7.5
½ cup ice cream	5–6
1 slice iced chocolate cake	4.2
1 plain doughnut	4
1 chocolate bar	4
1 brownie	3
1 tablespoon jam	3
1 tablespoon honey	3
1 cookie	1–3
1 tablespoon ketchup	.6

On a Diet Day #3, when you're in the mood for childhood games, associate sugar with hide and seek. You are "it," and you'd better find the sugar in your life if you want to win at the diet game. Sugar hides very successfully in many foods, but nowhere is its hidden presence more insidious than in children's cereals. One popular brand has 68 percent sugar. Now that you are a label reader, you can easily find out how much sugar is in a cereal by checking out the placement of sugar in the ingredients list. If you see sugar in the first four ingredients, tell the kids in your life that the coveted "Sugar Soggies" are off limits. However, beware of parental admonitions that have a reverse effect. My assistant, Libby, reports that she was so adamant about never buying her daughters one of the offending brands containing 40 percent sugar that, twenty years later, there are three grown women who still give the banished cereal to each other as a joke at Christmas.

At this point you are probably feeling pretty smug about the way you have replaced sinful sugar in your diet with artificial sweeteners. Until recently, I too congratulated myself on switching to diet soda and other "sugarless" products. I enjoyed pleasure without guilt until Gerri French, the dietitian who consulted on this book, had me read research that makes a strong case against artificial sweeteners. It seems that in people like me, who are "hyper-responders" (respond to the sight and smell of food), a chemical reaction occurs as if we had actually eaten the sugar, producing a lower level of blood sugar after a while. Apparently the sweet taste, whatever its source, signals the cells in the body to store carbohydrates and fats, causing the body to crave more and more food. In simple terms, artificial sweeteners may trigger hunger and cause us to eat more.

> The American Cancer Society reports that women who are long-term users of artificial sweeteners are more likely to gain weight, gain more weight, and, when losing, lose less weight than nonusers.

SUGAR SUBSTITUTES

All sweeteners fall into two groups, nutritive and nonnutritive. The term *nutritive sweetener* describes substances that occur in nature and provide energy or calories to the body. They include white sugar, raw sugar, brown sugar, fructose, honey, sorbitol, and aspartame. Nonnutritive sweeteners, manufactured in chemical laboratories, contribute no calories and are not metabolized by the body. In this group we find saccharin and cyclamate, which has been banned in this country by the FDA.

Nutritive. Aspartame has as many calories as sugar. However, it is two hundred times as sweet, so less is needed to make foods palatable. In a study, volunteers who drank aspartame-sweetened water were hungrier afterward than those who drank sugar-sweetened water, causing researchers to conclude that aspartame may produce chemical changes in the brain that motivate us to eat.

Nonnutritive. Saccharin is three hundred times as sweet as sugar and only two calories per teaspoon, but it leaves a bitter aftertaste. Although saccharin retains its sweet taste when heated, it still leaves an unpleasant, bitter aftertaste. Under suspicion by the FDA, saccharin is thought to cause tumors in rats.

> To use less sugar, add a little more vanilla and spices that tend to increase sweetness.

So now what are you supposed to do if sugar, in all its various forms, takes you for a wild ride? Aspartame and saccharin increase your motivation to eat and make you hungry, and cyclamates are banned. Even though the concept of moderation is hard to swallow on Diet Day #3, it is an essential principle to practice where sweets are concerned. Our best bet for combating a sweet tooth is eating a well-balanced diet on a regular schedule. Follow the menus and recipe suggestions given on this day to satisfy your childhood sweet tooth, and develop a taste for fruit.

DINING OUT

Picture yourself on a Diet Day #3 socializing at every stop along the party circuit. You'll zero in on any excuse for a coffee break and be tempted to drop in on every happy hour. By the time you realize the need to curtail your flight schedule, you may already be grounded on account of a heavy tail section. Let me show you how to check in with your control tower, so you can safely navigate the heavy social traffic on a typical Diet Day #3.

You will be faced with many choices today. If you are tempted to forsake your diet, keep your goal in mind. Count on your Diet Day #3 desire to look your best to keep you on target. Draw upon the optimistic attitude you woke up with this morning. This is the kind of day when you can get exactly what you want if you ask for it exactly as you want it. Don't be shy. Use the charm you have in abundance today to flatter the waiter into bringing you slimming substitutions and salad dressing on the side. Get ready to send your compliments to the chef when your entrée arrives sautéed delicately instead of buried in butter.

AT A COFFEE SHOP

If you're in the mood to go "booth sliding" in a typical American coffee shop, let me warn you that you'll find plenty to grease your "skids"! Most of the menu selections belong under the heading "fried and filled." And if you could slip into the kitchen, you might discover that the fat in the fryer and grease on the grill are lard.

> Fat finders: Does it coat the roof of your mouth with a film? Does it look slippery or shiny? Would it make a grease spot if it were in a paper bag? Does it crunch without being a raw vegetable or fruit? Will your hands be greasy if you touch it?

On a Diet Day #3 you have plenty of imagination. By making careful selections, you can create a nineties experience while grazing in a fifties diner.

Starters. Fresh fruit or tomato juice with lemon is better than canned fruit cocktail submerged in sugary syrup.

Soup. If you can see the bottom of the bowl when the soup is served, you are probably safe. Cream of anything is out, but bean is an acceptable choice so long as it isn't made with bacon or salt pork. Choose from clear soups with more vegetables than rice, noodles, or meat.

Salad. Green salad made with fresh vegetables and dressing on the side is better than molded fruit gelatin or coleslaw, potato, and macaroni concoctions dressed with mayonnaise. Believe me, it looks better on the salad than it will on you. If you see Thousand Island dressing on the menu, read "1,000 calories" and move on.

Even the simple fruit and cottage cheese salad requires careful scrutiny. Verify that the fruit is fresh before the waitress presents you with peaches canned in heavy syrup and maraschino cherries.

Main dish salads such as those called Chef's, Caesar, and Louis are acceptable with minor alterations. Ask the chef to give you three times the amount of turkey and forget the cheese and ham. Send a message that the dressing for Caesar and Louis are not invited to your table; you want fresh lemon instead. Avoid tuna or chicken salad, even if it's stuffed into a tomato instead of an avocado. The tuna, probably canned in oil, and the chicken are bound together with mayonnaise, and that spells calories!

Sandwiches. Fillings without mayonnaise are preferable; sliced turkey breast is the best. Pass on the roast beef, ham, pastrami, and corned beef.

Sourdough bread is a good choice because it is usually made without sugar or fat. Order sandwiches toasted, not grilled; cold, not heated and gravy-soaked; dry, not slathered in mayonnaise. Live it up with mustard or ketchup; and if you have to go overboard, throw caution to the wind with dill pickles, unless you must limit your sodium.

> A tomato slice at 4 calories is a better addition to a sandwich than ketchup at 16 calories per tablespoon.
>
> A large dill pickle has only 6 calories, while a sweet pickle has 146.

Avoid sandwiches with names like clubhouse, Reuben, croissant, patty melt, or Monte Cristo. The last is a misnomer; it should be called Monte Crisco.

Entrées. Entrées with simple names are safer than the ones with fancy names that cover up the fact that they are precooked, with low-cost ingredients. Order something as unadulterated and unadorned as the ambience of the coffee shop. Skip the fried shrimp! Fish should be poached or broiled—without butter, pleeeeze! Skip the country fried chicken and the stuffed and sauced varieties like Kiev and divan. Choose broiled instead of roasted, which implies basting with fat, and braised, which means stewed in its own glistening juice. Believe me, all that glitters or, in this case, glistens is not gold. Roast turkey is a good choice if you avoid the skin, stuffing, and gravy. The mashed potatoes are probably "fresh" out of a box. Even though they have preservatives, they are somewhat safe unless they were reconstituted with whole milk or cream and butter.

Skip meat loaf and meat balls, which are usually made with less expensive ground meat that is full of fat. Even though it drips out during cooking, it is reabsorbed into the meat while it sits in the pan. If you simply must order a hamburger, skip the cheese at 100 calories a slice. Ask them to "hold the mayo" and substitute sliced tomatoes for french fries.

Desserts. You have tasted them all before, so don't bore yourself with the standard menu items like carrot cake. There isn't enough vitamin A in it to improve your eyesight; there is, however, enough oil in the cake and butter and cream cheese in the frosting to lube your car. Select fresh fruit or sherbet. If you must indulge in something from the rotating, mirrored bakery case, taste someone else's dessert or take two bites of your own and salt the rest of it, rendering it inedible.

> A ½-cup serving of the richest ice cream is 269 calories; sherbet is 135 calories; sorbet is 117 calories.

Drinks. Water, iced tea, decaf coffee, diet soda, low-fat milk, and juice diluted with lots of ice cubes are the best choices. Skip the half-and-half on the table in favor of low-fat milk for your decaf, and forget the soda fountain specialties. Better to treat yourself when you get home to a root beer float made with diet root beer and half a cup of ice milk.

AT A DELI

On a Diet Day #3 rely on your creativity to come up with a designer deli sandwich to satisfy your cravings and your calorie allowance. Today your communication skills are finely tuned, so you won't have any trouble describing exactly what you want to eat. It's worth waiting in line for a custom sandwich because of the opportunity to meet people.

To qualify as a deli delight, your savory sandwich should have a high ratio of crunch to ooze. Factor in more vegetable components, such as lettuce, shredded cabbage, sprouts, celery, tomatoes, cucumber, dill pickle slices, and radishes. In the ooze department, ask for exotic mustards or horseradish, and make sure to order a large drink of seltzer or club soda to put out the fire.

1 tablespoon prepared horseradish	7 calories
1 tablespoon mustard	4 calories
1 tablespoon regular mayonnaise	100 calories

In the bread department, ask for sourdough, rye, white, or wheat insted of a kaiser roll, bagel, or croissant. Choose turkey over beef, ham, pastrami, or corned beef. Avoid mayonnaise-based fillings such as chicken or tuna salad. Forgo the cheese that is offered, unless you are choosing jack cheese, Swiss, or a low-fat cheese like part-skim mozzarella as the main ingredient in your sandwich.

1 ounce jack cheese	100 calories
1 ounce Swiss cheese	100 calories
1 ounce Cheddar cheese	100 calories
1 ounce part-skim mozzarella	80 calories

Pass on side dish salads like macaroni, potato, or coleslaw, and instead of the usual potato chips, insist sweetly on a big order of crisp and crunchy kosher dills.

Of course, it may take all the charm you can muster to talk your way into some of the more esoteric ingredients for your deli delight, so call ahead if you really want it your way. When you get it just the way you ordered it, be sure to make a display of your appreciation. On a Diet Day #3 you're in the mood to lay it on thick.

AT A SALAD BAR

You don't need to be a lawyer to pass this bar, but it helps if you know your facts. Most salad dressing ladles hold 4 tablespoons, which can account for 260 to 400 calories, depending on the kind of dressing you choose. At a salad bar, you're safer with oil dressings that drip off lettuce leaves rather than cream-based dressings that cling. Diet dressing at 40 calories per ladle is a better choice, unless you opt for lemon, wine vinegar, or rice vinegar—none of which has any calories. Think of it this way: the calories you save when you skip the dressing can be used for something tasty that has less fat and is better for you.

Before you fill up your plate haphazardly, survey the selections. Often the less expensive, higher-calorie salads come first. The fresher, less fattening items come next. Choose the smallest plate and fill it to overflowing with low-calorie, vitamin-rich red leaf lettuce, spinach, romaine, kale, and cabbage.

> Greens are low in calories, sodium, and fat.

Raw salad greens. A 3½-ounce serving ranges between 11 and 50 calories.

Iceberg lettuce, although the most popular, is the least nutritious.

Bibb, Boston, or Butter lettuce, with a sweet, delicate taste, is only slightly more nutritious.

Romaine makes a good showing, with vitamins A and C and some calcium.

Loose leaf lettuce, more mild than romaine, is somewhat less nutritious.

Arugula or Roquette spices up a salad and contributes more than the daily recommended allowance of vitamins A and C and one-third the calcium.

Chicory or Curly Endive and Radicchio are slightly bitter but provide the daily allowance of vitamin A and one-third of the vitamin C needed daily.

Escarole, an endive with wide leaves, provides less than half the daily allowance of vitamin A.

> The darker green-leaf vegetables are more nutritious.

> Increase the absorption of iron in greens by eating foods high in vitamin C, such as tomatoes and citrus.

Spinach provides more than the daily allowance of vitamin A, plus folacin and potassium, but its iron is not as well absorbed by the body as iron from animal sources.

Watercress, noted for its pungent flavor, provides the daily recommended allowance of vitamin A, two-thirds of vitamin C and some calcium.

Dandelion greens, whose young raw leaves in salads and larger leaves sautéed with other vegetables add a pungent taste, supply almost three times the vitamin A recommended and half the vitamin C, as well as some calcium.

> Greens, especially the cabbage family (turnips, chard, kale, and collards), may lower the risk of some forms of cancer.

Turnip greens, strong in flavor and providing more nutrition than the turnip root, offer one and a half times as much vitamin A and all the vitamin C required, in addition to one-fifth the calcium required.

Swiss chard, mild in flavor, provides more than half the vitamins A and C required, plus some calcium.

Kale, with its cabbagelike flavor, provides twice the vitamins A and C required and some calcium.

Collards, with a strong cabbage flavor, provide three-fourths of the vitamin A recommended and half of the vitamin C.

> To cook greens, steam or sauté in chicken broth briefly to preserve nutrients and texture.

Recommended Daily Allowance

Vitamin A	4,000–5,000 I.U.
Vitamin C	60 mg
Fiber	25 g
Calcium	1,000 mg
Iron	18 mg

Although salad greens are thought to be high in fiber by most people, in fact only dandelion greens and kale have more than 1 gram of fiber per 100-gram serving.

Give yourself a green light for the fresh vegetable selections, which will net you a mere 5 to 20 calories per ½ cup if you choose the right ones. Learn to see an imaginary yellow light for caution when you come to canned foods like corn or pickled beets. And come to a screeching halt when your mental red light warns you against items that are swimming in sauce, bound by mayonnaise, or of undetermined origin.

For protein, select cottage cheese, which also makes a tasty substitute for dressing, and garbanzo or kidney beans. Be careful of the oil dressing on the three-bean salad unless you are willing to spend the calories.

Just because you have planned to avoid the dressings, don't think you are out of the woods. You still have to get by the condiments. Pretend you don't see the bacon bits, banana chips, grated coconut and cheese, croutons, and guacamole. If the sunflower seeds are raw or dry-roasted, add a sprinkle for crunch.

Breadsticks and crackers that don't leave greasy marks on your napkin are all right, so long as you don't pick up some butter to go with them. Ignore the muffins, croissants, and buttered Texas toast.

At the fruit bar, choose fresh melon, citrus fruits, apples, pears, or kiwi. Grapes and pineapple are slightly higher in calorie because of their high sugar content. Skip the ambrosia-type fruit salad with dressing and the sweetened yogurts.

½ cantaloupe	60 calories
1 orange	65 calories
½ grapefruit	50 calories
1 large apple	100 calories
10 seedless grapes	66 calories
1 slice pineapple	50 calories

Soup is safe if it is relatively clear. Vegetable, minestrone, and chicken noodle are preferred over cream soups. Bean soup and chili are acceptble, in moderation.

No-calorie decaffeinated drinks are the best. If you need cream in your coffee, ask for low-fat milk.

AT A BUFFET

If you are buffaloed by the buffet, think positively, plan ahead, and enjoy the challenge. Make a deal with yourself. If you can stick to a simple green salad with cottage cheese, a slice of turkey instead of ham or prime rib, and some fresh fruit, promise yourself a reward. Turn your back on the hash browns and the stuffed baked potatoes loaded with fatty cheese.

AT A STEAK HOUSE

The unkindest cut in a steak house is the tenderest cut. Melt-in-your-mouth New York strip steaks and Delmonico are marbled with fat. The amount of fat left in the meat depends upon the cooking time—the more well done, the more fat has been rendered from the meat.

Look for London broil at 200 calories less per serving than the more marbled cuts, and order it cooked medium. If the portion weighs enough to feed a family of four, ask for a "people" bag; or better yet, ask the waiter to prepare a 3-ounce portion and wrap the rest to take home. You can't eat what doesn't appear on your plate!

A better choice than prime or choice beef is the broiled fish or chicken that invariably appears on a steak house menu. Or you could make a meal out of the shrimp cocktail or oysters on the half shell you find on the appetizer list.

> Half the calories in chicken are in the skin, so be sure to remove it before you eat.

Dress your own salad and forgo the vegetables unless you can order them steamed without butter.

When the waiter arrives with the dessert cart to describe the usual mud pies and cheesecake, pretend you don't see him. Take desperate measures to avoid his description of the raspberry sauce that comes on the cheesecake and mud pies, served with sauce and shaved chocolate. Hide under the table as if searching for your napkin, or make a sweeping exit in the direction of the ladies' room, until it's safe to return to your sorbet and decaf.

AT A SEAFOOD HOUSE

Fish by itself is not high in calories. It's all the trimmings and the fat added in cooking that you have to avoid.

> The Omega-3 fatty acids in fish such as trout, catfish, sardines, and salmon appear to lessen the chance of heart attacks.

Appetizers. If you choose carefully, one or two items from the appetizer list and a salad can make a fine meal. Look for steamed clams and dip them in lemon juice with a little butter instead of butter with a little lemon juice. "Pick and peel" shrimp or crab is a dieter's best choice, because you eat slowly if you eat as you pick. Consider shrimp cocktail with red sauce but no tartar sauce.

On the appetizer list, avoid selections like clams casino or oysters Rockefeller, which are topped with buttered bread crumbs.

> If you dip your fork in the sauce before you spear the shrimp, the last taste in your mouth is the sauce. You'll think you're getting more sauce than you really are. This works beautifully with salad dressings, too.

Soups. Tomato-based Manhattan clam chowder is a better choice than the New England variety made with butter, cream, and flour. Clear seafood gumbo, even with rice, is a better choice than creamy seafood bisque.

Salads. Shrimp or crab Louis with dressing on the side makes a whole meal. When a squeeze of fresh lemon enhances the taste of fresh seafood, why overpower its delicate flavors by smothering it in an oily dressing?

Entrées. Avoid combination seafood platters featuring fried fish and high-calorie concoctions like crab cakes. Skip anything stuffed, like sole filled with crab, which is loaded with butter. Pass on the white sauces, whether they are hot and bubbling with cheese or cold and full of sweet pickle relish and mayonnaise. If you cannot resist lobster, skip the Thermidor and Newburg versions and order it broiled without butter. Baked fish creole with tomatoes, herbs, and spices is a tasty low-calorie dish.

> The darker the flesh of the fish, the fattier the fish.

Calories in Fish per 3½-Ounce Serving

Ocean Fish		Freshwater Fish	
Salmon	163	Lake trout	169
Tuna	145	Catfish	157
Whitefish	121	Rainbow trout	154
Halibut	119		
Swordfish	118	**Shellfish**	
Flounder	94	Lobster	151
Striped bass	92	Shrimp	89
Grouper	89	Crab	86
Snapper	88	Scallops	80
Shark	87		
Sole	83		
Cod	74		

To gain the cooperation of the kitchen, tell your waiter that if your fish is cooked with butter, to which you are highly allergic, you will die right in the middle of the restaurant—very bad for business! Never mind how to get the fish off the grill without using butter; that's the chef's problem.

For future reference at home, the secret to getting fish off the grill is Pam and a white wine baste that keeps the fish moist. The alcohol calories from the wine evaporate in cooking.

Vegetables. Ask for steamed vegetables with no oil or butter. Rice is questionable, because it is usually cooked with butter or turned into a pilaf, which involves sautéing the rice before it is steamed. Instead, order a plain baked potato with lots of lemon and several turns of the pepper mill.

Desserts. If fresh fruit isn't available, choose sorbet instead of ice cream or creamy sherbet.

AT A HAPPY HOUR OR COCKTAIL PARTY

Before you go out. Don't starve the day of the party in anticipation of the feast. Not only will you slow down your metabolism, you will be even hungrier when you arrive and unable to resist overeating. Instead, your preparty strategy should include several small meals during the day, along with plenty of water.

Prior to going out, exercise in order to decrease your appetite. After a workout you're usually more aware of your body and will think twice about overeating. If possible, take a short nap to eliminate the chance that you might eat because you are tired. Just before you leave home, eat a small, nutritious snack and drink something hot, such as soup or decaf, so your appetite will be under control. Wear a tight belt or tight underclothes as a reminder not to overindulge.

Mentally rehearse the party and develop a plan. Will it be a cocktail party, an all-night Tex-Mex feast, or a sit-down dinner? Visualize the likely temptations and how you are going to avoid them. Picture yourself in control of your eating. This method works for me because I believe that thoughts are things, and what I think about I bring about.

To ensure the availability of "slim pickin's," offer to bring a vegetable platter you can eat. If the hostess seems hesitant, tell her you have already bought all the ingredients and it will be so gorgeous she won't need a centerpiece. Then go to the store and do yourself proud. While you're at it, pick up some of your favorite designer water and noncaloric drinks to take along, the more sophisticated the better. You don't want to be stuck drinking brandy Alexanders at 100 calories per sip if that's all they are serving.

Familiarize yourself with the calorie count of cocktail party food so you can make educated choices. Generally, plan to avoid cheeses of all types, especially Brie baked in pastry, cheese fondue, and quiche of all kinds. Steer clear of anything fried, such as mini egg rolls, chimechangas, fried wontons, and potato chips. Avoid things in oil; marinated artichoke hearts are 40 calories each, and stuffed grape leaves will cost you 50 calories apiece. The biggest offender is guacamole with corn chips, at 330 calories for ½ cup and 10 measly chips. For information on the calorie count of alcoholic beverages, see page 241.

At the party. On a Diet Day #3 it's easy to focus on the party guests and not the food. Be the belle of the ball. As you charm everyone with your scintillating conversation, heed the childhood admonishments that are playing in your head today. If your mother always told you not to talk with your mouth full, turn her admonitions into diet ammunition. Talk a lot and eat a little.

Stay out of the kitchen, where you might be asked to taste something. It's all right to help the hostess by passing food, so long as you clutch your no-cal drink in the other hand. If someone passes you the hors d'oeuvres, for heaven's sake don't whine about being on a diet. Remember, it's safer to pick from food that is passed, because it walks away from you, and cold hors d'oeuvres are usually less fattening.

At a sit-down dinner, don't make a big deal out of asking for small portions unless you can do so easily. Take a taste of each food and leave the rest. If you don't draw attention to your eating, neither will anyone else. Concentrate on the company, not the food.

DIET DOWNFALLS AND THEIR SOLUTIONS

On a Diet Day #3 you will hear all the parental messages from your childhood playing like audio tapes in your head. For instance, phrases like "Here's a lollipop for the brave little patient" or "Have a cookie, you'll feel better" may come back to haunt you today. In my case, I was a sickly child who grew up believing that my ill health was a result of not eating enough or properly. I spent my early adulthood purposely consuming three square meals daily from the four basic food groups, and all the junk food I liked, too. Consequently, I ended up healthy but fat! It's important for you to tap into your inner child on a Diet Day #3 to understand how you are manipulated as an adult by voices from your past. What food habits from childhood do you need to change?

A friend of my mother's confesses with great humor that she has never outgrown her ten o'clock bottle. Still in the habit of snacking before bedtime, this lively octogenarian has carried her childhood tape a long time. Milk and cookies at night or after-school treats are habits that can last a lifetime. Those of us with school-aged children at home are constantly bombarded with childhood food cues that can accumulate unattractively on an adult body. You don't need to give up those snacks if you include them, in moderation, as part of your total calorie count for the day.

> Figure out how to make low-calorie versions of the snacks you loved as a kid. Duplicate the taste, not the calories.

Today your inner child wants it when it wants it. Before you give in to your impulsive desires, the adult in you must ask, "Is it really worth it?" Calorie burning depends on many factors. Your age, sex, height, weight, your ratio of fat to lean body mass, the time of day you eat, your activity level all make a difference. However, assuming you weigh 150 pounds, are you willing to expend the time and effort it takes to walk off the following goodies?

	Minutes		Minutes
Banana split	143	Bagel and cream cheese	82
Cheeseburger	136	Danish	72
Burrito	123	Doughnut	54
Pancakes with butter, syrup	120	Beer	39
Cup of macaroni and cheese	113	Small slice of pizza	38
Cup of ice cream	97	Small bag of potato chips	38
Chocolate milkshake	93	Glass of white wine	22

The obvious alternative to food is gum. Choose sugarless, if sorbitol doesn't adversely affect you. According to your surroundings, you may be able to get away with the ultimate regression, bubble gum; or you may have to chew surreptitiously, avoiding so much as a snap or a pop that might tarnish your image.

Rely on toys if you want to fiddle your way through those tempting times at work when you are cornered in the coffee room with doughnuts and other delights. Whip out your little bag of jacks and entertain yourself and everyone around you. Chances are you will become so engrossed with your efforts at coordination, you will forget about eating and the urge will pass.

If you run out of childlike pursuits, which is highly unlikely on a Diet Day #3, capitalize on the increased interest you have in your appearance today. Go through the back issues of all your magazines and fill a folder with pictures of clothes you dream of wearing when you reach your ideal weight. Paste photographs of your face on the models bodies wearing your favorites, and use them to decorate your refrigerator door. Add a picture of yourself taken when you were pleased with your weight, and look at them every day.

I recommend erasing the old tapes and recording some new messages. Think before you reach. When someone offers you a dish of your favorite dessert ask yourself if you are really hungry. Savor one bite and tell yourself the second bite doesn't taste any different from the first.

Once you are aware of all the games you've been playing with food, start playing some alternative games and create new strategies to cope with the temptation food presents.

EXERCISE

On a Diet Day #3 you're a kid at heart and in the mood to play, not work, at exercise. To choose an activity that will burn off calories, draw on your fondest memories of childhood pastimes, such as biking, jumping rope, roller skating, and skipping, to name a few.

Take advantage of your desire to be social today by emphasizing the recreational aspect of exercise. Make an exercise date or plan a group outing that includes physical activity. To capitalize on your need to look your best on a Diet Day #3, dress for the occasion. *Whatever* exercise you choose, enjoy yourself. Invite your inner child to come out and play!

BICYCLING

If your bike played a big part in your childhood, you are likely to enjoy the sport as an adult. Whether you choose a stationary bike, a roadworthy multispeed racer, or an off-road mountain bike with knobby tires, bicycling will help you recapture the youthful image so important to you on a Diet Day #3.

> Bicycling for an hour at 5½ mph burns 210 calories; at 13 mph, 660 calories.

As a result of moving your heels up and down as you pedal, your calves will become trimmer and sleeker. Since the shinbone is connected to the thighbone and the thighbone is connected to the hipbone, your whole leg will benefit. As the long muscles in the front and back of your thighs develop, you may even be happier about your appearance in shorts or a bathing suit. Your upper body, particularly your shoulders and upper arms, benefit if you pull up on the handle bars.

On a Diet Day #3 you aren't averse to being the center of attention, so go for it. Put on your hot pink sweat suit and your Mickey Mouse T-shirt and give the neighbors something to talk about.

Although bicycling is long on aerobic conditioning and short on injuries as a non-weight-bearing activity, you should check with your doctor if you decide to become more than an occasional Diet Day #3 cyclist. To give the idea a test spin, borrow a bike from a neighborhood kid before you invest in the real thing. On a Diet Day #3 you can hear your mom telling you not to ride on the handlebars, so if you take the big step, purchase safety equipment, such as the helmet and the jazzy outfits with the tight pants that don't get caught in the spokes. If you are a member of a health club, you can join the beautiful people who ride stationary bikes in the window, a very appealing image on a Diet Day #3. Or buy your own two-wheeler to ride in front of your favorite TV sitcom at home. My eldest daughter, Jamie, watches her two favorite soap operas as she pedals. Or split your time between two favorite half-hour programs, one in the morning and one at night, like my friend Alexa. She puruses while she pedals, and she has kissed her weight problem good-bye. I like to talk on the telephone while I ride my stationary two-wheeler.

JUMPING ROPE

If you want to keep it simple, exercising with a jump rope is a good choice. Barring knee, ankle, or other orthopedic problems, you should have no trouble with this form of exercise, which requires little expense, space, or equipment. Jumping rope involves large muscles groups, is rhythmic, and can be continued for long periods of time in any weather. On a Diet Day #3, when your attention span isn't too long, jumping rope may be just what the doctor ordered. But be sure to ask!

If you are a beginner, try jumping with anything you can find around the house, until you are mildly fatigued. The dog's leash or an old clothesline will do. Later buy a cotton rope that won't sting when it hits the back of your legs or a real jump rope from a sporting goods store. Wear shoes that absorb the impact, and pick a forgiving surface such as a wood floor. Although carpet lessens the impact, it makes jumping difficult over a long period of time. At first, alternate feet instead of jumping on both at the same time. It's easier and will reduce your chances of injuries such as knee problems and shin splints. Build up slowly, and maintain your progress by recording your time.

> Depending upon weight and age, a beginner usually jumps 55 to 75 jumps per minute to burn 11 calories; 125 to 145 jumps per minute burn up 15 calories per minute.

TRAMPOLINING

If your knees have aged faster than your attitude, you can still jump if you use a small trampoline. Relatively inexpensive as exercise equipment goes, it's lots of fun and helps you to work up a good heart rate for aerobic effect. Because the springs of a trampoline assist your rebound, you will have to keep at it longer than if jumping on a hard surface to enjoy the same calorie-burning results. Check your target heart rate for maximum exercise benefit.

ROLLER SKATING

If you aren't hanging on to the rail for dear life, roller skating provides a good workout for the upper body as well as legs and cardiovascular system. Make sure your memory of your expertise isn't inflated, or you may fall flat on your face. Take a lesson from me. Don't show off wearing your kid's skates and skirt in front of your house. I don't recommend the kind of cellulite treatment I got when I fell on my asphalt . . . driveway, that is.

On the other hand, if you make your comeback appearance or maiden voyage on skates at the roller rink in the company of two strong, supportive friends, you may rediscover a truly entertaining form of exercise.

> Roller skating for an hour burns up 350 calories.

SKIPPING AND HOPPING

Remember skipping home from school to tell your mom you got 100 on the spelling test or more valentines than your archrival? A fast-paced step, hop, step, hop is exhilarating. Even my conservative friend Gregg enjoys skipping as an alternative to our evening walks.

Don't forget hopscotch! It's a great way to warm up or cool down from any exercise on a Diet Day #3. All you need are chalk, a sidewalk to write on, a pebble to mark your place, and a friend, imaginary or otherwise.

WALKING

If you choose walking for exercise on this Diet Day #3, grab your inner child by the hand. Take giant steps, and don't walk on the cracks or "you'll break your mother's back." And be optimistic. Walk a little farther than you did the last time. Or combine window-shopping and walking. Strolling won't do you as much good as a brisk walk, so pick up the pace on the street or check into fitness walking at the local mall. Most indoor facilities are open twenty-four hours.

> One hour of walking can burn 200 to 300 calories, depending on your pace.

RECIPES FOR DIET DAY #3

The following menus and recipes have been created to appeal to your social, outgoing mood on a Diet Day #3. To accommodate a schedule riddled by spontaneous interruptions, many suggestions are easy to prepare. Your inner child will delight in the low-calorie duplicates of childhood favorites, especially the treats designed to satisfy your sweet tooth.

A buffet, where you could be tempted by too many choices typical of a Diet Day #3, is the featured restaurant for dining out.

Food for Thought deals with the expansive overtone of the day, which might extend to the waistline if you aren't careful. Each message encourages you to chew on the positive characteristics of the day to nourish your soul as well as your body.

Menu 1

FOOD FOR THOUGHT

A smile is a curve that can set a lot of things straight.

BREAKFAST
(280 calories)

1 cup Cheerios
1 cup nonfat milk
1 6-inch banana

LUNCH
(160 calories)

½ can Campbell's Vegetarian Vegetable Alphabet Soup
*Bricks and Sticks**
*Gregarious Grape Drink**

SNACK
(115 calories)

*Root Beer Float**

DINNER
(315 calories)

¾ cup Chef Boyardee Dinosaurs
*Popeye Salad**
1 slice sourdough bread, no butter
1 can diet orange soda

BEDTIME SNACK
(140 calories)

12 Health Valley Oat Bran Animal crackers
1 cup nonfat milk

TOTAL CALORIES 1,010
PROTEIN 20%
CARBOHYDRATE 66%
FAT 14%

* Recipes follow.

BRICKS AND STICKS

1 ounce Laughing Cow Cheese (6 ⅙-ounce cubes)
12 pretzel sticks

Unwrap the cheese cubes and stick 2 pretzels in each.

Serves 1

GREGARIOUS GRAPE DRINK

2 tablespoons grape juice
8 ounces sparkling water
Ice cubes

Combine the grape juice and sparkling water in a tall glass with ice cubes.

Serves 1

ROOT BEER FLOAT

1 can diet root beer, chilled
½ cup vanilla Dreyer's Grand Light "Light" dairy dessert

Pour the root beer into a tall glass. Top with dairy dessert and serve with a spoon.

Serves 1

POPEYE SALAD

4 cups spinach, thoroughly washed and torn into bite-size pieces
1 cup frozen peas, thawed
1 carrot, grated
1 tomato, chopped
½ green bell pepper, chopped
4 mushrooms, sliced

Dressing

½ cup low-fat cottage cheese
4 tablespoons Wish-Bone Lite Classic Dijon Vinaigrette reduced-calorie dressing

Combine the salad ingredients in a large bowl. In a small bowl, mix the cottage cheese and dressing. Pour it over the salad and toss to serve.

Serves 4

Menu 2

FOOD FOR THOUGHT

Cheerfulness is what greases the axles of the world. Remember that if you hear yourself squeaking.

BREAKFAST
(240 calories)

*Nutty Fruit Sundae**

LUNCH
(360 calories)

*Grilled Tuna and Cheese Sandwich**
*Bunny Food**
1 cup Crystal Light fruit punch

SNACK
(90 calories)

Dole Fruit and Cream Bar

DINNER
(278 calories)

*Sloppy Serape**
*Green and White Trees**
*Orange Sparkler**

* Recipes follow.

CIRCUS SNACK
(110 calories)

1 can diet chocolate soda
3 peanut shells (9 peanuts)

TOTAL CALORIES 1,078
PROTEIN 22%
CARBOHYDRATE 55%
FAT 23%

* Recipes follow.

NUTTY FRUIT SUNDAE

½ apple, cored and chopped
½ banana, peeled and sliced
½ orange, peeled and chopped
½ cup nonfat plain yogurt
2 tablespoons Post Grape Nuts cereal

Place the fruit in a bowl. Top with yogurt and Grape Nuts.

Serves 1

GRILLED TUNA AND CHEESE SANDWICH

1 6½-ounce can water-packed white tuna, drained
1 teaspoon onion powder
2 carrots, grated
½ cup chopped tomato
2 tablespoons minced fresh parsley
1 teaspoon lemon juice
2 tablespoons nonfat plain yogurt
2 teaspoons diet mayonnaise
4 rice cakes
1 ounce Weight Watchers cheddar cheese, grated

In a bowl, mix together the tuna, onion powder, carrots, tomato, parsley, lemon juice, yogurt, and mayonnaise. Spread on rice cakes. Sprinkle the tops with cheese. Broil until the cheese melts.

Serves 2

BUNNY FOOD

1 carrot, peeled
1 stalk celery, washed and trimmed

Cut into sticks.

Serves 1

SLOPPY SERAPE

¾ cup Health Valley vegetarian chili, heated
1 corn tortilla, steamed

Wrap the chili in the tortilla, and wear a bib as you eat.

Serves 1

GREEN AND WHITE TREES

½ cup raw broccoli
½ cup raw cauliflower

Wash and trim the vegetables, leaving long stems on the florets to resemble trees.

Serves 1

ORANGE SPARKLER

2 tablespoons orange juice
8 ounces sparkling water
Ice cubes

Combine in a tall glass. Stir.

Serves 1

Menu 3

FOOD FOR THOUGHT

Make the most of the best and the least of the worst.

BREAKFAST

(220 calories)

*Berry Good Pancakes**

LUNCH

(205 calories)

*Lick the Bowl Soup**
Carrot Coins (1 carrot, sliced into medallions)
2 Pogen Krisprolls
1 can diet orange soda

SNACK

(190 calories)

*Ants on a Log**

DINNER

(315 calories)

*Musical Bowls Curry**
½ cup brown rice
Celestial Seasonings Mandarin Orange herb tea

DESSERT

(135 calories)

*Luscious Lemon Cheesecake**
Celestial Seasonings Lemon Zinger herb tea

TOTAL CALORIES 1,065
PROTEIN 26%
CARBOHYDRATE 49%
FAT 25%

* Recipes follow.

BERRY GOOD PANCAKES

2 4-inch pancakes made from Aunt Jemina Lite Buttermilk Complete Pancake Mix
¼ cup nonfat plain yogurt
½ cup berries of your choice, fresh or frozen without sugar

Make pancakes according to package directions. Top them with yogurt and berries.

Serves 1

LICK THE BOWL SOUP

1 leek, chopped
1 pound mushrooms, cleaned and sliced
1 bunch scallions, sliced
3 cups Swanson's Natural Goodness chicken broth
⅓ cup nonfat plain yogurt
2 tablespoons part-skim ricotta cheese
½ teaspoon lemon juice
⅛ teaspoon salt
⅛ teaspoon black pepper

Cut off the green top of the leek. Vertically slit open the white portion. Wash thoroughly under running water. Dry and chop.

In a 3-quart saucepan, combine the mushrooms, leek, scallions, and broth. Bring to a boil and simmer until the vegetables are tender, about 30 minutes.

Put half of the hot soup in the blender and purée. Transfer to clean saucepan and keep warm. To the remaining vegetable mixture add the yogurt, ricotta cheese, and lemon juice. Process in the blender until smooth. Add to the saucepan. Heat to serving temperature, but do not boil. To serve, season with salt and pepper.

Serves 4

ANTS ON A LOG

1 stalk celery
1½ teaspoons peanut butter
6 raisins

Wash and trim the celery. Fill with peanut butter and top with raisins.

Serves 1

MUSICAL BOWLS CURRY

12 ounces boneless, skinless chicken breast
1 tablespoon diet margarine
1 tablespoon flour
1 cup Swanson's Natural Goodness chicken broth
¼ cup nonfat milk
¼ cup chopped onions
2 cloves garlic, mashed
¼ teaspoon cinnamon
1 teaspoon curry powder
1 small apple, cored, peeled, and chopped
½ teaspoon grated lemon rind

Condiments

¼ cup sliced water chestnuts
¼ cup minced scallions
½ cup chopped celery
¼ cup diced seeded cucumber
⅛ cup raisins
⅛ cup peanuts

Broil the chicken breast for 6 minutes on each side, or until done, and keep hot. In a nonstick skillet, melt the margarine, add the flour, and cook until golden brown. Stir in the broth and milk and bring to a boil. Turn down the heat and add the onions, garlic, cinnamon, curry, and apple. Simmer over low heat for 15 to 20 minutes.

Put the curry mixture in a food processor or blender and process until smooth. Add the lemon rind. To serve, pour the sauce over the broiled chicken breasts and pass the condiments in separate bowls. To avoid confusion at the table, everyone should pass the bowls in the same direction.

Serves 4

LUSCIOUS LEMON CHEESECAKE

4 ounces part-skim ricotta cheese
12 ounces low-fat cottage cheese
2 eggs
4 tablespoons nonfat dry powdered milk
2 tablespoons sugar
1 teaspoon vanilla extract
⅛ teaspoon lemon extract
½ teaspoon grated lemon rind
2 egg whites
⅛ teaspoon cream of tartar

Using an electric beater, blend until smooth the ricotta cheese, cottage cheese, eggs, powdered milk, sugar, vanilla, lemon extract, and lemon rind.

In a separate bowl, beat the egg whites with cream of tartar until soft peaks form. Fold them into the cheese mixture until thoroughly blended.

Pour the batter into an 8-inch Pyrex pie dish that has been sprayed with Pam. Bake at 350° for 30 to 35 minutes, or until the top is lightly browned and a toothpick inserted in the center comes out clean. Let cool on a rack at room temperature, then refrigerate until well chilled.

Serves 6

Menu 4

EATING OUT AT A BUFFET AND SALAD BAR

FOOD FOR THOUGHT

Instead of grumbling because roses have thorns, be thankful that thorns have roses.

BREAKFAST BUFFET
(280 calories)

1 poached egg
1 mini bagel (3 inches across) **or** *1 English muffin, unbuttered*
Fresh fruit of the day

LUNCH AT A SALAD BAR
(340 calories)

2 cups leafy greens
2 tablespoons grated raw carrot
1 tablespoon grated raw zucchini
¼ cup raw cauliflower
¼ cup raw broccoli
2 tablespoons alfalfa sprouts
2 tablespoons sliced raw mushrooms
3 cucumber slices
2 radishes
2 jicama slices
2 tablespoons red kidney beans
1 teaspoon raisins
1 marinated artichoke heart
1 teaspoon raw sunflower seeds
1 teaspoon Parmesan cheese
2 tablespoons red wine vinegar
2 6-inch breadsticks
Iced tea with lemon

DINNER BUFFET
(400 calories)

3 ounces breast of turkey
½ baked potato or ½ cup wild rice
½ cup green beans
½ cup mushrooms vinaigrette
1 piece sourdough bread
½ cup melon balls
Decaffeinated coffee

TOTAL CALORIES 1,020
PROTEIN 26%
CARBOHYDRATE 59%
FAT 15%

DIET DAY #4

PLANNING AHEAD

This is a day in which you'll find yourself in a practical mood. You're ready to plan ahead and deal with details. Tasks associated with numbers, like weighing food and measuring portions, are appealing. And the urge to be thrifty is so strong today that you will actually enjoy balancing your checkbook and sticking to your budget. You'll be dreaming up casseroles to use up leftovers, and your heart will leap at the sight of a cents-off coupon in the morning paper. It's a great day to put yourself on a schedule, even down to the times you plan to eat. Make a list of the foods you need and go to the market. Reorganize your cupboards as you put away your groceries. Fill up the freezer by cooking ahead. Most important: capitalize on your thrifty mood by saving calories as well as money!

SUPERMARKET SURVIVAL

To emerge from a supermarket with your diet still intact, you need to plan ahead. Temptation lurks on every shelf, especially along the aisles in the middle of the store. There, arranged to catch your eye, all the processed, convenience foods lie in wait. Displays at the ends of the aisles feature stacks that overwhelm you into buying. Kids' favorites are strategically placed down where they can see and reach them, while the adult goodies are placed at grown-up eye level. The worst spot in the store is usually near the check-out counter, where you are forced to stand eyeball to eyeball with cute little packages of jelly beans and gumdrops. Ignore their siren call, and you'll be outsmarting the million-dollar advertising efforts of the food giants. And that's just the thing to make your frugal Diet Day #4 heart sing. If you can push that cart by a display that really makes you drool, give yourself a congratulatory pat on the pocketbook. Big business doesn't control your salivary glands, you do!

Strengthen your resolve to shop smart. Don't walk into a supermarket without a full stomach, a list, a pencil to mark off the items as you buy them, and a pack of sugarless gum. If you need glasses to read the fine print on the labels, bring them, too. If possible, shop by yourself. It's hard enough to say "no" to yourself; you don't need your children pleading for goodies as you round every aisle.

Arrange your list according to the layout of the store, to bypass the land mines in the bakery section and the freezer case. Confine your exploration to the outer perimeters of the market, where you will find the fresh produce, fresh fish and poultry, and the dairy case. Even in the so-called safety zone there will be temptations. Watch out for the individually wrapped candy in the big bins next to the potatoes. Be on the alert for the so-called real fruit yogurt next to the plain variety; those larger-than-life strawberries pictured on the carton are really pretty puny and loaded with sugar. You can make your own fruit yogurt that tastes and looks better.

> Homemade fruit yogurt: nonfat plain yogurt; unsweetened fruit (fresh, frozen, or canned in its own juice) or frozen fruit juice concentrate; vanilla, cinnamon, or nutmeg.

To maintain the high nutritional value of produce frozen at the peak of freshness, make sure you buy packages that are frozen solid, undamaged, and frost-free. Check bags of vegetables such as peas and corn to see that they are loose, not frozen in a lump, a sure sign of poor handling that allowed thawing and refreezing.

On a Diet Day #4 you are more than equal to the task of making wise choices in the face of an overwhelming number of tantalizing options. However, in your frugal mood, don't be caught in the trap of believing that all cents-off coupons are a good deal. Think about it: how often do you see a coupon for fresh fruit? Usually it's a come-on for a new convenience product high in sodium, preservatives, *calories,* and *price*. Look for coupons that offer savings on diet products, single-serving frozen vegetables, and household products you really need. If you are feeling too thrifty on a Diet Day #4 to buy skinless, boneless chicken breasts instead of less expensive whole chicken, ask yourself if it is really worth your time to skin and bone it. Of course, you can always collect the bones in a plastic bag in the freezer and use them to add flavor to soups. Another thrifty impulse you may have to curb on a Diet

Day #4 is the urge to stock up on the large, economy-size package of something you don't need in the first place.

> A maxim for dieters: if you don't buy it, you can't eat it.

Food shopping for a growing family often represents trouble for the dieter. Fortunately, on a Diet Day #4 you can appeal to the upstanding, truthful mood you are in, and admit that the cookies you are about to buy aren't really for the children. Tap into your "by the book" frame of mind and decide to set a good example for your family. If the high-calorie junk food is a problem for you, it probably isn't good for anyone at your house. Stock up on fresh fruit instead of the usual snacks, and put the whole crew on your healthy diet.

If a snack attack hits you while you are innocently traversing the aisles from diet soda to crackers in search of rice cakes, there are several diversionary tactics you can follow to extricate yourself from impending disaster. I rummage madly through my purse for a fresh piece of sugarless gum, trying not to foam at the mouth as I stare down at my favorite box of seasoned sesame sensations. Then I imagine the picture of a skull and crossbones on the offending cracker box. I just tell myself it's poison and keep on truckin'. If you consider your hunger an emergency, cruise by the refrigerator case for a diet soda to drink. Save the empty can so you can pay for it. Meanwhile, this is an opportune time to make a determined detour to the aisle where you will find five- and ten-pound sacks of flour. They are provided in all markets for the express purpose of showing you how much that amount of extra weight feels when you have to lug it around. (And you thought flour and sugar in big bags were for baking?) Pick up ten pounds of unbleached flour and carry it around the store under you arm, as a reminder of what you could be carrying permanently around your middle if you make a habit of giving in to your whims. If that lesson doesn't hit home, do what I did. Sidle up to the meat case and ring that little bell for the butcher. When he comes out, try to keep a straight face while you ask him to sell you three packages of fat, a one-pound, half-pound, and quarter-pound. Tell him to wrap it for freezing in clear plastic so you can see the stuff in all its corpulent glory. When I am tempted to munch, I take the one-pound package out of the freezer and picture that amount of fat loosely packed around my middle. Conjure up the vision of the congealed contents of the half-pound package clinging to each thigh or a quarter of a pound of the stuff hanging pendulously from each upper arm. Remember, *indulge* rhymes with *bulge*.

COOKING AHEAD

Now you're ready to cook up a storm, so long as you aren't too hungry or tired. Like food shopping, food preparation should never be undertaken on an empty stomach. Schedule your sessions in the kitchen for after a meal. Pour yourself a big glass of your favorite designer water and break out the sugarless gum. Put on an apron and tie it tightly enough to remind yourself that you are there to cook, not eat. Give up the notion that a proper cook tastes along the way to correct the seasonings. The recipes in this book are tested; trust me!

I distract myself from the food I am preparing by listening to the radio or watching television. While you are waiting for a pot to boil, keep busy with detailed tasks such as sharpening knives and alphabetizing your spices. On a Diet Day #4 you have systems on your mind, so it's an ideal time to clean the refrigerator or reorganize your cupboards. Be an efficiency expert; arrange the items in your kitchen for easy access. Store the ingredients you use most often toward the front of your cabinets. Hang measuring spoons and other utensils within easy reach, or keep them handy in a pretty container near the stove.

Take inventory. Do you have the proper equipment to make your kitchen an efficient workplace? Some tools for a fat-free kitchen are:

- Gravy separator to separate and discard fat
- Nonstick pans to fry without fat
- Hot-air popcorn popper or a paper bag and a microwave
- Measuring cups and spoons to keep you honest with oil and mayonnaise
- Food scale to measure servings accurately
- Vegetable cooking spray (Pam) to replace oil and butter in frying
- Grater to shred cheese (goes farther than sliced)

Some tools for a healthy kitchen:

- Metal steamer basket to preserve vitamins in cooked vegetables
- Cast-iron skillet to add iron, especially to high-acid foods like tomatoes
- Vegetable scrubber to wash edible peels so you can eat them and benefit from their vitamins and fiber

Some tools for a thrifty kitchen:

- Ice cube trays for making milk cubes, chicken broth cubes, spaghetti sauce cubes
- Blender or food processor to turn last night's vegetables into soup du jour
- Microwave to heat up leftovers

In spite of all your efforts to keep busy in the kitchen, the aromas of food cooking may trigger your impulse to eat, so turn on the fan over the stove or throw open the window even in the dead of winter. If the sight of food tempts you to taste, hide the seductive stuff under a lid. And if all else fails, put it on the back burner to simmer, and take your urge to eat for a walk.

STORAGE

Once you have completed the cooking phase, you are ready to get out the scale and the measuring cups. Check the recipes for serving sizes, and be accurate. I have found that the quickest way to sabotage a diet is to "eyeball" the amount of the servings. On a Diet Day #4 you're in the mood to be precise, so count those beans, level those cups, and check those ounces. Guesstimating will get you in trouble every time!

> Use your food scale. The difference between 4 and 6 ounces of skinless, boneless chicken breast is 65 calories.

If there are any leftovers that won't fit into your containers, feed them to the dog without hesitation! Think of all the years you have been eliminating waste by eating it. And what have you really accomplished? The elimination of your waist!

Your organizational skills are at an all-time high on a Diet Day #4, so you should be able to come up with a super system for labeling foods and arranging them in your freezer. The labels should be large enough for you to write the contents, date they were frozen, and number of the Diet Day for which they are planned.

When I prepare foods for freezer storage I use a gadget that heat-seals plastic bags that can be filled with food, frozen, and reheated by boiling the bag or heating in the microwave. Assorted small plastic containers are also useful for storage, but they need to be washed and they take up shelf space. Individual plastic bags for heat sealers are available in various sizes, but I like the convenience and low cost of the continuous rolls of plastic. I can heat-seal any size bag I want, depending on the amount of food I need to store.

If you are making a casserole in a dish that you do not wish to store in the freezer, line the dish with foil before you fill it for cooking. When the food has cooled, remove it, foil and all, from the dish. Wrap with additional foil and freeze. To reheat, remove the foil and place the frozen food in the original dish.

To allow for the expansion of liquids as they freeze, leave a ¾-inch space at the top of the container; otherwise, plastic bags and containers may pop open in the freezing process. Pressing the extra air out of a plastic bag before you seal it will keep food inside fresher, and the bag will take up less space in the freezer.

> Tomatoes and some fruit juices contain acid, which will cause tiny holes to form in aluminum foil over long periods of freezer storage. For best results, store these foods in plastic.

Decide what method you will use to reheat foods before you wrap them for freezing. Use foil for conventional ovens and plastic wrap, which can be loosened or pierced, for microwaving. Putting quantities of warm food in your freezer will cause the temperature to rise. Before freezing a large amount of food, cool it briefly at room temperature and chill it in the refrigerator. Remember, reheating frozen foods that have already been cooked adds to the total cooking time. For best texture and quality, undercook recipes that you intend to freeze and reheat.

In addition to cooked foods, you will have many fresh items to store. To preserve vitamins and freshness, each of the following fruits and vegetables is handled differently. Potatoes, onions, and garlic should be stored in a dark, well-ventilated cool place. Rinse and drain trimmed celery, leeks, scallions, and fresh herbs such as watercress and parsley and store them in sealed plastic bags. Parsley can also be stored in a covered water-filled container or minced and frozen. Leafy green vegetables should be washed, dried, wrapped in paper towels, and refrigerated in sealed plastic bags. A lettuce spinner comes in very handy for this process. Store mushrooms in a paper bag in the refrigerator, to allow air to circulate. Clean with a soft brush or paper towel just before using. Avoid washing mushrooms, as they absorb water very quickly and will become soggy. Vegetables that can be refrigerated unwashed in plastic bags are artichokes, asparagus, beets, broccoli, Brussels sprouts, cabbage, carrots, cauliflower, chayotes, Chinese pea pods, corn on the cob in the husk, cucumbers, eggplant, fennel, green beans, parsnips, peas in the pod, green and red peppers, rutabagas, summer squash, and turnips. Ripe fruits last several days without washing if they are refrigerated, loosely wrapped in plastic. Blemished or overripe fruit should be discarded so it won't spoil the rest. Leave berries unwashed in their store containers. No matter how carefully you store fresh produce, it will deteriorate after a while, so buy only what you can use within a few days.

Freeze foods in the most convenient, ready-to-use form. Chop onions and green peppers. Mince parsley. Form meat patties or make miniature meat loaves in aluminum cupcake liners or lined muffin tins.

After a couple of these Diet Day #4 stirring and storing marathons, you will have quite a selection of delicious meals and snacks stashed away for every Diet Day, #1 to #9. Having frozen food on hand to boil in a bag or heat quickly in the microwave will help you to stay on your diet, because it will minimize the time you spend in the kitchen cooking when you are hungry and most vulnerable.

If you are like me, the sight of food, even a familiar label, triggers an irresistible urge to eat. The other day I spotted in the refrigerator an open can of cat food that I had covered with the plastic top from my favorite cheese spread. No, I didn't eat the cat food, but my mouth instantly watered at the sight of the cheese spread logo. The moral of the story is you can't eat what you don't buy. Sometimes you can't avoid having irresistible food around, especially if you live with other people. Buy opaque storage containers for foods you can't resist, or cover the particularly appealing food with plain brown wrapper. Out of sight, out of mind!

DIET DOWNFALLS AND THEIR SOLUTIONS

A day filled with mundane details and schedules can be tedious and tiring. Like a good Boy Scout, be prepared. Eat as frequently as the menu allows, but be careful that you don't confuse lack of energy with hunger. Sit down and put your feet up. If you are routinely tired, you should see a physician; but often not eating on schedule, not getting proper rest, or too much sugar, caffeine, or alcohol is the problem. If you are a devoted fan of caffeinated beverages or any of the other offenders, try cutting down and see if your energy returns.

On a Diet Day #4 you may also confuse boredom with hunger. To give yourself a change of pace, pick up a project to take the place of eating and keep your hands busy. If you are at home and want to see results today, choose something like needlepoint, knitting, or a crossword puzzle. Whenever you feel restricted, move, even if it's doing isometric exercises at your desk. For a real energy boost, take a brisk walk around the block or up and down a few flights of stairs in the office building where you work.

If you come home tired and/or famished, bypass the kitchen and go straight to your room to take a shower and change your clothes. If the kids are underfoot, take just a minute to wash your face. It's okay to take care of yourself first, but it will be hard for you on a Diet Day #4, when your sense of family loyalty is strong. I am always reminded of the instructions given by the flight attendant on a plane: "If you are traveling with a child, adjust your own oxygen mask before you help your child." Most of the time it is better to get yourself under control before you try to assist your child. This is a good day to reexamine that time of the day when everyone comes home tired. You're in a planning mode anyway, so figure out what you can do to ease the transition period. Don't depend on food to give you a sense of satisfaction.

On a Diet Day #4 you are playing by the rules. The old tapes from childhood of your parents' maxims may come through loud and clear. I finally tore up my charter membership in the Clean Plate Club, and you have my permission to do the same. But bc careful, because this is the kind of day when you will feel honor bound to eat up the leftovers so they won't go to waste. It doesn't matter what you do with them—send them to the neighbors or feed them to the garbage disposal or your pets; just move them out.

If you are a slave to a schedule today and have no time to eat properly, you may fall into the biggest diet trap: ordering in junk food. Here's a diet maxim to believe in: Plan ahead or plan to fail. Isn't it odd that on a Diet Day #4, when you are so organized, you may have planned yourself into a corner in terms of your eating? Check the Diet Day #4 menus for low-preparation meals using convenience foods and the menu suggestions for eating out to avoid this common pitfall.

Take time to eat correctly. Sit down at a table. Don't forget: from this moment on, whenever you eat standing up, a trapdoor will open under your feet. Would I lie?

Eat slowly. Put your fork down between bites. Allow at least twenty minutes for a meal and ten minutes for a snack. If you are like me and eat quickly because you don't enjoy lukewarm food, start out with very hot food on a warm plate or use a microwave to reheat food that gets cold before you finish. Today you have the patience to chew until your jaw drops and savor each bite as if it were your last. Enjoy conversation with your meal, even if you have to talk to yourself.

> Did you know that it takes twenty minutes for your brain to receive the message from your stomach that it's full? It's easy to see how thousands of calories can disappear into your poor unsuspecting tummy before its pitiful cries of "enough, already" are heard.

The fact that your sense of design and balance is heightened on a Diet Day #4 affects your diet, believe it or not. Watch out! The uneven row of brownies or the jagged edge of a piece of pie might be downright irresistible. Instruct your family to be more precise and to cover up the contraband with foil so you can't see it.

On a Diet Day #4 perfection is in the air, and worry blows in with it. As your best-laid plans go out the window, don't let frustration drive you to eat.

REWARDS

Typical of Diet Day #4 behavior, you want to see tangible results for your efforts. If you are pushed to the max by your need to be perfect and are about to lose your marbles, I have the answer! Rush out to the toy store and buy some more. (I found elegant clear glass marbles, used for flower arranging, at floral supply and garden centers.) Then find two large glass jars. Keep your supply of marbles in one jar, and every time you successfully avoid a diet downfall, put a marble in the second jar. If you eat your popcorn plain while the rest of your family drowns theirs in butter, give yourself a marble. If you come home from the store without Twinkies and ice cream, give yourself a couple of marbles. When the second jar is full of the marbles you have earned for making good diet decisions, reward yourself (with something inedible, of course).

On a Diet Day #4 the kinds of rewards that will appeal to you are thrifty and practical: an afternoon spent at a sale, a peaceful nap, some pantry organizers to give you more space on the backs of cupboard doors, a new weekly planner, or a digital food scale.

RECORD KEEPING

The detail-oriented aspect of keeping records is great on a Diet Day #4. All you need are a pencil and a little spiral notebook. Keep your record with you in your purse or on the kitchen counter. Date each page and write down every mouthful of food you eat, the minute you eat it. If you wait until later or let a whole day go by, you won't remember. It also helps you to analyze your eating habits, if you note the reason for eating and where you ate. Were you really hungry or mad at your mother-in-law? Were you sitting in the parking lot of the grocery store eating salt-free tortilla chips or curled up in a ball like a couch potato after a hard day?

My assistant, Libby, confessed to me that she had eaten a whole bag of cookies while she put her groceries away. If she had been sitting at the table, writing down each cookie as she put it on her plate, she would have been more aware of what she was doing and might have avoided her mindless munching. As it is, she made the grave error of eating standing up in her kitchen, and you know what happened to her! As she climbed back up through the trapdoor from her basement, she decided to avoid future cookie-eating episodes by giving my daughter, Chelsea, the two other bags of cookies she had bought. Knowing me well, Libby wrapped the cookies in brown paper and duct tape, and labeled the package "writing paper" so I wouldn't be tempted.

> Watch yourself in a mirror while you are eating, especially snacking. If your frantic chomping isn't a pleasant sight, remember this moment when you are tempted in the future.

I reinforce my own good eating habits by writing down and circling food I *don't* eat, even though I want to. It helps me feel as if I am in control and keeps my hands busy until the urge passes. You can also use a different colored pen to record what you *don't* eat and give yourself a marble for every entry. Analyze your list to see what you crave and when, so you can understand what triggers your eating and become aware of patterns that may have been unconscious.

Hopping on your scale and recording your weight will appeal to you today, but it can be another diet trap. Resist the urge, on a Diet Day #4, to rely on your bathroom scale for evidence that your diet is working. Trust me: if you're following the Numbers Diet and the exercise plan, you *will* lose weight. Scales are not very accurate. Results vary depending upon carpet or other flooring in the bathroom, as well as a whole list of other factors over which you have little or no control. Shifts in fluid retention, your exercise level, elimination, and the time of day you weigh all influence what you see on the scale.

Instead of being a slave to your scale, weigh in at the beginning of a diet and no more often than once a week after that. Let your favorite pair of pants or belt and compliments from others be your indication that progress is or is not being made.

On the other hand, recording your exercise is a must. Regular, vigorous physical activity is the real secret to losing weight and an absolute essential to keeping it off. Use graph paper and give every date its own horizontal line. List the type of exercise you do and block out one square of the graph paper for every five minutes you exercise. Strive for a thirty-minute period twice a day to keep your body in high gear, efficiently burning up the food/fuel you put in it.

Exercise Activity Record

Each square represents 5 minutes at target heart rate

Date	Activity	Resting Pulse*	Target Heart Rate														

* (Beats per 10 seconds)

EXERCISE

The major excuse for not exercising is "no time." On a Diet Day #4 you are schedule-happy, so make exercise your top priority.

MARCHING

On a Diet Day #4 you've got rhythm! At the first hint of music your toes will start tapping, so take advantage of it. Tap into the patriotic sentiments that swell as well on a Diet Day #4, and you will agree that marching to a rousing John Philip Sousa composition is the perfect way to burn up several calories. Depending upon your height and weight, marching burns approximately five calories per minute.

Standing erect, put your hands on your hips. March in place, raising your knees as high as you can and pointing your toes downward as you raise your feet. When you master marching, gradually swing your arms in time with the music. If the spirit moves you, pretend you are waving "It's a Grand Old Flag" in a figure eight and hum a few bars.

Over a period of several Diet Day #4s, try to increase your marching time to at least ten minutes. If you get out of breath, it's a signal that you are marching too fast, raising your knees too high, and swinging your arms too vigorously. The object is to march slowly, at a steady pace, so you can last longer and burn fat, not just sugar. In addition, you will build muscle, which is important for the efficient burning of calories.

EXERCISE ON THE JOB

Later on a Diet Day #4 you may be tied down to your desk, either at home or at work, and buried in details. To eliminate the stress of bending over a pile of paper work, get up every hour for at least five minutes. Walk around or climb a few flights of stairs. At home, do a chore that allows you to move. While you are seated, change position frequently and prop your feet on a low stool to take the strain off your lower back.

> Use the best chair you can find to support your back and position it correctly.

Do the following exercises while sitting in a straight chair:

Move slowly and hold positions for about 10 seconds. Repeat three to ten times, depending on your comfort and level of ability and fitness.

Ankles. Using your left foot and pointing your toes, make ten circles clockwise and ten circles counterclockwise. Repeat with your right foot.

Back. Push your chair away from the desk and, bending from the waist, reach slowly for your toes. Now return slowly to an upright position, uncurling your back one vertebra at a time. If you're at the office among co-workers, pretend that you are picking up something you dropped.

Shoulders. Pretend you have an itch that needs to be scratched on your left shoulder blade. Sit up straight and reach above and behind your head slowly with your right hand to scratch the itch. Bend your left arm behind your back at the waist and try to grasp your right hand. Switch hands and repeat the process. Your shoulders will feel as if they are rotating backward.

Shoulders. Holding an imaginery broom handle horizontally and grasping it in both hands, raise it slowly above your head as high as you can, stretching your arms. Lower it behind your head and behind your shoulder blades, until your elbows are locked at your sides.

Neck. Keep your hands behind your neck and press your elbows as far back as you can, tucking your chin back.

Neck. Imagine that your head is on the continental divide, and north is straight ahead. Roll your head slowly to the north or straight down. Now slowly bring your head to the center position. Roll your head to the right or east, trying to touch your right ear to your right shoulder. Then slowly bring your head to the center position. Now slowly roll your head to the left or west, trying to touch your left ear to your left shoulder. Now roll your head up to the center position.

DANCING

Dance is an excellent alternative choice for exercise on a Diet Day #4. Capitalize on your nostalgic mood and get out the old Glenn Miller and Benny Goodman records or your Beatles tapes. Whether you "cut a rug" or "rock 'n' roll," let the music in your soul and the rhythm in your feet make those muscles work and those pounds and inches disappear.

RECIPES FOR DIET DAY #4

The following menus and recipes are planned to appeal to your practical mood on a Diet Day #4. Whether your schedule provides for time-consuming preparation, moderate preparation, or efficient last-minute preparation, you'll find simple recipes for basic foods like the ones Mother used to cook.

The diner or coffee shop is the featured restaurant today because it isn't too expensive for your frugal Diet Day #4 mood, and it provides a selection of all-American favorites that will stir your feelings of nostalgia and patriotism. Thrifty choices are included to help you pinch pennies, certain to be on your mind today.

Even the Food for Thought will reinforce Diet Day #4 themes: planning, perseverance, common sense, and quality. *The Numbers Diet* respects your conscientiously serious attitude today. Follow a Diet Day #4 menu and you will see tangible results for your efforts.

Menu 1

FOOD FOR THOUGHT

If your day is hemmed in by a plan, it is less likely to unravel.

BREAKFAST
(240 calories)

*Patriotic Pudding**
Decaffeinated Coffee

SNACK
(72 calories)

3 pretzel twists
Celestial Seasonings Country Peach Spice herb tea, iced

LUNCH
(345 calories)

*Grilled Cheese Sandwich**
*Penicillin and Pasta Soup**
*Carrot and Celery Sticks**
*Orange Spritzer**

* Recipes follow.

SNACK
(51 calories)

2 Hershey's Kisses
Decaffeinated coffee

DINNER
(250 calories)

*Sensible Spaghetti**
*Spinach and Mushroom Salad**
Bogus Burgundy (page 34)

DESSERT
(134 calories)

*Not Pudge Sundae**
Decaffeinated coffee

TOTAL CALORIES 1,092
PROTEIN 21%
CARBOHYDRATE 62%
FAT 17%

* Recipes follow.

PATRIOTIC PUDDING

½ cup egg substitute
1½ cups nonfat milk
1 tablespoon honey
1½ cups cooked brown rice (*not* instant)
1 tablespoon chopped dates
1 teaspoon vanilla extract
1 teaspoon cinnamon
Dash of nutmeg
½ teaspoon grated lemon rind
1 cup fresh or frozen blueberries
1 cup fresh or frozen raspberries

Mix the egg substitute, milk, and honey in a blender. In a large bowl, combine the cooked rice, egg mixture, and remaining ingredients except the berries. Pour into an 8-inch-square pan that has been sprayed with Pam. Sprinkle with nutmeg. Bake for 30 minutes at 350°. Turn the oven off, but leave the pudding in the oven for another 10 minutes. The pudding may still be loose, but it will solidify as it cools. Serve warm or cool with berries on top, making sure each serving has both red and blue berries.

Serves 4

GRILLED CHEESE SANDWICH

- 2 teaspoons Dijon mustard
- 2 slices "light" bread (not to exceed 40 calories each)
- 1½ ounces Weight Watchers mozzarella cheese, grated

Spread mustard on the bread slices and sprinkle on cheese. "Grill" both sides of the sandwich in a nonstick skillet sprayed with Pam until the cheese melts.

Serves 1

PENICILLIN AND PASTA SOUP

- 1 can Pritikin Chicken Vegetable Soup with Ribbon Pasta
- 2 tablespoons minced fresh parsley

Heat the soup according to directions on the can. Top with parsley.

Serves 2

CARROT AND CELERY STICKS

- 1 carrot, peeled and trimmed
- 1 stalk celery, washed and trimmed

Cut the vegetables into 3-inch sticks.

Serves 1

ORANGE SPRITZER

2 tablespoons orange juice
8 ounces sparkling water
Ice cubes

Combine in a tall glass.

Serves 1

SENSIBLE SPAGHETTI

12 ounces Turkey Store or Louis Rich ground turkey
½ medium onion, chopped
½ cup sliced mushrooms
⅛ teaspoon oregano
2 cups Pritikin Spaghetti Sauce with Mushrooms
2 cups cooked spaghetti

In a large nonstick skillet sprayed with Pam, brown the turkey, onion, and mushrooms until the turkey is cooked. Add the oregano and spaghetti sauce. Cover and simmer until hot. Pour the sauce over warm cooked spaghetti.

Serves 4

SPINACH AND MUSHROOM SALAD

Dressing
1½ teaspoons olive oil
4½ teaspoons lemon juice
1 tablespoon wine vinegar

4 cups spinach, thoroughly washed and torn into bite-size pieces
½ cup bean sprouts
2 ounces jicama, sliced
2 cooked egg whites, chopped
½ cup sliced mushrooms

1 carrot, grated
1 tomato, chopped

Shake the dressing ingredients in a glass jar with a tight lid. Pour over salad ingredients. Toss.

Serves 2

NOT PUDGE SUNDAE

½ cup vanilla Dreyer's Grand Light "Light" dairy dessert
1 tablespoon Hershey's chocolate syrup

Place the dairy dessert in a dish. Top with chocolate syrup.

Serves 1

Menu 2

FOOD FOR THOUGHT

Perseverance is not a long race; it is many short races, one after another.

BREAKFAST
(263 calories)

*All-American Danish**
*Old-fashioned Ovaltine**
Decaffeinated coffee

LUNCH
(295 calories)

*Penny-Pincher Sandwich**
1 cup nonfat milk
6 celery sticks

SNACK
(104 calories)

1 cup puffed wheat, dry
Alba 77 shake mix

* Recipes follow.

DINNER
(319 calories)

*Marvelous Meat Loaf**
*Pauper's Potatoes**
½ cup peas and carrots
Chianti Cup (page 26)

DESSERT
(64 calories)

*Baked Apple**

TOTAL CALORIES 1,045
PROTEIN 22%
CARBOHYDRATE 60%
FAT 18%

* Recipes follow.

ALL-AMERICAN DANISH

1 slice raisin bread
2 tablespoons yocotta (recipe follows)
1 teaspoon jam

Toast the raisin bread and top with yocotta and jam.

Serves 1

YOCOTTA

½ cup part-skim ricotta cheese
1 cup low-fat cottage cheese
1 cup nonfat plain yogurt

Combine in a blender or food processor and blend well. If necessary, add 1 to 3 tablespoons nonfat milk to make it the consistency of cream cheese. Store refrigerated for up to 1 week.

Makes 2½ cups

OLD-FASHIONED OVALTINE

1 tablespoon Ovaltine powder
1 cup nonfat milk

Stir Ovaltine powder into milk.

Serves 1

PENNY-PINCHER SANDWICH

1 tablespoon peanut butter
1 tablespoon jelly
2 slices "light" bread (not to exceed 40 calories per slice)

Spread peanut butter and jelly on a bread slice. Top with the other slice to make a sandwich.

Serves 1

MARVELOUS MEAT LOAF

2 pounds Turkey Store or Louis Rich ground turkey
½ cup grated carrots
½ cup finely chopped mushrooms
½ cup chopped onions
3 cloves garlic, mashed
1 cup Quaker Quick Oats
¼ cup grated Parmesan cheese
1 tablespoon Italian spices
1 tablespoon prepared horseradish
1 cup tomato sauce

Blend all ingredients together except ½ cup tomato sauce. Place in a large loaf pan sprayed with Pam. Cover and bake at 375° for 30 minutes. Remove the cover, top with the reserved tomato sauce, and cook, uncovered, for another 30 minutes, or until the meat pulls away from the sides of the pan.

Serves 8

PAUPER'S POTATOES

1 pound russet potatoes
¼ cup hot nonfat milk
1 tablespoon Butter Buds
Freshly ground black pepper

Peel the potatoes and boil until tender. Drain. Using an electric beater, beat the potatoes, milk, Butter Buds, and pepper until creamy.

Serves 4

BAKED APPLES

4 medium Granny Smith or pippin apples
1 can diet strawberry or black cherry soda
Cinnamon

Peel, core, and halve the apples. Sprinkle with cinnamon. To microwave, place them with the soda in a microwave-proof dish. Cover with plastic wrap, leaving a vent, and microwave on high for 5 to 10 minutes, until the apples are tender. To bake in a conventional oven, place them in a Pam-sprayed oven-proof dish. Cover with foil, pierce a vent in the foil, and bake at 350° for 30 minutes or longer.

Serves 4

Menu 3

FOOD FOR THOUGHT
Plan ahead or plan to fail.

BREAKFAST
(249 calories)

*Sausage Sandwich**
1 orange, sliced
Decaffeinated coffee

LUNCH
(357 calories)

*Waldorf Chicken Salad**
2 Ak-Mak crackers
Celestial Seasonings Cranberry Cove herb tea, iced

DINNER
(306 calories)

*Tuna Noodle Casserole**
*Confetti Coleslaw**
*Lemon Sparkler**

DESSERT
(176 calories)

*Apple Betty**
Celestial Seasonings Cinnamon Apple Spice herb tea

TOTAL CALORIES 1,088
PROTEIN 29%
CARBOHYDRATE 48%
FAT 23%

* Recipes follow.

SAUSAGE SANDWICH

2 ounces Turkey Store or Louis Rich turkey sausage
2 tablespoons Yocotta (page 112)
½ English muffin, toasted

Cook the sausage in a nonstick skillet. Spread Yocotta on the English muffin and top with sausage.

Serves 1

WALDORF CHICKEN SALAD

12 ounces boneless, skinless chicken breast, cooked and cubed
1 cup chopped celery
½ cup chopped red apples
½ cup chopped green apples
½ cup sliced water chestnuts
½ cup nonfat plain yogurt
1 tablespoon rice vinegar
1 teaspoon Dijon mustard
¼ teaspoon curry powder
2 teaspoons grated orange rind
Juice of 1 orange
Lettuce
2 tablespoons raisins
2 tablespoons toasted almonds

Combine the chicken, celery, apples, and water chestnuts. In a separate bowl, combine the yogurt, vinegar, mustard, curry powder, orange rind, and orange juice. Toss the chicken mixture with the dressing. To serve, place the salad on lettuce leaves and sprinkle with raisins and almonds.

Serves 4

TUNA NOODLE CASSEROLE

Sauce

⅓ cup Instant Soup Mix (page 137)
1¼ cups boiling water

1 medium onion, chopped
3 stalks celery, sliced
2 cloves garlic, mashed
1 teaspoon Dijon mustard
1 teaspoon Worcestershire sauce

- 2 6½-ounce cans water-packed white-meat tuna, drained
- 3 cups cooked rigatoni noodles
- ½ teaspoon paprika
- 1 tablespoon grated Parmesan cheese

Combine the soup mix and boiling water. Stir. Set aside.

In a saucepan, combine the onion, celery, garlic, mustard, Worcestershire sauce, and tuna. Stir to break up the tuna. Add the sauce. Stir over low heat for 5 minutes. Place the noodles in an 8-inch-square pan that has been sprayed with Pam. Pour the sauce over the noodles and gently stir, making sure all the noodles are coated with sauce. Sprinkle paprika and Parmesan on top. Bake, uncovered, in a 350° oven for 30 minutes.

Serves 4

CONFETTI COLESLAW

- 1½ cups shredded green cabbage
- 1½ cups shredded red cabbage
- ¾ cup grated carrots
- 1 8-ounce can diced pineapple packed in its own juice, drained and juice reserved
- 3 tablespoons currants or golden raisins
- 3 tablespoons low-fat cottage cheese
- 4½ teaspoons diet mayonnaise
- 1 teaspoon vinegar
- ¾ teaspoon fresh lemon juice
- 1½ teaspoons celery seed
- ⅛ teaspoon black pepper

In a large mixing bowl, combine the cabbage, carrots, pineapple, and currants. In a separate bowl, blend the cottage cheese, mayonnaise, vinegar, lemon juice, celery seed, pepper, and 1½ teaspoons of the reserved pineapple juice. Fold the dressing into the vegetable mixture. Chill thoroughly.

Serves 4

LEMON SPARKLER

1 teaspoon fresh lemon juice
8 ounces sparkling water
Ice cubes
Lemon slice

Combine the lemon juice and sparkling water in a tall glass with ice cubes. Garnish with the lemon slice.

Serves 1

APPLE BETTY

2 medium Granny Smith apples
Juice of 1 lemon
¼ cup orange juice
2 tablespoons diet margarine
1 tablespoon honey
1 tablespoon finely chopped walnuts
¾ cup Quaker Quick Oats
¼ cup Post Grape Nuts
1 tablespoon flour
1 teaspoon cinnamon
½ teaspoon nutmeg
⅛ teaspoon ground cloves

Peel, core, and slice the apples. Drizzle them with lemon and orange juice. Melt the margarine and honey together. In a bowl, combine the nuts, oats, Grape Nuts, flour, cinnamon, nutmeg, and cloves with the honey mixture. Spread half the apples in an 8-inch-square pan that has been sprayed with Pam. Crumble half the oat mixture over them. Add the remaining apples and top with the remaining oat mixture. Cover with foil and bake at 325° for 20 minutes. Uncover and bake for another 5 minutes, or until the apples are tender.

Serves 4

Menu 4

EATING OUT

FOOD FOR THOUGHT

The waste of time is the most extravagant and costly expense of all.

BREAKFAST

(275 calories)

1 poached egg
1 buttermilk biscuit
1 teaspoon jam
2 prunes or ½ grapefruit
Decaffeinated coffee

LUNCH

(232 calories)

½ cup cottage cheese
1½ cups seasonal fresh fruit
Bed of lettuce greens
6 saltines
Iced tea with lemon

SNACK

(120 calories)

Quaker Chewy Granola Bar

DINNER

(425 calories)

1 cup chili or beef stew
Mixed green salad with vinegar or lemon
1 corn muffin
½ cup applesauce **or** *½ cup sorbet*
Decaffeinated coffee

TOTAL CALORIES 1,052
PROTEIN 16%
CARBOHYDRATE 54%
FAT 30%

DIET DAY #5

ON THE GO

Change is in the air. Expect a varied schedule, punctuated by sudden interruptions. No grass will grow under your feet today. In fact, you'll be on the go to such an extent that you may not have time to eat, except on the run. This is a good day to pack your own portable snacks and quick meals to eat out of the trunk of your car. Otherwise you are at the mercy of fast-food restaurants and convenience markets, and you need a short course on which of their offerings will give you the most nutrition for the calories.

No two hours in this Diet Day #5 will be the same. To say you'll be busy is an understatement. Drawn to physical activity, you'll need to eat for energy. That requirement, together with a desire to satisfy your cravings for new and exciting foods, the spicier the better, will dictate the kinds of foods you choose.

You are acutely aware of everything today and don't want to miss any of it. To take advantage of every opportunity, keep your suitcase packed with a snack and expect the unexpected!

SURVIVING IN THE FAST-FOOD JUNGLE

On a Diet Day #5 you are likely to end up in the fast-food jungle, better known as Fat City! A way of American life, fast-food restaurants account for 40 percent of the dining establishments in the United States. Americans depend on them because our hectic schedules and fast-paced lifestyle make every day seem like a Diet Day #5. Shopping at a fast-food restaurant isn't like shopping at a grocery store, where you can rely on labels to make correct choices. At this time, fast-food establishments are not required to provide nutritional information, though some do make posters or pamphlets available. Some large chains have 800 numbers to call for nutritional information. Unfortunately, you are in such a hurry on a Diet Day #5 that you don't have the time, or the inclination, to call ahead!

First the good news about fast food for dieters:

Conveniently located on practically every corner, these restaurants offer reasonable cost, quick service most of the time, and consistent quality virtually worldwide. In comparison to other kinds of restaurants, fast-food outlets provide portion control, no alcohol to tempt you, no bread and butter or chips greeting you at the table, and no emphasis on desserts. The standard menu is predictable so you can preplan your order.

The bad news universal to fast food for dieters: too much fat, too much sodium, too much sugar, too many calories, and not enough fiber. About 40 to 60 percent of the calories in fast food come from fat, mainly because most of the food is fried.

If you allow yourself to fall off the diet bandwagon because you are in a hurry and eating away from home on a Diet Day #5, you could eat up enough calories to gain back pounds you have worked so hard to lose on the other days. Don't blow it today! Continue to use all the knowledge and meal-planning ability that work for you at home.

GENERAL GUIDELINES FOR ORDERING

Hamburgers. Avoid "deluxe," "whopper," "big," and other names that imply king-size burgers. The bigger, the more ingredients, and the more calories. It is better to order one or two plain hamburgers than to order one with the works. Hold the special sauce, which is full of fat. Skip the cheese at 100 calories per slice. Don't even think of adding bacon to your burger unless you want to look like the pig it came from.

Chicken Sandwich. This varies from establishment to establishment according to the way it is prepared. Almost always deep-fried in hydrogenated fat, the chicken is often dipped in batter, which acts like a sponge to soak up extra fat. The end result may net you 9 teaspoons of fat more than if you had ordered a hamburger *and* french fries.

> Wendy's grilled chicken sandwich has half the calories of Burger King's.

Chicken Pieces. Fried chicken pieces, sold under many names as cute as the little pieces themselves, are also dipped in batter and deep-fried. Because they are fried, the majority of their calories come from fat; and because there are so many little pieces, there are more surfaces on these crispy critters to soak up the fat. Add the accompanying dipping sauces, loaded with sugar, and you have ordered a high-calorie meal.

Fish Sandwich. People commonly make the mistake of thinking that fish sandwiches contain less calories than a hamburger. Wrong! The fish, like the offending chicken, is batter-fried and usually accompanied by a slice of cheese and fat-filled tartar sauce. Fifty percent of the calories in a fish sandwich come from fat, making it a poor choice. Of course, you could order your deep-sea devil without the cheese and the sauce, eat it on half a bun for an open-faced sandwich, and save lots of calories.

Salads. Several fast-food palaces offer packaged salads. Usually the grilled chicken salad is a better choice than the chef's salad because of the fat in the cheese and ham. Beware the accompanying packet of dressing. It could blow your calories for the day. Instead, ask for lemon or a packet of low-cal dressing.

Many chains now have salad bars, which are great if you choose fresh vegetables and fruit over canned. As you learned on Diet Day #3, the most dangerous items are the dressings and variety salads already mixed with mayonnaise- and oil-based dressings. Cottage cheese is usually available as a source of protein. Be especially careful to choose a low-cal dressing, and not too much of that.

Extras. Chili without cheese is available in many places and is a good choice if you balance the meal with salad on the side. Baked potatoes are a boon or a bust depending on how you top them; skip the butter, sour cream, or margarine and head for the salad bar, where you can top your tater with cottage cheese, fresh vegetables, and lemon. If you can find broiled chicken breasts at a fast-food restaurant, you've hit pay dirt!

Beverages. Low-calorie carbonated beverages are acceptable on occasion, but it's better to take advantage of the trend to provide nonfat and low-fat milk. Water, coffee, decaf, and hot and ice tea are always available. It goes without saying, a milk shake is a mistake.

Breakfast Foods. Breakfast at a fast-food chain can break your calorie fat bank if you aren't careful. The breakfast alone could use up 500 to 700 calories. Sausage is full of fat, as are croissants, which have butter built in. Choose a plain English muffin or plain toast with jelly. Order fresh fruit, if available, or fruit juice as a second choice.

SEASONINGS

On a sensual Diet Day #5 you are keenly aware of life through your five senses. You want to see, hear, touch, smell, and taste it all. Unfortunately, the most commonly used seasoning, salt, is an unhealthy choice, especially for a dieter.

SODIUM

Salt contains sodium, a mineral widely found in nature, which is necessary to maintain proper fluid balance in the body. Under normal conditions we get more than enough sodium in our diets from milk, meats, and certain vegetables. Although the body needs some sodium, it usually gets too much in the form of salt added to foods.

Consuming too much sodium has been linked with high blood pressure and kidney disease. Excess sodium causes a temporary buildup of fluids in your body, which makes it more difficult for your heart to pump blood through your cardiovascular system. Result: high blood pressure. In and of itself, hypertension is a painless disease; however, people with high blood pressure have a higher risk of stroke, heart attacks, and congestive heart failure. It's a good idea to shake your salt habit, not the saltshaker.

Processed convenience foods and fast foods are the source of excess sodium in our diets. When shopping with an eye toward reducing sodium, fresh is best; frozen is second best, and better than canned. For example, fresh vegetables contain approximately 1 to 5 milligrams of sodium per half cup, compared to 250 to 280 milligrams for a half cup of canned vegetables. Some salty foods, such as potato chips, are obvious sources of sodium; while other less obviously salty foods, such as some instant hot cereals, contain more sodium per ounce than potato chips.

Fortunately, it has become easier to cut down on sodium be-

> If you must use rice and pasta mixes occasionally, reduce their sodium impact on your diet by using only half of the seasoning packet.

cause manufacturers are responding to health-conscious Americans who request more low-sodium products. Ketchup, mustard, tomato products, spaghetti sauce, and a wide variety of vegetables all are available in low-sodium versions. If the food you want is not available in a low-sodium version, you can reduce the sodium in many foods simply by rinsing them with water. Besides providing low-sodium products, many food manufacturers now include the sodium content on the ingredients label.

Be a comparison shopper. Look at the difference in sodium content between:

	Mg
½ can low-sodium canned soup	30–70
½ can regular canned soup	500–600
½ cup rice or pasta	1–3
½ cup seasoned rice or pasta mix	600
¾ cup hot cereal	1
¾ cup instant hot cereal	280
½ cup unsalted nuts	1
½ cup salted nuts	230
1 cup milk or yogurt	120
1 cup buttermilk	319
1 ounce natural cheese	150–200
1 ounce processed American cheese	400
3 ounces fresh meat, fish, poultry	75
3 ounces shellfish	150
3 ounces ham	675
3 ounces luncheon meat	1,175
4 black olives	130
4 green olives	325
½ cup fresh vegetables	5
½ cup canned vegetables	250

SODIUM-FREE SEASONINGS

If "please pass the salt" is heard often at your table, remind your family that the use of salt is just a habit and usually is not related to the body's need for salt. Try removing the salt from your table and replacing it with a flavorful salt substitute. Experiment by cooking with herbs and spices, such as onion and garlic powder. Sauté foods in a nonstick pan with lemon juice for a nice browning effect and taste that replaces not only salt but fat, too. Instead of salting water when you cook pasta, add a bay leaf. Subtle flavors, once overpowered with salt, will emerge and you will enjoy new taste sensations, in addition to better health. As an added benefit, you can say good-bye to puffy eyes and ankles, and rings that don't fit.

On a Diet Day #5, when you are feeling adventurous and ready for a change, try adding a little spice to your life. Herbs and spices differ in that herbs are generally grown in temperate areas, while spices come from tropical zones.

HERBS

Herbs are a creative and healthy alternative to salt for flavoring foods. When used skillfully, they can turn an ordinary food into a gourmet delight. For best results when experimenting on a Diet Day #5, it's better to use one strong, flavorful herb and one milder flavor to complement the food. Never use two strong herbs in the same recipe. Use two to three times as much fresh herbs as dried, in which the flavor is more concentrated.

Strong herbs: bay leaves, mustard, rosemary, and sage.

Medium herbs: basil, celery seed and leaves, cumin, dill, fennel, garlic, marjoram, mint, oregano, savory, tarragon, thyme, and turmeric.

Mild, delicate herbs (great to blend with other herbs): chervil, chives, and parsley.

GROWING HERBS

Most herbs are easy to grow, and it's worth the effort when you know that fresh herbs are preferred by professional chefs.

For maximum flavor, herbs should be harvested in the morning, after the dew has evaporated but before the sunlight shines on them, and used that day.

Homegrown herbs can be harvested in large quantities, dried, and stored for future use. Hang bunches of cut herbs in a warm, dark, well-ventilated area, such as the attic, a closet, or a dry basement. However, make sure the temperature does not exceed 90 degrees, or the herbs will actually cook as they dry. As each variety becomes dry, store it in a labeled glass or plastic container for up to one year. Parsley, chives, tarragon, basil, mint, and sorrel can be fresh-frozen in individually marked plastic bags.

HARVESTING AND COOKING WITH FRESH HERBS

Use scissors rather than your fingers when plucking your plants. Finely chop leaves to create more cut surfaces and maximum flavor. Add finely chopped herbs directly to heated sauces and casseroles rather than sprinkling them on top. When making cold foods such as dips, spreads, dressings, and marinated vegetables, herbs should be added with the rest of the ingredients so their flavors can blend for several hours or overnight. On the other hand, add herbs to stews and soups about 45 minutes before the end of the cooking time, because the longer you cook a dish, the more the herb flavor is lost.

If you're trying a new herb on a Diet Day #5 and are unfamiliar with its flavor, mix it with nonfat plain yogurt. Ideally you should let it stand for at least an hour, to see if you like the taste before using it liberally. This is not always possible on a busy day, so use a light hand and experiment. You're in the mood for unexpected pleasures today.

USING DRIED HERBS

Dried herbs are stronger than fresh, and powdered herbs are stronger than crumbled. In general, ¼ teaspoon powdered herb equals 1 teaspoon crumbled equals 2 teaspoons fresh.

To powder an herb, put some dried leaves in a small, sturdy mortar and use a pestle to grind them.

Dried herbs lose their potency in about a year, so it's a good idea to date each jar as you buy it. Store herbs in their original plastic or glass containers or transfer products from their cardboard containers into tins or plastic bags. Most cooks mistakenly place herbs on the counter or in a cabinet near the stove for convenience. Heat and the humidity from cooking decrease their potency and shorten their shelf life, as does direct sunlight.

Fortunately, manufacturers have introduced new, smaller jars for herbs. Chances are you will use the contents before they become outdated.

When buying dried herbs, read the label carefully to be sure you aren't buying herbal blends with salt. If you want combinations, it's better to buy the herbs separately and make your own blends with less salt.

Some frugal gourmets find that it is less expensive to buy herbs individually. However, if you have tossed away your chef's apron, celebrate your freedom by purchasing herb mixtures. My favorite is fines herbes, which come in cute little crocks from France. I'm sure the crock costs more than the herbs, but it can be recycled as an adorable container for fresh flowers on your kitchen sink after you have used all the herbs. At a very high price, fines herbes is merely a mixture of parsley, chervil, and tarragon with a bit of basil, fennel, oregano, sage, or saffron. The bouquet garni mixtures contain bay, parsley, and thyme. Italian blend is a mixture of basil, marjoram, oregano, rosemary, sage, savory, and thyme. Barbecue blend is a mixture of cumin, garlic, hot pepper, and oregano.

MAKING HERB VINEGAR

If you love to cook and you miss baking goodies, start dabbling in potions using different herbs and vinegars. You can taste all the vinegar you want without ruining your diet.

For best results, line up your sterilized jars and bottles containing sprigs of fresh herbs. The vinegar should be heated, not boiled, in an enamel pan. Depending upon your preference, use white, red, or cider vinegar. Add the vinegar to the jars and bottles, cap securely, and let sit for two weeks before using.

SPICES

Spices, grown in tropical regions, have sharp tastes and strong aromas. Some are popular for their taste and others for their smell. Common spices include pepper, paprika, nutmeg, cloves, ginger, allspice, mace, and cinnamon. Spices have little in common except their use. For instance, cloves come from the bud, cinnamon from the bark, pepper and nutmeg from the fruit of their respective plants. Ginger comes from the root and mustard from the seed.

Spices, like herbs, lose their potency after a year, so purchase small amounts and be sure to date them.

> Cinnamon, vanilla, and allspice make foods seem sweeter.

CHOOSING FROZEN DINNERS

On a Diet Day #5 your busy schedule may call for the convenience of a frozen dinner. Fortunately, dieting Americans have more to choose from than the Salisbury steaks and macaroni and cheese of yesteryear. Many new entrées are aimed at health-conscious, weight-watching shoppers.

Just because a frozen dinner is labeled "light," "lite," or "lean" doesn't mean that it will make anything lighter about you besides your pocketbook. True, some frozen diet dinners have less calories than their chilly counterparts, but they may also have less food and more fat, sugar, salt, starchy fillers, flavor enhancers, and preservatives than you bargained for.

> Patronize the frozen-food manufacturers who are up front about their products, listing everything but the kitchen sink on both the nutrition and ingredients labels.

Be on the label alert! An ingredients label isn't enough. Avoid any brand that does not include a nutrition label. Few frozen dinners list fiber, cholesterol, and saturated/polyunsaturated fat information, or vitamins and minerals. What are they trying to hide? To find out, call (800) 555-1212 for the number of the manufacturer and ask them to send you their nutrition information.

To make sure the pretty picture on the outside isn't all you know about what you're eating on the inside, here's what to look for:

- Less than 850 milligrams of sodium per serving, unless you are extremely salt sensitive and need even less. Be on the lookout for some frozen diet dinners that improve their flavor with 2,000 milligrams per serving—more than you need for an entire day.
- Less than 10 grams of fat (primarily unsaturated) per 300-calorie serving, or 30 percent fat. Normally fish and chicken are low in fat, but many frozen dinners include *fried* chicken or *fried* fish. Don't assume that pasta, which is normally low in fat, is safe in a frozen dinner, because it's usually swimming in cream and butter sauce. Vegetarian dishes sound healthy but they may be full of oil, cheese, and other high-fat ingredients.
- Little or no added sugar under any of its aliases: molasses, fructose, honey, etc. When you cook dinner at home you don't put sugar on top of it, so why buy a frozen dinner from a manufacturer who does?
- Low in cholesterol, 300 milligrams or less per day is recommended. Many brands of frozen dinners don't include cholesterol information, so remember that 3 ounces of unadorned chicken or red meat has 25 percent of the daily maximum.
- Few additives. Be on red alert when you see the word *natural*. It doesn't mean a thing unless it's backed up with an ingredients list that passes the test.

A final word on frozen fare: just because a meat, fish, or poultry entrée, vegetable, and starch are included doesn't mean you are getting a completely balanced meal. The meal you choose may be low in fiber, calcium, and vitamins A and C. Add a glass of skim milk and a green salad to balance things out.

NUTRITION ON THE RUN

On any Diet Day it's good to have an emergency snack in the car, but on a Diet Day #5 you'll need your tailgate picnic supplies more than ever.

Supplies

Can openers, the V-shaped type to puncture juice cans and lift bottle caps and the hand-crank type to remove the entire lid of a can.

Plastic forks, spoons, knives

Paper cups, bowls, and plates

Paper napkins

Paper towels (good place mats and napkins, handy to sit on or for wiping off a bench)

Pocketknife

Premoistened towelettes

Snacks

Rice cakes (they stay fresher longer if you put them in a plastic container with a lid)

Small cans of unsweetened apple, pineapple, orange, or vegetable juice

Pop-top cans of tuna

Packages of Alba 77 shake mix

Small boxes of raisins

Individual snack packs of unsweetened applesauce

Crackers low in fat content (saltines, Ry-Krisp, or Wasa Crispbread Lite Rye)

Bottled water

Individual boxes of dry cereal (unsweetened type)

SNACK SHOPPING AT THE MINI MART

If you need a quick, nutritious snack as you are racing around on a Diet Day #5, and for some reason or another you don't have your tailgate party in your trunk, stop off at a mini mart.

This list does not give you carte blanche to go off the Numbers Diet, but if you are genuinely famished and caught empty-handed, these items are better than many alternatives:

Hard-cooked egg

Fresh fruit

Carton of nonfat or low-fat milk

Nonfat plain yogurt or low-fat "light" yogurt

Rice cakes
Bagels
Water-packed tuna
Water-packed fruit
Small carton of low-fat cottage cheese
Small container of part-skim ricotta cheese
Package of sliced turkey
Premade burrito (try to get a plain bean)
Cup of noodles (watch the sodium)
Cup of soup (low-sodium is preferable)
Little boxes of cereal (shredded wheat and Bran Chex are good snacks)
Box of raisins

Some good choices of sandwich meats, with their percentage of total calories from fat:

Oscar Meyer Oven Roasted Turkey Breast	18
Oscar Meyer Oven Roasted Chicken	21
Louis Rich Oven Roasted Turkey Breast	24
Louis Rich Turkey Pastrami (square)	25
Butterball Honey Cured Turkey Ham	26
Butterball Oven Roasted Turkey Breast	30
Butterball Turkey Pastrami	30

Choosing sandwich meats. The Earl of Sandwich must have had a Diet Day #5 in mind when he invented the ideal meal for people on the go. To make sure the middle layer of your handy meal is healthy, be a deli case detective. Many sandwich meats are high in fat, and most are loaded with sodium. Don't fall for labeling that would seduce you into believing the meat contains a low percentage of fat. One brand of turkey bologna that is advertised as 80 percent fat-free may be by weight, but it actually contains 77 percent of its calories in fat. Look for cold cuts that have 1 gram or less of fat per ounce, or state that they are at least 95 percent fat-free by weight.

The sandwich meat of choice is real honest-to-goodness turkey breast, not pressed turkey roll from the deli. Many of the turkey "breast" cold cuts from the market may be low in fat, but the meat has been processed and filled with additives such as modified food starch (also known as sugar). Depending upon whether the turkey roll is made primarily from dark or white meat, its fat content may vary. In addition, there may be gelatin and various sugars, flavorings, and fillings.

> In general, graham crackers, animal crackers, ginger snaps, and fig bars have less fat and sugar than many other cookies.

Choosing crackers and cookies. Besides calories and fat, crackers add sodium to our diets. If you are in too much of a hurry to read the label on a Diet Day #5, ask yourself if the cracker snack you're about to put in your mouth will taste salty or leave you with greasy fingers.

When you do read the labels, watch out for the saturated fats cracker makers rely on, such as lard and coconut, palm, and palm kernel oils. Also look for sodium content, keeping in mind that the total daily amount of sodium recommended is between 1,100 and 3,300 milligrams.

AIRLINE FOOD

The number 5 in numerology indicates travel. If you find yourself traveling by air on a Diet Day #5, here's how to manage your food.

Depending upon the length of the flight, and whether you can eat before your departure or after your arrival, you may need to eat on the plane. If you call at least thirty-six hours ahead, many airlines will honor requests for special meals. Once on board, give your name and seat number to the flight attendant.

The choices vary but usually include vegetarian meals, which feature cheese and milk; they are usually too high in fat calories. Sometimes a bean or grain dish is offered, but don't count on it. Just because it is vegetarian doesn't mean it is low in fat.

Diabetic or low-cholesterol selections are probably the best choice for a low-calorie meal. The usual offering is fish or chicken with salad, vegetables, and a roll. Sometimes you'll get what everyone else gets minus the dessert. The diabetic menu may include a slice of high-fat meat, potatoes, butter, roll, vegetable, and diet gelatin.

Seafood plate can be quite nice and filling. Usually served cold as a salad, its only drawback may be no fresh lemon. It's a good idea to carry a package of low-calorie dressing in your purse just in case you do get lettuce with your fish.

Fruit plate is usually small and not enough to eat on a long flight. Cottage cheese occasionally accompanies fresh fruit, but more often than not it arrives with squares of processed cheese.

If a meal is not offered on your short flight, count on the availability on board of club soda, diet drinks, water, tomato juice, coffee, decaf coffee, and tea. Skip the nuts that come with the beverage, and dip into the supply of diet munchies that you have brought along with you.

Of course, avoid wine, beer, and hard liquor. They add calories and increase your tendency to become dehydrated while flying. Since coffee and tea are diuretics, your best bet is water or a little bit of juice in a lot of water. (To avoid swollen feet and ankles on a long flight, drink plenty of water and pick an aisle seat so you can walk around.)

To protect yourself from less than terrific airline food and flight delays, fly with your own food. I always carry a package of Alba 77 to mix with water, small snack packs of unsweetened applesauce and a plastic spoon, individual packages of melba toast from a restaurant, and fresh fruit such as apples and bananas. The nutritious Instant Soup Mix (page 137) is excellent mixed with a cup of hot water. If you plan ahead, you can even take a broiled chicken breast or turkey sandwich with you.

ROOM-SERVICE FOOD

Next time you find yourself staying in a hotel, consider room service for breakfast. It beats the dining room because you won't be tempted at the last minute by the sight and smell of other people's food. In some hotels you can fill out your order the night before, when you are full of dinner and full of resolve. Leave the card on your door knob and *voilà,* your meal appears at the appointed hour.

If you call in your order, always be specific and ask them to repeat the order. Be sure to ask for ice water and, if you're like me, a large pot of herb tea or decaf coffee (tell them you're having an early party!). Ask for dry toast or a muffin, nonfat or low-fat milk for cereal and/or your coffee. Many hotel chains offer yogurt, unsugared cereal such as corn flakes, shredded wheat, or puffed rice or wheat in individual-size boxes, unsweetened granola, and hot oatmeal. Fresh fruit is always available.

> A cereal with 2 or more grams of fiber, 8 or less grams of sugar, and 2 or less grams of fat per serving is considered acceptable.

DIET DOWNFALLS AND THEIR SOLUTIONS

If you run out of gas on a busy Diet Day #5, be sure to fuel your body with the proper food. Don't revert to sugar, thinking it will give you the energy you need. The quick lift won't last. You'll be tired all over again, and trapped on the sugar roller coaster, unable to enjoy all the surprises that a Diet Day #5 has in store. Eat for energy by planning ahead. In anticipation of a busy day, prepare snacks the night before so you won't be caught short of the zip you need to take advantage of all the opportunities a Diet Day #5 has to offer.

With all you have to do today, you may think you don't have enough time to fix meals. Rely on the menus and recipes for a Diet Day #5. Between the suggestions for quick-to-fix foods and what to order at a fast-food restaurant or pick up at the mini mart, you should be able to keep going all day.

On a Diet Day #5 you may even think there's no time to eat food, much less prepare it. Eating on the run, even if you make wise food choices, is risky. It takes twenty minutes for your stomach to send the "full" signal to your brain. At the pace you're going on a Diet Day #5 you could easily fall by the wayside in five minutes and go off the deep end in twenty. So slow down and consume only the amount of food you planned to eat.

On your travels during a Diet Day #5, around town or around the world, stash safe snacks in your purse and pocket. Otherwise you're likely to track down the scent coming from a local bakery, rush to the store for the goody you see on a billboard, or fall victim to the food in a radio jingle.

Give in to your five senses, which are heightened on a Diet Day #5. Savor the sight of your food as well as the aroma, the taste, and the texture. Listen to the seductive snap of celery, and bathe your back teeth in the sweet, tart burst of flavor as you bite into a berry. On a Diet Day #5 you need an additional sense—common sense. Think before you eat!

EXERCISE

A busy Diet Day #5 is no excuse to skip exercise. Running around on errands in the car doesn't constitute exercise except for your accelerator foot.

You may have to be creative in your exercise to fit it into your activities. The most obvious exercise is walking instead of driving when you do your errands. Plan your route to drop items off at the cleaner's first and pick up bulky items just before you go home.

If that isn't feasible, take a walking coffee or lunch break. Use the stairs in your office building, apartment, or home for exercise. You'll be surprised how fast your heart rate will reach optimum level.

On a Diet Day #5 you already feel as if you are running around in circles, so why not go to the local high school and do a few fast laps around the track? If you take a battery-powered tape recorder you can make an oral list of other things you have to do. Forget pencil and paper. You may be in high gear, but the most anyone can do is walk and chew gum at the same time! Thirty minutes of purposeful circles will give you the lift you need to carry on with this active Diet Day #5 and keep you on your diet track.

Before you go to bed, unwind from your wacky Diet Day #5 with an evening stroll in your neighborhood. The additional thirty-minute walk will help you sleep better and rev up your metabolism.

RECIPES FOR DIET DAY #5

Fast food is featured throughout the menus for Diet Day #5. To speed you on your way, take advantage of frozen foods and quick-to-fix or make-ahead recipes.

You won't have to pull very far out of the fast lane to eat out, because there's a McDonald's on practically every corner.

Food for Thought encourages you to keep your eyes open and be flexible. You never know what unexpected pleasure awaits you on an exciting Diet Day #5.

Menu 1

FOOD FOR THOUGHT

A mind is like a parachute. It functions best when open.

BREAKFAST
(306 calories)

*Mug of Moo**
½ bagel
Decaffeinated Coffee

SNACK
(50 calories)

½ pear

LUNCH
(283 calories)

*Quick Cream of Vegetable Soup**
4 slices melba toast
Decaffeinated diet soda

SNACK
(107 calories)

1 Granny Smith apple
1 mini box (½ ounce) raisins

DINNER
(300 calories)

Healthy Choice or Armour Dinner Classics Lite frozen entrée
Wishful White Wine (page 25)

SNACK
(90 calories)

*McPopcorn**
Celestial Seasonings Sleepy Time herb tea

TOTAL CALORIES 1,136
PROTEIN 22%
CARBOHYDRATE 70%
FAT 8%

* Recipes follow.

MUG OF MOO

- 1 envelope Carnation Instant Breakfast (no sugar added)
- 8 ounces nonfat milk
- Ice cubes (optional)

Mix according to package directions. If using ice cubes, mix in a blender. Pour into a large mug.

Serves 1

QUICK CREAM OF VEGETABLE SOUP

- 1 cup frozen vegetables (any green or mixed vegetables)
- ⅓ cup Instant Soup Mix (recipe follows)
- 1¼ cups boiling water

Cook the vegetables according to package directions. Combine the soup mix and boiling water in a soup bowl. Stir to blend and add the vegetables.

Serves 1

INSTANT SOUP MIX

- ¼ cup instant oat bran cereal
- ¾ cup cornstarch
- 2 cups nonfat powdered milk
- ¼ cup instant chicken broth granules
- 2 tablespoons Lawry's Minced Onions with Green Onion Flakes
- ½ teaspoon dried basil
- 1 teaspoon dried thyme
- ½ teaspoon white pepper
- ¼ teaspoon garlic powder
- ⅛ teaspoon paprika
- ⅛ teaspoon dried dill

Combine all ingredients, mixing well. Place in an airtight container. Store at room temperature. To serve, mix ⅓ cup dry mix with 1¼ cups boiling water.

Serves 10

McPOPCORN

3 cups air-popped popcorn
1 tablespoon Molly McButter

Place hot popcorn in a large brown paper bag. Spray lightly with a fine mist of water. Add Molly McButter. Close the bag and shake to coat the popcorn. Serve immediately.

Serves 1

Menu 2

FOOD FOR THOUGHT
Expect a miracle!

BREAKFAST
(207 calories)

*Totable Potable**
½ cup Spoon Size Shredded Wheat, dry
Decaffeinated coffee

SNACK
(120 calories)

Quaker Chewy Granola Bar
Perrier

LUNCH
(240 calories)

*Pita Pocket Surprise**
Decaffeinated diet soda

SNACK
(40 calories)

1 tangerine
Celestial Seasonings Mandarin Orange Spice herb tea

DINNER
(408 calories)

*Crock Pot Chicken Cacciatore**
½ cup cooked pasta
*Roamin' 'n' Rushin' Salad**
Chianti Cup (page 26)

DESSERT
(25 calories)

Dole Fresh Lites frozen bar

TOTAL CALORIES 1,040
PROTEIN 27%
CARBOHYDRATE 54%
FAT 19%

* Recipes follow.

TOTABLE POTABLE

½ cup strawberries, fresh or frozen, without sugar
½ banana
1 cup nonfat milk
1 teaspoon wheat germ

Blend and serve immediately.

Serves 1

PITA POCKET SURPRISE

1 6½-ounce can water-packed white-meat tuna, drained
1 teaspoon chutney or orange marmalade
¼ cup grated carrots
1 scallion, minced
1 teaspoon lemon juice
6 ounces Spicy Hot V8 vegetable juice
8 almonds, chopped
1 6-inch pita bread

(Continued)

(Continued from page 139)

½ cup alfalfa sprouts
1 tomato, sliced

Combine the tuna, chutney, carrots, scallion, lemon juice, 3 ounces vegetable juice, and almonds and mash with a fork. Cut the pita bread in half. Fill each half with half of the tuna mixture; add sprouts and tomato slices. Drink the remaining 3 ounces of vegetable juice.

Serves 2

CROCK POT CHICKEN CACCIATORE

1 pound boneless, skinless chicken breast
1 cup mushrooms, cleaned and halved
2 cups tomato sauce
6 ounces tomato paste
1 onion, sliced
1 bell pepper, sliced
4 drops Tabasco sauce

Combine all of the ingredients in a slow cooker (crock pot). Cover and cook on low for up to 7 hours. If you do not have a crock pot, combine the ingredients, bring to a boil, reduce the heat, cover, and simmer for approximately 25 minutes, until the chicken is cooked.

Serves 4

ROAMIN' 'N' RUSHIN' SALAD

8 cups romaine lettuce, torn into bite-size pieces
1 cup alfalfa sprouts
1 red bell pepper, chopped
8 tablespoons Pritikin No-Oil Russian Dressing
Ground pepper to taste

In a bowl, combine all of the ingredients. Toss and serve.

Serves 4

Menu 3

FOOD FOR THOUGHT

Today is full of unexpected happiness waiting for you to discover it.

BREAKFAST
(243 calories)

*Go-Go Muffin**
Yoplait "Light" yogurt
Decaffeinated Coffee

SNACK
(60 calories)

1 small apple

LUNCH
(273 calories)

*Spicy Speedy Spud**
4 ounces Seneca 100% Natural Applesauce snack pack
Decaffeinated diet soda

SNACK
(50 calories)

*Finger Food**
Perrier

DINNER
(318 calories)

*Presto Pasta Salad**
Wishful White Wine (page 25)

DESSERT
(90 calories)

*Coffee Float**
Celestial Seasonings Sleepy Time herb tea

TOTAL CALORIES 1,034
PROTEIN 19%
CARBOHYDRATE 62%
FAT 19%

* Recipes follow.

GO-GO MUFFIN

Refrigerator Bran Muffins recipe (page 24)
1 prune, chopped

Fill a muffin cup one-quarter full of batter. Place the prune on top and fill the muffin cup half full of batter. Bake according to directions.

Serves 1

SPICY SPEEDY SPUD

1 6-ounce (4-inch) potato
¼ cup low-fat cottage cheese
1 tablespoon salsa
1 tablespoon fresh lemon juice

Scrub the potato and bake it in a conventional or microwave oven. Make a slice in the top of the potato and push in the ends to open the potato. Fill with cottage cheese and top with salsa and lemon juice.

Serves 1

FINGER FOOD

1 cup puffed rice, wheat, or corn

Munch as you would popcorn.

Serves 1

PRESTO PASTA SALAD

1 16-ounce bag frozen C&W Pasta Salad Fusilli, thawed (do *not* cook)
1 box frozen snow peas, thawed (do *not* cook)
8 ounces canned white-meat chicken or diced cooked chicken breast
½ cup Wish-Bone Lite Classic Dijon Vinaigrette reduced-calorie dressing

Place all of the ingredients in a bowl and toss. Cover and chill.

Serves 4

COFFEE FLOAT

1 cup decaffeinated coffee, iced or hot
½ cup vanilla Dreyer's Grand Light "Light" Dairy Dessert

To make an iced coffee float, refrigerate coffee left over from breakfast. Serve in a chilled tall glass, topped with dairy dessert.

To make a hot coffee float, pour hot coffee into a large mug and top with dairy dessert.

Serves 1

Menu 4

EATING OUT AT McDONALD'S

FOOD FOR THOUGHT

Unwelcome visitors sometimes bring unexpected blessings.

BREAKFAST

(307 calories)

Scrambled eggs
½ English muffin, unbuttered
Small orange juice
Decaffeinated coffee

LUNCH

(245 calories)

Oriental chicken salad
1 package chow mein noodles
1 package low-cal vinaigrette dressing
Iced tea with lemon

DINNER

(372 calories)

Hamburger (no sauce)
Side order of salad
1 package low-cal vinaigrette dressing
Diet Coke

DESSERT

(144 calories)

Small soft-serve cone

TOTAL CALORIES 1,068
PROTEIN 35%
CARBOHYDRATE 33%
FAT 32%

DIET DAY #6

KEEP THE HOME FIRES BURNING

On a Diet Day #6 love, home, and family are on your mind and your sense of responsibility is very strong. To achieve your goal of peace and harmony at all costs, you may be the one who is making adjustments today. You've heard of the A- and B-type personalities; well, on a Diet Day #6 you want to be the E-type personality: everything to everybody.

Chances are you are entertaining at home on a Diet Day #6. If you rely on the menus in the chapter, you'll find dishes to please the most discriminating gourmet on your guest list.

> Family holidays need not be planned entirely around food. Emphasize another activity besides eating.

On a Diet Day #6 you appreciate beauty in all its forms. Food should be a feast for the eyes as well as the palate. Arrange artful table settings using your best dishes and glassware. Even if you aren't entertaining, serve yourself sparkling water in a crystal goblet. Garnish everything in sight with sprinkles of nutmeg or paprika, and don't send a plate to the table without a sprig of parsley.

Today you are also interested in your own appearance. Play up your best features with accessories. Don't let a few extra pounds be an excuse for not looking your best. It should please you to know on a beauty-conscious Diet Day # 6 the Numbers Diet itself is the ultimate beauty treatment. You'll see the results not only in less pounds, but in clearer skin, improved posture, increased energy, and greater vitality. More water, calcium, complex carbohydrates, and exercise, combined with less stress, fat, sugar, salt, and caffeine, add up to a beautiful new you.

WHAT TRIGGERS YOUR EATING?

Home is where your heart is on a Diet Day #6, so watch out! If you are like me, you're likely to eat more when you are at home.

Often eating doesn't have anything to do with hunger: it has to do with appetite, which is defined as a craving or desire for food. If we understand what triggers appetite, we can control it. Circumstances in our environment, subconscious feelings, and ingrained habits lead us to eat. The key to controlled eating is found when we illuminate the hidden cues and see them for what they are.

Internal cues, linked to the metabolic process, are genuine hunger. Just like a hungry animal, you rummage around for food when your body tells your brain to eat. In addition, there are emotional reasons, such as anger, happiness, avoidance, boredom, and loneliness, that make you reach for food.

> Pay attention to negative self-talk. If you are telling yourself "I'm such a slob anyway" or "I might as well enjoy myself, I'll never lose weight," you need to reprogram yourself with positive self-talk.

External cues, such as sight and smell, are very powerful triggers for people like me, who are "hyper-responders" to food. Even if I have just eaten a four-course meal, I respond to the smell of Mexican food. I am reduced to a wretch without resolve at the sight of tortilla chips.

> Often during the writing of this book, my assistant, Libby, and I took a chicken tostada break at the local Mexican hangout. One day, even though we had vowed to avoid the chips, the waitress was too fast for us. There they were warm, crispy, and irresistible. As I reached for that fatal first fistful, Libby popped the menu over the bowl. It worked! Out of sight, out of mind.

And let's not forget that the taste of food can trigger a feeding frenzy. Faced with the opportunity to eat something you enjoy, you're not likely to stop at a small portion.

Hearing about food triggers appetite. I had to watch myself like a hawk while I was writing this book. It was bad enough just thinking and talking about food. Then I had to write about it! The final test was perfecting and taste-testing all the recipes. I solved the problem of temptation by keeping a liter of sparkling water on my computer table and eating regular small meals and snacks.

Plus, using the diary method I explained on Diet Day #4, I wrote down every bite I put into my mouth.

Not only must we contend with our own urges to eat, but we must stand up to the influence of other people. You feel obligated to eat the expensive dinner your date buys you, even though you're not that hungry. You worry that your hostess will think you don't like her triple-treat chocolate torte if you don't eat every crumb of the 1,000-calorie wedge she proudly plops onto your plate. People are forever asking you to "take just a bite" or "have some more"; "It's my grandmother's recipe," "I made it just for you," "try this." If it's hard for you to say "no," reread Diet Day #1 for tips on asserting yourself and Diet Day #2 for tips on tact.

Sometimes you eat out of habit, because it's normal mealtime. If you have a family, you are constantly tempted by cooking foods that aren't on your diet and tasting as you go. Eating with the family, you end up eating the wrong food, more than you want, when you aren't even hungry.

Sometimes we eat because we are lonely or bored. Better to pick up the phone, a book, or a project. Take a walk or go to a movie. Watch out for old patterns and old associations that trigger eating: popcorn at the movies, milk and cookies when you visit your mother's house, apple pie when you visit dear Granny, or your habitual TV snack. In a way, one thin sliver of pie is less damaging than a handful of Mom's oatmeal cookies and a glass of milk. The cookies and the milk never seem to come out even, and the temptation is to pour more and munch more.

To gain control of food, analyze your patterns of eating. On Diet Day #4 I told you about recording everything you ate or wanted to eat. Carry a small notebook with you for two weeks. In your diet diary jot down *what* you eat, *where* you eat, *why* you eat, *when* you eat, *with whom* you eat, and *how* you eat.

You will be amazed at what you discover. Your notes will illuminate patterns of unconscious behavior that have been hidden from you. By taking notes, you step back from the problem and become an observer. With a different perspective comes a better understanding of your environment. In your diet diary also make notes every time you want to eat but don't. Circle the foods you *thought* about eating. The circled items may point up a pattern.

What I am talking about here are not the metabolic changes that affect our appetite, but the internal, psychological triggers and external environmental cues that set us off. There's a difference between physiological hunger (real hunger) and psychological hunger. When you discover your weak spots by reading your diet diary, you can change your patterns.

> When a snack attack comes upon you, wait ten minutes before you respond. Perhaps the urge will pass or you will be distracted in the meantime.

The most compelling habit I had to deal with was eating when I was tired. I used to think that food, usually something sweet, would give me more energy. I discovered that the sugary snacks I was counting on to give me a lift were doing just the opposite. Today a balanced diet of 60 to 70 percent carbohydrates, 15 to 20 percent protein, and 25 to 30 percent fat keeps my engine revved up all day. An occasional catnap or a brisk walk revitalizes me better than the cinnamon gummy bears I used to eat. In addition, I have made it a hard and fast rule not to eat when I am upset or bored. Instead, I hop on my treadmill, take a walk outdoors, pick up my needlepoint, or do something else that gives me a change of scene and attitude. Do whatever it takes, but don't eat when you are upset, bored, lonely, depressed, or angry.

Here are some solutions that I discovered to break my poor eating habits. Perhaps some will work for you or suggest other ways you can overcome your diet dilemmas.

> Work on only two or three of these solutions at a time. When you have incorporated one into your life, start working on another one. Add your own ideas to my list.

1. For your "danger" times (mine are 10:00 A.M. and 3:00 P.M.), plan an activity that isn't compatible with eating. I return my business phone calls at these times. I know it's really tacky to talk and eat at the same time—especially when the person on the other end of the phone can hear every crunch amplified and every munch magnified!
2. Plan ahead to eat when you are hungriest. Eat a meal or snack during your danger hours.
3. Eat your meals and snacks on time so you don't become so famished that you eat more than you should.
4. Eat in a designated eating area (at the dining-room table is preferable).

5. Set a complete place for yourself, with a place mat, plate, and napkin, even when you eat a snack.
6. Eat slowly: twenty minutes for a meal and at least ten minutes for a snack.
7. Put your fork down between bites.
8. Ask someone else in the family to clear the table and do the dinner dishes if you need to break the habit of eating the leftovers.
9. Ask family members to prepare their own snacks, assuming they are old enough.
10. Delegate the grocery shopping to someone else. If you must do it yourself, eat a snack before you walk into the store, and make a list that you follow to a *t*.
11. It isn't always possible to keep trigger foods out of the house, especially if you have children, so it's important for you to learn how to deal with them. Rearrange the contents of your cupboards and refrigerator to keep trigger foods out of sight, out of mind. Turn boxes so you see only the product name, not the full picture.
12. Keep all of your food in the kitchen: no stashes in your bedroom, the den, etc. Keep emergency snacks in the trunk of your car to prevent forbidden fast-food snack attacks.
13. Don't keep food in your office desk drawer or eat at your desk.
14. If possible, keep water or a warm drink at your desk.
15. Limit your intake of foods containing caffeine and sugar. Get off the roller coaster!
16. Avoid reading or watching TV while you eat, to eliminate mindless munching.
17. Exercise every day.
18. Plan to exercise during your danger time. When I walk late every afternoon, it gives me more energy, a change of scene, and less appetite for dinner. My oldest daughter, Jamie, takes her aerobic dance class during her danger time.
19. If you brush your teeth after every meal or snack, you won't want to ruin that clean, fresh taste by eating.
20. And, last but most important, *don't eat standing up!*

Even though your heart is at home today, consider that it may not be the best place for your body. It may be too difficult to avoid overeating when you are home all day. If you are a full-time homemaker or retiree, find interesting activities outside your home.

Wherever you are, keep your mind off food and on people and projects that fill you up in more productive ways. Pull those food triggers and shoot down your bad habits. Have a full life instead of a full stomach!

CALCIUM AND OSTEOPOROSIS

Along with beautifying your surroundings on a Diet Day #6, looking your best and feeling terrific are also on your mind. Just as "happiness is an inside job," so is health.

One of the most important beauty foods for women is calcium. To move gracefully and maintain youthful posture, we must protect our bones from aging. When women reach thirty-five their bones experience a slowdown of remodeling, or the renewal process. The resulting loss of density and strength can lead, in extreme cases, to osteoporosis. Affecting 20 million, mostly women, this disease accounts for increased bone fractures over forty-five and "dowager's hump." Bones become porous and brittle. Although some loss of bone mass is considered part of the aging process, and low postmenopausal levels of estrogen are suspected of causing an increased loss of calcium in bones, something can be done to prevent osteoporosis. Even women deemed most likely to develop osteoporosis—because of combined factors of age, family history of the disease, inactive lifestyle, and use of alcohol and cigarettes—do have some recourse.

Your doctor is the best source of information on the subject, but you can take steps on your own to maintain strong bones by including adequate levels of calcium in your diet and scheduling regular exercise as part of your lifestyle. Taking calcium supplements without your doctor's approval is not advised, especially if you have a history of kidney stones.

> When you add just 1 tablespoon of powdered nonfat milk (15 calories) to a glass of nonfat milk, you add 52 milligrams of calcium to your diet.

Government studies show that half of all women over thirty-five in this country get less than two-thirds of the recommended 800 milligrams daily allowance for calcium. However, the latest medical studies indicate that premenopausal women may need as much as 1,000 milligrams daily, and postmenopausal women may need 1,500 milligrams daily.

The Numbers Diet includes many of the foods that are rich in calcium, such as skim milk, nonfat yogurt, part-skim ricotta cheese, leafy green vegetables, and canned salmon with bones. It is interesting to note that caffeine and stress are thought to be calcium robbers.

> Pink salmon is milder than firmer sockeye salmon, which flavor closely resembles its fresh counterpart's.

> Be sure to eat the calcium-rich leaves of broccoli as well as the florets.

Foods Rich in Calcium

Dairy Products	Mg
Nonfat skim milk	296 per cup
Cottage cheese	320 per 12 ounces
Ice milk	204 per cup
Nonfat yogurt	294 per cup
Meat, Poultry, and Seafood	
Canned salmon with bones	296 per cup
Crab	38 per 3 ounces
Raw oysters	226 per cup
Vegetables	
Broccoli, cooked	158 per stalk
Mustard greens	193 per cup
Spinach	200 per cup
Celery pieces	39 per cup
Carrots	45 per cup
Beets	29 per cup
Asparagus	37 per cup
Green beans	72 per cup

Vegetables (cont.)	Mg
Cauliflower, cooked	25 per cup
Pumpkin, canned	57 per cup
Sweet potato	52 each
Fruit	
Canned apricots	28 per cup
Dried apricots	100 per cup
Blackberries, raw	46 per cup
Grapefruit, fresh	20 per half
Orange, medium	54
Strawberries	31 per cup
Raspberries	27 per cup
Bread Products	
Bread	23 per slice
Buttermilk biscuit	34
Farina, cooked	147 per cup
Pancakes, plain	58 per cake
Pancakes, wheat-flour	27 per cake
Hard roll	24 each
Waffles, from mix	179 each
Sugars and Sweets	
Molasses, blackstrap	137 per tablespoon
Sherbet	31 per cup
Brown sugar	187 per cup
Nuts and Beans	
Almonds	160 per ½ cup
Tofu	128 per 3½ ounces
Walnuts	50 per ½ cup

> Almonds and walnuts are high in fat calories, so you are better off getting calcium from vegetables, salmon, and low-fat dairy products.

Along with a diet rich in calcium, exercise is a vital factor in maintaining proper bone growth and density. Exercise not only stimulates the development of bone mass, it slows down and may even halt bone loss. Medical research can't tell us exactly why this is so, but the best explanation I've read is that exercise creates stress on the bones. As a result, bones rise to the occasion by becoming stronger and thicker. Without proper exercise, bones become weaker and more porous. In addition, exercise increases blood flow to the bones, giving the skeleton nutrients that encourage bone growth and regeneration.

Although weight-bearing exercise, such as walking, jogging, jumping rope, marching, and aerobic types of dancing, were thought to be the best for bone development, experts now tell us that any muscle contraction across the bone is beneficial. Regular exercise will take years off the outside of your body and add years to the inside. On a Diet Day #6, when you're in the mood to remodel your home, remember that remodeling your bones on a continuous basis is serious business. Calcium and exercise are your keys to a beautiful body.

CELLULITE

The waffly-looking fat found on hips and thighs is a good topic for a Diet Day #6, when physical appearance is on your mind. Resistant to diet and exercise, cellulite is a combination of fat and water that have not been eliminated from the body.

Cellulite looks so bumpy because certain cells of the body have the capacity to store enormous amounts of fat. About half the fat is deposited in the cells immediately below the skin. Strands of fibrous tissue connect the skin to deeper tissue layers, and they also separate the fat cell compartments. When the fat cells increase in size, they apparently cause the compartments of fat to bulge and produce a waffled appearance.

Sex and heredity are the two most important determining factors of where we store fat. Men tend to deposit fat in the stomach region, acquiring beer bellies, while women accumulate fat in the breasts, hips, thighs, and derriere. Individuals vary in the patterns of fat distribution, and children seem to follow the same pattern as their parents.

Women seem to be more prone to waffled fat, or cellulite, because the connective tissue beneath women's skin creates large, round fat cell chambers, while in men the fat cell chambers are divided into small, polygonal shapes that don't bulge as readily when they are filled. In addition, certain outer layers of women's skin are thinner and more likely to reveal bulges. These outer layers become even thinner and less elastic with age.

We want the easy way out of our cellulite and are lured by expensive but unproven remedies. Thousands of women fall prey to pills, cactus fiber washcloths, loofah sponges, horsehair mitts, creams, lotions to be used in the shower, rollers, de-dimpler scrub brushes that are alleged to work like magic, not to mention exercise books and rubberized pants that are supposed to sweat the stuff off. Cellulite massage parlors have popped up around the country, appealing to some women with claims of a surefire European method. Other women turn to electrical muscle stimulators, vibrating machines, whirlpool baths, or vacuum cleaner–like tubes that shoot streams of water or air at the problem area. Some go to salons offering hormone injections, enzyme creams, thermal heat treatments, wax treatments, or vitamin and mineral supplements.

Before subjecting yourself to these barbaric treatments, you need to know that the only thing that will get thinner is your pocketbook, because there is no medical evidence that these remedies work. The truth is fat is fat wherever it is.

> Liposuction, intended for removing localized fatty deposits that are not affected by diet and exercise, is not a substitute for actual weight reduction.

Recently liposuction, as a way to remove saddlebags and love handles, has received attention in the press. Usually done under general anesthesia, this surgical procedure should be performed only by a competent board-certified plastic surgeon. At about $2,000 per body part, liposuction is expensive, and the results are not always successful.

Deep massage is another popular cellulite "cure." Although there is no medical proof that it removes cellulite, massage, when done correctly, does improve the circulation and helps to release waste products from the body.

Unfortunately, there are no magic solutions to cellulite. A sensible diet, hydrating your cells with eight glasses of water a day, and exercise are the only cures.

FRAUDULENT FLAB REMOVERS

Anyone who attended the fourth grade knows that Ponce de Leon, the Spanish explorer, allegedly sought a fountain of youth down among the alligators in Florida. Since then, diet sharks have come up with claims just as fantastic and elusive. Catering to the overweight, out-of-shape population who want to lose pounds and inches without dieting and exercising, the diet gurus are most successful at reducing our bank accounts. Millions of dollars are spent annually by diet hopefuls for pills that supposedly curb the appetite without side effects and let them lose weight by eating unlimited amounts of food. Dauntless dieters have endangered themselves by wearing custom-constructed rubber suits that supposedly induce weight loss while you sleep. *Sweat* dreams! A whole series of body-wrap schemes have come and gone, along with the tables that promised to jiggle off the offending flab. You'd think people would know better by now, but a new generation of well-advertised gimmicks greets every new generation of hopeful losers.

ELECTRICAL MUSCLE STIMULATOR

The latest in vanity-type quackery to appeal to armchair joggers is the electrical muscle stimulator. Billed as the method that provides "all the figure toning of 3,000 sit-ups without moving an inch," this machine contracts muscles by passing an electric current through electrodes or contact pads applied to the skin. Not only do these machines fail to fulfill their promises, they subject the dieter to dangerous electrical shocks and burns. They should never be used on pregnant women, people who have heart problems or wear a pacemaker, or anyone with cancer or epilepsy. Finally, the electrical muscle stimulator should not be placed where a strong current could pass through the brain, heart, or spinal column. The machines are definitely not safe for home use.

Like many gimmicks, the electrical muscle stimulators do have a legitimate use in physical therapy for relaxing muscle spasms, preventing blood clots in the leg muscles of bedridden patients, increasing blood circulation to a certain part of the body to promote healing following surgery, monitoring the range of motion of an arm or leg, and preventing or slowing muscle atrophy due to disuse from a disease or injury.

It may come as a shock to the charlatan, but these legitimate uses are a far cry from the promises of many salons, which include slimming and trimming, shaping and contouring, weight control, spot reducing, cellulite removal, bust development, wrinkle removal, and nonsurgical face lifts.

HERBAL WRAPS

With dreams of instant weight loss, the customer lies down and submits to being wrapped in warm herb-soaked gauze strips, then covered with a plastic sheet and a blanket. The resultant perspiration then causes the temporary reduction of pounds and inches by removing fluid. Potentially dangerous, the rapid loss of fluids may cause dehydration and electrolyte imbalance.

Wraps, whether "natural herb" or ordinary hot water, have no effect on fat deposits and will not dissolve fat. There is no truth to the myths that fat is magically broken down by perspiration, however profuse. The most magical part of herbal wraps is the instant reappearance of the lost weight and inches the moment you resume eating and drinking. The only permanent loss associated with this treatment is of your money.

GUAR GUM

The guar plant, grown in India and Sri Lanka, provides a natural gel-forming fiber that has been approved as a food additive by the Food and Drug Administration. Without taste or calories, guar is said to control appetite by slowing the time it takes for food to pass through the stomach, making you feel fuller longer. Side effects, such as bloating and diarrhea, which usually disappear in a few days, affect one in five people who take guar. People with colitis or difficulty in swallowing should not take guar, nor should people who have had surgery in the gastrointestinal tract. Used first in Europe, guar is now being prescribed by doctors for cholesterol reduction, stabilizing the blood sugar of diabetics, and weight reduction. Although guar may be abused by anorexics, it is not considered to be addicting, either physically or psychologically. Guar is available over the counter in drink-mix or capsule form.

DIET DOWNFALLS AND THEIR SOLUTIONS

Get out the crying towel. Everyone needs your help on a Diet Day #6. If you let other people's problems, over which you have no control, weigh you down, you may end up eating out of frustration.

If you give into the urge to entertain today, don't fall into the trap buying "special party foods." It is estimated that over half of all Americans are watching their weight, so bring on your low-calorie cuisine and delight your guests instead of adding to their diet dilemmas. Just because food is low in calories doesn't mean it has to be low in taste or eye appeal. Bring out your best china and crystal, your prettiest place mats and cloth napkins. Feast on the beauty and company, not just the food. Make a hundred calories look like a million by garnishing each plate with edible flowers or vegetable bouquets. Add lemon twists, thin slices cut across the center to the rind, with the ends twisted in opposite directions. Use a mushroom fluter and a carrot curler to make garnishing easier and more fun.

> Giving a birthday party? Of cakes, angel food is the lowest in calories and has no fat, compared to carrot cake, which is 50 percent fat.

> To avoid overeating, fill individual dinner plates in the kitchen instead of serving family style, from the table.

If you are spending more time in the kitchen today, you may find yourself tasting as you go. Keep a container of celery, carrot sticks, and radishes in the refrigerator, to munch on while you are cooking, and a glass of your favorite low-calorie drink at your elbow; otherwise you could consume a day's worth of calories before you ever get to the table.

On a typical Diet Day #6 you will probably be so busy taking care of everyone else that you forget about yourself. Be good to yourself. Take a bath, a hot shower, or a catnap before your guests arrive. Remember, they are coming to see you, not to see how clean your house is or how much effort you have put into the cooking.

Diet Day #6 goes along with motherhood and the cookie jar. Be sure your jar is filled with marbles so you can reward yourself for good eating habits (see Diet Day #4). Today's the day to turn in some of those marbles you've earned. Reward yourself with a beauty treatment, such as a pedicure, manicure, steam, and massage. Have your hair done.

EXERCISE

On a Diet Day #6 you have luxury and comfort on your mind. The last thing you want to do is work up an unladylike sweat. Personal appearance is so important to you today that you may be tempted to forgo your usual exercise routine if it threatens to spoil your hair or if the clothes you wear during exercise are uncomfortable or unbecoming. Another popular excuse on a Diet Day #6 is the weather, too hot or too cold.

MALL WALKING

Keep in mind that your all-important appearance will ultimately be affected adversely if you do not exercise regularly. Try some mall walking for temperature-controlled exercise. If your walking shoes are a neutral color, you can be a veritable fashion plate while you put in your thirty minutes "casing the joint." Walk at a fast clip and cover each side of every floor, using the stairs, not the escalator. If you arrive before the stores open, you'll be able to walk briskly, unimpeded by mommies, strollers, and little ankle biters. Later you can return to the stores that interest you and indulge in a favorite Diet Day #6 pastime, shopping for clothes.

REGULAR WALKING

To promote harmony and well-being on a Diet Day #6, invite your loved ones or dinner guests to walk with you in the evening after dinner. Enjoy the beauty in your neighborhood or drive to the high-rent district for a scenic sojourn. Persuade guest walkers to accompany you by offering to stop for nonfat frozen yogurt.

> Commercial frozen nonfat yogurt is about 20 calories per ounce.

Walking and food shouldn't become a habit unless you limit yourself to a noncaloric drink. In warm weather it's always a good idea to carry water or bring along money for a cold drink, especially if you are walking any distance.

TONING EXERCISES

A Diet Day #6 is a perfect time to emphasize toning exercises to improve your appearance. As you lose weight it's important to increase muscle tone to avoid the sags and bags that sometimes replace the rolls and bulges. Quick-weight-loss fad diets leave people looking emaciated, while the slower, steady weight loss and exercise program of *The Numbers Diet* will leave you looking younger and more vigorous.

Since most exercise activities stress the use of the lower body, upper-body toning needs special attention. Hand weights, used in conjunction with special exercises, are an excellent way to balance your workout. Heavy hands have a detachable weight at either end of the handle, for easy adjustment as you increase your level of fitness. Some hand weights are covered with terry cloth for a comfortable, moisture-absorbing grip.

Beginners should start with no more than one pound in each hand. Hold the weights firmly with your fingers, but not so firmly that you cut off circulation. Although many of these exercises may be done while walking, I suggest you master them first while standing still.

> If you want to try out the concept of hand weights, raid your cupboard for two soup cans.

TONING ARMS WITH HAND WEIGHTS

Holding a pound weight in each hand, with palms facing down, stretch both arms out to your sides. Make circles slowly with your hands. A more strenuous form of exercise is also beneficial for the upper arms, provided that you do not experience discomfort in your shoulders or hear unusual snapping or cracking from your shoulder joints. Keeping your elbows locked, slowly "flap your wings" like a butterfly ten to fifteen times, bringing them straight up over your head and then slowly moving them straight down to your sides, without rotating your wrists.

Still holding a pound weight in each hand, put your arms straight out in front of you at shoulder level, palms up this time. Keeping your upper arms stiff and straight, curl your hands toward your shoulders. Now curl them back, slowly straightening your arms. Repeat ten to fifteen times. This is a great way to tone the biceps, which inevitably seem to succumb to gravity over the years.

Another terrific exercise to firm the back of your upper arms is the motion of pulling a cord to start a gas lawn mower. Stand up and bend forward from the waist. To protect your lower back, rest one foot on a step or stationary object six inches from the floor. Keeping your arms close to the side of your body, bring your lower arms forward, bending at the elbows. Stay bent over, but straighten out your lower arm and push it back. Work up to twenty-five repetitions.

> Instead of putting on the feed bag while you watch TV, put on a leotard and do some toning exercises.

USING HAND WEIGHTS WHILE WALKING

To help propel yourself and increase your heart rate while walking, carry hand weights. With arms near your sides and elbows bent, move each arm forward and back in time with the opposite foot.

If you can walk, talk, and chew gum at the same time, incorporate the other arm exercises you've learned with walking.

ADDITIONAL TONING

Combat that common accumulation of fat on the outside of the upper thighs affectionately known as saddlebags. Lie down on the floor on your left side. Point your right toe down toward the floor. Keeping your knee locked, raise your right leg up straight about twelve inches off the floor. Slowly lower your right leg, keeping your toe pointed down, behind your left foot, which should be on the floor. Repeat this twenty-five to fifty times. As you become more advanced, do not allow your right leg to rest on the floor between leg lifts. You'll see and feel the results!

Turn over on your right side and repeat the same motion with your left leg. Repeat twenty-five to fifty times.

HOUSEWORK

Romantic it's not, but housework and gardening do burn off calories. Use some elbow grease and work hard. Instead of carrying supplies with you, deliberately make extra trips for yourself, especially up and down stairs. Use every opportunity to stretch and do repetitions of movements that work your muscles. Make sure you are lifting properly and carrying heavy objects carefully. Use your legs to spare your back when you lift.

> Housework burns off approximately 180 to 220 calories per hour.

AFTER HOURS EXERCISE

This is one exercise you will undoubtedly enjoy. On a Diet Day #6, when love and harmony are on your mind, make love for exercise.

A good romp in the hay burns off fifteen calories per minute while it lasts. Your performance will improve in this area as your fitness level increases from other exercise, giving you more incentive to keep it up.

Don't confuse heavy breathing and an increased heartbeat during sex with the same phenomena during exercise. It's only your hormones. In any event, enjoy yourself. A note to beginners: this is one exercise you don't have to stop when you begin to get tired.

RECIPES FOR DIET DAY #6

The hostess with the mostess will be comfortable with menus for a Diet Day #6. Every dish has eye appeal as well as taste appeal when company's coming.

Be sure to use the suggestions for dining out at an attractive restaurant to reinforce your need for beauty and harmony today.

Food for Thought reminds you to lead with your heart on a Diet Day #6 by bringing peace, joy, and love to everyone you meet.

Menu 1

FOOD FOR THOUGHT

Give others a piece of your heart, not a piece of your mind.

BREAKFAST
(260 calories)

*Lawful Waffle**
Yoplait "Light" yogurt
Decaffeinated coffee

LUNCH
(225 calories)

*Sumptuous Smoked Salmon Spread**
4 cocktail bread slices
*Pretty Pepper Salad**
Wishful White Wine (page 25)

SNACK
(150 calories)

½ pear
2 tablespoons dry-roasted mixed nuts
Celestial Seasonings Spearmint herb tea

DINNER
(330 calories)

*Fancy Fish**
*Wild Rice Pilaf**
½ cup steamed green beans
Perrier with lemon

DESSERT
(90 calories)

1 junior-size (3-ounce) frozen nonfat yogurt

TOTAL CALORIES 1,055
PROTEIN 25%
CARBOHYDRATE 49%
FAT 26%

* Recipes follow.

LAWFUL WAFFLE

1 Eggo Nutri-Grain frozen waffle
1 cup sliced strawberries or raspberries, fresh or frozen without sugar
2 tablespoons Rod's Light aerosol Whipped Cream

Heat the waffle according to package directions. Top with berries and whipped cream. If using frozen berries, thaw in a microwave and heat if desired.

Serves 1

SUMPTUOUS SMOKED SALMON SPREAD

1 7-ounce can best-quality smoked salmon
2 ounces low-fat cottage cheese
2 ounces part-skim ricotta cheese
1 tablespoon fresh lemon juice
1 tablespoon grated onion
1 teaspoon prepared horseradish
1 to 2 teaspoons liquid hickory smoke flavoring
2 tablespoons minced fresh parsley

Drain the salmon. Remove the skin but use the bones, because they are a good source of calcium. In a bowl, flake the salmon and combine it with the cheeses, lemon juice, onion, horseradish, liquid smoke, and parsley. Blend until smooth. Chill for several hours or overnight.

Serves 4

PRETTY PEPPER SALAD

¼ red bell pepper
¼ green bell pepper
6 radishes
2 tablespoons balsamic vinegar

Dice the peppers and slice the radishes. Toss with vinegar. Chill for up to 1 hour, or serve immediately.

Serves 1

FANCY FISH

1 pound fresh halibut, orange roughy, or a firm white fish
2 tablespoons orange juice concentrate, undiluted
4 teaspoons fresh lemon juice
¼ teaspoon dried dill
4 tablespoons minced fresh parsley
8 tablespoons white wine

Place the fish in a baking dish. In a bowl, combine the other ingredients; pour over the fish. Cover and refrigerate for 45 minutes, turning once. Spray a broiling pan with Pam. Broil the fish until flaky, 10 to 15 minutes, basting often with the marinade.

Serves 4

WILD RICE PILAF

¼ cup wild rice
1 tablespoon diet margarine
⅓ cup chopped onions
2 cups Swanson's Natural Goodness chicken broth
⅛ cup slivered almonds
4 dried apricot halves, chopped

Wash the wild rice under running water. In a nonstick skillet, melt the margarine and sauté the onions until golden brown. Add the wild rice and stir until it is glistening. Add the chicken broth and heat until near boiling. Cover, reduce the heat, and simmer for 20 to 30 minutes, until the broth is absorbed and the wild rice is tender. Place the wild rice, almonds, and apricots in a Pam-sprayed baking dish. Cover and bake in a 325° oven for 15 minutes.

Serves 4

MENU 2

FOOD FOR THOUGHT

What your heart knows today, your head will understand tomorrow.

BREAKFAST

(200 calories)

*Apricot Cream Crèpes**
Decaffeinated coffee

SNACK

(70 calories)

2 Pogen Krisprolls
Celestial Seasonings Grandma's Tummy Mint tea

LUNCH

(300 calories)

*Black Bean Soup**
*Snow Pea Snap**
2 Wasa Crispbread Savory Sesame Crackers
Celestial Seasonings Country Peach Spice herb tea, iced

SNACK

(50 calories)

1 sliced kiwi or ½ cup fresh pineapple
Celestial Seasonings Almond Sunset herb tea

DINNER

(300 calories)

*Florentine Stuffed Chicken Breast**
*Beauty and the Beet Slaw**
Dilly Dash Potatoes (page 53)
Wishful White Wine (page 25)

DESSERT

(150 calories)

*"To Die For" Chocolate Mousse**
*Crème de Café**

* Recipe follows.

TOTAL CALORIES 1,070
PROTEIN 29%
CARBOHYDRATE 54%
FAT 17%

APRICOT CREAM CRÊPES

Crêpes

2 tablespoons nonfat plain yogurt
⅔ cup part-skim ricotta cheese
½ cup nonfat milk
6 tablespoons whole-wheat flour
2 teaspoons sugar
¼ teaspoon baking powder
1 teaspoon vanilla extract
3 egg whites
⅛ teaspoon cream of tartar

Filling

2 cups Yocotta (page 112)
2 cups canned apricots, packed in "light" syrup, drained

To make crêpes, put the yogurt and ricotta cheese in a blender. Whirl. Add the milk, flour, sugar, baking powder, and vanilla. Blend until smooth. In a small bowl, beat the egg whites with cream of tartar until soft peaks form. Gently fold them into the batter. Spray a nonstick skillet with Pam. Place one-eighth of the batter in the pan and rotate it quickly. Allow to brown lightly until golden. Turn and brown lightly on the other side. Repeat to make 8 crêpes.

To assemble the crêpes, in the center of each place ¼ cup yocotta and ¼ cup apricots. Roll gently, placing seam side down.

Serves 4 (2 per serving)

BLACK BEAN SOUP

1 large onion, chopped
1 clove garlic, minced
3 tablespoons Swanson's Natural Goodness chicken broth
2 stalks celery, sliced
1 carrot, sliced thin
2 cups cooked black beans, cooking liquid reserved
2 tablespoons tomato paste
½ teaspoon cumin
¼ teaspoon cayenne pepper
¼ cup nonfat plain yogurt
1 scallion, minced

In a heavy skillet, sauté the onion and garlic in broth. Cook over low heat until they are transparent. Add the celery and carrot. Cook until the carrot is done, 4 to 6 minutes. Add the beans to the vegetable mixture. Stir in the tomato paste, the reserved cooking liquid, cumin, and cayenne pepper. Simmer the soup for 30 minutes. If you prefer a smoother consistency, purée in a food processor or blender. Divide the soup into bowls and top with yogurt and scallion.

Serves 4

SNOW PEA SNAP

1 cup snow peas

Wash and trim the snow peas. Serve chilled and raw.

Serves 1

FLORENTINE STUFFED CHICKEN BREASTS

4 4-ounce boneless, skinless chicken breasts
½ cup diced onion
2 cloves garlic, minced
½ cup chopped mushrooms
½ cup frozen chopped spinach, thawed and well drained
¼ cup minced fresh parsley
½ cup low-fat cottage cheese
2 tablespoons grated Parmesan cheese
1 tablespoon soft bread crumbs
½ cup dry white wine

Pound each chicken breast to a thickness of ¼ inch. In a nonstick skillet sprayed with Pam, sauté the onion, garlic, and mushrooms until tender. Combine the mixture with the spinach, parsley, cottage cheese, Parmesan cheese, and bread crumbs. Spread one-quarter of the spinach mixture over each breast. Carefully roll the chicken breasts to enclose the filling, and secure with toothpicks. Transfer the chicken rolls to a baking dish. Add wine to the dish, cover with foil, and bake for 30 to 40 minutes at 350°. Remove the toothpicks before serving.

Serves 4

BEAUTY AND THE BEET SLAW

3 medium raw beets
1 carrot
1 tablespoon mayonnaise
2 tablespoons nonfat plain yogurt
Grated rind of 1 lemon
2 tablespoons orange juice
1 tablespoon fresh lemon juice
½ cup canned juice-packed crushed pineapple, drained

Grate the beets and carrots in a food processor. In a bowl, combine the mayonnaise, yogurt, lemon rind, orange juice, and lemon juice. Fold in the beets, carrots, and pineapple. Chill.

Serves 4

"TO DIE FOR" CHOCOLATE MOUSSE

2 tablespoons *plus* 1/3 cup nonfat milk
3½ teaspoons unflavored Knox gelatin
1 egg, separated
1 tablespoon unsweetened cocoa powder
2 tablespoons *plus* 1½ teaspoons sugar
1 teaspoon vanilla extract
½ cup low-fat cottage cheese
¼ cup part-skim ricotta cheese
1 tablespoon Kahlua liqueur
⅛ teaspoon cream of tartar

Place 2 tablespoons milk in the container of a blender; sprinkle gelatin over it and let stand for 2 minutes. In a saucepan, heat 1/3 cup milk to a boil. Pour the heated milk into the blender. Cover and blend at high speed for 10 seconds. Set aside for 5 minutes. To the gelatin mixture add the egg yolk, cocoa, sugar, vanilla, cheeses, and liqueur. Whirl until smooth. Pour into a bowl and refrigerate until slightly thickened. In a separate bowl, beat the egg white with cream of tartar until soft peaks form. Gently fold into the cheese mixture, blending thoroughly. Pour into 4 custard cups. Refrigerate for several hours or overnight.

Serves 4

CRÈME DE CAFÉ

⅛ teaspoon vanilla extract or a 1-inch piece of vanilla bean
1 cup hot decaffeinated coffee
¼ cup canned evaporated skim milk

Add vanilla to the hot coffee, or brew decaf with the vanilla bean on top of the grounds. Serve with evaporated milk.

Serves 1

Menu 3

FOOD FOR THOUGHT
Make your house a home today.

BREAKFAST IN BED
(248 calories)

*Quiche**
*Apple Banana Bread**
Decaffeinated coffee
Newspaper (to read, not to eat)

LUNCH
(357 calories)

*Salade Niçoise**
1 small whole-wheat roll
Perrier with lemon

SNACK
(50 calories)

½ cup fresh papaya with lime
Celestial Seasonings Cranberry Cove herb tea

DINNER
(290 calories)

*Savory Stuffed Squash**
*Razzle-Dazzle Salad**
*Wine Spritzer**

DESSERT
(160 calories)

*Elegant Apple Tart**
Celestial Seasonings Roastaroma herb tea

TOTAL CALORIES 1,105
PROTEIN 18%
CARBOHYDRATE 63%
FAT 19%

* Recipe follows.

QUICHE

½ cup chopped onions
½ cup chopped mushrooms
½ cup grated zucchini
1 clove garlic, minced
4 tablespoons tomato sauce
4 tablespoons minced fresh parsley
2 tablespoons grated Parmesan cheese
¾ cup egg substitute
⅛ teaspoon black pepper

In a nonstick skillet sprayed with Pam, sauté the onions, mushrooms, zucchini, and garlic in tomato sauce. Add the parsley, cheese, egg substitute, and pepper. Spray nonstick muffin tins with Pam. Spoon the mixture into 8 muffin cups and bake in a 425° oven for 15 minutes, until the filling is almost dry and a toothpick inserted in the center comes out clean. The quiche will become more solid upon cooling. Serve warm or at room temperature.

Serves 4 (2 per serving)

WARMHEARTED APPLESAUCE

2 cups unsweetened applesauce
8 Red Hot cinnamon candies

Heat the applesauce and candies over low heat or in a microwave. Stir to partially dissolve the candies and blend their flavor with the applesauce. Serve warm.

Serves 4

APPLE BANANA BREAD

2 ripe bananas, mashed
½ cup egg substitute
2 teaspoons vanilla extract
2 teaspoons cinnamon
½ teaspoon nutmeg
¼ cup honey
1¾ cups whole-wheat flour
¼ cup Quaker Old Fashioned Oats, ground fine in a food processor
2 teaspoons baking powder
1 teaspoon baking soda
½ teaspoon salt
6 tablespoons golden raisins
2 apples, cored, peeled, and finely chopped

In a bowl, combine the banana, egg substitue, vanilla, cinnamon, nutmeg, and honey. In a separate bowl, combine the flour, oats, baking powder, baking soda, and salt. Stir into the banana mixture. Mix until smooth. Fold in the raisins and apples. Spray a nonstick loaf pan with Pam. Spoon the mixture into the pan and bake in a preheated 375° oven for 40 to 45 minutes, or until a toothpick comes out clean. Allow to cool on a rack at room temperature. When cool, refrigerate for several hours. Slice and wrap each slice individually, label, and freeze.

Serves 12

SALADE NIÇOISE

Dressing

2 tablespoons Dijon mustard
3 cloves garlic, mashed
2 tablespoons fresh lemon juice
⅓ cup red wine vinegar
2 tablespoons olive oil

½ small red onion, thinly sliced
1½ tablespoons red wine vinegar
2 small thin-skinned red potatoes, scrubbed
12 ounces green beans, strings removed
8 black olives
12 cherry tomatoes
4 hard-cooked eggs, halved
1 tablespoon capers, drained
1 6½-ounce can water-packed white-meat tuna, drained
4 cups crisp romaine lettuce, torn into bite-size pieces

In a small jar, mix the mustard, garlic, lemon juice, and vinegar. Stir in the oil. Cover tightly and chill. Shake before using.

Combine the onion and vinegar in a bowl and set aside. Steam the potatoes and green beans until tender. Immerse in ice-cold water, drain, and chill. On a platter arrange side by side, in spoke fashion, the potatoes, beans, olives, tomatoes, and eggs, topped with capers. Drain the onion, discard the vinegar, and arrange the onion with the vegetables. Break the tuna into chunks and mound in a small glass bowl in the center of the platter. Arrange the romaine on 4 salad plates. Divide the dressing into 4 small dishes and pass the salad.

Serves 4

RAZZLE-DAZZLE SALAD

8 cups crisp romaine lettuce, torn into bite-size pieces
2 tomatoes, chopped
½ green bell pepper, chopped
2 tablespoons diced red onion
2 tablespoons minced fresh parsley
½ cup bean sprouts
1 cup shredded red cabbage
4 tablespoons raspberry vinegar

Combine in a bowl. Toss and serve.

Serves 4

SAVORY STUFFED SQUASH

2 small acorn squash
¼ cup Swanson's Natural Goodness chicken broth
½ cup chopped onions
1 cup chopped apples
1 cup chopped celery
3 cups cooked brown rice (*not* instant or quick)
1½ cups cooked lentils (see note)
2 tablespoons chutney or jam
1 tablespoon raisins
¼ cup nonfat plain yogurt
1 tablespoon Dijon mustard
1 tablespoon fresh lemon juice
2 tablespoons chopped walnuts
1 teaspoon cinnamon

Cut the squash in half lengthwise (through the stem to the flower end). Scoop out and discard the seeds and strings. Steam the squash until tender in a pot with ½ inch water. Or to microwave, place the squash, cut side down, on a paper towel in the microwave. Microwave on full power until tender, approximately 15 minutes. Scoop out the pulp and reserve 1 cup of it.

In a nonstick skillet sprayed with Pam, heat the chicken broth and sauté the onions, apples, and celery together for about 5 minutes, or until the onions are translucent. In a large bowl, combine the apple mixture with the rice, lentils, and reserved squash pulp. Add the chutney, raisins, yogurt, mustard, lemon juice, nuts, and cinnamon. Toss all ingredients together. Fill the squash cavities with the stuffing. Sprinkle lightly with additional cinnamon. Bake at 350° for 20 minutes. To microwave, cover loosely with plastic wrap and cook on high for 3 minutes. Turn and cook on high for 1 more minute. Stir the filling to check the temperature, and cook longer if necessary.

Serves 4

Note: To cook lentils, wash ¾ cup dried lentils until the water runs clear. Combine in a pot with 2 cups water and bring to a boil. Turn the heat down to low, cover, and simmer for 1 hour. Drain and reserve the lentils.

WINE SPRITZER

2 tablespoons white wine, chilled
6 ounces sparkling water, chilled

Blend and serve in a chilled wine goblet.

Serves 1

ELEGANT APPLE TART

1¼ cups whole-wheat flour
6 tablespoons diet margarine
2 tablespoons ice water
4 green pippin apples, peeled, cored, and sliced thin
2 tablespoons sugar
1 teaspoon cinnamon
½ teaspoon grated lemon rind
2 tablespoons apricot preserves

Place the flour in mixing bowl. Add the margarine and mix with a fork until crumbly. Sprinkle ice water over the mixture and combine with a fork until the dough is moistened evenly. Form the dough into a ball. Cover with plastic wrap and refrigerate for 30 minutes. Roll the dough out on a lightly floured surface. Place in a 10-inch pie plate, making sure to bring dough up the sides ½ inch. Prick with a fork. In a bowl, combine the apples, sugar, cinnamon, and lemon rind. Toss. Arrange the apple mixture on the dough. Bake in a 400° oven for 30 minutes, or until the apples are tender and pastry is golden brown. Melt the preserves in a microwave or in a small saucepan. Drizzle over the tart.

Serves 8

Menu 4

DINING OUT

FOOD FOR THOUGHT

Of all the things you wear, your expression is the most important.

BREAKFAST

(290 calories)

½ spinach and mushroom omelet
1 slice whole-wheat toast
1 teaspoon jam
½ grapefruit or ¼ melon or 1 cup berries
Decaffeinated coffee

LUNCH

(323 calories)

Shrimp Louis made with 2 cups lettuce, 2 ounces shrimp,
3 asparagus spears, 1 hard-cooked egg, 1 tomato
1 tablespoon Thousand Island dressing diluted with lemon juice
1 sourdough roll
Iced tea

DINNER

(407 calories)

3 ounces beef brochette
½ cup steamed green beans
6 ounces tomato juice with lemon
Perrier with lemon

DESSERT

(135 calories)

½ cup sorbet
Decaffeinated coffee

TOTAL CALORIES 1,155
PROTEIN 25%
CARBOHYDRATE 48%
FAT 27%

DIET DAY #7

BACK TO NATURE

Anything natural or connected with the great out-of-doors has appeal for you on a Diet Day #7. You want fresh, healthy foods today and are very particular about what you eat.

In an analytical frame of mind, you are in the mood to understand the theories behind the Numbers Diet. The perfectionist side of your personality shows today. Not only will you follow your diet precisely, but you probably won't cheat.

Some time alone, perferably spent outdoors, is high on your list of priorities. This is a good day to take a mental vacation. Journey within yourself and relax. Recharge your batteries so you can hit it on all eight cylinders tomorrow.

WATER

This is a good day to consider the body's most essential natural requirement, water. With all the commercial soft drinks available, not to mention beer, wine, coffee, and tea, we have almost forgotten to drink plain water. One of nature's major elements, water is used for other terrific things like swimming, sprinkling the lawn, watering the vegetables we eat, and keeping ourselves, our clothes, and even Rover clean. We forget that the most important thing we should do with water is drink it. The only liquid consumed by the body that doesn't require energy to metabolize or excrete, water has no calories, yet it is essential to good health, and paramount for weight control.

Approximately seven-tenths of a human body is water, which explains its vital role in our diet. The average woman's body weight consists of 55 to 65 percent water, while a man's body weight consists of 65 to 75 percent water. The difference is explained by the fact that women have a larger percentage of body fat, which holds less water than muscle. Babies are even more dependent on water than adults, because 85 percent of their body weight comes from water.

A healthy person can survive for weeks with no food, but only a few days without water. Water is the only nutrient required daily to keep our bodies functioning efficiently. It accounts for 92 percent of blood plasma and 60 percent of blood cells. Water is the basic substance in blood that carries oxygen and nutrients throughout the body. Essential for the kidney function of excreting toxins and waste, water acts as a filter. Ten to seventeen ounces of water, approximately two glasses, must pass through the kidneys daily just to get rid of metabolic wastes.

Contrary to popular belief, water does not help us to burn fat faster, but it is necessary to break down the stored fats and to help burn sugar for energy. Water also combines with our digestive juices to break down the foods we eat into usable form. Studies have shown that a decrease in water intake will cause a body's fat deposits to increase, while an increase in water intake can actually reduce fat deposits. During weight loss the body needs to process more water in order to wash away toxins and flush out the metabolized body fat.

> I remember how my ankles used to swell when I was a teenage sun worshipper. I never understood why I looked as if I had elephantiasis every summer. Now I realize that I didn't drink enough water while I was sweating in the sun.

If we become dehydrated, either by not drinking enough water or from excess perspiration, the kidneys behave as if they are in the Sahara desert by holding back every drop of water in order to survive, and fluid retention results.

In order to get rid of extra fluids retained by the body, you must drink lots of water. The more salt you eat, the more water your body retains, to dilute the salt. The only way to get rid of the stored water is to drink more water, washing away the excess sodium.

> Water acts as an air conditioner in the summer to cool us, and a heater in the winter to warm us. Believe it or not, if you want to stay warm in winter, drink lots of water.

Without adequate water to serve as a lubricant, eyes become irritated, nasal passages become dry, and the digestive system suffers. Water constitutes 80 percent of our muscle mass and is essential to maintaining proper muscle tone. Water gives muscles their natural ability to contract and prevents the sagging skin that sometimes accompanies weight loss. Shrinking cells are buoyed by water, which plumps up the skin and leaves it clear, healthy, and resilient.

> If you think drinking plain water is unappetizing, flavor it with a slice of lemon and serve it in a crystal goblet.

Water is essential for good elimination. Solid wastes move more rapidly and easily through the intestines if there is adequate water for them to absorb. If the kidneys don't get enough water, they pass the buck to the liver, whose primary function is to metabolize stored fat into usable energy for the body. When the liver is burdened by doing the kidneys' job, the liver metabolizes less fat, which slows down your weight loss. In other words, more stored fat is used for fuel when your liver isn't moonlighting for a pair of water-starved kidneys. Water literally flushes your system, so drink up.

Water in sufficient quantities decreases your appetite. On the other hand, a body with insufficient water causes the hypothalamus, a regulatory gland, to signal thirst, which you sometimes confuse with hunger. As a result, you end up eating instead of drinking.

To prevent a water shortage in your body:

- Drink at least 6 to 8 glasses of water a day.
- Drink before you feel thirsty.
- In hot, humid weather, increase your water consumption.
- Don't rely on any liquid other than water to satisfy the daily requirement of 6 to 8 glasses. Caffeine, found in coffee, tea, and some diet sodas, is a mild diuretic and actually causes water loss.

> To avoid dehydration while traveling by air, and the accompanying symptoms of jet lag, drink water before, during, and after the flight.

KINDS OF WATER

Is bottled water better? The answer depends on your personal preference and the condition of the tap water where you live. Consider taste, price, convenience, and sodium content before you decide which water is best for your body.

Hard water. From the tap, it contains calcium, magnesium, and salts.

Softened water. It contains sodium, often copper, iron, and zinc.

Distilled water. All the minerals have been removed by processing. It is usually used in appliances such as steam irons.

Commercially bottled water. For drinking, this may be natural spring water or well water, or processed water straight out of the municipal water supply.

Imported mineral water. Although it comes from a foreign country, imported water must meet U.S. sanitary requirements. Check to see if the sodium level is within your range.

Seltzer. Filtered tap water is carbonated with carbon dioxide when forced through a special cartridge that is part of a seltzer bottle.

Club soda. This is tap water, filtered and carbonated, with minerals and mineral salts added for flavoring.

Natural sparkling water. This too contains carbon dioxide, directly from a spring or reinjected during processing for a natural bubbling quality.

In this book I recommend water with 1 to 2 tablespoons of juice as flavoring, or herb tea, hot or iced.

FIBER

On a Diet Day #7 you are interested in natural foods and preventive medicine.

Fiber is nature's foremost fighter in the battle against our killer diseases: certain forms of cancer, high cholesterol, diabetes, obesity, and heart disease. Despite this knowledge, Americans consume much less fiber than they should, because the foods we eat are refined and processed to be prepared quickly and eaten on the run. The part of plants not digested by our bodies, fiber is "nature's broom" and comes in two basic kinds, each with different advantages.

WATER-SOLUBLE FIBER

High-fiber foods with water-soluble fiber take more time to digest. They are released slowly into the bloodstream, which helps to prevent dramatic swings in blood sugar levels. Also credited with lowering blood cholesterol and triglycerides, water-soluble fiber is found in apples and other fruits and vegetables, barley, dried beans, peas and nuts, and oats, as in oat bran and oatmeal.

WATER-INSOLUBLE FIBER

This is credited with being the key element in keeping our digestive machinery healthy and running smoothly. It is found in wheat bran, whole grains, and certain fresh vegetables.

Some fiber is like a sponge that absorbs excess water in our gastrointestinal tracts. Fiber needs water to make it work properly —all the more reason to drink 8 glasses of water a day.

> Fiber and water together are nature's laxatives. Try a glass of warm water and the unstrained juice of one lemon every morning for a safe, gentle natural laxative.

There are many advantages to getting adequate fiber in your diet. Fiber promotes weight control. Foods with fiber, such as fresh fruit and vegetables, are more filling and satisfying. They add bulk, which takes longer to eat and chew. During the twenty minutes it takes for the brain to register that the stomach is full, you can consume less chewy, high-fiber food than slippery high-fat food that goes down easily at a high calorie clip. If you eat high-fiber food instead of high-calorie, high-fat food, you can decrease the total number of calories you eat in one day. In addition, high-fiber foods promote quick elimination, which may discourage absorption of fats in the other foods you eat in a meal with the high-fiber foods. I'm not suggesting that you can avoid being stuck with the butter fat from the ice cream if you eat a chocolate sundae after a heaping plate of brown rice and raw carrots. I am saying it's a good idea to adjust your diet to include more fiber and less fat. There are no free tickets to guilt-free fatty-food feasts.

There are easy ways to add extra fiber to your diet:

- Fill Parmesan cheese–type containers with oat bran and wheat germ. Add a sprinkle to breakfast cereal, yogurt, or salad.
- Use whole-wheat pasta instead of egg pasta.
- Substitute whole-wheat flour for half of the white flour in muffins and breads.
- Use whole-grain bread for sandwiches and toast.
- Eat fresh fruits and vegetables every day. Whenever possible, eat their skins.

OAT BRAN

The expression "feeling your oats" comes from ranchers who noticed how energetic their horses were shortly after eating their grain. It's good for you, too.

Until recently, wheat bran, as a high-fiber preventive of colon cancer, has been the darling of nutritionists. Up-and-coming oat bran is now winning the popularity contest, due to reports of its role in reducing cholesterol.

Oat bran is really a misnomer, because it is actually more than the husk of the crushed oat grain left after milling. Also included are three or four layers of aleurone, in which many of the vitamins (such as thiamine), minerals (such as iron and phosphorus), and protein of oat bran are concentrated.

Lighter in color, texture, and flavor than wheat bran, oat bran is popular for use in baked goods because they more closely resemble those made with traditional refined flour, making oat bran ideal for people who are just becoming familiar with grains other than wheat. Unlike wheat bran, oat bran is soluble in water because of its high concentration of water-soluble gums. These gums give cooked oats their sticky texture.

Slightly more expensive than wheat bran, oat bran sold as cereal can replace flour in muffins, breads, and cookies. Oat bran sold in bulk at health food stores and co-ops is a little coarser. It can be ground to a finer texture in a blender or food processor. In recipes that call for baking powder, try using half oat bran and half wheat flour.

The natural oils in bran can become rancid, so check whatever oat bran product you buy before you store it. Like wheat flour, oat bran should be tightly sealed in a glass or plastic container. It can be refrigerated for up to three months, or stored in the freezer for six months.

Other oat products, such as Quaker Old-Fashioned Oats, quick oats, and instant oats, are also good for you. Refining wheat flour is nutritional robbery, but processing oats by flattening, cracking, or cutting doesn't seem to deplete any of the nutrients, probably because no parts are discarded. For example, Quaker Old-Fashioned Oats, or rolled oats, which cook in about five minutes, are oat kernels that have been mashed flat by steel rollers, Quaker Quick Oats, which cook in one minute, are rolled oats that have been cut up. Instant Quaker Oats, which are reconstituted right in the bowl with boiling water, are minced even finer. All three products have the same vitamin and mineral levels and comparable fiber.

> Recent studies indicate that rice bran (brown rice) is also helpful in lowering cholesterol.

USING OAT BRAN PRODUCTS

Oat bran or ground oat flour may be substituted for refined flour in baked goods. Because oat bran and oat flour contain no gluten, you cannot use them to replace more than one-third of the wheat flour without sacrificing texture in the finished product.

When you cook with oat bran, here are some secrets for success:

- Preheat your oven to the correct temperature.
- Mix the batter with the fewest possible strokes.
- All ingredients (including nuts, flour, liquid, oil) should be at room temperature, not ice cold.
- To substitute rolled oats for whole-wheat flour, use 1½ cups rolled oats for each cup of flour.
- Substitute 1½ cups regular oats for 1¼ cups quick oats. Instant oats do not make a satisfactory substitute for wheat flour.
- Use oat products as an extender or instead of bread crumbs, or as stuffings and fillings. You can add ½ cup oats to 1 pound of meat or poultry if you increase the liquid by 2 tablespoons.

- Coat skinned chicken in oat bran before baking to seal in the juices and add a nice crunchy replacement for the skin.
- Replace chopped nuts in a recipe with rolled oats. Reduce the amount of flour by half the volume of the added toasted or rolled oats. For example, if you add ½ cup oats, omit ¼ cup flour.
- You can make oat flour by putting rolled oats in the food processor and processing with a steel blade.
- Make your own Shake and Bake by brushing fish or poultry with nonfat milk and coating with rolled or quick oats to which you have added herbs and spices. Use rolled oats in chicken recipes that call for cooking times of longer than 30 minutes. Quick oats work better in fish recipes, which require shorter cooking times.
- Use 2 tablespoons of rolled oats to thicken a sloppy joe mixture based on 1 pound of ground turkey or beef.
- To make a great topping to use on fresh fruit or yogurt, mix rolled oats with a little diet margarine and cinnamon and toast in a 350° oven for 15 minutes. Stir twice, and remove from the oven when brown.

LEGUMES

Packed with protein, vitamins, and minerals, dried legumes are one of the most complete foods. They are inexpensive, easy to store, low in calories, high in fiber, low in cholesterol, and versatile. Although most dried beans require overnight soaking and/or long cooking, dried peas and lentils don't need to be soaked and can be prepared in under an hour.

The fiber in legumes acts as a cleaning agent in the stomach and lower intestine, removing fats, cholesterol, residual food material, and potential carcinogens. Legumes in your daily diet promote healthy digestion and regularity.

As a complex carbohydrate, legumes release energy slowly and steadily for maximum body strength and endurance. Combined with grains such as rice, wheat, and corn, legumes provide protein quality equivalent to beef, with less fat, cholesterol, and calories.

Soaking dried beans overnight (at least 6 hours) covered with cold water (which is then discarded) prevents the flatulence sometimes associated with them. Add fresh water and bring to a boil over high heat. Then turn the heat to a simmer and cook, partially covered, until the beans are tender. Check occasionally and add water if necessary to keep the beans from burning.

A quick method calls for washing beans and boiling them with water for 5 minutes. Turn off the heat and allow the beans to stand. At the end of 1 hour, reheat in the same water to the boiling point. Simmer, partially covered, for 1 hour, until the beans are tender. Cooking times vary according to the type of bean used.

Although some recipes call for bicarbonate of soda, do not add it, because the vitamin B will be destroyed and the beans will have a high concentration of sodium.

If salt is added in the beginning, cooking will be delayed, since the salt prevents the water from being absorbed. For tender beans, do not add tomatoes, spices, molasses, or wine at the beginning of the process, as the acid in these foods tends to toughen the outside covering of the legumes.

YOGURT

Nonfat plain yogurt is a dieter's dream. Full of protein and calcium, it can be turned into soups, salad dressings, dips, sauces, and desserts. Knowing you can have yogurt substitutes makes it easier to give up cream soups, mayonnaise, whipped cream, ice cream, and puddings. Its tangy flavor is an acquired taste, but once you get used to it, you'll appreciate the versatility of yogurt.

Many brands of yogurt are loaded with calories from fat and sugar. Vanilla- and lemon-flavored yogurt have less calories than fruit-added yogurts, but the lowest in calories is nonfat plain yogurt. With more nutrients per ounce than the flavored versions, nonfat plain yogurt is the best choice. Check labels carefully.

The liquid in yogurt accounts for the tart flavor. To produce yogurt "cheese," a thicker, more condensed product with a milder flavor, the liquid can be drained by placing the yogurt in a colander lined with cheesecloth or paper coffee filters. Place a container under the colander to catch the liquid as it drains. Since it takes at least 4 to 8 hours, this procedure is better accomplished in the refrigerator, to prevent spoilage. The finished product is more like sour cream than yogurt and is a great substitute for sour cream or mayonnaise. Yogurt "cheese" can be also be thinned with skim milk for use in creamy salad dressings and soups.

COOKING WITH YOGURT

When used as a sour cream substitute in recipes that call for heating, yogurt and yogurt cheese must be stabilized to avoid curdling. Add 1 tablespoon flour or cornstarch per cup of yogurt, prior to heating. Yogurt "cheese" produces a thicker, milder-tasting product for heated recipes.

IDEAS FOR USING YOGURT

- Extend mayonnaise with yogurt for the same flavor and less calories. One part mayonnaise to two parts yogurt makes a mixture that still tastes enough like mayonnaise for use in recipes where the mayonnaise flavor is important, such as chicken, tuna, egg, potato, or Waldorf salad.
- Combine yogurt with puréed beans for a tasty reduced-calorie dip or pâté.
- Top baked potatoes and garnish soups with yogurt in place of sour cream.
- Instead of mayonnaise and buttermilk, yogurt can be mixed with a teaspoon of dry Ranch House dressing mix to produce the flavor of the dressing without the calories and increase the nutritional value of your salad by adding protein and calcium.
- Dilute commercial "light" dressings with nonfat plain yogurt for a more nutritious variety of the original dressing.
- Mix "no oil" vinaigrette dressings (Pritikin is excellent) with nonfat plain yogurt for a creamy vinaigrette. Add some mashed fresh garlic. *Voilà!* You've never had a healthier, creamier garlic dressing.
- Blend equal parts of cottage cheese and nonfat plain yogurt with seasonings, such as dill. Spread on rice cakes for a snack or top baked potatoes for a main dish.
- Combine yogurt with packaged dry taco mix seasoning for a zippy south-of-the-border dressing.
- Mix yogurt with fresh lemon juice, paprika, and a dash of cayenne to make a tasty dip for artichokes, or a sauce that brings out the flavor of steamed broccoli or asparagus.
- Mix yogurt with diced fresh fruit for a homemade fresh fruit yogurt sundae much lower in calories than sugar-laden commercial varieties.

- Swirl 1 tablespoon frozen orange juice or apple juice concentrate into ½ cup nonfat plain yogurt for a smooth, cool treat.
- Mix yogurt with frozen berries that have been warmed in the microwave to release juices for a luscious "fire and ice" treat.
- Blend yogurt with ricotta and all-fruit jam (no sugar added) for a sweet toast-topper.
- Combine a small amount of peanut butter with nonfat yogurt and use to stuff stalks of celery.
- Add dry Crystal Light powders to yogurt for use as "frosting" on rice cakes or crackers for a snack.
- Add "sweet" spices, such as cinnamon or ready-mixed apple pie or pumpkin pie spice, to yogurt and use as a spread. Adding a teaspoon of honey will add only 16 calories.
- Make your own low-calorie vanilla yogurt by adding pure vanilla extract (the best is the type purchased from your pharmacist) and a little honey. If you aren't concerned about using artificial sweeteners, add a small amount of sugar substitute to taste. Vanilla extract intensifies the sweet taste of artificial sweeteners, so add sweetener sparingly.
- Dilute high-calorie commercial fruit and flavored yogurts with the nonfat plain yogurt.
- Sprinkle a crumbled no-sugar-added cereal or cookie on nonfat plain yogurt for added flavor and nutty texture.

VEGETARIAN DIETS

A Diet Day #7 is a good time to satisfy your curiosity about vegetarian diets because you are attracted to the idea of eating natural foods.

The addition of meatless dishes and whole menus to the restaurant scene tells us that vegetarians have become part of the mainstream. The important thing you, as a dieter, should know is that the term *vegetarian* is not synonymous with *low-calorie*. Many vegetarian dishes served in restaurants are loaded with cheese, which is high in fat calories.

There are several kinds of vegetarians:

- Lacto-ovo vegetarians, who don't eat meat, seafood, or poultry but do eat dairy products and eggs, make up 90 percent of the 8 million vegetarians in the United States.

- Lacto-vegetarians don't eat meat, poultry, seafood, or eggs, but do eat dairy products.
- Vegans, or strict vegetarians, don't eat any food of animal origin—meat, poultry, seafood, eggs, or dairy products.

HEALTH BENEFITS OF A VEGETARIAN DIET

By eating less meat and more fresh fruits and vegetables, legumes (dried beans, peas, and lentils), whole grains, and nonfat dairy products you can reduce the amount of fat in your diet, increase the amount of fiber in your diet, lower triglycerides (blood fat), lower serum cholesterol, lower weight, and lower blood pressure.

You can get high-quality, complete protein from a vegetarian diet by eating combinations of grains, legumes, seeds, and nuts. These vegetable sources of protein can be augmented by low-fat dairy products and eggs, according to the category of vegetarian diet you follow.

Complete protein combinations:
Whole grains + legumes
Whole grains + dairy products (milk, yogurt, cheese)
Nuts and seeds + legumes

The main sources of vegetable protein are:

Grains: Barley, brown rice, buckwheat, bulgur wheat, cornmeal, millet, oats, rye, wheat, and corn.

Legumes: Beans (white, red, lima, kidney, black), lentils, mung beans, peanuts, peas (black-eyed and split), soybeans, and soybean curd (tofu).

Seeds: Sesame, sunflower, and pumpkin.

Nuts: Almonds, Brazil nuts, cashews, pecans, walnuts, and pine nuts.

Some people mistakenly believe that vegetarians are anemic. Actually, vegetarians and meat eaters alike can avoid nutritional problems if they eat sensibly and include a wide variety of foods in their diet. Although meat, poultry, and fish are excellent sources of protein and iron, as well as B vitamins and other nutrients, legumes and grains, in the right combinations, can provide enough complete protein for a balanced diet. Whole-grain products supply the B vitamins, iron, and other minerals, while eating foods rich in vitamin C, like tomato sauce over pasta, help the body utilize available iron from other foods. If eggs and cheese constitute a large part of a vegetarian's diet, high cholesterol may become a problem.

FASTING

On a Diet Day #7, when you are in the mood to take a sabbatical, the question of fasting may be on your mind.

There are basically two types of fasting: a one-day liquid fast of juice and water and an extended liquid-protein fast that is medically supervised.

ONE-DAY FAST

Some people believe that fasting on juice or water for one day a week is beneficial because it supposedly cleanses the body and rests the digestive tract. Others fast one day a week for religious purposes.

Personally, I do not approve of this practice. If skipping breakfast and lunch wreaks havoc on your metabolism, why subject it to an all-day fast? Remember, lack of food sends your body into starvation mode, reducing your metabolism, the rate at which you burn calories. Even after you resume eating, the body plays it safe by continuing to burn calories slowly to preserve body fat. The body stores extra fat in the event that food becomes scarce again. A weekly one-day fast is counterproductive to weight loss.

MEDICALLY SUPERVISED FAST

Recent attention has been focused on celebrities who have lost over fifty pounds on medically supervised fasts of liquid protein. Protein powders made by pharmaceutical companies come in premeasured packets that, when mixed with water, provide 400 to 600 calories per day. Even though some of these products are available over the counter, dieters are cautioned not to use them without medical supervision.

Liquid protein is an effective way to lose weight. However, unless the medically supervised program includes behavior modification to permanently change your eating habits and establish regular exercise, maintaining weight loss is unlikely.

In certain cases, medically supervised liquid protein fasts do have merit. Liquid protein fasts are expensive; the more popular programs cost $100 or more per week. And dieters must realize that the price they are paying for losing on liquid protein is very high in metabolic terms, too. Fasting on liquid protein may slow down the metabolism so that once the dieter resumes eating regular food, his daily calorie allowance may have to be lowered drastically in order to maintain weight loss. The key to keeping the metabolism high is exercising, which maintains muscle mass while losing fat. It's essential to continue to exercise during the maintenance period, which is the rest of your life.

There is no free lunch. If you aren't careful, you may pay even when you don't eat.

DIET DOWNFALLS AND THEIR SOLUTIONS

In your desire to spend some time alone on a Diet Day #7, you may be eating by yourself. Be sure you don't use that as an excuse to eat unwisely. On the other hand, if you are feeling lonely or misunderstood, as sometimes happens on a Diet Day #7, don't eat as an escape from your feelings. You'll only make matters worse and wind up feeling guilty.

If worry creeps into your thoughts, don't let your hands creep into the cookie jar. Instead, keep them busy making a list of all the things you worried about in the recent past. How many of these potential disasters really happened, and how much time did you waste worrying about them? If you find yourself worrying about "what happens if," get busy and take some concrete steps to prepare yourself for the disaster that's on your mind. If you're chewing your nails and every cracker in the house because a family member is ill or coming home late, busy yourself doing something for the one you love.

Use your analytical mood to figure out why you are feeling the way you are. Spend some time examining your diet diary to see where you can make changes in your eating habits.

If you experience a typical Diet Day #7 attack of perfectionism, don't be too hard on yourself. It's fine to spend time thinking about how you gained weight so long as you move on to take positive steps to control your weight. Give yourself credit for past accomplishments.

The solution to Diet Day #7 downfalls is spending special time on yourself. Don't worry or feel guilty while you are relaxing. You deserve a day off! You will be far more productive tomorrow as a result. See today as the Sabbath or period of rest, but not a Sabbath from dieting. Just as academic professionals renew themselves with a sabbatical every seven years, you can afford to spend part of a Diet Day #7 on yourself.

Take a walk in a quiet setting, or spend some time near water. It is very restoring to the soul. Plant an herb garden, read a good inspirational book or a novel with a happy ending, or listen to positive-thinking tapes.

EXERCISE

Although you want to be a part of nature today, you are also feeling refined. For instance, you might enjoy gardening today, but you'd probably be more comfortable wearing gloves. Instead of being knee-deep in mud, you would be happier kneeling on an outdoor cushion, trimming plants to perfect their shapes and doing some weeding.

> Mowing the lawn, even with a power mower, burns off 250 calories.

STRETCHING

A Diet Day #7 calls for quiet, solitary exercise in the out-of-doors, weather permitting. Stretching fills the bill today. Pick an inspirational setting with a view or beautiful surroundings. Free your mind of distracting thoughts and set the mood with music that calms and relaxes you. Be sure to breathe deeply and move slowly.

Back stretch. Using a mat, kneel on all fours so that your hands are flat on the floor and your knees and lower legs are flat on the floor. Your arms should be straight and shoulder width apart. Like a cat, slowly arch your back up. Now slowly raise your head, lowering your back until it forms a reverse arch. Now drop your head, rounding your back upward again. Closing your eyes during this stretch will help you concentrate on how your body feels. Repeat the process slowly ten times.

Hamstring stretch. Lie facedown on your mat, arms raised and bent at elbow, your head resting facedown on your arms. Close your eyes. Relax and breathe deeply. Bending at the knee, curl your right lower leg up as far as you can bring it toward your derriere. Lower your right leg onto the floor. Now repeat the process with your left leg. Repeat the process ten times.

Shoulder, chest stretch. Stand up straight, facing a wall. Stretching your arms at shoulder level, place the palms of your hands, fingers pointing up, at shoulder width on the wall. With your hands still on the wall, walk backward slowly, taking small steps. Keep your feet flat on the floor. You will feel the backs of your legs pull slightly. Hold this position while you bend your arms at the elbows. Keeping your back straight, lean forward until your nose practically touches the wall. Straighten out your arms and repeat the process slowly ten times.

POOL EXERCISE

On a Diet Day #7 you take to water like a duck. A pool is a terrific place to exercise. The support of the water decreases your body weight by 80 percent, allowing you to move effortlessly and do many exercises that would be difficult out of the water. At the same time, you get a good workout because you must intensify your movements due to the water's resistance.

Kicking. Holding on to the edge of the pool or using a styrofoam kickboard, stretch out your body. With your knees straight, do little flutter kicks from the hip. Point your toes. Kick for as long as you are comfortable.

Upper arms. Standing in water up to your neck, place your feet apart to shoulder width. Stretch your arms straight out to the sides. With your palms facing down, bring your arms down to your sides. Then raise them back up to shoulder level. Repeat twenty-five times.

Lower body. Stand in shoulder-deep water, facing the side of the pool. Stand at arm's distance from the side of the pool, hands on hips. Beginning with your right leg, raise your knee to your chest as far as you can. Lower slowly. Now bring your left knee up to your chest as far as it will go. Repeat the process twenty-five times.

Knee raises are fun to do with your hands on the sides of your waist as you prance up and down like a pony hopping about in the water.

ROWING

If you can't actually row on a lake today, try a rowing machine. Pick a quiet corner at home or at the gym on a Diet Day #7, when you are thinking of the great outdoors and peace and solitude. Remember to start slowly, avoiding stressful bouncing motions. Row smoothly and imagine yourself on the water.

> Rowing for one hour burns 250 calories.

WALKING

On a Diet Day #7 you need to get off the beaten path for some solitude. If there is a beautiful park in your area with gentle hills to climb, this would be a good change of scene for a walk. Exercise in a natural setting will revitalize you and remove you from the hustle and bustle you want to avoid today. Your only companion should be a Walkman playing classical music.

YOGA

Combining stretching and meditation, this ancient form of exercise is ideal on a Diet Day #7. Taught in classes or on video tapes, yoga has become a very popular antidote to the stress of modern civilization.

> Ice skating for one hour burns 300 to 350 calories. The more your skating improves, the faster you will skate and the more calories you will burn.

ICE SKATING

The cool temperature of an indoor ice skating rink approximates the out-of-doors, a setting that will refresh you on a Diet Day #7.

If skating is part of your past, or you want to take lessons, it's a great sport, especially today. Out there on the ice you can be in your own world, skating to the music and oblivious to the other skaters. The repetition of moving around and around the rink has a meditative effect, which will rest your mind while your body gets a good aerobic workout.

RECIPES FOR DIET DAY #7

Fresh and unadorned, many of the foods in today's menus are raw or just as nature made them. "Health" foods are introduced, as well as a vegetarian day.

You'll enjoy a visit to a health food restaurant and have an opportunity to try out some foods you may not have eaten before.

Food for Thought addresses the contemplative side of a Diet Day #7 and encourages you to take time for yourself today.

Menu 1

FOOD FOR THOUGHT

The pessimist sees the difficulty in every opportunity; the optimist, the opportunity in every difficulty.

BREAKFAST

(166 calories)

*Cream of Oats Cereal with Blueberries**
Celestial Seasonings Roastaroma herb tea

SNACK

(90 calories)

Yoplait "Light" yogurt
Celestial Seasonings Strawberry Fields herb tea

LUNCH
(403 calories)

*Super Soup**
2 Pogen Krisprolls
1 ounce string cheese
*Zucchini Zircles**
Celestial Seasonings Cranberry Cove herb tea, iced

DINNER
(334 calories)

*Vegetarian Chili**
1 steamed corn tortilla
*Orange and Green Salad**
Perrier with lemon

DESSERT
(25 calories)

Dole Fresh Lites frozen bar
Celestial Seasonings Chamomile herb tea

TOTAL CALORIES 1,018
PROTEIN 22%
CARBOHYDRATE 61%
FAT 17%

* Recipes follow.

CREAM OF OATS CEREAL WITH BLUEBERRIES

½ cup Quaker Oat Bran cereal
¼ cup canned evaporated skim milk
½ cup frozen blueberries, thawed

Prepare a ½-cup serving of the cereal according to package directions. Top with skim milk and berries.

Serves 1

SUPER SOUP

2 tablespoons diet margarine
1 medium onion, chopped
1 tablespoon whole-wheat flour
½ teaspoon curry powder
2 cups Swanson's Natural Goodness chicken broth
1 medium russet potato, peeled and cubed
1 cup chopped bok choy or Chinese cabbage
1 cup chopped mustard greens
1 carrot, sliced thin
1 stalk celery, sliced
¼ cup green beans, sliced into 1-inch pieces
⅛ teaspoon sage
1 13-ounce can evaporated skim milk
1 cup diced cooked chicken breast
2 teaspoons diced fresh ginger
⅛ teaspoon black pepper
2 teaspoons fresh lemon juice

Melt the margarine in a large saucepan. Add the onion and sauté over medium heat for 5 to 10 minutes. Stir in the flour and curry. Cook over medium heat for 3 minutes. Add ½ cup chicken broth and stir with a whisk until smooth. Add the remainder of the broth and the potato, bok choy, mustard greens, carrot, celery, green beans, and sage. Cover and simmer for 30 minutes. Add the milk and chicken. Cover and simmer for 10 minutes more. Add the seasonings and lemon juice.

Serves 4

ZUCCHINI ZIRCLES

1 medium zucchini
Fresh lemon juice
Dried dill

Wash, trim, and slice the zucchini to make 1 cup slices. Toss with lemon juice and dill.

Serves 1

VEGETARIAN CHILI

1 medium onion, chopped
3 cloves garlic, minced
¼ cup Swanson's Natural Goodness chicken broth
½ pound mushrooms, quartered
1 carrot, sliced thin
1 tablespoon chili powder
1 cup canned kidney beans, drained
1 cup canned pinto beans, drained
1 28-ounce can tomatoes, drained and chopped
6 ounces tomato paste
8 ounces tomato sauce
Cayenne pepper to taste
1 tablespoon minced fresh cilantro

Sauté the onion and garlic in chicken broth until the onion is translucent. Add the mushrooms, carrots, and chili powder. Cook for 3 minutes. Add the beans and tomato products. Reduce the heat to low and simmer, stirring occasionally, until the chili is thick and carrots are cooked, about 25 to 30 minutes. Season with cayenne pepper. Serve topped with cilantro.

Serves 4

ORANGE AND GREEN SALAD

1 carrot, peeled and grated
8 cups Boston or bibb lettuce, torn into bite-size pieces
1 cup frozen peas, thawed
½ cucumber, peeled, seeded, and sliced
1 cup alfalfa sprouts
8 tablespoons Wish-Bone Lite Classic Dijon Vinaigrette reduced-calorie dressing

Toss the vegetables with the dressing.

Serves 4

MENU 2

FOOD FOR THOUGHT

Be like the wise man who is not always silent but knows when to be.

BREAKFAST

(250 calories)

*Great Granola with Yogurt and Berries**
Decaffeinated coffee

LUNCH

(231 calories)

*Chicken Broccoli Salad**
2 Pogen Krisprolls
Sparkling water with lemon slice

SNACK

(140 calories)

1 apple
1 ounce string cheese
Celestial Seasonings Wildforest Blackberry herb tea

DINNER

(233 calories)

*Ratatouille**
½ cup brown rice
Bogus Burgundy (page 34)

DESSERT

(190 calories)

*Peach Snow**
Celestial Seasonings Country Peach Spice herb tea

TOTAL CALORIES 1,044
PROTEIN 26%
CARBOHYDRATE 56%
FAT 18%

* Recipes follow.

GREAT GRANOLA WITH YOGURT AND BERRIES

½ cup Great Granola (recipe follows)
6 ounces nonfat plain yogurt
½ cup berries of your choice, fresh or frozen

Sprinkle granola over yogurt and top with berries.

Serves 1

GREAT GRANOLA

2 cups Quaker Old Fashioned Oats
1 cup unsweetened oat bran flakes
1 cup unsweetened wheat flakes
⅓ cup nonfat dry powdered milk
¼ cup slivered almonds
2 teaspoons cinnamon
½ teaspoon nutmeg
⅛ teaspoon ground cloves
¼ cup apple juice
½ cup orange juice
2 tablespoons vanilla extract
¼ cup currants
5 dried apricot halves, chopped

Combine the oats, bran flakes, wheat flakes, powdered milk, almonds, cinnamon, nutmeg, and cloves. In a separate bowl, combine the apple juice, orange juice, and vanilla. Stir well. Pour the juice mixture into the dry mixture and mix well. Spread in a nonstick baking pan sprayed with Pam. Bake at 275° for 1 hour, stirring every 15 minutes. Remove from the oven and let cool on a rack. Stir in the currants and apricots. Store in a tightly covered container at room temperature.

Serves 12 (½ cup per serving)

CHICKEN BROCCOLI SALAD

Dressing

2 tablespoons mayonnaise
4 tablespoons nonfat plain yogurt
1 tablespoon liquid from jar of green olives
Juice of 1 lemon
⅛ teaspoon white pepper

2 heads broccoli, trimmed and cut into small florets (5 cups)
2 scallions, minced
2 pimiento-stuffed green olives, minced
1 3-ounce can sliced water chestnuts, drained
2 hard-cooked egg whites, chopped
8 ounces cooked chicken breast, diced

In a small bowl, mix the mayonnaise, yogurt, olive liquid, lemon juice, and pepper. In a large bowl, toss the broccoli florets, scallions, olives, water chestnuts, egg whites, and chicken with the dressing. Cover and chill.

Serves 4

RATATOUILLE

1 small eggplant, peeled and cut into 1-inch cubes
1 cup sliced zucchini
1 cup chopped tomatoes
1 cup chopped green bell pepper
1 cup chopped onion
1 carrot, grated
2 cloves garlic, minced
1½ tablespoons Italian seasoning
⅛ teaspoon cumin
¼ cup water
¼ cup white wine
Dash of butter-flavor salt
16 ounces tofu, drained, patted dry, and cubed

2 tablespoons grated Parmesan cheese
¼ teaspoon dried, crushed red pepper flakes (optional)

Combine all of the ingredients except the tofu, Parmesan cheese, and pepper flakes in a heavy 4-quart saucepan. Cover and cook over low heat for 15 minutes. Add the tofu and simmer for another 15 minutes, until the vegetables are tender and the tofu has absorbed some of the flavor from the tomato mixture. To serve, sprinkle with Parmesan cheese and, if desired, pepper flakes.

Serves 4

PEACH SNOW

16 ounces nonfat plain yogurt
6 milk cubes (see note)
2 whole peaches, pitted, or 1 cup frozen unsweetened peaches
2 tablespoons peach nectar
2 tablespoons sugar
2 teaspoons vanilla extract

Combine the yogurt, milk cubes, peaches, peach nectar, sugar, and vanilla in a blender. Whirl until smooth. Serve immediately.

Serves 4

Note: To make 6 milk cubes, pour 1¼ cups nonfat milk into 6 sections of an ice cube tray and freeze until solid.

Menu 3

FOOD FOR THOUGHT

Silence is one of the great arts of conversation.

BREAKFAST

(300 calories)

*Apple Oat Bran Muffin**
*Felicitous Fruit**
Celestial Seasonings Cinnamon Apple Spice herb tea

LUNCH

(390 calories)

*Laudable Lentil Soup**
*Florentine Flat**
Celestial Seasonings Spearmint herb tea

DINNER

(294 calories)

*Healthful Halibut**
*Corn on the Cob**
*Cucumber Salad**
Celestial Seasonings Orange Zinger herb tea

DESSERT

(120 calories)

*Tropical Tofrutti**
Celestial Seasonings Almond Sunset herb tea

TOTAL CALORIES 1,104
PROTEIN 28%
CARBOHYDRATES 58%
FAT 14%

* Recipe follows.

APPLE OAT BRAN MUFFINS

Dry Ingredients

1 cup whole-wheat flour
½ cup Quaker Old Fashioned Oats
½ cup Quaker Oat Bran cereal
3 tablespoons golden raisins
2 teaspoons cinnamon
1 teaspoon baking soda
1 teaspoon pumpkin pie spice

Liquid Ingredients

2 tablespoons orange juice
2 egg whites
1 cup buttermilk (may use reconstituted powdered buttermilk)
1 tablespoon honey

Grated rind of 1 orange
1 apple, cored and grated (approximately 1 cup)

Mix the dry ingredients together. In a separate bowl, mix the liquid ingredients together and stir in the orange rind and apple. Then stir the liquid ingredients into the dry ingredients and mix just until blended. Put the batter in nonstick muffin tins that have been sprayed with Pam. Bake in a preheated 350° oven for 25 minutes, or until a toothpick inserted in the center of a muffin comes out clean. The muffins can be frozen.

Makes 12 muffins

FLORENTINE FLAT

1 whole sheet onion matzoh cracker
1 serving Florentine Spread (recipe follows)

Break the matzoh into serving-size rectangles and spread with Florentine spread.

Serves 1

FLORENTINE SPREAD

½ cup low-fat cottage cheese
8 ounces frozen chopped spinach, thawed and drained
¼ cup minced scallions
¼ cup minced fresh parsley
2 tablespoons chopped water chestnuts
¼ cup cooked crab meat
½ teaspoon black pepper
2 tablespoons diet mayonnaise
2 tablespoons nonfat plain yogurt
1 teaspoon fresh lemon or lime juice
¼ teaspoon Worcestershire Sauce

Purée the cottage cheese in a food processor or blender. Combine with the remaining ingredients in a medium-size bowl and mix with a fork. Cover and chill.

Serves 4

LAUDABLE LENTIL SOUP

1 cup dried lentils
½ cup chopped onion
¾ cup sliced carrots
1 small sweet potato, diced
4 cups water
2 cloves garlic, mashed
⅛ teaspoon white pepper
¼ teaspoon marjoram
1 teaspoon vinegar
½ cup frozen chopped spinach, thawed and drained

Combine all of the ingredients except the spinach in a saucepan. Heat until near boiling. Reduce the heat, add the spinach, cover, and simmer until the lentils are tender, approximately 1 hour.

Serves 4

FELICITOUS FRUIT

½ cup diced fresh fruit
¼ cup nonfat plain yogurt
¼ cup low-fat cottage cheese
Cinnamon

Place diced fruit of your choice in a small bowl. Combine the yogurt and cottage cheese and spoon on as a topping over the fruit. Sprinkle with cinnamon.

Serves 1

HEALTHFUL HALIBUT

1 pound fresh halibut, cut into 4 pieces
4 tablespoons white wine
Juice of 1 lemon
2 tablespoons minced fresh parsley
2 teaspoons Lawry's Minced Onions with Green Onion Flakes

Spray a baking dish with Pam. Arrange the halibut in it and cover with wine, lemon juice, parsley, and onion flakes. Bake at 350° until the fish flakes with a fork. The cooking time depends on the thickness of the fish.

Serves 4

CORN ON THE COB

2 large ears corn
Molly McButter
Pepper

Remove the husks and silk from the corn. Wash each ear and break in half. Steam. Sprinkle with Molly McButter and pepper.

Serves 4

CUCUMBER SALAD

Dressing

1 cup nonfat plain yogurt
2 tablespoons rice vinegar
2 teaspoons diet mayonnaise
⅛ teaspoon white pepper

2 cups iceberg lettuce, torn into bite-size pieces
2 cucumbers, seeded and finely sliced
2 tablespoons minced scallion
½ cup chopped red bell pepper

In a bowl, combine the dressing ingredients. Pour over the salad mixture and toss gently.

Serves 4

TROPICAL TOFRUTTI

2 8-ounce cans juice-packed crushed pineapple
1 6-ounce jar baby food pears
8 ounces tofu, drained and patted dry
1 teaspoon vanilla extract
Dash of nutmeg

Drain both cans of pineapple, reserving ⅓ cup of the juice. Mix the pears, tofu, half of one can of pineapple, vanilla, and reserved juice in a blender. Divide the remaining pineapple into 4 custard cups. Pour the tofu mixture over the pineapple. Refrigerate for at least 1 hour. To serve, sprinkle nutmeg on top.

Serves 4

Menu 4

EATING OUT AT A HEALTH FOOD RESTAURANT

FOOD FOR THOUGHT

We mutter, we sputter, we fume, and we spurt. We mumble and grumble, our feelings get hurt. We can't understand things, we moan and we groan, when all that we need is a moment alone.

BREAKFAST

(234 calories)

2 4-inch whole-wheat pancakes
1 cup strawberries
2 ounces turkey sausage
Herb tea

LUNCH

(400 calories)

Vegetarian plate made with 1 cup steamed vegetables and 2 ounces melted cheese
½ cup cooked whole-wheat pasta
Sparkling mineral water with lemon

DINNER

(300 calories)

Broiled garden burger on bun
Green salad with 2 tablespoons no-oil dressing or ½ cup rice
½ cup beans
Green salad with 1 tablespoon house dressing mixed with 1 tablespoon vinegar
Mineral water

DESSERT

(90 calories)

½ cup Yoplait Soft frozen yogurt

TOTAL CALORIES 1,024
PROTEIN 23%
CARBOHYDRATE 49%
FAT 28%

DIET DAY #8

SUCCESS AND STRESS

In numerology the number 8 means money, power, and success. A Diet Day #8 is apt to be a high-powered, stressful day. You may be on a tight schedule and need to make every minute count. Rely on your executive skills and *The Numbers Diet* for energy. Delegate everything but responsibility for your own health.

Pay attention to your emotional well-being, as well as your diet. To keep on an even keel, divide your day into eight hours of work, eight hours of play, and eight hours of sleep.

Status and achievement are top priorities today and make great motivation when it comes to diet. No one has to tell you on a Diet Day #8 that nothing tastes as good as being thin feels. Be a weight manager today by first controlling what goes into your mouth and ultimately controlling your weight. You've got what it takes to succeed. Today your diet—tomorrow the world!

CHOLESTEROL

Success, and the lifestyle that goes with it, includes living off the fat of the land or eating high on the hog. We now know that expensive, status foods like fat-marbled prime meat, rich sauces like béarnaise, and premium ice creams contribute to the demise of many a successful person.

It's okay to be rich—just don't eat rich, fat-filled foods.

Cholesterol is the fatty substance present in all animal cells. Vital to life, cholesterol is needed for many body functions such as hormone production and proper functioning of the old gray matter, the brain. Next time cholesterol is getting a bad press, keep in mind how dull life would be without hormones and brainpower.

On the other hand, if your bloodstream has too much cholesterol clinging to the walls of your blood vessels, especially those near the heart, you face increased risk of heart disease. Unhealthy, high levels of cholesterol can be caused by eating too much of it in foods or eating too many saturated fats, those that are solid at room temperature. According to the American Heart Association, cholesterol intake should be less than 100 milligrams per 1,000 calories, not to exceed 300 milligrams per day.

Cholesterol, like cowboys, comes in two forms. The high-minded guys in the white hats are called HDL (high-density lipoprotein) and the low-down, rotten scoundrels in the black hats are called the LDL (low-density lipoprotein). The good guys, the HDL, protect the body against the bad guys, the LDL, reducing the total cholesterol in the bloodstream. Allowed to accumulate, the LDL becomes the plaque in our arteries, which restricts blood flow and increases the risk of heart disease.

Cholesterol is only part of the story. Triglycerides are another kind of fat, whose vital function is to transport nutrients through the bloodstream; but, like cholesterol, too many triglycerides can accumulate and put the body at risk. Triglyceride levels become elevated when we take in too many simple carbohydrates such as sugar, or too much alcohol; or when we eat only one large meal a day, causing fat overload.

Understanding cholesterol and triglycerides is only half the information you need about fats. Let me introduce you to polyunsaturated, monounsaturated, and especially their sinister sister, saturated. All fats contain combinations of these three.

Saturated Fats tend to increase levels of cholesterol in the blood. They are solid, both at room temperature and under refrigeration. Predominantly found in animal fats, saturated fats are also found in two tropical oils, palm and coconut. Other foods high in saturated fats are cream, butter, hard cheese, coconut, coconut oil, egg yolk, lard, animal fat, whole milk, palm oil, poultry skin, solid vegetable shortening, and hydrogenated (hardened) fat or oil.

Monounsaturated fats are somewhat solid. Liquid at room temperature, they become viscous under refrigeration. When certain monounsaturated fats are used in place of, not in addition to, saturated fats, they may increase HDL, the good cholesterol. Some foods that are high in monounsaturated fats are almonds, avocados, olives, olive oil, peanut butter (natural, made without hydrogenated oils), peanuts, pecans, and sesame seeds and sesame oil. Olive oil and avocados have been recommended in low-cholesterol diets, but peanut oil has not.

Polyunsaturated fats, oils liquid both at room temperature and under refrigeration, may decrease total cholesterol, but their potential for lowering HDL is not as great as that of primarily monounsaturated olive oil, which is preferred. Polyunsaturated fats are found in vegetable oils such as corn, cottonseed, safflower, soybean, sunflower, and walnut.

Finally, there is one more term related to fats you need to understand.

Hydrogenation is a process that hardens liquid oils, making them solid in form, like lard or butter, for use in cooking. The more solid they become, the more saturated they become, turning into significant contributors to heart disease. For this reason, soft tub margarine is preferred to stick margarine.

STRESS

The success and power of a Diet Day #8 require effort on your part, especially when the stakes are high; and money, while welcome in large quantities, requires responsible management.

The emotions caused by stress are often said to be the underlying cause of our weight problems. Eating as a reaction to stress creates further stress by causing overweight, which in turn leads to more overeating, creating a vicious circle.

If stress triggers your eating, you need to understand the source of the stress so you can eliminate it or learn to cope with it in more productive ways.

In numerology, stress generated by pressures of and desire for success has number 8 written all over it. More than any other day, Diet Day #8 finds you wanting the status symbols of our society. The TV commercial touting the ''in'' perfume, the illustrations of the posh house in *Rich Residences of the Thin and Famous,* the size 6 designer clothes you would love to wear, and the neighbor's new car assume great importance in your life today. Dissatisfied because they can't have it all, some people overspend, but those of us who eat under stress are likely to treat ourselves to a hot fudge sundae. When the material things we want seem out of reach, the ice cream is within easy reach to make us feel better temporarily.

Outside stress, caused by family, friends, career, and relationships, often creates inner stress. No matter how difficult other people make our lives, we seem to be our own worst enemy! We are often harder on ourselves than the strictest parent or most tyrannical boss.

In numerology, a number calculated from your birth date tells you how to take advantage of your greatest opportunities in life.

When I "do" numbers, I teach people how to convert their names into numbers. These numbers help them to understand themselves, their loved ones, and co-workers. From their birth dates I show them how to benefit from the cycles in their lives.

Women, especially, take care of everyone else but themselves. One year, after my agent had booked me to do numbers at a record number of holiday parties, I decided to relax on a cruise to Mexico. My daughters were rather young at the time, so I left them with a baby-sitter. While I was away, my middle daughter, Brooke, dislocated her knee, the plumbing overflowed, and the brand-new wool carpet in my bedroom was ruined. There I was, stuck on a ship in the middle of the Pacific, trying unsuccessfully to solve the situation with expensive ship-to-shore phone calls. In my frustration, I ate everything in sight—an easy task on a cruise ship, where food is available in abundance twenty-four hours a day. I'm not sure what the term *sea swell* means scientifically, but it certainly described my condition as I waddled down the gangplank when I returned to Los Angeles. Eating hadn't solved the problems that were causing me stress. In fact, eating had made me feel worse. I still had to deal with Brooke's knee, the carpet, and the plumber's bill, *plus* lose those ten extra pounds.

A busy executive who can't turn his brain off over the weekend often comes back to work on Monday more frazzled than he was on Friday. If you can't relax on your days off and vacations, you just add to the stress that caused you to need the time off in the first place.

Eating is so handy, and for many people it relieves stress temporarily. There are, however, healthier ways to handle stress. First, understand how stress affects your body. Three stages of stress have been identified: alarm, resistance, and exhaustion. For example, a rude driver cuts you off on the freeway. Anger and fear for your safety cause hormones to be released into your bloodstream. Your face becomes flushed, you break out in a cold sweat, and every muscle in your body becomes tight. Once the incident is over and the danger passes, your body begins to repair itself in a second stage called resistance. Ideally, you can recuperate during the final stage by resting.

> Most people don't realize that stress causes the body to retain fluids.

Today most of us spend hours on and off the "road of life" under pressure-cooker conditions. Repeated stress becomes a constant state of distress, which leads to common stress-related diseases such as migraine headaches, high blood pressure, backache, insomnia, and obesity, to name a few.

What causes stress in *your* life? Some sources can be eliminated, but the secret to surviving life's pressures is learning to deal with them in ways that contribute to your overall well-being. *Eating what's eating you is not the answer.*

We need some techniques that will help solve problems, not create new ones. Remember, awareness is gradual and changing patterns doesn't happen overnight. Even when we do mend our ways, we need to be on guard against those situations that cause us to regress under stress—to our old eating patterns.

EAT PROPERLY

A healthy diet gives you more energy to deal with stress by keeping your blood sugar stable. On a particularly stressful day like some Diet Day #8s, eat all of your allotted meals and snacks. Don't ride the sugar roller coaster when you're already on the emotional roller coaster.

The usual sweets, such as candy bars, aren't the only offenders. Sometimes even drinking fruit juice elevates the blood sugar rapidly, because juices are absorbed into the bloodstream quickly. A stress-buster snack of fresh fruit contains enough fiber to slow down the sugar absorption and gives you chewing satisfaction.

Meals and snacks should combine complex carbohydrates and

protein. Complex carbohydrates (vegetables, bread, pasta, etc.) release glucose slowly into the bloodstream over a longer period of time. Adequate complex carbohydrates in your diet go a long way toward preventing headaches and that sluggish, tired feeling.

> Carbohydrates do reduce stress, by triggering the brain to produce serotonin, 1½ to 2 ounces of low-fat complex carbohydrates will do their job in 20 minutes.

Avoid alcohol. It only complicates your problems by lowering blood sugar levels and taxing your liver. In addition, alcohol robs the body of B vitamins, which contribute to good mental health. You need all your wits about you when you are under stress.

Caffeine, found in coffee, tea, chocolate, and cola, may produce symptoms that are similar to hypoglycemia (low blood sugar). The symptoms are headaches, irritability, rapid heartbeat, and anxiety. If you already have the shakes because you are nervous over a stressful situation, you don't need "coffee nerves" on top of that.

Get your Diet Day #8 off to a good start. Be prepared to eat right by keeping a shopping list in the kitchen so you'll always have the proper food on hand. Cook ahead and use your freezer. Prepare for the morning the night before. Get a head start on breakfast, set two alarm clocks if you have to, and lay out your clothes.

GET ENOUGH REST

Burning the candle at both ends does not relieve stress, it creates more. Figure out how many hours of sleep you need and make sure you get it. Learn to pace yourself. If you are behaving like the rabbit in the story "The Tortoise and the Hare," take your lesson from the tortoise.

GET ENOUGH EXERCISE

In the busiest, most stressful day, make time to exercise. Don't skip your regular exercise or pass up an opportunity to exercise on the spur of the moment. At the end of a stressful day, a bedtime stroll guarantees a good night's sleep and a fresh start in the morning.

SIMPLIFY YOUR LIFE

Helena Davis, my first numerology teacher, always told me, "Less is more." She was a firm believer in the maxim "Simplicity is happiness."

Use your management skills on a Diet Day #8 to reorder your priorities and delegate work to others. Ask yourself some serious questions. Do your goals for success come with a price tag that's too high? Is it really worth all the work and stress to get to where you think you want to go? Is the view from the top really that great? How can you simplify your life?

I used to entertain a lot, spending all day cleaning and cooking. My daughters hated it when we had company, because I expected everyone to "hop to" and became resentful if they didn't. I finally had to ask myself, "Is it necessary to go to all this work for friends?" When I streamlined my approach to parties with simpler food and a more casual eye for housecleaning, I reduced the stress associated with entertaining. What little help I needed my girls gave more cheerfully, because I was more relaxed and my requests were more reasonable.

SCHEDULE A REALISTIC DAY

Don't try to cram twenty-six hours into a twenty-four-hour day. Allow enough time between tasks or appointments so you don't have to worry, rush, and apologize for being late. Don't bite off more than you can chew on a Diet Day #8. Be honest with yourself. Some things can wait and others can't. Procrastination creates stress on its own, so get your priorities straight.

Schedule some "down" time for yourself. In these high-tech times, it's easy to equate yourself with all the other machines you turn on in the morning and off at night. You're still human, and don't you forget it!

DISTINGUISH BETWEEN WANT AND SHOULD

I'll never forget the day I realized I was so busy doing things I *should* do that I didn't have time to do the things I *wanted* to do. You can reduce stress in your life in direct proportion to the numbers of "shoulds" you eliminate and the number of "wants" you include in your day.

As I get older and more mellow, it's not the things I've *done* that make me have regrets, but the things I *haven't* done. Take it from me, don't wait! If you've always dreamed of learning to sail, to ski, to play tennis, to needlepoint, to ice skate, do it now!

BE A TODAY PERSON

There is a little enamel Halycon box I covet. On it is the phrase "There are two days we shouldn't worry about—yesterday and tomorrow." If you concentrate on the precious moment of today, tomorrow usually takes care of itself. In the words of my minister friend, Dr. Frank Richelieu, "Be a today person. Enjoy every minute of it. Don't spoil the present with recriminations for the past and fear of the future."

Don't be like the vacationer who spends the whole time thinking about how little of the trip is left instead of enjoying each day.

Focus on the task at hand and tackle the hardest job first, when you are fresh. Give it your all and you will be rewarded with a sense of accomplishment and the calm assurance of having done your job well.

DON'T MAKE MOUNTAINS OUT OF MOLEHILLS

Ask yourself if you're majoring in minor things. Are you one of those people who waste energy by magnifying their sorrows? If you catch yourself using phrases like "I could have died!", "I want to kill him!", "You make me livid," "I'm so furious," "I'm absolutely devastated!", consider how these exaggerations tend to escalate stressful situations. Appraise life's situations with a steady head and keep a lid on your emotions. Make sure your outburst is warranted by the occasion. Otherwise, you may be getting worked up over nothing.

HOW TO SUCCEED AT EXERCISE

Psych yourself up by reviewing the benefits of exercise. You are going to have more energy and find it easier to lose weight and keep it off when you make exercise a part of your daily routine. You will build muscles that burn calories faster than your unexercised body does now. As you lose weight, exercising will help you tone muscle to maintain a firm body. Exercise will decrease your appetite, lower stress, help you think more clearly and concentrate better. Your heart and lungs will function more efficiently to protect you against cardiovascular disease. Exercise promotes relaxation and sound sleep. In addition, you will enjoy more variety in your life through the new activities you try and the different people you meet while exercising. So what are you waiting for? With your doctor's blessing, it's time to get started.

It's not the last fifteen minutes of your workout that are hard; it's getting started.

Changing our sedentary habits isn't easy. I visited my mother recently at her retirement home. As a new convert to exercise, I missed my thirty-minute walk, so I decided to push her wheelchair into the physical therapy room, where she could sit and talk to me while I pedaled on the stationary bicycle. After about five minutes she said to me, "Well, Jean, I never thought I'd see the day when you would consciously choose to exercise." Neither did I. It took me forty-six years. I changed because I wanted to, and you can too.

Unrealistic long-term goals will discourage you before you begin, so start out nice and easy. Don't overdo your first time out. Build up gradually. If you miss exercising one day, you haven't blown your entire workout program. The simple truth is that you missed one day, and you will exercise tomorrow.

> My attorney friend prepares himself to cope with the pressure-cooker atmosphere in the courtroom by exercising with a personal trainer at 7:00 A.M. three days a week.

Exercise commitments are sometimes easier to keep when others are involved, and it's more fun with company. The right person can help to keep you motivated. You will think twice about letting a friend down, whereas you might break a commitment to yourself. On the other hand, don't put the responsibility for exercising entirely on your friend's shoulders. If she's sick or tired, find another friend or keep going on your own and encourage her to come back. My first gym buddy, Tammy, who could hardly wait to get me into a program, lost interest and I had to go it alone. By now I have lots of gym buddies who are interested in the same thing I am, fun and exercise for good health.

Buy a dog, which will nudge you out of the house for a walk every day.

Put exercise on your calendar. To succeed at exercise, I schedule my walking and visits to the gym just like business or dentist's appointments. Take exercise seriously! Gradually exercise will become its own reward, and you'll be so convinced of its benefits you won't want to stop.

Fit exercise into your daily routine. Some people I know exercise at lunchtime to break up the monotony of a long day. A business man I know is so relaxed after his midday "Y" break, his staff purposely approaches him at that time with "sticky" questions. He admits he feels more alert and better able to cope with business after exercising at lunch. If I've been out all day, I can catch an aerobics class on my way home because I keep a set of exercise clothes in my car. I know if I get all the way home, I will take off my shoes, lose my momentum, and never make it to the gym. My psychologist friend has a stationary bike in his office and pedals between patients as well as at the end of the day.

The first time you notice how great you feel after exercise, take a moment to jot down your feelings. Next time you're tempted to skip exercising, or if you've been away from it and can't get going again, read your notes and remind yourself how much better you'll feel if you get started again.

When you are planning to be out of town on business or vacation, pack your workout clothes. If you belong to a gym, ask about reciprocal privileges at clubs in cities you will be visiting. Choose a hotel with gym facilities on the premises or privileges nearby. When you are in a strange city, it's more enjoyable to spend the evening with a group of people at a gym than it is to be lonely in your hotel room. Plan vacations that include a time and place for exercise.

Walk to work if you can. My former publicist used to walk all the way from the East Seventies to her office at Eighteenth Street in Manhattan. While she walked, she planned her day, dreamed of creative solutions to problems, and kept slim all at the same time.

My trademark attorney walks between his Greenwich Village condo and his office on the East Side, even in the snow. He says walking to work gives him an opportunity to think through his cases, and walking home gives him a chance to unwind after a stressful day.

If you work at home, include your children when you exercise. When my girls were little, I used the excuse that I was too busy and didn't have a baby-sitter. Nonsense! Had I wanted to, I could have pushed a stroller or pulled a little red wagon. I could have logged two round trips each day walking the girls to and from school. No telling how many pounds I could have lost walking up and down that hill. I chose to be a chunky chauffeur instead.

My physician friend has a standing date with his wife and kids every evening. They tell him their news while he pedals on his stationary bike.

Family exercise habits influence children's later attitude toward fitness. Kinder Gym and Mommy and Me programs help parents stay fit right along with their children. Take walks together. Play catch and eventually develop the facility to play several sports together.

Be prepared to exercise comfortably and safely. In hot weather, schedule your exercise during cooler morning or evening hours. Drink plenty of water before, during, and after exercise. Wear absorbent cottons and loose-fitting, comfortable clothing. In any weather, layers of light clothing are practical because you can peel them off as you become warmer. Avoid clothing designed to make you perspire. The increased water loss and rise in body temperature cause overheated conditions that can lead to heatstroke or sunstroke. If you become dizzy, light-headed, or excessively tired, suspect heatstroke or sunstroke. Seek medical attention immediately.

During cold weather wear gloves and a hat to retain body heat while exercising outdoors.

Wear a minimum amount of makeup so your face can perspire naturally. Sunscreen will allow your skin to "breathe" and, along with a hat or sun visor, is recommended to prevent the sun's aging effects.

Prevent accidents by wearing the right clothing for your sport, such as a bicycle helmet, gloves, reflective tape if you're out at night, and chain guards on your long pants. Remember what your mother always told you: walk facing oncoming traffic. Be sure you know what you're doing; get proper instruction for using equipment and doing exercises. Never exercise to the point of absolute exhaustion. Listen to your doctor, your instructor, and most important, your own body.

DIET DOWNFALLS AND THEIR SOLUTIONS

To handle the stresses of power and success associated with a Diet Day #8, you've got to keep your emotions and nutrition in balance.

If you dine with movers and shakers, notice that the most successful movers order Perrier and broiled fish for a power lunch. The shakers order martinis and drink too much coffee after lunch.

If the pace becomes frantic and the stakes are so high they give you acrophobia, don't allow yourself to become upset. Relieve the pressure by delegating some of the responsibility and use your executive skills to manage your emotions.

Don't let success go to your head or your stomach. It's okay to wheel and deal like King Midas, but remember not to eat like a king.

EXERCISE

You can delegate everything on your schedule today but your exercise.

On a Diet Day #8 you're on your way to the top, climbing the ladder of success, so why not make that your exercise? Stair-climbing machines are available for you to try at gyms. Or get off the treadmill at work by climbing on a treadmill at the gym or at home.

STAIR CLIMBING

Walking up stairs is good for your gluteus maximus, affectionately known as your "duff," especially if you put your whole foot on each stair. The calf muscles of your legs benefit especially if you climb stairs placing only your toes on each stair. Your inner thighs get a good workout if you climb two or three stairs at a time. Walking down stairs works the rear muscles as well as the muscles in the front of your legs, especially the quadriceps in your thighs.

Use the stairs at home, in your office or apartment house, or outdoors at a park or public building. Carrying something will increase your workout, so grab the hand weights or the groceries.

TREADMILL

Every morning I roll out of bed onto my treadmill, right in front of a small television set. It's a great exercise to wake up with because I catch the morning news and get my day off to a rolling start.

Wear shoes on a treadmill and use caution. Don't crank up the motor or adjust the incline at too steep an angle at first.

BUSINESS-RELATED EXERCISE

On a Diet Day #8, a day associated with business, many a deal gets closed on the golf course or between sets of tennis. But these occasional sports should be considered extras. Your real exercise program is made up of a thirty-minute workout at least five days a week.

Other business-related "exercise," like passing the buck, throwing your weight around, and pushing your luck, may cause you to work up a head of steam, but unfortunately, they are either too stressful or too slothful to be recommended as calorie-burning activities.

RECIPES FOR DIET DAY #8

Foods associated with "the good life" are featured on a Diet Day #8 in healthy but high-tone menus. Stress-buster meals assure a continuous supply of nutritious foods to keep you charging on a demanding Diet Day #8.

If a power lunch is on your calendar today, check the menu for eating out. To find more suggestions for restaurant ordering see chapters 3 and 9.

Food for Thought reminds you not to underestimate your potential on this high-powered day, or any other day.

Menu 1

FOOD FOR THOUGHT

Swallowing your pride occasionally will never give you indigestion.

BREAKFAST

(342 calories)

*Magnificent Muffin**
*Sophisticated Smoothie**
Decaffeinated coffee

LUNCH

(305 calories)

*Broccoli Bisque**
*Cheddar Butter**
6 Carr's Water Biscuits
Wishful White Wine (page 25)

SNACK

(52 calories)

*Cream Cheese and Cucumber**
Celestial Seasonings Mellow Mint herb tea

DINNER

(265 calories)

*Fettucine Alfonso**
*Red and Green Salad**
Chianti Cup (page 26)

DESSERT

(67 calories)

*Ritzy Raspberries**
Celestial Seasonings Raspberry Patch herb tea

TOTAL CALORIES 1,031
PROTEIN 19%
CARBOHYDRATE 59%
FAT 22%

* Recipe follows.

MAGNIFICENT MUFFIN

1 teaspoon jam
Refrigerator Bran Muffins recipe (page 24)

Fill 1 muffin cup one-quarter full of batter. Place the jam on top of the batter and fill the muffin cup half full of batter. Bake according to directions.

Serves 1

SOPHISTICATED SMOOTHIE

8 ounces nonfat milk
3 ice cubes
1 ripe banana
½ teaspoon vanilla extract

Blend all of the ingredients in a blender until smooth. Serve immediately.

Serves 1

BROCCOLI BISQUE

1 cup frozen chopped broccoli, cooked
⅓ cup Instant Soup Mix (page 137)
1¼ cups boiling water

Cook the broccoli according to package directions. Place the dry soup mix in a bowl. Pour boiling water into the dry mixture gradually, stirring until smooth. Add the hot broccoli.

Serves 1

CHEDDAR BUTTER

1 ounce Weight Watchers cheddar cheese, grated
¼ cup part-skim ricotta cheese
¼ cup low-fat cottage cheese
½ teaspoon Dijon mustard
½ clove garlic, minced

Blend all ingredients together until smooth. Cover and chill. Keeps 1 to 2 weeks, depending upon the freshness of the cheeses.

Serves 4 (2 tablespoons per serving)

CREAM CHEESE AND CUCUMBER

½ cucumber, peeled
2 tablespoons Philadelphia brand "Light" pasteurized cream cheese
Dried dill

Cut the cucumber in half lengthwise. Scoop out the seeds with a spoon and fill each cavity with cream cheese. Top with a sprinkle of dill.

Serves 1

RITZY RASPBERRIES

1 cup fresh raspberries
1 teaspoon kirsch liqueur

Rinse and drain the raspberries. Add the liqueur and chill for no longer than 1 hour.

Serves 1

FETTUCCINE ALFONSO

Sauce

1 large head cauliflower
1 medium onion, chopped
8 ounces Swanson's Natural Goodness chicken broth
4 ounces nonfat milk
¼ teaspoon white pepper
1 teaspoon fresh lemon juice
1 cup part-skim ricotta cheese
⅛ teaspoon butter-flavor salt
2 cups cooked fettuccine noodles

Remove the center stem from the cauliflower. Cut up and steam the cauliflower and onion until tender. Drain. In a blender, process half of the cauliflower and onion with half of the chicken broth and milk. Repeat blending process, using the remaining sauce ingredients and lemon juice. In a saucepan, whisk the cauliflower mixture into the ricotta cheese. Heat and blend until smooth. Pour over hot noodles.

Serves 4

Note: The sauce is also delicious served chilled as a vichyssoise. Garnish with chopped fresh chives and a squeeze of lemon.

RED AND GREEN SALAD

Dressing

1 tablespoon olive oil
3 tablespoons fresh lemon juice
1 tablespoon red wine vinegar
1 tablespoon grated Parmesan cheese

2 tomatoes, peeled and chopped
2 tablespoons chopped scallion
¼ cup chopped green bell pepper
¼ cup chopped red bell pepper
4 cups spinach, thoroughly washed and torn into bite-size pieces
2 tablespoons minced fresh parsley

In a small bowl, combine the dressing ingredients. Stir well. Pour over the salad mixture. Toss lightly.

Serves 4

Menu 2

FOOD FOR THOUGHT
You've got what it takes! Weight no more.

BREAKFAST
(240 calories)

*Penthouse Pumpkin Pudding**
1 orange, sliced
Celestial Seasonings Sunburst C herb tea

SNACK
(50 calories)

1 ½-ounce package Weight Watcher Apple Fruit Snack

* Recipe follows

LUNCH
(237 calories)

*Tomato Bisque**
½ cup raw snow peas
½ cup jicama with lemon
½ bagel
Celestial Seasonings Emperor's Choice herb tea, iced

SNACK
(25 calories)

Dole Fresh Lites frozen bar
Celestial Seasonings Cinnamon Rose herb tea

DINNER
(340 calories)

*Seafood Brochette**
*Palatial Pilaf**
1 cup steamed broccoli
Wishful White Wine (page 25)

DESSERT
(154 calories)

*Raspberries on a Cloud**
Celestial Seasonings Raspberry Patch herb tea

TOTAL CALORIES 1,046
PROTEIN 23%
CARBOHYDRATE 62%
FAT 15%

* Recipe follows

PENTHOUSE PUMPKIN PUDDING

4 slices oatmeal bread
8 ounces tofu, drained and patted dry
8 ounces canned pumpkin
1 tablespoon orange marmalade
½ cup egg substitute
½ cup nonfat milk
3 tablespoons brown sugar
1 teaspoon vanilla extract
⅛ teaspoon nutmeg
2 teaspoons cinnamon
2 teaspoons pumpkin pie spice

Spray an 8-inch square baking dish with Pam. Cut the bread into 1-inch cubes and place in the baking dish. Combine all of the other ingredients in a food processor or blender and blend. Pour the pumpkin mixture over the bread in the baking dish. Place the baking dish in a baking pan that is slightly larger than the baking dish. Pour hot water into the larger pan to a depth of about ½ inch. Bake at 375° until a knife inserted in the center of the pudding comes out clean, approximately 1 hour. Serve warm or chilled.

Serves 4

TOMATO BISQUE

2½ cups Spicy Hot V8 vegetable juice
2 cups nonfat plain yogurt
1 dash Worcestershire sauce
2 sprinkles Molly McButter
2 tablespoons minced scallion
¼ teaspoon white pepper
4 hard-cooked egg whites, sieved

Blend the vegetable juice with yogurt in a blender. Add the Worcestershire sauce, Molly McButter, scallion, and pepper. Chill. Sprinkle sieved egg white on top of each serving. Serve cold.

Serves 4

SEAFOOD BROCHETTE

4 ounces medium shrimp, shelled, deveined, and cleaned
8 ounces scallops
2 medium zucchini, skin intact, thickly sliced
1 small onion, thinly sliced
6 tablespoons butter
½ teaspoon thyme
⅛ teaspoon turmeric
⅛ teaspoon white pepper
½ cup white wine
2 large tomatoes, peeled, cored, and quartered
2 cloves garlic, minced
2 tablespoons basil
½ teaspoon sugar

Arrange the shrimp, scallops, and zucchini in an interesting pattern on 4 skewers. Place the onion in a Pam-sprayed 9 × 13-inch baking dish. Melt 2 tablespoons butter. Add the thyme, turmeric, and pepper to the melted butter and use the mixture to coat the food on the skewers. Set the skewers on top of the onion slices and broil for 4 or 5 minutes, until the shrimp turn pink. Remove the brochettes and set aside, keeping warm. In a pan, combine the wine, tomatoes, garlic, basil, and sugar. Cook over high heat for 1 minute. Reduce the heat and add the remaining 4 tablespoons butter. Simmer for 1 minute. On 4 serving plates, arrange the onions and skewered brochettes. Divide the tomato wedges and sauce evenly and pour over the onions and brochettes.

Serves 4

PALATIAL PILAF

¼ cup chopped celery
½ medium onion, chopped
½ cup sliced mushrooms
1½ cups Swanson's Natural Goodness chicken broth
¼ cup barley
¼ cup dried lentils
⅛ teaspoon oregano
⅛ teaspoon black pepper

In a nonstick frying pan, sauté the celery, onion, and mushrooms in 2 tablespoons chicken broth. Stir constantly until the vegetables are tender. Add the barley and lentils and cook for 2 minutes. Add the seasonings and the remainder of the chicken broth. Bring to a boil. Cover, reduce the heat, and simmer for 45 minutes.

Serves 4

RASPBERRIES ON A CLOUD

Raspberry Sauce

1 10-ounce package frozen raspberries, thawed
2 tablespoons sugar
1 teaspoon cornstarch
3 tablespoons water

Cloud

1 cup part-skim ricotta cheese
½ cup low-fat cottage cheese
¼ cup nonfat plain yogurt
2 tablespoons honey
1 tablespoon skim milk
1 teaspoon vanilla extract
Mint leaves (optional)

Put the raspberries in a strainer and mash with a spoon. Discard the seeds. Place the raspberries and sugar in a small saucepan. In a dish, mix the cornstarch and water. Stir and add to the raspberries. Cook over medium heat, stirring constantly, until the mixture comes to a boil and is thick. Refrigerate for several hours.

Combine all of the cloud ingredients in a blender or food processor and blend until creamy. Cover and chill for at least 1 hour. Place the cloud mixture in 4 goblets. Spoon on the raspberry mixture. If desired, garnish with mint leaves.

Serves 4

Menu 3

FOOD FOR THOUGHT
Attitudes are often more important than facts.

BREAKFAST
(260 calories)

*Silver Dollar Pancakes**
¾ cup fresh or frozen strawberries, no sugar added
Decaffeinated coffee

LUNCH
(250 calories)

Crab-Stuffed Tomato
2 Pogen Krisprolls
Celestial Seasonings Lemon Zinger herb tea, iced

SNACK
(80 calories)

¼ cantaloupe with 2 tablespoons sorbet
Celestial Seasonings Mandarin Orange herb tea

DINNER
(343 calories)

*Asparagus Vinaigrette with Sliced Breast of Chicken**
*Pure Gold Puffs**
1 slice French bread baguette
Wishful White Wine (page 25)

DESSERT
(105 calories)

*Midas Macaroons**
Celestial Seasonings Almond Sunset herb tea

TOTAL CALORIES 1,038
PROTEIN 29%
CARBOHYDRATE 48%
FAT 23%

* Recipe follows

SILVER DOLLAR PANCAKES

½ teaspoon grated lemon rind
4 tablespoons nonfat plain yogurt
1⅓ cups part-skim ricotta cheese
½ cup nonfat milk
12 tablespoons whole-wheat flour
4 teaspoons sugar
½ teaspoon baking powder
2 teaspoons vanilla extract
4 egg whites
¼ teaspoon cream of tartar

Place the lemon rind, yogurt, and ricotta cheese in blender. Add the milk, flour, sugar, baking powder, and vanilla. Whirl until smooth. If the mixture is too thick, add 1 to 2 tablespoons more milk. In a small bowl, beat the egg whites and cream of tartar until soft peaks form. Carefully fold the egg whites into the batter. Spray a nonstick skillet with Pam. Fry the pancakes until golden on each side.

Serves 4

CRAB-STUFFED TOMATO

4 tomatoes

Filling

2 cups cooked crab meat (see note)
2 tablespoons mayonnaise
1 tablespoon nonfat plain yogurt
2 tablespoons fresh lemon juice
½ cup canned artichoke hearts (not marinated), chopped
2 tablespoons chopped pimiento
2 teaspoons Dijon mustard
4 scallions, minced
2 stalks celery, chopped
⅛ teaspoon black pepper

8 cups crisp romaine lettuce, torn into bite-size pieces

(Continued)

(Continued from page 231)
Peel and core the tomatoes. Slice almost to the bottom into 6 sections. Combine all of the filling ingredients. Chill. Serve in tomatoes that have been placed on a bed of lettuce.

Serves 4

Note: Fresh, frozen, or canned crab meat is preferred in that order. Fresh or frozen imitation crab meat is also acceptable. The fish used in imitation crab meat is usually pollock, a white, low-fat fish that is tasty. The unfortunate part of the imitation crab is that it is highly saturated with sodium and artificial coloring has been added to make it resemble real crab. Imitation crab also tastes a little sweeter than real crab.

ASPARAGUS VINAIGRETTE WITH SLICED BREAST OF CHICKEN

12 ounces skinless, boneless chicken breast
1½ pounds asparagus

Dressing

1 clove garlic, mashed
⅛ teaspoon salt
½ teaspoon white pepper
2 teaspoons Dijon mustard
3 tablespoons fresh lemon juice
4 tablespoons Swanson's Natural Goodness chicken broth
1 tablespoon sesame oil

4 cups spinach, thoroughly washed and torn into bite-size pieces

Bake the chicken in a 350° oven for approximately 45 minutes, or until done. Chill. Clean the asparagus and cut off the tough ends of the stalks and discard. Steam the asparagus for 5 to 10 minutes, until tender yet slightly crisp. Chill. In a bowl, combine the dressing ingredients. Place in a tightly covered jar and refrigerate. When the chicken is cooled, slice thin. Place the spinach on 4 salad plates. On top of that place the asparagus spears and chicken. Shake the dressing well. Drizzle 3 tablespoons dressing over each serving.

Serves 4

PURE GOLD PUFFS

2 cups cooked carrots
¼ teaspoon nutmeg

Purée the carrots in a blender or food processor. Using a pastry bag, form 4 decorative servings on individual warmed dinner plates. Sprinkle with nutmeg and serve immediately.

Serves 4

MIDAS MACAROONS

1 cup Spoon Size Shredded Wheat
1 cup Quaker Old Fashioned Oats
¼ cup chopped almonds
¼ cup frozen orange juice concentrate, undiluted
1 tablespoon raspberry jam
1 teaspoon almond flavoring
1 teaspoon vanilla extract
2 egg whites

Grind the shredded wheat in a food processor. In a large bowl, combine the processed shredded wheat with oats and almonds. In another bowl, combine the orange juice concentrate, jam, almond flavoring, and vanilla. In another bowl, beat the egg whites until stiff. Carefully fold the egg whites into the orange juice mixture, then fold all of that into the cereal mixture. Drop by teaspoonfuls onto a nonstick baking sheet that has been sprayed with Pam. Bake at 350° for 15 minutes.

Makes 12 cookies (3 per serving)

Menu 4

EATING OUT

FOOD FOR THOUGHT

Behold the turtle; he doesn't accomplish anything until he sticks his neck out.

BREAKFAST

(290 calories)

Egg unbenedict made with ½ English muffin (unbuttered), 1 poached egg, 1 slice Canadian bacon, 1 tablespoon hollandaise sauce
1 cup fresh fruit
Decaffeinated coffee

LUNCH

(380 calories)

1 cup consommé
1 slice spinach and cheese quiche (do not eat the crust)
Green salad with red wine vinegar
Iced tea

DINNER

(300 calories)

3 ounces broiled lobster with lemon
1 cup steamed fresh vegetables
½ cup rice or 1 dinner roll
Perrier with lemon

DESSERT

(100 calories)

½ cup sorbet
Decaffeinated coffee

TOTAL CALORIES 1,070
PROTEIN 20%
CARBOHYDRATE 50%
FAT 30%

DIET DAY #9

SEEING THE BIG PICTURE

In numerology, the number 9 indicates an interest in travel and the world at large. You'll seek out foreign flavors and crowds. Nine also signifies completion: a Diet Day #9 is the end of a nine-day cycle. It's time to tie up loose ends and finish projects. As you look back over the past nine days, review your mistakes and learn from them. Forgive yourself for any diet digressions and get ready to begin again.

Look at the big picture today, especially where diet is concerned. You didn't gain weight overnight, and you won't lose it overnight, either. If you are disappointed over the rate at which you are losing, remember that each daily loss, no matter how small, will add up to an impressive total if you keep at it.

Operate from the typical Diet Day #9 generosity you feel by giving away what is no longer useful to you. All the foods in your cupboard that didn't pass the label test on Diet Day #2 can be donated to a worthy cause. Fill another box with the clothes that are too big and take them to a thrift shop. Be generous with praise as well. Express appreciation to the people who have helped you stay on your diet, and share the support you have received with another dieter.

A Diet Day #9 is a great day to spread the word about the Numbers Diet. Tell others how much better you feel now that you have incorporated sensible food and regular exercise into your life. Bolster your spirits and self-esteem by projecting the positive image of a diet-conscious weight manager. Celebrate your accomplishments. You have gained insight, not weight, during the last nine days.

The overriding principle for a Diet Day #9 can be summed up in the phrase "what goes around comes around." What you give out will come back to you. Play by the rules today, especially the golden rule, and you will be rewarded.

BREAKING BAD HABITS

For over twenty years I have used numerology to take advantage of the overtones of each day. Knowing that a Diet Day #9 is the perfect time to put an end to a bad habit makes it easier for me to make the commitment. I am also encouraged by the knowledge that while I am ending an unproductive behavior on a Diet Day #9, I can replace it with a new, beneficial behavior on a Diet Day #1.

> Numerology can also explain the overtones of each month and year.

Experts agree that success in quitting smoking, drinking, nail biting, or overeating depends upon replacing that activity with another that is pleasing and beneficial. For every Diet Day, there are suggestions for activities to combat diet downfalls. Use your newfound knowledge to determine what behavior you need to change and what foods you need to give up.

Be reasonable. When you eliminate some fats from your diet (to reduce your intake to 20 to 30 percent of your total daily calories), cut out fats you don't like and leave yourself some of the fats you do enjoy.

Be realistic. If you backslide, remember: you're only human, like the rest of us. Don't use one mistake as a reason to berate yourself. Learn from that mistake and give yourself credit for starting anew.

Be good to yourself. Why are you "treating" yourself with a bad habit when you could be pampering your whole body with a good one?

Reach out. The real secret to self-fulfillment comes from giving to others. Enjoy the satisfaction of making this world a better place, and see if that doesn't fill you up even better than food.

In addition to sugar, salt, and fat, consider breaking a caffeine or alcohol habit on a Diet Day #9 if either of these substances is causing you to miss out on a healthy lifestyle.

CAFFEINE

If you're a zombie until you've had your first cup of coffee, perhaps it's time to start asking yourself if it's worth it. Caffeine is an accepted part of the daily diet in many cultures and one of the most widely used stimulants the world around. Coffee is found all over the world and, thanks to the English, the sun still never sets on a cup of tea so strong it will hold a spoon upright. Together with chocolate, colas are responsible for early childhood addiction to caffeine.

Using even small amounts of caffeine can disturb your sleep, give you the jitters, cause irritability and nervousness, and account for stomach irritation, digestive disturbances, and prostate problems. Blood sugar is affected, causing highs and lows like those associated with sugar. Caffeine affects the cardiovascular system by raising the blood pressure and resting heart rate. Furthermore, abnormal heart rhythms and heart palpitations are often attributed to caffeine use. Worst of all for women, caffeine robs our bones of calcium, making us more prone to osteoporosis. In addition, caffeine is said to be linked with fibrocystic breast disease (breast lumps). In 1980 the FDA advised pregnant women to lower their consumption of caffeine, because it crosses the placental barrier.

Try not to have more than 16 ounces of caffeine drinks per day.

To eliminate caffeine without withdrawal symptoms, cut down slowly. Drink increasingly smaller servings of caffeinated beverages, replacing them with more healthy liquids.

As a dieter, you should be aware of what caffeine does to your body and how it affects your hunger patterns. Since coffee is the most popular form of caffeine, let's use it as an example. Once that steaming aromatic brew hits your system, the caffeine in coffee stimulates your liver to release glucose (sugar) into your blood. The result is a thirty-minute rush of quick energy. You're awake and raring to go for the time being. At the end of thirty minutes, the caffeine wears off and you crave another cup, which further drains your liver of sugar, which could be going to your brain as fuel instead.

It doesn't take much caffeine to give us a rush, only 150 to 250 milligrams, or the amount in one to two cups of brewed coffee. Although coffee, tea, cola sodas, and chocolate contain caffeine, so do common over-the-counter and prescription medications for headache, cold, allergy, stay-awake, and sleeping medication and diet preparations. The FDA reports that more than a thousand over-the-counter medications contain caffeine. To raise your caffeine IQ, check out the amount of caffeine in the products you use.

COFFEE

The amount of caffeine in coffee depends on how it's brewed and for how long, whether it's instant or ground. Decaffeinated brands have a few milligrams of caffeine.

TEA

Tea contains approximately one-third the caffeine of brewed coffee, but the longer it is steeped, the higher the caffeine level. Herbal teas without caffeine make good substitutes.

SODAS AND COLAS

Cola drinks contain the highest levels of caffeine. Check the label on your favorite variety and consider the caffeine-free version as an alternative.

CHOCOLATE

The high level of caffeine in the cocoa bean accounts for the caffeine in chocolate. One cup of hot chocolate contains approximately as much caffeine as ¼ cup of brewed coffee. The amount of baking chocolate used in one serving of ice cream, candy, or a brownie contains one-third the caffeine in a cup of coffee.

Caffeine Content of Beverages and Foods

	Mg
Coffee (per cup)	
Brewed, drip method	115
Brewed, percolator	80
Instant	65
Decaffeinated, brewed	3
Decaffeinated, instant	2
Tea (per cup)	
Brewed, major U.S. brands	40
Brewed, imported brands	60
Instant	30
Iced	70
Chocolate Drinks (per cup)	
Cocoa beverage	4
Chocolate milk	5

	Mg
Chocolate (per ounce)	
Dark chocolate, semisweet	20
Baker's chocolate	26
Chocolate-flavored syrup	4
Soft Drinks (12 ounces)	
Coca-Cola	63
Mountain Dew	55
Diet Coke	45.6
Dr Pepper	39.6
Pepsi-Cola	38.4
Diet Pepsi	36

Caffeine Content of Nonprescription Drugs (Per Dose)

	Mg
Alertness	
No-Doz	100
Vivarin	200
Pain Relief	
Anacin, maximum strength	32
Vanquish	33
Excedrin	65
Midol	32.4

	Mg
Diuretic	
Aqua-ban	100
Cold/Allergy Preparations	
Many cold preparations	30

ALCOHOL

All you ever wanted to know about alcohol . . . and were sorry you asked. According to the experts, one drink a day won't hurt a healthy person. However, excessive amounts of alcohol, which is toxic to the brain, heart, liver, and gastrointestinal tract, can lead to an anesthetizing of the brain. Control and judgment become impaired after 5 or 6 ounces. After 22 ounces, coma and death can occur. Aside from liver disease, cancer, gastrointestinal injury due to excess stomach acidity, impaired sexual performance, birth defects, sleep disturbance, gout, impaired ability to fight bacterial infections, interference in the body's ability to digest essential nutrients, hypoglycemia, headaches, nausea, dizziness, and general instability, the real reason no weight manager in her right mind would take more than one glass of white wine is calorie content. The alcohol in one drink or in a glass of wine is 100 calories. I don't know about you, but when I'm hungry I can think of 100 things that taste 100 times better than an alcoholic beverge. Except on special occasions, why consume 100 empty calories of alcohol when you could eat 100 calories' worth of nutritious foods that taste delicious?

> There are 100 calories in 3½ ounces of wine, but most wineglasses hold 6 to 7 ounces.

Check the table on opposite page for the calorie count of popular alcoholic beverages and decide if any one of them is worth ingesting on a regular basis.

A hundred calories, the amount in an average alcoholic beverage, is a lot when you are on a 1,000- to 1,200-calorie diet to lose weight. To be properly nourished on such a low-calorie diet, you must make every calorie count. Why waste one-tenth of your allotment on booze?

If you miss the sociability that the cocktail hour affords, join in with club soda or mineral water. If you feel you need the relaxation alcohol provides to disengage your brain, take a nap, a walk, meditate, go for a massage, or make love!

Calorie Count of Alcoholic Beverages

Beverage	Amount	Calories
Beer	12 ounces	140–150
Light beer	12 ounces	70–95
Sherry, dry	3 ounces	110
Sherry, sweet	3 ounces	150
Sweet or fortified wine	3 ounces	120–160
Red or white wine	3½ ounces	100
Gin, rum, vodka, whiskey		
80 proof	1½ ounces	97
86 proof	1½ ounces	105
90 proof	1½ ounces	110
94 proof	1½ ounces	116
100 proof	1½ ounces	124
Daiquiri	4 ounces	260
Eggnog	4 ounces	196–330
Manhattan	1 cocktail	160
Martini	1 cocktail	140
Old-fashioned	1 cocktail	185
Gimlet	1 cocktail	320
Mai-Tai	1 cocktail	260
Piña colada	1 cocktail	260
Liqueur	1 ounce	70–115
Brandy and Cognac	1 ounce	65
Mixers		
Tom Collins	8 ounces	112
Seltzer, club soda, mineral water	8 ounces	0
Cola	8 ounces	96
Ginger ale	8 ounces	72

TOFU

Is tofu for you? You bet! On a Diet Day #9 your urge for the exotic will make that strange white stuff seem intriguing. Tofu is a versatile, low-cost source of low-fat, low-calorie protein. It just looks funny to most Americans, but it has been a staple food in many Asian countries, including China and Japan, where few people are overweight and the incidence of heart disease is low.

Tofu is made from cooked soybeans, water, and added minerals to make it into the firm custardlike blocks you see in the dairy case or produce section. Available in hard or firm, regular or medium, and soft for different uses, tofu can be purchased in heat-sealed packages that have a prolonged shelf life and require refrigeration only after opening. Tofu is inexpensive, costing about a dollar per pound.

By itself, tofu does not have much flavor, but it readily absorbs all the delicious flavors from other ingredients in a recipe. Tofu can be diced, sliced, crumbled, and puréed. It can be grilled, boiled, steamed, deep-fried (don't you dare!), baked, broiled, sautéed, or barbecued. It's ideal for use in soups, salads, dressings, dips, and casseroles, and as a substitute for mayonnaise, yogurt, and cheese, as well as a nutritional extender to "beef up" the food value of a recipe. It's even a good egg substitute, since it does not contain cholesterol and is a significant source of protein. Your success in using tofu to replace eggs completely in a recipe will depend on what they do. Tofu can bind foods together as egg whites do, but it won't thicken as egg yolks do. It cannot be whipped.

STORING TOFU

Most types of tofu need to be refrigerated. The heat-sealed variety requires refrigeration only after opening. Tofu is usually shipped and stored in water. Check the shelf-life date on the label to ensure freshness.

Once you open your tofu, keep it up to a week in water, which should be changed every two days.

Tofu in leftover cooked dishes lasts longer under refrigeration than tofu in uncooked salads and spreads. The secret is buying small amounts and using it all up so leftovers do not become a factor.

Freezing tofu gives it a more chewy texture, which is great for meat and chili-type dishes. Thaw and drain frozen packaged tofu. Rinse in fresh water and squeeze dry before using in recipes.

Look for prepared tofu products, especially in health food stores. Convenience products such as tofu salads, spreads, burritos, and lasagna are also available and provide a chance to sample this strange new stuff before you try cooking with it at home.

Remember, tofu as an ingredient in foods does not guarantee reduced calories, so check the labels. For instance, commercially made tofu-based ice cream may be free of cholesterol, but it can be loaded with sugar and hidden calories. Four ounces may contain anywhere from 130 to 270 calories, compared to frozen nonfat yogurt at 80 to 100 calories.

FLAB-U-LESS WAY TO FRY

On a Diet Day #9 your imagination wanders to foreign lands, even though your body has to stay home. Here's a Chinese method of cooking called stir frying, which you can adapt to foods of any culture.

Whether you are a novice or an expert cook, stir frying is a simple method to learn. The traditional utensil is a wok, a curved metal pan, but if you don't have one, you can just as easily use a nonstick frying pan. In fact, a nonstick surface is preferable, because you can substitute chicken broth, vegetable stock, lemon juice, water, or white wine for the oil normally used in a wok.

It's important to have all the ingredients for a dish cut into bite-size pieces and ready to use, because stir frying is done quickly. Vegetables cut on the diagonal are pretty and they cook faster. The more dense the food, such as celery, water chestnuts, and carrots, the thinner you slice it. Crunchy foods, such as bean sprouts and snow peas, can be left whole or diced to provide interesting texture. Dry vegetables thoroughly after washing them to eliminate excess moisture, which might cause vegetables to become mushy.

Prepare ingredients up to a day in advance, wrap in separate paper towels and plastic bags, and store in the crisper drawer of the refrigerator. Meats and poultry should be sliced thin uniformly so all the pieces will cook in the same amount of time. Meat should be cut against the grain, but chicken is shredded or cut with the grain.

If a recipe calls for tofu, follow directions carefully. Sauté tofu separately to avoid crumbling, remove, and keep hot to add back to the finished dish. In recipes such as scrambled bean sprouts that call for tofu instead of eggs, cook the tofu along with other ingredients. If you are using seafood in your stir fry, use firm fish such as halibut, shrimp, and lobster. Delicate varieties such as cod or sole will crumble when stir-fried.

To stir fry, heat the nonstick skillet or wok over medium high heat. The Chinese cook over gas burners, which I prefer, but you can also use an electric stove. Be sure your pan is large enough to stir and cook ingredients quickly. If food is more than 1 inch deep, the ingredients will become soggy. When the pan is hot enough to make a drop of water dance, add about 2 tablespoons of "legal" liquid. Immediately rotate the pan to distribute the liquid and add the ingredient that will require the longest cooking time (such as chicken or fish). Avoid covering the wok or skillet, unless you wanted steamed mush!

DIET DOWNFALLS AND THEIR SOLUTIONS

Looking back through my diet history, I discovered that I usually fell off my diet train on a Diet Day #9. The tendency is to give up today because it is the end of a cycle. Whatever you do, don't quit, and don't get on the scale today. If you haven't lost, you'll be tempted to throw in the towel. If you have lost, you may be tempted to relax and eat a "little something" that isn't on the Numbers Diet. When you cheat, the tendency is to say "I ate something I shouldn't have, so the day is shot; I may as well stay off my diet just for today and start back on it tomorrow." Sometimes tomorrow never comes, so it's better to get back on course immediately. Don't get tripped up by a slipup.

In a Diet Day #9 fit of generosity you may get carried away worrying about others. Saboteurs lurk around every corner. Every time you put yourself down, you drive yourself to eat for consolation, abandoning your diet. Every time you listen to a friend who means well but gives you misinformation about diet, you risk getting off the diet track. Every time you let your mother ply you with goodies or chide you for not "eating right," your diet resolve weakens. Beware the envious friend who feels competitive and may lead you astray if she thinks you're becoming an attractive threat. Get ready to reassure the man in your life that the new you still has eyes only for him. And if your newly acquired shape suddenly triggers attention from other men, don't subconsciously retreat behind a few added pounds of unattractive fat for safety.

If you suspect that you or others in your life are creating diet dilemmas, look beneath the surface and try to understand the dynamics of what's happening. You may have to change your negative self-talk to positive pep talks and deal more honestly with the people in your life. If you invest too much in other people and what they think, you may be tempted to eat something just to make another person happy. It's okay to focus on people, but not on food. Don't give food powers it wasn't meant to have. Eat for your own best interests, not someone else's.

Don't feel you have to keep goodies in the house for your children, the way I used to. In the end I realized I did them no service by providing the means for them to establish bad eating habits.

Don't let your philanthropic mood be your undoing today. If you buy Girl Scout cookies and "earn your way to camp" chocolate bars from those cute kids outside the supermarket, you'll just eat the stuff. Contrary to popular belief, these goodies do have calories, even though they benefit a good cause.

> In true Diet Day #9 charity, donate money for a box of Girl Scout cookies, but leave the box for the scout to sell again or eat herself.

DINING OUT

Give in to your cravings for exotic flavors on a Diet Day #9.

AT A CHINESE RESTAURANT

Long on rice and vegetables and short on meat, Chinese food seems like a good choice if you are cautious about the selections you make. Contrary to popular opinion, Chinese food can be high in calories. Beware the hidden facts. Put your waiter to the test by asking how things are prepared. Ask if beef and chicken are deep-fried before they are added to vegetables in the dishes with exotic names. Ask if some dishes can be prepared with chicken broth instead of oil. If you're sensitive to sodium, request that the dish be prepared without soy sauce or MSG.

> Don't be deceived by the small plates or lose track of how many times you fill yours.

Appetizers. Egg drop soup or wonton soup is better than sizzling rice soup. Do I need to tell you what makes those little rice kernels sizzle? Each one is coated in oil and fried so it will speak to you when the waiter dumps it into the hot soup.

Barbecued pork spareribs, deep-fried shrimp, egg rolls, fried wontons, and egg foo yong, at too many calories per crispy fried crunch, are off limits.

Rice. Steamed is preferred over fried rice, for obvious reasons.

Entrées. Sweet and sour is out, but moo goo gai pan (chicken with mushrooms and assorted vegetables) and almond gai ding (diced chicken with almonds and vegetables) tie for first choice. Chop suey is better than chow mein, which is traditionally served with fried noodles. If you are dining in a first-class Chinese restaurant or your favorite local hangout where you are a valued customer, ask for chicken or shrimp stir-fried without oil, in broth with vegetables.

> Use chopsticks to help you eat less over a longer period of time.

Desserts. Opt for fresh sliced oranges instead of syrupy lichee nuts or crackling apples or bananas, another bit of Oriental magic, performed by submerging freshly fried fruit in ice water. On a Diet Day #9 you are in a talkative mood, so keep yourself occupied during dessert by telling your friends who are eating this stuff how it is prepared.

Since fortune cookies are made from egg whites and flour, they are acceptable assuming you don't keep eating them until you find a fortune you like. Confucius says: "Drink lots of tea and stay up all night!"

AT A MEXICAN RESTAURANT

A seemingly healthy cuisine, on the one hand, because it traditionally combines beans, rice, and corn for a complete protein, Mexican cooking uses lard in many dishes, such as refried beans. Call several restaurants until you find one that does not use lard or will prepare your meal to order without it.

Appetizers. If you succumb to a margarita, you are sacrificing 350 calories. It's better to choose a light beer at 70 to 95 calories, and best to confine your festivity to a diet soft drink or sparkling water, if available.

Nachos, combination plates, and "fiesta" platters are designed to wipe out your calorie allowance for two days in one sitting, even if you are sharing an order. In addition, the ever-present bowl of irresistible chips is dynamite. Each one is 16 calories, and you know how easy it is to polish off the entire bowl by yourself.

> I love salsa, which is low in calories, so I bring my own tortilla triangle chips (page 28) from home in a plastic bag.

Salads. Keep your salad simple and green, with the dressing on the side. Before you give in to avocado, remember that one-eighth of an avocado is 50 calories. Salsa fresca (fresh salsa) makes a great topping for salads, especially a main dish chicken tostada.

Soups. Albondigas, seasoned beef broth with vegetables and meatballs, makes a whole meal, but watch out for extra fat.

> If you are with family or understanding friends, surreptitiously slip a couple of ice cubes into your soup, let the excess fat congeal on the cubes, and daintily hide them on your plate.

Gazpacho, tomato-based vegetable soup served chilled, is a very refreshing low-calorie item so long as you ignore the accompanying sour cream in favor of the Mexican parsley called cilantro.

Entrées. You can still enjoy the Mexican flavor if you order a soft burrito, taco, or tostada instead of the deep-fried versions. Chicken and fish entrées are preferable to beef. Go easy on the cheese, which comes with practically everything, and order tortillas made with cornmeal instead of flour. Make your own soft taco from the side order menu: corn tortillas, beans without cheese, rice, and salsa.

Cenas (dinners) featuring pescado (fish) that is baked or broiled, Vera Cruz style, are fine for the diner who can handle three-alarm fires. Picado pollo (breast of chicken sautéed with vegetables) is probably low enough in calories if you skip the skin, and a small serving of machaca (usually flank steak that has been seasoned and shredded) won't break your calorie bank. Also consider pollo a la romano, which is boned chicken in wine sauce. Order à la carte so you won't be tempted by the rice and beans, which are a whole meal in themselves.

Desserts. Famous for their flan (caramel custard), Mexican restaurants can be a test for dieters. Mexican coffee, spiked with Kahlua and cream, is also off limits. Settle for coffee with cinnamon, your choice of sugar substitute, and a dash of low-fat milk.

AT AN ITALIAN RESTAURANT

Do as the Romans do and you may regret it. Watch out for their cream soups and hidden fats. At 100 calories per tablespoon, olive oil and/or butter lurk in garlic bread, antipasto, pesto sauce, Caesar salad dressing, roasted sweet peppers with anchovies or tuna, cheese entrées, and bread crumb mixtures with cheese.

Appetizers. Select fresh melon without the prosciutto (very salty Italian ham).

Salads. Order without meats, cheese, or olives. Ask for lemon wedges or a cruet of vinegar, and treat yourself to a dusting of Parmesan cheese and a few twists of freshly ground pepper.

Soups. Minestrone is good if there isn't too much oil in it. Cioppino (seafood soup) is an excellent choice because you have to work at liberating the shellfish before you can eat it. Skip the cream soups.

Pizza. It's okay if you ask for a thick crust, request more vegetables and less cheese, and skip the pepperoni and sausage. The rational behind the thick crust is that you will be satisfied with one piece instead of several.

Pasta. Whole-wheat pasta is preferred, but egg pasta will do. The colored pasta is pretty to look at, but it's usually made with insignificant amounts of vegetable nutrients and won't add much to your good health.

Entrées. Order mussels with marinara sauce, veal or chicken piccata (request lots of lemon and very little butter), pasta marinara, ravioli, manicotti with cheese on top, and linguine with red clam sauce. Chicken marsala and chicken cacciatore are acceptable choices if you remove the skin. Also good diet fare are muscoli della rivera (steamed mussels in red sauce), zuppa de vongole (clams steamed in white wine and shallots), calamari barcaiola (squid in white wine with tomatoes and shallots), and linguine alle vongole (linguine in red clam sauce).

Sauces. Red, tomato-based, meatless sauces are better than white sauces, which are loaded with cream, butter, and cheese.

> Red sauce with meat is acceptable on pasta if you are ordering it as an entrée.

Breads. So long as you don't slather them with butter, Italian bread and breadsticks are permissible in small quantities.

Vegetables. Often dressed with olive oil, cheese, and seasonings, Italian vegetable dishes can be high-calorie. Stick with a green salad and control the oil in the dressing by making it yourself on the salad, using red wine vinegar and a dash of olive oil.

Desserts. Fresh fruit, without the usual splash of Italian liqueur, is your best bet. If you don't let the waiter sweet-talk you into cannoli, tortoni, or spumoni, you can let your resolve melt for a small scoop of gelato or Italian ice.

Coffee. Finish off your evening with a decaf cappuccino made with low-fat milk.

AT A FRENCH RESTAURANT

The French pride themselves on exquisite preparation of high-quality fresh foods, and their portions are notoriously small. Unfortunately, they use butter, heavy cream, eggs, and flour in liberal quantities to make delectable sauces such as hollandaise, béchamel, mornay, and béarnaise. To avoid the fat, try a wine sauce, one made with tomato or vegetables such as coulis or piquante, and have it served on the side. Most dishes are made to order, so you can specify your preference for baked, broiled, steamed, or poached foods.

Appetizers. Try huitres hors d'oeuvres (oysters on the half shell) and salad d'artichauts et griolles (artichoke and mushroom salad), coupled with crusty French bread sans le beurre (without butter). Stay away from the pâté, because the butter and organ meats from which they are made are high in cholesterol and calories. Avoid quiche, because the fat-laden crust and the fillings made with butter, egg, cream, and cheese will set you back several diet days. Onion soup is on the approved list so long as you pass on the crusty crouton and melted cheese topping.

Salads. Salade verte (mixed greens) is safe, providing you order the vinaigrette dressing on the side. Fortunately the salade Niçoise (greens with olives, eggs, tuna, and anchovies) is just as appetizing undressed.

Caesar salad and salads served with creamy Roquefort cheese dressing are off limits. However, you can have the Roquefort taste if you ask for a green salad, a cruet of vinegar and one of oil, and the cheese on the side. Vinegar with a dash of oil and a sprinkle of cheese will give you the flavor without so much fat.

Bread. Cultivate a taste for French bread without butter, and concentrate on the crust; it's tastier and takes longer to chew.

Vegetables. Steamed to perfection by the French, vegetables can reach new heights of culinary glory. Ask for twice as many vegetables when you decline the sauce that goes with them, and remember, flattery will get you anything from a French waiter.

Entrées. Although duck is standard French fare, it is off limits because of its high fat content. Poached fish in white wine is always a good choice. Bouillabaisse sans aïoli (without garlic mayonnaise) is even better, because you'll barely have time to eat it after you have pried the seafood out of its shells. Quenelles (poached fish dumplings made with egg whites) are acceptable, as is pot-au-feu (stewed chicken in broth) so long as the broth has been defatted.

Desserts. Run, do not walk, when you see the dessert cart approach, laden with French pastries. Opt for French-roast coffee and a walk in the moonlight with someone romantic.

EXERCISE

Given your interest in ethnic foods today, the single most important exercise on a Diet Day #9 is pushing yourself away from the table.

Solo exercise and exercise for exercise's sake are not high on your list. On a Diet Day #9 you are better off doing physical activities that include others and making exercise a *part* of what you do and not an end in itself.

FOLK DANCING

If you can't be a world traveler today, pick a restaurant that features foreign music as well as food and stay for the dancing. Let the strains of a mariachi band and the Mexican hat dance transport you south of the border. Or pluck that rose out of the vase on the table, plant it between your teeth, and do a fancy flamenco.

Every culture has its traditional dance. Sign up for a class and master the Scottish sword dance or the Filipino stick dance. Grab a grass skirt and rotate that pelvis with the hula or Tahitian dancing. Scoop up your scarves and do your best belly dance. Call your local temple and join in doing the horah.

If you're a mother with young children, put them in their little red wagon and pull them around the block and pretend you are pulling a rickshaw in Japan.

PHILANTHROPIC EXERCISE

Participate in a walk-a-thon, car wash, or cleanup project. Organize a charity event that benefits a worthy cause at your gym or workplace. Ask people to get sponsors for a certain number of minutes on a stationary bike and stage a bike-a-thon. Or plan your own private exercise routine for the most important cause, yourself. On a Diet Day #9 don't forget that charity begins at home.

RECIPES FOR DIET DAY #9

Treat your taste buds to a touch of exotica with foreign flavors on a Diet Day #9. These menus provide low-calorie diet delectables from around the world, from spicy Mexican chilies to cool, creamy flan. Dine out south of the border style and enjoy all your Mexican favorites.

Food for Thought adds to your mental diet with wise words on love, gratitude, generosity, and hope.

Menu 1

ORIENTAL

FOOD FOR THOUGHT

There is no limit to what a person can do if he doesn't care who gets the credit.

BREAKFAST

(296 calories)

*Eggs Oriental**
*Mandarin Oranges Mimosa**
Celestial Seasonings Mandarin Orange Spice herb tea

LUNCH

(315 calories)

*Rickshaw Soup**
*Ginger Broccoli**
Celestial Seasonings Ginseng Plus herb tea

DINNER

(370 calories)

*Cashew Chicken**
½ cup steamed white rice
*Stir-fried Vegetables**
Celestial Seasonings Almond Sunset herb tea

DESSERT

(93 calories)

2 fortune cookies
Celestial Seasonings Emperor's Choice herb tea

TOTAL CALORIES 1,074
PROTEIN 29%
CARBOHYDRATE 49%
FAT 22%

* Recipe follows.

EGGS ORIENTAL

2 tablespoons Swanson's Natural Goodness chicken broth
1 clove garlic, minced
2 cups cooked brown rice (*not* instant brown rice, which will get gummy)
1 cup egg substitute
¼ cup sliced water chestnuts
½ cup green peas, fresh or frozen and thawed
2 tablespoons minced scallion
¼ teaspoon sesame oil
1 teaspoon slivered almonds
1 teaspoon soy sauce

Heat the broth in a large nonstick pan. Add the garlic and stir fry until heated. Add the rice and stir until the grains are coated with broth. In a separate nonstick pan sprayed with Pam, scramble the egg substitute. Gently fold the scrambled eggs into the rice. Add the water chestnuts and peas and stir fry until heated. Add the scallion, oil, and almonds. Taste before adding soy sauce.

Serves 4

RICKSHAW SOUP

8 ounces boneless, skinless chicken breast, sliced
6 tablespoons fresh lemon juice
1 tablespoon soy sauce
6 cups Swanson's Natural Goodness chicken broth
1 cup broccoli florets
4 scallions, sliced
1 cup sliced mushrooms
¼ cup cooked ramen noodles or short pieces of spaghetti

In a nonstick frying pan, brown the chicken in lemon juice and soy sauce. Set aside. In a large saucepan, combine the other ingredients. Heat until near boiling. Reduce the heat, add the chicken, and simmer until it is hot. Serve.

Serves 4

MANDARIN ORANGES MIMOSA

2 cups mandarin oranges, canned in "lite" syrup, drained
Dash of orange-flower water

Combine and chill.

Serves 4

GINGER BROCCOLI

¼ cup Swanson's Natural Goodness chicken broth
2 tablespoons grated fresh ginger
1 clove garlic, minced
4 cups broccoli, steamed but still crisp
2 tablespoons or more water
½ teaspoon sesame oil

In a skillet, heat the broth. Add the ginger and garlic and cook until heated. Add the broccoli and cook for about 2 minutes. Add water, if needed. Add sesame oil. Toss the broccoli in the liquid. Cover and steam for 1 minute, until the broccoli is crisp yet tender.

Serves 4

CASHEW CHICKEN

1 egg white
½ teaspoon sesame oil
2 teaspoons cornstarch
12 ounces boneless, skinless chicken breast, cubed
1 tablespoon safflower oil
2 tablespoons Swanson's Natural Goodness chicken broth
1 carrot, sliced
1 cup sliced celery
2 slices fresh ginger, minced
2 scallions, sliced
1 tablespoon cashews

½ cup sliced water chestnuts
Dash of white pepper

Combine the egg white, sesame oil, and cornstarch. Marinate the chicken cubes in the mixture for 15 minutes. Heat safflower oil in a nonstick frying pan over high heat. Add the chicken and stir fry until the meat is white and firm. Remove the chicken; set aside and keep warm. Add the broth to the pan and stir fry the carrot, celery, and ginger for 2 minutes. Add the scallions, cashews, water chestnuts, and pepper. Return the chicken to the pan and stir until all the ingredients are hot enough to serve.

Serves 4

STIR-FRIED VEGETABLES

½ cup Swanson's Natural Goodness chicken broth
1 tablespoon white wine or sherry
1 teaspoon soy sauce
1½ teaspoons cornstarch
1 clove garlic, mashed
1 tablespoon grated fresh ginger
2 carrots, sliced thin
1 stalk celery, sliced
1 cup sliced mushrooms
3 cups chopped greens (bok choy, Chinese cabbage, spinach, Swiss chard, collards)
1 cup bean sprouts

Mix ¼ cup chicken broth with the wine, soy sauce, and cornstarch and set aside. Heat the remaining ¼ cup broth in a large nonstick skillet. Add the garlic, ginger, carrots, and celery. Stir fry for 2 minutes. Add the mushrooms and cook for 2 additional minutes. Add the greens and cook until they turn bright green. Toss the bean sprouts with the vegetables. Add the soy sauce mixture and cook until slightly thickened.

Serves 4

Menu 2

MEXICAN

FOOD FOR THOUGHT
The best is yet to come.

BREAKFAST
(280 calories)

*Chili Cheese Corn Bread**
*Spanish Scramble**
Decaffeinated coffee

LUNCH
(282 calories)

*Tostada**
Celestial Seasonings Orange Zinger herb tea, iced

DINNER
(357 calories)

*Enchiladas**
*Spicy Spanish Rice**
*Sangria**

DESSERT
(160 calories)

*Flan**
*Café Olé**

TOTAL CALORIES 1,079
PROTEIN 22%
CARBOHYDRATE 55%
FAT 23%

* Recipe follows.

CHILI CHEESE CORN BREAD

½ cup whole-wheat flour
2 teaspoons baking powder
1 teaspoon baking soda
1½ cups yellow cornmeal
⅓ cup packed dark brown sugar
1 large egg or ¼ cup egg substitute
1 cup nonfat plain yogurt
¼ cup diced green chilies
¼ cup grated Weight Watchers cheddar cheese

In a mixing bowl, combine the flour, baking powder, baking soda, cornmeal, and sugar. In another bowl, blend the egg and yogurt. Add the liquid ingredients to the dry. Mix until the dry ingredients are moistened. Add the chilies and the cheese. Spray an 8-inch-square pan with Pam and spread the mixture in it. Bake at 350° for 30 to 35 minutes, or until a toothpick inserted in the center comes out clean.

Serves 8

SPANISH SCRAMBLE

4 ounces tofu, drained and patted dry
2 tablespoons spicy salsa
1 clove garlic, minced
¼ cup minced onion
½ cup sliced mushrooms
½ cup chopped bell pepper
2 whole eggs plus 2 egg whites, or ¾ cup egg substitute
1 teaspoon chili powder (optional)
1 tomato, chopped

Cut the tofu into small cubes, mix with the salsa, and set aside. Sauté the garlic, onion, mushrooms, and pepper in a Pam-sprayed nonstick skillet. Cook until the onion is translucent. Lightly beat the eggs and egg whites; add them to the vegetables, along with the chili powder, if desired, and scramble. Add the tomato and tofu mixture and stir gently. Cover and cook over low heat until heated through.

Serves 4

TOSTADA

1 corn tortilla
Chili powder to taste
½ cup canned vegetarian refried beans, heated
1 tablespoon diced green chilies
2 tablespoons salsa
¼ cup grated carrots
½ cup shredded lettuce
1 tablespoon nonfat plain yogurt

Mist the tortilla with a fine spray of water. Sprinkle on the chili powder and heat in a 350° oven until crisp. Place the toasted tortilla on a plate. Top with beans, chilies, salsa, carrots, and lettuce. Garnish with yogurt.

Serves 1

ENCHILADAS

16 ounces tofu, drained and patted dry
⅛ teaspoon chili powder
1 3½-ounce can diced green chilies
½ cup frozen peas, thawed
1 tablespoon chopped fresh cilantro
8 ounces canned Rosarita Enchilada Sauce
8 corn tortillas
3 ounces Weight Watchers part-skim jack cheese, grated

Combine the tofu, chili powder, chilies, peas, and cilantro. Heat the enchilada sauce. Dip the tortillas, one at a time, in the hot sauce. Place each on a plate and spoon one-eighth of the tofu mixture down the center. Roll up and place, seam side down, in a single row in a 9 x 13 x 2-inch baking dish. Pour the remaining sauce over the top. Sprinkle with cheese and bake in a 375° oven for 20 minutes, or until heated through.

Serves 4

SPICY SPANISH RICE

½ cup chopped onions
1 clove garlic, minced
¼ cup Swanson's Natural Goodness chicken broth
½ cup chopped bell pepper
1 8-ounce can stewed tomatoes, drained
⅛ teaspoon cumin
⅛ teaspoon black pepper
3 cups cooked brown rice (*not* quick or instant)
1 tablespoon minced fresh cilantro

In a nonstick skillet, sauté the onions and garlic in the broth. Cook until the onions are translucent. Add the bell pepper and cook for 2 minutes. Add the tomatoes, cumin, black pepper, and rice and stir until blended. Cover and simmer until the mixture is heated through. To serve, garnish with cilantro.

Serves 4

SANGRIA

1 tablespoon orange juice, chilled
1 tablespoon cranberry juice, chilled
8 ounces sparkling water, chilled

Combine in a wineglass.

Serves 1

CAFÉ OLÉ

1 tablespoon evaporated nonfat milk
1 cup decaffeinated coffee brewed with ⅛ teaspoon cinnamon
Cinnamon stick

Add evaporated milk to the coffee and serve with a cinnamon stick.

Serves 1

FLAN

1 small (9-ounce) box Jell-O Sugar Free Instant Vanilla Pudding
2 cups nonfat milk
1 teaspoon liquid imitation butter flavoring
2 teaspoons liquid imitation brandy flavoring
2 teaspoons Kahlua liqueur

Prepare the pudding with the milk according to the directions on the box. Add the flavorings and liqueur. Pour into 4 custard cups. Refrigerate.

Serves 4

Menu 3

ITALIAN

FOOD FOR THOUGHT
Forget what you give, but remember what you receive.

BREAKFAST
(200 calories)

*Frittata**
2 Stella D'oro anisette toasts
½ cup melon
Decaffeinated coffee

LUNCH
(363 calories)

*Minestrone Soup**
*Parmesan Bread**
Celestial Seasonings Almond Sunset herb tea

DINNER
(359 calories)

*Lasagna**
*Insalata di Spinaci**
Bogus Burgundy (page 34)

DESSERT

(150 calories)

*Cannoli Cream**
Celestial Seasonings Amaretto Nights herb tea

TOTAL CALORIES 1,072
PROTEIN 23%
CARBOHYDRATE 53%
FAT 24%

* Recipe follows.

MINESTRONE SOUP

1 14½-ounce can Swanson's Natural Goodness chicken broth plus 1 can water
1 16-ounce can juice-packed peeled tomatoes (no salt added), mashed and undrained
2 stalks celery with leaves, sliced
2 medium zucchini, sliced
¼ cup diced green pepper
1 carrot, sliced
2 scallions, sliced (including green tops)
1½ ounces vermicelli, broken into short lengths
1 clove garlic, speared with a toothpick
½ teaspoon basil
½ teaspoon oregano
2 tablespoons minced fresh parsley
¼ teaspoon black pepper
1 8¾-ounce can garbanzo beans, undrained
6 large spinach leaves, chopped

In a 2-quart pan, bring to a boil the broth and water, tomatoes, celery, zucchini, green pepper, carrot, scallions, pasta, garlic, basil, oregano, parsley and black pepper. Boil, uncovered, until the pasta is cooked, approximately 5 minutes. During the last few minutes of cooking add the garbanzo beans and spinach. Remove the garlic and serve.

Serves 4

FRITATTA

1 cup low-fat cottage cheese
½ cup egg substitute
½ cup chopped mushrooms
2 tablespoons minced fresh parsley
1 tablespoon Quaker Oat Bran Cereal
1 tablespoon grated Parmesan cheese
2 teaspoons Italian herbs
1 10-ounce package frozen chopped spinach, thawed and well drained

In a large bowl, mix the cottage cheese, egg substitute, mushrooms, parsley, cereal, Parmesan, and herbs. Add the spinach. Pour into a Pam-sprayed baking dish. Bake in a 350° oven for 30 minutes, or until firm.

Serves 4

PARMESAN BREAD

Parmesan Butter

¼ cup part-skim ricotta cheese
¼ cup low-fat cottage cheese
2 tablespoons grated Parmesan cheese
1 tablespoon finely minced fresh parsley
½ teaspoon fresh basil or ¼ teaspoon dried
1 scallion, mince fine

8 slices Italian bread

Blend the Parmesan butter ingredients together. Cover and chill. (Keeps up to 1 week.)

Spread 1 tablespoon of the butter on each slice of bread. Serve at room temperature or lightly toasted.

Serves 4

LASAGNA

Tomato Sauce

¼ cup white wine or chicken broth
1 cup chopped onions
2 cloves garlic, minced
1 cup chopped mushrooms
1 28-ounce can tomatoes, undrained and chopped
1 8-ounce can tomato sauce
1 6-ounce can tomato paste
1 carrot, grated
¼ cup minced fresh parsley
1 tablespoon Italian seasoning
⅛ teaspoon Chinese five-spice powder
2 tablespoons grated Parmesan cheese
8 ounces lasagna noodles

Filling

8 ounces low-fat cottage cheese
8 ounces part-skim ricotta cheese
8 ounces tofu
2 ounces part-skim mozzarella cheese, grated

In a large saucepan, heat the wine and sauté the onions, garlic, and mushrooms until tender. Add the tomato products, carrot, parsley, Italian seasoning, five-spice powder, and 1 tablespoon Parmesan cheese. Let the sauce simmer, uncovered, while you prepare the remaining ingredients.

Bring a large pot of water to a boil. Carefully add the noodles to the water and cook until tender but still a bit chewy (al dente). Drain the noodles, rinse with cold water, and separate them.

Combine the cottage cheese, ricotta cheese, tofu, and mozzarella cheese.

Spray a 13 x 9 x 2-inch pan with Pam. Spoon in a thin layer of sauce to cover the bottom of the pan. Add a layer of noodles (4 noodles), half of the filling, more sauce, another layer of noodles, and the rest of the filling. Top with the remaining sauce. Sprinkle with the remaining Parmesan cheese. Cover with foil and bake in

(Continued)

(Continued from page 263)
a 375° oven for 35 minutes. Uncover and cook for another 15 minutes, or until bubbling. Remove from the oven and let stand for 10 minutes before cutting to serve. This dish freezes well.

Serves 8

INSALATA DI SPINACI

Dressing

1 tablespoon olive oil
3 tablespoons fresh lemon juice
3 tablespoons red wine vinegar
1 tablespoon grated Parmesan cheese
Black pepper

8 cups spinach, thoroughly washed and torn into bite-size pieces

Combine the dressing ingredients in a screw-top jar and shake to mix well. Pour over the spinach and toss.

Serves 4

CANNOLI CREAM

8 ounces part-skim ricotta cheese
⅛ cup nonfat milk
1 tablespoon orange marmalade
½ teaspoon sugar
¼ teaspoon rum extract
2 tablespoons golden raisins
2 tablespoons slivered almonds

In a food processor or blender, blend the ricotta cheese, milk, marmalade, sugar, and rum extract until smooth. Stir in the raisins. Refrigerate for 1 hour or longer. Place the almonds in a nonstick skillet and shake over medium heat for 5 to 10 minutes, until lightly toasted. Stir them into the cheese mixture just before serving.

Serves 4

Menu 4

EATING OUT AT A MEXICAN RESTAURANT

FOOD FOR THOUGHT

Be of love a little more careful than of anything else.

BREAKFAST

(320 calories)

Huevos rancheros made with
1 poached egg, ½ cup refried beans, ½ cup salsa,
1 steamed corn tortilla
Decaffeinated coffee

LUNCH

(333 calories)

Bean burrito
Green salad with lemon juice

DINNER

(350 calories)

Chicken tostada
½ cup refried beans
¼ cup salsa
1 steamed corn tortilla
Iced tea with lemon

DESSERT

(25 calories)

Dole Fresh Lites frozen bar

TOTAL CALORIES 1,028
PROTEIN 21%
CARBOHYDRATE 50%
FAT 29%

MAINTENANCE

When you have lost the number of pounds you want to lose, the next step is to stabilize your weight and keep it off. Because the Numbers Diet is nutritionally sound, you can stay on it safely even after you have reached your ideal weight. The amounts of protein and fat in the Numbers Diet are more than adequate, but when you achieve your ideal weight you may add more carbohydrates (fruits, vegetables, grains). To stabilize your weight, begin by gradually adding one serving of carbohydrates at a time until you determine how much food your body needs to maintain your weight without gaining. When you add an extra piece of fruit or a half cup of rice or half a baked potato or a cup of vegetables, your weight may vary by a pound or two. Adjust your calorie intake accordingly.

By now you have learned that drinking eight glasses of water a day, and exercising a minimum of five times per week, is as important as eating properly. Adopt the Numbers Diet as a way of life. Remember, your body is now smaller and requires less calories. Exercise is necessary to maintain a high rate of metabolism. In addition, you want to increase the ratio of muscle mass to body fat so your body burns calories more efficiently. Exercise is the key. It's very simple: you *will* be able to eat more *if* you exercise more. If you stop exercising now, as you begin to increase your calorie intake, you *will* gain weight.

Diet may be a four-letter word, but it doesn't have to be a *negative* word if you continually look for healthy, positive thoughts to include on your mental menu.

Recently my minister and friend, Dr. Frank Richelieu, inspired me with his thoughts on numbers and simple arithmetic. He reminded me that math, like numerology, is based on just ten digits that combine in various ways to make all numbers. Arithmetic problems are merely arrangements of the same ten digits with instructions next to them. Once you understand how to add, subtract, multiply, and divide, finding the answer is easy.

Life, like numbers, is made up of relatively few elements, and once you know the rules, you can solve life's problems. According to Dr. Richelieu, we need to rearrange our lives and circumstances, just like the numbers in a math problem.

This book gives you the basic rules and the knowledge with which to cope with your food cravings plus solve your diet downfalls as they occur on Diet Day Numbers 1 through 9.

Along with eating correctly and exercising, you can take a mathematician's approach to life. *Add* positive goals to your priorities, *subtract* unhealthy habits, *add* good foods to your diet, and *multiply* their benefits every day you stick with the Numbers Diet. *Divide* your long-term goal into manageable short-term goals.

Your weight problem is not unsurmountable. In the words of Dr. Richelieu, "A problem is not an obstacle but a challenge. To find the answer, work the problem in a new way."

The Numbers Diet gives you a new way to look at weight management. Using the wisdom of the ages, a positive attitude, and up-to-date information on diet and exercise, you have what it takes to be a loser and love it.

May you continue to make the most of the best and the least of the worst, and multiply your happiness as you subtract those pounds and inches.

CHARTS

The Diet Day Number Charts are correct for use "as is" in the years 1990, 1998, and 2007. To learn how to find your Diet Day Number, see page 1.

To use the charts in other years, change the number in the chart (center) to the number on the right.

In the Years	Number in Chart	Becomes
1991, 2000, 2009	1	3
	2	4
	3	5
	4	6
	5	7
	6	8
	7	9
	8	1
	9	2
1992, 2001, 2010	1	4
	2	5
	3	6
	4	7
	5	8
	6	9
	7	1
	8	2
	9	3
1993, 2002, 2011	1	5
	2	6
	3	7
	4	8
	5	9
	6	1
	7	2
	8	3
	9	4

KW

Dr. L. H. Grunthal, Jr.
1022 Park St.
Jacksonville, Florida 32204

NAME:

MEAT-VEGETABLE DIET

I. BREAKFAST

½ grapefruit or unsweetened grapefruit juice
2 eggs, any style, 2 slices of bacon, minimum.
Coffee, or tea, no cream or sugar

II. LUNCH

½ grapefruit
meat any style, any amount
salad, as much as you can eat with any dressing that contains no sugar.
coffee or tea

III. DINNER

½ grapefruit
meat, any style, any amount, with gravy providing that it is not thickened with flour, of course you may substitute fish for meat.
Any green, yellow or red vegetables. Eat as much

IV. BEDTIME SNACK — Tomato juice or skimmed milk.

****

1. Eat moderate amounts only. Eat meals at regular intervals and same time each day.
2. Don't eliminate anything; for example; don't skip bacon at breakfast or omit the salad at dinner. It is this combination of foods that burns up accumulated fats.
3. The grapefruit is important because it acts as a catalyst that starts the fat burning process.
4. Cut down on coffee. It is thought to affect the insulin balance that hinders the burning process. Try to limit yourself to one cup at each meal.
5. No eating between meals. If you can eat the combination of foods suggested you won't be hungry between meals.
6. Note that this diet completely eliminates sugar and starches which form lipoids and lipoids are what form fat. You can fry your eggs in margarine and use margarine on your vegetables.
7. Note that with this diet you may eat what your family eats except deserts, breads, and white vegetables. While your family eats this you may have more meat, salads or vegetables. The more you can eat of the proper combination, the more you lose.
8. It's best to broil or bake meats. Nothing fried.

7/19/67

Weight now: 241

Lose 30-35 pounds next 3 to 4 months.

1994, 2003, 2012	1	6
	2	7
	3	8
	4	9
	5	1
	6	2
	7	3
	8	4
	9	5
1995, 2004, 2013	1	7
	2	8
	3	9
	4	1
	5	2
	6	3
	7	4
	8	5
	9	6
1996, 2005, 2014	1	8
	2	9
	3	1
	4	2
	5	3
	6	4
	7	5
	8	6
	9	7
1997, 2006, 2015	1	9
	2	1
	3	2
	4	3
	5	4
	6	5

	7	6
	8	7
	9	8
1998, 2007, 2016	Use the charts "as is"	
1999, 2008, 2017	1	2
	2	3
	3	4
	4	5
	5	6
	6	7
	7	8
	8	9
	9	1

JANUARY 1

	1	2	3	4	5	6	7	8	9	10	11	12	13	14	15	16	17	18	19	20	21	22	23	24	25	26	27	28	29	30	31
Jan	5	6	7	8	9	1	2	3	4	5	6	7	8	9	1	2	3	4	5	6	7	8	9	1	2	3	4	5	6	7	8
Feb	6	7	8	9	1	2	3	4	5	6	7	8	9	1	2	3	4	5	6	7	8	9	1	2	3	4	5	6	7		
Mar	7	8	9	1	2	3	4	5	6	7	8	9	1	2	3	4	5	6	7	8	9	1	2	3	4	5	6	7	8	9	1
Apr	8	9	1	2	3	4	5	6	7	8	9	1	2	3	4	5	6	7	8	9	1	2	3	4	5	6	7	8	9	1	
May	9	1	2	3	4	5	6	7	8	9	1	2	3	4	5	6	7	8	9	1	2	3	4	5	6	7	8	9	1	2	3
Jun	1	2	3	4	5	6	7	8	9	1	2	3	4	5	6	7	8	9	1	2	3	4	5	6	7	8	9	1	2	3	
Jul	2	3	4	5	6	7	8	9	1	2	3	4	5	6	7	8	9	1	2	3	4	5	6	7	8	9	1	2	3	4	5
Aug	3	4	5	6	7	8	9	1	2	3	4	5	6	7	8	9	1	2	3	4	5	6	7	8	9	1	2	3	4	5	6
Sep	4	5	6	7	8	9	1	2	3	4	5	6	7	8	9	1	2	3	4	5	6	7	8	9	1	2	3	4	5	6	
Oct	5	6	7	8	9	1	2	3	4	5	6	7	8	9	1	2	3	4	5	6	7	8	9	1	2	3	4	5	6	7	8
Nov	6	7	8	9	1	2	3	4	5	6	7	8	9	1	2	3	4	5	6	7	8	9	1	2	3	4	5	6	7	8	
Dec	7	8	9	1	2	3	4	5	6	7	8	9	1	2	3	4	5	6	7	8	9	1	2	3	4	5	6	7	8	9	1

JANUARY 2

	1	2	3	4	5	6	7	8	9	10	11	12	13	14	15	16	17	18	19	20	21	22	23	24	25	26	27	28	29	30	31
Jan	5	7	8	9	1	2	3	4	5	6	7	8	9	1	2	3	4	5	6	7	8	9	1	2	3	4	5	6	7	8	9
Feb	7	8	9	1	2	3	4	5	6	7	8	9	1	2	3	4	5	6	7	8	9	1	2	3	4	5	6	7	8		
Mar	8	9	1	2	3	4	5	6	7	8	9	1	2	3	4	5	6	7	8	9	1	2	3	4	5	6	7	8	9	1	2
Apr	9	1	2	3	4	5	6	7	8	9	1	2	3	4	5	6	7	8	9	1	2	3	4	5	6	7	8	9	1	2	
May	1	2	3	4	5	6	7	8	9	1	2	3	4	5	6	7	8	9	1	2	3	4	5	6	7	8	9	1	2	3	4
Jun	2	3	4	5	6	7	8	9	1	2	3	4	5	6	7	8	9	1	2	3	4	5	6	7	8	9	1	2	3	4	
Jul	3	4	5	6	7	8	9	1	2	3	4	5	6	7	8	9	1	2	3	4	5	6	7	8	9	1	2	3	4	5	6
Aug	4	5	6	7	8	9	1	2	3	4	5	6	7	8	9	1	2	3	4	5	6	7	8	9	1	2	3	4	5	6	7
Sep	5	6	7	8	9	1	2	3	4	5	6	7	8	9	1	2	3	4	5	6	7	8	9	1	2	3	4	5	6	7	
Oct	6	7	8	9	1	2	3	4	5	6	7	8	9	1	2	3	4	5	6	7	8	9	1	2	3	4	5	6	7	8	9
Nov	7	8	9	1	2	3	4	5	6	7	8	9	1	2	3	4	5	6	7	8	9	1	2	3	4	5	6	7	8	9	
Dec	8	9	1	2	3	4	5	6	7	8	9	1	2	3	4	5	6	7	8	9	1	2	3	4	5	6	7	8	9	1	2

JANUARY 3

	1	2	3	4	5	6	7	8	9	10	11	12	13	14	15	16	17	18	19	20	21	22	23	24	25	26	27	28	29	30	31
Jan	6	7	9	1	2	3	4	5	6	7	8	9	1	2	3	4	5	6	7	8	9	1	2	3	4	5	6	7	8	9	1
Feb	8	9	1	2	3	4	5	6	7	8	9	1	2	3	4	5	6	7	8	9	1	2	3	4	5	6	7	8	9		
Mar	9	1	2	3	4	5	6	7	8	9	1	2	3	4	5	6	7	8	9	1	2	3	4	5	6	7	8	9	1	2	3
Apr	1	2	3	4	5	6	7	8	9	1	2	3	4	5	6	7	8	9	1	2	3	4	5	6	7	8	9	1	2	3	
May	2	3	4	5	6	7	8	9	1	2	3	4	5	6	7	8	9	1	2	3	4	5	6	7	8	9	1	2	3	4	5
Jun	3	4	5	6	7	8	9	1	2	3	4	5	6	7	8	9	1	2	3	4	5	6	7	8	9	1	2	3	4	5	
Jul	4	5	6	7	8	9	1	2	3	4	5	6	7	8	9	1	2	3	4	5	6	7	8	9	1	2	3	4	5	6	7
Aug	5	6	7	8	9	1	2	3	4	5	6	7	8	9	1	2	3	4	5	6	7	8	9	1	2	3	4	5	6	7	8
Sep	6	7	8	9	1	2	3	4	5	6	7	8	9	1	2	3	4	5	6	7	8	9	1	2	3	4	5	6	7	8	
Oct	7	8	9	1	2	3	4	5	6	7	8	9	1	2	3	4	5	6	7	8	9	1	2	3	4	5	6	7	8	9	1
Nov	8	9	1	2	3	4	5	6	7	8	9	1	2	3	4	5	6	7	8	9	1	2	3	4	5	6	7	8	9	1	
Dec	9	1	2	3	4	5	6	7	8	9	1	2	3	4	5	6	7	8	9	1	2	3	4	5	6	7	8	9	1	2	3

JANUARY 4

	1	2	3	4	5	6	7	8	9	10	11	12	13	14	15	16	17	18	19	20	21	22	23	24	25	26	27	28	29	30	31
Jan	7	8	9	2	3	4	5	6	7	8	9	1	2	3	4	5	6	7	8	9	1	2	3	4	5	6	7	8	9	1	2
Feb	9	1	2	3	4	5	6	7	8	9	1	2	3	4	5	6	7	8	9	1	2	3	4	5	6	7	8	9	1		
Mar	1	2	3	4	5	6	7	8	9	1	2	3	4	5	6	7	8	9	1	2	3	4	5	6	7	8	9	1	2	3	4
Apr	2	3	4	5	6	7	8	9	1	2	3	4	5	6	7	8	9	1	2	3	4	5	6	7	8	9	1	2	3	4	
May	3	4	5	6	7	8	9	1	2	3	4	5	6	7	8	9	1	2	3	4	5	6	7	8	9	1	2	3	4	5	6
Jun	4	5	6	7	8	9	1	2	3	4	5	6	7	8	9	1	2	3	4	5	6	7	8	9	1	2	3	4	5	6	
Jul	5	6	7	8	9	1	2	3	4	5	6	7	8	9	1	2	3	4	5	6	7	8	9	1	2	3	4	5	6	7	8
Aug	6	7	8	9	1	2	3	4	5	6	7	8	9	1	2	3	4	5	6	7	8	9	1	2	3	4	5	6	7	8	9
Sep	7	8	9	1	2	3	4	5	6	7	8	9	1	2	3	4	5	6	7	8	9	1	2	3	4	5	6	7	8	9	
Oct	8	9	1	2	3	4	5	6	7	8	9	1	2	3	4	5	6	7	8	9	1	2	3	4	5	6	7	8	9	1	2
Nov	9	1	2	3	4	5	6	7	8	9	1	2	3	4	5	6	7	8	9	1	2	3	4	5	6	7	8	9	1	2	
Dec	1	2	3	4	5	6	7	8	9	1	2	3	4	5	6	7	8	9	1	2	3	4	5	6	7	8	9	1	2	3	4

JANUARY 5

	1	2	3	4	5	6	7	8	9	10	11	12	13	14	15	16	17	18	19	20	21	22	23	24	25	26	27	28	29	30	31
Jan	8	9	1	2	4	5	6	7	8	9	1	2	3	4	5	6	7	8	9	1	2	3	4	5	6	7	8	9	1	2	3
Feb	1	2	3	4	5	6	7	8	9	1	2	3	4	5	6	7	8	9	1	2	3	4	5	6	7	8	9	1	2		
Mar	2	3	4	5	6	7	8	9	1	2	3	4	5	6	7	8	9	1	2	3	4	5	6	7	8	9	1	2	3	4	5
Apr	3	4	5	6	7	8	9	1	2	3	4	5	6	7	8	9	1	2	3	4	5	6	7	8	9	1	2	3	4	5	
May	4	5	6	7	8	9	1	2	3	4	5	6	7	8	9	1	2	3	4	5	6	7	8	9	1	2	3	4	5	6	7
Jun	5	6	7	8	9	1	2	3	4	5	6	7	8	9	1	2	3	4	5	6	7	8	9	1	2	3	4	5	6	7	
Jul	6	7	8	9	1	2	3	4	5	6	7	8	9	1	2	3	4	5	6	7	8	9	1	2	3	4	5	6	7	8	9
Aug	7	8	9	1	2	3	4	5	6	7	8	9	1	2	3	4	5	6	7	8	9	1	2	3	4	5	6	7	8	9	1
Sep	8	9	1	2	3	4	5	6	7	8	9	1	2	3	4	5	6	7	8	9	1	2	3	4	5	6	7	8	9	1	
Oct	9	1	2	3	4	5	6	7	8	9	1	2	3	4	5	6	7	8	9	1	2	3	4	5	6	7	8	9	1	2	3
Nov	1	2	3	4	5	6	7	8	9	1	2	3	4	5	6	7	8	9	1	2	3	4	5	6	7	8	9	1	2	3	
Dec	2	3	4	5	6	7	8	9	1	2	3	4	5	6	7	8	9	1	2	3	4	5	6	7	8	9	1	2	3	4	5

JANUARY 6

	1	2	3	4	5	6	7	8	9	10	11	12	13	14	15	16	17	18	19	20	21	22	23	24	25	26	27	28	29	30	31
Jan	9	1	2	3	4	6	7	8	9	1	2	3	4	5	6	7	8	9	1	2	3	4	5	6	7	8	9	1	2	3	4
Feb	2	3	4	5	6	7	8	9	1	2	3	4	5	6	7	8	9	1	2	3	4	5	6	7	8	9	1	2	3		
Mar	3	4	5	6	7	8	9	1	2	3	4	5	6	7	8	9	1	2	3	4	5	6	7	8	9	1	2	3	4	5	6
Apr	4	5	6	7	8	9	1	2	3	4	5	6	7	8	9	1	2	3	4	5	6	7	8	9	1	2	3	4	5	6	
May	5	6	7	8	9	1	2	3	4	5	6	7	8	9	1	2	3	4	5	6	7	8	9	1	2	3	4	5	6	7	8
Jun	6	7	8	9	1	2	3	4	5	6	7	8	9	1	2	3	4	5	6	7	8	9	1	2	3	4	5	6	7	8	
Jul	7	8	9	1	2	3	4	5	6	7	8	9	1	2	3	4	5	6	7	8	9	1	2	3	4	5	6	7	8	9	1
Aug	8	9	1	2	3	4	5	6	7	8	9	1	2	3	4	5	6	7	8	9	1	2	3	4	5	6	7	8	9	1	2
Sep	9	1	2	3	4	5	6	7	8	9	1	2	3	4	5	6	7	8	9	1	2	3	4	5	6	7	8	9	1	2	
Oct	1	2	3	4	5	6	7	8	9	1	2	3	4	5	6	7	8	9	1	2	3	4	5	6	7	8	9	1	2	3	4
Nov	2	3	4	5	6	7	8	9	1	2	3	4	5	6	7	8	9	1	2	3	4	5	6	7	8	9	1	2	3	4	
Dec	3	4	5	6	7	8	9	1	2	3	4	5	6	7	8	9	1	2	3	4	5	6	7	8	9	1	2	3	4	5	6

JANUARY 7

	1	2	3	4	5	6	7	8	9	10	11	12	13	14	15	16	17	18	19	20	21	22	23	24	25	26	27	28	29	30	31
Jan	1	2	3	4	5	6	8	9	1	2	3	4	5	6	7	8	9	1	2	3	4	5	6	7	8	9	1	2	3	4	5
Feb	3	4	5	6	7	8	9	1	2	3	4	5	6	7	8	9	1	2	3	4	5	6	7	8	9	1	2	3	4		
Mar	4	5	6	7	8	9	1	2	3	4	5	6	7	8	9	1	2	3	4	5	6	7	8	9	1	2	3	4	5	6	7
Apr	5	6	7	8	9	1	2	3	4	5	6	7	8	9	1	2	3	4	5	6	7	8	9	1	2	3	4	5	6	7	
May	6	7	8	9	1	2	3	4	5	6	7	8	9	1	2	3	4	5	6	7	8	9	1	2	3	4	5	6	7	8	9
Jun	7	8	9	1	2	3	4	5	6	7	8	9	1	2	3	4	5	6	7	8	9	1	2	3	4	5	6	7	8	9	
Jul	8	9	1	2	3	4	5	6	7	8	9	1	2	3	4	5	6	7	8	9	1	2	3	4	5	6	7	8	9	1	2
Aug	9	1	2	3	4	5	6	7	8	9	1	2	3	4	5	6	7	8	9	1	2	3	4	5	6	7	8	9	1	2	3
Sep	1	2	3	4	5	6	7	8	9	1	2	3	4	5	6	7	8	9	1	2	3	4	5	6	7	8	9	1	2	3	
Oct	2	3	4	5	6	7	8	9	1	2	3	4	5	6	7	8	9	1	2	3	4	5	6	7	8	9	1	2	3	4	5
Nov	3	4	5	6	7	8	9	1	2	3	4	5	6	7	8	9	1	2	3	4	5	6	7	8	9	1	2	3	4	5	
Dec	4	5	6	7	8	9	1	2	3	4	5	6	7	8	9	1	2	3	4	5	6	7	8	9	1	2	3	4	5	6	7

JANUARY 8

	1	2	3	4	5	6	7	8	9	10	11	12	13	14	15	16	17	18	19	20	21	22	23	24	25	26	27	28	29	30	31
Jan	2	3	4	5	6	7	8	1	2	3	4	5	6	7	8	9	1	2	3	4	5	6	7	8	9	1	2	3	4	5	6
Feb	4	5	6	7	8	9	1	2	3	4	5	6	7	8	9	1	2	3	4	5	6	7	8	9	1	2	3	4	5		
Mar	5	6	7	8	9	1	2	3	4	5	6	7	8	9	1	2	3	4	5	6	7	8	9	1	2	3	4	5	6	7	8
Apr	6	7	8	9	1	2	3	4	5	6	7	8	9	1	2	3	4	5	6	7	8	9	1	2	3	4	5	6	7	8	
May	7	8	9	1	2	3	4	5	6	7	8	9	1	2	3	4	5	6	7	8	9	1	2	3	4	5	6	7	8	9	1
Jun	8	9	1	2	3	4	5	6	7	8	9	1	2	3	4	5	6	7	8	9	1	2	3	4	5	6	7	8	9	1	
Jul	9	1	2	3	4	5	6	7	8	9	1	2	3	4	5	6	7	8	9	1	2	3	4	5	6	7	8	9	1	2	3
Aug	1	2	3	4	5	6	7	8	9	1	2	3	4	5	6	7	8	9	1	2	3	4	5	6	7	8	9	1	2	3	4
Sep	2	3	4	5	6	7	8	9	1	2	3	4	5	6	7	8	9	1	2	3	4	5	6	7	8	9	1	2	3	4	
Oct	3	4	5	6	7	8	9	1	2	3	4	5	6	7	8	9	1	2	3	4	5	6	7	8	9	1	2	3	4	5	6
Nov	4	5	6	7	8	9	1	2	3	4	5	6	7	8	9	1	2	3	4	5	6	7	8	9	1	2	3	4	5	6	
Dec	5	6	7	8	9	1	2	3	4	5	6	7	8	9	1	2	3	4	5	6	7	8	9	1	2	3	4	5	6	7	8

JANUARY 9

	1	2	3	4	5	6	7	8	9	10	11	12	13	14	15	16	17	18	19	20	21	22	23	24	25	26	27	28	29	30	31
Jan	3	4	5	6	7	8	9	1	3	4	5	6	7	8	9	1	2	3	4	5	6	7	8	9	1	2	3	4	5	6	7
Feb	5	6	7	8	9	1	2	3	4	5	6	7	8	9	1	2	3	4	5	6	7	8	9	1	2	3	4	5	6		
Mar	6	7	8	9	1	2	3	4	5	6	7	8	9	1	2	3	4	5	6	7	8	9	1	2	3	4	5	6	7	8	9
Apr	7	8	9	1	2	3	4	5	6	7	8	9	1	2	3	4	5	6	7	8	9	1	2	3	4	5	6	7	8	9	
May	8	9	1	2	3	4	5	6	7	8	9	1	2	3	4	5	6	7	8	9	1	2	3	4	5	6	7	8	9	1	2
Jun	9	1	2	3	4	5	6	7	8	9	1	2	3	4	5	6	7	8	9	1	2	3	4	5	6	7	8	9	1	2	
Jul	1	2	3	4	5	6	7	8	9	1	2	3	4	5	6	7	8	9	1	2	3	4	5	6	7	8	9	1	2	3	4
Aug	2	3	4	5	6	7	8	9	1	2	3	4	5	6	7	8	9	1	2	3	4	5	6	7	8	9	1	2	3	4	5
Sep	3	4	5	6	7	8	9	1	2	3	4	5	6	7	8	9	1	2	3	4	5	6	7	8	9	1	2	3	4	5	
Oct	4	5	6	7	8	9	1	2	3	4	5	6	7	8	9	1	2	3	4	5	6	7	8	9	1	2	3	4	5	6	7
Nov	5	6	7	8	9	1	2	3	4	5	6	7	8	9	1	2	3	4	5	6	7	8	9	1	2	3	4	5	6	7	
Dec	6	7	8	9	1	2	3	4	5	6	7	8	9	1	2	3	4	5	6	7	8	9	1	2	3	4	5	6	7	8	9

JANUARY 10

	1	2	3	4	5	6	7	8	9	10	11	12	13	14	15	16	17	18	19	20	21	22	23	24	25	26	27	28	29	30	31
Jan	4	5	6	7	8	9	1	2	3	5	6	7	8	9	1	2	3	4	5	6	7	8	9	1	2	3	4	5	6	7	8
Feb	6	7	8	9	1	2	3	4	5	6	7	8	9	1	2	3	4	5	6	7	8	9	1	2	3	4	5	6	7		
Mar	7	8	9	1	2	3	4	5	6	7	8	9	1	2	3	4	5	6	7	8	9	1	2	3	4	5	6	7	8	9	1
Apr	8	9	1	2	3	4	5	6	7	8	9	1	2	3	4	5	6	7	8	9	1	2	3	4	5	6	7	8	9	1	
May	9	1	2	3	4	5	6	7	8	9	1	2	3	4	5	6	7	8	9	1	2	3	4	5	6	7	8	9	1	2	3
Jun	1	2	3	4	5	6	7	8	9	1	2	3	4	5	6	7	8	9	1	2	3	4	5	6	7	8	9	1	2	3	
Jul	2	3	4	5	6	7	8	9	1	2	3	4	5	6	7	8	9	1	2	3	4	5	6	7	8	9	1	2	3	4	5
Aug	3	4	5	6	7	8	9	1	2	3	4	5	6	7	8	9	1	2	3	4	5	6	7	8	9	1	2	3	4	5	6
Sep	4	5	6	7	8	9	1	2	3	4	5	6	7	8	9	1	2	3	4	5	6	7	8	9	1	2	3	4	5	6	
Oct	5	6	7	8	9	1	2	3	4	5	6	7	8	9	1	2	3	4	5	6	7	8	9	1	2	3	4	5	6	7	8
Nov	6	7	8	9	1	2	3	4	5	6	7	8	9	1	2	3	4	5	6	7	8	9	1	2	3	4	5	6	7	8	
Dec	7	8	9	1	2	3	4	5	6	7	8	9	1	2	3	4	5	6	7	8	9	1	2	3	4	5	6	7	8	9	1

JANUARY 11

	1	2	3	4	5	6	7	8	9	10	11	12	13	14	15	16	17	18	19	20	21	22	23	24	25	26	27	28	29	30	31
Jan	5	6	7	8	9	1	2	3	4	5	7	8	9	1	2	3	4	5	6	7	8	9	1	2	3	4	5	6	7	8	9
Feb	7	8	9	1	2	3	4	5	6	7	8	9	1	2	3	4	5	6	7	8	9	1	2	3	4	5	6	7	8		
Mar	8	9	1	2	3	4	5	6	7	8	9	1	2	3	4	5	6	7	8	9	1	2	3	4	5	6	7	8	9	1	2
Apr	9	1	2	3	4	5	6	7	8	9	1	2	3	4	5	6	7	8	9	1	2	3	4	5	6	7	8	9	1	2	
May	1	2	3	4	5	6	7	8	9	1	2	3	4	5	6	7	8	9	1	2	3	4	5	6	7	8	9	1	2	3	4
Jun	2	3	4	5	6	7	8	9	1	2	3	4	5	6	7	8	9	1	2	3	4	5	6	7	8	9	1	2	3	4	
Jul	3	4	5	6	7	8	9	1	2	3	4	5	6	7	8	9	1	2	3	4	5	6	7	8	9	1	2	3	4	5	6
Aug	4	5	6	7	8	9	1	2	3	4	5	6	7	8	9	1	2	3	4	5	6	7	8	9	1	2	3	4	5	6	7
Sep	5	6	7	8	9	1	2	3	4	5	6	7	8	9	1	2	3	4	5	6	7	8	9	1	2	3	4	5	6	7	
Oct	6	7	8	9	1	2	3	4	5	6	7	8	9	1	2	3	4	5	6	7	8	9	1	2	3	4	5	6	7	8	9
Nov	7	8	9	1	2	3	4	5	6	7	8	9	1	2	3	4	5	6	7	8	9	1	2	3	4	5	6	7	8	9	
Dec	8	9	1	2	3	4	5	6	7	8	9	1	2	3	4	5	6	7	8	9	1	2	3	4	5	6	7	8	9	1	2

JANUARY 12

	1	2	3	4	5	6	7	8	9	10	11	12	13	14	15	16	17	18	19	20	21	22	23	24	25	26	27	28	29	30	31
Jan	6	7	8	9	1	2	3	4	5	6	7	9	1	2	3	4	5	6	7	8	9	1	2	3	4	5	6	7	8	9	1
Feb	8	9	1	2	3	4	5	6	7	8	9	1	2	3	4	5	6	7	8	9	1	2	3	4	5	6	7	8	9		
Mar	9	1	2	3	4	5	6	7	8	9	1	2	3	4	5	6	7	8	9	1	2	3	4	5	6	7	8	9	1	2	3
Apr	1	2	3	4	5	6	7	8	9	1	2	3	4	5	6	7	8	9	1	2	3	4	5	6	7	8	9	1	2	3	
May	2	3	4	5	6	7	8	9	1	2	3	4	5	6	7	8	9	1	2	3	4	5	6	7	8	9	1	2	3	4	5
Jun	3	4	5	6	7	8	9	1	2	3	4	5	6	7	8	9	1	2	3	4	5	6	7	8	9	1	2	3	4	5	
Jul	4	5	6	7	8	9	1	2	3	4	5	6	7	8	9	1	2	3	4	5	6	7	8	9	1	2	3	4	5	6	7
Aug	5	6	7	8	9	1	2	3	4	5	6	7	8	9	1	2	3	4	5	6	7	8	9	1	2	3	4	5	6	7	8
Sep	6	7	8	9	1	2	3	4	5	6	7	8	9	1	2	3	4	5	6	7	8	9	1	2	3	4	5	6	7	8	
Oct	7	8	9	1	2	3	4	5	6	7	8	9	1	2	3	4	5	6	7	8	9	1	2	3	4	5	6	7	8	9	1
Nov	8	9	1	2	3	4	5	6	7	8	9	1	2	3	4	5	6	7	8	9	1	2	3	4	5	6	7	8	9	1	
Dec	9	1	2	3	4	5	6	7	8	9	1	2	3	4	5	6	7	8	9	1	2	3	4	5	6	7	8	9	1	2	3

JANUARY 13

	1	2	3	4	5	6	7	8	9	10	11	12	13	14	15	16	17	18	19	20	21	22	23	24	25	26	27	28	29	30	31
Jan	7	8	9	1	2	3	4	5	6	7	8	9	2	3	4	5	6	7	8	9	1	2	3	4	5	6	7	8	9	1	2
Feb	9	1	2	3	4	5	6	7	8	9	1	2	3	4	5	6	7	8	9	1	2	3	4	5	6	7	8	9	1		
Mar	1	2	3	4	5	6	7	8	9	1	2	3	4	5	6	7	8	9	1	2	3	4	5	6	7	8	9	1	2	3	4
Apr	2	3	4	5	6	7	8	9	1	2	3	4	5	6	7	8	9	1	2	3	4	5	6	7	8	9	1	2	3	4	
May	3	4	5	6	7	8	9	1	2	3	4	5	6	7	8	9	1	2	3	4	5	6	7	8	9	1	2	3	4	5	6
Jun	4	5	6	7	8	9	1	2	3	4	5	6	7	8	9	1	2	3	4	5	6	7	8	9	1	2	3	4	5	6	
Jul	5	6	7	8	9	1	2	3	4	5	6	7	8	9	1	2	3	4	5	6	7	8	9	1	2	3	4	5	6	7	8
Aug	6	7	8	9	1	2	3	4	5	6	7	8	9	1	2	3	4	5	6	7	8	9	1	2	3	4	5	6	7	8	9
Sep	7	8	9	1	2	3	4	5	6	7	8	9	1	2	3	4	5	6	7	8	9	1	2	3	4	5	6	7	8	9	
Oct	8	9	1	2	3	4	5	6	7	8	9	1	2	3	4	5	6	7	8	9	1	2	3	4	5	6	7	8	9	1	2
Nov	9	1	2	3	4	5	6	7	8	9	1	2	3	4	5	6	7	8	9	1	2	3	4	5	6	7	8	9	1	2	
Dec	1	2	3	4	5	6	7	8	9	1	2	3	4	5	6	7	8	9	1	2	3	4	5	6	7	8	9	1	2	3	4

JANUARY 14

	1	2	3	4	5	6	7	8	9	10	11	12	13	14	15	16	17	18	19	20	21	22	23	24	25	26	27	28	29	30	31
Jan	8	9	1	2	3	4	5	6	7	8	9	1	2	4	5	6	7	8	9	1	2	3	4	5	6	7	8	9	1	2	3
Feb	1	2	3	4	5	6	7	8	9	1	2	3	4	5	6	7	8	9	1	2	3	4	5	6	7	8	9	1	2		
Mar	2	3	4	5	6	7	8	9	1	2	3	4	5	6	7	8	9	1	2	3	4	5	6	7	8	9	1	2	3	4	5
Apr	3	4	5	6	7	8	9	1	2	3	4	5	6	7	8	9	1	2	3	4	5	6	7	8	9	1	2	3	4	5	
May	4	5	6	7	8	9	1	2	3	4	5	6	7	8	9	1	2	3	4	5	6	7	8	9	1	2	3	4	5	6	7
Jun	5	6	7	8	9	1	2	3	4	5	6	7	8	9	1	2	3	4	5	6	7	8	9	1	2	3	4	5	6	7	
Jul	6	7	8	9	1	2	3	4	5	6	7	8	9	1	2	3	4	5	6	7	8	9	1	2	3	4	5	6	7	8	9
Aug	7	8	9	1	2	3	4	5	6	7	8	9	1	2	3	4	5	6	7	8	9	1	2	3	4	5	6	7	8	9	1
Sep	8	9	1	2	3	4	5	6	7	8	9	1	2	3	4	5	6	7	8	9	1	2	3	4	5	6	7	8	9	1	
Oct	9	1	2	3	4	5	6	7	8	9	1	2	3	4	5	6	7	8	9	1	2	3	4	5	6	7	8	9	1	2	3
Nov	1	2	3	4	5	6	7	8	9	1	2	3	4	5	6	7	8	9	1	2	3	4	5	6	7	8	9	1	2	3	
Dec	2	3	4	5	6	7	8	9	1	2	3	4	5	6	7	8	9	1	2	3	4	5	6	7	8	9	1	2	3	4	5

JANUARY 15

	1	2	3	4	5	6	7	8	9	10	11	12	13	14	15	16	17	18	19	20	21	22	23	24	25	26	27	28	29	30	31
Jan	9	1	2	3	4	5	6	7	8	9	1	2	3	4	6	7	8	9	1	2	3	4	5	6	7	8	9	1	2	3	4
Feb	2	3	4	5	6	7	8	9	1	2	3	4	5	6	7	8	9	1	2	3	4	5	6	7	8	9	1	2	3		
Mar	3	4	5	6	7	8	9	1	2	3	4	5	6	7	8	9	1	2	3	4	5	6	7	8	9	1	2	3	4	5	6
Apr	4	5	6	7	8	9	1	2	3	4	5	6	7	8	9	1	2	3	4	5	6	7	8	9	1	2	3	4	5	6	
May	5	6	7	8	9	1	2	3	4	5	6	7	8	9	1	2	3	4	5	6	7	8	9	1	2	3	4	5	6	7	8
Jun	6	7	8	9	1	2	3	4	5	6	7	8	9	1	2	3	4	5	6	7	8	9	1	2	3	4	5	6	7	8	
Jul	7	8	9	1	2	3	4	5	6	7	8	9	1	2	3	4	5	6	7	8	9	1	2	3	4	5	6	7	8	9	1
Aug	8	9	1	2	3	4	5	6	7	8	9	1	2	3	4	5	6	7	8	9	1	2	3	4	5	6	7	8	9	1	2
Sep	9	1	2	3	4	5	6	7	8	9	1	2	3	4	5	6	7	8	9	1	2	3	4	5	6	7	8	9	1	2	
Oct	1	2	3	4	5	6	7	8	9	1	2	3	4	5	6	7	8	9	1	2	3	4	5	6	7	8	9	1	2	3	4
Nov	2	3	4	5	6	7	8	9	1	2	3	4	5	6	7	8	9	1	2	3	4	5	6	7	8	9	1	2	3	4	
Dec	3	4	5	6	7	8	9	1	2	3	4	5	6	7	8	9	1	2	3	4	5	6	7	8	9	1	2	3	4	5	6

JANUARY 16

	1	2	3	4	5	6	7	8	9	10	11	12	13	14	15	16	17	18	19	20	21	22	23	24	25	26	27	28	29	30	31
Jan	1	2	3	4	5	6	7	8	9	1	2	3	4	5	6	8	9	1	2	3	4	5	6	7	8	9	1	2	3	4	5
Feb	3	4	5	6	7	8	9	1	2	3	4	5	6	7	8	9	1	2	3	4	5	6	7	8	9	1	2	3	4		
Mar	4	5	6	7	8	9	1	2	3	4	5	6	7	8	9	1	2	3	4	5	6	7	8	9	1	2	3	4	5	6	7
Apr	5	6	7	8	9	1	2	3	4	5	6	7	8	9	1	2	3	4	5	6	7	8	9	1	2	3	4	5	6	7	
May	6	7	8	9	1	2	3	4	5	6	7	8	9	1	2	3	4	5	6	7	8	9	1	2	3	4	5	6	7	8	9
Jun	7	8	9	1	2	3	4	5	6	7	8	9	1	2	3	4	5	6	7	8	9	1	2	3	4	5	6	7	8	9	
Jul	8	9	1	2	3	4	5	6	7	8	9	1	2	3	4	5	6	7	8	9	1	2	3	4	5	6	7	8	9	1	2
Aug	9	1	2	3	4	5	6	7	8	9	1	2	3	4	5	6	7	8	9	1	2	3	4	5	6	7	8	9	1	2	3
Sep	1	2	3	4	5	6	7	8	9	1	2	3	4	5	6	7	8	9	1	2	3	4	5	6	7	8	9	1	2	3	
Oct	2	3	4	5	6	7	8	9	1	2	3	4	5	6	7	8	9	1	2	3	4	5	6	7	8	9	1	2	3	4	5
Nov	3	4	5	6	7	8	9	1	2	3	4	5	6	7	8	9	1	2	3	4	5	6	7	8	9	1	2	3	4	5	
Dec	4	5	6	7	8	9	1	2	3	4	5	6	7	8	9	1	2	3	4	5	6	7	8	9	1	2	3	4	5	6	7

JANUARY 17

	1	2	3	4	5	6	7	8	9	10	11	12	13	14	15	16	17	18	19	20	21	22	23	24	25	26	27	28	29	30	31
Jan	2	3	4	5	6	7	8	9	1	2	3	4	5	6	7	8	1	2	3	4	5	6	7	8	9	1	2	3	4	5	6
Feb	4	5	6	7	8	9	1	2	3	4	5	6	7	8	9	1	2	3	4	5	6	7	8	9	1	2	3	4	5		
Mar	5	6	7	8	9	1	2	3	4	5	6	7	8	9	1	2	3	4	5	6	7	8	9	1	2	3	4	5	6	7	8
Apr	6	7	8	9	1	2	3	4	5	6	7	8	9	1	2	3	4	5	6	7	8	9	1	2	3	4	5	6	7	8	
May	7	8	9	1	2	3	4	5	6	7	8	9	1	2	3	4	5	6	7	8	9	1	2	3	4	5	6	7	8	9	1
Jun	8	9	1	2	3	4	5	6	7	8	9	1	2	3	4	5	6	7	8	9	1	2	3	4	5	6	7	8	9	1	
Jul	9	1	2	3	4	5	6	7	8	9	1	2	3	4	5	6	7	8	9	1	2	3	4	5	6	7	8	9	1	2	3
Aug	1	2	3	4	5	6	7	8	9	1	2	3	4	5	6	7	8	9	1	2	3	4	5	6	7	8	9	1	2	3	4
Sep	2	3	4	5	6	7	8	9	1	2	3	4	5	6	7	8	9	1	2	3	4	5	6	7	8	9	1	2	3	4	
Oct	3	4	5	6	7	8	9	1	2	3	4	5	6	7	8	9	1	2	3	4	5	6	7	8	9	1	2	3	4	5	6
Nov	4	5	6	7	8	9	1	2	3	4	5	6	7	8	9	1	2	3	4	5	6	7	8	9	1	2	3	4	5	6	
Dec	5	6	7	8	9	1	2	3	4	5	6	7	8	9	1	2	3	4	5	6	7	8	9	1	2	3	4	5	6	7	8

JANUARY 18

	1	2	3	4	5	6	7	8	9	10	11	12	13	14	15	16	17	18	19	20	21	22	23	24	25	26	27	28	29	30	31
Jan	3	4	5	6	7	8	9	1	2	3	4	5	6	7	8	9	1	3	4	5	6	7	8	9	1	2	3	4	5	6	7
Feb	5	6	7	8	9	1	2	3	4	5	6	7	8	9	1	2	3	4	5	6	7	8	9	1	2	3	4	5	6		
Mar	6	7	8	9	1	2	3	4	5	6	7	8	9	1	2	3	4	5	6	7	8	9	1	2	3	4	5	6	7	8	9
Apr	7	8	9	1	2	3	4	5	6	7	8	9	1	2	3	4	5	6	7	8	9	1	2	3	4	5	6	7	8	9	
May	8	9	1	2	3	4	5	6	7	8	9	1	2	3	4	5	6	7	8	9	1	2	3	4	5	6	7	8	9	1	2
Jun	9	1	2	3	4	5	6	7	8	9	1	2	3	4	5	6	7	8	9	1	2	3	4	5	6	7	8	9	1	2	
Jul	1	2	3	4	5	6	7	8	9	1	2	3	4	5	6	7	8	9	1	2	3	4	5	6	7	8	9	1	2	3	4
Aug	2	3	4	5	6	7	8	9	1	2	3	4	5	6	7	8	9	1	2	3	4	5	6	7	8	9	1	2	3	4	5
Sep	3	4	5	6	7	8	9	1	2	3	4	5	6	7	8	9	1	2	3	4	5	6	7	8	9	1	2	3	4	5	
Oct	4	5	6	7	8	9	1	2	3	4	5	6	7	8	9	1	2	3	4	5	6	7	8	9	1	2	3	4	5	6	7
Nov	5	6	7	8	9	1	2	3	4	5	6	7	8	9	1	2	3	4	5	6	7	8	9	1	2	3	4	5	6	7	
Dec	6	7	8	9	1	2	3	4	5	6	7	8	9	1	2	3	4	5	6	7	8	9	1	2	3	4	5	6	7	8	9

JANUARY 19

	1	2	3	4	5	6	7	8	9	10	11	12	13	14	15	16	17	18	19	20	21	22	23	24	25	26	27	28	29	30	31
Jan	4	5	6	7	8	9	1	2	3	4	5	6	7	8	9	1	2	3	5	6	7	8	9	1	2	3	4	5	6	7	8
Feb	6	7	8	9	1	2	3	4	5	6	7	8	9	1	2	3	4	5	6	7	8	9	1	2	3	4	5	6	7		
Mar	7	8	9	1	2	3	4	5	6	7	8	9	1	2	3	4	5	6	7	8	9	1	2	3	4	5	6	7	8	9	1
Apr	8	9	1	2	3	4	5	6	7	8	9	1	2	3	4	5	6	7	8	9	1	2	3	4	5	6	7	8	9	1	
May	9	1	2	3	4	5	6	7	8	9	1	2	3	4	5	6	7	8	9	1	2	3	4	5	6	7	8	9	1	2	3
Jun	1	2	3	4	5	6	7	8	9	1	2	3	4	5	6	7	8	9	1	2	3	4	5	6	7	8	9	1	2	3	
Jul	2	3	4	5	6	7	8	9	1	2	3	4	5	6	7	8	9	1	2	3	4	5	6	7	8	9	1	2	3	4	5
Aug	3	4	5	6	7	8	9	1	2	3	4	5	6	7	8	9	1	2	3	4	5	6	7	8	9	1	2	3	4	5	6
Sep	4	5	6	7	8	9	1	2	3	4	5	6	7	8	9	1	2	3	4	5	6	7	8	9	1	2	3	4	5	6	
Oct	5	6	7	8	9	1	2	3	4	5	6	7	8	9	1	2	3	4	5	6	7	8	9	1	2	3	4	5	6	7	8
Nov	6	7	8	9	1	2	3	4	5	6	7	8	9	1	2	3	4	5	6	7	8	9	1	2	3	4	5	6	7	8	
Dec	7	8	9	1	2	3	4	5	6	7	8	9	1	2	3	4	5	6	7	8	9	1	2	3	4	5	6	7	8	9	1

JANUARY 20

	1	2	3	4	5	6	7	8	9	10	11	12	13	14	15	16	17	18	19	20	21	22	23	24	25	26	27	28	29	30	31
Jan	5	6	7	8	9	1	2	3	4	5	6	7	8	9	1	2	3	4	5	7	8	9	1	2	3	4	5	6	7	8	9
Feb	7	8	9	1	2	3	4	5	6	7	8	9	1	2	3	4	5	6	7	8	9	1	2	3	4	5	6	7	8		
Mar	8	9	1	2	3	4	5	6	7	8	9	1	2	3	4	5	6	7	8	9	1	2	3	4	5	6	7	8	9	1	2
Apr	9	1	2	3	4	5	6	7	8	9	1	2	3	4	5	6	7	8	9	1	2	3	4	5	6	7	8	9	1	2	
May	1	2	3	4	5	6	7	8	9	1	2	3	4	5	6	7	8	9	1	2	3	4	5	6	7	8	9	1	2	3	4
Jun	2	3	4	5	6	7	8	9	1	2	3	4	5	6	7	8	9	1	2	3	4	5	6	7	8	9	1	2	3	4	
Jul	3	4	5	6	7	8	9	1	2	3	4	5	6	7	8	9	1	2	3	4	5	6	7	8	9	1	2	3	4	5	6
Aug	4	5	6	7	8	9	1	2	3	4	5	6	7	8	9	1	2	3	4	5	6	7	8	9	1	2	3	4	5	6	7
Sep	5	6	7	8	9	1	2	3	4	5	6	7	8	9	1	2	3	4	5	6	7	8	9	1	2	3	4	5	6	7	
Oct	6	7	8	9	1	2	3	4	5	6	7	8	9	1	2	3	4	5	6	7	8	9	1	2	3	4	5	6	7	8	9
Nov	7	8	9	1	2	3	4	5	6	7	8	9	1	2	3	4	5	6	7	8	9	1	2	3	4	5	6	7	8	9	
Dec	8	9	1	2	3	4	5	6	7	8	9	1	2	3	4	5	6	7	8	9	1	2	3	4	5	6	7	8	9	1	2

JANUARY 21

	1	2	3	4	5	6	7	8	9	10	11	12	13	14	15	16	17	18	19	20	21	22	23	24	25	26	27	28	29	30	31
Jan	6	7	8	9	1	2	3	4	5	6	7	8	9	1	2	3	4	5	6	7	9	1	2	3	4	5	6	7	8	9	1
Feb	8	9	1	2	3	4	5	6	7	8	9	1	2	3	4	5	6	7	8	9	1	2	3	4	5	6	7	8	9		
Mar	9	1	2	3	4	5	6	7	8	9	1	2	3	4	5	6	7	8	9	1	2	3	4	5	6	7	8	9	1	2	3
Apr	1	2	3	4	5	6	7	8	9	1	2	3	4	5	6	7	8	9	1	2	3	4	5	6	7	8	9	1	2	3	
May	2	3	4	5	6	7	8	9	1	2	3	4	5	6	7	8	9	1	2	3	4	5	6	7	8	9	1	2	3	4	5
Jun	3	4	5	6	7	8	9	1	2	3	4	5	6	7	8	9	1	2	3	4	5	6	7	8	9	1	2	3	4	5	
Jul	4	5	6	7	8	9	1	2	3	4	5	6	7	8	9	1	2	3	4	5	6	7	8	9	1	2	3	4	5	6	7
Aug	5	6	7	8	9	1	2	3	4	5	6	7	8	9	1	2	3	4	5	6	7	8	9	1	2	3	4	5	6	7	8
Sep	6	7	8	9	1	2	3	4	5	6	7	8	9	1	2	3	4	5	6	7	8	9	1	2	3	4	5	6	7	8	
Oct	7	8	9	1	2	3	4	5	6	7	8	9	1	2	3	4	5	6	7	8	9	1	2	3	4	5	6	7	8	9	1
Nov	8	9	1	2	3	4	5	6	7	8	9	1	2	3	4	5	6	7	8	9	1	2	3	4	5	6	7	8	9	1	
Dec	9	1	2	3	4	5	6	7	8	9	1	2	3	4	5	6	7	8	9	1	2	3	4	5	6	7	8	9	1	2	3

JANUARY 22

	1	2	3	4	5	6	7	8	9	10	11	12	13	14	15	16	17	18	19	20	21	22	23	24	25	26	27	28	29	30	31
Jan	7	8	9	1	2	3	4	5	6	7	8	9	1	2	3	4	5	6	7	8	9	2	3	4	5	6	7	8	9	1	2
Feb	9	1	2	3	4	5	6	7	8	9	1	2	3	4	5	6	7	8	9	1	2	3	4	5	6	7	8	9	1		
Mar	1	2	3	4	5	6	7	8	9	1	2	3	4	5	6	7	8	9	1	2	3	4	5	6	7	8	9	1	2	3	4
Apr	2	3	4	5	6	7	8	9	1	2	3	4	5	6	7	8	9	1	2	3	4	5	6	7	8	9	1	2	3	4	
May	3	4	5	6	7	8	9	1	2	3	4	5	6	7	8	9	1	2	3	4	5	6	7	8	9	1	2	3	4	5	6
Jun	4	5	6	7	8	9	1	2	3	4	5	6	7	8	9	1	2	3	4	5	6	7	8	9	1	2	3	4	5	6	
Jul	5	6	7	8	9	1	2	3	4	5	6	7	8	9	1	2	3	4	5	6	7	8	9	1	2	3	4	5	6	7	8
Aug	6	7	8	9	1	2	3	4	5	6	7	8	9	1	2	3	4	5	6	7	8	9	1	2	3	4	5	6	7	8	9
Sep	7	8	9	1	2	3	4	5	6	7	8	9	1	2	3	4	5	6	7	8	9	1	2	3	4	5	6	7	8	9	
Oct	8	9	1	2	3	4	5	6	7	8	9	1	2	3	4	5	6	7	8	9	1	2	3	4	5	6	7	8	9	1	2
Nov	9	1	2	3	4	5	6	7	8	9	1	2	3	4	5	6	7	8	9	1	2	3	4	5	6	7	8	9	1	2	
Dec	1	2	3	4	5	6	7	8	9	1	2	3	4	5	6	7	8	9	1	2	3	4	5	6	7	8	9	1	2	3	4

JANUARY 23

	1	2	3	4	5	6	7	8	9	10	11	12	13	14	15	16	17	18	19	20	21	22	23	24	25	26	27	28	29	30	31
Jan	8	9	1	2	3	4	5	6	7	8	9	1	2	3	4	5	6	7	8	9	1	2	4	5	6	7	8	9	1	2	3
Feb	1	2	3	4	5	6	7	8	9	1	2	3	4	5	6	7	8	9	1	2	3	4	5	6	7	8	9	1	2		
Mar	2	3	4	5	6	7	8	9	1	2	3	4	5	6	7	8	9	1	2	3	4	5	6	7	8	9	1	2	3	4	5
Apr	3	4	5	6	7	8	9	1	2	3	4	5	6	7	8	9	1	2	3	4	5	6	7	8	9	1	2	3	4	5	
May	4	5	6	7	8	9	1	2	3	4	5	6	7	8	9	1	2	3	4	5	6	7	8	9	1	2	3	4	5	6	7
Jun	5	6	7	8	9	1	2	3	4	5	6	7	8	9	1	2	3	4	5	6	7	8	9	1	2	3	4	5	6	7	
Jul	6	7	8	9	1	2	3	4	5	6	7	8	9	1	2	3	4	5	6	7	8	9	1	2	3	4	5	6	7	8	9
Aug	7	8	9	1	2	3	4	5	6	7	8	9	1	2	3	4	5	6	7	8	9	1	2	3	4	5	6	7	8	9	1
Sep	8	9	1	2	3	4	5	6	7	8	9	1	2	3	4	5	6	7	8	9	1	2	3	4	5	6	7	8	9	1	
Oct	9	1	2	3	4	5	6	7	8	9	1	2	3	4	5	6	7	8	9	1	2	3	4	5	6	7	8	9	1	2	3
Nov	1	2	3	4	5	6	7	8	9	1	2	3	4	5	6	7	8	9	1	2	3	4	5	6	7	8	9	1	2	3	
Dec	2	3	4	5	6	7	8	9	1	2	3	4	5	6	7	8	9	1	2	3	4	5	6	7	8	9	1	2	3	4	5

JANUARY 24

	1	2	3	4	5	6	7	8	9	10	11	12	13	14	15	16	17	18	19	20	21	22	23	24	25	26	27	28	29	30	31
Jan	9	1	2	3	4	5	6	7	8	9	1	2	3	4	5	6	7	8	9	1	2	3	4	6	7	8	9	1	2	3	4
Feb	2	3	4	5	6	7	8	9	1	2	3	4	5	6	7	8	9	1	2	3	4	5	6	7	8	9	1	2	3		
Mar	3	4	5	6	7	8	9	1	2	3	4	5	6	7	8	9	1	2	3	4	5	6	7	8	9	1	2	3	4	5	6
Apr	4	5	6	7	8	9	1	2	3	4	5	6	7	8	9	1	2	3	4	5	6	7	8	9	1	2	3	4	5	6	
May	5	6	7	8	9	1	2	3	4	5	6	7	8	9	1	2	3	4	5	6	7	8	9	1	2	3	4	5	6	7	8
Jun	6	7	8	9	1	2	3	4	5	6	7	8	9	1	2	3	4	5	6	7	8	9	1	2	3	4	5	6	7	8	
Jul	7	8	9	1	2	3	4	5	6	7	8	9	1	2	3	4	5	6	7	8	9	1	2	3	4	5	6	7	8	9	1
Aug	8	9	1	2	3	4	5	6	7	8	9	1	2	3	4	5	6	7	8	9	1	2	3	4	5	6	7	8	9	1	2
Sep	9	1	2	3	4	5	6	7	8	9	1	2	3	4	5	6	7	8	9	1	2	3	4	5	6	7	8	9	1	2	
Oct	1	2	3	4	5	6	7	8	9	1	2	3	4	5	6	7	8	9	1	2	3	4	5	6	7	8	9	1	2	3	4
Nov	2	3	4	5	6	7	8	9	1	2	3	4	5	6	7	8	9	1	2	3	4	5	6	7	8	9	1	2	3	4	
Dec	3	4	5	6	7	8	9	1	2	3	4	5	6	7	8	9	1	2	3	4	5	6	7	8	9	1	2	3	4	5	6

JANUARY 25

	1	2	3	4	5	6	7	8	9	10	11	12	13	14	15	16	17	18	19	20	21	22	23	24	25	26	27	28	29	30	31
Jan	1	2	3	4	5	6	7	8	9	1	2	3	4	5	6	7	8	9	1	2	3	4	5	6	8	9	1	2	3	4	5
Feb	3	4	5	6	7	8	9	1	2	3	4	5	6	7	8	9	1	2	3	4	5	6	7	8	9	1	2	3	4		
Mar	4	5	6	7	8	9	1	2	3	4	5	6	7	8	9	1	2	3	4	5	6	7	8	9	1	2	3	4	5	6	7
Apr	5	6	7	8	9	1	2	3	4	5	6	7	8	9	1	2	3	4	5	6	7	8	9	1	2	3	4	5	6	7	
May	6	7	8	9	1	2	3	4	5	6	7	8	9	1	2	3	4	5	6	7	8	9	1	2	3	4	5	6	7	8	9
Jun	7	8	9	1	2	3	4	5	6	7	8	9	1	2	3	4	5	6	7	8	9	1	2	3	4	5	6	7	8	9	
Jul	8	9	1	2	3	4	5	6	7	8	9	1	2	3	4	5	6	7	8	9	1	2	3	4	5	6	7	8	9	1	2
Aug	9	1	2	3	4	5	6	7	8	9	1	2	3	4	5	6	7	8	9	1	2	3	4	5	6	7	8	9	1	2	3
Sep	1	2	3	4	5	6	7	8	9	1	2	3	4	5	6	7	8	9	1	2	3	4	5	6	7	8	9	1	2	3	
Oct	2	3	4	5	6	7	8	9	1	2	3	4	5	6	7	8	9	1	2	3	4	5	6	7	8	9	1	2	3	4	5
Nov	3	4	5	6	7	8	9	1	2	3	4	5	6	7	8	9	1	2	3	4	5	6	7	8	9	1	2	3	4	5	
Dec	4	5	6	7	8	9	1	2	3	4	5	6	7	8	9	1	2	3	4	5	6	7	8	9	1	2	3	4	5	6	7

JANUARY 26

	1	2	3	4	5	6	7	8	9	10	11	12	13	14	15	16	17	18	19	20	21	22	23	24	25	26	27	28	29	30	31
Jan	2	3	4	5	6	7	8	9	1	2	3	4	5	6	7	8	9	1	2	3	4	5	6	7	8	1	2	3	4	5	6
Feb	4	5	6	7	8	9	1	2	3	4	5	6	7	8	9	1	2	3	4	5	6	7	8	9	1	2	3	4	5		
Mar	5	6	7	8	9	1	2	3	4	5	6	7	8	9	1	2	3	4	5	6	7	8	9	1	2	3	4	5	6	7	8
Apr	6	7	8	9	1	2	3	4	5	6	7	8	9	1	2	3	4	5	6	7	8	9	1	2	3	4	5	6	7	8	
May	7	8	9	1	2	3	4	5	6	7	8	9	1	2	3	4	5	6	7	8	9	1	2	3	4	5	6	7	8	9	1
Jun	8	9	1	2	3	4	5	6	7	8	9	1	2	3	4	5	6	7	8	9	1	2	3	4	5	6	7	8	9	1	
Jul	9	1	2	3	4	5	6	7	8	9	1	2	3	4	5	6	7	8	9	1	2	3	4	5	6	7	8	9	1	2	3
Aug	1	2	3	4	5	6	7	8	9	1	2	3	4	5	6	7	8	9	1	2	3	4	5	6	7	8	9	1	2	3	4
Sep	2	3	4	5	6	7	8	9	1	2	3	4	5	6	7	8	9	1	2	3	4	5	6	7	8	9	1	2	3	4	
Oct	3	4	5	6	7	8	9	1	2	3	4	5	6	7	8	9	1	2	3	4	5	6	7	8	9	1	2	3	4	5	6
Nov	4	5	6	7	8	9	1	2	3	4	5	6	7	8	9	1	2	3	4	5	6	7	8	9	1	2	3	4	5	6	
Dec	5	6	7	8	9	1	2	3	4	5	6	7	8	9	1	2	3	4	5	6	7	8	9	1	2	3	4	5	6	7	8

JANUARY 27

	1	2	3	4	5	6	7	8	9	10	11	12	13	14	15	16	17	18	19	20	21	22	23	24	25	26	27	28	29	30	31
Jan	3	4	5	6	7	8	9	1	2	3	4	5	6	7	8	9	1	2	3	4	5	6	7	8	9	1	3	4	5	6	7
Feb	5	6	7	8	9	1	2	3	4	5	6	7	8	9	1	2	3	4	5	6	7	8	9	1	2	3	4	5	6		
Mar	6	7	8	9	1	2	3	4	5	6	7	8	9	1	2	3	4	5	6	7	8	9	1	2	3	4	5	6	7	8	9
Apr	7	8	9	1	2	3	4	5	6	7	8	9	1	2	3	4	5	6	7	8	9	1	2	3	4	5	6	7	8	9	
May	8	9	1	2	3	4	5	6	7	8	9	1	2	3	4	5	6	7	8	9	1	2	3	4	5	6	7	8	9	1	2
Jun	9	1	2	3	4	5	6	7	8	9	1	2	3	4	5	6	7	8	9	1	2	3	4	5	6	7	8	9	1	2	
Jul	1	2	3	4	5	6	7	8	9	1	2	3	4	5	6	7	8	9	1	2	3	4	5	6	7	8	9	1	2	3	4
Aug	2	3	4	5	6	7	8	9	1	2	3	4	5	6	7	8	9	1	2	3	4	5	6	7	8	9	1	2	3	4	5
Sep	3	4	5	6	7	8	9	1	2	3	4	5	6	7	8	9	1	2	3	4	5	6	7	8	9	1	2	3	4	5	
Oct	4	5	6	7	8	9	1	2	3	4	5	6	7	8	9	1	2	3	4	5	6	7	8	9	1	2	3	4	5	6	7
Nov	5	6	7	8	9	1	2	3	4	5	6	7	8	9	1	2	3	4	5	6	7	8	9	1	2	3	4	5	6	7	
Dec	6	7	8	9	1	2	3	4	5	6	7	8	9	1	2	3	4	5	6	7	8	9	1	2	3	4	5	6	7	8	9

JANUARY 28

	1	2	3	4	5	6	7	8	9	10	11	12	13	14	15	16	17	18	19	20	21	22	23	24	25	26	27	28	29	30	31
Jan	4	5	6	7	8	9	1	2	3	4	5	6	7	8	9	1	2	3	4	5	6	7	8	9	1	2	3	5	6	7	8
Feb	6	7	8	9	1	2	3	4	5	6	7	8	9	1	2	3	4	5	6	7	8	9	1	2	3	4	5	6	7		
Mar	7	8	9	1	2	3	4	5	6	7	8	9	1	2	3	4	5	6	7	8	9	1	2	3	4	5	6	7	8	9	1
Apr	8	9	1	2	3	4	5	6	7	8	9	1	2	3	4	5	6	7	8	9	1	2	3	4	5	6	7	8	9	1	
May	9	1	2	3	4	5	6	7	8	9	1	2	3	4	5	6	7	8	9	1	2	3	4	5	6	7	8	9	1	2	3
Jun	1	2	3	4	5	6	7	8	9	1	2	3	4	5	6	7	8	9	1	2	3	4	5	6	7	8	9	1	2	3	
Jul	2	3	4	5	6	7	8	9	1	2	3	4	5	6	7	8	9	1	2	3	4	5	6	7	8	9	1	2	3	4	5
Aug	3	4	5	6	7	8	9	1	2	3	4	5	6	7	8	9	1	2	3	4	5	6	7	8	9	1	2	3	4	5	6
Sep	4	5	6	7	8	9	1	2	3	4	5	6	7	8	9	1	2	3	4	5	6	7	8	9	1	2	3	4	5	6	
Oct	5	6	7	8	9	1	2	3	4	5	6	7	8	9	1	2	3	4	5	6	7	8	9	1	2	3	4	5	6	7	8
Nov	6	7	8	9	1	2	3	4	5	6	7	8	9	1	2	3	4	5	6	7	8	9	1	2	3	4	5	6	7	8	
Dec	7	8	9	1	2	3	4	5	6	7	8	9	1	2	3	4	5	6	7	8	9	1	2	3	4	5	6	7	8	9	1

JANUARY 29

	1	2	3	4	5	6	7	8	9	10	11	12	13	14	15	16	17	18	19	20	21	22	23	24	25	26	27	28	29	30	31
Jan	5	6	7	8	9	1	2	3	4	5	6	7	8	9	1	2	3	4	5	6	7	8	9	1	2	3	4	5	7	8	9
Feb	7	8	9	1	2	3	4	5	6	7	8	9	1	2	3	4	5	6	7	8	9	1	2	3	4	5	6	7	8		
Mar	8	9	1	2	3	4	5	6	7	8	9	1	2	3	4	5	6	7	8	9	1	2	3	4	5	6	7	8	9	1	2
Apr	9	1	2	3	4	5	6	7	8	9	1	2	3	4	5	6	7	8	9	1	2	3	4	5	6	7	8	9	1	2	
May	1	2	3	4	5	6	7	8	9	1	2	3	4	5	6	7	8	9	1	2	3	4	5	6	7	8	9	1	2	3	4
Jun	2	3	4	5	6	7	8	9	1	2	3	4	5	6	7	8	9	1	2	3	4	5	6	7	8	9	1	2	3	4	
Jul	3	4	5	6	7	8	9	1	2	3	4	5	6	7	8	9	1	2	3	4	5	6	7	8	9	1	2	3	4	5	6
Aug	4	5	6	7	8	9	1	2	3	4	5	6	7	8	9	1	2	3	4	5	6	7	8	9	1	2	3	4	5	6	7
Sep	5	6	7	8	9	1	2	3	4	5	6	7	8	9	1	2	3	4	5	6	7	8	9	1	2	3	4	5	6	7	
Oct	6	7	8	9	1	2	3	4	5	6	7	8	9	1	2	3	4	5	6	7	8	9	1	2	3	4	5	6	7	8	9
Nov	7	8	9	1	2	3	4	5	6	7	8	9	1	2	3	4	5	6	7	8	9	1	2	3	4	5	6	7	8	9	
Dec	8	9	1	2	3	4	5	6	7	8	9	1	2	3	4	5	6	7	8	9	1	2	3	4	5	6	7	8	9	1	2

JANUARY 30

	1	2	3	4	5	6	7	8	9	10	11	12	13	14	15	16	17	18	19	20	21	22	23	24	25	26	27	28	29	30	31
Jan	6	7	8	9	1	2	3	4	5	6	7	8	9	1	2	3	4	5	6	7	8	9	1	2	3	4	5	6	7	9	1
Feb	8	9	1	2	3	4	5	6	7	8	9	1	2	3	4	5	6	7	8	9	1	2	3	4	5	6	7	8	9		
Mar	9	1	2	3	4	5	6	7	8	9	1	2	3	4	5	6	7	8	9	1	2	3	4	5	6	7	8	9	1	2	3
Apr	1	2	3	4	5	6	7	8	9	1	2	3	4	5	6	7	8	9	1	2	3	4	5	6	7	8	9	1	2	3	
May	2	3	4	5	6	7	8	9	1	2	3	4	5	6	7	8	9	1	2	3	4	5	6	7	8	9	1	2	3	4	5
Jun	3	4	5	6	7	8	9	1	2	3	4	5	6	7	8	9	1	2	3	4	5	6	7	8	9	1	2	3	4	5	
Jul	4	5	6	7	8	9	1	2	3	4	5	6	7	8	9	1	2	3	4	5	6	7	8	9	1	2	3	4	5	6	7
Aug	5	6	7	8	9	1	2	3	4	5	6	7	8	9	1	2	3	4	5	6	7	8	9	1	2	3	4	5	6	7	8
Sep	6	7	8	9	1	2	3	4	5	6	7	8	9	1	2	3	4	5	6	7	8	9	1	2	3	4	5	6	7	8	
Oct	7	8	9	1	2	3	4	5	6	7	8	9	1	2	3	4	5	6	7	8	9	1	2	3	4	5	6	7	8	9	1
Nov	8	9	1	2	3	4	5	6	7	8	9	1	2	3	4	5	6	7	8	9	1	2	3	4	5	6	7	8	9	1	
Dec	9	1	2	3	4	5	6	7	8	9	1	2	3	4	5	6	7	8	9	1	2	3	4	5	6	7	8	9	1	2	3

JANUARY 31

	1	2	3	4	5	6	7	8	9	10	11	12	13	14	15	16	17	18	19	20	21	22	23	24	25	26	27	28	29	30	31
Jan	7	8	9	1	2	3	4	5	6	7	8	9	1	2	3	4	5	6	7	8	9	1	2	3	4	5	6	7	8	9	2
Feb	9	1	2	3	4	5	6	7	8	9	1	2	3	4	5	6	7	8	9	1	2	3	4	5	6	7	8	9	1		
Mar	1	2	3	4	5	6	7	8	9	1	2	3	4	5	6	7	8	9	1	2	3	4	5	6	7	8	9	1	2	3	4
Apr	2	3	4	5	6	7	8	9	1	2	3	4	5	6	7	8	9	1	2	3	4	5	6	7	8	9	1	2	3	4	
May	3	4	5	6	7	8	9	1	2	3	4	5	6	7	8	9	1	2	3	4	5	6	7	8	9	1	2	3	4	5	6
Jun	4	5	6	7	8	9	1	2	3	4	5	6	7	8	9	1	2	3	4	5	6	7	8	9	1	2	3	4	5	6	
Jul	5	6	7	8	9	1	2	3	4	5	6	7	8	9	1	2	3	4	5	6	7	8	9	1	2	3	4	5	6	7	8
Aug	6	7	8	9	1	2	3	4	5	6	7	8	9	1	2	3	4	5	6	7	8	9	1	2	3	4	5	6	7	8	9
Sep	7	8	9	1	2	3	4	5	6	7	8	9	1	2	3	4	5	6	7	8	9	1	2	3	4	5	6	7	8	9	
Oct	8	9	1	2	3	4	5	6	7	8	9	1	2	3	4	5	6	7	8	9	1	2	3	4	5	6	7	8	9	1	2
Nov	9	1	2	3	4	5	6	7	8	9	1	2	3	4	5	6	7	8	9	1	2	3	4	5	6	7	8	9	1	2	
Dec	1	2	3	4	5	6	7	8	9	1	2	3	4	5	6	7	8	9	1	2	3	4	5	6	7	8	9	1	2	3	4

FEBRUARY 1

	1	2	3	4	5	6	7	8	9	10	11	12	13	14	15	16	17	18	19	20	21	22	23	24	25	26	27	28	29	30	31
Jan	5	6	7	8	9	1	2	3	4	5	6	7	8	9	1	2	3	4	5	6	7	8	9	1	2	3	4	5	6	7	8
Feb	7	8	9	1	2	3	4	5	6	7	8	9	1	2	3	4	5	6	7	8	9	1	2	3	4	5	6	7	8		
Mar	8	9	1	2	3	4	5	6	7	8	9	1	2	3	4	5	6	7	8	9	1	2	3	4	5	6	7	8	9	1	2
Apr	9	1	2	3	4	5	6	7	8	9	1	2	3	4	5	6	7	8	9	1	2	3	4	5	6	7	8	9	1	2	
May	1	2	3	4	5	6	7	8	9	1	2	3	4	5	6	7	8	9	1	2	3	4	5	6	7	8	9	1	2	3	4
Jun	2	3	4	5	6	7	8	9	1	2	3	4	5	6	7	8	9	1	2	3	4	5	6	7	8	9	1	2	3	4	
Jul	3	4	5	6	7	8	9	1	2	3	4	5	6	7	8	9	1	2	3	4	5	6	7	8	9	1	2	3	4	5	6
Aug	4	5	6	7	8	9	1	2	3	4	5	6	7	8	9	1	2	3	4	5	6	7	8	9	1	2	3	4	5	6	7
Sep	5	6	7	8	9	1	2	3	4	5	6	7	8	9	1	2	3	4	5	6	7	8	9	1	2	3	4	5	6	7	
Oct	6	7	8	9	1	2	3	4	5	6	7	8	9	1	2	3	4	5	6	7	8	9	1	2	3	4	5	6	7	8	9
Nov	7	8	9	1	2	3	4	5	6	7	8	9	1	2	3	4	5	6	7	8	9	1	2	3	4	5	6	7	8	9	
Dec	8	9	1	2	3	4	5	6	7	8	9	1	2	3	4	5	6	7	8	9	1	2	3	4	5	6	7	8	9	1	2

FEBRUARY 2

	1	2	3	4	5	6	7	8	9	10	11	12	13	14	15	16	17	18	19	20	21	22	23	24	25	26	27	28	29	30	31
Jan	6	7	8	9	1	2	3	4	5	6	7	8	9	1	2	3	4	5	6	7	8	9	1	2	3	4	5	6	7	8	9
Feb	7	9	1	2	3	4	5	6	7	8	9	1	2	3	4	5	6	7	8	9	1	2	3	4	5	6	7	8	9		
Mar	9	1	2	3	4	5	6	7	8	9	1	2	3	4	5	6	7	8	9	1	2	3	4	5	6	7	8	9	1	2	3
Apr	1	2	3	4	5	6	7	8	9	1	2	3	4	5	6	7	8	9	1	2	3	4	5	6	7	8	9	1	2	3	
May	2	3	4	5	6	7	8	9	1	2	3	4	5	6	7	8	9	1	2	3	4	5	6	7	8	9	1	2	3	4	5
Jun	3	4	5	6	7	8	9	1	2	3	4	5	6	7	8	9	1	2	3	4	5	6	7	8	9	1	2	3	4	5	
Jul	4	5	6	7	8	9	1	2	3	4	5	6	7	8	9	1	2	3	4	5	6	7	8	9	1	2	3	4	5	6	7
Aug	5	6	7	8	9	1	2	3	4	5	6	7	8	9	1	2	3	4	5	6	7	8	9	1	2	3	4	5	6	7	8
Sep	6	7	8	9	1	2	3	4	5	6	7	8	9	1	2	3	4	5	6	7	8	9	1	2	3	4	5	6	7	8	
Oct	7	8	9	1	2	3	4	5	6	7	8	9	1	2	3	4	5	6	7	8	9	1	2	3	4	5	6	7	8	9	1
Nov	8	9	1	2	3	4	5	6	7	8	9	1	2	3	4	5	6	7	8	9	1	2	3	4	5	6	7	8	9	1	
Dec	9	1	2	3	4	5	6	7	8	9	1	2	3	4	5	6	7	8	9	1	2	3	4	5	6	7	8	9	1	2	3

FEBRUARY 3

	1	2	3	4	5	6	7	8	9	10	11	12	13	14	15	16	17	18	19	20	21	22	23	24	25	26	27	28	29	30	31
Jan	7	8	9	1	2	3	4	5	6	7	8	9	1	2	3	4	5	6	7	8	9	1	2	3	4	5	6	7	8	9	1
Feb	8	9	2	3	4	5	6	7	8	9	1	2	3	4	5	6	7	8	9	1	2	3	4	5	6	7	8	9	1		
Mar	1	2	3	4	5	6	7	8	9	1	2	3	4	5	6	7	8	9	1	2	3	4	5	6	7	8	9	1	2	3	4
Apr	2	3	4	5	6	7	8	9	1	2	3	4	5	6	7	8	9	1	2	3	4	5	6	7	8	9	1	2	3	4	
May	3	4	5	6	7	8	9	1	2	3	4	5	6	7	8	9	1	2	3	4	5	6	7	8	9	1	2	3	4	5	6
Jun	4	5	6	7	8	9	1	2	3	4	5	6	7	8	9	1	2	3	4	5	6	7	8	9	1	2	3	4	5	6	
Jul	5	6	7	8	9	1	2	3	4	5	6	7	8	9	1	2	3	4	5	6	7	8	9	1	2	3	4	5	6	7	8
Aug	6	7	8	9	1	2	3	4	5	6	7	8	9	1	2	3	4	5	6	7	8	9	1	2	3	4	5	6	7	8	9
Sep	7	8	9	1	2	3	4	5	6	7	8	9	1	2	3	4	5	6	7	8	9	1	2	3	4	5	6	7	8	9	
Oct	8	9	1	2	3	4	5	6	7	8	9	1	2	3	4	5	6	7	8	9	1	2	3	4	5	6	7	8	9	1	2
Nov	9	1	2	3	4	5	6	7	8	9	1	2	3	4	5	6	7	8	9	1	2	3	4	5	6	7	8	9	1	2	
Dec	1	2	3	4	5	6	7	8	9	1	2	3	4	5	6	7	8	9	1	2	3	4	5	6	7	8	9	1	2	3	4

FEBRUARY 4

	1	2	3	4	5	6	7	8	9	10	11	12	13	14	15	16	17	18	19	20	21	22	23	24	25	26	27	28	29	30	31
Jan	8	9	1	2	3	4	5	6	7	8	9	1	2	3	4	5	6	7	8	9	1	2	3	4	5	6	7	8	9	1	2
Feb	9	1	2	4	5	6	7	8	9	1	2	3	4	5	6	7	8	9	1	2	3	4	5	6	7	8	9	1	2		
Mar	2	3	4	5	6	7	8	9	1	2	3	4	5	6	7	8	9	1	2	3	4	5	6	7	8	9	1	2	3	4	5
Apr	3	4	5	6	7	8	9	1	2	3	4	5	6	7	8	9	1	2	3	4	5	6	7	8	9	1	2	3	4	5	
May	4	5	6	7	8	9	1	2	3	4	5	6	7	8	9	1	2	3	4	5	6	7	8	9	1	2	3	4	5	6	7
Jun	5	6	7	8	9	1	2	3	4	5	6	7	8	9	1	2	3	4	5	6	7	8	9	1	2	3	4	5	6	7	
Jul	6	7	8	9	1	2	3	4	5	6	7	8	9	1	2	3	4	5	6	7	8	9	1	2	3	4	5	6	7	8	9
Aug	7	8	9	1	2	3	4	5	6	7	8	9	1	2	3	4	5	6	7	8	9	1	2	3	4	5	6	7	8	9	1
Sep	8	9	1	2	3	4	5	6	7	8	9	1	2	3	4	5	6	7	8	9	1	2	3	4	5	6	7	8	9	1	
Oct	9	1	2	3	4	5	6	7	8	9	1	2	3	4	5	6	7	8	9	1	2	3	4	5	6	7	8	9	1	2	3
Nov	1	2	3	4	5	6	7	8	9	1	2	3	4	5	6	7	8	9	1	2	3	4	5	6	7	8	9	1	2	3	
Dec	2	3	4	5	6	7	8	9	1	2	3	4	5	6	7	8	9	1	2	3	4	5	6	7	8	9	1	2	3	4	5

FEBRUARY 5

	1	2	3	4	5	6	7	8	9	10	11	12	13	14	15	16	17	18	19	20	21	22	23	24	25	26	27	28	29	30	31
Jan	9	1	2	3	4	5	6	7	8	9	1	2	3	4	5	6	7	8	9	1	2	3	4	5	6	7	8	9	1	2	3
Feb	1	2	3	4	6	7	8	9	1	2	3	4	5	6	7	8	9	1	2	3	4	5	6	7	8	9	1	2	3		
Mar	3	4	5	6	7	8	9	1	2	3	4	5	6	7	8	9	1	2	3	4	5	6	7	8	9	1	2	3	4	5	6
Apr	4	5	6	7	8	9	1	2	3	4	5	6	7	8	9	1	2	3	4	5	6	7	8	9	1	2	3	4	5	6	
May	5	6	7	8	9	1	2	3	4	5	6	7	8	9	1	2	3	4	5	6	7	8	9	1	2	3	4	5	6	7	8
Jun	6	7	8	9	1	2	3	4	5	6	7	8	9	1	2	3	4	5	6	7	8	9	1	2	3	4	5	6	7	8	
Jul	7	8	9	1	2	3	4	5	6	7	8	9	1	2	3	4	5	6	7	8	9	1	2	3	4	5	6	7	8	9	1
Aug	8	9	1	2	3	4	5	6	7	8	9	1	2	3	4	5	6	7	8	9	1	2	3	4	5	6	7	8	9	1	2
Sep	9	1	2	3	4	5	6	7	8	9	1	2	3	4	5	6	7	8	9	1	2	3	4	5	6	7	8	9	1	2	
Oct	1	2	3	4	5	6	7	8	9	1	2	3	4	5	6	7	8	9	1	2	3	4	5	6	7	8	9	1	2	3	4
Nov	2	3	4	5	6	7	8	9	1	2	3	4	5	6	7	8	9	1	2	3	4	5	6	7	8	9	1	2	3	4	
Dec	3	4	5	6	7	8	9	1	2	3	4	5	6	7	8	9	1	2	3	4	5	6	7	8	9	1	2	3	4	5	6

FEBRUARY 6

	1	2	3	4	5	6	7	8	9	10	11	12	13	14	15	16	17	18	19	20	21	22	23	24	25	26	27	28	29	30	31
Jan	1	2	3	4	5	6	7	8	9	1	2	3	4	5	6	7	8	9	1	2	3	4	5	6	7	8	9	1	2	3	4
Feb	2	3	4	5	6	8	9	1	2	3	4	5	6	7	8	9	1	2	3	4	5	6	7	8	9	1	2	3	4		
Mar	4	5	6	7	8	9	1	2	3	4	5	6	7	8	9	1	2	3	4	5	6	7	8	9	1	2	3	4	5	6	7
Apr	5	6	7	8	9	1	2	3	4	5	6	7	8	9	1	2	3	4	5	6	7	8	9	1	2	3	4	5	6	7	
May	6	7	8	9	1	2	3	4	5	6	7	8	9	1	2	3	4	5	6	7	8	9	1	2	3	4	5	6	7	8	9
Jun	7	8	9	1	2	3	4	5	6	7	8	9	1	2	3	4	5	6	7	8	9	1	2	3	4	5	6	7	8	9	
Jul	8	9	1	2	3	4	5	6	7	8	9	1	2	3	4	5	6	7	8	9	1	2	3	4	5	6	7	8	9	1	2
Aug	9	1	2	3	4	5	6	7	8	9	1	2	3	4	5	6	7	8	9	1	2	3	4	5	6	7	8	9	1	2	3
Sep	1	2	3	4	5	6	7	8	9	1	2	3	4	5	6	7	8	9	1	2	3	4	5	6	7	8	9	1	2	3	
Oct	2	3	4	5	6	7	8	9	1	2	3	4	5	6	7	8	9	1	2	3	4	5	6	7	8	9	1	2	3	4	5
Nov	3	4	5	6	7	8	9	1	2	3	4	5	6	7	8	9	1	2	3	4	5	6	7	8	9	1	2	3	4	5	
Dec	4	5	6	7	8	9	1	2	3	4	5	6	7	8	9	1	2	3	4	5	6	7	8	9	1	2	3	4	5	6	7

FEBRUARY 7

	1	2	3	4	5	6	7	8	9	10	11	12	13	14	15	16	17	18	19	20	21	22	23	24	25	26	27	28	29	30	31
Jan	2	3	4	5	6	7	8	9	1	2	3	4	5	6	7	8	9	1	2	3	4	5	6	7	8	9	1	2	3	4	5
Feb	3	4	5	6	7	8	1	2	3	4	5	6	7	8	9	1	2	3	4	5	6	7	8	9	1	2	3	4	5		
Mar	5	6	7	8	9	1	2	3	4	5	6	7	8	9	1	2	3	4	5	6	7	8	9	1	2	3	4	5	6	7	8
Apr	6	7	8	9	1	2	3	4	5	6	7	8	9	1	2	3	4	5	6	7	8	9	1	2	3	4	5	6	7	8	
May	7	8	9	1	2	3	4	5	6	7	8	9	1	2	3	4	5	6	7	8	9	1	2	3	4	5	6	7	8	9	1
Jun	8	9	1	2	3	4	5	6	7	8	9	1	2	3	4	5	6	7	8	9	1	2	3	4	5	6	7	8	9	1	
Jul	9	1	2	3	4	5	6	7	8	9	1	2	3	4	5	6	7	8	9	1	2	3	4	5	6	7	8	9	1	2	3
Aug	1	2	3	4	5	6	7	8	9	1	2	3	4	5	6	7	8	9	1	2	3	4	5	6	7	8	9	1	2	3	4
Sep	2	3	4	5	6	7	8	9	1	2	3	4	5	6	7	8	9	1	2	3	4	5	6	7	8	9	1	2	3	4	
Oct	3	4	5	6	7	8	9	1	2	3	4	5	6	7	8	9	1	2	3	4	5	6	7	8	9	1	2	3	4	5	6
Nov	4	5	6	7	8	9	1	2	3	4	5	6	7	8	9	1	2	3	4	5	6	7	8	9	1	2	3	4	5	6	
Dec	5	6	7	8	9	1	2	3	4	5	6	7	8	9	1	2	3	4	5	6	7	8	9	1	2	3	4	5	6	7	8

FEBRUARY 8

	1	2	3	4	5	6	7	8	9	10	11	12	13	14	15	16	17	18	19	20	21	22	23	24	25	26	27	28	29	30	31
Jan	3	4	5	6	7	8	9	1	2	3	4	5	6	7	8	9	1	2	3	4	5	6	7	8	9	1	2	3	4	5	6
Feb	4	5	6	7	8	9	1	3	4	5	6	7	8	9	1	2	3	4	5	6	7	8	9	1	2	3	4	5	6		
Mar	6	7	8	9	1	2	3	4	5	6	7	8	9	1	2	3	4	5	6	7	8	9	1	2	3	4	5	6	7	8	9
Apr	7	8	9	1	2	3	4	5	6	7	8	9	1	2	3	4	5	6	7	8	9	1	2	3	4	5	6	7	8	9	
May	8	9	1	2	3	4	5	6	7	8	9	1	2	3	4	5	6	7	8	9	1	2	3	4	5	6	7	8	9	1	2
Jun	9	1	2	3	4	5	6	7	8	9	1	2	3	4	5	6	7	8	9	1	2	3	4	5	6	7	8	9	1	2	
Jul	1	2	3	4	5	6	7	8	9	1	2	3	4	5	6	7	8	9	1	2	3	4	5	6	7	8	9	1	2	3	4
Aug	2	3	4	5	6	7	8	9	1	2	3	4	5	6	7	8	9	1	2	3	4	5	6	7	8	9	1	2	3	4	5
Sep	3	4	5	6	7	8	9	1	2	3	4	5	6	7	8	9	1	2	3	4	5	6	7	8	9	1	2	3	4	5	
Oct	4	5	6	7	8	9	1	2	3	4	5	6	7	8	9	1	2	3	4	5	6	7	8	9	1	2	3	4	5	6	7
Nov	5	6	7	8	9	1	2	3	4	5	6	7	8	9	1	2	3	4	5	6	7	8	9	1	2	3	4	5	6	7	
Dec	6	7	8	9	1	2	3	4	5	6	7	8	9	1	2	3	4	5	6	7	8	9	1	2	3	4	5	6	7	8	9

FEBRUARY 9

	1	2	3	4	5	6	7	8	9	10	11	12	13	14	15	16	17	18	19	20	21	22	23	24	25	26	27	28	29	30	31
Jan	4	5	6	7	8	9	1	2	3	4	5	6	7	8	9	1	2	3	4	5	6	7	8	9	1	2	3	4	5	6	7
Feb	5	6	7	8	9	1	2	3	5	6	7	8	9	1	2	3	4	5	6	7	8	9	1	2	3	4	5	6	7		
Mar	7	8	9	1	2	3	4	5	6	7	8	9	1	2	3	4	5	6	7	8	9	1	2	3	4	5	6	7	8	9	1
Apr	8	9	1	2	3	4	5	6	7	8	9	1	2	3	4	5	6	7	8	9	1	2	3	4	5	6	7	8	9	1	
May	9	1	2	3	4	5	6	7	8	9	1	2	3	4	5	6	7	8	9	1	2	3	4	5	6	7	8	9	1	2	3
Jun	1	2	3	4	5	6	7	8	9	1	2	3	4	5	6	7	8	9	1	2	3	4	5	6	7	8	9	1	2	3	
Jul	2	3	4	5	6	7	8	9	1	2	3	4	5	6	7	8	9	1	2	3	4	5	6	7	8	9	1	2	3	4	5
Aug	3	4	5	6	7	8	9	1	2	3	4	5	6	7	8	9	1	2	3	4	5	6	7	8	9	1	2	3	4	5	6
Sep	4	5	6	7	8	9	1	2	3	4	5	6	7	8	9	1	2	3	4	5	6	7	8	9	1	2	3	4	5	6	
Oct	5	6	7	8	9	1	2	3	4	5	6	7	8	9	1	2	3	4	5	6	7	8	9	1	2	3	4	5	6	7	8
Nov	6	7	8	9	1	2	3	4	5	6	7	8	9	1	2	3	4	5	6	7	8	9	1	2	3	4	5	6	7	8	
Dec	7	8	9	1	2	3	4	5	6	7	8	9	1	2	3	4	5	6	7	8	9	1	2	3	4	5	6	7	8	9	1

FEBRUARY 10

	1	2	3	4	5	6	7	8	9	10	11	12	13	14	15	16	17	18	19	20	21	22	23	24	25	26	27	28	29	30	31
Jan	5	6	7	8	9	1	2	3	4	5	6	7	8	9	1	2	3	4	5	6	7	8	9	1	2	3	4	5	6	7	8
Feb	6	7	8	9	1	2	3	4	5	7	8	9	1	2	3	4	5	6	7	8	9	1	2	3	4	5	6	7	8		
Mar	8	9	1	2	3	4	5	6	7	8	9	1	2	3	4	5	6	7	8	9	1	2	3	4	5	6	7	8	9	1	2
Apr	9	1	2	3	4	5	6	7	8	9	1	2	3	4	5	6	7	8	9	1	2	3	4	5	6	7	8	9	1	2	
May	1	2	3	4	5	6	7	8	9	1	2	3	4	5	6	7	8	9	1	2	3	4	5	6	7	8	9	1	2	3	4
Jun	2	3	4	5	6	7	8	9	1	2	3	4	5	6	7	8	9	1	2	3	4	5	6	7	8	9	1	2	3	4	
Jul	3	4	5	6	7	8	9	1	2	3	4	5	6	7	8	9	1	2	3	4	5	6	7	8	9	1	2	3	4	5	6
Aug	4	5	6	7	8	9	1	2	3	4	5	6	7	8	9	1	2	3	4	5	6	7	8	9	1	2	3	4	5	6	7
Sep	5	6	7	8	9	1	2	3	4	5	6	7	8	9	1	2	3	4	5	6	7	8	9	1	2	3	4	5	6	7	
Oct	6	7	8	9	1	2	3	4	5	6	7	8	9	1	2	3	4	5	6	7	8	9	1	2	3	4	5	6	7	8	9
Nov	7	8	9	1	2	3	4	5	6	7	8	9	1	2	3	4	5	6	7	8	9	1	2	3	4	5	6	7	8	9	
Dec	8	9	1	2	3	4	5	6	7	8	9	1	2	3	4	5	6	7	8	9	1	2	3	4	5	6	7	8	9	1	2

FEBRUARY 11

	1	2	3	4	5	6	7	8	9	10	11	12	13	14	15	16	17	18	19	20	21	22	23	24	25	26	27	28	29	30	31
Jan	6	7	8	9	1	2	3	4	5	6	7	8	9	1	2	3	4	5	6	7	8	9	1	2	3	4	5	6	7	8	9
Feb	7	8	9	1	2	3	4	5	6	7	9	1	2	3	4	5	6	7	8	9	1	2	3	4	5	6	7	8	9		
Mar	9	1	2	3	4	5	6	7	8	9	1	2	3	4	5	6	7	8	9	1	2	3	4	5	6	7	8	9	1	2	3
Apr	1	2	3	4	5	6	7	8	9	1	2	3	4	5	6	7	8	9	1	2	3	4	5	6	7	8	9	1	2	3	
May	2	3	4	5	6	7	8	9	1	2	3	4	5	6	7	8	9	1	2	3	4	5	6	7	8	9	1	2	3	4	5
Jun	3	4	5	6	7	8	9	1	2	3	4	5	6	7	8	9	1	2	3	4	5	6	7	8	9	1	2	3	4	5	
Jul	4	5	6	7	8	9	1	2	3	4	5	6	7	8	9	1	2	3	4	5	6	7	8	9	1	2	3	4	5	6	7
Aug	5	6	7	8	9	1	2	3	4	5	6	7	8	9	1	2	3	4	5	6	7	8	9	1	2	3	4	5	6	7	8
Sep	6	7	8	9	1	2	3	4	5	6	7	8	9	1	2	3	4	5	6	7	8	9	1	2	3	4	5	6	7	8	
Oct	7	8	9	1	2	3	4	5	6	7	8	9	1	2	3	4	5	6	7	8	9	1	2	3	4	5	6	7	8	9	1
Nov	8	9	1	2	3	4	5	6	7	8	9	1	2	3	4	5	6	7	8	9	1	2	3	4	5	6	7	8	9	1	
Dec	9	1	2	3	4	5	6	7	8	9	1	2	3	4	5	6	7	8	9	1	2	3	4	5	6	7	8	9	1	2	3

FEBRUARY 12

	1	2	3	4	5	6	7	8	9	10	11	12	13	14	15	16	17	18	19	20	21	22	23	24	25	26	27	28	29	30	31
Jan	7	8	9	1	2	3	4	5	6	7	8	9	1	2	3	4	5	6	7	8	9	1	2	3	4	5	6	7	8	9	1
Feb	8	9	1	2	3	4	5	6	7	8	9	2	3	4	5	6	7	8	9	1	2	3	4	5	6	7	8	9	1		
Mar	1	2	3	4	5	6	7	8	9	1	2	3	4	5	6	7	8	9	1	2	3	4	5	6	7	8	9	1	2	3	4
Apr	2	3	4	5	6	7	8	9	1	2	3	4	5	6	7	8	9	1	2	3	4	5	6	7	8	9	1	2	3	4	
May	3	4	5	6	7	8	9	1	2	3	4	5	6	7	8	9	1	2	3	4	5	6	7	8	9	1	2	3	4	5	6
Jun	4	5	6	7	8	9	1	2	3	4	5	6	7	8	9	1	2	3	4	5	6	7	8	9	1	2	3	4	5	6	
Jul	5	6	7	8	9	1	2	3	4	5	6	7	8	9	1	2	3	4	5	6	7	8	9	1	2	3	4	5	6	7	8
Aug	6	7	8	9	1	2	3	4	5	6	7	8	9	1	2	3	4	5	6	7	8	9	1	2	3	4	5	6	7	8	9
Sep	7	8	9	1	2	3	4	5	6	7	8	9	1	2	3	4	5	6	7	8	9	1	2	3	4	5	6	7	8	9	
Oct	8	9	1	2	3	4	5	6	7	8	9	1	2	3	4	5	6	7	8	9	1	2	3	4	5	6	7	8	9	1	2
Nov	9	1	2	3	4	5	6	7	8	9	1	2	3	4	5	6	7	8	9	1	2	3	4	5	6	7	8	9	1	2	
Dec	1	2	3	4	5	6	7	8	9	1	2	3	4	5	6	7	8	9	1	2	3	4	5	6	7	8	9	1	2	3	4

FEBRUARY 13

	1	2	3	4	5	6	7	8	9	10	11	12	13	14	15	16	17	18	19	20	21	22	23	24	25	26	27	28	29	30	31
Jan	8	9	1	2	3	4	5	6	7	8	9	1	2	3	4	5	6	7	8	9	1	2	3	4	5	6	7	8	9	1	2
Feb	9	1	2	3	4	5	6	7	8	9	1	2	4	5	6	7	8	9	1	2	3	4	5	6	7	8	9	1	2		
Mar	2	3	4	5	6	7	8	9	1	2	3	4	5	6	7	8	9	1	2	3	4	5	6	7	8	9	1	2	3	4	5
Apr	3	4	5	6	7	8	9	1	2	3	4	5	6	7	8	9	1	2	3	4	5	6	7	8	9	1	2	3	4	5	
May	4	5	6	7	8	9	1	2	3	4	5	6	7	8	9	1	2	3	4	5	6	7	8	9	1	2	3	4	5	6	7
Jun	5	6	7	8	9	1	2	3	4	5	6	7	8	9	1	2	3	4	5	6	7	8	9	1	2	3	4	5	6	7	
Jul	6	7	8	9	1	2	3	4	5	6	7	8	9	1	2	3	4	5	6	7	8	9	1	2	3	4	5	6	7	8	9
Aug	7	8	9	1	2	3	4	5	6	7	8	9	1	2	3	4	5	6	7	8	9	1	2	3	4	5	6	7	8	9	1
Sep	8	9	1	2	3	4	5	6	7	8	9	1	2	3	4	5	6	7	8	9	1	2	3	4	5	6	7	8	9	1	
Oct	9	1	2	3	4	5	6	7	8	9	1	2	3	4	5	6	7	8	9	1	2	3	4	5	6	7	8	9	1	2	3
Nov	1	2	3	4	5	6	7	8	9	1	2	3	4	5	6	7	8	9	1	2	3	4	5	6	7	8	9	1	2	3	
Dec	2	3	4	5	6	7	8	9	1	2	3	4	5	6	7	8	9	1	2	3	4	5	6	7	8	9	1	2	3	4	5

FEBRUARY 14

	1	2	3	4	5	6	7	8	9	10	11	12	13	14	15	16	17	18	19	20	21	22	23	24	25	26	27	28	29	30	31
Jan	9	1	2	3	4	5	6	7	8	9	1	2	3	4	5	6	7	8	9	1	2	3	4	5	6	7	8	9	1	2	3
Feb	1	2	3	4	5	6	7	8	9	1	2	3	4	6	7	8	9	1	2	3	4	5	6	7	8	9	1	2	3		
Mar	3	4	5	6	7	8	9	1	2	3	4	5	6	7	8	9	1	2	3	4	5	6	7	8	9	1	2	3	4	5	6
Apr	4	5	6	7	8	9	1	2	3	4	5	6	7	8	9	1	2	3	4	5	6	7	8	9	1	2	3	4	5	6	
May	5	6	7	8	9	1	2	3	4	5	6	7	8	9	1	2	3	4	5	6	7	8	9	1	2	3	4	5	6	7	8
Jun	6	7	8	9	1	2	3	4	5	6	7	8	9	1	2	3	4	5	6	7	8	9	1	2	3	4	5	6	7	8	
Jul	7	8	9	1	2	3	4	5	6	7	8	9	1	2	3	4	5	6	7	8	9	1	2	3	4	5	6	7	8	9	1
Aug	8	9	1	2	3	4	5	6	7	8	9	1	2	3	4	5	6	7	8	9	1	2	3	4	5	6	7	8	9	1	2
Sep	9	1	2	3	4	5	6	7	8	9	1	2	3	4	5	6	7	8	9	1	2	3	4	5	6	7	8	9	1	2	
Oct	1	2	3	4	5	6	7	8	9	1	2	3	4	5	6	7	8	9	1	2	3	4	5	6	7	8	9	1	2	3	4
Nov	2	3	4	5	6	7	8	9	1	2	3	4	5	6	7	8	9	1	2	3	4	5	6	7	8	9	1	2	3	4	
Dec	3	4	5	6	7	8	9	1	2	3	4	5	6	7	8	9	1	2	3	4	5	6	7	8	9	1	2	3	4	5	6

FEBRUARY 15

	1	2	3	4	5	6	7	8	9	10	11	12	13	14	15	16	17	18	19	20	21	22	23	24	25	26	27	28	29	30	31
Jan	1	2	3	4	5	6	7	8	9	1	2	3	4	5	6	7	8	9	1	2	3	4	5	6	7	8	9	1	2	3	4
Feb	2	3	4	5	6	7	8	9	1	2	3	4	5	6	8	9	1	2	3	4	5	6	7	8	9	1	2	3	4		
Mar	4	5	6	7	8	9	1	2	3	4	5	6	7	8	9	1	2	3	4	5	6	7	8	9	1	2	3	4	5	6	7
Apr	5	6	7	8	9	1	2	3	4	5	6	7	8	9	1	2	3	4	5	6	7	8	9	1	2	3	4	5	6	7	
May	6	7	8	9	1	2	3	4	5	6	7	8	9	1	2	3	4	5	6	7	8	9	1	2	3	4	5	6	7	8	9
Jun	7	8	9	1	2	3	4	5	6	7	8	9	1	2	3	4	5	6	7	8	9	1	2	3	4	5	6	7	8	9	
Jul	8	9	1	2	3	4	5	6	7	8	9	1	2	3	4	5	6	7	8	9	1	2	3	4	5	6	7	8	9	1	2
Aug	9	1	2	3	4	5	6	7	8	9	1	2	3	4	5	6	7	8	9	1	2	3	4	5	6	7	8	9	1	2	3
Sep	1	2	3	4	5	6	7	8	9	1	2	3	4	5	6	7	8	9	1	2	3	4	5	6	7	8	9	1	2	3	
Oct	2	3	4	5	6	7	8	9	1	2	3	4	5	6	7	8	9	1	2	3	4	5	6	7	8	9	1	2	3	4	5
Nov	3	4	5	6	7	8	9	1	2	3	4	5	6	7	8	9	1	2	3	4	5	6	7	8	9	1	2	3	4	5	
Dec	4	5	6	7	8	9	1	2	3	4	5	6	7	8	9	1	2	3	4	5	6	7	8	9	1	2	3	4	5	6	7

FEBRUARY 16

	1	2	3	4	5	6	7	8	9	10	11	12	13	14	15	16	17	18	19	20	21	22	23	24	25	26	27	28	29	30	31
Jan	2	3	4	5	6	7	8	9	1	2	3	4	5	6	7	8	9	1	2	3	4	5	6	7	8	9	1	2	3	4	5
Feb	3	4	5	6	7	8	9	1	2	3	4	5	6	7	8	1	2	3	4	5	6	7	8	9	1	2	3	4	5		
Mar	5	6	7	8	9	1	2	3	4	5	6	7	8	9	1	2	3	4	5	6	7	8	9	1	2	3	4	5	6	7	8
Apr	6	7	8	9	1	2	3	4	5	6	7	8	9	1	2	3	4	5	6	7	8	9	1	2	3	4	5	6	7	8	
May	7	8	9	1	2	3	4	5	6	7	8	9	1	2	3	4	5	6	7	8	9	1	2	3	4	5	6	7	8	9	1
Jun	8	9	1	2	3	4	5	6	7	8	9	1	2	3	4	5	6	7	8	9	1	2	3	4	5	6	7	8	9	1	
Jul	9	1	2	3	4	5	6	7	8	9	1	2	3	4	5	6	7	8	9	1	2	3	4	5	6	7	8	9	1	2	3
Aug	1	2	3	4	5	6	7	8	9	1	2	3	4	5	6	7	8	9	1	2	3	4	5	6	7	8	9	1	2	3	4
Sep	2	3	4	5	6	7	8	9	1	2	3	4	5	6	7	8	9	1	2	3	4	5	6	7	8	9	1	2	3	4	
Oct	3	4	5	6	7	8	9	1	2	3	4	5	6	7	8	9	1	2	3	4	5	6	7	8	9	1	2	3	4	5	6
Nov	4	5	6	7	8	9	1	2	3	4	5	6	7	8	9	1	2	3	4	5	6	7	8	9	1	2	3	4	5	6	
Dec	5	6	7	8	9	1	2	3	4	5	6	7	8	9	1	2	3	4	5	6	7	8	9	1	2	3	4	5	6	7	8

FEBRUARY 17

	1	2	3	4	5	6	7	8	9	10	11	12	13	14	15	16	17	18	19	20	21	22	23	24	25	26	27	28	29	30	31
Jan	3	4	5	6	7	8	9	1	2	3	4	5	6	7	8	9	1	2	3	4	5	6	7	8	9	1	2	3	4	5	6
Feb	4	5	6	7	8	9	1	2	3	4	5	6	7	8	9	1	3	4	5	6	7	8	9	1	2	3	4	5	6		
Mar	6	7	8	9	1	2	3	4	5	6	7	8	9	1	2	3	4	5	6	7	8	9	1	2	3	4	5	6	7	8	9
Apr	7	8	9	1	2	3	4	5	6	7	8	9	1	2	3	4	5	6	7	8	9	1	2	3	4	5	6	7	8	9	
May	8	9	1	2	3	4	5	6	7	8	9	1	2	3	4	5	6	7	8	9	1	2	3	4	5	6	7	8	9	1	2
Jun	9	1	2	3	4	5	6	7	8	9	1	2	3	4	5	6	7	8	9	1	2	3	4	5	6	7	8	9	1	2	
Jul	1	2	3	4	5	6	7	8	9	1	2	3	4	5	6	7	8	9	1	2	3	4	5	6	7	8	9	1	2	3	4
Aug	2	3	4	5	6	7	8	9	1	2	3	4	5	6	7	8	9	1	2	3	4	5	6	7	8	9	1	2	3	4	5
Sep	3	4	5	6	7	8	9	1	2	3	4	5	6	7	8	9	1	2	3	4	5	6	7	8	9	1	2	3	4	5	
Oct	4	5	6	7	8	9	1	2	3	4	5	6	7	8	9	1	2	3	4	5	6	7	8	9	1	2	3	4	5	6	7
Nov	5	6	7	8	9	1	2	3	4	5	6	7	8	9	1	2	3	4	5	6	7	8	9	1	2	3	4	5	6	7	
Dec	6	7	8	9	1	2	3	4	5	6	7	8	9	1	2	3	4	5	6	7	8	9	1	2	3	4	5	6	7	8	9

Change to [illegible]

FEBRUARY 18

	1	2	3	4	5	6	7	8	9	10	11	12	13	14	15	16	17	18	19	20	21	22	23	24	25	26	27	28	29	30	31
Jan	4	5	6	7	8	9	1	2	3	4	5	6	7	8	9	1	2	3	4	5	6	7	8	9	1	2	3	4	5	6	7
Feb	5	6	7	8	9	1	2	3	4	5	6	7	8	9	1	2	3	5	6	7	8	9	1	2	3	4	5	6	7		
Mar	7	8	9	1	2	3	4	5	6	7	8	9	1	2	3	4	5	6	7	8	9	1	2	3	4	5	6	7	8	9	1
Apr	8	9	1	2	3	4	5	6	7	8	9	1	2	3	4	5	6	7	8	9	1	2	3	4	5	6	7	8	9	1	
May	9	1	2	3	4	5	6	7	8	9	1	2	3	4	5	6	7	8	9	1	2	3	4	5	6	7	8	9	1	2	3
Jun	1	2	3	4	5	6	7	8	9	1	2	3	4	5	6	7	8	9	1	2	3	4	5	6	7	8	9	1	2	3	
Jul	2	3	4	5	6	7	8	9	1	2	3	4	5	6	7	8	9	1	2	3	4	5	6	7	8	9	1	2	3	4	5
Aug	3	4	5	6	7	8	9	1	2	3	4	5	6	7	8	9	1	2	3	4	5	6	7	8	9	1	2	3	4	5	6
Sep	4	5	6	7	8	9	1	2	3	4	5	6	7	8	9	1	2	3	4	5	6	7	8	9	1	2	3	4	5	6	
Oct	5	6	7	8	9	1	2	3	4	5	6	7	8	9	1	2	3	4	5	6	7	8	9	1	2	3	4	5	6	7	8
Nov	6	7	8	9	1	2	3	4	5	6	7	8	9	1	2	3	4	5	6	7	8	9	1	2	3	4	5	6	7	8	
Dec	7	8	9	1	2	3	4	5	6	7	8	9	1	2	3	4	5	6	7	8	9	1	2	3	4	5	6	7	8	9	1

FEBRUARY 19

	1	2	3	4	5	6	7	8	9	10	11	12	13	14	15	16	17	18	19	20	21	22	23	24	25	26	27	28	29	30	31
Jan	5	6	7	8	9	1	2	3	4	5	6	7	8	9	1	2	3	4	5	6	7	8	9	1	2	3	4	5	6	7	8
Feb	6	7	8	9	1	2	3	4	5	6	7	8	9	1	2	3	4	5	7	8	9	1	2	3	4	5	6	7	8		
Mar	8	9	1	2	3	4	5	6	7	8	9	1	2	3	4	5	6	7	8	9	1	2	3	4	5	6	7	8	9	1	2
Apr	9	1	2	3	4	5	6	7	8	9	1	2	3	4	5	6	7	8	9	1	2	3	4	5	6	7	8	9	1	2	
May	1	2	3	4	5	6	7	8	9	1	2	3	4	5	6	7	8	9	1	2	3	4	5	6	7	8	9	1	2	3	4
Jun	2	3	4	5	6	7	8	9	1	2	3	4	5	6	7	8	9	1	2	3	4	5	6	7	8	9	1	2	3	4	
Jul	3	4	5	6	7	8	9	1	2	3	4	5	6	7	8	9	1	2	3	4	5	6	7	8	9	1	2	3	4	5	6
Aug	4	5	6	7	8	9	1	2	3	4	5	6	7	8	9	1	2	3	4	5	6	7	8	9	1	2	3	4	5	6	7
Sep	5	6	7	8	9	1	2	3	4	5	6	7	8	9	1	2	3	4	5	6	7	8	9	1	2	3	4	5	6	7	
Oct	6	7	8	9	1	2	3	4	5	6	7	8	9	1	2	3	4	5	6	7	8	9	1	2	3	4	5	6	7	8	9
Nov	7	8	9	1	2	3	4	5	6	7	8	9	1	2	3	4	5	6	7	8	9	1	2	3	4	5	6	7	8	9	
Dec	8	9	1	2	3	4	5	6	7	8	9	1	2	3	4	5	6	7	8	9	1	2	3	4	5	6	7	8	9	1	2

FEBRUARY 20

	1	2	3	4	5	6	7	8	9	10	11	12	13	14	15	16	17	18	19	20	21	22	23	24	25	26	27	28	29	30	31
Jan	6	7	8	9	1	2	3	4	5	6	7	8	9	1	2	3	4	5	6	7	8	9	1	2	3	4	5	6	7	8	9
Feb	7	8	9	1	2	3	4	5	6	7	8	9	1	2	3	4	5	6	7	9	1	2	3	4	5	6	7	8	9		
Mar	9	1	2	3	4	5	6	7	8	9	1	2	3	4	5	6	7	8	9	1	2	3	4	5	6	7	8	9	1	2	3
Apr	1	2	3	4	5	6	7	8	9	1	2	3	4	5	6	7	8	9	1	2	3	4	5	6	7	8	9	1	2	3	
May	2	3	4	5	6	7	8	9	1	2	3	4	5	6	7	8	9	1	2	3	4	5	6	7	8	9	1	2	3	4	5
Jun	3	4	5	6	7	8	9	1	2	3	4	5	6	7	8	9	1	2	3	4	5	6	7	8	9	1	2	3	4	5	
Jul	4	5	6	7	8	9	1	2	3	4	5	6	7	8	9	1	2	3	4	5	6	7	8	9	1	2	3	4	5	6	7
Aug	5	6	7	8	9	1	2	3	4	5	6	7	8	9	1	2	3	4	5	6	7	8	9	1	2	3	4	5	6	7	8
Sep	6	7	8	9	1	2	3	4	5	6	7	8	9	1	2	3	4	5	6	7	8	9	1	2	3	4	5	6	7	8	
Oct	7	8	9	1	2	3	4	5	6	7	8	9	1	2	3	4	5	6	7	8	9	1	2	3	4	5	6	7	8	9	1
Nov	8	9	1	2	3	4	5	6	7	8	9	1	2	3	4	5	6	7	8	9	1	2	3	4	5	6	7	8	9	1	
Dec	9	1	2	3	4	5	6	7	8	9	1	2	3	4	5	6	7	8	9	1	2	3	4	5	6	7	8	9	1	2	3

FEBRUARY 21

	1	2	3	4	5	6	7	8	9	10	11	12	13	14	15	16	17	18	19	20	21	22	23	24	25	26	27	28	29	30	31
Jan	7	8	9	1	2	3	4	5	6	7	8	9	1	2	3	4	5	6	7	8	9	1	2	3	4	5	6	7	8	9	1
Feb	8	9	1	2	3	4	5	6	7	8	9	1	2	3	4	5	6	7	8	9	2	3	4	5	6	7	8	9	1		
Mar	1	2	3	4	5	6	7	8	9	1	2	3	4	5	6	7	8	9	1	2	3	4	5	6	7	8	9	1	2	3	4
Apr	2	3	4	5	6	7	8	9	1	2	3	4	5	6	7	8	9	1	2	3	4	5	6	7	8	9	1	2	3	4	
May	3	4	5	6	7	8	9	1	2	3	4	5	6	7	8	9	1	2	3	4	5	6	7	8	9	1	2	3	4	5	6
Jun	4	5	6	7	8	9	1	2	3	4	5	6	7	8	9	1	2	3	4	5	6	7	8	9	1	2	3	4	5	6	
Jul	5	6	7	8	9	1	2	3	4	5	6	7	8	9	1	2	3	4	5	6	7	8	9	1	2	3	4	5	6	7	8
Aug	6	7	8	9	1	2	3	4	5	6	7	8	9	1	2	3	4	5	6	7	8	9	1	2	3	4	5	6	7	8	9
Sep	7	8	9	1	2	3	4	5	6	7	8	9	1	2	3	4	5	6	7	8	9	1	2	3	4	5	6	7	8	9	
Oct	8	9	1	2	3	4	5	6	7	8	9	1	2	3	4	5	6	7	8	9	1	2	3	4	5	6	7	8	9	1	2
Nov	9	1	2	3	4	5	6	7	8	9	1	2	3	4	5	6	7	8	9	1	2	3	4	5	6	7	8	9	1	2	
Dec	1	2	3	4	5	6	7	8	9	1	2	3	4	5	6	7	8	9	1	2	3	4	5	6	7	8	9	1	2	3	4

FEBRUARY 22

	1	2	3	4	5	6	7	8	9	10	11	12	13	14	15	16	17	18	19	20	21	22	23	24	25	26	27	28	29	30	31
Jan	8	9	1	2	3	4	5	6	7	8	9	1	2	3	4	5	6	7	8	9	1	2	3	4	5	6	7	8	9	1	2
Feb	9	1	2	3	4	5	6	7	8	9	1	2	3	4	5	6	7	8	9	1	2	4	5	6	7	8	9	1	2		
Mar	2	3	4	5	6	7	8	9	1	2	3	4	5	6	7	8	9	1	2	3	4	5	6	7	8	9	1	2	3	4	5
Apr	3	4	5	6	7	8	9	1	2	3	4	5	6	7	8	9	1	2	3	4	5	6	7	8	9	1	2	3	4	5	
May	4	5	6	7	8	9	1	2	3	4	5	6	7	8	9	1	2	3	4	5	6	7	8	9	1	2	3	4	5	6	7
Jun	5	6	7	8	9	1	2	3	4	5	6	7	8	9	1	2	3	4	5	6	7	8	9	1	2	3	4	5	6	7	
Jul	6	7	8	9	1	2	3	4	5	6	7	8	9	1	2	3	4	5	6	7	8	9	1	2	3	4	5	6	7	8	9
Aug	7	8	9	1	2	3	4	5	6	7	8	9	1	2	3	4	5	6	7	8	9	1	2	3	4	5	6	7	8	9	1
Sep	8	9	1	2	3	4	5	6	7	8	9	1	2	3	4	5	6	7	8	9	1	2	3	4	5	6	7	8	9	1	
Oct	9	1	2	3	4	5	6	7	8	9	1	2	3	4	5	6	7	8	9	1	2	3	4	5	6	7	8	9	1	2	3
Nov	1	2	3	4	5	6	7	8	9	1	2	3	4	5	6	7	8	9	1	2	3	4	5	6	7	8	9	1	2	3	
Dec	2	3	4	5	6	7	8	9	1	2	3	4	5	6	7	8	9	1	2	3	4	5	6	7	8	9	1	2	3	4	5

FEBRUARY 23

	1	2	3	4	5	6	7	8	9	10	11	12	13	14	15	16	17	18	19	20	21	22	23	24	25	26	27	28	29	30	31
Jan	9	1	2	3	4	5	6	7	8	9	1	2	3	4	5	6	7	8	9	1	2	3	4	5	6	7	8	9	1	2	3
Feb	1	2	3	4	5	6	7	8	9	1	2	3	4	5	6	7	8	9	1	2	3	4	6	7	8	9	1	2	3		
Mar	3	4	5	6	7	8	9	1	2	3	4	5	6	7	8	9	1	2	3	4	5	6	7	8	9	1	2	3	4	5	6
Apr	4	5	6	7	8	9	1	2	3	4	5	6	7	8	9	1	2	3	4	5	6	7	8	9	1	2	3	4	5	6	
May	5	6	7	8	9	1	2	3	4	5	6	7	8	9	1	2	3	4	5	6	7	8	9	1	2	3	4	5	6	7	8
Jun	6	7	8	9	1	2	3	4	5	6	7	8	9	1	2	3	4	5	6	7	8	9	1	2	3	4	5	6	7	8	
Jul	7	8	9	1	2	3	4	5	6	7	8	9	1	2	3	4	5	6	7	8	9	1	2	3	4	5	6	7	8	9	1
Aug	8	9	1	2	3	4	5	6	7	8	9	1	2	3	4	5	6	7	8	9	1	2	3	4	5	6	7	8	9	1	2
Sep	9	1	2	3	4	5	6	7	8	9	1	2	3	4	5	6	7	8	9	1	2	3	4	5	6	7	8	9	1	2	
Oct	1	2	3	4	5	6	7	8	9	1	2	3	4	5	6	7	8	9	1	2	3	4	5	6	7	8	9	1	2	3	4
Nov	2	3	4	5	6	7	8	9	1	2	3	4	5	6	7	8	9	1	2	3	4	5	6	7	8	9	1	2	3	4	
Dec	3	4	5	6	7	8	9	1	2	3	4	5	6	7	8	9	1	2	3	4	5	6	7	8	9	1	2	3	4	5	6

FEBRUARY 24

	1	2	3	4	5	6	7	8	9	10	11	12	13	14	15	16	17	18	19	20	21	22	23	24	25	26	27	28	29	30	31
Jan	1	2	3	4	5	6	7	8	9	1	2	3	4	5	6	7	8	9	1	2	3	4	5	6	7	8	9	1	2	3	4
Feb	2	3	4	5	6	7	8	9	1	2	3	4	5	6	7	8	9	1	2	3	4	5	6	8	9	1	2	3	4		
Mar	4	5	6	7	8	9	1	2	3	4	5	6	7	8	9	1	2	3	4	5	6	7	8	9	1	2	3	4	5	6	7
Apr	5	6	7	8	9	1	2	3	4	5	6	7	8	9	1	2	3	4	5	6	7	8	9	1	2	3	4	5	6	7	
May	6	7	8	9	1	2	3	4	5	6	7	8	9	1	2	3	4	5	6	7	8	9	1	2	3	4	5	6	7	8	9
Jun	7	8	9	1	2	3	4	5	6	7	8	9	1	2	3	4	5	6	7	8	9	1	2	3	4	5	6	7	8	9	
Jul	8	9	1	2	3	4	5	6	7	8	9	1	2	3	4	5	6	7	8	9	1	2	3	4	5	6	7	8	9	1	2
Aug	9	1	2	3	4	5	6	7	8	9	1	2	3	4	5	6	7	8	9	1	2	3	4	5	6	7	8	9	1	2	3
Sep	1	2	3	4	5	6	7	8	9	1	2	3	4	5	6	7	8	9	1	2	3	4	5	6	7	8	9	1	2	3	
Oct	2	3	4	5	6	7	8	9	1	2	3	4	5	6	7	8	9	1	2	3	4	5	6	7	8	9	1	2	3	4	5
Nov	3	4	5	6	7	8	9	1	2	3	4	5	6	7	8	9	1	2	3	4	5	6	7	8	9	1	2	3	4	5	
Dec	4	5	6	7	8	9	1	2	3	4	5	6	7	8	9	1	2	3	4	5	6	7	8	9	1	2	3	4	5	6	7

FEBRUARY 25

	1	2	3	4	5	6	7	8	9	10	11	12	13	14	15	16	17	18	19	20	21	22	23	24	25	26	27	28	29	30	31
Jan	2	3	4	5	6	7	8	9	1	2	3	4	5	6	7	8	9	1	2	3	4	5	6	7	8	9	1	2	3	4	5
Feb	3	4	5	6	7	8	9	1	2	3	4	5	6	7	8	9	1	2	3	4	5	6	7	8	1	2	3	4	5		
Mar	5	6	7	8	9	1	2	3	4	5	6	7	8	9	1	2	3	4	5	6	7	8	9	1	2	3	4	5	6	7	8
Apr	6	7	8	9	1	2	3	4	5	6	7	8	9	1	2	3	4	5	6	7	8	9	1	2	3	4	5	6	7	8	
May	7	8	9	1	2	3	4	5	6	7	8	9	1	2	3	4	5	6	7	8	9	1	2	3	4	5	6	7	8	9	1
Jun	8	9	1	2	3	4	5	6	7	8	9	1	2	3	4	5	6	7	8	9	1	2	3	4	5	6	7	8	9	1	
Jul	9	1	2	3	4	5	6	7	8	9	1	2	3	4	5	6	7	8	9	1	2	3	4	5	6	7	8	9	1	2	3
Aug	1	2	3	4	5	6	7	8	9	1	2	3	4	5	6	7	8	9	1	2	3	4	5	6	7	8	9	1	2	3	4
Sep	2	3	4	5	6	7	8	9	1	2	3	4	5	6	7	8	9	1	2	3	4	5	6	7	8	9	1	2	3	4	
Oct	3	4	5	6	7	8	9	1	2	3	4	5	6	7	8	9	1	2	3	4	5	6	7	8	9	1	2	3	4	5	6
Nov	4	5	6	7	8	9	1	2	3	4	5	6	7	8	9	1	2	3	4	5	6	7	8	9	1	2	3	4	5	6	
Dec	5	6	7	8	9	1	2	3	4	5	6	7	8	9	1	2	3	4	5	6	7	8	9	1	2	3	4	5	6	7	8

FEBRUARY 26

	1	2	3	4	5	6	7	8	9	10	11	12	13	14	15	16	17	18	19	20	21	22	23	24	25	26	27	28	29	30	31
Jan	3	4	5	6	7	8	9	1	2	3	4	5	6	7	8	9	1	2	3	4	5	6	7	8	9	1	2	3	4	5	6
Feb	4	5	6	7	8	9	1	2	3	4	5	6	7	8	9	1	2	3	4	5	6	7	8	9	1	3	4	5	6		
Mar	6	7	8	9	1	2	3	4	5	6	7	8	9	1	2	3	4	5	6	7	8	9	1	2	3	4	5	6	7	8	9
Apr	7	8	9	1	2	3	4	5	6	7	8	9	1	2	3	4	5	6	7	8	9	1	2	3	4	5	6	7	8	9	
May	8	9	1	2	3	4	5	6	7	8	9	1	2	3	4	5	6	7	8	9	1	2	3	4	5	6	7	8	9	1	2
Jun	9	1	2	3	4	5	6	7	8	9	1	2	3	4	5	6	7	8	9	1	2	3	4	5	6	7	8	9	1	2	
Jul	1	2	3	4	5	6	7	8	9	1	2	3	4	5	6	7	8	9	1	2	3	4	5	6	7	8	9	1	2	3	4
Aug	2	3	4	5	6	7	8	9	1	2	3	4	5	6	7	8	9	1	2	3	4	5	6	7	8	9	1	2	3	4	5
Sep	3	4	5	6	7	8	9	1	2	3	4	5	6	7	8	9	1	2	3	4	5	6	7	8	9	1	2	3	4	5	
Oct	4	5	6	7	8	9	1	2	3	4	5	6	7	8	9	1	2	3	4	5	6	7	8	9	1	2	3	4	5	6	7
Nov	5	6	7	8	9	1	2	3	4	5	6	7	8	9	1	2	3	4	5	6	7	8	9	1	2	3	4	5	6	7	
Dec	6	7	8	9	1	2	3	4	5	6	7	8	9	1	2	3	4	5	6	7	8	9	1	2	3	4	5	6	7	8	9

FEBRUARY 27

	1	2	3	4	5	6	7	8	9	10	11	12	13	14	15	16	17	18	19	20	21	22	23	24	25	26	27	28	29	30	31
Jan	4	5	6	7	8	9	1	2	3	4	5	6	7	8	9	1	2	3	4	5	6	7	8	9	1	2	3	4	5	6	7
Feb	5	6	7	8	9	1	2	3	4	5	6	7	8	9	1	2	3	4	5	6	7	8	9	1	2	3	5	6	7		
Mar	7	8	9	1	2	3	4	5	6	7	8	9	1	2	3	4	5	6	7	8	9	1	2	3	4	5	6	7	8	9	1
Apr	8	9	1	2	3	4	5	6	7	8	9	1	2	3	4	5	6	7	8	9	1	2	3	4	5	6	7	8	9	1	
May	9	1	2	3	4	5	6	7	8	9	1	2	3	4	5	6	7	8	9	1	2	3	4	5	6	7	8	9	1	2	3
Jun	1	2	3	4	5	6	7	8	9	1	2	3	4	5	6	7	8	9	1	2	3	4	5	6	7	8	9	1	2	3	
Jul	2	3	4	5	6	7	8	9	1	2	3	4	5	6	7	8	9	1	2	3	4	5	6	7	8	9	1	2	3	4	5
Aug	3	4	5	6	7	8	9	1	2	3	4	5	6	7	8	9	1	2	3	4	5	6	7	8	9	1	2	3	4	5	6
Sep	4	5	6	7	8	9	1	2	3	4	5	6	7	8	9	1	2	3	4	5	6	7	8	9	1	2	3	4	5	6	
Oct	5	6	7	8	9	1	2	3	4	5	6	7	8	9	1	2	3	4	5	6	7	8	9	1	2	3	4	5	6	7	8
Nov	6	7	8	9	1	2	3	4	5	6	7	8	9	1	2	3	4	5	6	7	8	9	1	2	3	4	5	6	7	8	
Dec	7	8	9	1	2	3	4	5	6	7	8	9	1	2	3	4	5	6	7	8	9	1	2	3	4	5	6	7	8	9	1

FEBRUARY 28

	1	2	3	4	5	6	7	8	9	10	11	12	13	14	15	16	17	18	19	20	21	22	23	24	25	26	27	28	29	30	31
Jan	5	6	7	8	9	1	2	3	4	5	6	7	8	9	1	2	3	4	5	6	7	8	9	1	2	3	4	5	6	7	8
Feb	6	7	8	9	1	2	3	4	5	6	7	8	9	1	2	3	4	5	6	7	8	9	1	2	3	4	5	7	8		
Mar	8	9	1	2	3	4	5	6	7	8	9	1	2	3	4	5	6	7	8	9	1	2	3	4	5	6	7	8	9	1	2
Apr	9	1	2	3	4	5	6	7	8	9	1	2	3	4	5	6	7	8	9	1	2	3	4	5	6	7	8	9	1	2	
May	1	2	3	4	5	6	7	8	9	1	2	3	4	5	6	7	8	9	1	2	3	4	5	6	7	8	9	1	2	3	4
Jun	2	3	4	5	6	7	8	9	1	2	3	4	5	6	7	8	9	1	2	3	4	5	6	7	8	9	1	2	3	4	
Jul	3	4	5	6	7	8	9	1	2	3	4	5	6	7	8	9	1	2	3	4	5	6	7	8	9	1	2	3	4	5	6
Aug	4	5	6	7	8	9	1	2	3	4	5	6	7	8	9	1	2	3	4	5	6	7	8	9	1	2	3	4	5	6	7
Sep	5	6	7	8	9	1	2	3	4	5	6	7	8	9	1	2	3	4	5	6	7	8	9	1	2	3	4	5	6	7	
Oct	6	7	8	9	1	2	3	4	5	6	7	8	9	1	2	3	4	5	6	7	8	9	1	2	3	4	5	6	7	8	9
Nov	7	8	9	1	2	3	4	5	6	7	8	9	1	2	3	4	5	6	7	8	9	1	2	3	4	5	6	7	8	9	
Dec	8	9	1	2	3	4	5	6	7	8	9	1	2	3	4	5	6	7	8	9	1	2	3	4	5	6	7	8	9	1	2

FEBRUARY 29

	1	2	3	4	5	6	7	8	9	10	11	12	13	14	15	16	17	18	19	20	21	22	23	24	25	26	27	28	29	30	31
Jan	6	7	8	9	1	2	3	4	5	6	7	8	9	1	2	3	4	5	6	7	8	9	1	2	3	4	5	6	7	8	9
Feb	7	8	9	1	2	3	4	5	6	7	8	9	1	2	3	4	5	6	7	8	9	1	2	3	4	5	6	7	9		
Mar	9	1	2	3	4	5	6	7	8	9	1	2	3	4	5	6	7	8	9	1	2	3	4	5	6	7	8	9	1	2	3
Apr	1	2	3	4	5	6	7	8	9	1	2	3	4	5	6	7	8	9	1	2	3	4	5	6	7	8	9	1	2	3	
May	2	3	4	5	6	7	8	9	1	2	3	4	5	6	7	8	9	1	2	3	4	5	6	7	8	9	1	2	3	4	5
Jun	3	4	5	6	7	8	9	1	2	3	4	5	6	7	8	9	1	2	3	4	5	6	7	8	9	1	2	3	4	5	
Jul	4	5	6	7	8	9	1	2	3	4	5	6	7	8	9	1	2	3	4	5	6	7	8	9	1	2	3	4	5	6	7
Aug	5	6	7	8	9	1	2	3	4	5	6	7	8	9	1	2	3	4	5	6	7	8	9	1	2	3	4	5	6	7	8
Sep	6	7	8	9	1	2	3	4	5	6	7	8	9	1	2	3	4	5	6	7	8	9	1	2	3	4	5	6	7	8	
Oct	7	8	9	1	2	3	4	5	6	7	8	9	1	2	3	4	5	6	7	8	9	1	2	3	4	5	6	7	8	9	1
Nov	8	9	1	2	3	4	5	6	7	8	9	1	2	3	4	5	6	7	8	9	1	2	3	4	5	6	7	8	9	1	
Dec	9	1	2	3	4	5	6	7	8	9	1	2	3	4	5	6	7	8	9	1	2	3	4	5	6	7	8	9	1	2	3

MARCH 1

	1	2	3	4	5	6	7	8	9	10	11	12	13	14	15	16	17	18	19	20	21	22	23	24	25	26	27	28	29	30	31
Jan	6	7	8	9	1	2	3	4	5	6	7	8	9	1	2	3	4	5	6	7	8	9	1	2	3	4	5	6	7	8	9
Feb	7	8	9	1	2	3	4	5	6	7	8	9	1	2	3	4	5	6	7	8	9	1	2	3	4	5	6	7	8		
Mar	9	1	2	3	4	5	6	7	8	9	1	2	3	4	5	6	7	8	9	1	2	3	4	5	6	7	8	9	1	2	3
Apr	1	2	3	4	5	6	7	8	9	1	2	3	4	5	6	7	8	9	1	2	3	4	5	6	7	8	9	1	2	3	
May	2	3	4	5	6	7	8	9	1	2	3	4	5	6	7	8	9	1	2	3	4	5	6	7	8	9	1	2	3	4	5
Jun	3	4	5	6	7	8	9	1	2	3	4	5	6	7	8	9	1	2	3	4	5	6	7	8	9	1	2	3	4	5	
Jul	4	5	6	7	8	9	1	2	3	4	5	6	7	8	9	1	2	3	4	5	6	7	8	9	1	2	3	4	5	6	7
Aug	5	6	7	8	9	1	2	3	4	5	6	7	8	9	1	2	3	4	5	6	7	8	9	1	2	3	4	5	6	7	8
Sep	6	7	8	9	1	2	3	4	5	6	7	8	9	1	2	3	4	5	6	7	8	9	1	2	3	4	5	6	7	8	
Oct	7	8	9	1	2	3	4	5	6	7	8	9	1	2	3	4	5	6	7	8	9	1	2	3	4	5	6	7	8	9	1
Nov	8	9	1	2	3	4	5	6	7	8	9	1	2	3	4	5	6	7	8	9	1	2	3	4	5	6	7	8	9	1	
Dec	9	1	2	3	4	5	6	7	8	9	1	2	3	4	5	6	7	8	9	1	2	3	4	5	6	7	8	9	1	2	3

MARCH 2

	1	2	3	4	5	6	7	8	9	10	11	12	13	14	15	16	17	18	19	20	21	22	23	24	25	26	27	28	29	30	31
Jan	7	8	9	1	2	3	4	5	6	7	8	9	1	2	3	4	5	6	7	8	9	1	2	3	4	5	6	7	8	9	1
Feb	8	9	1	2	3	4	5	6	7	8	9	1	2	3	4	5	6	7	8	9	1	2	3	4	5	6	7	8	9		
Mar	9	2	3	4	5	6	7	8	9	1	2	3	4	5	6	7	8	9	1	2	3	4	5	6	7	8	9	1	2	3	4
Apr	2	3	4	5	6	7	8	9	1	2	3	4	5	6	7	8	9	1	2	3	4	5	6	7	8	9	1	2	3	4	
May	3	4	5	6	7	8	9	1	2	3	4	5	6	7	8	9	1	2	3	4	5	6	7	8	9	1	2	3	4	5	6
Jun	4	5	6	7	8	9	1	2	3	4	5	6	7	8	9	1	2	3	4	5	6	7	8	9	1	2	3	4	5	6	
Jul	5	6	7	8	9	1	2	3	4	5	6	7	8	9	1	2	3	4	5	6	7	8	9	1	2	3	4	5	6	7	8
Aug	6	7	8	9	1	2	3	4	5	6	7	8	9	1	2	3	4	5	6	7	8	9	1	2	3	4	5	6	7	8	9
Sep	7	8	9	1	2	3	4	5	6	7	8	9	1	2	3	4	5	6	7	8	9	1	2	3	4	5	6	7	8	9	
Oct	8	9	1	2	3	4	5	6	7	8	9	1	2	3	4	5	6	7	8	9	1	2	3	4	5	6	7	8	9	1	2
Nov	9	1	2	3	4	5	6	7	8	9	1	2	3	4	5	6	7	8	9	1	2	3	4	5	6	7	8	9	1	2	
Dec	1	2	3	4	5	6	7	8	9	1	2	3	4	5	6	7	8	9	1	2	3	4	5	6	7	8	9	1	2	3	4

MARCH 3

	1	2	3	4	5	6	7	8	9	10	11	12	13	14	15	16	17	18	19	20	21	22	23	24	25	26	27	28	29	30	31
Jan	8	9	1	2	3	4	5	6	7	8	9	1	2	3	4	5	6	7	8	9	1	2	3	4	5	6	7	8	9	1	2
Feb	9	1	2	3	4	5	6	7	8	9	1	2	3	4	5	6	7	8	9	1	2	3	4	5	6	7	8	9	1		
Mar	1	2	4	5	6	7	8	9	1	2	3	4	5	6	7	8	9	1	2	3	4	5	6	7	8	9	1	2	3	4	5
Apr	3	4	5	6	7	8	9	1	2	3	4	5	6	7	8	9	1	2	3	4	5	6	7	8	9	1	2	3	4	5	
May	4	5	6	7	8	9	1	2	3	4	5	6	7	8	9	1	2	3	4	5	6	7	8	9	1	2	3	4	5	6	7
Jun	5	6	7	8	9	1	2	3	4	5	6	7	8	9	1	2	3	4	5	6	7	8	9	1	2	3	4	5	6	7	
Jul	6	7	8	9	1	2	3	4	5	6	7	8	9	1	2	3	4	5	6	7	8	9	1	2	3	4	5	6	7	8	9
Aug	7	8	9	1	2	3	4	5	6	7	8	9	1	2	3	4	5	6	7	8	9	1	2	3	4	5	6	7	8	9	1
Sep	8	9	1	2	3	4	5	6	7	8	9	1	2	3	4	5	6	7	8	9	1	2	3	4	5	6	7	8	9	1	
Oct	9	1	2	3	4	5	6	7	8	9	1	2	3	4	5	6	7	8	9	1	2	3	4	5	6	7	8	9	1	2	3
Nov	1	2	3	4	5	6	7	8	9	1	2	3	4	5	6	7	8	9	1	2	3	4	5	6	7	8	9	1	2	3	
Dec	2	3	4	5	6	7	8	9	1	2	3	4	5	6	7	8	9	1	2	3	4	5	6	7	8	9	1	2	3	4	5

MARCH 4

	1	2	3	4	5	6	7	8	9	10	11	12	13	14	15	16	17	18	19	20	21	22	23	24	25	26	27	28	29	30	31
Jan	9	1	2	3	4	5	6	7	8	9	1	2	3	4	5	6	7	8	9	1	2	3	4	5	6	7	8	9	1	2	3
Feb	1	2	3	4	5	6	7	8	9	1	2	3	4	5	6	7	8	9	1	2	3	4	5	6	7	8	9	1	2		
Mar	2	3	4	6	7	8	9	1	2	3	4	5	6	7	8	9	1	2	3	4	5	6	7	8	9	1	2	3	4	5	6
Apr	4	5	6	7	8	9	1	2	3	4	5	6	7	8	9	1	2	3	4	5	6	7	8	9	1	2	3	4	5	6	
May	5	6	7	8	9	1	2	3	4	5	6	7	8	9	1	2	3	4	5	6	7	8	9	1	2	3	4	5	6	7	8
Jun	6	7	8	9	1	2	3	4	5	6	7	8	9	1	2	3	4	5	6	7	8	9	1	2	3	4	5	6	7	8	
Jul	7	8	9	1	2	3	4	5	6	7	8	9	1	2	3	4	5	6	7	8	9	1	2	3	4	5	6	7	8	9	1
Aug	8	9	1	2	3	4	5	6	7	8	9	1	2	3	4	5	6	7	8	9	1	2	3	4	5	6	7	8	9	1	2
Sep	9	1	2	3	4	5	6	7	8	9	1	2	3	4	5	6	7	8	9	1	2	3	4	5	6	7	8	9	1	2	
Oct	1	2	3	4	5	6	7	8	9	1	2	3	4	5	6	7	8	9	1	2	3	4	5	6	7	8	9	1	2	3	4
Nov	2	3	4	5	6	7	8	9	1	2	3	4	5	6	7	8	9	1	2	3	4	5	6	7	8	9	1	2	3	4	
Dec	3	4	5	6	7	8	9	1	2	3	4	5	6	7	8	9	1	2	3	4	5	6	7	8	9	1	2	3	4	5	6

MARCH 5

	1	2	3	4	5	6	7	8	9	10	11	12	13	14	15	16	17	18	19	20	21	22	23	24	25	26	27	28	29	30	31
Jan	1	2	3	4	5	6	7	8	9	1	2	3	4	5	6	7	8	9	1	2	3	4	5	6	7	8	9	1	2	3	4
Feb	2	3	4	5	6	7	8	9	1	2	3	4	5	6	7	8	9	1	2	3	4	5	6	7	8	9	1	2	3		
Mar	3	4	5	6	8	9	1	2	3	4	5	6	7	8	9	1	2	3	4	5	6	7	8	9	1	2	3	4	5	6	7
Apr	5	6	7	8	9	1	2	3	4	5	6	7	8	9	1	2	3	4	5	6	7	8	9	1	2	3	4	5	6	7	
May	6	7	8	9	1	2	3	4	5	6	7	8	9	1	2	3	4	5	6	7	8	9	1	2	3	4	5	6	7	8	9
Jun	7	8	9	1	2	3	4	5	6	7	8	9	1	2	3	4	5	6	7	8	9	1	2	3	4	5	6	7	8	9	
Jul	8	9	1	2	3	4	5	6	7	8	9	1	2	3	4	5	6	7	8	9	1	2	3	4	5	6	7	8	9	1	2
Aug	9	1	2	3	4	5	6	7	8	9	1	2	3	4	5	6	7	8	9	1	2	3	4	5	6	7	8	9	1	2	3
Sep	1	2	3	4	5	6	7	8	9	1	2	3	4	5	6	7	8	9	1	2	3	4	5	6	7	8	9	1	2	3	
Oct	2	3	4	5	6	7	8	9	1	2	3	4	5	6	7	8	9	1	2	3	4	5	6	7	8	9	1	2	3	4	5
Nov	3	4	5	6	7	8	9	1	2	3	4	5	6	7	8	9	1	2	3	4	5	6	7	8	9	1	2	3	4	5	
Dec	4	5	6	7	8	9	1	2	3	4	5	6	7	8	9	1	2	3	4	5	6	7	8	9	1	2	3	4	5	6	7

MARCH 6

	1	2	3	4	5	6	7	8	9	10	11	12	13	14	15	16	17	18	19	20	21	22	23	24	25	26	27	28	29	30	31
Jan	2	3	4	5	6	7	8	9	1	2	3	4	5	6	7	8	9	1	2	3	4	5	6	7	8	9	1	2	3	4	5
Feb	3	4	5	6	7	8	9	1	2	3	4	5	6	7	8	9	1	2	3	4	5	6	7	8	9	1	2	3	4		
Mar	4	5	6	7	8	1	2	3	4	5	6	7	8	9	1	2	3	4	5	6	7	8	9	1	2	3	4	5	6	7	8
Apr	6	7	8	9	1	2	3	4	5	6	7	8	9	1	2	3	4	5	6	7	8	9	1	2	3	4	5	6	7	8	
May	7	8	9	1	2	3	4	5	6	7	8	9	1	2	3	4	5	6	7	8	9	1	2	3	4	5	6	7	8	9	1
Jun	8	9	1	2	3	4	5	6	7	8	9	1	2	3	4	5	6	7	8	9	1	2	3	4	5	6	7	8	9	1	
Jul	9	1	2	3	4	5	6	7	8	9	1	2	3	4	5	6	7	8	9	1	2	3	4	5	6	7	8	9	1	2	3
Aug	1	2	3	4	5	6	7	8	9	1	2	3	4	5	6	7	8	9	1	2	3	4	5	6	7	8	9	1	2	3	4
Sep	2	3	4	5	6	7	8	9	1	2	3	4	5	6	7	8	9	1	2	3	4	5	6	7	8	9	1	2	3	4	
Oct	3	4	5	6	7	8	9	1	2	3	4	5	6	7	8	9	1	2	3	4	5	6	7	8	9	1	2	3	4	5	6
Nov	4	5	6	7	8	9	1	2	3	4	5	6	7	8	9	1	2	3	4	5	6	7	8	9	1	2	3	4	5	6	
Dec	5	6	7	8	9	1	2	3	4	5	6	7	8	9	1	2	3	4	5	6	7	8	9	1	2	3	4	5	6	7	8

MARCH 7

	1	2	3	4	5	6	7	8	9	10	11	12	13	14	15	16	17	18	19	20	21	22	23	24	25	26	27	28	29	30	31
Jan	3	4	5	6	7	8	9	1	2	3	4	5	6	7	8	9	1	2	3	4	5	6	7	8	9	1	2	3	4	5	6
Feb	4	5	6	7	8	9	1	2	3	4	5	6	7	8	9	1	2	3	4	5	6	7	8	9	1	2	3	4	5		
Mar	5	6	7	8	9	1	3	4	5	6	7	8	9	1	2	3	4	5	6	7	8	9	1	2	3	4	5	6	7	8	9
Apr	7	8	9	1	2	3	4	5	6	7	8	9	1	2	3	4	5	6	7	8	9	1	2	3	4	5	6	7	8	9	
May	8	9	1	2	3	4	5	6	7	8	9	1	2	3	4	5	6	7	8	9	1	2	3	4	5	6	7	8	9	1	2
Jun	9	1	2	3	4	5	6	7	8	9	1	2	3	4	5	6	7	8	9	1	2	3	4	5	6	7	8	9	1	2	
Jul	1	2	3	4	5	6	7	8	9	1	2	3	4	5	6	7	8	9	1	2	3	4	5	6	7	8	9	1	2	3	4
Aug	2	3	4	5	6	7	8	9	1	2	3	4	5	6	7	8	9	1	2	3	4	5	6	7	8	9	1	2	3	4	5
Sep	3	4	5	6	7	8	9	1	2	3	4	5	6	7	8	9	1	2	3	4	5	6	7	8	9	1	2	3	4	5	
Oct	4	5	6	7	8	9	1	2	3	4	5	6	7	8	9	1	2	3	4	5	6	7	8	9	1	2	3	4	5	6	7
Nov	5	6	7	8	9	1	2	3	4	5	6	7	8	9	1	2	3	4	5	6	7	8	9	1	2	3	4	5	6	7	
Dec	6	7	8	9	1	2	3	4	5	6	7	8	9	1	2	3	4	5	6	7	8	9	1	2	3	4	5	6	7	8	9

MARCH 8

	1	2	3	4	5	6	7	8	9	10	11	12	13	14	15	16	17	18	19	20	21	22	23	24	25	26	27	28	29	30	31
Jan	4	5	6	7	8	9	1	2	3	4	5	6	7	8	9	1	2	3	4	5	6	7	8	9	1	2	3	4	5	6	7
Feb	5	6	7	8	9	1	2	3	4	5	6	7	8	9	1	2	3	4	5	6	7	8	9	1	2	3	4	5	6		
Mar	6	7	8	9	1	2	3	5	6	7	8	9	1	2	3	4	5	6	7	8	9	1	2	3	4	5	6	7	8	9	1
Apr	8	9	1	2	3	4	5	6	7	8	9	1	2	3	4	5	6	7	8	9	1	2	3	4	5	6	7	8	9	1	
May	9	1	2	3	4	5	6	7	8	9	1	2	3	4	5	6	7	8	9	1	2	3	4	5	6	7	8	9	1	2	3
Jun	1	2	3	4	5	6	7	8	9	1	2	3	4	5	6	7	8	9	1	2	3	4	5	6	7	8	9	1	2	3	
Jul	2	3	4	5	6	7	8	9	1	2	3	4	5	6	7	8	9	1	2	3	4	5	6	7	8	9	1	2	3	4	5
Aug	3	4	5	6	7	8	9	1	2	3	4	5	6	7	8	9	1	2	3	4	5	6	7	8	9	1	2	3	4	5	6
Sep	4	5	6	7	8	9	1	2	3	4	5	6	7	8	9	1	2	3	4	5	6	7	8	9	1	2	3	4	5	6	
Oct	5	6	7	8	9	1	2	3	4	5	6	7	8	9	1	2	3	4	5	6	7	8	9	1	2	3	4	5	6	7	8
Nov	6	7	8	9	1	2	3	4	5	6	7	8	9	1	2	3	4	5	6	7	8	9	1	2	3	4	5	6	7	8	
Dec	7	8	9	1	2	3	4	5	6	7	8	9	1	2	3	4	5	6	7	8	9	1	2	3	4	5	6	7	8	9	1

MARCH 9

	1	2	3	4	5	6	7	8	9	10	11	12	13	14	15	16	17	18	19	20	21	22	23	24	25	26	27	28	29	30	31
Jan	5	6	7	8	9	1	2	3	4	5	6	7	8	9	1	2	3	4	5	6	7	8	9	1	2	3	4	5	6	7	8
Feb	6	7	8	9	1	2	3	4	5	6	7	8	9	1	2	3	4	5	6	7	8	9	1	2	3	4	5	6	7		
Mar	7	8	9	1	2	3	4	5	7	8	9	1	2	3	4	5	6	7	8	9	1	2	3	4	5	6	7	8	9	1	2
Apr	9	1	2	3	4	5	6	7	8	9	1	2	3	4	5	6	7	8	9	1	2	3	4	5	6	7	8	9	1	2	
May	1	2	3	4	5	6	7	8	9	1	2	3	4	5	6	7	8	9	1	2	3	4	5	6	7	8	9	1	2	3	4
Jun	2	3	4	5	6	7	8	9	1	2	3	4	5	6	7	8	9	1	2	3	4	5	6	7	8	9	1	2	3	4	
Jul	3	4	5	6	7	8	9	1	2	3	4	5	6	7	8	9	1	2	3	4	5	6	7	8	9	1	2	3	4	5	6
Aug	4	5	6	7	8	9	1	2	3	4	5	6	7	8	9	1	2	3	4	5	6	7	8	9	1	2	3	4	5	6	7
Sep	5	6	7	8	9	1	2	3	4	5	6	7	8	9	1	2	3	4	5	6	7	8	9	1	2	3	4	5	6	7	
Oct	6	7	8	9	1	2	3	4	5	6	7	8	9	1	2	3	4	5	6	7	8	9	1	2	3	4	5	6	7	8	9
Nov	7	8	9	1	2	3	4	5	6	7	8	9	1	2	3	4	5	6	7	8	9	1	2	3	4	5	6	7	8	9	
Dec	8	9	1	2	3	4	5	6	7	8	9	1	2	3	4	5	6	7	8	9	1	2	3	4	5	6	7	8	9	1	2

MARCH 10

	1	2	3	4	5	6	7	8	9	10	11	12	13	14	15	16	17	18	19	20	21	22	23	24	25	26	27	28	29	30	31
Jan	6	7	8	9	1	2	3	4	5	6	7	8	9	1	2	3	4	5	6	7	8	9	1	2	3	4	5	6	7	8	9
Feb	7	8	9	1	2	3	4	5	6	7	8	9	1	2	3	4	5	6	7	8	9	1	2	3	4	5	6	7	8		
Mar	8	9	1	2	3	4	5	6	7	9	1	2	3	4	5	6	7	8	9	1	2	3	4	5	6	7	8	9	1	2	3
Apr	1	2	3	4	5	6	7	8	9	1	2	3	4	5	6	7	8	9	1	2	3	4	5	6	7	8	9	1	2	3	
May	2	3	4	5	6	7	8	9	1	2	3	4	5	6	7	8	9	1	2	3	4	5	6	7	8	9	1	2	3	4	5
Jun	3	4	5	6	7	8	9	1	2	3	4	5	6	7	8	9	1	2	3	4	5	6	7	8	9	1	2	3	4	5	
Jul	4	5	6	7	8	9	1	2	3	4	5	6	7	8	9	1	2	3	4	5	6	7	8	9	1	2	3	4	5	6	7
Aug	5	6	7	8	9	1	2	3	4	5	6	7	8	9	1	2	3	4	5	6	7	8	9	1	2	3	4	5	6	7	8
Sep	6	7	8	9	1	2	3	4	5	6	7	8	9	1	2	3	4	5	6	7	8	9	1	2	3	4	5	6	7	8	
Oct	7	8	9	1	2	3	4	5	6	7	8	9	1	2	3	4	5	6	7	8	9	1	2	3	4	5	6	7	8	9	1
Nov	8	9	1	2	3	4	5	6	7	8	9	1	2	3	4	5	6	7	8	9	1	2	3	4	5	6	7	8	9	1	
Dec	9	1	2	3	4	5	6	7	8	9	1	2	3	4	5	6	7	8	9	1	2	3	4	5	6	7	8	9	1	2	3

MARCH 11

	1	2	3	4	5	6	7	8	9	10	11	12	13	14	15	16	17	18	19	20	21	22	23	24	25	26	27	28	29	30	31
Jan	7	8	9	1	2	3	4	5	6	7	8	9	1	2	3	4	5	6	7	8	9	1	2	3	4	5	6	7	8	9	1
Feb	8	9	1	2	3	4	5	6	7	8	9	1	2	3	4	5	6	7	8	9	1	2	3	4	5	6	7	8	9		
Mar	9	1	2	3	4	5	6	7	8	9	2	3	4	5	6	7	8	9	1	2	3	4	5	6	7	8	9	1	2	3	4
Apr	2	3	4	5	6	7	8	9	1	2	3	4	5	6	7	8	9	1	2	3	4	5	6	7	8	9	1	2	3	4	
May	3	4	5	6	7	8	9	1	2	3	4	5	6	7	8	9	1	2	3	4	5	6	7	8	9	1	2	3	4	5	6
Jun	4	5	6	7	8	9	1	2	3	4	5	6	7	8	9	1	2	3	4	5	6	7	8	9	1	2	3	4	5	6	
Jul	5	6	7	8	9	1	2	3	4	5	6	7	8	9	1	2	3	4	5	6	7	8	9	1	2	3	4	5	6	7	8
Aug	6	7	8	9	1	2	3	4	5	6	7	8	9	1	2	3	4	5	6	7	8	9	1	2	3	4	5	6	7	8	9
Sep	7	8	9	1	2	3	4	5	6	7	8	9	1	2	3	4	5	6	7	8	9	1	2	3	4	5	6	7	8	9	
Oct	8	9	1	2	3	4	5	6	7	8	9	1	2	3	4	5	6	7	8	9	1	2	3	4	5	6	7	8	9	1	2
Nov	9	1	2	3	4	5	6	7	8	9	1	2	3	4	5	6	7	8	9	1	2	3	4	5	6	7	8	9	1	2	
Dec	1	2	3	4	5	6	7	8	9	1	2	3	4	5	6	7	8	9	1	2	3	4	5	6	7	8	9	1	2	3	4

MARCH 12

	1	2	3	4	5	6	7	8	9	10	11	12	13	14	15	16	17	18	19	20	21	22	23	24	25	26	27	28	29	30	31
Jan	8	9	1	2	3	4	5	6	7	8	9	1	2	3	4	5	6	7	8	9	1	2	3	4	5	6	7	8	9	1	2
Feb	9	1	2	3	4	5	6	7	8	9	1	2	3	4	5	6	7	8	9	1	2	3	4	5	6	7	8	9	1		
Mar	1	2	3	4	5	6	7	8	9	1	2	4	5	6	7	8	9	1	2	3	4	5	6	7	8	9	1	2	3	4	5
Apr	3	4	5	6	7	8	9	1	2	3	4	5	6	7	8	9	1	2	3	4	5	6	7	8	9	1	2	3	4	5	
May	4	5	6	7	8	9	1	2	3	4	5	6	7	8	9	1	2	3	4	5	6	7	8	9	1	2	3	4	5	6	7
Jun	5	6	7	8	9	1	2	3	4	5	6	7	8	9	1	2	3	4	5	6	7	8	9	1	2	3	4	5	6	7	
Jul	6	7	8	9	1	2	3	4	5	6	7	8	9	1	2	3	4	5	6	7	8	9	1	2	3	4	5	6	7	8	9
Aug	7	8	9	1	2	3	4	5	6	7	8	9	1	2	3	4	5	6	7	8	9	1	2	3	4	5	6	7	8	9	1
Sep	8	9	1	2	3	4	5	6	7	8	9	1	2	3	4	5	6	7	8	9	1	2	3	4	5	6	7	8	9	1	
Oct	9	1	2	3	4	5	6	7	8	9	1	2	3	4	5	6	7	8	9	1	2	3	4	5	6	7	8	9	1	2	3
Nov	1	2	3	4	5	6	7	8	9	1	2	3	4	5	6	7	8	9	1	2	3	4	5	6	7	8	9	1	2	3	
Dec	2	3	4	5	6	7	8	9	1	2	3	4	5	6	7	8	9	1	2	3	4	5	6	7	8	9	1	2	3	4	5

MARCH 13

	1	2	3	4	5	6	7	8	9	10	11	12	13	14	15	16	17	18	19	20	21	22	23	24	25	26	27	28	29	30	31
Jan	9	1	2	3	4	5	6	7	8	9	1	2	3	4	5	6	7	8	9	1	2	3	4	5	6	7	8	9	1	2	3
Feb	1	2	3	4	5	6	7	8	9	1	2	3	4	5	6	7	8	9	1	2	3	4	5	6	7	8	9	1	2		
Mar	2	3	4	5	6	7	8	9	1	2	3	4	6	7	8	9	1	2	3	4	5	6	7	8	9	1	2	3	4	5	6
Apr	4	5	6	7	8	9	1	2	3	4	5	6	7	8	9	1	2	3	4	5	6	7	8	9	1	2	3	4	5	6	
May	5	6	7	8	9	1	2	3	4	5	6	7	8	9	1	2	3	4	5	6	7	8	9	1	2	3	4	5	6	7	8
Jun	6	7	8	9	1	2	3	4	5	6	7	8	9	1	2	3	4	5	6	7	8	9	1	2	3	4	5	6	7	8	
Jul	7	8	9	1	2	3	4	5	6	7	8	9	1	2	3	4	5	6	7	8	9	1	2	3	4	5	6	7	8	9	1
Aug	8	9	1	2	3	4	5	6	7	8	9	1	2	3	4	5	6	7	8	9	1	2	3	4	5	6	7	8	9	1	2
Sep	9	1	2	3	4	5	6	7	8	9	1	2	3	4	5	6	7	8	9	1	2	3	4	5	6	7	8	9	1	2	
Oct	1	2	3	4	5	6	7	8	9	1	2	3	4	5	6	7	8	9	1	2	3	4	5	6	7	8	9	1	2	3	4
Nov	2	3	4	5	6	7	8	9	1	2	3	4	5	6	7	8	9	1	2	3	4	5	6	7	8	9	1	2	3	4	
Dec	3	4	5	6	7	8	9	1	2	3	4	5	6	7	8	9	1	2	3	4	5	6	7	8	9	1	2	3	4	5	6

MARCH 14

	1	2	3	4	5	6	7	8	9	10	11	12	13	14	15	16	17	18	19	20	21	22	23	24	25	26	27	28	29	30	31
Jan	1	2	3	4	5	6	7	8	9	1	2	3	4	5	6	7	8	9	1	2	3	4	5	6	7	8	9	1	2	3	4
Feb	2	3	4	5	6	7	8	9	1	2	3	4	5	6	7	8	9	1	2	3	4	5	6	7	8	9	1	2	3		
Mar	3	4	5	6	7	8	9	1	2	3	4	5	6	8	9	1	2	3	4	5	6	7	8	9	1	2	3	4	5	6	7
Apr	5	6	7	8	9	1	2	3	4	5	6	7	8	9	1	2	3	4	5	6	7	8	9	1	2	3	4	5	6	7	
May	6	7	8	9	1	2	3	4	5	6	7	8	9	1	2	3	4	5	6	7	8	9	1	2	3	4	5	6	7	8	9
Jun	7	8	9	1	2	3	4	5	6	7	8	9	1	2	3	4	5	6	7	8	9	1	2	3	4	5	6	7	8	9	
Jul	8	9	1	2	3	4	5	6	7	8	9	1	2	3	4	5	6	7	8	9	1	2	3	4	5	6	7	8	9	1	2
Aug	9	1	2	3	4	5	6	7	8	9	1	2	3	4	5	6	7	8	9	1	2	3	4	5	6	7	8	9	1	2	3
Sep	1	2	3	4	5	6	7	8	9	1	2	3	4	5	6	7	8	9	1	2	3	4	5	6	7	8	9	1	2	3	
Oct	2	3	4	5	6	7	8	9	1	2	3	4	5	6	7	8	9	1	2	3	4	5	6	7	8	9	1	2	3	4	5
Nov	3	4	5	6	7	8	9	1	2	3	4	5	6	7	8	9	1	2	3	4	5	6	7	8	9	1	2	3	4	5	
Dec	4	5	6	7	8	9	1	2	3	4	5	6	7	8	9	1	2	3	4	5	6	7	8	9	1	2	3	4	5	6	7

MARCH 15

	1	2	3	4	5	6	7	8	9	10	11	12	13	14	15	16	17	18	19	20	21	22	23	24	25	26	27	28	29	30	31
Jan	2	3	4	5	6	7	8	9	1	2	3	4	5	6	7	8	9	1	2	3	4	5	6	7	8	9	1	2	3	4	5
Feb	3	4	5	6	7	8	9	1	2	3	4	5	6	7	8	9	1	2	3	4	5	6	7	8	9	1	2	3	4		
Mar	4	5	6	7	8	9	1	2	3	4	5	6	7	8	1	2	3	4	5	6	7	8	9	1	2	3	4	5	6	7	8
Apr	6	7	8	9	1	2	3	4	5	6	7	8	9	1	2	3	4	5	6	7	8	9	1	2	3	4	5	6	7	8	
May	7	8	9	1	2	3	4	5	6	7	8	9	1	2	3	4	5	6	7	8	9	1	2	3	4	5	6	7	8	9	1
Jun	8	9	1	2	3	4	5	6	7	8	9	1	2	3	4	5	6	7	8	9	1	2	3	4	5	6	7	8	9	1	
Jul	9	1	2	3	4	5	6	7	8	9	1	2	3	4	5	6	7	8	9	1	2	3	4	5	6	7	8	9	1	2	3
Aug	1	2	3	4	5	6	7	8	9	1	2	3	4	5	6	7	8	9	1	2	3	4	5	6	7	8	9	1	2	3	4
Sep	2	3	4	5	6	7	8	9	1	2	3	4	5	6	7	8	9	1	2	3	4	5	6	7	8	9	1	2	3	4	
Oct	3	4	5	6	7	8	9	1	2	3	4	5	6	7	8	9	1	2	3	4	5	6	7	8	9	1	2	3	4	5	6
Nov	4	5	6	7	8	9	1	2	3	4	5	6	7	8	9	1	2	3	4	5	6	7	8	9	1	2	3	4	5	6	
Dec	5	6	7	8	9	1	2	3	4	5	6	7	8	9	1	2	3	4	5	6	7	8	9	1	2	3	4	5	6	7	8

MARCH 16

	1	2	3	4	5	6	7	8	9	10	11	12	13	14	15	16	17	18	19	20	21	22	23	24	25	26	27	28	29	30	31
Jan	3	4	5	6	7	8	9	1	2	3	4	5	6	7	8	9	1	2	3	4	5	6	7	8	9	1	2	3	4	5	6
Feb	4	5	6	7	8	9	1	2	3	4	5	6	7	8	9	1	2	3	4	5	6	7	8	9	1	2	3	4	5		
Mar	5	6	7	8	9	1	2	3	4	5	6	7	8	9	1	3	4	5	6	7	8	9	1	2	3	4	5	6	7	8	9
Apr	7	8	9	1	2	3	4	5	6	7	8	9	1	2	3	4	5	6	7	8	9	1	2	3	4	5	6	7	8	9	
May	8	9	1	2	3	4	5	6	7	8	9	1	2	3	4	5	6	7	8	9	1	2	3	4	5	6	7	8	9	1	2
Jun	9	1	2	3	4	5	6	7	8	9	1	2	3	4	5	6	7	8	9	1	2	3	4	5	6	7	8	9	1	2	
Jul	1	2	3	4	5	6	7	8	9	1	2	3	4	5	6	7	8	9	1	2	3	4	5	6	7	8	9	1	2	3	4
Aug	2	3	4	5	6	7	8	9	1	2	3	4	5	6	7	8	9	1	2	3	4	5	6	7	8	9	1	2	3	4	5
Sep	3	4	5	6	7	8	9	1	2	3	4	5	6	7	8	9	1	2	3	4	5	6	7	8	9	1	2	3	4	5	
Oct	4	5	6	7	8	9	1	2	3	4	5	6	7	8	9	1	2	3	4	5	6	7	8	9	1	2	3	4	5	6	7
Nov	5	6	7	8	9	1	2	3	4	5	6	7	8	9	1	2	3	4	5	6	7	8	9	1	2	3	4	5	6	7	
Dec	6	7	8	9	1	2	3	4	5	6	7	8	9	1	2	3	4	5	6	7	8	9	1	2	3	4	5	6	7	8	9

MARCH 17

	1	2	3	4	5	6	7	8	9	10	11	12	13	14	15	16	17	18	19	20	21	22	23	24	25	26	27	28	29	30	31
Jan	4	5	6	7	8	9	1	2	3	4	5	6	7	8	9	1	2	3	4	5	6	7	8	9	1	2	3	4	5	6	7
Feb	5	6	7	8	9	1	2	3	4	5	6	7	8	9	1	2	3	4	5	6	7	8	9	1	2	3	4	5	6		
Mar	6	7	8	9	1	2	3	4	5	6	7	8	9	1	2	3	5	6	7	8	9	1	2	3	4	5	6	7	8	9	1
Apr	8	9	1	2	3	4	5	6	7	8	9	1	2	3	4	5	6	7	8	9	1	2	3	4	5	6	7	8	9	1	
May	9	1	2	3	4	5	6	7	8	9	1	2	3	4	5	6	7	8	9	1	2	3	4	5	6	7	8	9	1	2	3
Jun	1	2	3	4	5	6	7	8	9	1	2	3	4	5	6	7	8	9	1	2	3	4	5	6	7	8	9	1	2	3	
Jul	2	3	4	5	6	7	8	9	1	2	3	4	5	6	7	8	9	1	2	3	4	5	6	7	8	9	1	2	3	4	5
Aug	3	4	5	6	7	8	9	1	2	3	4	5	6	7	8	9	1	2	3	4	5	6	7	8	9	1	2	3	4	5	6
Sep	4	5	6	7	8	9	1	2	3	4	5	6	7	8	9	1	2	3	4	5	6	7	8	9	1	2	3	4	5	6	
Oct	5	6	7	8	9	1	2	3	4	5	6	7	8	9	1	2	3	4	5	6	7	8	9	1	2	3	4	5	6	7	8
Nov	6	7	8	9	1	2	3	4	5	6	7	8	9	1	2	3	4	5	6	7	8	9	1	2	3	4	5	6	7	8	
Dec	7	8	9	1	2	3	4	5	6	7	8	9	1	2	3	4	5	6	7	8	9	1	2	3	4	5	6	7	8	9	1

MARCH 18

	1	2	3	4	5	6	7	8	9	10	11	12	13	14	15	16	17	18	19	20	21	22	23	24	25	26	27	28	29	30	31
Jan	5	6	7	8	9	1	2	3	4	5	6	7	8	9	1	2	3	4	5	6	7	8	9	1	2	3	4	5	6	7	8
Feb	6	7	8	9	1	2	3	4	5	6	7	8	9	1	2	3	4	5	6	7	8	9	1	2	3	4	5	6	7		
Mar	7	8	9	1	2	3	4	5	6	7	8	9	1	2	3	4	5	7	8	9	1	2	3	4	5	6	7	8	9	1	2
Apr	9	1	2	3	4	5	6	7	8	9	1	2	3	4	5	6	7	8	9	1	2	3	4	5	6	7	8	9	1	2	
May	1	2	3	4	5	6	7	8	9	1	2	3	4	5	6	7	8	9	1	2	3	4	5	6	7	8	9	1	2	3	4
Jun	2	3	4	5	6	7	8	9	1	2	3	4	5	6	7	8	9	1	2	3	4	5	6	7	8	9	1	2	3	4	
Jul	3	4	5	6	7	8	9	1	2	3	4	5	6	7	8	9	1	2	3	4	5	6	7	8	9	1	2	3	4	5	6
Aug	4	5	6	7	8	9	1	2	3	4	5	6	7	8	9	1	2	3	4	5	6	7	8	9	1	2	3	4	5	6	7
Sep	5	6	7	8	9	1	2	3	4	5	6	7	8	9	1	2	3	4	5	6	7	8	9	1	2	3	4	5	6	7	
Oct	6	7	8	9	1	2	3	4	5	6	7	8	9	1	2	3	4	5	6	7	8	9	1	2	3	4	5	6	7	8	9
Nov	7	8	9	1	2	3	4	5	6	7	8	9	1	2	3	4	5	6	7	8	9	1	2	3	4	5	6	7	8	9	
Dec	8	9	1	2	3	4	5	6	7	8	9	1	2	3	4	5	6	7	8	9	1	2	3	4	5	6	7	8	9	1	2

MARCH 19

	1	2	3	4	5	6	7	8	9	10	11	12	13	14	15	16	17	18	19	20	21	22	23	24	25	26	27	28	29	30	31
Jan	6	7	8	9	1	2	3	4	5	6	7	8	9	1	2	3	4	5	6	7	8	9	1	2	3	4	5	6	7	8	9
Feb	7	8	9	1	2	3	4	5	6	7	8	9	1	2	3	4	5	6	7	8	9	1	2	3	4	5	6	7	8		
Mar	8	9	1	2	3	4	5	6	7	8	9	1	2	3	4	5	6	7	9	1	2	3	4	5	6	7	8	9	1	2	3
Apr	1	2	3	4	5	6	7	8	9	1	2	3	4	5	6	7	8	9	1	2	3	4	5	6	7	8	9	1	2	3	
May	2	3	4	5	6	7	8	9	1	2	3	4	5	6	7	8	9	1	2	3	4	5	6	7	8	9	1	2	3	4	5
Jun	3	4	5	6	7	8	9	1	2	3	4	5	6	7	8	9	1	2	3	4	5	6	7	8	9	1	2	3	4	5	
Jul	4	5	6	7	8	9	1	2	3	4	5	6	7	8	9	1	2	3	4	5	6	7	8	9	1	2	3	4	5	6	7
Aug	5	6	7	8	9	1	2	3	4	5	6	7	8	9	1	2	3	4	5	6	7	8	9	1	2	3	4	5	6	7	8
Sep	6	7	8	9	1	2	3	4	5	6	7	8	9	1	2	3	4	5	6	7	8	9	1	2	3	4	5	6	7	8	
Oct	7	8	9	1	2	3	4	5	6	7	8	9	1	2	3	4	5	6	7	8	9	1	2	3	4	5	6	7	8	9	1
Nov	8	9	1	2	3	4	5	6	7	8	9	1	2	3	4	5	6	7	8	9	1	2	3	4	5	6	7	8	9	1	
Dec	9	1	2	3	4	5	6	7	8	9	1	2	3	4	5	6	7	8	9	1	2	3	4	5	6	7	8	9	1	2	3

MARCH 20

	1	2	3	4	5	6	7	8	9	10	11	12	13	14	15	16	17	18	19	20	21	22	23	24	25	26	27	28	29	30	31
Jan	7	8	9	1	2	3	4	5	6	7	8	9	1	2	3	4	5	6	7	8	9	1	2	3	4	5	6	7	8	9	1
Feb	8	9	1	2	3	4	5	6	7	8	9	1	2	3	4	5	6	7	8	9	1	2	3	4	5	6	7	8	9		
Mar	9	1	2	3	4	5	6	7	8	9	1	2	3	4	5	6	7	8	9	2	3	4	5	6	7	8	9	1	2	3	4
Apr	2	3	4	5	6	7	8	9	1	2	3	4	5	6	7	8	9	1	2	3	4	5	6	7	8	9	1	2	3	4	
May	3	4	5	6	7	8	9	1	2	3	4	5	6	7	8	9	1	2	3	4	5	6	7	8	9	1	2	3	4	5	6
Jun	4	5	6	7	8	9	1	2	3	4	5	6	7	8	9	1	2	3	4	5	6	7	8	9	1	2	3	4	5	6	
Jul	5	6	7	8	9	1	2	3	4	5	6	7	8	9	1	2	3	4	5	6	7	8	9	1	2	3	4	5	6	7	8
Aug	6	7	8	9	1	2	3	4	5	6	7	8	9	1	2	3	4	5	6	7	8	9	1	2	3	4	5	6	7	8	9
Sep	7	8	9	1	2	3	4	5	6	7	8	9	1	2	3	4	5	6	7	8	9	1	2	3	4	5	6	7	8	9	
Oct	8	9	1	2	3	4	5	6	7	8	9	1	2	3	4	5	6	7	8	9	1	2	3	4	5	6	7	8	9	1	2
Nov	9	1	2	3	4	5	6	7	8	9	1	2	3	4	5	6	7	8	9	1	2	3	4	5	6	7	8	9	1	2	
Dec	1	2	3	4	5	6	7	8	9	1	2	3	4	5	6	7	8	9	1	2	3	4	5	6	7	8	9	1	2	3	4

MARCH 21

	1	2	3	4	5	6	7	8	9	10	11	12	13	14	15	16	17	18	19	20	21	22	23	24	25	26	27	28	29	30	31
Jan	8	9	1	2	3	4	5	6	7	8	9	1	2	3	4	5	6	7	8	9	1	2	3	4	5	6	7	8	9	1	2
Feb	9	1	2	3	4	5	6	7	8	9	1	2	3	4	5	6	7	8	9	1	2	3	4	5	6	7	8	9	1		
Mar	1	2	3	4	5	6	7	8	9	1	2	3	4	5	6	7	8	9	1	2	4	5	6	7	8	9	1	2	3	4	5
Apr	3	4	5	6	7	8	9	1	2	3	4	5	6	7	8	9	1	2	3	4	5	6	7	8	9	1	2	3	4	5	
May	4	5	6	7	8	9	1	2	3	4	5	6	7	8	9	1	2	3	4	5	6	7	8	9	1	2	3	4	5	6	7
Jun	5	6	7	8	9	1	2	3	4	5	6	7	8	9	1	2	3	4	5	6	7	8	9	1	2	3	4	5	6	7	
Jul	6	7	8	9	1	2	3	4	5	6	7	8	9	1	2	3	4	5	6	7	8	9	1	2	3	4	5	6	7	8	9
Aug	7	8	9	1	2	3	4	5	6	7	8	9	1	2	3	4	5	6	7	8	9	1	2	3	4	5	6	7	8	9	1
Sep	8	9	1	2	3	4	5	6	7	8	9	1	2	3	4	5	6	7	8	9	1	2	3	4	5	6	7	8	9	1	
Oct	9	1	2	3	4	5	6	7	8	9	1	2	3	4	5	6	7	8	9	1	2	3	4	5	6	7	8	9	1	2	3
Nov	1	2	3	4	5	6	7	8	9	1	2	3	4	5	6	7	8	9	1	2	3	4	5	6	7	8	9	1	2	3	
Dec	2	3	4	5	6	7	8	9	1	2	3	4	5	6	7	8	9	1	2	3	4	5	6	7	8	9	1	2	3	4	5

MARCH 22

	1	2	3	4	5	6	7	8	9	10	11	12	13	14	15	16	17	18	19	20	21	22	23	24	25	26	27	28	29	30	31
Jan	9	1	2	3	4	5	6	7	8	9	1	2	3	4	5	6	7	8	9	1	2	3	4	5	6	7	8	9	1	2	3
Feb	1	2	3	4	5	6	7	8	9	1	2	3	4	5	6	7	8	9	1	2	3	4	5	6	7	8	9	1	2		
Mar	2	3	4	5	6	7	8	9	1	2	3	4	5	6	7	8	9	1	2	3	4	6	7	8	9	1	2	3	4	5	6
Apr	4	5	6	7	8	9	1	2	3	4	5	6	7	8	9	1	2	3	4	5	6	7	8	9	1	2	3	4	5	6	
May	5	6	7	8	9	1	2	3	4	5	6	7	8	9	1	2	3	4	5	6	7	8	9	1	2	3	4	5	6	7	8
Jun	6	7	8	9	1	2	3	4	5	6	7	8	9	1	2	3	4	5	6	7	8	9	1	2	3	4	5	6	7	8	
Jul	7	8	9	1	2	3	4	5	6	7	8	9	1	2	3	4	5	6	7	8	9	1	2	3	4	5	6	7	8	9	1
Aug	8	9	1	2	3	4	5	6	7	8	9	1	2	3	4	5	6	7	8	9	1	2	3	4	5	6	7	8	9	1	2
Sep	9	1	2	3	4	5	6	7	8	9	1	2	3	4	5	6	7	8	9	1	2	3	4	5	6	7	8	9	1	2	
Oct	1	2	3	4	5	6	7	8	9	1	2	3	4	5	6	7	8	9	1	2	3	4	5	6	7	8	9	1	2	3	4
Nov	2	3	4	5	6	7	8	9	1	2	3	4	5	6	7	8	9	1	2	3	4	5	6	7	8	9	1	2	3	4	
Dec	3	4	5	6	7	8	9	1	2	3	4	5	6	7	8	9	1	2	3	4	5	6	7	8	9	1	2	3	4	5	6

MARCH 23

	1	2	3	4	5	6	7	8	9	10	11	12	13	14	15	16	17	18	19	20	21	22	23	24	25	26	27	28	29	30	31
Jan	1	2	3	4	5	6	7	8	9	1	2	3	4	5	6	7	8	9	1	2	3	4	5	6	7	8	9	1	2	3	4
Feb	2	3	4	5	6	7	8	9	1	2	3	4	5	6	7	8	9	1	2	3	4	5	6	7	8	9	1	2	3		
Mar	3	4	5	6	7	8	9	1	2	3	4	5	6	7	8	9	1	2	3	4	5	6	8	9	1	2	3	4	5	6	7
Apr	5	6	7	8	9	1	2	3	4	5	6	7	8	9	1	2	3	4	5	6	7	8	9	1	2	3	4	5	6	7	
May	6	7	8	9	1	2	3	4	5	6	7	8	9	1	2	3	4	5	6	7	8	9	1	2	3	4	5	6	7	8	9
Jun	7	8	9	1	2	3	4	5	6	7	8	9	1	2	3	4	5	6	7	8	9	1	2	3	4	5	6	7	8	9	
Jul	8	9	1	2	3	4	5	6	7	8	9	1	2	3	4	5	6	7	8	9	1	2	3	4	5	6	7	8	9	1	2
Aug	9	1	2	3	4	5	6	7	8	9	1	2	3	4	5	6	7	8	9	1	2	3	4	5	6	7	8	9	1	2	3
Sep	1	2	3	4	5	6	7	8	9	1	2	3	4	5	6	7	8	9	1	2	3	4	5	6	7	8	9	1	2	3	
Oct	2	3	4	5	6	7	8	9	1	2	3	4	5	6	7	8	9	1	2	3	4	5	6	7	8	9	1	2	3	4	5
Nov	3	4	5	6	7	8	9	1	2	3	4	5	6	7	8	9	1	2	3	4	5	6	7	8	9	1	2	3	4	5	
Dec	4	5	6	7	8	9	1	2	3	4	5	6	7	8	9	1	2	3	4	5	6	7	8	9	1	2	3	4	5	6	7

MARCH 24

	1	2	3	4	5	6	7	8	9	10	11	12	13	14	15	16	17	18	19	20	21	22	23	24	25	26	27	28	29	30	31
Jan	2	3	4	5	6	7	8	9	1	2	3	4	5	6	7	8	9	1	2	3	4	5	6	7	8	9	1	2	3	4	5
Feb	3	4	5	6	7	8	9	1	2	3	4	5	6	7	8	9	1	2	3	4	5	6	7	8	9	1	2	3	4		
Mar	4	5	6	7	8	9	1	2	3	4	5	6	7	8	9	1	2	3	4	5	6	7	8	1	2	3	4	5	6	7	8
Apr	6	7	8	9	1	2	3	4	5	6	7	8	9	1	2	3	4	5	6	7	8	9	1	2	3	4	5	6	7	8	
May	7	8	9	1	2	3	4	5	6	7	8	9	1	2	3	4	5	6	7	8	9	1	2	3	4	5	6	7	8	9	1
Jun	8	9	1	2	3	4	5	6	7	8	9	1	2	3	4	5	6	7	8	9	1	2	3	4	5	6	7	8	9	1	
Jul	9	1	2	3	4	5	6	7	8	9	1	2	3	4	5	6	7	8	9	1	2	3	4	5	6	7	8	9	1	2	3
Aug	1	2	3	4	5	6	7	8	9	1	2	3	4	5	6	7	8	9	1	2	3	4	5	6	7	8	9	1	2	3	4
Sep	2	3	4	5	6	7	8	9	1	2	3	4	5	6	7	8	9	1	2	3	4	5	6	7	8	9	1	2	3	4	
Oct	3	4	5	6	7	8	9	1	2	3	4	5	6	7	8	9	1	2	3	4	5	6	7	8	9	1	2	3	4	5	6
Nov	4	5	6	7	8	9	1	2	3	4	5	6	7	8	9	1	2	3	4	5	6	7	8	9	1	2	3	4	5	6	
Dec	5	6	7	8	9	1	2	3	4	5	6	7	8	9	1	2	3	4	5	6	7	8	9	1	2	3	4	5	6	7	8

MARCH 25

	1	2	3	4	5	6	7	8	9	10	11	12	13	14	15	16	17	18	19	20	21	22	23	24	25	26	27	28	29	30	31
Jan	3	4	5	6	7	8	9	1	2	3	4	5	6	7	8	9	1	2	3	4	5	6	7	8	9	1	2	3	4	5	6
Feb	4	5	6	7	8	9	1	2	3	4	5	6	7	8	9	1	2	3	4	5	6	7	8	9	1	2	3	4	5		
Mar	5	6	7	8	9	1	2	3	4	5	6	7	8	9	1	2	3	4	5	6	7	8	9	1	3	4	5	6	7	8	9
Apr	7	8	9	1	2	3	4	5	6	7	8	9	1	2	3	4	5	6	7	8	9	1	2	3	4	5	6	7	8	9	
May	8	9	1	2	3	4	5	6	7	8	9	1	2	3	4	5	6	7	8	9	1	2	3	4	5	6	7	8	9	1	2
Jun	9	1	2	3	4	5	6	7	8	9	1	2	3	4	5	6	7	8	9	1	2	3	4	5	6	7	8	9	1	2	
Jul	1	2	3	4	5	6	7	8	9	1	2	3	4	5	6	7	8	9	1	2	3	4	5	6	7	8	9	1	2	3	4
Aug	2	3	4	5	6	7	8	9	1	2	3	4	5	6	7	8	9	1	2	3	4	5	6	7	8	9	1	2	3	4	5
Sep	3	4	5	6	7	8	9	1	2	3	4	5	6	7	8	9	1	2	3	4	5	6	7	8	9	1	2	3	4	5	
Oct	4	5	6	7	8	9	1	2	3	4	5	6	7	8	9	1	2	3	4	5	6	7	8	9	1	2	3	4	5	6	7
Nov	5	6	7	8	9	1	2	3	4	5	6	7	8	9	1	2	3	4	5	6	7	8	9	1	2	3	4	5	6	7	
Dec	6	7	8	9	1	2	3	4	5	6	7	8	9	1	2	3	4	5	6	7	8	9	1	2	3	4	5	6	7	8	9

MARCH 26

	1	2	3	4	5	6	7	8	9	10	11	12	13	14	15	16	17	18	19	20	21	22	23	24	25	26	27	28	29	30	31
Jan	4	5	6	7	8	9	1	2	3	4	5	6	7	8	9	1	2	3	4	5	6	7	8	9	1	2	3	4	5	6	7
Feb	5	6	7	8	9	1	2	3	4	5	6	7	8	9	1	2	3	4	5	6	7	8	9	1	2	3	4	5	6		
Mar	6	7	8	9	1	2	3	4	5	6	7	8	9	1	2	3	4	5	6	7	8	9	1	2	3	5	6	7	8	9	1
Apr	8	9	1	2	3	4	5	6	7	8	9	1	2	3	4	5	6	7	8	9	1	2	3	4	5	6	7	8	9	1	
May	9	1	2	3	4	5	6	7	8	9	1	2	3	4	5	6	7	8	9	1	2	3	4	5	6	7	8	9	1	2	3
Jun	1	2	3	4	5	6	7	8	9	1	2	3	4	5	6	7	8	9	1	2	3	4	5	6	7	8	9	1	2	3	
Jul	2	3	4	5	6	7	8	9	1	2	3	4	5	6	7	8	9	1	2	3	4	5	6	7	8	9	1	2	3	4	5
Aug	3	4	5	6	7	8	9	1	2	3	4	5	6	7	8	9	1	2	3	4	5	6	7	8	9	1	2	3	4	5	6
Sep	4	5	6	7	8	9	1	2	3	4	5	6	7	8	9	1	2	3	4	5	6	7	8	9	1	2	3	4	5	6	
Oct	5	6	7	8	9	1	2	3	4	5	6	7	8	9	1	2	3	4	5	6	7	8	9	1	2	3	4	5	6	7	8
Nov	6	7	8	9	1	2	3	4	5	6	7	8	9	1	2	3	4	5	6	7	8	9	1	2	3	4	5	6	7	8	
Dec	7	8	9	1	2	3	4	5	6	7	8	9	1	2	3	4	5	6	7	8	9	1	2	3	4	5	6	7	8	9	1

MARCH 27

	1	2	3	4	5	6	7	8	9	10	11	12	13	14	15	16	17	18	19	20	21	22	23	24	25	26	27	28	29	30	31
Jan	5	6	7	8	9	1	2	3	4	5	6	7	8	9	1	2	3	4	5	6	7	8	9	1	2	3	4	5	6	7	8
Feb	6	7	8	9	1	2	3	4	5	6	7	8	9	1	2	3	4	5	6	7	8	9	1	2	3	4	5	6	7		
Mar	7	8	9	1	2	3	4	5	6	7	8	9	1	2	3	4	5	6	7	8	9	1	2	3	4	5	7	8	9	1	2
Apr	9	1	2	3	4	5	6	7	8	9	1	2	3	4	5	6	7	8	9	1	2	3	4	5	6	7	8	9	1	2	
May	1	2	3	4	5	6	7	8	9	1	2	3	4	5	6	7	8	9	1	2	3	4	5	6	7	8	9	1	2	3	4
Jun	2	3	4	5	6	7	8	9	1	2	3	4	5	6	7	8	9	1	2	3	4	5	6	7	8	9	1	2	3	4	
Jul	3	4	5	6	7	8	9	1	2	3	4	5	6	7	8	9	1	2	3	4	5	6	7	8	9	1	2	3	4	5	6
Aug	4	5	6	7	8	9	1	2	3	4	5	6	7	8	9	1	2	3	4	5	6	7	8	9	1	2	3	4	5	6	7
Sep	5	6	7	8	9	1	2	3	4	5	6	7	8	9	1	2	3	4	5	6	7	8	9	1	2	3	4	5	6	7	
Oct	6	7	8	9	1	2	3	4	5	6	7	8	9	1	2	3	4	5	6	7	8	9	1	2	3	4	5	6	7	8	9
Nov	7	8	9	1	2	3	4	5	6	7	8	9	1	2	3	4	5	6	7	8	9	1	2	3	4	5	6	7	8	9	
Dec	8	9	1	2	3	4	5	6	7	8	9	1	2	3	4	5	6	7	8	9	1	2	3	4	5	6	7	8	9	1	2

MARCH 28

	1	2	3	4	5	6	7	8	9	10	11	12	13	14	15	16	17	18	19	20	21	22	23	24	25	26	27	28	29	30	31
Jan	6	7	8	9	1	2	3	4	5	6	7	8	9	1	2	3	4	5	6	7	8	9	1	2	3	4	5	6	7	8	9
Feb	7	8	9	1	2	3	4	5	6	7	8	9	1	2	3	4	5	6	7	8	9	1	2	3	4	5	6	7	8		
Mar	8	9	1	2	3	4	5	6	7	8	9	1	2	3	4	5	6	7	8	9	1	2	3	4	5	6	7	9	1	2	3
Apr	1	2	3	4	5	6	7	8	9	1	2	3	4	5	6	7	8	9	1	2	3	4	5	6	7	8	9	1	2	3	
May	2	3	4	5	6	7	8	9	1	2	3	4	5	6	7	8	9	1	2	3	4	5	6	7	8	9	1	2	3	4	5
Jun	3	4	5	6	7	8	9	1	2	3	4	5	6	7	8	9	1	2	3	4	5	6	7	8	9	1	2	3	4	5	
Jul	4	5	6	7	8	9	1	2	3	4	5	6	7	8	9	1	2	3	4	5	6	7	8	9	1	2	3	4	5	6	7
Aug	5	6	7	8	9	1	2	3	4	5	6	7	8	9	1	2	3	4	5	6	7	8	9	1	2	3	4	5	6	7	8
Sep	6	7	8	9	1	2	3	4	5	6	7	8	9	1	2	3	4	5	6	7	8	9	1	2	3	4	5	6	7	8	
Oct	7	8	9	1	2	3	4	5	6	7	8	9	1	2	3	4	5	6	7	8	9	1	2	3	4	5	6	7	8	9	1
Nov	8	9	1	2	3	4	5	6	7	8	9	1	2	3	4	5	6	7	8	9	1	2	3	4	5	6	7	8	9	1	
Dec	9	1	2	3	4	5	6	7	8	9	1	2	3	4	5	6	7	8	9	1	2	3	4	5	6	7	8	9	1	2	3

MARCH 29

	1	2	3	4	5	6	7	8	9	10	11	12	13	14	15	16	17	18	19	20	21	22	23	24	25	26	27	28	29	30	31
Jan	7	8	9	1	2	3	4	5	6	7	8	9	1	2	3	4	5	6	7	8	9	1	2	3	4	5	6	7	8	9	1
Feb	8	9	1	2	3	4	5	6	7	8	9	1	2	3	4	5	6	7	8	9	1	2	3	4	5	6	7	8	9		
Mar	9	1	2	3	4	5	6	7	8	9	1	2	3	4	5	6	7	8	9	1	2	3	4	5	6	7	8	9	2	3	4
Apr	2	3	4	5	6	7	8	9	1	2	3	4	5	6	7	8	9	1	2	3	4	5	6	7	8	9	1	2	3	4	
May	3	4	5	6	7	8	9	1	2	3	4	5	6	7	8	9	1	2	3	4	5	6	7	8	9	1	2	3	4	5	6
Jun	4	5	6	7	8	9	1	2	3	4	5	6	7	8	9	1	2	3	4	5	6	7	8	9	1	2	3	4	5	6	
Jul	5	6	7	8	9	1	2	3	4	5	6	7	8	9	1	2	3	4	5	6	7	8	9	1	2	3	4	5	6	7	8
Aug	6	7	8	9	1	2	3	4	5	6	7	8	9	1	2	3	4	5	6	7	8	9	1	2	3	4	5	6	7	8	9
Sep	7	8	9	1	2	3	4	5	6	7	8	9	1	2	3	4	5	6	7	8	9	1	2	3	4	5	6	7	8	9	
Oct	8	9	1	2	3	4	5	6	7	8	9	1	2	3	4	5	6	7	8	9	1	2	3	4	5	6	7	8	9	1	2
Nov	9	1	2	3	4	5	6	7	8	9	1	2	3	4	5	6	7	8	9	1	2	3	4	5	6	7	8	9	1	2	
Dec	1	2	3	4	5	6	7	8	9	1	2	3	4	5	6	7	8	9	1	2	3	4	5	6	7	8	9	1	2	3	4

MARCH 30

	1	2	3	4	5	6	7	8	9	10	11	12	13	14	15	16	17	18	19	20	21	22	23	24	25	26	27	28	29	30	31
Jan	8	9	1	2	3	4	5	6	7	8	9	1	2	3	4	5	6	7	8	9	1	2	3	4	5	6	7	8	9	1	2
Feb	9	1	2	3	4	5	6	7	8	9	1	2	3	4	5	6	7	8	9	1	2	3	4	5	6	7	8	9	1		
Mar	1	2	3	4	5	6	7	8	9	1	2	3	4	5	6	7	8	9	1	2	3	4	5	6	7	8	9	1	2	4	5
Apr	3	4	5	6	7	8	9	1	2	3	4	5	6	7	8	9	1	2	3	4	5	6	7	8	9	1	2	3	4	5	
May	4	5	6	7	8	9	1	2	3	4	5	6	7	8	9	1	2	3	4	5	6	7	8	9	1	2	3	4	5	6	7
Jun	5	6	7	8	9	1	2	3	4	5	6	7	8	9	1	2	3	4	5	6	7	8	9	1	2	3	4	5	6	7	
Jul	6	7	8	9	1	2	3	4	5	6	7	8	9	1	2	3	4	5	6	7	8	9	1	2	3	4	5	6	7	8	9
Aug	7	8	9	1	2	3	4	5	6	7	8	9	1	2	3	4	5	6	7	8	9	1	2	3	4	5	6	7	8	9	1
Sep	8	9	1	2	3	4	5	6	7	8	9	1	2	3	4	5	6	7	8	9	1	2	3	4	5	6	7	8	9	1	
Oct	9	1	2	3	4	5	6	7	8	9	1	2	3	4	5	6	7	8	9	1	2	3	4	5	6	7	8	9	1	2	3
Nov	1	2	3	4	5	6	7	8	9	1	2	3	4	5	6	7	8	9	1	2	3	4	5	6	7	8	9	1	2	3	
Dec	2	3	4	5	6	7	8	9	1	2	3	4	5	6	7	8	9	1	2	3	4	5	6	7	8	9	1	2	3	4	5

MARCH 31

	1	2	3	4	5	6	7	8	9	10	11	12	13	14	15	16	17	18	19	20	21	22	23	24	25	26	27	28	29	30	31
Jan	9	1	2	3	4	5	6	7	8	9	1	2	3	4	5	6	7	8	9	1	2	3	4	5	6	7	8	9	1	2	3
Feb	1	2	3	4	5	6	7	8	9	1	2	3	4	5	6	7	8	9	1	2	3	4	5	6	7	8	9	1	2		
Mar	2	3	4	5	6	7	8	9	1	2	3	4	5	6	7	8	9	1	2	3	4	5	6	7	8	9	1	2	3	4	6
Apr	4	5	6	7	8	9	1	2	3	4	5	6	7	8	9	1	2	3	4	5	6	7	8	9	1	2	3	4	5	6	
May	5	6	7	8	9	1	2	3	4	5	6	7	8	9	1	2	3	4	5	6	7	8	9	1	2	3	4	5	6	7	8
Jun	6	7	8	9	1	2	3	4	5	6	7	8	9	1	2	3	4	5	6	7	8	9	1	2	3	4	5	6	7	8	
Jul	7	8	9	1	2	3	4	5	6	7	8	9	1	2	3	4	5	6	7	8	9	1	2	3	4	5	6	7	8	9	1
Aug	8	9	1	2	3	4	5	6	7	8	9	1	2	3	4	5	6	7	8	9	1	2	3	4	5	6	7	8	9	1	2
Sep	9	1	2	3	4	5	6	7	8	9	1	2	3	4	5	6	7	8	9	1	2	3	4	5	6	7	8	9	1	2	
Oct	1	2	3	4	5	6	7	8	9	1	2	3	4	5	6	7	8	9	1	2	3	4	5	6	7	8	9	1	2	3	4
Nov	2	3	4	5	6	7	8	9	1	2	3	4	5	6	7	8	9	1	2	3	4	5	6	7	8	9	1	2	3	4	
Dec	3	4	5	6	7	8	9	1	2	3	4	5	6	7	8	9	1	2	3	4	5	6	7	8	9	1	2	3	4	5	6

APRIL 1

	1	2	3	4	5	6	7	8	9	10	11	12	13	14	15	16	17	18	19	20	21	22	23	24	25	26	27	28	29	30	31
Jan	7	8	9	1	2	3	4	5	6	7	8	9	1	2	3	4	5	6	7	8	9	1	2	3	4	5	6	7	8	9	1
Feb	8	9	1	2	3	4	5	6	7	8	9	1	2	3	4	5	6	7	8	9	1	2	3	4	5	6	7	8	9		
Mar	9	1	2	3	4	5	6	7	8	9	1	2	3	4	5	6	7	8	9	1	2	3	4	5	6	7	8	9	1	2	3
Apr	2	3	4	5	6	7	8	9	1	2	3	4	5	6	7	8	9	1	2	3	4	5	6	7	8	9	1	2	3	4	
May	3	4	5	6	7	8	9	1	2	3	4	5	6	7	8	9	1	2	3	4	5	6	7	8	9	1	2	3	4	5	6
Jun	4	5	6	7	8	9	1	2	3	4	5	6	7	8	9	1	2	3	4	5	6	7	8	9	1	2	3	4	5	6	
Jul	5	6	7	8	9	1	2	3	4	5	6	7	8	9	1	2	3	4	5	6	7	8	9	1	2	3	4	5	6	7	8
Aug	6	7	8	9	1	2	3	4	5	6	7	8	9	1	2	3	4	5	6	7	8	9	1	2	3	4	5	6	7	8	9
Sep	7	8	9	1	2	3	4	5	6	7	8	9	1	2	3	4	5	6	7	8	9	1	2	3	4	5	6	7	8	9	
Oct	8	9	1	2	3	4	5	6	7	8	9	1	2	3	4	5	6	7	8	9	1	2	3	4	5	6	7	8	9	1	2
Nov	9	1	2	3	4	5	6	7	8	9	1	2	3	4	5	6	7	8	9	1	2	3	4	5	6	7	8	9	1	2	
Dec	1	2	3	4	5	6	7	8	9	1	2	3	4	5	6	7	8	9	1	2	3	4	5	6	7	8	9	1	2	3	4

APRIL 2

	1	2	3	4	5	6	7	8	9	10	11	12	13	14	15	16	17	18	19	20	21	22	23	24	25	26	27	28	29	30	31
Jan	8	9	1	2	3	4	5	6	7	8	9	1	2	3	4	5	6	7	8	9	1	2	3	4	5	6	7	8	9	1	2
Feb	9	1	2	3	4	5	6	7	8	9	1	2	3	4	5	6	7	8	9	1	2	3	4	5	6	7	8	9	1		
Mar	1	2	3	4	5	6	7	8	9	1	2	3	4	5	6	7	8	9	1	2	3	4	5	6	7	8	9	1	2	3	4
Apr	2	4	5	6	7	8	9	1	2	3	4	5	6	7	8	9	1	2	3	4	5	6	7	8	9	1	2	3	4	5	
May	4	5	6	7	8	9	1	2	3	4	5	6	7	8	9	1	2	3	4	5	6	7	8	9	1	2	3	4	5	6	7
Jun	5	6	7	8	9	1	2	3	4	5	6	7	8	9	1	2	3	4	5	6	7	8	9	1	2	3	4	5	6	7	
Jul	6	7	8	9	1	2	3	4	5	6	7	8	9	1	2	3	4	5	6	7	8	9	1	2	3	4	5	6	7	8	9
Aug	7	8	9	1	2	3	4	5	6	7	8	9	1	2	3	4	5	6	7	8	9	1	2	3	4	5	6	7	8	9	1
Sep	8	9	1	2	3	4	5	6	7	8	9	1	2	3	4	5	6	7	8	9	1	2	3	4	5	6	7	8	9	1	
Oct	9	1	2	3	4	5	6	7	8	9	1	2	3	4	5	6	7	8	9	1	2	3	4	5	6	7	8	9	1	2	3
Nov	1	2	3	4	5	6	7	8	9	1	2	3	4	5	6	7	8	9	1	2	3	4	5	6	7	8	9	1	2	3	
Dec	2	3	4	5	6	7	8	9	1	2	3	4	5	6	7	8	9	1	2	3	4	5	6	7	8	9	1	2	3	4	5

APRIL 3

	1	2	3	4	5	6	7	8	9	10	11	12	13	14	15	16	17	18	19	20	21	22	23	24	25	26	27	28	29	30	31
Jan	9	1	2	3	4	5	6	7	8	9	1	2	3	4	5	6	7	8	9	1	2	3	4	5	6	7	8	9	1	2	3
Feb	1	2	3	4	5	6	7	8	9	1	2	3	4	5	6	7	8	9	1	2	3	4	5	6	7	8	9	1	2		
Mar	2	3	4	5	6	7	8	9	1	2	3	4	5	6	7	8	9	1	2	3	4	5	6	7	8	9	1	2	3	4	5
Apr	3	4	6	7	8	9	1	2	3	4	5	6	7	8	9	1	2	3	4	5	6	7	8	9	1	2	3	4	5	6	
May	5	6	7	8	9	1	2	3	4	5	6	7	8	9	1	2	3	4	5	6	7	8	9	1	2	3	4	5	6	7	8
Jun	6	7	8	9	1	2	3	4	5	6	7	8	9	1	2	3	4	5	6	7	8	9	1	2	3	4	5	6	7	8	
Jul	7	8	9	1	2	3	4	5	6	7	8	9	1	2	3	4	5	6	7	8	9	1	2	3	4	5	6	7	8	9	1
Aug	8	9	1	2	3	4	5	6	7	8	9	1	2	3	4	5	6	7	8	9	1	2	3	4	5	6	7	8	9	1	2
Sep	9	1	2	3	4	5	6	7	8	9	1	2	3	4	5	6	7	8	9	1	2	3	4	5	6	7	8	9	1	2	
Oct	1	2	3	4	5	6	7	8	9	1	2	3	4	5	6	7	8	9	1	2	3	4	5	6	7	8	9	1	2	3	4
Nov	2	3	4	5	6	7	8	9	1	2	3	4	5	6	7	8	9	1	2	3	4	5	6	7	8	9	1	2	3	4	
Dec	3	4	5	6	7	8	9	1	2	3	4	5	6	7	8	9	1	2	3	4	5	6	7	8	9	1	2	3	4	5	6

APRIL 4

	1	2	3	4	5	6	7	8	9	10	11	12	13	14	15	16	17	18	19	20	21	22	23	24	25	26	27	28	29	30	31
Jan	1	2	3	4	5	6	7	8	9	1	2	3	4	5	6	7	8	9	1	2	3	4	5	6	7	8	9	1	2	3	4
Feb	2	3	4	5	6	7	8	9	1	2	3	4	5	6	7	8	9	1	2	3	4	5	6	7	8	9	1	2	3		
Mar	3	4	5	6	7	8	9	1	2	3	4	5	6	7	8	9	1	2	3	4	5	6	7	8	9	1	2	3	4	5	6
Apr	4	5	6	8	9	1	2	3	4	5	6	7	8	9	1	2	3	4	5	6	7	8	9	1	2	3	4	5	6	7	
May	6	7	8	9	1	2	3	4	5	6	7	8	9	1	2	3	4	5	6	7	8	9	1	2	3	4	5	6	7	8	9
Jun	7	8	9	1	2	3	4	5	6	7	8	9	1	2	3	4	5	6	7	8	9	1	2	3	4	5	6	7	8	9	
Jul	8	9	1	2	3	4	5	6	7	8	9	1	2	3	4	5	6	7	8	9	1	2	3	4	5	6	7	8	9	1	2
Aug	9	1	2	3	4	5	6	7	8	9	1	2	3	4	5	6	7	8	9	1	2	3	4	5	6	7	8	9	1	2	3
Sep	1	2	3	4	5	6	7	8	9	1	2	3	4	5	6	7	8	9	1	2	3	4	5	6	7	8	9	1	2	3	
Oct	2	3	4	5	6	7	8	9	1	2	3	4	5	6	7	8	9	1	2	3	4	5	6	7	8	9	1	2	3	4	5
Nov	3	4	5	6	7	8	9	1	2	3	4	5	6	7	8	9	1	2	3	4	5	6	7	8	9	1	2	3	4	5	
Dec	4	5	6	7	8	9	1	2	3	4	5	6	7	8	9	1	2	3	4	5	6	7	8	9	1	2	3	4	5	6	7

APRIL 5

	1	2	3	4	5	6	7	8	9	10	11	12	13	14	15	16	17	18	19	20	21	22	23	24	25	26	27	28	29	30	31
Jan	2	3	4	5	6	7	8	9	1	2	3	4	5	6	7	8	9	1	2	3	4	5	6	7	8	9	1	2	3	4	5
Feb	3	4	5	6	7	8	9	1	2	3	4	5	6	7	8	9	1	2	3	4	5	6	7	8	9	1	2	3	4		
Mar	4	5	6	7	8	9	1	2	3	4	5	6	7	8	9	1	2	3	4	5	6	7	8	9	1	2	3	4	5	6	7
Apr	5	6	7	8	1	2	3	4	5	6	7	8	9	1	2	3	4	5	6	7	8	9	1	2	3	4	5	6	7	8	
May	7	8	9	1	2	3	4	5	6	7	8	9	1	2	3	4	5	6	7	8	9	1	2	3	4	5	6	7	8	9	1
Jun	8	9	1	2	3	4	5	6	7	8	9	1	2	3	4	5	6	7	8	9	1	2	3	4	5	6	7	8	9	1	
Jul	9	1	2	3	4	5	6	7	8	9	1	2	3	4	5	6	7	8	9	1	2	3	4	5	6	7	8	9	1	2	3
Aug	1	2	3	4	5	6	7	8	9	1	2	3	4	5	6	7	8	9	1	2	3	4	5	6	7	8	9	1	2	3	4
Sep	2	3	4	5	6	7	8	9	1	2	3	4	5	6	7	8	9	1	2	3	4	5	6	7	8	9	1	2	3	4	
Oct	3	4	5	6	7	8	9	1	2	3	4	5	6	7	8	9	1	2	3	4	5	6	7	8	9	1	2	3	4	5	6
Nov	4	5	6	7	8	9	1	2	3	4	5	6	7	8	9	1	2	3	4	5	6	7	8	9	1	2	3	4	5	6	
Dec	5	6	7	8	9	1	2	3	4	5	6	7	8	9	1	2	3	4	5	6	7	8	9	1	2	3	4	5	6	7	8

APRIL 6

	1	2	3	4	5	6	7	8	9	10	11	12	13	14	15	16	17	18	19	20	21	22	23	24	25	26	27	28	29	30	31
Jan	3	4	5	6	7	8	9	1	2	3	4	5	6	7	8	9	1	2	3	4	5	6	7	8	9	1	2	3	4	5	6
Feb	4	5	6	7	8	9	1	2	3	4	5	6	7	8	9	1	2	3	4	5	6	7	8	9	1	2	3	4	5		
Mar	5	6	7	8	9	1	2	3	4	5	6	7	8	9	1	2	3	4	5	6	7	8	9	1	2	3	4	5	6	7	8
Apr	6	7	8	9	1	3	4	5	6	7	8	9	1	2	3	4	5	6	7	8	9	1	2	3	4	5	6	7	8	9	
May	8	9	1	2	3	4	5	6	7	8	9	1	2	3	4	5	6	7	8	9	1	2	3	4	5	6	7	8	9	1	2
Jun	9	1	2	3	4	5	6	7	8	9	1	2	3	4	5	6	7	8	9	1	2	3	4	5	6	7	8	9	1	2	
Jul	1	2	3	4	5	6	7	8	9	1	2	3	4	5	6	7	8	9	1	2	3	4	5	6	7	8	9	1	2	3	4
Aug	2	3	4	5	6	7	8	9	1	2	3	4	5	6	7	8	9	1	2	3	4	5	6	7	8	9	1	2	3	4	5
Sep	3	4	5	6	7	8	9	1	2	3	4	5	6	7	8	9	1	2	3	4	5	6	7	8	9	1	2	3	4	5	
Oct	4	5	6	7	8	9	1	2	3	4	5	6	7	8	9	1	2	3	4	5	6	7	8	9	1	2	3	4	5	6	7
Nov	5	6	7	8	9	1	2	3	4	5	6	7	8	9	1	2	3	4	5	6	7	8	9	1	2	3	4	5	6	7	
Dec	6	7	8	9	1	2	3	4	5	6	7	8	9	1	2	3	4	5	6	7	8	9	1	2	3	4	5	6	7	8	9

APRIL 7

	1	2	3	4	5	6	7	8	9	10	11	12	13	14	15	16	17	18	19	20	21	22	23	24	25	26	27	28	29	30	31
Jan	4	5	6	7	8	9	1	2	3	4	5	6	7	8	9	1	2	3	4	5	6	7	8	9	1	2	3	4	5	6	7
Feb	5	6	7	8	9	1	2	3	4	5	6	7	8	9	1	2	3	4	5	6	7	8	9	1	2	3	4	5	6		
Mar	6	7	8	9	1	2	3	4	5	6	7	8	9	1	2	3	4	5	6	7	8	9	1	2	3	4	5	6	7	8	9
Apr	7	8	9	1	2	3	5	6	7	8	9	1	2	3	4	5	6	7	8	9	1	2	3	4	5	6	7	8	9	1	
May	9	1	2	3	4	5	6	7	8	9	1	2	3	4	5	6	7	8	9	1	2	3	4	5	6	7	8	9	1	2	3
Jun	1	2	3	4	5	6	7	8	9	1	2	3	4	5	6	7	8	9	1	2	3	4	5	6	7	8	9	1	2	3	
Jul	2	3	4	5	6	7	8	9	1	2	3	4	5	6	7	8	9	1	2	3	4	5	6	7	8	9	1	2	3	4	5
Aug	3	4	5	6	7	8	9	1	2	3	4	5	6	7	8	9	1	2	3	4	5	6	7	8	9	1	2	3	4	5	6
Sep	4	5	6	7	8	9	1	2	3	4	5	6	7	8	9	1	2	3	4	5	6	7	8	9	1	2	3	4	5	6	
Oct	5	6	7	8	9	1	2	3	4	5	6	7	8	9	1	2	3	4	5	6	7	8	9	1	2	3	4	5	6	7	8
Nov	6	7	8	9	1	2	3	4	5	6	7	8	9	1	2	3	4	5	6	7	8	9	1	2	3	4	5	6	7	8	
Dec	7	8	9	1	2	3	4	5	6	7	8	9	1	2	3	4	5	6	7	8	9	1	2	3	4	5	6	7	8	9	1

APRIL 8

	1	2	3	4	5	6	7	8	9	10	11	12	13	14	15	16	17	18	19	20	21	22	23	24	25	26	27	28	29	30	31
Jan	5	6	7	8	9	1	2	3	4	5	6	7	8	9	1	2	3	4	5	6	7	8	9	1	2	3	4	5	6	7	8
Feb	6	7	8	9	1	2	3	4	5	6	7	8	9	1	2	3	4	5	6	7	8	9	1	2	3	4	5	6	7		
Mar	7	8	9	1	2	3	4	5	6	7	8	9	1	2	3	4	5	6	7	8	9	1	2	3	4	5	6	7	8	9	1
Apr	8	9	1	2	3	4	5	7	8	9	1	2	3	4	5	6	7	8	9	1	2	3	4	5	6	7	8	9	1	2	
May	1	2	3	4	5	6	7	8	9	1	2	3	4	5	6	7	8	9	1	2	3	4	5	6	7	8	9	1	2	3	4
Jun	2	3	4	5	6	7	8	9	1	2	3	4	5	6	7	8	9	1	2	3	4	5	6	7	8	9	1	2	3	4	
Jul	3	4	5	6	7	8	9	1	2	3	4	5	6	7	8	9	1	2	3	4	5	6	7	8	9	1	2	3	4	5	6
Aug	4	5	6	7	8	9	1	2	3	4	5	6	7	8	9	1	2	3	4	5	6	7	8	9	1	2	3	4	5	6	7
Sep	5	6	7	8	9	1	2	3	4	5	6	7	8	9	1	2	3	4	5	6	7	8	9	1	2	3	4	5	6	7	
Oct	6	7	8	9	1	2	3	4	5	6	7	8	9	1	2	3	4	5	6	7	8	9	1	2	3	4	5	6	7	8	9
Nov	7	8	9	1	2	3	4	5	6	7	8	9	1	2	3	4	5	6	7	8	9	1	2	3	4	5	6	7	8	9	
Dec	8	9	1	2	3	4	5	6	7	8	9	1	2	3	4	5	6	7	8	9	1	2	3	4	5	6	7	8	9	1	2

APRIL 9

	1	2	3	4	5	6	7	8	9	10	11	12	13	14	15	16	17	18	19	20	21	22	23	24	25	26	27	28	29	30	31
Jan	6	7	8	9	1	2	3	4	5	6	7	8	9	1	2	3	4	5	6	7	8	9	1	2	3	4	5	6	7	8	9
Feb	7	8	9	1	2	3	4	5	6	7	8	9	1	2	3	4	5	6	7	8	9	1	2	3	4	5	6	7	8		
Mar	8	9	1	2	3	4	5	6	7	8	9	1	2	3	4	5	6	7	8	9	1	2	3	4	5	6	7	8	9	1	2
Apr	9	1	2	3	4	5	6	7	9	1	2	3	4	5	6	7	8	9	1	2	3	4	5	6	7	8	9	1	2	3	
May	2	3	4	5	6	7	8	9	1	2	3	4	5	6	7	8	9	1	2	3	4	5	6	7	8	9	1	2	3	4	5
Jun	3	4	5	6	7	8	9	1	2	3	4	5	6	7	8	9	1	2	3	4	5	6	7	8	9	1	2	3	4	5	
Jul	4	5	6	7	8	9	1	2	3	4	5	6	7	8	9	1	2	3	4	5	6	7	8	9	1	2	3	4	5	6	7
Aug	5	6	7	8	9	1	2	3	4	5	6	7	8	9	1	2	3	4	5	6	7	8	9	1	2	3	4	5	6	7	8
Sep	6	7	8	9	1	2	3	4	5	6	7	8	9	1	2	3	4	5	6	7	8	9	1	2	3	4	5	6	7	8	
Oct	7	8	9	1	2	3	4	5	6	7	8	9	1	2	3	4	5	6	7	8	9	1	2	3	4	5	6	7	8	9	1
Nov	8	9	1	2	3	4	5	6	7	8	9	1	2	3	4	5	6	7	8	9	1	2	3	4	5	6	7	8	9	1	
Dec	9	1	2	3	4	5	6	7	8	9	1	2	3	4	5	6	7	8	9	1	2	3	4	5	6	7	8	9	1	2	3

APRIL 10

	1	2	3	4	5	6	7	8	9	10	11	12	13	14	15	16	17	18	19	20	21	22	23	24	25	26	27	28	29	30	31
Jan	7	8	9	1	2	3	4	5	6	7	8	9	1	2	3	4	5	6	7	8	9	1	2	3	4	5	6	7	8	9	1
Feb	8	9	1	2	3	4	5	6	7	8	9	1	2	3	4	5	6	7	8	9	1	2	3	4	5	6	7	8	9		
Mar	9	1	2	3	4	5	6	7	8	9	1	2	3	4	5	6	7	8	9	1	2	3	4	5	6	7	8	9	1	2	3
Apr	1	2	3	4	5	6	7	8	9	2	3	4	5	6	7	8	9	1	2	3	4	5	6	7	8	9	1	2	3	4	
May	3	4	5	6	7	8	9	1	2	3	4	5	6	7	8	9	1	2	3	4	5	6	7	8	9	1	2	3	4	5	6
Jun	4	5	6	7	8	9	1	2	3	4	5	6	7	8	9	1	2	3	4	5	6	7	8	9	1	2	3	4	5	6	
Jul	5	6	7	8	9	1	2	3	4	5	6	7	8	9	1	2	3	4	5	6	7	8	9	1	2	3	4	5	6	7	8
Aug	6	7	8	9	1	2	3	4	5	6	7	8	9	1	2	3	4	5	6	7	8	9	1	2	3	4	5	6	7	8	9
Sep	7	8	9	1	2	3	4	5	6	7	8	9	1	2	3	4	5	6	7	8	9	1	2	3	4	5	6	7	8	9	
Oct	8	9	1	2	3	4	5	6	7	8	9	1	2	3	4	5	6	7	8	9	1	2	3	4	5	6	7	8	9	1	2
Nov	9	1	2	3	4	5	6	7	8	9	1	2	3	4	5	6	7	8	9	1	2	3	4	5	6	7	8	9	1	2	
Dec	1	2	3	4	5	6	7	8	9	1	2	3	4	5	6	7	8	9	1	2	3	4	5	6	7	8	9	1	2	3	4

APRIL 11

	1	2	3	4	5	6	7	8	9	10	11	12	13	14	15	16	17	18	19	20	21	22	23	24	25	26	27	28	29	30	31
Jan	8	9	1	2	3	4	5	6	7	8	9	1	2	3	4	5	6	7	8	9	1	2	3	4	5	6	7	8	9	1	2
Feb	9	1	2	3	4	5	6	7	8	9	1	2	3	4	5	6	7	8	9	1	2	3	4	5	6	7	8	9	1		
Mar	1	2	3	4	5	6	7	8	9	1	2	3	4	5	6	7	8	9	1	2	3	4	5	6	7	8	9	1	2	3	4
Apr	2	3	4	5	6	7	8	9	1	2	4	5	6	7	8	9	1	2	3	4	5	6	7	8	9	1	2	3	4	5	
May	4	5	6	7	8	9	1	2	3	4	5	6	7	8	9	1	2	3	4	5	6	7	8	9	1	2	3	4	5	6	7
Jun	5	6	7	8	9	1	2	3	4	5	6	7	8	9	1	2	3	4	5	6	7	8	9	1	2	3	4	5	6	7	
Jul	6	7	8	9	1	2	3	4	5	6	7	8	9	1	2	3	4	5	6	7	8	9	1	2	3	4	5	6	7	8	9
Aug	7	8	9	1	2	3	4	5	6	7	8	9	1	2	3	4	5	6	7	8	9	1	2	3	4	5	6	7	8	9	1
Sep	8	9	1	2	3	4	5	6	7	8	9	1	2	3	4	5	6	7	8	9	1	2	3	4	5	6	7	8	9	1	
Oct	9	1	2	3	4	5	6	7	8	9	1	2	3	4	5	6	7	8	9	1	2	3	4	5	6	7	8	9	1	2	3
Nov	1	2	3	4	5	6	7	8	9	1	2	3	4	5	6	7	8	9	1	2	3	4	5	6	7	8	9	1	2	3	
Dec	2	3	4	5	6	7	8	9	1	2	3	4	5	6	7	8	9	1	2	3	4	5	6	7	8	9	1	2	3	4	5

APRIL 12

	1	2	3	4	5	6	7	8	9	10	11	12	13	14	15	16	17	18	19	20	21	22	23	24	25	26	27	28	29	30	31
Jan	9	1	2	3	4	5	6	7	8	9	1	2	3	4	5	6	7	8	9	1	2	3	4	5	6	7	8	9	1	2	3
Feb	1	2	3	4	5	6	7	8	9	1	2	3	4	5	6	7	8	9	1	2	3	4	5	6	7	8	9	1	2		
Mar	2	3	4	5	6	7	8	9	1	2	3	4	5	6	7	8	9	1	2	3	4	5	6	7	8	9	1	2	3	4	5
Apr	3	4	5	6	7	8	9	1	2	3	4	6	7	8	9	1	2	3	4	5	6	7	8	9	1	2	3	4	5	6	
May	5	6	7	8	9	1	2	3	4	5	6	7	8	9	1	2	3	4	5	6	7	8	9	1	2	3	4	5	6	7	8
Jun	6	7	8	9	1	2	3	4	5	6	7	8	9	1	2	3	4	5	6	7	8	9	1	2	3	4	5	6	7	8	
Jul	7	8	9	1	2	3	4	5	6	7	8	9	1	2	3	4	5	6	7	8	9	1	2	3	4	5	6	7	8	9	1
Aug	8	9	1	2	3	4	5	6	7	8	9	1	2	3	4	5	6	7	8	9	1	2	3	4	5	6	7	8	9	1	2
Sep	9	1	2	3	4	5	6	7	8	9	1	2	3	4	5	6	7	8	9	1	2	3	4	5	6	7	8	9	1	2	
Oct	1	2	3	4	5	6	7	8	9	1	2	3	4	5	6	7	8	9	1	2	3	4	5	6	7	8	9	1	2	3	4
Nov	2	3	4	5	6	7	8	9	1	2	3	4	5	6	7	8	9	1	2	3	4	5	6	7	8	9	1	2	3	4	
Dec	3	4	5	6	7	8	9	1	2	3	4	5	6	7	8	9	1	2	3	4	5	6	7	8	9	1	2	3	4	5	6

APRIL 13

	1	2	3	4	5	6	7	8	9	10	11	12	13	14	15	16	17	18	19	20	21	22	23	24	25	26	27	28	29	30	31
Jan	1	2	3	4	5	6	7	8	9	1	2	3	4	5	6	7	8	9	1	2	3	4	5	6	7	8	9	1	2	3	4
Feb	2	3	4	5	6	7	8	9	1	2	3	4	5	6	7	8	9	1	2	3	4	5	6	7	8	9	1	2	3		
Mar	3	4	5	6	7	8	9	1	2	3	4	5	6	7	8	9	1	2	3	4	5	6	7	8	9	1	2	3	4	5	6
Apr	4	5	6	7	8	9	1	2	3	4	5	6	8	9	1	2	3	4	5	6	7	8	9	1	2	3	4	5	6	7	
May	6	7	8	9	1	2	3	4	5	6	7	8	9	1	2	3	4	5	6	7	8	9	1	2	3	4	5	6	7	8	9
Jun	7	8	9	1	2	3	4	5	6	7	8	9	1	2	3	4	5	6	7	8	9	1	2	3	4	5	6	7	8	9	
Jul	8	9	1	2	3	4	5	6	7	8	9	1	2	3	4	5	6	7	8	9	1	2	3	4	5	6	7	8	9	1	2
Aug	9	1	2	3	4	5	6	7	8	9	1	2	3	4	5	6	7	8	9	1	2	3	4	5	6	7	8	9	1	2	3
Sep	1	2	3	4	5	6	7	8	9	1	2	3	4	5	6	7	8	9	1	2	3	4	5	6	7	8	9	1	2	3	
Oct	2	3	4	5	6	7	8	9	1	2	3	4	5	6	7	8	9	1	2	3	4	5	6	7	8	9	1	2	3	4	5
Nov	3	4	5	6	7	8	9	1	2	3	4	5	6	7	8	9	1	2	3	4	5	6	7	8	9	1	2	3	4	5	
Dec	4	5	6	7	8	9	1	2	3	4	5	6	7	8	9	1	2	3	4	5	6	7	8	9	1	2	3	4	5	6	7

APRIL 14

	1	2	3	4	5	6	7	8	9	10	11	12	13	14	15	16	17	18	19	20	21	22	23	24	25	26	27	28	29	30	31
Jan	2	3	4	5	6	7	8	9	1	2	3	4	5	6	7	8	9	1	2	3	4	5	6	7	8	9	1	2	3	4	5
Feb	3	4	5	6	7	8	9	1	2	3	4	5	6	7	8	9	1	2	3	4	5	6	7	8	9	1	2	3	4		
Mar	4	5	6	7	8	9	1	2	3	4	5	6	7	8	9	1	2	3	4	5	6	7	8	9	1	2	3	4	5	6	7
Apr	5	6	7	8	9	1	2	3	4	5	6	7	8	1	2	3	4	5	6	7	8	9	1	2	3	4	5	6	7	8	
May	7	8	9	1	2	3	4	5	6	7	8	9	1	2	3	4	5	6	7	8	9	1	2	3	4	5	6	7	8	9	1
Jun	8	9	1	2	3	4	5	6	7	8	9	1	2	3	4	5	6	7	8	9	1	2	3	4	5	6	7	8	9	1	
Jul	9	1	2	3	4	5	6	7	8	9	1	2	3	4	5	6	7	8	9	1	2	3	4	5	6	7	8	9	1	2	3
Aug	1	2	3	4	5	6	7	8	9	1	2	3	4	5	6	7	8	9	1	2	3	4	5	6	7	8	9	1	2	3	4
Sep	2	3	4	5	6	7	8	9	1	2	3	4	5	6	7	8	9	1	2	3	4	5	6	7	8	9	1	2	3	4	
Oct	3	4	5	6	7	8	9	1	2	3	4	5	6	7	8	9	1	2	3	4	5	6	7	8	9	1	2	3	4	5	6
Nov	4	5	6	7	8	9	1	2	3	4	5	6	7	8	9	1	2	3	4	5	6	7	8	9	1	2	3	4	5	6	
Dec	5	6	7	8	9	1	2	3	4	5	6	7	8	9	1	2	3	4	5	6	7	8	9	1	2	3	4	5	6	7	8

APRIL 15

	1	2	3	4	5	6	7	8	9	10	11	12	13	14	15	16	17	18	19	20	21	22	23	24	25	26	27	28	29	30	31
Jan	3	4	5	6	7	8	9	1	2	3	4	5	6	7	8	9	1	2	3	4	5	6	7	8	9	1	2	3	4	5	6
Feb	4	5	6	7	8	9	1	2	3	4	5	6	7	8	9	1	2	3	4	5	6	7	8	9	1	2	3	4	5		
Mar	5	6	7	8	9	1	2	3	4	5	6	7	8	9	1	2	3	4	5	6	7	8	9	1	2	3	4	5	6	7	8
Apr	6	7	8	9	1	2	3	4	5	6	7	8	9	1	3	4	5	6	7	8	9	1	2	3	4	5	6	7	8	9	
May	8	9	1	2	3	4	5	6	7	8	9	1	2	3	4	5	6	7	8	9	1	2	3	4	5	6	7	8	9	1	2
Jun	9	1	2	3	4	5	6	7	8	9	1	2	3	4	5	6	7	8	9	1	2	3	4	5	6	7	8	9	1	2	
Jul	1	2	3	4	5	6	7	8	9	1	2	3	4	5	6	7	8	9	1	2	3	4	5	6	7	8	9	1	2	3	4
Aug	2	3	4	5	6	7	8	9	1	2	3	4	5	6	7	8	9	1	2	3	4	5	6	7	8	9	1	2	3	4	5
Sep	3	4	5	6	7	8	9	1	2	3	4	5	6	7	8	9	1	2	3	4	5	6	7	8	9	1	2	3	4	5	
Oct	4	5	6	7	8	9	1	2	3	4	5	6	7	8	9	1	2	3	4	5	6	7	8	9	1	2	3	4	5	6	7
Nov	5	6	7	8	9	1	2	3	4	5	6	7	8	9	1	2	3	4	5	6	7	8	9	1	2	3	4	5	6	7	
Dec	6	7	8	9	1	2	3	4	5	6	7	8	9	1	2	3	4	5	6	7	8	9	1	2	3	4	5	6	7	8	9

APRIL 16

	1	2	3	4	5	6	7	8	9	10	11	12	13	14	15	16	17	18	19	20	21	22	23	24	25	26	27	28	29	30	31
Jan	4	5	6	7	8	9	1	2	3	4	5	6	7	8	9	1	2	3	4	5	6	7	8	9	1	2	3	4	5	6	7
Feb	5	6	7	8	9	1	2	3	4	5	6	7	8	9	1	2	3	4	5	6	7	8	9	1	2	3	4	5	6		
Mar	6	7	8	9	1	2	3	4	5	6	7	8	9	1	2	3	4	5	6	7	8	9	1	2	3	4	5	6	7	8	9
Apr	7	8	9	1	2	3	4	5	6	7	8	9	1	2	3	5	6	7	8	9	1	2	3	4	5	6	7	8	9	1	
May	9	1	2	3	4	5	6	7	8	9	1	2	3	4	5	6	7	8	9	1	2	3	4	5	6	7	8	9	1	2	3
Jun	1	2	3	4	5	6	7	8	9	1	2	3	4	5	6	7	8	9	1	2	3	4	5	6	7	8	9	1	2	3	
Jul	2	3	4	5	6	7	8	9	1	2	3	4	5	6	7	8	9	1	2	3	4	5	6	7	8	9	1	2	3	4	5
Aug	3	4	5	6	7	8	9	1	2	3	4	5	6	7	8	9	1	2	3	4	5	6	7	8	9	1	2	3	4	5	6
Sep	4	5	6	7	8	9	1	2	3	4	5	6	7	8	9	1	2	3	4	5	6	7	8	9	1	2	3	4	5	6	
Oct	5	6	7	8	9	1	2	3	4	5	6	7	8	9	1	2	3	4	5	6	7	8	9	1	2	3	4	5	6	7	8
Nov	6	7	8	9	1	2	3	4	5	6	7	8	9	1	2	3	4	5	6	7	8	9	1	2	3	4	5	6	7	8	
Dec	7	8	9	1	2	3	4	5	6	7	8	9	1	2	3	4	5	6	7	8	9	1	2	3	4	5	6	7	8	9	1

APRIL 17

	1	2	3	4	5	6	7	8	9	10	11	12	13	14	15	16	17	18	19	20	21	22	23	24	25	26	27	28	29	30	31
Jan	5	6	7	8	9	1	2	3	4	5	6	7	8	9	1	2	3	4	5	6	7	8	9	1	2	3	4	5	6	7	8
Feb	6	7	8	9	1	2	3	4	5	6	7	8	9	1	2	3	4	5	6	7	8	9	1	2	3	4	5	6	7		
Mar	7	8	9	1	2	3	4	5	6	7	8	9	1	2	3	4	5	6	7	8	9	1	2	3	4	5	6	7	8	9	1
Apr	8	9	1	2	3	4	5	6	7	8	9	1	2	3	4	5	7	8	9	1	2	3	4	5	6	7	8	9	1	2	
May	1	2	3	4	5	6	7	8	9	1	2	3	4	5	6	7	8	9	1	2	3	4	5	6	7	8	9	1	2	3	4
Jun	2	3	4	5	6	7	8	9	1	2	3	4	5	6	7	8	9	1	2	3	4	5	6	7	8	9	1	2	3	4	
Jul	3	4	5	6	7	8	9	1	2	3	4	5	6	7	8	9	1	2	3	4	5	6	7	8	9	1	2	3	4	5	6
Aug	4	5	6	7	8	9	1	2	3	4	5	6	7	8	9	1	2	3	4	5	6	7	8	9	1	2	3	4	5	6	7
Sep	5	6	7	8	9	1	2	3	4	5	6	7	8	9	1	2	3	4	5	6	7	8	9	1	2	3	4	5	6	7	
Oct	6	7	8	9	1	2	3	4	5	6	7	8	9	1	2	3	4	5	6	7	8	9	1	2	3	4	5	6	7	8	9
Nov	7	8	9	1	2	3	4	5	6	7	8	9	1	2	3	4	5	6	7	8	9	1	2	3	4	5	6	7	8	9	
Dec	8	9	1	2	3	4	5	6	7	8	9	1	2	3	4	5	6	7	8	9	1	2	3	4	5	6	7	8	9	1	2

APRIL 18

	1	2	3	4	5	6	7	8	9	10	11	12	13	14	15	16	17	18	19	20	21	22	23	24	25	26	27	28	29	30	31
Jan	6	7	8	9	1	2	3	4	5	6	7	8	9	1	2	3	4	5	6	7	8	9	1	2	3	4	5	6	7	8	9
Feb	7	8	9	1	2	3	4	5	6	7	8	9	1	2	3	4	5	6	7	8	9	1	2	3	4	5	6	7	8		
Mar	8	9	1	2	3	4	5	6	7	8	9	1	2	3	4	5	6	7	8	9	1	2	3	4	5	6	7	8	9	1	2
Apr	9	1	2	3	4	5	6	7	8	9	1	2	3	4	5	6	7	9	1	2	3	4	5	6	7	8	9	1	2	3	
May	2	3	4	5	6	7	8	9	1	2	3	4	5	6	7	8	9	1	2	3	4	5	6	7	8	9	1	2	3	4	5
Jun	3	4	5	6	7	8	9	1	2	3	4	5	6	7	8	9	1	2	3	4	5	6	7	8	9	1	2	3	4	5	
Jul	4	5	6	7	8	9	1	2	3	4	5	6	7	8	9	1	2	3	4	5	6	7	8	9	1	2	3	4	5	6	7
Aug	5	6	7	8	9	1	2	3	4	5	6	7	8	9	1	2	3	4	5	6	7	8	9	1	2	3	4	5	6	7	8
Sep	6	7	8	9	1	2	3	4	5	6	7	8	9	1	2	3	4	5	6	7	8	9	1	2	3	4	5	6	7	8	
Oct	7	8	9	1	2	3	4	5	6	7	8	9	1	2	3	4	5	6	7	8	9	1	2	3	4	5	6	7	8	9	1
Nov	8	9	1	2	3	4	5	6	7	8	9	1	2	3	4	5	6	7	8	9	1	2	3	4	5	6	7	8	9	1	
Dec	9	1	2	3	4	5	6	7	8	9	1	2	3	4	5	6	7	8	9	1	2	3	4	5	6	7	8	9	1	2	3

APRIL 19

	1	2	3	4	5	6	7	8	9	10	11	12	13	14	15	16	17	18	19	20	21	22	23	24	25	26	27	28	29	30	31
Jan	7	8	9	1	2	3	4	5	6	7	8	9	1	2	3	4	5	6	7	8	9	1	2	3	4	5	6	7	8	9	1
Feb	8	9	1	2	3	4	5	6	7	8	9	1	2	3	4	5	6	7	8	9	1	2	3	4	5	6	7	8	9		
Mar	9	1	2	3	4	5	6	7	8	9	1	2	3	4	5	6	7	8	9	1	2	3	4	5	6	7	8	9	1	2	3
Apr	1	2	3	4	5	6	7	8	9	1	2	3	4	5	6	7	8	9	2	3	4	5	6	7	8	9	1	2	3	4	
May	3	4	5	6	7	8	9	1	2	3	4	5	6	7	8	9	1	2	3	4	5	6	7	8	9	1	2	3	4	5	6
Jun	4	5	6	7	8	9	1	2	3	4	5	6	7	8	9	1	2	3	4	5	6	7	8	9	1	2	3	4	5	6	
Jul	5	6	7	8	9	1	2	3	4	5	6	7	8	9	1	2	3	4	5	6	7	8	9	1	2	3	4	5	6	7	8
Aug	6	7	8	9	1	2	3	4	5	6	7	8	9	1	2	3	4	5	6	7	8	9	1	2	3	4	5	6	7	8	9
Sep	7	8	9	1	2	3	4	5	6	7	8	9	1	2	3	4	5	6	7	8	9	1	2	3	4	5	6	7	8	9	
Oct	8	9	1	2	3	4	5	6	7	8	9	1	2	3	4	5	6	7	8	9	1	2	3	4	5	6	7	8	9	1	2
Nov	9	1	2	3	4	5	6	7	8	9	1	2	3	4	5	6	7	8	9	1	2	3	4	5	6	7	8	9	1	2	
Dec	1	2	3	4	5	6	7	8	9	1	2	3	4	5	6	7	8	9	1	2	3	4	5	6	7	8	9	1	2	3	4

APRIL 20

	1	2	3	4	5	6	7	8	9	10	11	12	13	14	15	16	17	18	19	20	21	22	23	24	25	26	27	28	29	30	31
Jan	8	9	1	2	3	4	5	6	7	8	9	1	2	3	4	5	6	7	8	9	1	2	3	4	5	6	7	8	9	1	2
Feb	9	1	2	3	4	5	6	7	8	9	1	2	3	4	5	6	7	8	9	1	2	3	4	5	6	7	8	9	1		
Mar	1	2	3	4	5	6	7	8	9	1	2	3	4	5	6	7	8	9	1	2	3	4	5	6	7	8	9	1	2	3	4
Apr	2	3	4	5	6	7	8	9	1	2	3	4	5	6	7	8	9	1	2	4	5	6	7	8	9	1	2	3	4	5	
May	4	5	6	7	8	9	1	2	3	4	5	6	7	8	9	1	2	3	4	5	6	7	8	9	1	2	3	4	5	6	7
Jun	5	6	7	8	9	1	2	3	4	5	6	7	8	9	1	2	3	4	5	6	7	8	9	1	2	3	4	5	6	7	
Jul	6	7	8	9	1	2	3	4	5	6	7	8	9	1	2	3	4	5	6	7	8	9	1	2	3	4	5	6	7	8	9
Aug	7	8	9	1	2	3	4	5	6	7	8	9	1	2	3	4	5	6	7	8	9	1	2	3	4	5	6	7	8	9	1
Sep	8	9	1	2	3	4	5	6	7	8	9	1	2	3	4	5	6	7	8	9	1	2	3	4	5	6	7	8	9	1	
Oct	9	1	2	3	4	5	6	7	8	9	1	2	3	4	5	6	7	8	9	1	2	3	4	5	6	7	8	9	1	2	3
Nov	1	2	3	4	5	6	7	8	9	1	2	3	4	5	6	7	8	9	1	2	3	4	5	6	7	8	9	1	2	3	
Dec	2	3	4	5	6	7	8	9	1	2	3	4	5	6	7	8	9	1	2	3	4	5	6	7	8	9	1	2	3	4	5

APRIL 21

	1	2	3	4	5	6	7	8	9	10	11	12	13	14	15	16	17	18	19	20	21	22	23	24	25	26	27	28	29	30	31
Jan	9	1	2	3	4	5	6	7	8	9	1	2	3	4	5	6	7	8	9	1	2	3	4	5	6	7	8	9	1	2	3
Feb	1	2	3	4	5	6	7	8	9	1	2	3	4	5	6	7	8	9	1	2	3	4	5	6	7	8	9	1	2		
Mar	2	3	4	5	6	7	8	9	1	2	3	4	5	6	7	8	9	1	2	3	4	5	6	7	8	9	1	2	3	4	5
Apr	3	4	5	6	7	8	9	1	2	3	4	5	6	7	8	9	1	2	3	4	6	7	8	9	1	2	3	4	5	6	
May	5	6	7	8	9	1	2	3	4	5	6	7	8	9	1	2	3	4	5	6	7	8	9	1	2	3	4	5	6	7	8
Jun	6	7	8	9	1	2	3	4	5	6	7	8	9	1	2	3	4	5	6	7	8	9	1	2	3	4	5	6	7	8	
Jul	7	8	9	1	2	3	4	5	6	7	8	9	1	2	3	4	5	6	7	8	9	1	2	3	4	5	6	7	8	9	1
Aug	8	9	1	2	3	4	5	6	7	8	9	1	2	3	4	5	6	7	8	9	1	2	3	4	5	6	7	8	9	1	2
Sep	9	1	2	3	4	5	6	7	8	9	1	2	3	4	5	6	7	8	9	1	2	3	4	5	6	7	8	9	1	2	
Oct	1	2	3	4	5	6	7	8	9	1	2	3	4	5	6	7	8	9	1	2	3	4	5	6	7	8	9	1	2	3	4
Nov	2	3	4	5	6	7	8	9	1	2	3	4	5	6	7	8	9	1	2	3	4	5	6	7	8	9	1	2	3	4	
Dec	3	4	5	6	7	8	9	1	2	3	4	5	6	7	8	9	1	2	3	4	5	6	7	8	9	1	2	3	4	5	6

APRIL 22

	1	2	3	4	5	6	7	8	9	10	11	12	13	14	15	16	17	18	19	20	21	22	23	24	25	26	27	28	29	30	31
Jan	1	2	3	4	5	6	7	8	9	1	2	3	4	5	6	7	8	9	1	2	3	4	5	6	7	8	9	1	2	3	4
Feb	2	3	4	5	6	7	8	9	1	2	3	4	5	6	7	8	9	1	2	3	4	5	6	7	8	9	1	2	3		
Mar	3	4	5	6	7	8	9	1	2	3	4	5	6	7	8	9	1	2	3	4	5	6	7	8	9	1	2	3	4	5	6
Apr	4	5	6	7	8	9	1	2	3	4	5	6	7	8	9	1	2	3	4	5	6	8	9	1	2	3	4	5	6	7	
May	6	7	8	9	1	2	3	4	5	6	7	8	9	1	2	3	4	5	6	7	8	9	1	2	3	4	5	6	7	8	9
Jun	7	8	9	1	2	3	4	5	6	7	8	9	1	2	3	4	5	6	7	8	9	1	2	3	4	5	6	7	8	9	
Jul	8	9	1	2	3	4	5	6	7	8	9	1	2	3	4	5	6	7	8	9	1	2	3	4	5	6	7	8	9	1	2
Aug	9	1	2	3	4	5	6	7	8	9	1	2	3	4	5	6	7	8	9	1	2	3	4	5	6	7	8	9	1	2	3
Sep	1	2	3	4	5	6	7	8	9	1	2	3	4	5	6	7	8	9	1	2	3	4	5	6	7	8	9	1	2	3	
Oct	2	3	4	5	6	7	8	9	1	2	3	4	5	6	7	8	9	1	2	3	4	5	6	7	8	9	1	2	3	4	5
Nov	3	4	5	6	7	8	9	1	2	3	4	5	6	7	8	9	1	2	3	4	5	6	7	8	9	1	2	3	4	5	
Dec	4	5	6	7	8	9	1	2	3	4	5	6	7	8	9	1	2	3	4	5	6	7	8	9	1	2	3	4	5	6	7

APRIL 23

	1	2	3	4	5	6	7	8	9	10	11	12	13	14	15	16	17	18	19	20	21	22	23	24	25	26	27	28	29	30	31
Jan	2	3	4	5	6	7	8	9	1	2	3	4	5	6	7	8	9	1	2	3	4	5	6	7	8	9	1	2	3	4	5
Feb	3	4	5	6	7	8	9	1	2	3	4	5	6	7	8	9	1	2	3	4	5	6	7	8	9	1	2	3	4		
Mar	4	5	6	7	8	9	1	2	3	4	5	6	7	8	9	1	2	3	4	5	6	7	8	9	1	2	3	4	5	6	7
Apr	5	6	7	8	9	1	2	3	4	5	6	7	8	9	1	2	3	4	5	6	7	8	1	2	3	4	5	6	7	8	
May	7	8	9	1	2	3	4	5	6	7	8	9	1	2	3	4	5	6	7	8	9	1	2	3	4	5	6	7	8	9	1
Jun	8	9	1	2	3	4	5	6	7	8	9	1	2	3	4	5	6	7	8	9	1	2	3	4	5	6	7	8	9	1	
Jul	9	1	2	3	4	5	6	7	8	9	1	2	3	4	5	6	7	8	9	1	2	3	4	5	6	7	8	9	1	2	3
Aug	1	2	3	4	5	6	7	8	9	1	2	3	4	5	6	7	8	9	1	2	3	4	5	6	7	8	9	1	2	3	4
Sep	2	3	4	5	6	7	8	9	1	2	3	4	5	6	7	8	9	1	2	3	4	5	6	7	8	9	1	2	3	4	
Oct	3	4	5	6	7	8	9	1	2	3	4	5	6	7	8	9	1	2	3	4	5	6	7	8	9	1	2	3	4	5	6
Nov	4	5	6	7	8	9	1	2	3	4	5	6	7	8	9	1	2	3	4	5	6	7	8	9	1	2	3	4	5	6	
Dec	5	6	7	8	9	1	2	3	4	5	6	7	8	9	1	2	3	4	5	6	7	8	9	1	2	3	4	5	6	7	8

APRIL 24

	1	2	3	4	5	6	7	8	9	10	11	12	13	14	15	16	17	18	19	20	21	22	23	24	25	26	27	28	29	30	31
Jan	3	4	5	6	7	8	9	1	2	3	4	5	6	7	8	9	1	2	3	4	5	6	7	8	9	1	2	3	4	5	6
Feb	4	5	6	7	8	9	1	2	3	4	5	6	7	8	9	1	2	3	4	5	6	7	8	9	1	2	3	4	5		
Mar	5	6	7	8	9	1	2	3	4	5	6	7	8	9	1	2	3	4	5	6	7	8	9	1	2	3	4	5	6	7	8
Apr	6	7	8	9	1	2	3	4	5	6	7	8	9	1	2	3	4	5	6	7	8	9	1	3	4	5	6	7	8	9	
May	8	9	1	2	3	4	5	6	7	8	9	1	2	3	4	5	6	7	8	9	1	2	3	4	5	6	7	8	9	1	2
Jun	9	1	2	3	4	5	6	7	8	9	1	2	3	4	5	6	7	8	9	1	2	3	4	5	6	7	8	9	1	2	
Jul	1	2	3	4	5	6	7	8	9	1	2	3	4	5	6	7	8	9	1	2	3	4	5	6	7	8	9	1	2	3	4
Aug	2	3	4	5	6	7	8	9	1	2	3	4	5	6	7	8	9	1	2	3	4	5	6	7	8	9	1	2	3	4	5
Sep	3	4	5	6	7	8	9	1	2	3	4	5	6	7	8	9	1	2	3	4	5	6	7	8	9	1	2	3	4	5	
Oct	4	5	6	7	8	9	1	2	3	4	5	6	7	8	9	1	2	3	4	5	6	7	8	9	1	2	3	4	5	6	7
Nov	5	6	7	8	9	1	2	3	4	5	6	7	8	9	1	2	3	4	5	6	7	8	9	1	2	3	4	5	6	7	
Dec	6	7	8	9	1	2	3	4	5	6	7	8	9	1	2	3	4	5	6	7	8	9	1	2	3	4	5	6	7	8	9

APRIL 25

	1	2	3	4	5	6	7	8	9	10	11	12	13	14	15	16	17	18	19	20	21	22	23	24	25	26	27	28	29	30	31
Jan	4	5	6	7	8	9	1	2	3	4	5	6	7	8	9	1	2	3	4	5	6	7	8	9	1	2	3	4	5	6	7
Feb	5	6	7	8	9	1	2	3	4	5	6	7	8	9	1	2	3	4	5	6	7	8	9	1	2	3	4	5	6		
Mar	6	7	8	9	1	2	3	4	5	6	7	8	9	1	2	3	4	5	6	7	8	9	1	2	3	4	5	6	7	8	9
Apr	7	8	9	1	2	3	4	5	6	7	8	9	1	2	3	4	5	6	7	8	9	1	2	3	5	6	7	8	9	1	
May	9	1	2	3	4	5	6	7	8	9	1	2	3	4	5	6	7	8	9	1	2	3	4	5	6	7	8	9	1	2	3
Jun	1	2	3	4	5	6	7	8	9	1	2	3	4	5	6	7	8	9	1	2	3	4	5	6	7	8	9	1	2	3	
Jul	2	3	4	5	6	7	8	9	1	2	3	4	5	6	7	8	9	1	2	3	4	5	6	7	8	9	1	2	3	4	5
Aug	3	4	5	6	7	8	9	1	2	3	4	5	6	7	8	9	1	2	3	4	5	6	7	8	9	1	2	3	4	5	6
Sep	4	5	6	7	8	9	1	2	3	4	5	6	7	8	9	1	2	3	4	5	6	7	8	9	1	2	3	4	5	6	
Oct	5	6	7	8	9	1	2	3	4	5	6	7	8	9	1	2	3	4	5	6	7	8	9	1	2	3	4	5	6	7	8
Nov	6	7	8	9	1	2	3	4	5	6	7	8	9	1	2	3	4	5	6	7	8	9	1	2	3	4	5	6	7	8	
Dec	7	8	9	1	2	3	4	5	6	7	8	9	1	2	3	4	5	6	7	8	9	1	2	3	4	5	6	7	8	9	1

APRIL 26

	1	2	3	4	5	6	7	8	9	10	11	12	13	14	15	16	17	18	19	20	21	22	23	24	25	26	27	28	29	30	31
Jan	5	6	7	8	9	1	2	3	4	5	6	7	8	9	1	2	3	4	5	6	7	8	9	1	2	3	4	5	6	7	8
Feb	6	7	8	9	1	2	3	4	5	6	7	8	9	1	2	3	4	5	6	7	8	9	1	2	3	4	5	6	7		
Mar	7	8	9	1	2	3	4	5	6	7	8	9	1	2	3	4	5	6	7	8	9	1	2	3	4	5	6	7	8	9	1
Apr	8	9	1	2	3	4	5	6	7	8	9	1	2	3	4	5	6	7	8	9	1	2	3	4	5	7	8	9	1	2	
May	1	2	3	4	5	6	7	8	9	1	2	3	4	5	6	7	8	9	1	2	3	4	5	6	7	8	9	1	2	3	4
Jun	2	3	4	5	6	7	8	9	1	2	3	4	5	6	7	8	9	1	2	3	4	5	6	7	8	9	1	2	3	4	
Jul	3	4	5	6	7	8	9	1	2	3	4	5	6	7	8	9	1	2	3	4	5	6	7	8	9	1	2	3	4	5	6
Aug	4	5	6	7	8	9	1	2	3	4	5	6	7	8	9	1	2	3	4	5	6	7	8	9	1	2	3	4	5	6	7
Sep	5	6	7	8	9	1	2	3	4	5	6	7	8	9	1	2	3	4	5	6	7	8	9	1	2	3	4	5	6	7	
Oct	6	7	8	9	1	2	3	4	5	6	7	8	9	1	2	3	4	5	6	7	8	9	1	2	3	4	5	6	7	8	9
Nov	7	8	9	1	2	3	4	5	6	7	8	9	1	2	3	4	5	6	7	8	9	1	2	3	4	5	6	7	8	9	
Dec	8	9	1	2	3	4	5	6	7	8	9	1	2	3	4	5	6	7	8	9	1	2	3	4	5	6	7	8	9	1	2

APRIL 27

	1	2	3	4	5	6	7	8	9	10	11	12	13	14	15	16	17	18	19	20	21	22	23	24	25	26	27	28	29	30	31
Jan	6	7	8	9	1	2	3	4	5	6	7	8	9	1	2	3	4	5	6	7	8	9	1	2	3	4	5	6	7	8	9
Feb	7	8	9	1	2	3	4	5	6	7	8	9	1	2	3	4	5	6	7	8	9	1	2	3	4	5	6	7	8		
Mar	8	9	1	2	3	4	5	6	7	8	9	1	2	3	4	5	6	7	8	9	1	2	3	4	5	6	7	8	9	1	2
Apr	9	1	2	3	4	5	6	7	8	9	1	2	3	4	5	6	7	8	9	1	2	3	4	5	6	7	9	1	2	3	
May	2	3	4	5	6	7	8	9	1	2	3	4	5	6	7	8	9	1	2	3	4	5	6	7	8	9	1	2	3	4	5
Jun	3	4	5	6	7	8	9	1	2	3	4	5	6	7	8	9	1	2	3	4	5	6	7	8	9	1	2	3	4	5	
Jul	4	5	6	7	8	9	1	2	3	4	5	6	7	8	9	1	2	3	4	5	6	7	8	9	1	2	3	4	5	6	7
Aug	5	6	7	8	9	1	2	3	4	5	6	7	8	9	1	2	3	4	5	6	7	8	9	1	2	3	4	5	6	7	8
Sep	6	7	8	9	1	2	3	4	5	6	7	8	9	1	2	3	4	5	6	7	8	9	1	2	3	4	5	6	7	8	
Oct	7	8	9	1	2	3	4	5	6	7	8	9	1	2	3	4	5	6	7	8	9	1	2	3	4	5	6	7	8	9	1
Nov	8	9	1	2	3	4	5	6	7	8	9	1	2	3	4	5	6	7	8	9	1	2	3	4	5	6	7	8	9	1	
Dec	9	1	2	3	4	5	6	7	8	9	1	2	3	4	5	6	7	8	9	1	2	3	4	5	6	7	8	9	1	2	3

APRIL 28

	1	2	3	4	5	6	7	8	9	10	11	12	13	14	15	16	17	18	19	20	21	22	23	24	25	26	27	28	29	30	31
Jan	7	8	9	1	2	3	4	5	6	7	8	9	1	2	3	4	5	6	7	8	9	1	2	3	4	5	6	7	8	9	1
Feb	8	9	1	2	3	4	5	6	7	8	9	1	2	3	4	5	6	7	8	9	1	2	3	4	5	6	7	8	9		
Mar	9	1	2	3	4	5	6	7	8	9	1	2	3	4	5	6	7	8	9	1	2	3	4	5	6	7	8	9	1	2	3
Apr	1	2	3	4	5	6	7	8	9	1	2	3	4	5	6	7	8	9	1	2	3	4	5	6	7	8	9	2	3	4	
May	3	4	5	6	7	8	9	1	2	3	4	5	6	7	8	9	1	2	3	4	5	6	7	8	9	1	2	3	4	5	6
Jun	4	5	6	7	8	9	1	2	3	4	5	6	7	8	9	1	2	3	4	5	6	7	8	9	1	2	3	4	5	6	
Jul	5	6	7	8	9	1	2	3	4	5	6	7	8	9	1	2	3	4	5	6	7	8	9	1	2	3	4	5	6	7	8
Aug	6	7	8	9	1	2	3	4	5	6	7	8	9	1	2	3	4	5	6	7	8	9	1	2	3	4	5	6	7	8	9
Sep	7	8	9	1	2	3	4	5	6	7	8	9	1	2	3	4	5	6	7	8	9	1	2	3	4	5	6	7	8	9	
Oct	8	9	1	2	3	4	5	6	7	8	9	1	2	3	4	5	6	7	8	9	1	2	3	4	5	6	7	8	9	1	2
Nov	9	1	2	3	4	5	6	7	8	9	1	2	3	4	5	6	7	8	9	1	2	3	4	5	6	7	8	9	1	2	
Dec	1	2	3	4	5	6	7	8	9	1	2	3	4	5	6	7	8	9	1	2	3	4	5	6	7	8	9	1	2	3	4

APRIL 29

	1	2	3	4	5	6	7	8	9	10	11	12	13	14	15	16	17	18	19	20	21	22	23	24	25	26	27	28	29	30	31
Jan	8	9	1	2	3	4	5	6	7	8	9	1	2	3	4	5	6	7	8	9	1	2	3	4	5	6	7	8	9	1	2
Feb	9	1	2	3	4	5	6	7	8	9	1	2	3	4	5	6	7	8	9	1	2	3	4	5	6	7	8	9	1		
Mar	1	2	3	4	5	6	7	8	9	1	2	3	4	5	6	7	8	9	1	2	3	4	5	6	7	8	9	1	2	3	4
Apr	2	3	4	5	6	7	8	9	1	2	3	4	5	6	7	8	9	1	2	3	4	5	6	7	8	9	1	2	4	5	
May	4	5	6	7	8	9	1	2	3	4	5	6	7	8	9	1	2	3	4	5	6	7	8	9	1	2	3	4	5	6	7
Jun	5	6	7	8	9	1	2	3	4	5	6	7	8	9	1	2	3	4	5	6	7	8	9	1	2	3	4	5	6	7	
Jul	6	7	8	9	1	2	3	4	5	6	7	8	9	1	2	3	4	5	6	7	8	9	1	2	3	4	5	6	7	8	9
Aug	7	8	9	1	2	3	4	5	6	7	8	9	1	2	3	4	5	6	7	8	9	1	2	3	4	5	6	7	8	9	1
Sep	8	9	1	2	3	4	5	6	7	8	9	1	2	3	4	5	6	7	8	9	1	2	3	4	5	6	7	8	9	1	
Oct	9	1	2	3	4	5	6	7	8	9	1	2	3	4	5	6	7	8	9	1	2	3	4	5	6	7	8	9	1	2	3
Nov	1	2	3	4	5	6	7	8	9	1	2	3	4	5	6	7	8	9	1	2	3	4	5	6	7	8	9	1	2	3	
Dec	2	3	4	5	6	7	8	9	1	2	3	4	5	6	7	8	9	1	2	3	4	5	6	7	8	9	1	2	3	4	5

APRIL 30

	1	2	3	4	5	6	7	8	9	10	11	12	13	14	15	16	17	18	19	20	21	22	23	24	25	26	27	28	29	30	31
Jan	9	1	2	3	4	5	6	7	8	9	1	2	3	4	5	6	7	8	9	1	2	3	4	5	6	7	8	9	1	2	3
Feb	1	2	3	4	5	6	7	8	9	1	2	3	4	5	6	7	8	9	1	2	3	4	5	6	7	8	9	1	2		
Mar	2	3	4	5	6	7	8	9	1	2	3	4	5	6	7	8	9	1	2	3	4	5	6	7	8	9	1	2	3	4	5
Apr	3	4	5	6	7	8	9	1	2	3	4	5	6	7	8	9	1	2	3	4	5	6	7	8	9	1	2	3	4	6	
May	5	6	7	8	9	1	2	3	4	5	6	7	8	9	1	2	3	4	5	6	7	8	9	1	2	3	4	5	6	7	8
Jun	6	7	8	9	1	2	3	4	5	6	7	8	9	1	2	3	4	5	6	7	8	9	1	2	3	4	5	6	7	8	
Jul	7	8	9	1	2	3	4	5	6	7	8	9	1	2	3	4	5	6	7	8	9	1	2	3	4	5	6	7	8	9	1
Aug	8	9	1	2	3	4	5	6	7	8	9	1	2	3	4	5	6	7	8	9	1	2	3	4	5	6	7	8	9	1	2
Sep	9	1	2	3	4	5	6	7	8	9	1	2	3	4	5	6	7	8	9	1	2	3	4	5	6	7	8	9	1	2	
Oct	1	2	3	4	5	6	7	8	9	1	2	3	4	5	6	7	8	9	1	2	3	4	5	6	7	8	9	1	2	3	4
Nov	2	3	4	5	6	7	8	9	1	2	3	4	5	6	7	8	9	1	2	3	4	5	6	7	8	9	1	2	3	4	
Dec	3	4	5	6	7	8	9	1	2	3	4	5	6	7	8	9	1	2	3	4	5	6	7	8	9	1	2	3	4	5	6

MAY 1

	1	2	3	4	5	6	7	8	9	10	11	12	13	14	15	16	17	18	19	20	21	22	23	24	25	26	27	28	29	30	31
Jan	8	9	1	2	3	4	5	6	7	8	9	1	2	3	4	5	6	7	8	9	1	2	3	4	5	6	7	8	9	1	2
Feb	9	1	2	3	4	5	6	7	8	9	1	2	3	4	5	6	7	8	9	1	2	3	4	5	6	7	8	9	1		
Mar	1	2	3	4	5	6	7	8	9	1	2	3	4	5	6	7	8	9	1	2	3	4	5	6	7	8	9	1	2	3	4
Apr	2	3	4	5	6	7	8	9	1	2	3	4	5	6	7	8	9	1	2	3	4	5	6	7	8	9	1	2	3	4	
May	4	5	6	7	8	9	1	2	3	4	5	6	7	8	9	1	2	3	4	5	6	7	8	9	1	2	3	4	5	6	7
Jun	5	6	7	8	9	1	2	3	4	5	6	7	8	9	1	2	3	4	5	6	7	8	9	1	2	3	4	5	6	7	
Jul	6	7	8	9	1	2	3	4	5	6	7	8	9	1	2	3	4	5	6	7	8	9	1	2	3	4	5	6	7	8	9
Aug	7	8	9	1	2	3	4	5	6	7	8	9	1	2	3	4	5	6	7	8	9	1	2	3	4	5	6	7	8	9	1
Sep	8	9	1	2	3	4	5	6	7	8	9	1	2	3	4	5	6	7	8	9	1	2	3	4	5	6	7	8	9	1	
Oct	9	1	2	3	4	5	6	7	8	9	1	2	3	4	5	6	7	8	9	1	2	3	4	5	6	7	8	9	1	2	3
Nov	1	2	3	4	5	6	7	8	9	1	2	3	4	5	6	7	8	9	1	2	3	4	5	6	7	8	9	1	2	3	
Dec	2	3	4	5	6	7	8	9	1	2	3	4	5	6	7	8	9	1	2	3	4	5	6	7	8	9	1	2	3	4	5

MAY 2

	1	2	3	4	5	6	7	8	9	10	11	12	13	14	15	16	17	18	19	20	21	22	23	24	25	26	27	28	29	30	31
Jan	9	1	2	3	4	5	6	7	8	9	1	2	3	4	5	6	7	8	9	1	2	3	4	5	6	7	8	9	1	2	3
Feb	1	2	3	4	5	6	7	8	9	1	2	3	4	5	6	7	8	9	1	2	3	4	5	6	7	8	9	1	2		
Mar	2	3	4	5	6	7	8	9	1	2	3	4	5	6	7	8	9	1	2	3	4	5	6	7	8	9	1	2	3	4	5
Apr	3	4	5	6	7	8	9	1	2	3	4	5	6	7	8	9	1	2	3	4	5	6	7	8	9	1	2	3	4	5	
May	4	6	7	8	9	1	2	3	4	5	6	7	8	9	1	2	3	4	5	6	7	8	9	1	2	3	4	5	6	7	8
Jun	6	7	8	9	1	2	3	4	5	6	7	8	9	1	2	3	4	5	6	7	8	9	1	2	3	4	5	6	7	8	
Jul	7	8	9	1	2	3	4	5	6	7	8	9	1	2	3	4	5	6	7	8	9	1	2	3	4	5	6	7	8	9	1
Aug	8	9	1	2	3	4	5	6	7	8	9	1	2	3	4	5	6	7	8	9	1	2	3	4	5	6	7	8	9	1	2
Sep	9	1	2	3	4	5	6	7	8	9	1	2	3	4	5	6	7	8	9	1	2	3	4	5	6	7	8	9	1	2	
Oct	1	2	3	4	5	6	7	8	9	1	2	3	4	5	6	7	8	9	1	2	3	4	5	6	7	8	9	1	2	3	4
Nov	2	3	4	5	6	7	8	9	1	2	3	4	5	6	7	8	9	1	2	3	4	5	6	7	8	9	1	2	3	4	
Dec	3	4	5	6	7	8	9	1	2	3	4	5	6	7	8	9	1	2	3	4	5	6	7	8	9	1	2	3	4	5	6

MAY 3

	1	2	3	4	5	6	7	8	9	10	11	12	13	14	15	16	17	18	19	20	21	22	23	24	25	26	27	28	29	30	31
Jan	1	2	3	4	5	6	7	8	9	1	2	3	4	5	6	7	8	9	1	2	3	4	5	6	7	8	9	1	2	3	4
Feb	2	3	4	5	6	7	8	9	1	2	3	4	5	6	7	8	9	1	2	3	4	5	6	7	8	9	1	2	3		
Mar	3	4	5	6	7	8	9	1	2	3	4	5	6	7	8	9	1	2	3	4	5	6	7	8	9	1	2	3	4	5	6
Apr	4	5	6	7	8	9	1	2	3	4	5	6	7	8	9	1	2	3	4	5	6	7	8	9	1	2	3	4	5	6	
May	5	6	8	9	1	2	3	4	5	6	7	8	9	1	2	3	4	5	6	7	8	9	1	2	3	4	5	6	7	8	9
Jun	7	8	9	1	2	3	4	5	6	7	8	9	1	2	3	4	5	6	7	8	9	1	2	3	4	5	6	7	8	9	
Jul	8	9	1	2	3	4	5	6	7	8	9	1	2	3	4	5	6	7	8	9	1	2	3	4	5	6	7	8	9	1	2
Aug	9	1	2	3	4	5	6	7	8	9	1	2	3	4	5	6	7	8	9	1	2	3	4	5	6	7	8	9	1	2	3
Sep	1	2	3	4	5	6	7	8	9	1	2	3	4	5	6	7	8	9	1	2	3	4	5	6	7	8	9	1	2	3	
Oct	2	3	4	5	6	7	8	9	1	2	3	4	5	6	7	8	9	1	2	3	4	5	6	7	8	9	1	2	3	4	5
Nov	3	4	5	6	7	8	9	1	2	3	4	5	6	7	8	9	1	2	3	4	5	6	7	8	9	1	2	3	4	5	
Dec	4	5	6	7	8	9	1	2	3	4	5	6	7	8	9	1	2	3	4	5	6	7	8	9	1	2	3	4	5	6	7

MAY 4

	1	2	3	4	5	6	7	8	9	10	11	12	13	14	15	16	17	18	19	20	21	22	23	24	25	26	27	28	29	30	31
Jan	2	3	4	5	6	7	8	9	1	2	3	4	5	6	7	8	9	1	2	3	4	5	6	7	8	9	1	2	3	4	5
Feb	3	4	5	6	7	8	9	1	2	3	4	5	6	7	8	9	1	2	3	4	5	6	7	8	9	1	2	3	4		
Mar	4	5	6	7	8	9	1	2	3	4	5	6	7	8	9	1	2	3	4	5	6	7	8	9	1	2	3	4	5	6	7
Apr	5	6	7	8	9	1	2	3	4	5	6	7	8	9	1	2	3	4	5	6	7	8	9	1	2	3	4	5	6	7	
May	6	7	8	1	2	3	4	5	6	7	8	9	1	2	3	4	5	6	7	8	9	1	2	3	4	5	6	7	8	9	1
Jun	8	9	1	2	3	4	5	6	7	8	9	1	2	3	4	5	6	7	8	9	1	2	3	4	5	6	7	8	9	1	
Jul	9	1	2	3	4	5	6	7	8	9	1	2	3	4	5	6	7	8	9	1	2	3	4	5	6	7	8	9	1	2	3
Aug	1	2	3	4	5	6	7	8	9	1	2	3	4	5	6	7	8	9	1	2	3	4	5	6	7	8	9	1	2	3	4
Sep	2	3	4	5	6	7	8	9	1	2	3	4	5	6	7	8	9	1	2	3	4	5	6	7	8	9	1	2	3	4	
Oct	3	4	5	6	7	8	9	1	2	3	4	5	6	7	8	9	1	2	3	4	5	6	7	8	9	1	2	3	4	5	6
Nov	4	5	6	7	8	9	1	2	3	4	5	6	7	8	9	1	2	3	4	5	6	7	8	9	1	2	3	4	5	6	
Dec	5	6	7	8	9	1	2	3	4	5	6	7	8	9	1	2	3	4	5	6	7	8	9	1	2	3	4	5	6	7	8

MAY 5

	1	2	3	4	5	6	7	8	9	10	11	12	13	14	15	16	17	18	19	20	21	22	23	24	25	26	27	28	29	30	31
Jan	3	4	5	6	7	8	9	1	2	3	4	5	6	7	8	9	1	2	3	4	5	6	7	8	9	1	2	3	4	5	6
Feb	4	5	6	7	8	9	1	2	3	4	5	6	7	8	9	1	2	3	4	5	6	7	8	9	1	2	3	4	5		
Mar	5	6	7	8	9	1	2	3	4	5	6	7	8	9	1	2	3	4	5	6	7	8	9	1	2	3	4	5	6	7	8
Apr	6	7	8	9	1	2	3	4	5	6	7	8	9	1	2	3	4	5	6	7	8	9	1	2	3	4	5	6	7	8	
May	7	8	9	1	3	4	5	6	7	8	9	1	2	3	4	5	6	7	8	9	1	2	3	4	5	6	7	8	9	1	2
Jun	9	1	2	3	4	5	6	7	8	9	1	2	3	4	5	6	7	8	9	1	2	3	4	5	6	7	8	9	1	2	
Jul	1	2	3	4	5	6	7	8	9	1	2	3	4	5	6	7	8	9	1	2	3	4	5	6	7	8	9	1	2	3	4
Aug	2	3	4	5	6	7	8	9	1	2	3	4	5	6	7	8	9	1	2	3	4	5	6	7	8	9	1	2	3	4	5
Sep	3	4	5	6	7	8	9	1	2	3	4	5	6	7	8	9	1	2	3	4	5	6	7	8	9	1	2	3	4	5	
Oct	4	5	6	7	8	9	1	2	3	4	5	6	7	8	9	1	2	3	4	5	6	7	8	9	1	2	3	4	5	6	7
Nov	5	6	7	8	9	1	2	3	4	5	6	7	8	9	1	2	3	4	5	6	7	8	9	1	2	3	4	5	6	7	
Dec	6	7	8	9	1	2	3	4	5	6	7	8	9	1	2	3	4	5	6	7	8	9	1	2	3	4	5	6	7	8	9

MAY 6

	1	2	3	4	5	6	7	8	9	10	11	12	13	14	15	16	17	18	19	20	21	22	23	24	25	26	27	28	29	30	31
Jan	4	5	6	7	8	9	1	2	3	4	5	6	7	8	9	1	2	3	4	5	6	7	8	9	1	2	3	4	5	6	7
Feb	5	6	7	8	9	1	2	3	4	5	6	7	8	9	1	2	3	4	5	6	7	8	9	1	2	3	4	5	6		
Mar	6	7	8	9	1	2	3	4	5	6	7	8	9	1	2	3	4	5	6	7	8	9	1	2	3	4	5	6	7	8	9
Apr	7	8	9	1	2	3	4	5	6	7	8	9	1	2	3	4	5	6	7	8	9	1	2	3	4	5	6	7	8	9	
May	8	9	1	2	3	5	6	7	8	9	1	2	3	4	5	6	7	8	9	1	2	3	4	5	6	7	8	9	1	2	3
Jun	1	2	3	4	5	6	7	8	9	1	2	3	4	5	6	7	8	9	1	2	3	4	5	6	7	8	9	1	2	3	
Jul	2	3	4	5	6	7	8	9	1	2	3	4	5	6	7	8	9	1	2	3	4	5	6	7	8	9	1	2	3	4	5
Aug	3	4	5	6	7	8	9	1	2	3	4	5	6	7	8	9	1	2	3	4	5	6	7	8	9	1	2	3	4	5	6
Sep	4	5	6	7	8	9	1	2	3	4	5	6	7	8	9	1	2	3	4	5	6	7	8	9	1	2	3	4	5	6	
Oct	5	6	7	8	9	1	2	3	4	5	6	7	8	9	1	2	3	4	5	6	7	8	9	1	2	3	4	5	6	7	8
Nov	6	7	8	9	1	2	3	4	5	6	7	8	9	1	2	3	4	5	6	7	8	9	1	2	3	4	5	6	7	8	
Dec	7	8	9	1	2	3	4	5	6	7	8	9	1	2	3	4	5	6	7	8	9	1	2	3	4	5	6	7	8	9	1

MAY 7

	1	2	3	4	5	6	7	8	9	10	11	12	13	14	15	16	17	18	19	20	21	22	23	24	25	26	27	28	29	30	31
Jan	5	6	7	8	9	1	2	3	4	5	6	7	8	9	1	2	3	4	5	6	7	8	9	1	2	3	4	5	6	7	8
Feb	6	7	8	9	1	2	3	4	5	6	7	8	9	1	2	3	4	5	6	7	8	9	1	2	3	4	5	6	7		
Mar	7	8	9	1	2	3	4	5	6	7	8	9	1	2	3	4	5	6	7	8	9	1	2	3	4	5	6	7	8	9	1
Apr	8	9	1	2	3	4	5	6	7	8	9	1	2	3	4	5	6	7	8	9	1	2	3	4	5	6	7	8	9	1	
May	9	1	2	3	4	5	7	8	9	1	2	3	4	5	6	7	8	9	1	2	3	4	5	6	7	8	9	1	2	3	4
Jun	2	3	4	5	6	7	8	9	1	2	3	4	5	6	7	8	9	1	2	3	4	5	6	7	8	9	1	2	3	4	
Jul	3	4	5	6	7	8	9	1	2	3	4	5	6	7	8	9	1	2	3	4	5	6	7	8	9	1	2	3	4	5	6
Aug	4	5	6	7	8	9	1	2	3	4	5	6	7	8	9	1	2	3	4	5	6	7	8	9	1	2	3	4	5	6	7
Sep	5	6	7	8	9	1	2	3	4	5	6	7	8	9	1	2	3	4	5	6	7	8	9	1	2	3	4	5	6	7	
Oct	6	7	8	9	1	2	3	4	5	6	7	8	9	1	2	3	4	5	6	7	8	9	1	2	3	4	5	6	7	8	9
Nov	7	8	9	1	2	3	4	5	6	7	8	9	1	2	3	4	5	6	7	8	9	1	2	3	4	5	6	7	8	9	
Dec	8	9	1	2	3	4	5	6	7	8	9	1	2	3	4	5	6	7	8	9	1	2	3	4	5	6	7	8	9	1	2

MAY 8

	1	2	3	4	5	6	7	8	9	10	11	12	13	14	15	16	17	18	19	20	21	22	23	24	25	26	27	28	29	30	31
Jan	6	7	8	9	1	2	3	4	5	6	7	8	9	1	2	3	4	5	6	7	8	9	1	2	3	4	5	6	7	8	9
Feb	7	8	9	1	2	3	4	5	6	7	8	9	1	2	3	4	5	6	7	8	9	1	2	3	4	5	6	7	8		
Mar	8	9	1	2	3	4	5	6	7	8	9	1	2	3	4	5	6	7	8	9	1	2	3	4	5	6	7	8	9	1	2
Apr	9	1	2	3	4	5	6	7	8	9	1	2	3	4	5	6	7	8	9	1	2	3	4	5	6	7	8	9	1	2	
May	1	2	3	4	5	6	7	9	1	2	3	4	5	6	7	8	9	1	2	3	4	5	6	7	8	9	1	2	3	4	5
Jun	3	4	5	6	7	8	9	1	2	3	4	5	6	7	8	9	1	2	3	4	5	6	7	8	9	1	2	3	4	5	
Jul	4	5	6	7	8	9	1	2	3	4	5	6	7	8	9	1	2	3	4	5	6	7	8	9	1	2	3	4	5	6	7
Aug	5	6	7	8	9	1	2	3	4	5	6	7	8	9	1	2	3	4	5	6	7	8	9	1	2	3	4	5	6	7	8
Sep	6	7	8	9	1	2	3	4	5	6	7	8	9	1	2	3	4	5	6	7	8	9	1	2	3	4	5	6	7	8	
Oct	7	8	9	1	2	3	4	5	6	7	8	9	1	2	3	4	5	6	7	8	9	1	2	3	4	5	6	7	8	9	1
Nov	8	9	1	2	3	4	5	6	7	8	9	1	2	3	4	5	6	7	8	9	1	2	3	4	5	6	7	8	9	1	
Dec	9	1	2	3	4	5	6	7	8	9	1	2	3	4	5	6	7	8	9	1	2	3	4	5	6	7	8	9	1	2	3

MAY 9

	1	2	3	4	5	6	7	8	9	10	11	12	13	14	15	16	17	18	19	20	21	22	23	24	25	26	27	28	29	30	31
Jan	7	8	9	1	2	3	4	5	6	7	8	9	1	2	3	4	5	6	7	8	9	1	2	3	4	5	6	7	8	9	1
Feb	8	9	1	2	3	4	5	6	7	8	9	1	2	3	4	5	6	7	8	9	1	2	3	4	5	6	7	8	9		
Mar	9	1	2	3	4	5	6	7	8	9	1	2	3	4	5	6	7	8	9	1	2	3	4	5	6	7	8	9	1	2	3
Apr	1	2	3	4	5	6	7	8	9	1	2	3	4	5	6	7	8	9	1	2	3	4	5	6	7	8	9	1	2	3	
May	2	3	4	5	6	7	8	9	2	3	4	5	6	7	8	9	1	2	3	4	5	6	7	8	9	1	2	3	4	5	6
Jun	4	5	6	7	8	9	1	2	3	4	5	6	7	8	9	1	2	3	4	5	6	7	8	9	1	2	3	4	5	6	
Jul	5	6	7	8	9	1	2	3	4	5	6	7	8	9	1	2	3	4	5	6	7	8	9	1	2	3	4	5	6	7	8
Aug	6	7	8	9	1	2	3	4	5	6	7	8	9	1	2	3	4	5	6	7	8	9	1	2	3	4	5	6	7	8	9
Sep	7	8	9	1	2	3	4	5	6	7	8	9	1	2	3	4	5	6	7	8	9	1	2	3	4	5	6	7	8	9	
Oct	8	9	1	2	3	4	5	6	7	8	9	1	2	3	4	5	6	7	8	9	1	2	3	4	5	6	7	8	9	1	2
Nov	9	1	2	3	4	5	6	7	8	9	1	2	3	4	5	6	7	8	9	1	2	3	4	5	6	7	8	9	1	2	
Dec	1	2	3	4	5	6	7	8	9	1	2	3	4	5	6	7	8	9	1	2	3	4	5	6	7	8	9	1	2	3	4

MAY 10

	1	2	3	4	5	6	7	8	9	10	11	12	13	14	15	16	17	18	19	20	21	22	23	24	25	26	27	28	29	30	31
Jan	8	9	1	2	3	4	5	6	7	8	9	1	2	3	4	5	6	7	8	9	1	2	3	4	5	6	7	8	9	1	2
Feb	9	1	2	3	4	5	6	7	8	9	1	2	3	4	5	6	7	8	9	1	2	3	4	5	6	7	8	9	1		
Mar	1	2	3	4	5	6	7	8	9	1	2	3	4	5	6	7	8	9	1	2	3	4	5	6	7	8	9	1	2	3	4
Apr	2	3	4	5	6	7	8	9	1	2	3	4	5	6	7	8	9	1	2	3	4	5	6	7	8	9	1	2	3	4	
May	3	4	5	6	7	8	9	1	2	4	5	6	7	8	9	1	2	3	4	5	6	7	8	9	1	2	3	4	5	6	7
Jun	5	6	7	8	9	1	2	3	4	5	6	7	8	9	1	2	3	4	5	6	7	8	9	1	2	3	4	5	6	7	
Jul	6	7	8	9	1	2	3	4	5	6	7	8	9	1	2	3	4	5	6	7	8	9	1	2	3	4	5	6	7	8	9
Aug	7	8	9	1	2	3	4	5	6	7	8	9	1	2	3	4	5	6	7	8	9	1	2	3	4	5	6	7	8	9	1
Sep	8	9	1	2	3	4	5	6	7	8	9	1	2	3	4	5	6	7	8	9	1	2	3	4	5	6	7	8	9	1	
Oct	9	1	2	3	4	5	6	7	8	9	1	2	3	4	5	6	7	8	9	1	2	3	4	5	6	7	8	9	1	2	3
Nov	1	2	3	4	5	6	7	8	9	1	2	3	4	5	6	7	8	9	1	2	3	4	5	6	7	8	9	1	2	3	
Dec	2	3	4	5	6	7	8	9	1	2	3	4	5	6	7	8	9	1	2	3	4	5	6	7	8	9	1	2	3	4	5

MAY 11

	1	2	3	4	5	6	7	8	9	10	11	12	13	14	15	16	17	18	19	20	21	22	23	24	25	26	27	28	29	30	31
Jan	9	1	2	3	4	5	6	7	8	9	1	2	3	4	5	6	7	8	9	1	2	3	4	5	6	7	8	9	1	2	3
Feb	1	2	3	4	5	6	7	8	9	1	2	3	4	5	6	7	8	9	1	2	3	4	5	6	7	8	9	1	2		
Mar	2	3	4	5	6	7	8	9	1	2	3	4	5	6	7	8	9	1	2	3	4	5	6	7	8	9	1	2	3	4	5
Apr	3	4	5	6	7	8	9	1	2	3	4	5	6	7	8	9	1	2	3	4	5	6	7	8	9	1	2	3	4	5	
May	4	5	6	7	8	9	1	2	3	4	6	7	8	9	1	2	3	4	5	6	7	8	9	1	2	3	4	5	6	7	8
Jun	6	7	8	9	1	2	3	4	5	6	7	8	9	1	2	3	4	5	6	7	8	9	1	2	3	4	5	6	7	8	
Jul	7	8	9	1	2	3	4	5	6	7	8	9	1	2	3	4	5	6	7	8	9	1	2	3	4	5	6	7	8	9	1
Aug	8	9	1	2	3	4	5	6	7	8	9	1	2	3	4	5	6	7	8	9	1	2	3	4	5	6	7	8	9	1	2
Sep	9	1	2	3	4	5	6	7	8	9	1	2	3	4	5	6	7	8	9	1	2	3	4	5	6	7	8	9	1	2	
Oct	1	2	3	4	5	6	7	8	9	1	2	3	4	5	6	7	8	9	1	2	3	4	5	6	7	8	9	1	2	3	4
Nov	2	3	4	5	6	7	8	9	1	2	3	4	5	6	7	8	9	1	2	3	4	5	6	7	8	9	1	2	3	4	
Dec	3	4	5	6	7	8	9	1	2	3	4	5	6	7	8	9	1	2	3	4	5	6	7	8	9	1	2	3	4	5	6

MAY 12

	1	2	3	4	5	6	7	8	9	10	11	12	13	14	15	16	17	18	19	20	21	22	23	24	25	26	27	28	29	30	31
Jan	1	2	3	4	5	6	7	8	9	1	2	3	4	5	6	7	8	9	1	2	3	4	5	6	7	8	9	1	2	3	4
Feb	2	3	4	5	6	7	8	9	1	2	3	4	5	6	7	8	9	1	2	3	4	5	6	7	8	9	1	2	3		
Mar	3	4	5	6	7	8	9	1	2	3	4	5	6	7	8	9	1	2	3	4	5	6	7	8	9	1	2	3	4	5	6
Apr	4	5	6	7	8	9	1	2	3	4	5	6	7	8	9	1	2	3	4	5	6	7	8	9	1	2	3	4	5	6	
May	5	6	7	8	9	1	2	3	4	5	6	8	9	1	2	3	4	5	6	7	8	9	1	2	3	4	5	6	7	8	9
Jun	7	8	9	1	2	3	4	5	6	7	8	9	1	2	3	4	5	6	7	8	9	1	2	3	4	5	6	7	8	9	
Jul	8	9	1	2	3	4	5	6	7	8	9	1	2	3	4	5	6	7	8	9	1	2	3	4	5	6	7	8	9	1	2
Aug	9	1	2	3	4	5	6	7	8	9	1	2	3	4	5	6	7	8	9	1	2	3	4	5	6	7	8	9	1	2	3
Sep	1	2	3	4	5	6	7	8	9	1	2	3	4	5	6	7	8	9	1	2	3	4	5	6	7	8	9	1	2	3	
Oct	2	3	4	5	6	7	8	9	1	2	3	4	5	6	7	8	9	1	2	3	4	5	6	7	8	9	1	2	3	4	5
Nov	3	4	5	6	7	8	9	1	2	3	4	5	6	7	8	9	1	2	3	4	5	6	7	8	9	1	2	3	4	5	
Dec	4	5	6	7	8	9	1	2	3	4	5	6	7	8	9	1	2	3	4	5	6	7	8	9	1	2	3	4	5	6	7

MAY 13

	1	2	3	4	5	6	7	8	9	10	11	12	13	14	15	16	17	18	19	20	21	22	23	24	25	26	27	28	29	30	31
Jan	2	3	4	5	6	7	8	9	1	2	3	4	5	6	7	8	9	1	2	3	4	5	6	7	8	9	1	2	3	4	5
Feb	3	4	5	6	7	8	9	1	2	3	4	5	6	7	8	9	1	2	3	4	5	6	7	8	9	1	2	3	4		
Mar	4	5	6	7	8	9	1	2	3	4	5	6	7	8	9	1	2	3	4	5	6	7	8	9	1	2	3	4	5	6	7
Apr	5	6	7	8	9	1	2	3	4	5	6	7	8	9	1	2	3	4	5	6	7	8	9	1	2	3	4	5	6	7	
May	6	7	8	9	1	2	3	4	5	6	7	8	1	2	3	4	5	6	7	8	9	1	2	3	4	5	6	7	8	9	1
Jun	8	9	1	2	3	4	5	6	7	8	9	1	2	3	4	5	6	7	8	9	1	2	3	4	5	6	7	8	9	1	
Jul	9	1	2	3	4	5	6	7	8	9	1	2	3	4	5	6	7	8	9	1	2	3	4	5	6	7	8	9	1	2	3
Aug	1	2	3	4	5	6	7	8	9	1	2	3	4	5	6	7	8	9	1	2	3	4	5	6	7	8	9	1	2	3	4
Sep	2	3	4	5	6	7	8	9	1	2	3	4	5	6	7	8	9	1	2	3	4	5	6	7	8	9	1	2	3	4	
Oct	3	4	5	6	7	8	9	1	2	3	4	5	6	7	8	9	1	2	3	4	5	6	7	8	9	1	2	3	4	5	6
Nov	4	5	6	7	8	9	1	2	3	4	5	6	7	8	9	1	2	3	4	5	6	7	8	9	1	2	3	4	5	6	
Dec	5	6	7	8	9	1	2	3	4	5	6	7	8	9	1	2	3	4	5	6	7	8	9	1	2	3	4	5	6	7	8

MAY 14

	1	2	3	4	5	6	7	8	9	10	11	12	13	14	15	16	17	18	19	20	21	22	23	24	25	26	27	28	29	30	31
Jan	3	4	5	6	7	8	9	1	2	3	4	5	6	7	8	9	1	2	3	4	5	6	7	8	9	1	2	3	4	5	6
Feb	4	5	6	7	8	9	1	2	3	4	5	6	7	8	9	1	2	3	4	5	6	7	8	9	1	2	3	4	5		
Mar	5	6	7	8	9	1	2	3	4	5	6	7	8	9	1	2	3	4	5	6	7	8	9	1	2	3	4	5	6	7	8
Apr	6	7	8	9	1	2	3	4	5	6	7	8	9	1	2	3	4	5	6	7	8	9	1	2	3	4	5	6	7	8	
May	7	8	9	1	2	3	4	5	6	7	8	9	1	3	4	5	6	7	8	9	1	2	3	4	5	6	7	8	9	1	2
Jun	9	1	2	3	4	5	6	7	8	9	1	2	3	4	5	6	7	8	9	1	2	3	4	5	6	7	8	9	1	2	
Jul	1	2	3	4	5	6	7	8	9	1	2	3	4	5	6	7	8	9	1	2	3	4	5	6	7	8	9	1	2	3	4
Aug	2	3	4	5	6	7	8	9	1	2	3	4	5	6	7	8	9	1	2	3	4	5	6	7	8	9	1	2	3	4	5
Sep	3	4	5	6	7	8	9	1	2	3	4	5	6	7	8	9	1	2	3	4	5	6	7	8	9	1	2	3	4	5	
Oct	4	5	6	7	8	9	1	2	3	4	5	6	7	8	9	1	2	3	4	5	6	7	8	9	1	2	3	4	5	6	7
Nov	5	6	7	8	9	1	2	3	4	5	6	7	8	9	1	2	3	4	5	6	7	8	9	1	2	3	4	5	6	7	
Dec	6	7	8	9	1	2	3	4	5	6	7	8	9	1	2	3	4	5	6	7	8	9	1	2	3	4	5	6	7	8	9

MAY 15

	1	2	3	4	5	6	7	8	9	10	11	12	13	14	15	16	17	18	19	20	21	22	23	24	25	26	27	28	29	30	31
Jan	4	5	6	7	8	9	1	2	3	4	5	6	7	8	9	1	2	3	4	5	6	7	8	9	1	2	3	4	5	6	7
Feb	5	6	7	8	9	1	2	3	4	5	6	7	8	9	1	2	3	4	5	6	7	8	9	1	2	3	4	5	6		
Mar	6	7	8	9	1	2	3	4	5	6	7	8	9	1	2	3	4	5	6	7	8	9	1	2	3	4	5	6	7	8	9
Apr	7	8	9	1	2	3	4	5	6	7	8	9	1	2	3	4	5	6	7	8	9	1	2	3	4	5	6	7	8	9	
May	8	9	1	2	3	4	5	6	7	8	9	1	2	3	5	6	7	8	9	1	2	3	4	5	6	7	8	9	1	2	3
Jun	1	2	3	4	5	6	7	8	9	1	2	3	4	5	6	7	8	9	1	2	3	4	5	6	7	8	9	1	2	3	
Jul	2	3	4	5	6	7	8	9	1	2	3	4	5	6	7	8	9	1	2	3	4	5	6	7	8	9	1	2	3	4	5
Aug	3	4	5	6	7	8	9	1	2	3	4	5	6	7	8	9	1	2	3	4	5	6	7	8	9	1	2	3	4	5	6
Sep	4	5	6	7	8	9	1	2	3	4	5	6	7	8	9	1	2	3	4	5	6	7	8	9	1	2	3	4	5	6	
Oct	5	6	7	8	9	1	2	3	4	5	6	7	8	9	1	2	3	4	5	6	7	8	9	1	2	3	4	5	6	7	8
Nov	6	7	8	9	1	2	3	4	5	6	7	8	9	1	2	3	4	5	6	7	8	9	1	2	3	4	5	6	7	8	
Dec	7	8	9	1	2	3	4	5	6	7	8	9	1	2	3	4	5	6	7	8	9	1	2	3	4	5	6	7	8	9	1

MAY 16

	1	2	3	4	5	6	7	8	9	10	11	12	13	14	15	16	17	18	19	20	21	22	23	24	25	26	27	28	29	30	31
Jan	5	6	7	8	9	1	2	3	4	5	6	7	8	9	1	2	3	4	5	6	7	8	9	1	2	3	4	5	6	7	8
Feb	6	7	8	9	1	2	3	4	5	6	7	8	9	1	2	3	4	5	6	7	8	9	1	2	3	4	5	6	7		
Mar	7	8	9	1	2	3	4	5	6	7	8	9	1	2	3	4	5	6	7	8	9	1	2	3	4	5	6	7	8	9	1
Apr	8	9	1	2	3	4	5	6	7	8	9	1	2	3	4	5	6	7	8	9	1	2	3	4	5	6	7	8	9	1	
May	9	1	2	3	4	5	6	7	8	9	1	2	3	4	5	7	8	9	1	2	3	4	5	6	7	8	9	1	2	3	4
Jun	2	3	4	5	6	7	8	9	1	2	3	4	5	6	7	8	9	1	2	3	4	5	6	7	8	9	1	2	3	4	
Jul	3	4	5	6	7	8	9	1	2	3	4	5	6	7	8	9	1	2	3	4	5	6	7	8	9	1	2	3	4	5	6
Aug	4	5	6	7	8	9	1	2	3	4	5	6	7	8	9	1	2	3	4	5	6	7	8	9	1	2	3	4	5	6	7
Sep	5	6	7	8	9	1	2	3	4	5	6	7	8	9	1	2	3	4	5	6	7	8	9	1	2	3	4	5	6	7	
Oct	6	7	8	9	1	2	3	4	5	6	7	8	9	1	2	3	4	5	6	7	8	9	1	2	3	4	5	6	7	8	9
Nov	7	8	9	1	2	3	4	5	6	7	8	9	1	2	3	4	5	6	7	8	9	1	2	3	4	5	6	7	8	9	
Dec	8	9	1	2	3	4	5	6	7	8	9	1	2	3	4	5	6	7	8	9	1	2	3	4	5	6	7	8	9	1	2

MAY 17

	1	2	3	4	5	6	7	8	9	10	11	12	13	14	15	16	17	18	19	20	21	22	23	24	25	26	27	28	29	30	31
Jan	6	7	8	9	1	2	3	4	5	6	7	8	9	1	2	3	4	5	6	7	8	9	1	2	3	4	5	6	7	8	9
Feb	7	8	9	1	2	3	4	5	6	7	8	9	1	2	3	4	5	6	7	8	9	1	2	3	4	5	6	7	8		
Mar	8	9	1	2	3	4	5	6	7	8	9	1	2	3	4	5	6	7	8	9	1	2	3	4	5	6	7	8	9	1	2
Apr	9	1	2	3	4	5	6	7	8	9	1	2	3	4	5	6	7	8	9	1	2	3	4	5	6	7	8	9	1	2	
May	1	2	3	4	5	6	7	8	9	1	2	3	4	5	6	7	9	1	2	3	4	5	6	7	8	9	1	2	3	4	5
Jun	3	4	5	6	7	8	9	1	2	3	4	5	6	7	8	9	1	2	3	4	5	6	7	8	9	1	2	3	4	5	
Jul	4	5	6	7	8	9	1	2	3	4	5	6	7	8	9	1	2	3	4	5	6	7	8	9	1	2	3	4	5	6	7
Aug	5	6	7	8	9	1	2	3	4	5	6	7	8	9	1	2	3	4	5	6	7	8	9	1	2	3	4	5	6	7	8
Sep	6	7	8	9	1	2	3	4	5	6	7	8	9	1	2	3	4	5	6	7	8	9	1	2	3	4	5	6	7	8	
Oct	7	8	9	1	2	3	4	5	6	7	8	9	1	2	3	4	5	6	7	8	9	1	2	3	4	5	6	7	8	9	1
Nov	8	9	1	2	3	4	5	6	7	8	9	1	2	3	4	5	6	7	8	9	1	2	3	4	5	6	7	8	9	1	
Dec	9	1	2	3	4	5	6	7	8	9	1	2	3	4	5	6	7	8	9	1	2	3	4	5	6	7	8	9	1	2	3

MAY 18

	1	2	3	4	5	6	7	8	9	10	11	12	13	14	15	16	17	18	19	20	21	22	23	24	25	26	27	28	29	30	31
Jan	7	8	9	1	2	3	4	5	6	7	8	9	1	2	3	4	5	6	7	8	9	1	2	3	4	5	6	7	8	9	1
Feb	8	9	1	2	3	4	5	6	7	8	9	1	2	3	4	5	6	7	8	9	1	2	3	4	5	6	7	8	9		
Mar	9	1	2	3	4	5	6	7	8	9	1	2	3	4	5	6	7	8	9	1	2	3	4	5	6	7	8	9	1	2	3
Apr	1	2	3	4	5	6	7	8	9	1	2	3	4	5	6	7	8	9	1	2	3	4	5	6	7	8	9	1	2	3	
May	2	3	4	5	6	7	8	9	1	2	3	4	5	6	7	8	9	2	3	4	5	6	7	8	9	1	2	3	4	5	6
Jun	4	5	6	7	8	9	1	2	3	4	5	6	7	8	9	1	2	3	4	5	6	7	8	9	1	2	3	4	5	6	
Jul	5	6	7	8	9	1	2	3	4	5	6	7	8	9	1	2	3	4	5	6	7	8	9	1	2	3	4	5	6	7	8
Aug	6	7	8	9	1	2	3	4	5	6	7	8	9	1	2	3	4	5	6	7	8	9	1	2	3	4	5	6	7	8	9
Sep	7	8	9	1	2	3	4	5	6	7	8	9	1	2	3	4	5	6	7	8	9	1	2	3	4	5	6	7	8	9	
Oct	8	9	1	2	3	4	5	6	7	8	9	1	2	3	4	5	6	7	8	9	1	2	3	4	5	6	7	8	9	1	2
Nov	9	1	2	3	4	5	6	7	8	9	1	2	3	4	5	6	7	8	9	1	2	3	4	5	6	7	8	9	1	2	
Dec	1	2	3	4	5	6	7	8	9	1	2	3	4	5	6	7	8	9	1	2	3	4	5	6	7	8	9	1	2	3	4

MAY 19

	1	2	3	4	5	6	7	8	9	10	11	12	13	14	15	16	17	18	19	20	21	22	23	24	25	26	27	28	29	30	31
Jan	8	9	1	2	3	4	5	6	7	8	9	1	2	3	4	5	6	7	8	9	1	2	3	4	5	6	7	8	9	1	2
Feb	9	1	2	3	4	5	6	7	8	9	1	2	3	4	5	6	7	8	9	1	2	3	4	5	6	7	8	9	1		
Mar	1	2	3	4	5	6	7	8	9	1	2	3	4	5	6	7	8	9	1	2	3	4	5	6	7	8	9	1	2	3	4
Apr	2	3	4	5	6	7	8	9	1	2	3	4	5	6	7	8	9	1	2	3	4	5	6	7	8	9	1	2	3	4	
May	3	4	5	6	7	8	9	1	2	3	4	5	6	7	8	9	1	2	4	5	6	7	8	9	1	2	3	4	5	6	7
Jun	5	6	7	8	9	1	2	3	4	5	6	7	8	9	1	2	3	4	5	6	7	8	9	1	2	3	4	5	6	7	
Jul	6	7	8	9	1	2	3	4	5	6	7	8	9	1	2	3	4	5	6	7	8	9	1	2	3	4	5	6	7	8	9
Aug	7	8	9	1	2	3	4	5	6	7	8	9	1	2	3	4	5	6	7	8	9	1	2	3	4	5	6	7	8	9	1
Sep	8	9	1	2	3	4	5	6	7	8	9	1	2	3	4	5	6	7	8	9	1	2	3	4	5	6	7	8	9	1	
Oct	9	1	2	3	4	5	6	7	8	9	1	2	3	4	5	6	7	8	9	1	2	3	4	5	6	7	8	9	1	2	3
Nov	1	2	3	4	5	6	7	8	9	1	2	3	4	5	6	7	8	9	1	2	3	4	5	6	7	8	9	1	2	3	
Dec	2	3	4	5	6	7	8	9	1	2	3	4	5	6	7	8	9	1	2	3	4	5	6	7	8	9	1	2	3	4	5

MAY 20

	1	2	3	4	5	6	7	8	9	10	11	12	13	14	15	16	17	18	19	20	21	22	23	24	25	26	27	28	29	30	31
Jan	9	1	2	3	4	5	6	7	8	9	1	2	3	4	5	6	7	8	9	1	2	3	4	5	6	7	8	9	1	2	3
Feb	1	2	3	4	5	6	7	8	9	1	2	3	4	5	6	7	8	9	1	2	3	4	5	6	7	8	9	1	2		
Mar	2	3	4	5	6	7	8	9	1	2	3	4	5	6	7	8	9	1	2	3	4	5	6	7	8	9	1	2	3	4	5
Apr	3	4	5	6	7	8	9	1	2	3	4	5	6	7	8	9	1	2	3	4	5	6	7	8	9	1	2	3	4	5	
May	4	5	6	7	8	9	1	2	3	4	5	6	7	8	9	1	2	3	4	6	7	8	9	1	2	3	4	5	6	7	8
Jun	6	7	8	9	1	2	3	4	5	6	7	8	9	1	2	3	4	5	6	7	8	9	1	2	3	4	5	6	7	8	
Jul	7	8	9	1	2	3	4	5	6	7	8	9	1	2	3	4	5	6	7	8	9	1	2	3	4	5	6	7	8	9	1
Aug	8	9	1	2	3	4	5	6	7	8	9	1	2	3	4	5	6	7	8	9	1	2	3	4	5	6	7	8	9	1	2
Sep	9	1	2	3	4	5	6	7	8	9	1	2	3	4	5	6	7	8	9	1	2	3	4	5	6	7	8	9	1	2	
Oct	1	2	3	4	5	6	7	8	9	1	2	3	4	5	6	7	8	9	1	2	3	4	5	6	7	8	9	1	2	3	4
Nov	2	3	4	5	6	7	8	9	1	2	3	4	5	6	7	8	9	1	2	3	4	5	6	7	8	9	1	2	3	4	
Dec	3	4	5	6	7	8	9	1	2	3	4	5	6	7	8	9	1	2	3	4	5	6	7	8	9	1	2	3	4	5	6

MAY 21

	1	2	3	4	5	6	7	8	9	10	11	12	13	14	15	16	17	18	19	20	21	22	23	24	25	26	27	28	29	30	31
Jan	1	2	3	4	5	6	7	8	9	1	2	3	4	5	6	7	8	9	1	2	3	4	5	6	7	8	9	1	2	3	4
Feb	2	3	4	5	6	7	8	9	1	2	3	4	5	6	7	8	9	1	2	3	4	5	6	7	8	9	1	2	3		
Mar	3	4	5	6	7	8	9	1	2	3	4	5	6	7	8	9	1	2	3	4	5	6	7	8	9	1	2	3	4	5	6
Apr	4	5	6	7	8	9	1	2	3	4	5	6	7	8	9	1	2	3	4	5	6	7	8	9	1	2	3	4	5	6	
May	5	6	7	8	9	1	2	3	4	5	6	7	8	9	1	2	3	4	5	6	8	9	1	2	3	4	5	6	7	8	9
Jun	7	8	9	1	2	3	4	5	6	7	8	9	1	2	3	4	5	6	7	8	9	1	2	3	4	5	6	7	8	9	
Jul	8	9	1	2	3	4	5	6	7	8	9	1	2	3	4	5	6	7	8	9	1	2	3	4	5	6	7	8	9	1	2
Aug	9	1	2	3	4	5	6	7	8	9	1	2	3	4	5	6	7	8	9	1	2	3	4	5	6	7	8	9	1	2	3
Sep	1	2	3	4	5	6	7	8	9	1	2	3	4	5	6	7	8	9	1	2	3	4	5	6	7	8	9	1	2	3	
Oct	2	3	4	5	6	7	8	9	1	2	3	4	5	6	7	8	9	1	2	3	4	5	6	7	8	9	1	2	3	4	5
Nov	3	4	5	6	7	8	9	1	2	3	4	5	6	7	8	9	1	2	3	4	5	6	7	8	9	1	2	3	4	5	
Dec	4	5	6	7	8	9	1	2	3	4	5	6	7	8	9	1	2	3	4	5	6	7	8	9	1	2	3	4	5	6	7

MAY 22

	1	2	3	4	5	6	7	8	9	10	11	12	13	14	15	16	17	18	19	20	21	22	23	24	25	26	27	28	29	30	31
Jan	2	3	4	5	6	7	8	9	1	2	3	4	5	6	7	8	9	1	2	3	4	5	6	7	8	9	1	2	3	4	5
Feb	3	4	5	6	7	8	9	1	2	3	4	5	6	7	8	9	1	2	3	4	5	6	7	8	9	1	2	3	4		
Mar	4	5	6	7	8	9	1	2	3	4	5	6	7	8	9	1	2	3	4	5	6	7	8	9	1	2	3	4	5	6	7
Apr	5	6	7	8	9	1	2	3	4	5	6	7	8	9	1	2	3	4	5	6	7	8	9	1	2	3	4	5	6	7	
May	6	7	8	9	1	2	3	4	5	6	7	8	9	1	2	3	4	5	6	7	8	1	2	3	4	5	6	7	8	9	1
Jun	8	9	1	2	3	4	5	6	7	8	9	1	2	3	4	5	6	7	8	9	1	2	3	4	5	6	7	8	9	1	
Jul	9	1	2	3	4	5	6	7	8	9	1	2	3	4	5	6	7	8	9	1	2	3	4	5	6	7	8	9	1	2	3
Aug	1	2	3	4	5	6	7	8	9	1	2	3	4	5	6	7	8	9	1	2	3	4	5	6	7	8	9	1	2	3	4
Sep	2	3	4	5	6	7	8	9	1	2	3	4	5	6	7	8	9	1	2	3	4	5	6	7	8	9	1	2	3	4	
Oct	3	4	5	6	7	8	9	1	2	3	4	5	6	7	8	9	1	2	3	4	5	6	7	8	9	1	2	3	4	5	6
Nov	4	5	6	7	8	9	1	2	3	4	5	6	7	8	9	1	2	3	4	5	6	7	8	9	1	2	3	4	5	6	
Dec	5	6	7	8	9	1	2	3	4	5	6	7	8	9	1	2	3	4	5	6	7	8	9	1	2	3	4	5	6	7	8

MAY 23

	1	2	3	4	5	6	7	8	9	10	11	12	13	14	15	16	17	18	19	20	21	22	23	24	25	26	27	28	29	30	31
Jan	3	4	5	6	7	8	9	1	2	3	4	5	6	7	8	9	1	2	3	4	5	6	7	8	9	1	2	3	4	5	6
Feb	4	5	6	7	8	9	1	2	3	4	5	6	7	8	9	1	2	3	4	5	6	7	8	9	1	2	3	4	5		
Mar	5	6	7	8	9	1	2	3	4	5	6	7	8	9	1	2	3	4	5	6	7	8	9	1	2	3	4	5	6	7	8
Apr	6	7	8	9	1	2	3	4	5	6	7	8	9	1	2	3	4	5	6	7	8	9	1	2	3	4	5	6	7	8	
May	7	8	9	1	2	3	4	5	6	7	8	9	1	2	3	4	5	6	7	8	9	1	3	4	5	6	7	8	9	1	2
Jun	9	1	2	3	4	5	6	7	8	9	1	2	3	4	5	6	7	8	9	1	2	3	4	5	6	7	8	9	1	2	
Jul	1	2	3	4	5	6	7	8	9	1	2	3	4	5	6	7	8	9	1	2	3	4	5	6	7	8	9	1	2	3	4
Aug	2	3	4	5	6	7	8	9	1	2	3	4	5	6	7	8	9	1	2	3	4	5	6	7	8	9	1	2	3	4	5
Sep	3	4	5	6	7	8	9	1	2	3	4	5	6	7	8	9	1	2	3	4	5	6	7	8	9	1	2	3	4	5	
Oct	4	5	6	7	8	9	1	2	3	4	5	6	7	8	9	1	2	3	4	5	6	7	8	9	1	2	3	4	5	6	7
Nov	5	6	7	8	9	1	2	3	4	5	6	7	8	9	1	2	3	4	5	6	7	8	9	1	2	3	4	5	6	7	
Dec	6	7	8	9	1	2	3	4	5	6	7	8	9	1	2	3	4	5	6	7	8	9	1	2	3	4	5	6	7	8	9

MAY 24

	1	2	3	4	5	6	7	8	9	10	11	12	13	14	15	16	17	18	19	20	21	22	23	24	25	26	27	28	29	30	31
Jan	4	5	6	7	8	9	1	2	3	4	5	6	7	8	9	1	2	3	4	5	6	7	8	9	1	2	3	4	5	6	7
Feb	5	6	7	8	9	1	2	3	4	5	6	7	8	9	1	2	3	4	5	6	7	8	9	1	2	3	4	5	6		
Mar	6	7	8	9	1	2	3	4	5	6	7	8	9	1	2	3	4	5	6	7	8	9	1	2	3	4	5	6	7	8	9
Apr	7	8	9	1	2	3	4	5	6	7	8	9	1	2	3	4	5	6	7	8	9	1	2	3	4	5	6	7	8	9	
May	8	9	1	2	3	4	5	6	7	8	9	1	2	3	4	5	6	7	8	9	1	2	3	5	6	7	8	9	1	2	3
Jun	1	2	3	4	5	6	7	8	9	1	2	3	4	5	6	7	8	9	1	2	3	4	5	6	7	8	9	1	2	3	
Jul	2	3	4	5	6	7	8	9	1	2	3	4	5	6	7	8	9	1	2	3	4	5	6	7	8	9	1	2	3	4	5
Aug	3	4	5	6	7	8	9	1	2	3	4	5	6	7	8	9	1	2	3	4	5	6	7	8	9	1	2	3	4	5	6
Sep	4	5	6	7	8	9	1	2	3	4	5	6	7	8	9	1	2	3	4	5	6	7	8	9	1	2	3	4	5	6	
Oct	5	6	7	8	9	1	2	3	4	5	6	7	8	9	1	2	3	4	5	6	7	8	9	1	2	3	4	5	6	7	8
Nov	6	7	8	9	1	2	3	4	5	6	7	8	9	1	2	3	4	5	6	7	8	9	1	2	3	4	5	6	7	8	
Dec	7	8	9	1	2	3	4	5	6	7	8	9	1	2	3	4	5	6	7	8	9	1	2	3	4	5	6	7	8	9	1

MAY 25

	1	2	3	4	5	6	7	8	9	10	11	12	13	14	15	16	17	18	19	20	21	22	23	24	25	26	27	28	29	30	31
Jan	5	6	7	8	9	1	2	3	4	5	6	7	8	9	1	2	3	4	5	6	7	8	9	1	2	3	4	5	6	7	8
Feb	6	7	8	9	1	2	3	4	5	6	7	8	9	1	2	3	4	5	6	7	8	9	1	2	3	4	5	6	7		
Mar	7	8	9	1	2	3	4	5	6	7	8	9	1	2	3	4	5	6	7	8	9	1	2	3	4	5	6	7	8	9	1
Apr	8	9	1	2	3	4	5	6	7	8	9	1	2	3	4	5	6	7	8	9	1	2	3	4	5	6	7	8	9	1	
May	9	1	2	3	4	5	6	7	8	9	1	2	3	4	5	6	7	8	9	1	2	3	4	5	7	8	9	1	2	3	4
Jun	2	3	4	5	6	7	8	9	1	2	3	4	5	6	7	8	9	1	2	3	4	5	6	7	8	9	1	2	3	4	
Jul	3	4	5	6	7	8	9	1	2	3	4	5	6	7	8	9	1	2	3	4	5	6	7	8	9	1	2	3	4	5	6
Aug	4	5	6	7	8	9	1	2	3	4	5	6	7	8	9	1	2	3	4	5	6	7	8	9	1	2	3	4	5	6	7
Sep	5	6	7	8	9	1	2	3	4	5	6	7	8	9	1	2	3	4	5	6	7	8	9	1	2	3	4	5	6	7	
Oct	6	7	8	9	1	2	3	4	5	6	7	8	9	1	2	3	4	5	6	7	8	9	1	2	3	4	5	6	7	8	9
Nov	7	8	9	1	2	3	4	5	6	7	8	9	1	2	3	4	5	6	7	8	9	1	2	3	4	5	6	7	8	9	
Dec	8	9	1	2	3	4	5	6	7	8	9	1	2	3	4	5	6	7	8	9	1	2	3	4	5	6	7	8	9	1	2

MAY 26

	1	2	3	4	5	6	7	8	9	10	11	12	13	14	15	16	17	18	19	20	21	22	23	24	25	26	27	28	29	30	31
Jan	6	7	8	9	1	2	3	4	5	6	7	8	9	1	2	3	4	5	6	7	8	9	1	2	3	4	5	6	7	8	9
Feb	7	8	9	1	2	3	4	5	6	7	8	9	1	2	3	4	5	6	7	8	9	1	2	3	4	5	6	7	8		
Mar	8	9	1	2	3	4	5	6	7	8	9	1	2	3	4	5	6	7	8	9	1	2	3	4	5	6	7	8	9	1	2
Apr	9	1	2	3	4	5	6	7	8	9	1	2	3	4	5	6	7	8	9	1	2	3	4	5	6	7	8	9	1	2	
May	1	2	3	4	5	6	7	8	9	1	2	3	4	5	6	7	8	9	1	2	3	4	5	6	7	9	1	2	3	4	5
Jun	3	4	5	6	7	8	9	1	2	3	4	5	6	7	8	9	1	2	3	4	5	6	7	8	9	1	2	3	4	5	
Jul	4	5	6	7	8	9	1	2	3	4	5	6	7	8	9	1	2	3	4	5	6	7	8	9	1	2	3	4	5	6	7
Aug	5	6	7	8	9	1	2	3	4	5	6	7	8	9	1	2	3	4	5	6	7	8	9	1	2	3	4	5	6	7	8
Sep	6	7	8	9	1	2	3	4	5	6	7	8	9	1	2	3	4	5	6	7	8	9	1	2	3	4	5	6	7	8	
Oct	7	8	9	1	2	3	4	5	6	7	8	9	1	2	3	4	5	6	7	8	9	1	2	3	4	5	6	7	8	9	1
Nov	8	9	1	2	3	4	5	6	7	8	9	1	2	3	4	5	6	7	8	9	1	2	3	4	5	6	7	8	9	1	
Dec	9	1	2	3	4	5	6	7	8	9	1	2	3	4	5	6	7	8	9	1	2	3	4	5	6	7	8	9	1	2	3

MAY 27

	1	2	3	4	5	6	7	8	9	10	11	12	13	14	15	16	17	18	19	20	21	22	23	24	25	26	27	28	29	30	31
Jan	7	8	9	1	2	3	4	5	6	7	8	9	1	2	3	4	5	6	7	8	9	1	2	3	4	5	6	7	8	9	1
Feb	8	9	1	2	3	4	5	6	7	8	9	1	2	3	4	5	6	7	8	9	1	2	3	4	5	6	7	8	9		
Mar	9	1	2	3	4	5	6	7	8	9	1	2	3	4	5	6	7	8	9	1	2	3	4	5	6	7	8	9	1	2	3
Apr	1	2	3	4	5	6	7	8	9	1	2	3	4	5	6	7	8	9	1	2	3	4	5	6	7	8	9	1	2	3	
May	2	3	4	5	6	7	8	9	1	2	3	4	5	6	7	8	9	1	2	3	4	5	6	7	8	9	2	3	4	5	6
Jun	4	5	6	7	8	9	1	2	3	4	5	6	7	8	9	1	2	3	4	5	6	7	8	9	1	2	3	4	5	6	
Jul	5	6	7	8	9	1	2	3	4	5	6	7	8	9	1	2	3	4	5	6	7	8	9	1	2	3	4	5	6	7	8
Aug	6	7	8	9	1	2	3	4	5	6	7	8	9	1	2	3	4	5	6	7	8	9	1	2	3	4	5	6	7	8	9
Sep	7	8	9	1	2	3	4	5	6	7	8	9	1	2	3	4	5	6	7	8	9	1	2	3	4	5	6	7	8	9	
Oct	8	9	1	2	3	4	5	6	7	8	9	1	2	3	4	5	6	7	8	9	1	2	3	4	5	6	7	8	9	1	2
Nov	9	1	2	3	4	5	6	7	8	9	1	2	3	4	5	6	7	8	9	1	2	3	4	5	6	7	8	9	1	2	
Dec	1	2	3	4	5	6	7	8	9	1	2	3	4	5	6	7	8	9	1	2	3	4	5	6	7	8	9	1	2	3	4

MAY 28

	1	2	3	4	5	6	7	8	9	10	11	12	13	14	15	16	17	18	19	20	21	22	23	24	25	26	27	28	29	30	31
Jan	8	9	1	2	3	4	5	6	7	8	9	1	2	3	4	5	6	7	8	9	1	2	3	4	5	6	7	8	9	1	2
Feb	9	1	2	3	4	5	6	7	8	9	1	2	3	4	5	6	7	8	9	1	2	3	4	5	6	7	8	9	1		
Mar	1	2	3	4	5	6	7	8	9	1	2	3	4	5	6	7	8	9	1	2	3	4	5	6	7	8	9	1	2	3	4
Apr	2	3	4	5	6	7	8	9	1	2	3	4	5	6	7	8	9	1	2	3	4	5	6	7	8	9	1	2	3	4	
May	3	4	5	6	7	8	9	1	2	3	4	5	6	7	8	9	1	2	3	4	5	6	7	8	9	1	2	4	5	6	7
Jun	5	6	7	8	9	1	2	3	4	5	6	7	8	9	1	2	3	4	5	6	7	8	9	1	2	3	4	5	6	7	
Jul	6	7	8	9	1	2	3	4	5	6	7	8	9	1	2	3	4	5	6	7	8	9	1	2	3	4	5	6	7	8	9
Aug	7	8	9	1	2	3	4	5	6	7	8	9	1	2	3	4	5	6	7	8	9	1	2	3	4	5	6	7	8	9	1
Sep	8	9	1	2	3	4	5	6	7	8	9	1	2	3	4	5	6	7	8	9	1	2	3	4	5	6	7	8	9	1	
Oct	9	1	2	3	4	5	6	7	8	9	1	2	3	4	5	6	7	8	9	1	2	3	4	5	6	7	8	9	1	2	3
Nov	1	2	3	4	5	6	7	8	9	1	2	3	4	5	6	7	8	9	1	2	3	4	5	6	7	8	9	1	2	3	
Dec	2	3	4	5	6	7	8	9	1	2	3	4	5	6	7	8	9	1	2	3	4	5	6	7	8	9	1	2	3	4	5

MAY 29

	1	2	3	4	5	6	7	8	9	10	11	12	13	14	15	16	17	18	19	20	21	22	23	24	25	26	27	28	29	30	31
Jan	9	1	2	3	4	5	6	7	8	9	1	2	3	4	5	6	7	8	9	1	2	3	4	5	6	7	8	9	1	2	3
Feb	1	2	3	4	5	6	7	8	9	1	2	3	4	5	6	7	8	9	1	2	3	4	5	6	7	8	9	1	2		
Mar	2	3	4	5	6	7	8	9	1	2	3	4	5	6	7	8	9	1	2	3	4	5	6	7	8	9	1	2	3	4	5
Apr	3	4	5	6	7	8	9	1	2	3	4	5	6	7	8	9	1	2	3	4	5	6	7	8	9	1	2	3	4	5	
May	4	5	6	7	8	9	1	2	3	4	5	6	7	8	9	1	2	3	4	5	6	7	8	9	1	2	3	4	6	7	8
Jun	6	7	8	9	1	2	3	4	5	6	7	8	9	1	2	3	4	5	6	7	8	9	1	2	3	4	5	6	7	8	
Jul	7	8	9	1	2	3	4	5	6	7	8	9	1	2	3	4	5	6	7	8	9	1	2	3	4	5	6	7	8	9	1
Aug	8	9	1	2	3	4	5	6	7	8	9	1	2	3	4	5	6	7	8	9	1	2	3	4	5	6	7	8	9	1	2
Sep	9	1	2	3	4	5	6	7	8	9	1	2	3	4	5	6	7	8	9	1	2	3	4	5	6	7	8	9	1	2	
Oct	1	2	3	4	5	6	7	8	9	1	2	3	4	5	6	7	8	9	1	2	3	4	5	6	7	8	9	1	2	3	4
Nov	2	3	4	5	6	7	8	9	1	2	3	4	5	6	7	8	9	1	2	3	4	5	6	7	8	9	1	2	3	4	
Dec	3	4	5	6	7	8	9	1	2	3	4	5	6	7	8	9	1	2	3	4	5	6	7	8	9	1	2	3	4	5	6

MAY 30

	1	2	3	4	5	6	7	8	9	10	11	12	13	14	15	16	17	18	19	20	21	22	23	24	25	26	27	28	29	30	31
Jan	1	2	3	4	5	6	7	8	9	1	2	3	4	5	6	7	8	9	1	2	3	4	5	6	7	8	9	1	2	3	4
Feb	2	3	4	5	6	7	8	9	1	2	3	4	5	6	7	8	9	1	2	3	4	5	6	7	8	9	1	2	3		
Mar	3	4	5	6	7	8	9	1	2	3	4	5	6	7	8	9	1	2	3	4	5	6	7	8	9	1	2	3	4	5	6
Apr	4	5	6	7	8	9	1	2	3	4	5	6	7	8	9	1	2	3	4	5	6	7	8	9	1	2	3	4	5	6	
May	5	6	8	7	9	1	2	3	4	5	6	7	8	9	1	2	3	4	5	6	7	8	9	1	2	3	4	5	6	8	9
Jun	7	8	9	1	2	3	4	5	6	7	8	9	1	2	3	4	5	6	7	8	9	1	2	3	4	5	6	7	8	9	
Jul	8	9	1	2	3	4	5	6	7	8	9	1	2	3	4	5	6	7	8	9	1	2	3	4	5	6	7	8	9	1	2
Aug	9	1	2	3	4	5	6	7	8	9	1	2	3	4	5	6	7	8	9	1	2	3	4	5	6	7	8	9	1	2	3
Sep	1	2	3	4	5	6	7	8	9	1	2	3	4	5	6	7	8	9	1	2	3	4	5	6	7	8	9	1	2	3	
Oct	2	3	4	5	6	7	8	9	1	2	3	4	5	6	7	8	9	1	2	3	4	5	6	7	8	9	1	2	3	4	5
Nov	3	4	5	6	7	8	9	1	2	3	4	5	6	7	8	9	1	2	3	4	5	6	7	8	9	1	2	3	4	5	
Dec	4	5	6	7	8	9	1	2	3	4	5	6	7	8	9	1	2	3	4	5	6	7	8	9	1	2	3	4	5	6	7

MAY 31

	1	2	3	4	5	6	7	8	9	10	11	12	13	14	15	16	17	18	19	20	21	22	23	24	25	26	27	28	29	30	31
Jan	2	3	4	5	6	7	8	9	1	2	3	4	5	6	7	8	9	1	2	3	4	5	6	7	8	9	1	2	3	4	5
Feb	3	4	5	6	7	8	9	1	2	3	4	5	6	7	8	9	1	2	3	4	5	6	7	8	9	1	2	3	4		
Mar	4	5	6	7	8	9	1	2	3	4	5	6	7	8	9	1	2	3	4	5	6	7	8	9	1	2	3	4	5	6	7
Apr	5	6	7	8	9	1	2	3	4	5	6	7	8	9	1	2	3	4	5	6	7	8	9	1	2	3	4	5	6	7	
May	6	7	8	9	1	2	3	4	5	6	7	8	9	1	2	3	4	5	6	7	8	9	1	2	3	4	5	6	7	8	1
Jun	8	9	1	2	3	4	5	6	7	8	9	1	2	3	4	5	6	7	8	9	1	2	3	4	5	6	7	8	9	1	
Jul	9	1	2	3	4	5	6	7	8	9	1	2	3	4	5	6	7	8	9	1	2	3	4	5	6	7	8	9	1	2	3
Aug	1	2	3	4	5	6	7	8	9	1	2	3	4	5	6	7	8	9	1	2	3	4	5	6	7	8	9	1	2	3	4
Sep	2	3	4	5	6	7	8	9	1	2	3	4	5	6	7	8	9	1	2	3	4	5	6	7	8	9	1	2	3	4	
Oct	3	4	5	6	7	8	9	1	2	3	4	5	6	7	8	9	1	2	3	4	5	6	7	8	9	1	2	3	4	5	6
Nov	4	5	6	7	8	9	1	2	3	4	5	6	7	8	9	1	2	3	4	5	6	7	8	9	1	2	3	4	5	6	
Dec	5	6	7	8	9	1	2	3	4	5	6	7	8	9	1	2	3	4	5	6	7	8	9	1	2	3	4	5	6	7	8

JUNE 1

	1	2	3	4	5	6	7	8	9	10	11	12	13	14	15	16	17	18	19	20	21	22	23	24	25	26	27	28	29	30	31
Jan	9	1	2	3	4	5	6	7	8	9	1	2	3	4	5	6	7	8	9	1	2	3	4	5	6	7	8	9	1	2	3
Feb	1	2	3	4	5	6	7	8	9	1	2	3	4	5	6	7	8	9	1	2	3	4	5	6	7	8	9	1	2		
Mar	2	3	4	5	6	7	8	9	1	2	3	4	5	6	7	8	9	1	2	3	4	5	6	7	8	9	1	2	3	4	5
Apr	3	4	5	6	7	8	9	1	2	3	4	5	6	7	8	9	1	2	3	4	5	6	7	8	9	1	2	3	4	5	
May	4	5	6	7	8	9	1	2	3	4	5	6	7	8	9	1	2	3	4	5	6	7	8	9	1	2	3	4	5	6	7
Jun	6	7	8	9	1	2	3	4	5	6	7	8	9	1	2	3	4	5	6	7	8	9	1	2	3	4	5	6	7	8	
Jul	7	8	9	1	2	3	4	5	6	7	8	9	1	2	3	4	5	6	7	8	9	1	2	3	4	5	6	7	8	9	1
Aug	8	9	1	2	3	4	5	6	7	8	9	1	2	3	4	5	6	7	8	9	1	2	3	4	5	6	7	8	9	1	2
Sep	9	1	2	3	4	5	6	7	8	9	1	2	3	4	5	6	7	8	9	1	2	3	4	5	6	7	8	9	1	2	
Oct	1	2	3	4	5	6	7	8	9	1	2	3	4	5	6	7	8	9	1	2	3	4	5	6	7	8	9	1	2	3	4
Nov	2	3	4	5	6	7	8	9	1	2	3	4	5	6	7	8	9	1	2	3	4	5	6	7	8	9	1	2	3	4	
Dec	3	4	5	6	7	8	9	1	2	3	4	5	6	7	8	9	1	2	3	4	5	6	7	8	9	1	2	3	4	5	6

JUNE 2

	1	2	3	4	5	6	7	8	9	10	11	12	13	14	15	16	17	18	19	20	21	22	23	24	25	26	27	28	29	30	31
Jan	1	2	3	4	5	6	7	8	9	1	2	3	4	5	6	7	8	9	1	2	3	4	5	6	7	8	9	1	2	3	4
Feb	2	3	4	5	6	7	8	9	1	2	3	4	5	6	7	8	9	1	2	3	4	5	6	7	8	9	1	2	3		
Mar	3	4	5	6	7	8	9	1	2	3	4	5	6	7	8	9	1	2	3	4	5	6	7	8	9	1	2	3	4	5	6
Apr	4	5	6	7	8	9	1	2	3	4	5	6	7	8	9	1	2	3	4	5	6	7	8	9	1	2	3	4	5	6	
May	5	6	7	8	9	1	2	3	4	5	6	7	8	9	1	2	3	4	5	6	7	8	9	1	2	3	4	5	6	7	8
Jun	6	8	9	1	2	3	4	5	6	7	8	9	1	2	3	4	5	6	7	8	9	1	2	3	4	5	6	7	8	9	
Jul	8	9	1	2	3	4	5	6	7	8	9	1	2	3	4	5	6	7	8	9	1	2	3	4	5	6	7	8	9	1	2
Aug	9	1	2	3	4	5	6	7	8	9	1	2	3	4	5	6	7	8	9	1	2	3	4	5	6	7	8	9	1	2	3
Sep	1	2	3	4	5	6	7	8	9	1	2	3	4	5	6	7	8	9	1	2	3	4	5	6	7	8	9	1	2	3	
Oct	2	3	4	5	6	7	8	9	1	2	3	4	5	6	7	8	9	1	2	3	4	5	6	7	8	9	1	2	3	4	5
Nov	3	4	5	6	7	8	9	1	2	3	4	5	6	7	8	9	1	2	3	4	5	6	7	8	9	1	2	3	4	5	
Dec	4	5	6	7	8	9	1	2	3	4	5	6	7	8	9	1	2	3	4	5	6	7	8	9	1	2	3	4	5	6	7

JUNE 3

	1	2	3	4	5	6	7	8	9	10	11	12	13	14	15	16	17	18	19	20	21	22	23	24	25	26	27	28	29	30	31
Jan	2	3	4	5	6	7	8	9	1	2	3	4	5	6	7	8	9	1	2	3	4	5	6	7	8	9	1	2	3	4	5
Feb	3	4	5	6	7	8	9	1	2	3	4	5	6	7	8	9	1	2	3	4	5	6	7	8	9	1	2	3	4		
Mar	4	5	6	7	8	9	1	2	3	4	5	6	7	8	9	1	2	3	4	5	6	7	8	9	1	2	3	4	5	6	7
Apr	5	6	7	8	9	1	2	3	4	5	6	7	8	9	1	2	3	4	5	6	7	8	9	1	2	3	4	5	6	7	
May	6	7	8	9	1	2	3	4	5	6	7	8	9	1	2	3	4	5	6	7	8	9	1	2	3	4	5	6	7	8	9
Jun	7	8	1	2	3	4	5	6	7	8	9	1	2	3	4	5	6	7	8	9	1	2	3	4	5	6	7	8	9	1	
Jul	9	1	2	3	4	5	6	7	8	9	1	2	3	4	5	6	7	8	9	1	2	3	4	5	6	7	8	9	1	2	3
Aug	1	2	3	4	5	6	7	8	9	1	2	3	4	5	6	7	8	9	1	2	3	4	5	6	7	8	9	1	2	3	4
Sep	2	3	4	5	6	7	8	9	1	2	3	4	5	6	7	8	9	1	2	3	4	5	6	7	8	9	1	2	3	4	
Oct	3	4	5	6	7	8	9	1	2	3	4	5	6	7	8	9	1	2	3	4	5	6	7	8	9	1	2	3	4	5	6
Nov	4	5	6	7	8	9	1	2	3	4	5	6	7	8	9	1	2	3	4	5	6	7	8	9	1	2	3	4	5	6	
Dec	5	6	7	8	9	1	2	3	4	5	6	7	8	9	1	2	3	4	5	6	7	8	9	1	2	3	4	5	6	7	8

JUNE 4

	1	2	3	4	5	6	7	8	9	10	11	12	13	14	15	16	17	18	19	20	21	22	23	24	25	26	27	28	29	30	31
Jan	3	4	5	6	7	8	9	1	2	3	4	5	6	7	8	9	1	2	3	4	5	6	7	8	9	1	2	3	4	5	6
Feb	4	5	6	7	8	9	1	2	3	4	5	6	7	8	9	1	2	3	4	5	6	7	8	9	1	2	3	4	5		
Mar	5	6	7	8	9	1	2	3	4	5	6	7	8	9	1	2	3	4	5	6	7	8	9	1	2	3	4	5	6	7	8
Apr	6	7	8	9	1	2	3	4	5	6	7	8	9	1	2	3	4	5	6	7	8	9	1	2	3	4	5	6	7	8	
May	7	8	9	1	2	3	4	5	6	7	8	9	1	2	3	4	5	6	7	8	9	1	2	3	4	5	6	7	8	9	1
Jun	8	9	1	3	4	5	6	7	8	9	1	2	3	4	5	6	7	8	9	1	2	3	4	5	6	7	8	9	1	2	
Jul	1	2	3	4	5	6	7	8	9	1	2	3	4	5	6	7	8	9	1	2	3	4	5	6	7	8	9	1	2	3	4
Aug	2	3	4	5	6	7	8	9	1	2	3	4	5	6	7	8	9	1	2	3	4	5	6	7	8	9	1	2	3	4	5
Sep	3	4	5	6	7	8	9	1	2	3	4	5	6	7	8	9	1	2	3	4	5	6	7	8	9	1	2	3	4	5	
Oct	4	5	6	7	8	9	1	2	3	4	5	6	7	8	9	1	2	3	4	5	6	7	8	9	1	2	3	4	5	6	7
Nov	5	6	7	8	9	1	2	3	4	5	6	7	8	9	1	2	3	4	5	6	7	8	9	1	2	3	4	5	6	7	
Dec	6	7	8	9	1	2	3	4	5	6	7	8	9	1	2	3	4	5	6	7	8	9	1	2	3	4	5	6	7	8	9

JUNE 5

	1	2	3	4	5	6	7	8	9	10	11	12	13	14	15	16	17	18	19	20	21	22	23	24	25	26	27	28	29	30	31
Jan	4	5	6	7	8	9	1	2	3	4	5	6	7	8	9	1	2	3	4	5	6	7	8	9	1	2	3	4	5	6	7
Feb	5	6	7	8	9	1	2	3	4	5	6	7	8	9	1	2	3	4	5	6	7	8	9	1	2	3	4	5	6		
Mar	6	7	8	9	1	2	3	4	5	6	7	8	9	1	2	3	4	5	6	7	8	9	1	2	3	4	5	6	7	8	9
Apr	7	8	9	1	2	3	4	5	6	7	8	9	1	2	3	4	5	6	7	8	9	1	2	3	4	5	6	7	8	9	
May	8	9	1	2	3	4	5	6	7	8	9	1	2	3	4	5	6	7	8	9	1	2	3	4	5	6	7	8	9	1	2
Jun	9	1	2	3	5	6	7	8	9	1	2	3	4	5	6	7	8	9	1	2	3	4	5	6	7	8	9	1	2	3	
Jul	2	3	4	5	6	7	8	9	1	2	3	4	5	6	7	8	9	1	2	3	4	5	6	7	8	9	1	2	3	4	5
Aug	3	4	5	6	7	8	9	1	2	3	4	5	6	7	8	9	1	2	3	4	5	6	7	8	9	1	2	3	4	5	6
Sep	4	5	6	7	8	9	1	2	3	4	5	6	7	8	9	1	2	3	4	5	6	7	8	9	1	2	3	4	5	6	
Oct	5	6	7	8	9	1	2	3	4	5	6	7	8	9	1	2	3	4	5	6	7	8	9	1	2	3	4	5	6	7	8
Nov	6	7	8	9	1	2	3	4	5	6	7	8	9	1	2	3	4	5	6	7	8	9	1	2	3	4	5	6	7	8	
Dec	7	8	9	1	2	3	4	5	6	7	8	9	1	2	3	4	5	6	7	8	9	1	2	3	4	5	6	7	8	9	1

JUNE 6

	1	2	3	4	5	6	7	8	9	10	11	12	13	14	15	16	17	18	19	20	21	22	23	24	25	26	27	28	29	30	31
Jan	5	6	7	8	9	1	2	3	4	5	6	7	8	9	1	2	3	4	5	6	7	8	9	1	2	3	4	5	6	7	8
Feb	6	7	8	9	1	2	3	4	5	6	7	8	9	1	2	3	4	5	6	7	8	9	1	2	3	4	5	6	7		
Mar	7	8	9	1	2	3	4	5	6	7	8	9	1	2	3	4	5	6	7	8	9	1	2	3	4	5	6	7	8	9	1
Apr	8	9	1	2	3	4	5	6	7	8	9	1	2	3	4	5	6	7	8	9	1	2	3	4	5	6	7	8	9	1	
May	9	1	2	3	4	5	6	7	8	9	1	2	3	4	5	6	7	8	9	1	2	3	4	5	6	7	8	9	1	2	3
Jun	1	2	3	4	5	7	8	9	1	2	3	4	5	6	7	8	9	1	2	3	4	5	6	7	8	9	1	2	3	4	
Jul	3	4	5	6	7	8	9	1	2	3	4	5	6	7	8	9	1	2	3	4	5	6	7	8	9	1	2	3	4	5	6
Aug	4	5	6	7	8	9	1	2	3	4	5	6	7	8	9	1	2	3	4	5	6	7	8	9	1	2	3	4	5	6	7
Sep	5	6	7	8	9	1	2	3	4	5	6	7	8	9	1	2	3	4	5	6	7	8	9	1	2	3	4	5	6	7	
Oct	6	7	8	9	1	2	3	4	5	6	7	8	9	1	2	3	4	5	6	7	8	9	1	2	3	4	5	6	7	8	9
Nov	7	8	9	1	2	3	4	5	6	7	8	9	1	2	3	4	5	6	7	8	9	1	2	3	4	5	6	7	8	9	
Dec	8	9	1	2	3	4	5	6	7	8	9	1	2	3	4	5	6	7	8	9	1	2	3	4	5	6	7	8	9	1	2

JUNE 7

	1	2	3	4	5	6	7	8	9	10	11	12	13	14	15	16	17	18	19	20	21	22	23	24	25	26	27	28	29	30	31
Jan	6	7	8	9	1	2	3	4	5	6	7	8	9	1	2	3	4	5	6	7	8	9	1	2	3	4	5	6	7	8	9
Feb	7	8	9	1	2	3	4	5	6	7	8	9	1	2	3	4	5	6	7	8	9	1	2	3	4	5	6	7	8		
Mar	8	9	1	2	3	4	5	6	7	8	9	1	2	3	4	5	6	7	8	9	1	2	3	4	5	6	7	8	9	1	2
Apr	9	1	2	3	4	5	6	7	8	9	1	2	3	4	5	6	7	8	9	1	2	3	4	5	6	7	8	9	1	2	
May	1	2	3	4	5	6	7	8	9	1	2	3	4	5	6	7	8	9	1	2	3	4	5	6	7	8	9	1	2	3	4
Jun	2	3	4	5	6	7	9	1	2	3	4	5	6	7	8	9	1	2	3	4	5	6	7	8	9	1	2	3	4	5	
Jul	4	5	6	7	8	9	1	2	3	4	5	6	7	8	9	1	2	3	4	5	6	7	8	9	1	2	3	4	5	6	7
Aug	5	6	7	8	9	1	2	3	4	5	6	7	8	9	1	2	3	4	5	6	7	8	9	1	2	3	4	5	6	7	8
Sep	6	7	8	9	1	2	3	4	5	6	7	8	9	1	2	3	4	5	6	7	8	9	1	2	3	4	5	6	7	8	
Oct	7	8	9	1	2	3	4	5	6	7	8	9	1	2	3	4	5	6	7	8	9	1	2	3	4	5	6	7	8	9	1
Nov	8	9	1	2	3	4	5	6	7	8	9	1	2	3	4	5	6	7	8	9	1	2	3	4	5	6	7	8	9	1	
Dec	9	1	2	3	4	5	6	7	8	9	1	2	3	4	5	6	7	8	9	1	2	3	4	5	6	7	8	9	1	2	3

JUNE 8

	1	2	3	4	5	6	7	8	9	10	11	12	13	14	15	16	17	18	19	20	21	22	23	24	25	26	27	28	29	30	31
Jan	7	8	9	1	2	3	4	5	6	7	8	9	1	2	3	4	5	6	7	8	9	1	2	3	4	5	6	7	8	9	1
Feb	8	9	1	2	3	4	5	6	7	8	9	1	2	3	4	5	6	7	8	9	1	2	3	4	5	6	7	8	9		
Mar	9	1	2	3	4	5	6	7	8	9	1	2	3	4	5	6	7	8	9	1	2	3	4	5	6	7	8	9	1	2	3
Apr	1	2	3	4	5	6	7	8	9	1	2	3	4	5	6	7	8	9	1	2	3	4	5	6	7	8	9	1	2	3	
May	2	3	4	5	6	7	8	9	1	2	3	4	5	6	7	8	9	1	2	3	4	5	6	7	8	9	1	2	3	4	5
Jun	3	4	5	6	7	8	9	2	3	4	5	6	7	8	9	1	2	3	4	5	6	7	8	9	1	2	3	4	5	6	
Jul	5	6	7	8	9	1	2	3	4	5	6	7	8	9	1	2	3	4	5	6	7	8	9	1	2	3	4	5	6	7	8
Aug	6	7	8	9	1	2	3	4	5	6	7	8	9	1	2	3	4	5	6	7	8	9	1	2	3	4	5	6	7	8	9
Sep	7	8	9	1	2	3	4	5	6	7	8	9	1	2	3	4	5	6	7	8	9	1	2	3	4	5	6	7	8	9	
Oct	8	9	1	2	3	4	5	6	7	8	9	1	2	3	4	5	6	7	8	9	1	2	3	4	5	6	7	8	9	1	2
Nov	9	1	2	3	4	5	6	7	8	9	1	2	3	4	5	6	7	8	9	1	2	3	4	5	6	7	8	9	1	2	
Dec	1	2	3	4	5	6	7	8	9	1	2	3	4	5	6	7	8	9	1	2	3	4	5	6	7	8	9	1	2	3	4

JUNE 9

	1	2	3	4	5	6	7	8	9	10	11	12	13	14	15	16	17	18	19	20	21	22	23	24	25	26	27	28	29	30	31
Jan	8	9	1	2	3	4	5	6	7	8	9	1	2	3	4	5	6	7	8	9	1	2	3	4	5	6	7	8	9	1	2
Feb	9	1	2	3	4	5	6	7	8	9	1	2	3	4	5	6	7	8	9	1	2	3	4	5	6	7	8	9	1		
Mar	1	2	3	4	5	6	7	8	9	1	2	3	4	5	6	7	8	9	1	2	3	4	5	6	7	8	9	1	2	3	4
Apr	2	3	4	5	6	7	8	9	1	2	3	4	5	6	7	8	9	1	2	3	4	5	6	7	8	9	1	2	3	4	
May	3	4	5	6	7	8	9	1	2	3	4	5	6	7	8	9	1	2	3	4	5	6	7	8	9	1	2	3	4	5	6
Jun	4	5	6	7	8	9	1	2	4	5	6	7	8	9	1	2	3	4	5	6	7	8	9	1	2	3	4	5	6	7	
Jul	6	7	8	9	1	2	3	4	5	6	7	8	9	1	2	3	4	5	6	7	8	9	1	2	3	4	5	6	7	8	9
Aug	7	8	9	1	2	3	4	5	6	7	8	9	1	2	3	4	5	6	7	8	9	1	2	3	4	5	6	7	8	9	1
Sep	8	9	1	2	3	4	5	6	7	8	9	1	2	3	4	5	6	7	8	9	1	2	3	4	5	6	7	8	9	1	
Oct	9	1	2	3	4	5	6	7	8	9	1	2	3	4	5	6	7	8	9	1	2	3	4	5	6	7	8	9	1	2	3
Nov	1	2	3	4	5	6	7	8	9	1	2	3	4	5	6	7	8	9	1	2	3	4	5	6	7	8	9	1	2	3	
Dec	2	3	4	5	6	7	8	9	1	2	3	4	5	6	7	8	9	1	2	3	4	5	6	7	8	9	1	2	3	4	5

JUNE 10

	1	2	3	4	5	6	7	8	9	10	11	12	13	14	15	16	17	18	19	20	21	22	23	24	25	26	27	28	29	30	31
Jan	9	1	2	3	4	5	6	7	8	9	1	2	3	4	5	6	7	8	9	1	2	3	4	5	6	7	8	9	1	2	3
Feb	1	2	3	4	5	6	7	8	9	1	2	3	4	5	6	7	8	9	1	2	3	4	5	6	7	8	9	1	2		
Mar	2	3	4	5	6	7	8	9	1	2	3	4	5	6	7	8	9	1	2	3	4	5	6	7	8	9	1	2	3	4	5
Apr	3	4	5	6	7	8	9	1	2	3	4	5	6	7	8	9	1	2	3	4	5	6	7	8	9	1	2	3	4	5	
May	4	5	6	7	8	9	1	2	3	4	5	6	7	8	9	1	2	3	4	5	6	7	8	9	1	2	3	4	5	6	7
Jun	5	6	7	8	9	1	2	3	4	6	7	8	9	1	2	3	4	5	6	7	8	9	1	2	3	4	5	6	7	8	
Jul	7	8	9	1	2	3	4	5	6	7	8	9	1	2	3	4	5	6	7	8	9	1	2	3	4	5	6	7	8	9	1
Aug	8	9	1	2	3	4	5	6	7	8	9	1	2	3	4	5	6	7	8	9	1	2	3	4	5	6	7	8	9	1	2
Sep	9	1	2	3	4	5	6	7	8	9	1	2	3	4	5	6	7	8	9	1	2	3	4	5	6	7	8	9	1	2	
Oct	1	2	3	4	5	6	7	8	9	1	2	3	4	5	6	7	8	9	1	2	3	4	5	6	7	8	9	1	2	3	4
Nov	2	3	4	5	6	7	8	9	1	2	3	4	5	6	7	8	9	1	2	3	4	5	6	7	8	9	1	2	3	4	
Dec	3	4	5	6	7	8	9	1	2	3	4	5	6	7	8	9	1	2	3	4	5	6	7	8	9	1	2	3	4	5	6

JUNE 11

	1	2	3	4	5	6	7	8	9	10	11	12	13	14	15	16	17	18	19	20	21	22	23	24	25	26	27	28	29	30	31
Jan	1	2	3	4	5	6	7	8	9	1	2	3	4	5	6	7	8	9	1	2	3	4	5	6	7	8	9	1	2	3	4
Feb	2	3	4	5	6	7	8	9	1	2	3	4	5	6	7	8	9	1	2	3	4	5	6	7	8	9	1	2	3		
Mar	3	4	5	6	7	8	9	1	2	3	4	5	6	7	8	9	1	2	3	4	5	6	7	8	9	1	2	3	4	5	6
Apr	4	5	6	7	8	9	1	2	3	4	5	6	7	8	9	1	2	3	4	5	6	7	8	9	1	2	3	4	5	6	
May	5	6	7	8	9	1	2	3	4	5	6	7	8	9	1	2	3	4	5	6	7	8	9	1	2	3	4	5	6	7	8
Jun	6	7	8	9	1	2	3	4	5	6	8	9	1	2	3	4	5	6	7	8	9	1	2	3	4	5	6	7	8	9	
Jul	8	9	1	2	3	4	5	6	7	8	9	1	2	3	4	5	6	7	8	9	1	2	3	4	5	6	7	8	9	1	2
Aug	9	1	2	3	4	5	6	7	8	9	1	2	3	4	5	6	7	8	9	1	2	3	4	5	6	7	8	9	1	2	3
Sep	1	2	3	4	5	6	7	8	9	1	2	3	4	5	6	7	8	9	1	2	3	4	5	6	7	8	9	1	2	3	
Oct	2	3	4	5	6	7	8	9	1	2	3	4	5	6	7	8	9	1	2	3	4	5	6	7	8	9	1	2	3	4	5
Nov	3	4	5	6	7	8	9	1	2	3	4	5	6	7	8	9	1	2	3	4	5	6	7	8	9	1	2	3	4	5	
Dec	4	5	6	7	8	9	1	2	3	4	5	6	7	8	9	1	2	3	4	5	6	7	8	9	1	2	3	4	5	6	7

JUNE 12

	1	2	3	4	5	6	7	8	9	10	11	12	13	14	15	16	17	18	19	20	21	22	23	24	25	26	27	28	29	30	31
Jan	2	3	4	5	6	7	8	9	1	2	3	4	5	6	7	8	9	1	2	3	4	5	6	7	8	9	1	2	3	4	5
Feb	3	4	5	6	7	8	9	1	2	3	4	5	6	7	8	9	1	2	3	4	5	6	7	8	9	1	2	3	4		
Mar	4	5	6	7	8	9	1	2	3	4	5	6	7	8	9	1	2	3	4	5	6	7	8	9	1	2	3	4	5	6	7
Apr	5	6	7	8	9	1	2	3	4	5	6	7	8	9	1	2	3	4	5	6	7	8	9	1	2	3	4	5	6	7	
May	6	7	8	9	1	2	3	4	5	6	7	8	9	1	2	3	4	5	6	7	8	9	1	2	3	4	5	6	7	8	9
Jun	7	8	9	1	2	3	4	5	6	7	8	1	2	3	4	5	6	7	8	9	1	2	3	4	5	6	7	8	9	1	
Jul	9	1	2	3	4	5	6	7	8	9	1	2	3	4	5	6	7	8	9	1	2	3	4	5	6	7	8	9	1	2	3
Aug	1	2	3	4	5	6	7	8	9	1	2	3	4	5	6	7	8	9	1	2	3	4	5	6	7	8	9	1	2	3	4
Sep	2	3	4	5	6	7	8	9	1	2	3	4	5	6	7	8	9	1	2	3	4	5	6	7	8	9	1	2	3	4	
Oct	3	4	5	6	7	8	9	1	2	3	4	5	6	7	8	9	1	2	3	4	5	6	7	8	9	1	2	3	4	5	6
Nov	4	5	6	7	8	9	1	2	3	4	5	6	7	8	9	1	2	3	4	5	6	7	8	9	1	2	3	4	5	6	
Dec	5	6	7	8	9	1	2	3	4	5	6	7	8	9	1	2	3	4	5	6	7	8	9	1	2	3	4	5	6	7	8

JUNE 13

	1	2	3	4	5	6	7	8	9	10	11	12	13	14	15	16	17	18	19	20	21	22	23	24	25	26	27	28	29	30	31
Jan	3	4	5	6	7	8	9	1	2	3	4	5	6	7	8	9	1	2	3	4	5	6	7	8	9	1	2	3	4	5	6
Feb	4	5	6	7	8	9	1	2	3	4	5	6	7	8	9	1	2	3	4	5	6	7	8	9	1	2	3	4	5		
Mar	5	6	7	8	9	1	2	3	4	5	6	7	8	9	1	2	3	4	5	6	7	8	9	1	2	3	4	5	6	7	8
Apr	6	7	8	9	1	2	3	4	5	6	7	8	9	1	2	3	4	5	6	7	8	9	1	2	3	4	5	6	7	8	
May	7	8	9	1	2	3	4	5	6	7	8	9	1	2	3	4	5	6	7	8	9	1	2	3	4	5	6	7	8	9	1
Jun	8	9	1	2	3	4	5	6	7	8	9	1	3	4	5	6	7	8	9	1	2	3	4	5	6	7	8	9	1	2	
Jul	1	2	3	4	5	6	7	8	9	1	2	3	4	5	6	7	8	9	1	2	3	4	5	6	7	8	9	1	2	3	4
Aug	2	3	4	5	6	7	8	9	1	2	3	4	5	6	7	8	9	1	2	3	4	5	6	7	8	9	1	2	3	4	5
Sep	3	4	5	6	7	8	9	1	2	3	4	5	6	7	8	9	1	2	3	4	5	6	7	8	9	1	2	3	4	5	
Oct	4	5	6	7	8	9	1	2	3	4	5	6	7	8	9	1	2	3	4	5	6	7	8	9	1	2	3	4	5	6	7
Nov	5	6	7	8	9	1	2	3	4	5	6	7	8	9	1	2	3	4	5	6	7	8	9	1	2	3	4	5	6	7	
Dec	6	7	8	9	1	2	3	4	5	6	7	8	9	1	2	3	4	5	6	7	8	9	1	2	3	4	5	6	7	8	9

JUNE 14

	1	2	3	4	5	6	7	8	9	10	11	12	13	14	15	16	17	18	19	20	21	22	23	24	25	26	27	28	29	30	31
Jan	4	5	6	7	8	9	1	2	3	4	5	6	7	8	9	1	2	3	4	5	6	7	8	9	1	2	3	4	5	6	7
Feb	5	6	7	8	9	1	2	3	4	5	6	7	8	9	1	2	3	4	5	6	7	8	9	1	2	3	4	5	6		
Mar	6	7	8	9	1	2	3	4	5	6	7	8	9	1	2	3	4	5	6	7	8	9	1	2	3	4	5	6	7	8	9
Apr	7	8	9	1	2	3	4	5	6	7	8	9	1	2	3	4	5	6	7	8	9	1	2	3	4	5	6	7	8	9	
May	8	9	1	2	3	4	5	6	7	8	9	1	2	3	4	5	6	7	8	9	1	2	3	4	5	6	7	8	9	1	2
Jun	9	1	2	3	4	5	6	7	8	9	1	2	3	5	6	7	8	9	1	2	3	4	5	6	7	8	9	1	2	3	
Jul	2	3	4	5	6	7	8	9	1	2	3	4	5	6	7	8	9	1	2	3	4	5	6	7	8	9	1	2	3	4	5
Aug	3	4	5	6	7	8	9	1	2	3	4	5	6	7	8	9	1	2	3	4	5	6	7	8	9	1	2	3	4	5	6
Sep	4	5	6	7	8	9	1	2	3	4	5	6	7	8	9	1	2	3	4	5	6	7	8	9	1	2	3	4	5	6	
Oct	5	6	7	8	9	1	2	3	4	5	6	7	8	9	1	2	3	4	5	6	7	8	9	1	2	3	4	5	6	7	8
Nov	6	7	8	9	1	2	3	4	5	6	7	8	9	1	2	3	4	5	6	7	8	9	1	2	3	4	5	6	7	8	
Dec	7	8	9	1	2	3	4	5	6	7	8	9	1	2	3	4	5	6	7	8	9	1	2	3	4	5	6	7	8	9	1

JUNE 15

	1	2	3	4	5	6	7	8	9	10	11	12	13	14	15	16	17	18	19	20	21	22	23	24	25	26	27	28	29	30	31
Jan	5	6	7	8	9	1	2	3	4	5	6	7	8	9	1	2	3	4	5	6	7	8	9	1	2	3	4	5	6	7	8
Feb	6	7	8	9	1	2	3	4	5	6	7	8	9	1	2	3	4	5	6	7	8	9	1	2	3	4	5	6	7		
Mar	7	8	9	1	2	3	4	5	6	7	8	9	1	2	3	4	5	6	7	8	9	1	2	3	4	5	6	7	8	9	1
Apr	8	9	1	2	3	4	5	6	7	8	9	1	2	3	4	5	6	7	8	9	1	2	3	4	5	6	7	8	9	1	
May	9	1	2	3	4	5	6	7	8	9	1	2	3	4	5	6	7	8	9	1	2	3	4	5	6	7	8	9	1	2	3
Jun	1	2	3	4	5	6	7	8	9	1	2	3	4	5	7	8	9	1	2	3	4	5	6	7	8	9	1	2	3	4	
Jul	3	4	5	6	7	8	9	1	2	3	4	5	6	7	8	9	1	2	3	4	5	6	7	8	9	1	2	3	4	5	6
Aug	4	5	6	7	8	9	1	2	3	4	5	6	7	8	9	1	2	3	4	5	6	7	8	9	1	2	3	4	5	6	7
Sep	5	6	7	8	9	1	2	3	4	5	6	7	8	9	1	2	3	4	5	6	7	8	9	1	2	3	4	5	6	7	
Oct	6	7	8	9	1	2	3	4	5	6	7	8	9	1	2	3	4	5	6	7	8	9	1	2	3	4	5	6	7	8	9
Nov	7	8	9	1	2	3	4	5	6	7	8	9	1	2	3	4	5	6	7	8	9	1	2	3	4	5	6	7	8	9	
Dec	8	9	1	2	3	4	5	6	7	8	9	1	2	3	4	5	6	7	8	9	1	2	3	4	5	6	7	8	9	1	2

JUNE 16

	1	2	3	4	5	6	7	8	9	10	11	12	13	14	15	16	17	18	19	20	21	22	23	24	25	26	27	28	29	30	31
Jan	6	7	8	9	1	2	3	4	5	6	7	8	9	1	2	3	4	5	6	7	8	9	1	2	3	4	5	6	7	8	9
Feb	7	8	9	1	2	3	4	5	6	7	8	9	1	2	3	4	5	6	7	8	9	1	2	3	4	5	6	7	8		
Mar	8	9	1	2	3	4	5	6	7	8	9	1	2	3	4	5	6	7	8	9	1	2	3	4	5	6	7	8	9	1	2
Apr	9	1	2	3	4	5	6	7	8	9	1	2	3	4	5	6	7	8	9	1	2	3	4	5	6	7	8	9	1	2	
May	1	2	3	4	5	6	7	8	9	1	2	3	4	5	6	7	8	9	1	2	3	4	5	6	7	8	9	1	2	3	4
Jun	2	3	4	5	6	7	8	9	1	2	3	4	5	6	7	9	1	2	3	4	5	6	7	8	9	1	2	3	4	5	
Jul	4	5	6	7	8	9	1	2	3	4	5	6	7	8	9	1	2	3	4	5	6	7	8	9	1	2	3	4	5	6	7
Aug	5	6	7	8	9	1	2	3	4	5	6	7	8	9	1	2	3	4	5	6	7	8	9	1	2	3	4	5	6	7	8
Sep	6	7	8	9	1	2	3	4	5	6	7	8	9	1	2	3	4	5	6	7	8	9	1	2	3	4	5	6	7	8	
Oct	7	8	9	1	2	3	4	5	6	7	8	9	1	2	3	4	5	6	7	8	9	1	2	3	4	5	6	7	8	9	1
Nov	8	9	1	2	3	4	5	6	7	8	9	1	2	3	4	5	6	7	8	9	1	2	3	4	5	6	7	8	9	1	
Dec	9	1	2	3	4	5	6	7	8	9	1	2	3	4	5	6	7	8	9	1	2	3	4	5	6	7	8	9	1	2	3

JUNE 17

	1	2	3	4	5	6	7	8	9	10	11	12	13	14	15	16	17	18	19	20	21	22	23	24	25	26	27	28	29	30	31
Jan	7	8	9	1	2	3	4	5	6	7	8	9	1	2	3	4	5	6	7	8	9	1	2	3	4	5	6	7	8	9	1
Feb	8	9	1	2	3	4	5	6	7	8	9	1	2	3	4	5	6	7	8	9	1	2	3	4	5	6	7	8	9		
Mar	9	1	2	3	4	5	6	7	8	9	1	2	3	4	5	6	7	8	9	1	2	3	4	5	6	7	8	9	1	2	3
Apr	1	2	3	4	5	6	7	8	9	1	2	3	4	5	6	7	8	9	1	2	3	4	5	6	7	8	9	1	2	3	
May	2	3	4	5	6	7	8	9	1	2	3	4	5	6	7	8	9	1	2	3	4	5	6	7	8	9	1	2	3	4	5
Jun	3	4	5	6	7	8	9	1	2	3	4	5	6	7	8	9	2	3	4	5	6	7	8	9	1	2	3	4	5	6	
Jul	5	6	7	8	9	1	2	3	4	5	6	7	8	9	1	2	3	4	5	6	7	8	9	1	2	3	4	5	6	7	8
Aug	6	7	8	9	1	2	3	4	5	6	7	8	9	1	2	3	4	5	6	7	8	9	1	2	3	4	5	6	7	8	9
Sep	7	8	9	1	2	3	4	5	6	7	8	9	1	2	3	4	5	6	7	8	9	1	2	3	4	5	6	7	8	9	
Oct	8	9	1	2	3	4	5	6	7	8	9	1	2	3	4	5	6	7	8	9	1	2	3	4	5	6	7	8	9	1	2
Nov	9	1	2	3	4	5	6	7	8	9	1	2	3	4	5	6	7	8	9	1	2	3	4	5	6	7	8	9	1	2	
Dec	1	2	3	4	5	6	7	8	9	1	2	3	4	5	6	7	8	9	1	2	3	4	5	6	7	8	9	1	2	3	4

JUNE 18

	1	2	3	4	5	6	7	8	9	10	11	12	13	14	15	16	17	18	19	20	21	22	23	24	25	26	27	28	29	30	31
Jan	8	9	1	2	3	4	5	6	7	8	9	1	2	3	4	5	6	7	8	9	1	2	3	4	5	6	7	8	9	1	2
Feb	9	1	2	3	4	5	6	7	8	9	1	2	3	4	5	6	7	8	9	1	2	3	4	5	6	7	8	9	1		
Mar	1	2	3	4	5	6	7	8	9	1	2	3	4	5	6	7	8	9	1	2	3	4	5	6	7	8	9	1	2	3	4
Apr	2	3	4	5	6	7	8	9	1	2	3	4	5	6	7	8	9	1	2	3	4	5	6	7	8	9	1	2	3	4	
May	3	4	5	6	7	8	9	1	2	3	4	5	6	7	8	9	1	2	3	4	5	6	7	8	9	1	2	3	4	5	6
Jun	4	5	6	7	8	9	1	2	3	4	5	6	7	8	9	1	2	4	5	6	7	8	9	1	2	3	4	5	6	7	
Jul	6	7	8	9	1	2	3	4	5	6	7	8	9	1	2	3	4	5	6	7	8	9	1	2	3	4	5	6	7	8	9
Aug	7	8	9	1	2	3	4	5	6	7	8	9	1	2	3	4	5	6	7	8	9	1	2	3	4	5	6	7	8	9	1
Sep	8	9	1	2	3	4	5	6	7	8	9	1	2	3	4	5	6	7	8	9	1	2	3	4	5	6	7	8	9	1	
Oct	9	1	2	3	4	5	6	7	8	9	1	2	3	4	5	6	7	8	9	1	2	3	4	5	6	7	8	9	1	2	3
Nov	1	2	3	4	5	6	7	8	9	1	2	3	4	5	6	7	8	9	1	2	3	4	5	6	7	8	9	1	2	3	
Dec	2	3	4	5	6	7	8	9	1	2	3	4	5	6	7	8	9	1	2	3	4	5	6	7	8	9	1	2	3	4	5

JUNE 19

	1	2	3	4	5	6	7	8	9	10	11	12	13	14	15	16	17	18	19	20	21	22	23	24	25	26	27	28	29	30	31
Jan	9	1	2	3	4	5	6	7	8	9	1	2	3	4	5	6	7	8	9	1	2	3	4	5	6	7	8	9	1	2	3
Feb	1	2	3	4	5	6	7	8	9	1	2	3	4	5	6	7	8	9	1	2	3	4	5	6	7	8	9	1	2		
Mar	2	3	4	5	6	7	8	9	1	2	3	4	5	6	7	8	9	1	2	3	4	5	6	7	8	9	1	2	3	4	5
Apr	3	4	5	6	7	8	9	1	2	3	4	5	6	7	8	9	1	2	3	4	5	6	7	8	9	1	2	3	4	5	
May	4	5	6	7	8	9	1	2	3	4	5	6	7	8	9	1	2	3	4	5	6	7	8	9	1	2	3	4	5	6	7
Jun	5	6	7	8	9	1	2	3	4	5	6	7	8	9	1	2	3	4	6	7	8	9	1	2	3	4	5	6	7	8	
Jul	7	8	9	1	2	3	4	5	6	7	8	9	1	2	3	4	5	6	7	8	9	1	2	3	4	5	6	7	8	9	1
Aug	8	9	1	2	3	4	5	6	7	8	9	1	2	3	4	5	6	7	8	9	1	2	3	4	5	6	7	8	9	1	2
Sep	9	1	2	3	4	5	6	7	8	9	1	2	3	4	5	6	7	8	9	1	2	3	4	5	6	7	8	9	1	2	
Oct	1	2	3	4	5	6	7	8	9	1	2	3	4	5	6	7	8	9	1	2	3	4	5	6	7	8	9	1	2	3	4
Nov	2	3	4	5	6	7	8	9	1	2	3	4	5	6	7	8	9	1	2	3	4	5	6	7	8	9	1	2	3	4	
Dec	3	4	5	6	7	8	9	1	2	3	4	5	6	7	8	9	1	2	3	4	5	6	7	8	9	1	2	3	4	5	6

JUNE 20

	1	2	3	4	5	6	7	8	9	10	11	12	13	14	15	16	17	18	19	20	21	22	23	24	25	26	27	28	29	30	31
Jan	1	2	3	4	5	6	7	8	9	1	2	3	4	5	6	7	8	9	1	2	3	4	5	6	7	8	9	1	2	3	4
Feb	2	3	4	5	6	7	8	9	1	2	3	4	5	6	7	8	9	1	2	3	4	5	6	7	8	9	1	2	3		
Mar	3	4	5	6	7	8	9	1	2	3	4	5	6	7	8	9	1	2	3	4	5	6	7	8	9	1	2	3	4	5	6
Apr	4	5	6	7	8	9	1	2	3	4	5	6	7	8	9	1	2	3	4	5	6	7	8	9	1	2	3	4	5	6	
May	5	6	7	8	9	1	2	3	4	5	6	7	8	9	1	2	3	4	5	6	7	8	9	1	2	3	4	5	6	7	8
Jun	6	7	8	9	1	2	3	4	5	6	7	8	9	1	2	3	4	5	6	8	9	1	2	3	4	5	6	7	8	9	
Jul	8	9	1	2	3	4	5	6	7	8	9	1	2	3	4	5	6	7	8	9	1	2	3	4	5	6	7	8	9	1	2
Aug	9	1	2	3	4	5	6	7	8	9	1	2	3	4	5	6	7	8	9	1	2	3	4	5	6	7	8	9	1	2	3
Sep	1	2	3	4	5	6	7	8	9	1	2	3	4	5	6	7	8	9	1	2	3	4	5	6	7	8	9	1	2	3	
Oct	2	3	4	5	6	7	8	9	1	2	3	4	5	6	7	8	9	1	2	3	4	5	6	7	8	9	1	2	3	4	5
Nov	3	4	5	6	7	8	9	1	2	3	4	5	6	7	8	9	1	2	3	4	5	6	7	8	9	1	2	3	4	5	
Dec	4	5	6	7	8	9	1	2	3	4	5	6	7	8	9	1	2	3	4	5	6	7	8	9	1	2	3	4	5	6	7

JUNE 21

	1	2	3	4	5	6	7	8	9	10	11	12	13	14	15	16	17	18	19	20	21	22	23	24	25	26	27	28	29	30	31
Jan	2	3	4	5	6	7	8	9	1	2	3	4	5	6	7	8	9	1	2	3	4	5	6	7	8	9	1	2	3	4	5
Feb	3	4	5	6	7	8	9	1	2	3	4	5	6	7	8	9	1	2	3	4	5	6	7	8	9	1	2	3	4		
Mar	4	5	6	7	8	9	1	2	3	4	5	6	7	8	9	1	2	3	4	5	6	7	8	9	1	2	3	4	5	6	7
Apr	5	6	7	8	9	1	2	3	4	5	6	7	8	9	1	2	3	4	5	6	7	8	9	1	2	3	4	5	6	7	
May	6	7	8	9	1	2	3	4	5	6	7	8	9	1	2	3	4	5	6	7	8	9	1	2	3	4	5	6	7	8	9
Jun	7	8	9	1	2	3	4	5	6	7	8	9	1	2	3	4	5	6	7	8	1	2	3	4	5	6	7	8	9	1	
Jul	9	1	2	3	4	5	6	7	8	9	1	2	3	4	5	6	7	8	9	1	2	3	4	5	6	7	8	9	1	2	3
Aug	1	2	3	4	5	6	7	8	9	1	2	3	4	5	6	7	8	9	1	2	3	4	5	6	7	8	9	1	2	3	4
Sep	2	3	4	5	6	7	8	9	1	2	3	4	5	6	7	8	9	1	2	3	4	5	6	7	8	9	1	2	3	4	
Oct	3	4	5	6	7	8	9	1	2	3	4	5	6	7	8	9	1	2	3	4	5	6	7	8	9	1	2	3	4	5	6
Nov	4	5	6	7	8	9	1	2	3	4	5	6	7	8	9	1	2	3	4	5	6	7	8	9	1	2	3	4	5	6	
Dec	5	6	7	8	9	1	2	3	4	5	6	7	8	9	1	2	3	4	5	6	7	8	9	1	2	3	4	5	6	7	8

JUNE 22

	1	2	3	4	5	6	7	8	9	10	11	12	13	14	15	16	17	18	19	20	21	22	23	24	25	26	27	28	29	30	31
Jan	3	4	5	6	7	8	9	1	2	3	4	5	6	7	8	9	1	2	3	4	5	6	7	8	9	1	2	3	4	5	6
Feb	4	5	6	7	8	9	1	2	3	4	5	6	7	8	9	1	2	3	4	5	6	7	8	9	1	2	3	4	5		
Mar	5	6	7	8	9	1	2	3	4	5	6	7	8	9	1	2	3	4	5	6	7	8	9	1	2	3	4	5	6	7	8
Apr	6	7	8	9	1	2	3	4	5	6	7	8	9	1	2	3	4	5	6	7	8	9	1	2	3	4	5	6	7	8	
May	7	8	9	1	2	3	4	5	6	7	8	9	1	2	3	4	5	6	7	8	9	1	2	3	4	5	6	7	8	9	1
Jun	8	9	1	2	3	4	5	6	7	8	9	1	2	3	4	5	6	7	8	9	1	3	4	5	6	7	8	9	1	2	
Jul	1	2	3	4	5	6	7	8	9	1	2	3	4	5	6	7	8	9	1	2	3	4	5	6	7	8	9	1	2	3	4
Aug	2	3	4	5	6	7	8	9	1	2	3	4	5	6	7	8	9	1	2	3	4	5	6	7	8	9	1	2	3	4	5
Sep	3	4	5	6	7	8	9	1	2	3	4	5	6	7	8	9	1	2	3	4	5	6	7	8	9	1	2	3	4	5	
Oct	4	5	6	7	8	9	1	2	3	4	5	6	7	8	9	1	2	3	4	5	6	7	8	9	1	2	3	4	5	6	7
Nov	5	6	7	8	9	1	2	3	4	5	6	7	8	9	1	2	3	4	5	6	7	8	9	1	2	3	4	5	6	7	
Dec	6	7	8	9	1	2	3	4	5	6	7	8	9	1	2	3	4	5	6	7	8	9	1	2	3	4	5	6	7	8	9

JUNE 23

	1	2	3	4	5	6	7	8	9	10	11	12	13	14	15	16	17	18	19	20	21	22	23	24	25	26	27	28	29	30	31
Jan	4	5	6	7	8	9	1	2	3	4	5	6	7	8	9	1	2	3	4	5	6	7	8	9	1	2	3	4	5	6	7
Feb	5	6	7	8	9	1	2	3	4	5	6	7	8	9	1	2	3	4	5	6	7	8	9	1	2	3	4	5	6		
Mar	6	7	8	9	1	2	3	4	5	6	7	8	9	1	2	3	4	5	6	7	8	9	1	2	3	4	5	6	7	8	9
Apr	7	8	9	1	2	3	4	5	6	7	8	9	1	2	3	4	5	6	7	8	9	1	2	3	4	5	6	7	8	9	
May	8	9	1	2	3	4	5	6	7	8	9	1	2	3	4	5	6	7	8	9	1	2	3	4	5	6	7	8	9	1	2
Jun	9	1	2	3	4	5	6	7	8	9	1	2	3	4	5	6	7	8	9	1	2	3	5	6	7	8	9	1	2	3	
Jul	2	3	4	5	6	7	8	9	1	2	3	4	5	6	7	8	9	1	2	3	4	5	6	7	8	9	1	2	3	4	5
Aug	3	4	5	6	7	8	9	1	2	3	4	5	6	7	8	9	1	2	3	4	5	6	7	8	9	1	2	3	4	5	6
Sep	4	5	6	7	8	9	1	2	3	4	5	6	7	8	9	1	2	3	4	5	6	7	8	9	1	2	3	4	5	6	
Oct	5	6	7	8	9	1	2	3	4	5	6	7	8	9	1	2	3	4	5	6	7	8	9	1	2	3	4	5	6	7	8
Nov	6	7	8	9	1	2	3	4	5	6	7	8	9	1	2	3	4	5	6	7	8	9	1	2	3	4	5	6	7	8	
Dec	7	8	9	1	2	3	4	5	6	7	8	9	1	2	3	4	5	6	7	8	9	1	2	3	4	5	6	7	8	9	1

JUNE 24

	1	2	3	4	5	6	7	8	9	10	11	12	13	14	15	16	17	18	19	20	21	22	23	24	25	26	27	28	29	30	31
Jan	5	6	7	8	9	1	2	3	4	5	6	7	8	9	1	2	3	4	5	6	7	8	9	1	2	3	4	5	6	7	8
Feb	6	7	8	9	1	2	3	4	5	6	7	8	9	1	2	3	4	5	6	7	8	9	1	2	3	4	5	6	7		
Mar	7	8	9	1	2	3	4	5	6	7	8	9	1	2	3	4	5	6	7	8	9	1	2	3	4	5	6	7	8	9	1
Apr	8	9	1	2	3	4	5	6	7	8	9	1	2	3	4	5	6	7	8	9	1	2	3	4	5	6	7	8	9	1	
May	9	1	2	3	4	5	6	7	8	9	1	2	3	4	5	6	7	8	9	1	2	3	4	5	6	7	8	9	1	2	3
Jun	1	2	3	4	5	6	7	8	9	1	2	3	4	5	6	7	8	9	1	2	3	4	5	7	8	9	1	2	3	4	
Jul	3	4	5	6	7	8	9	1	2	3	4	5	6	7	8	9	1	2	3	4	5	6	7	8	9	1	2	3	4	5	6
Aug	4	5	6	7	8	9	1	2	3	4	5	6	7	8	9	1	2	3	4	5	6	7	8	9	1	2	3	4	5	6	7
Sep	5	6	7	8	9	1	2	3	4	5	6	7	8	9	1	2	3	4	5	6	7	8	9	1	2	3	4	5	6	7	
Oct	6	7	8	9	1	2	3	4	5	6	7	8	9	1	2	3	4	5	6	7	8	9	1	2	3	4	5	6	7	8	9
Nov	7	8	9	1	2	3	4	5	6	7	8	9	1	2	3	4	5	6	7	8	9	1	2	3	4	5	6	7	8	9	
Dec	8	9	1	2	3	4	5	6	7	8	9	1	2	3	4	5	6	7	8	9	1	2	3	4	5	6	7	8	9	1	2

JUNE 25

	1	2	3	4	5	6	7	8	9	10	11	12	13	14	15	16	17	18	19	20	21	22	23	24	25	26	27	28	29	30	31
Jan	6	7	8	9	1	2	3	4	5	6	7	8	9	1	2	3	4	5	6	7	8	9	1	2	3	4	5	6	7	8	9
Feb	7	8	9	1	2	3	4	5	6	7	8	9	1	2	3	4	5	6	7	8	9	1	2	3	4	5	6	7	8		
Mar	8	9	1	2	3	4	5	6	7	8	9	1	2	3	4	5	6	7	8	9	1	2	3	4	5	6	7	8	9	1	2
Apr	9	1	2	3	4	5	6	7	8	9	1	2	3	4	5	6	7	8	9	1	2	3	4	5	6	7	8	9	1	2	
May	1	2	3	4	5	6	7	8	9	1	2	3	4	5	6	7	8	9	1	2	3	4	5	6	7	8	9	1	2	3	4
Jun	2	3	4	5	6	7	8	9	1	2	3	4	5	6	7	8	9	1	2	3	4	5	6	7	9	1	2	3	4	5	
Jul	4	5	6	7	8	9	1	2	3	4	5	6	7	8	9	1	2	3	4	5	6	7	8	9	1	2	3	4	5	6	7
Aug	5	6	7	8	9	1	2	3	4	5	6	7	8	9	1	2	3	4	5	6	7	8	9	1	2	3	4	5	6	7	8
Sep	6	7	8	9	1	2	3	4	5	6	7	8	9	1	2	3	4	5	6	7	8	9	1	2	3	4	5	6	7	8	
Oct	7	8	9	1	2	3	4	5	6	7	8	9	1	2	3	4	5	6	7	8	9	1	2	3	4	5	6	7	8	9	1
Nov	8	9	1	2	3	4	5	6	7	8	9	1	2	3	4	5	6	7	8	9	1	2	3	4	5	6	7	8	9	1	
Dec	9	1	2	3	4	5	6	7	8	9	1	2	3	4	5	6	7	8	9	1	2	3	4	5	6	7	8	9	1	2	3

JUNE 26

	1	2	3	4	5	6	7	8	9	10	11	12	13	14	15	16	17	18	19	20	21	22	23	24	25	26	27	28	29	30	31
Jan	7	8	9	1	2	3	4	5	6	7	8	9	1	2	3	4	5	6	7	8	9	1	2	3	4	5	6	7	8	9	1
Feb	8	9	1	2	3	4	5	6	7	8	9	1	2	3	4	5	6	7	8	9	1	2	3	4	5	6	7	8	9		
Mar	9	1	2	3	4	5	6	7	8	9	1	2	3	4	5	6	7	8	9	1	2	3	4	5	6	7	8	9	1	2	3
Apr	1	2	3	4	5	6	7	8	9	1	2	3	4	5	6	7	8	9	1	2	3	4	5	6	7	8	9	1	2	3	
May	2	3	4	5	6	7	8	9	1	2	3	4	5	6	7	8	9	1	2	3	4	5	6	7	8	9	1	2	3	4	5
Jun	3	4	5	6	7	8	9	1	2	3	4	5	6	7	8	9	1	2	3	4	5	6	7	8	9	2	3	4	5	6	
Jul	5	6	7	8	9	1	2	3	4	5	6	7	8	9	1	2	3	4	5	6	7	8	9	1	2	3	4	5	6	7	8
Aug	6	7	8	9	1	2	3	4	5	6	7	8	9	1	2	3	4	5	6	7	8	9	1	2	3	4	5	6	7	8	9
Sep	7	8	9	1	2	3	4	5	6	7	8	9	1	2	3	4	5	6	7	8	9	1	2	3	4	5	6	7	8	9	
Oct	8	9	1	2	3	4	5	6	7	8	9	1	2	3	4	5	6	7	8	9	1	2	3	4	5	6	7	8	9	1	2
Nov	9	1	2	3	4	5	6	7	8	9	1	2	3	4	5	6	7	8	9	1	2	3	4	5	6	7	8	9	1	2	
Dec	1	2	3	4	5	6	7	8	9	1	2	3	4	5	6	7	8	9	1	2	3	4	5	6	7	8	9	1	2	3	4

JUNE 27

	1	2	3	4	5	6	7	8	9	10	11	12	13	14	15	16	17	18	19	20	21	22	23	24	25	26	27	28	29	30	31
Jan	8	9	1	2	3	4	5	6	7	8	9	1	2	3	4	5	6	7	8	9	1	2	3	4	5	6	7	8	9	1	2
Feb	9	1	2	3	4	5	6	7	8	9	1	2	3	4	5	6	7	8	9	1	2	3	4	5	6	7	8	9	1		
Mar	1	2	3	4	5	6	7	8	9	1	2	3	4	5	6	7	8	9	1	2	3	4	5	6	7	8	9	1	2	3	4
Apr	2	3	4	5	6	7	8	9	1	2	3	4	5	6	7	8	9	1	2	3	4	5	6	7	8	9	1	2	3	4	
May	3	4	5	6	7	8	9	1	2	3	4	5	6	7	8	9	1	2	3	4	5	6	7	8	9	1	2	3	4	5	6
Jun	4	5	6	7	8	9	1	2	3	4	5	6	7	8	9	1	2	3	4	5	6	7	8	9	1	2	4	5	6	7	
Jul	6	7	8	9	1	2	3	4	5	6	7	8	9	1	2	3	4	5	6	7	8	9	1	2	3	4	5	6	7	8	9
Aug	7	8	9	1	2	3	4	5	6	7	8	9	1	2	3	4	5	6	7	8	9	1	2	3	4	5	6	7	8	9	1
Sep	8	9	1	2	3	4	5	6	7	8	9	1	2	3	4	5	6	7	8	9	1	2	3	4	5	6	7	8	9	1	
Oct	9	1	2	3	4	5	6	7	8	9	1	2	3	4	5	6	7	8	9	1	2	3	4	5	6	7	8	9	1	2	3
Nov	1	2	3	4	5	6	7	8	9	1	2	3	4	5	6	7	8	9	1	2	3	4	5	6	7	8	9	1	2	3	
Dec	2	3	4	5	6	7	8	9	1	2	3	4	5	6	7	8	9	1	2	3	4	5	6	7	8	9	1	2	3	4	5

JUNE 28

	1	2	3	4	5	6	7	8	9	10	11	12	13	14	15	16	17	18	19	20	21	22	23	24	25	26	27	28	29	30	31
Jan	9	1	2	3	4	5	6	7	8	9	1	2	3	4	5	6	7	8	9	1	2	3	4	5	6	7	8	9	1	2	3
Feb	1	2	3	4	5	6	7	8	9	1	2	3	4	5	6	7	8	9	1	2	3	4	5	6	7	8	9	1	2		
Mar	2	3	4	5	6	7	8	9	1	2	3	4	5	6	7	8	9	1	2	3	4	5	6	7	8	9	1	2	3	4	5
Apr	3	4	5	6	7	8	9	1	2	3	4	5	6	7	8	9	1	2	3	4	5	6	7	8	9	1	2	3	4	5	
May	4	5	6	7	8	9	1	2	3	4	5	6	7	8	9	1	2	3	4	5	6	7	8	9	1	2	3	4	5	6	7
Jun	5	6	7	8	9	1	2	3	4	5	6	7	8	9	1	2	3	4	5	6	7	8	9	1	2	3	4	6	7	8	
Jul	7	8	9	1	2	3	4	5	6	7	8	9	1	2	3	4	5	6	7	8	9	1	2	3	4	5	6	7	8	9	1
Aug	8	9	1	2	3	4	5	6	7	8	9	1	2	3	4	5	6	7	8	9	1	2	3	4	5	6	7	8	9	1	2
Sep	9	1	2	3	4	5	6	7	8	9	1	2	3	4	5	6	7	8	9	1	2	3	4	5	6	7	8	9	1	2	
Oct	1	2	3	4	5	6	7	8	9	1	2	3	4	5	6	7	8	9	1	2	3	4	5	6	7	8	9	1	2	3	4
Nov	2	3	4	5	6	7	8	9	1	2	3	4	5	6	7	8	9	1	2	3	4	5	6	7	8	9	1	2	3	4	
Dec	3	4	5	6	7	8	9	1	2	3	4	5	6	7	8	9	1	2	3	4	5	6	7	8	9	1	2	3	4	5	6

JUNE 29

	1	2	3	4	5	6	7	8	9	10	11	12	13	14	15	16	17	18	19	20	21	22	23	24	25	26	27	28	29	30	31
Jan	1	2	3	4	5	6	7	8	9	1	2	3	4	5	6	7	8	9	1	2	3	4	5	6	7	8	9	1	2	3	4
Feb	2	3	4	5	6	7	8	9	1	2	3	4	5	6	7	8	9	1	2	3	4	5	6	7	8	9	1	2	3		
Mar	3	4	5	6	7	8	9	1	2	3	4	5	6	7	8	9	1	2	3	4	5	6	7	8	9	1	2	3	4	5	6
Apr	4	5	6	7	8	9	1	2	3	4	5	6	7	8	9	1	2	3	4	5	6	7	8	9	1	2	3	4	5	6	
May	5	6	7	8	9	1	2	3	4	5	6	7	8	9	1	2	3	4	5	6	7	8	9	1	2	3	4	5	6	7	8
Jun	6	7	8	9	1	2	3	4	5	6	7	8	9	1	2	3	4	5	6	7	8	9	1	2	3	4	5	6	8	9	
Jul	8	9	1	2	3	4	5	6	7	8	9	1	2	3	4	5	6	7	8	9	1	2	3	4	5	6	7	8	9	1	2
Aug	9	1	2	3	4	5	6	7	8	9	1	2	3	4	5	6	7	8	9	1	2	3	4	5	6	7	8	9	1	2	3
Sep	1	2	3	4	5	6	7	8	9	1	2	3	4	5	6	7	8	9	1	2	3	4	5	6	7	8	9	1	2	3	
Oct	2	3	4	5	6	7	8	9	1	2	3	4	5	6	7	8	9	1	2	3	4	5	6	7	8	9	1	2	3	4	5
Nov	3	4	5	6	7	8	9	1	2	3	4	5	6	7	8	9	1	2	3	4	5	6	7	8	9	1	2	3	4	5	
Dec	4	5	6	7	8	9	1	2	3	4	5	6	7	8	9	1	2	3	4	5	6	7	8	9	1	2	3	4	5	6	7

JUNE 30

	1	2	3	4	5	6	7	8	9	10	11	12	13	14	15	16	17	18	19	20	21	22	23	24	25	26	27	28	29	30	31
Jan	2	3	4	5	6	7	8	9	1	2	3	4	5	6	7	8	9	1	2	3	4	5	6	7	8	9	1	2	3	4	5
Feb	3	4	5	6	7	8	9	1	2	3	4	5	6	7	8	9	1	2	3	4	5	6	7	8	9	1	2	3	4		
Mar	4	5	6	7	8	9	1	2	3	4	5	6	7	8	9	1	2	3	4	5	6	7	8	9	1	2	3	4	5	6	7
Apr	5	6	7	8	9	1	2	3	4	5	6	7	8	9	1	2	3	4	5	6	7	8	9	1	2	3	4	5	6	7	
May	6	7	8	9	1	2	3	4	5	6	7	8	9	1	2	3	4	5	6	7	8	9	1	2	3	4	5	6	7	8	9
Jun	7	8	9	1	2	3	4	5	6	7	8	9	1	2	3	4	5	6	7	8	9	1	2	3	4	5	6	7	8	1	
Jul	9	1	2	3	4	5	6	7	8	9	1	2	3	4	5	6	7	8	9	1	2	3	4	5	6	7	8	9	1	2	3
Aug	1	2	3	4	5	6	7	8	9	1	2	3	4	5	6	7	8	9	1	2	3	4	5	6	7	8	9	1	2	3	4
Sep	2	3	4	5	6	7	8	9	1	2	3	4	5	6	7	8	9	1	2	3	4	5	6	7	8	9	1	2	3	4	
Oct	3	4	5	6	7	8	9	1	2	3	4	5	6	7	8	9	1	2	3	4	5	6	7	8	9	1	2	3	4	5	6
Nov	4	5	6	7	8	9	1	2	3	4	5	6	7	8	9	1	2	3	4	5	6	7	8	9	1	2	3	4	5	6	
Dec	5	6	7	8	9	1	2	3	4	5	6	7	8	9	1	2	3	4	5	6	7	8	9	1	2	3	4	5	6	7	8

JULY 1

	1	2	3	4	5	6	7	8	9	10	11	12	13	14	15	16	17	18	19	20	21	22	23	24	25	26	27	28	29	30	31
Jan	1	2	3	4	5	6	7	8	9	1	2	3	4	5	6	7	8	9	1	2	3	4	5	6	7	8	9	1	2	3	4
Feb	2	3	4	5	6	7	8	9	1	2	3	4	5	6	7	8	9	1	2	3	4	5	6	7	8	9	1	2	3		
Mar	3	4	5	6	7	8	9	1	2	3	4	5	6	7	8	9	1	2	3	4	5	6	7	8	9	1	2	3	4	5	6
Apr	4	5	6	7	8	9	1	2	3	4	5	6	7	8	9	1	2	3	4	5	6	7	8	9	1	2	3	4	5	6	
May	5	6	7	8	9	1	2	3	4	5	6	7	8	9	1	2	3	4	5	6	7	8	9	1	2	3	4	5	6	7	8
Jun	6	7	8	9	1	2	3	4	5	6	7	8	9	1	2	3	4	5	6	7	8	9	1	2	3	4	5	6	7	8	
Jul	8	9	1	2	3	4	5	6	7	8	9	1	2	3	4	5	6	7	8	9	1	2	3	4	5	6	7	8	9	1	2
Aug	9	1	2	3	4	5	6	7	8	9	1	2	3	4	5	6	7	8	9	1	2	3	4	5	6	7	8	9	1	2	3
Sep	1	2	3	4	5	6	7	8	9	1	2	3	4	5	6	7	8	9	1	2	3	4	5	6	7	8	9	1	2	3	
Oct	2	3	4	5	6	7	8	9	1	2	3	4	5	6	7	8	9	1	2	3	4	5	6	7	8	9	1	2	3	4	5
Nov	3	4	5	6	7	8	9	1	2	3	4	5	6	7	8	9	1	2	3	4	5	6	7	8	9	1	2	3	4	5	
Dec	4	5	6	7	8	9	1	2	3	4	5	6	7	8	9	1	2	3	4	5	6	7	8	9	1	2	3	4	5	6	7

JULY 2

	1	2	3	4	5	6	7	8	9	10	11	12	13	14	15	16	17	18	19	20	21	22	23	24	25	26	27	28	29	30	31
Jan	2	3	4	5	6	7	8	9	1	2	3	4	5	6	7	8	9	1	2	3	4	5	6	7	8	9	1	2	3	4	5
Feb	3	4	5	6	7	8	9	1	2	3	4	5	6	7	8	9	1	2	3	4	5	6	7	8	9	1	2	3	4		
Mar	4	5	6	7	8	9	1	2	3	4	5	6	7	8	9	1	2	3	4	5	6	7	8	9	1	2	3	4	5	6	7
Apr	5	6	7	8	9	1	2	3	4	5	6	7	8	9	1	2	3	4	5	6	7	8	9	1	2	3	4	5	6	7	
May	6	7	8	9	1	2	3	4	5	6	7	8	9	1	2	3	4	5	6	7	8	9	1	2	3	4	5	6	7	8	9
Jun	7	8	9	1	2	3	4	5	6	7	8	9	1	2	3	4	5	6	7	8	9	1	2	3	4	5	6	7	8	9	
Jul	8	1	2	3	4	5	6	7	8	9	1	2	3	4	5	6	7	8	9	1	2	3	4	5	6	7	8	9	1	2	3
Aug	1	2	3	4	5	6	7	8	9	1	2	3	4	5	6	7	8	9	1	2	3	4	5	6	7	8	9	1	2	3	4
Sep	2	3	4	5	6	7	8	9	1	2	3	4	5	6	7	8	9	1	2	3	4	5	6	7	8	9	1	2	3	4	
Oct	3	4	5	6	7	8	9	1	2	3	4	5	6	7	8	9	1	2	3	4	5	6	7	8	9	1	2	3	4	5	6
Nov	4	5	6	7	8	9	1	2	3	4	5	6	7	8	9	1	2	3	4	5	6	7	8	9	1	2	3	4	5	6	
Dec	5	6	7	8	9	1	2	3	4	5	6	7	8	9	1	2	3	4	5	6	7	8	9	1	2	3	4	5	6	7	8

JULY 3

	1	2	3	4	5	6	7	8	9	10	11	12	13	14	15	16	17	18	19	20	21	22	23	24	25	26	27	28	29	30	31
Jan	3	4	5	6	7	8	9	1	2	3	4	5	6	7	8	9	1	2	3	4	5	6	7	8	9	1	2	3	4	5	6
Feb	4	5	6	7	8	9	1	2	3	4	5	6	7	8	9	1	2	3	4	5	6	7	8	9	1	2	3	4	5		
Mar	5	6	7	8	9	1	2	3	4	5	6	7	8	9	1	2	3	4	5	6	7	8	9	1	2	3	4	5	6	7	8
Apr	6	7	8	9	1	2	3	4	5	6	7	8	9	1	2	3	4	5	6	7	8	9	1	2	3	4	5	6	7	8	
May	7	8	9	1	2	3	4	5	6	7	8	9	1	2	3	4	5	6	7	8	9	1	2	3	4	5	6	7	8	9	1
Jun	8	9	1	2	3	4	5	6	7	8	9	1	2	3	4	5	6	7	8	9	1	2	3	4	5	6	7	8	9	1	
Jul	9	1	3	4	5	6	7	8	9	1	2	3	4	5	6	7	8	9	1	2	3	4	5	6	7	8	9	1	2	3	4
Aug	2	3	4	5	6	7	8	9	1	2	3	4	5	6	7	8	9	1	2	3	4	5	6	7	8	9	1	2	3	4	5
Sep	3	4	5	6	7	8	9	1	2	3	4	5	6	7	8	9	1	2	3	4	5	6	7	8	9	1	2	3	4	5	
Oct	4	5	6	7	8	9	1	2	3	4	5	6	7	8	9	1	2	3	4	5	6	7	8	9	1	2	3	4	5	6	7
Nov	5	6	7	8	9	1	2	3	4	5	6	7	8	9	1	2	3	4	5	6	7	8	9	1	2	3	4	5	6	7	
Dec	6	7	8	9	1	2	3	4	5	6	7	8	9	1	2	3	4	5	6	7	8	9	1	2	3	4	5	6	7	8	9

JULY 4

	1	2	3	4	5	6	7	8	9	10	11	12	13	14	15	16	17	18	19	20	21	22	23	24	25	26	27	28	29	30	31
Jan	4	5	6	7	8	9	1	2	3	4	5	6	7	8	9	1	2	3	4	5	6	7	8	9	1	2	3	4	5	6	7
Feb	5	6	7	8	9	1	2	3	4	5	6	7	8	9	1	2	3	4	5	6	7	8	9	1	2	3	4	5	6		
Mar	6	7	8	9	1	2	3	4	5	6	7	8	9	1	2	3	4	5	6	7	8	9	1	2	3	4	5	6	7	8	9
Apr	7	8	9	1	2	3	4	5	6	7	8	9	1	2	3	4	5	6	7	8	9	1	2	3	4	5	6	7	8	9	
May	8	9	1	2	3	4	5	6	7	8	9	1	2	3	4	5	6	7	8	9	1	2	3	4	5	6	7	8	9	1	2
Jun	9	1	2	3	4	5	6	7	8	9	1	2	3	4	5	6	7	8	9	1	2	3	4	5	6	7	8	9	1	2	
Jul	1	2	3	5	6	7	8	9	1	2	3	4	5	6	7	8	9	1	2	3	4	5	6	7	8	9	1	2	3	4	5
Aug	3	4	5	6	7	8	9	1	2	3	4	5	6	7	8	9	1	2	3	4	5	6	7	8	9	1	2	3	4	5	6
Sep	4	5	6	7	8	9	1	2	3	4	5	6	7	8	9	1	2	3	4	5	6	7	8	9	1	2	3	4	5	6	
Oct	5	6	7	8	9	1	2	3	4	5	6	7	8	9	1	2	3	4	5	6	7	8	9	1	2	3	4	5	6	7	8
Nov	6	7	8	9	1	2	3	4	5	6	7	8	9	1	2	3	4	5	6	7	8	9	1	2	3	4	5	6	7	8	
Dec	7	8	9	1	2	3	4	5	6	7	8	9	1	2	3	4	5	6	7	8	9	1	2	3	4	5	6	7	8	9	1

JULY 5

	1	2	3	4	5	6	7	8	9	10	11	12	13	14	15	16	17	18	19	20	21	22	23	24	25	26	27	28	29	30	31
Jan	5	6	7	8	9	1	2	3	4	5	6	7	8	9	1	2	3	4	5	6	7	8	9	1	2	3	4	5	6	7	8
Feb	6	7	8	9	1	2	3	4	5	6	7	8	9	1	2	3	4	5	6	7	8	9	1	2	3	4	5	6	7		
Mar	7	8	9	1	2	3	4	5	6	7	8	9	1	2	3	4	5	6	7	8	9	1	2	3	4	5	6	7	8	9	1
Apr	8	9	1	2	3	4	5	6	7	8	9	1	2	3	4	5	6	7	8	9	1	2	3	4	5	6	7	8	9	1	
May	9	1	2	3	4	5	6	7	8	9	1	2	3	4	5	6	7	8	9	1	2	3	4	5	6	7	8	9	1	2	3
Jun	1	2	3	4	5	6	7	8	9	1	2	3	4	5	6	7	8	9	1	2	3	4	5	6	7	8	9	1	2	3	
Jul	2	3	4	5	7	8	9	1	2	3	4	5	6	7	8	9	1	2	3	4	5	6	7	8	9	1	2	3	4	5	6
Aug	4	5	6	7	8	9	1	2	3	4	5	6	7	8	9	1	2	3	4	5	6	7	8	9	1	2	3	4	5	6	7
Sep	5	6	7	8	9	1	2	3	4	5	6	7	8	9	1	2	3	4	5	6	7	8	9	1	2	3	4	5	6	7	
Oct	6	7	8	9	1	2	3	4	5	6	7	8	9	1	2	3	4	5	6	7	8	9	1	2	3	4	5	6	7	8	9
Nov	7	8	9	1	2	3	4	5	6	7	8	9	1	2	3	4	5	6	7	8	9	1	2	3	4	5	6	7	8	9	
Dec	8	9	1	2	3	4	5	6	7	8	9	1	2	3	4	5	6	7	8	9	1	2	3	4	5	6	7	8	9	1	2

JULY 6

	1	2	3	4	5	6	7	8	9	10	11	12	13	14	15	16	17	18	19	20	21	22	23	24	25	26	27	28	29	30	31
Jan	6	7	8	9	1	2	3	4	5	6	7	8	9	1	2	3	4	5	6	7	8	9	1	2	3	4	5	6	7	8	9
Feb	7	8	9	1	2	3	4	5	6	7	8	9	1	2	3	4	5	6	7	8	9	1	2	3	4	5	6	7	8		
Mar	8	9	1	2	3	4	5	6	7	8	9	1	2	3	4	5	6	7	8	9	1	2	3	4	5	6	7	8	9	1	2
Apr	9	1	2	3	4	5	6	7	8	9	1	2	3	4	5	6	7	8	9	1	2	3	4	5	6	7	8	9	1	2	
May	1	2	3	4	5	6	7	8	9	1	2	3	4	5	6	7	8	9	1	2	3	4	5	6	7	8	9	1	2	3	4
Jun	2	3	4	5	6	7	8	9	1	2	3	4	5	6	7	8	9	1	2	3	4	5	6	7	8	9	1	2	3	4	
Jul	3	4	5	6	7	9	1	2	3	4	5	6	7	8	9	1	2	3	4	5	6	7	8	9	1	2	3	4	5	6	7
Aug	5	6	7	8	9	1	2	3	4	5	6	7	8	9	1	2	3	4	5	6	7	8	9	1	2	3	4	5	6	7	8
Sep	6	7	8	9	1	2	3	4	5	6	7	8	9	1	2	3	4	5	6	7	8	9	1	2	3	4	5	6	7	8	
Oct	7	8	9	1	2	3	4	5	6	7	8	9	1	2	3	4	5	6	7	8	9	1	2	3	4	5	6	7	8	9	1
Nov	8	9	1	2	3	4	5	6	7	8	9	1	2	3	4	5	6	7	8	9	1	2	3	4	5	6	7	8	9	1	
Dec	9	1	2	3	4	5	6	7	8	9	1	2	3	4	5	6	7	8	9	1	2	3	4	5	6	7	8	9	1	2	3

JULY 7

	1	2	3	4	5	6	7	8	9	10	11	12	13	14	15	16	17	18	19	20	21	22	23	24	25	26	27	28	29	30	31
Jan	7	8	9	1	2	3	4	5	6	7	8	9	1	2	3	4	5	6	7	8	9	1	2	3	4	5	6	7	8	9	1
Feb	8	9	1	2	3	4	5	6	7	8	9	1	2	3	4	5	6	7	8	9	1	2	3	4	5	6	7	8	9		
Mar	9	1	2	3	4	5	6	7	8	9	1	2	3	4	5	6	7	8	9	1	2	3	4	5	6	7	8	9	1	2	3
Apr	1	2	3	4	5	6	7	8	9	1	2	3	4	5	6	7	8	9	1	2	3	4	5	6	7	8	9	1	2	3	
May	2	3	4	5	6	7	8	9	1	2	3	4	5	6	7	8	9	1	2	3	4	5	6	7	8	9	1	2	3	4	5
Jun	3	4	5	6	7	8	9	1	2	3	4	5	6	7	8	9	1	2	3	4	5	6	7	8	9	1	2	3	4	5	
Jul	4	5	6	7	8	9	2	3	4	5	6	7	8	9	1	2	3	4	5	6	7	8	9	1	2	3	4	5	6	7	8
Aug	6	7	8	9	1	2	3	4	5	6	7	8	9	1	2	3	4	5	6	7	8	9	1	2	3	4	5	6	7	8	9
Sep	7	8	9	1	2	3	4	5	6	7	8	9	1	2	3	4	5	6	7	8	9	1	2	3	4	5	6	7	8	9	
Oct	8	9	1	2	3	4	5	6	7	8	9	1	2	3	4	5	6	7	8	9	1	2	3	4	5	6	7	8	9	1	2
Nov	9	1	2	3	4	5	6	7	8	9	1	2	3	4	5	6	7	8	9	1	2	3	4	5	6	7	8	9	1	2	
Dec	1	2	3	4	5	6	7	8	9	1	2	3	4	5	6	7	8	9	1	2	3	4	5	6	7	8	9	1	2	3	4

JULY 8

	1	2	3	4	5	6	7	8	9	10	11	12	13	14	15	16	17	18	19	20	21	22	23	24	25	26	27	28	29	30	31
Jan	8	9	1	2	3	4	5	6	7	8	9	1	2	3	4	5	6	7	8	9	1	2	3	4	5	6	7	8	9	1	2
Feb	9	1	2	3	4	5	6	7	8	9	1	2	3	4	5	6	7	8	9	1	2	3	4	5	6	7	8	9	1		
Mar	1	2	3	4	5	6	7	8	9	1	2	3	4	5	6	7	8	9	1	2	3	4	5	6	7	8	9	1	2	3	4
Apr	2	3	4	5	6	7	8	9	1	2	3	4	5	6	7	8	9	1	2	3	4	5	6	7	8	9	1	2	3	4	
May	3	4	5	6	7	8	9	1	2	3	4	5	6	7	8	9	1	2	3	4	5	6	7	8	9	1	2	3	4	5	6
Jun	4	5	6	7	8	9	1	2	3	4	5	6	7	8	9	1	2	3	4	5	6	7	8	9	1	2	3	4	5	6	
Jul	5	6	7	8	9	1	2	4	5	6	7	8	9	1	2	3	4	5	6	7	8	9	1	2	3	4	5	6	7	8	9
Aug	7	8	9	1	2	3	4	5	6	7	8	9	1	2	3	4	5	6	7	8	9	1	2	3	4	5	6	7	8	9	1
Sep	8	9	1	2	3	4	5	6	7	8	9	1	2	3	4	5	6	7	8	9	1	2	3	4	5	6	7	8	9	1	
Oct	9	1	2	3	4	5	6	7	8	9	1	2	3	4	5	6	7	8	9	1	2	3	4	5	6	7	8	9	1	2	3
Nov	1	2	3	4	5	6	7	8	9	1	2	3	4	5	6	7	8	9	1	2	3	4	5	6	7	8	9	1	2	3	
Dec	2	3	4	5	6	7	8	9	1	2	3	4	5	6	7	8	9	1	2	3	4	5	6	7	8	9	1	2	3	4	5

JULY 9

	1	2	3	4	5	6	7	8	9	10	11	12	13	14	15	16	17	18	19	20	21	22	23	24	25	26	27	28	29	30	31
Jan	9	1	2	3	4	5	6	7	8	9	1	2	3	4	5	6	7	8	9	1	2	3	4	5	6	7	8	9	1	2	3
Feb	1	2	3	4	5	6	7	8	9	1	2	3	4	5	6	7	8	9	1	2	3	4	5	6	7	8	9	1	2		
Mar	2	3	4	5	6	7	8	9	1	2	3	4	5	6	7	8	9	1	2	3	4	5	6	7	8	9	1	2	3	4	5
Apr	3	4	5	6	7	8	9	1	2	3	4	5	6	7	8	9	1	2	3	4	5	6	7	8	9	1	2	3	4	5	
May	4	5	6	7	8	9	1	2	3	4	5	6	7	8	9	1	2	3	4	5	6	7	8	9	1	2	3	4	5	6	7
Jun	5	6	7	8	9	1	2	3	4	5	6	7	8	9	1	2	3	4	5	6	7	8	9	1	2	3	4	5	6	7	
Jul	6	7	8	9	1	2	3	4	6	7	8	9	1	2	3	4	5	6	7	8	9	1	2	3	4	5	6	7	8	9	1
Aug	8	9	1	2	3	4	5	6	7	8	9	1	2	3	4	5	6	7	8	9	1	2	3	4	5	6	7	8	9	1	2
Sep	9	1	2	3	4	5	6	7	8	9	1	2	3	4	5	6	7	8	9	1	2	3	4	5	6	7	8	9	1	2	
Oct	1	2	3	4	5	6	7	8	9	1	2	3	4	5	6	7	8	9	1	2	3	4	5	6	7	8	9	1	2	3	4
Nov	2	3	4	5	6	7	8	9	1	2	3	4	5	6	7	8	9	1	2	3	4	5	6	7	8	9	1	2	3	4	
Dec	3	4	5	6	7	8	9	1	2	3	4	5	6	7	8	9	1	2	3	4	5	6	7	8	9	1	2	3	4	5	6

JULY 10

	1	2	3	4	5	6	7	8	9	10	11	12	13	14	15	16	17	18	19	20	21	22	23	24	25	26	27	28	29	30	31
Jan	1	2	3	4	5	6	7	8	9	1	2	3	4	5	6	7	8	9	1	2	3	4	5	6	7	8	9	1	2	3	4
Feb	2	3	4	5	6	7	8	9	1	2	3	4	5	6	7	8	9	1	2	3	4	5	6	7	8	9	1	2	3		
Mar	3	4	5	6	7	8	9	1	2	3	4	5	6	7	8	9	1	2	3	4	5	6	7	8	9	1	2	3	4	5	6
Apr	4	5	6	7	8	9	1	2	3	4	5	6	7	8	9	1	2	3	4	5	6	7	8	9	1	2	3	4	5	6	
May	5	6	7	8	9	1	2	3	4	5	6	7	8	9	1	2	3	4	5	6	7	8	9	1	2	3	4	5	6	7	8
Jun	6	7	8	9	1	2	3	4	5	6	7	8	9	1	2	3	4	5	6	7	8	9	1	2	3	4	5	6	7	8	
Jul	7	8	9	1	2	3	4	5	6	8	9	1	2	3	4	5	6	7	8	9	1	2	3	4	5	6	7	8	9	1	2
Aug	9	1	2	3	4	5	6	7	8	9	1	2	3	4	5	6	7	8	9	1	2	3	4	5	6	7	8	9	1	2	3
Sep	1	2	3	4	5	6	7	8	9	1	2	3	4	5	6	7	8	9	1	2	3	4	5	6	7	8	9	1	2	3	
Oct	2	3	4	5	6	7	8	9	1	2	3	4	5	6	7	8	9	1	2	3	4	5	6	7	8	9	1	2	3	4	5
Nov	3	4	5	6	7	8	9	1	2	3	4	5	6	7	8	9	1	2	3	4	5	6	7	8	9	1	2	3	4	5	
Dec	4	5	6	7	8	9	1	2	3	4	5	6	7	8	9	1	2	3	4	5	6	7	8	9	1	2	3	4	5	6	7

JULY 11

	1	2	3	4	5	6	7	8	9	10	11	12	13	14	15	16	17	18	19	20	21	22	23	24	25	26	27	28	29	30	31
Jan	2	3	4	5	6	7	8	9	1	2	3	4	5	6	7	8	9	1	2	3	4	5	6	7	8	9	1	2	3	4	5
Feb	3	4	5	6	7	8	9	1	2	3	4	5	6	7	8	9	1	2	3	4	5	6	7	8	9	1	2	3	4		
Mar	4	5	6	7	8	9	1	2	3	4	5	6	7	8	9	1	2	3	4	5	6	7	8	9	1	2	3	4	5	6	7
Apr	5	6	7	8	9	1	2	3	4	5	6	7	8	9	1	2	3	4	5	6	7	8	9	1	2	3	4	5	6	7	
May	6	7	8	9	1	2	3	4	5	6	7	8	9	1	2	3	4	5	6	7	8	9	1	2	3	4	5	6	7	8	9
Jun	7	8	9	1	2	3	4	5	6	7	8	9	1	2	3	4	5	6	7	8	9	1	2	3	4	5	6	7	8	9	
Jul	8	9	1	2	3	4	5	6	7	8	1	2	3	4	5	6	7	8	9	1	2	3	4	5	6	7	8	9	1	2	3
Aug	1	2	3	4	5	6	7	8	9	1	2	3	4	5	6	7	8	9	1	2	3	4	5	6	7	8	9	1	2	3	4
Sep	2	3	4	5	6	7	8	9	1	2	3	4	5	6	7	8	9	1	2	3	4	5	6	7	8	9	1	2	3	4	
Oct	3	4	5	6	7	8	9	1	2	3	4	5	6	7	8	9	1	2	3	4	5	6	7	8	9	1	2	3	4	5	6
Nov	4	5	6	7	8	9	1	2	3	4	5	6	7	8	9	1	2	3	4	5	6	7	8	9	1	2	3	4	5	6	
Dec	5	6	7	8	9	1	2	3	4	5	6	7	8	9	1	2	3	4	5	6	7	8	9	1	2	3	4	5	6	7	8

JULY 12

	1	2	3	4	5	6	7	8	9	10	11	12	13	14	15	16	17	18	19	20	21	22	23	24	25	26	27	28	29	30	31
Jan	3	4	5	6	7	8	9	1	2	3	4	5	6	7	8	9	1	2	3	4	5	6	7	8	9	1	2	3	4	5	6
Feb	4	5	6	7	8	9	1	2	3	4	5	6	7	8	9	1	2	3	4	5	6	7	8	9	1	2	3	4	5		
Mar	5	6	7	8	9	1	2	3	4	5	6	7	8	9	1	2	3	4	5	6	7	8	9	1	2	3	4	5	6	7	8
Apr	6	7	8	9	1	2	3	4	5	6	7	8	9	1	2	3	4	5	6	7	8	9	1	2	3	4	5	6	7	8	
May	7	8	9	1	2	3	4	5	6	7	8	9	1	2	3	4	5	6	7	8	9	1	2	3	4	5	6	7	8	9	1
Jun	8	9	1	2	3	4	5	6	7	8	9	1	2	3	4	5	6	7	8	9	1	2	3	4	5	6	7	8	9	1	
Jul	9	1	2	3	4	5	6	7	8	9	1	3	4	5	6	7	8	9	1	2	3	4	5	6	7	8	9	1	2	3	4
Aug	2	3	4	5	6	7	8	9	1	2	3	4	5	6	7	8	9	1	2	3	4	5	6	7	8	9	1	2	3	4	5
Sep	3	4	5	6	7	8	9	1	2	3	4	5	6	7	8	9	1	2	3	4	5	6	7	8	9	1	2	3	4	5	
Oct	4	5	6	7	8	9	1	2	3	4	5	6	7	8	9	1	2	3	4	5	6	7	8	9	1	2	3	4	5	6	7
Nov	5	6	7	8	9	1	2	3	4	5	6	7	8	9	1	2	3	4	5	6	7	8	9	1	2	3	4	5	6	7	
Dec	6	7	8	9	1	2	3	4	5	6	7	8	9	1	2	3	4	5	6	7	8	9	1	2	3	4	5	6	7	8	9

JULY 13

	1	2	3	4	5	6	7	8	9	10	11	12	13	14	15	16	17	18	19	20	21	22	23	24	25	26	27	28	29	30	31
Jan	4	5	6	7	8	9	1	2	3	4	5	6	7	8	9	1	2	3	4	5	6	7	8	9	1	2	3	4	5	6	7
Feb	5	6	7	8	9	1	2	3	4	5	6	7	8	9	1	2	3	4	5	6	7	8	9	1	2	3	4	5	6		
Mar	6	7	8	9	1	2	3	4	5	6	7	8	9	1	2	3	4	5	6	7	8	9	1	2	3	4	5	6	7	8	9
Apr	7	8	9	1	2	3	4	5	6	7	8	9	1	2	3	4	5	6	7	8	9	1	2	3	4	5	6	7	8	9	
May	8	9	1	2	3	4	5	6	7	8	9	1	2	3	4	5	6	7	8	9	1	2	3	4	5	6	7	8	9	1	2
Jun	9	1	2	3	4	5	6	7	8	9	1	2	3	4	5	6	7	8	9	1	2	3	4	5	6	7	8	9	1	2	
Jul	1	2	3	4	5	6	7	8	9	1	2	3	5	6	7	8	9	1	2	3	4	5	6	7	8	9	1	2	3	4	5
Aug	3	4	5	6	7	8	9	1	2	3	4	5	6	7	8	9	1	2	3	4	5	6	7	8	9	1	2	3	4	5	6
Sep	4	5	6	7	8	9	1	2	3	4	5	6	7	8	9	1	2	3	4	5	6	7	8	9	1	2	3	4	5	6	
Oct	5	6	7	8	9	1	2	3	4	5	6	7	8	9	1	2	3	4	5	6	7	8	9	1	2	3	4	5	6	7	8
Nov	6	7	8	9	1	2	3	4	5	6	7	8	9	1	2	3	4	5	6	7	8	9	1	2	3	4	5	6	7	8	
Dec	7	8	9	1	2	3	4	5	6	7	8	9	1	2	3	4	5	6	7	8	9	1	2	3	4	5	6	7	8	9	1

JULY 14

	1	2	3	4	5	6	7	8	9	10	11	12	13	14	15	16	17	18	19	20	21	22	23	24	25	26	27	28	29	30	31
Jan	5	6	7	8	9	1	2	3	4	5	6	7	8	9	1	2	3	4	5	6	7	8	9	1	2	3	4	5	6	7	8
Feb	6	7	8	9	1	2	3	4	5	6	7	8	9	1	2	3	4	5	6	7	8	9	1	2	3	4	5	6	7		
Mar	7	8	9	1	2	3	4	5	6	7	8	9	1	2	3	4	5	6	7	8	9	1	2	3	4	5	6	7	8	9	1
Apr	8	9	1	2	3	4	5	6	7	8	9	1	2	3	4	5	6	7	8	9	1	2	3	4	5	6	7	8	9	1	
May	9	1	2	3	4	5	6	7	8	9	1	2	3	4	5	6	7	8	9	1	2	3	4	5	6	7	8	9	1	2	3
Jun	1	2	3	4	5	6	7	8	9	1	2	3	4	5	6	7	8	9	1	2	3	4	5	6	7	8	9	1	2	3	
Jul	2	3	4	5	6	7	8	9	1	2	3	4	5	7	8	9	1	2	3	4	5	6	7	8	9	1	2	3	4	5	6
Aug	4	5	6	7	8	9	1	2	3	4	5	6	7	8	9	1	2	3	4	5	6	7	8	9	1	2	3	4	5	6	7
Sep	5	6	7	8	9	1	2	3	4	5	6	7	8	9	1	2	3	4	5	6	7	8	9	1	2	3	4	5	6	7	
Oct	6	7	8	9	1	2	3	4	5	6	7	8	9	1	2	3	4	5	6	7	8	9	1	2	3	4	5	6	7	8	9
Nov	7	8	9	1	2	3	4	5	6	7	8	9	1	2	3	4	5	6	7	8	9	1	2	3	4	5	6	7	8	9	
Dec	8	9	1	2	3	4	5	6	7	8	9	1	2	3	4	5	6	7	8	9	1	2	3	4	5	6	7	8	9	1	2

JULY 15

	1	2	3	4	5	6	7	8	9	10	11	12	13	14	15	16	17	18	19	20	21	22	23	24	25	26	27	28	29	30	31
Jan	6	7	8	9	1	2	3	4	5	6	7	8	9	1	2	3	4	5	6	7	8	9	1	2	3	4	5	6	7	8	9
Feb	7	8	9	1	2	3	4	5	6	7	8	9	1	2	3	4	5	6	7	8	9	1	2	3	4	5	6	7	8		
Mar	8	9	1	2	3	4	5	6	7	8	9	1	2	3	4	5	6	7	8	9	1	2	3	4	5	6	7	8	9	1	2
Apr	9	1	2	3	4	5	6	7	8	9	1	2	3	4	5	6	7	8	9	1	2	3	4	5	6	7	8	9	1	2	
May	1	2	3	4	5	6	7	8	9	1	2	3	4	5	6	7	8	9	1	2	3	4	5	6	7	8	9	1	2	3	4
Jun	2	3	4	5	6	7	8	9	1	2	3	4	5	6	7	8	9	1	2	3	4	5	6	7	8	9	1	2	3	4	
Jul	3	4	5	6	7	8	9	1	2	3	4	5	6	7	9	1	2	3	4	5	6	7	8	9	1	2	3	4	5	6	7
Aug	5	6	7	8	9	1	2	3	4	5	6	7	8	9	1	2	3	4	5	6	7	8	9	1	2	3	4	5	6	7	8
Sep	6	7	8	9	1	2	3	4	5	6	7	8	9	1	2	3	4	5	6	7	8	9	1	2	3	4	5	6	7	8	
Oct	7	8	9	1	2	3	4	5	6	7	8	9	1	2	3	4	5	6	7	8	9	1	2	3	4	5	6	7	8	9	1
Nov	8	9	1	2	3	4	5	6	7	8	9	1	2	3	4	5	6	7	8	9	1	2	3	4	5	6	7	8	9	1	
Dec	9	1	2	3	4	5	6	7	8	9	1	2	3	4	5	6	7	8	9	1	2	3	4	5	6	7	8	9	1	2	3

JULY 16

	1	2	3	4	5	6	7	8	9	10	11	12	13	14	15	16	17	18	19	20	21	22	23	24	25	26	27	28	29	30	31
Jan	7	8	9	1	2	3	4	5	6	7	8	9	1	2	3	4	5	6	7	8	9	1	2	3	4	5	6	7	8	9	1
Feb	8	9	1	2	3	4	5	6	7	8	9	1	2	3	4	5	6	7	8	9	1	2	3	4	5	6	7	8	9		
Mar	9	1	2	3	4	5	6	7	8	9	1	2	3	4	5	6	7	8	9	1	2	3	4	5	6	7	8	9	1	2	3
Apr	1	2	3	4	5	6	7	8	9	1	2	3	4	5	6	7	8	9	1	2	3	4	5	6	7	8	9	1	2	3	
May	2	3	4	5	6	7	8	9	1	2	3	4	5	6	7	8	9	1	2	3	4	5	6	7	8	9	1	2	3	4	5
Jun	3	4	5	6	7	8	9	1	2	3	4	5	6	7	8	9	1	2	3	4	5	6	7	8	9	1	2	3	4	5	
Jul	4	5	6	7	8	9	1	2	3	4	5	6	7	8	9	2	3	4	5	6	7	8	9	1	2	3	4	5	6	7	8
Aug	6	7	8	9	1	2	3	4	5	6	7	8	9	1	2	3	4	5	6	7	8	9	1	2	3	4	5	6	7	8	9
Sep	7	8	9	1	2	3	4	5	6	7	8	9	1	2	3	4	5	6	7	8	9	1	2	3	4	5	6	7	8	9	
Oct	8	9	1	2	3	4	5	6	7	8	9	1	2	3	4	5	6	7	8	9	1	2	3	4	5	6	7	8	9	1	2
Nov	9	1	2	3	4	5	6	7	8	9	1	2	3	4	5	6	7	8	9	1	2	3	4	5	6	7	8	9	1	2	
Dec	1	2	3	4	5	6	7	8	9	1	2	3	4	5	6	7	8	9	1	2	3	4	5	6	7	8	9	1	2	3	4

JULY 17

	1	2	3	4	5	6	7	8	9	10	11	12	13	14	15	16	17	18	19	20	21	22	23	24	25	26	27	28	29	30	31
Jan	8	9	1	2	3	4	5	6	7	8	9	1	2	3	4	5	6	7	8	9	1	2	3	4	5	6	7	8	9	1	2
Feb	9	1	2	3	4	5	6	7	8	9	1	2	3	4	5	6	7	8	9	1	2	3	4	5	6	7	8	9	1		
Mar	1	2	3	4	5	6	7	8	9	1	2	3	4	5	6	7	8	9	1	2	3	4	5	6	7	8	9	1	2	3	4
Apr	2	3	4	5	6	7	8	9	1	2	3	4	5	6	7	8	9	1	2	3	4	5	6	7	8	9	1	2	3	4	
May	3	4	5	6	7	8	9	1	2	3	4	5	6	7	8	9	1	2	3	4	5	6	7	8	9	1	2	3	4	5	6
Jun	4	5	6	7	8	9	1	2	3	4	5	6	7	8	9	1	2	3	4	5	6	7	8	9	1	2	3	4	5	6	
Jul	5	6	7	8	9	1	2	3	4	5	6	7	8	9	1	2	4	5	6	7	8	9	1	2	3	4	5	6	7	8	9
Aug	7	8	9	1	2	3	4	5	6	7	8	9	1	2	3	4	5	6	7	8	9	1	2	3	4	5	6	7	8	9	1
Sep	8	9	1	2	3	4	5	6	7	8	9	1	2	3	4	5	6	7	8	9	1	2	3	4	5	6	7	8	9	1	
Oct	9	1	2	3	4	5	6	7	8	9	1	2	3	4	5	6	7	8	9	1	2	3	4	5	6	7	8	9	1	2	3
Nov	1	2	3	4	5	6	7	8	9	1	2	3	4	5	6	7	8	9	1	2	3	4	5	6	7	8	9	1	2	3	
Dec	2	3	4	5	6	7	8	9	1	2	3	4	5	6	7	8	9	1	2	3	4	5	6	7	8	9	1	2	3	4	5

JULY 18

	1	2	3	4	5	6	7	8	9	10	11	12	13	14	15	16	17	18	19	20	21	22	23	24	25	26	27	28	29	30	31
Jan	9	1	2	3	4	5	6	7	8	9	1	2	3	4	5	6	7	8	9	1	2	3	4	5	6	7	8	9	1	2	3
Feb	1	2	3	4	5	6	7	8	9	1	2	3	4	5	6	7	8	9	1	2	3	4	5	6	7	8	9	1	2		
Mar	2	3	4	5	6	7	8	9	1	2	3	4	5	6	7	8	9	1	2	3	4	5	6	7	8	9	1	2	3	4	5
Apr	3	4	5	6	7	8	9	1	2	3	4	5	6	7	8	9	1	2	3	4	5	6	7	8	9	1	2	3	4	5	
May	4	5	6	7	8	9	1	2	3	4	5	6	7	8	9	1	2	3	4	5	6	7	8	9	1	2	3	4	5	6	7
Jun	5	6	7	8	9	1	2	3	4	5	6	7	8	9	1	2	3	4	5	6	7	8	9	1	2	3	4	5	6	7	
Jul	6	7	8	9	1	2	3	4	5	6	7	8	9	1	2	3	4	6	7	8	9	1	2	3	4	5	6	7	8	9	1
Aug	8	9	1	2	3	4	5	6	7	8	9	1	2	3	4	5	6	7	8	9	1	2	3	4	5	6	7	8	9	1	2
Sep	9	1	2	3	4	5	6	7	8	9	1	2	3	4	5	6	7	8	9	1	2	3	4	5	6	7	8	9	1	2	
Oct	1	2	3	4	5	6	7	8	9	1	2	3	4	5	6	7	8	9	1	2	3	4	5	6	7	8	9	1	2	3	4
Nov	2	3	4	5	6	7	8	9	1	2	3	4	5	6	7	8	9	1	2	3	4	5	6	7	8	9	1	2	3	4	
Dec	3	4	5	6	7	8	9	1	2	3	4	5	6	7	8	9	1	2	3	4	5	6	7	8	9	1	2	3	4	5	6

JULY 19

	1	2	3	4	5	6	7	8	9	10	11	12	13	14	15	16	17	18	19	20	21	22	23	24	25	26	27	28	29	30	31
Jan	1	2	3	4	5	6	7	8	9	1	2	3	4	5	6	7	8	9	1	2	3	4	5	6	7	8	9	1	2	3	4
Feb	2	3	4	5	6	7	8	9	1	2	3	4	5	6	7	8	9	1	2	3	4	5	6	7	8	9	1	2	3		
Mar	3	4	5	6	7	8	9	1	2	3	4	5	6	7	8	9	1	2	3	4	5	6	7	8	9	1	2	3	4	5	6
Apr	4	5	6	7	8	9	1	2	3	4	5	6	7	8	9	1	2	3	4	5	6	7	8	9	1	2	3	4	5	6	
May	5	6	7	8	9	1	2	3	4	5	6	7	8	9	1	2	3	4	5	6	7	8	9	1	2	3	4	5	6	7	8
Jun	6	7	8	9	1	2	3	4	5	6	7	8	9	1	2	3	4	5	6	7	8	9	1	2	3	4	5	6	7	8	
Jul	7	8	9	1	2	3	4	5	6	7	8	9	1	2	3	4	5	6	8	9	1	2	3	4	5	6	7	8	9	1	2
Aug	9	1	2	3	4	5	6	7	8	9	1	2	3	4	5	6	7	8	9	1	2	3	4	5	6	7	8	9	1	2	3
Sep	1	2	3	4	5	6	7	8	9	1	2	3	4	5	6	7	8	9	1	2	3	4	5	6	7	8	9	1	2	3	
Oct	2	3	4	5	6	7	8	9	1	2	3	4	5	6	7	8	9	1	2	3	4	5	6	7	8	9	1	2	3	4	5
Nov	3	4	5	6	7	8	9	1	2	3	4	5	6	7	8	9	1	2	3	4	5	6	7	8	9	1	2	3	4	5	
Dec	4	5	6	7	8	9	1	2	3	4	5	6	7	8	9	1	2	3	4	5	6	7	8	9	1	2	3	4	5	6	7

JULY 20

	1	2	3	4	5	6	7	8	9	10	11	12	13	14	15	16	17	18	19	20	21	22	23	24	25	26	27	28	29	30	31
Jan	2	3	4	5	6	7	8	9	1	2	3	4	5	6	7	8	9	1	2	3	4	5	6	7	8	9	1	2	3	4	5
Feb	3	4	5	6	7	8	9	1	2	3	4	5	6	7	8	9	1	2	3	4	5	6	7	8	9	1	2	3	4		
Mar	4	5	6	7	8	9	1	2	3	4	5	6	7	8	9	1	2	3	4	5	6	7	8	9	1	2	3	4	5	6	7
Apr	5	6	7	8	9	1	2	3	4	5	6	7	8	9	1	2	3	4	5	6	7	8	9	1	2	3	4	5	6	7	
May	6	7	8	9	1	2	3	4	5	6	7	8	9	1	2	3	4	5	6	7	8	9	1	2	3	4	5	6	7	8	9
Jun	7	8	9	1	2	3	4	5	6	7	8	9	1	2	3	4	5	6	7	8	9	1	2	3	4	5	6	7	8	9	
Jul	8	9	1	2	3	4	5	6	7	8	9	1	2	3	4	5	6	7	8	1	2	3	4	5	6	7	8	9	1	2	3
Aug	1	2	3	4	5	6	7	8	9	1	2	3	4	5	6	7	8	9	1	2	3	4	5	6	7	8	9	1	2	3	4
Sep	2	3	4	5	6	7	8	9	1	2	3	4	5	6	7	8	9	1	2	3	4	5	6	7	8	9	1	2	3	4	
Oct	3	4	5	6	7	8	9	1	2	3	4	5	6	7	8	9	1	2	3	4	5	6	7	8	9	1	2	3	4	5	6
Nov	4	5	6	7	8	9	1	2	3	4	5	6	7	8	9	1	2	3	4	5	6	7	8	9	1	2	3	4	5	6	
Dec	5	6	7	8	9	1	2	3	4	5	6	7	8	9	1	2	3	4	5	6	7	8	9	1	2	3	4	5	6	7	8

JULY 21

	1	2	3	4	5	6	7	8	9	10	11	12	13	14	15	16	17	18	19	20	21	22	23	24	25	26	27	28	29	30	31
Jan	3	4	5	6	7	8	9	1	2	3	4	5	6	7	8	9	1	2	3	4	5	6	7	8	9	1	2	3	4	5	6
Feb	4	5	6	7	8	9	1	2	3	4	5	6	7	8	9	1	2	3	4	5	6	7	8	9	1	2	3	4	5		
Mar	5	6	7	8	9	1	2	3	4	5	6	7	8	9	1	2	3	4	5	6	7	8	9	1	2	3	4	5	6	7	8
Apr	6	7	8	9	1	2	3	4	5	6	7	8	9	1	2	3	4	5	6	7	8	9	1	2	3	4	5	6	7	8	
May	7	8	9	1	2	3	4	5	6	7	8	9	1	2	3	4	5	6	7	8	9	1	2	3	4	5	6	7	8	9	1
Jun	8	9	1	2	3	4	5	6	7	8	9	1	2	3	4	5	6	7	8	9	1	2	3	4	5	6	7	8	9	1	
Jul	9	1	2	3	4	5	6	7	8	9	1	2	3	4	5	6	7	8	9	1	3	4	5	6	7	8	9	1	2	3	4
Aug	2	3	4	5	6	7	8	9	1	2	3	4	5	6	7	8	9	1	2	3	4	5	6	7	8	9	1	2	3	4	5
Sep	3	4	5	6	7	8	9	1	2	3	4	5	6	7	8	9	1	2	3	4	5	6	7	8	9	1	2	3	4	5	
Oct	4	5	6	7	8	9	1	2	3	4	5	6	7	8	9	1	2	3	4	5	6	7	8	9	1	2	3	4	5	6	7
Nov	5	6	7	8	9	1	2	3	4	5	6	7	8	9	1	2	3	4	5	6	7	8	9	1	2	3	4	5	6	7	
Dec	6	7	8	9	1	2	3	4	5	6	7	8	9	1	2	3	4	5	6	7	8	9	1	2	3	4	5	6	7	8	9

JULY 22

	1	2	3	4	5	6	7	8	9	10	11	12	13	14	15	16	17	18	19	20	21	22	23	24	25	26	27	28	29	30	31
Jan	4	5	6	7	8	9	1	2	3	4	5	6	7	8	9	1	2	3	4	5	6	7	8	9	1	2	3	4	5	6	7
Feb	5	6	7	8	9	1	2	3	4	5	6	7	8	9	1	2	3	4	5	6	7	8	9	1	2	3	4	5	6		
Mar	6	7	8	9	1	2	3	4	5	6	7	8	9	1	2	3	4	5	6	7	8	9	1	2	3	4	5	6	7	8	9
Apr	7	8	9	1	2	3	4	5	6	7	8	9	1	2	3	4	5	6	7	8	9	1	2	3	4	5	6	7	8	9	
May	8	9	1	2	3	4	5	6	7	8	9	1	2	3	4	5	6	7	8	9	1	2	3	4	5	6	7	8	9	1	2
Jun	9	1	2	3	4	5	6	7	8	9	1	2	3	4	5	6	7	8	9	1	2	3	4	5	6	7	8	9	1	2	
Jul	1	2	3	4	5	6	7	8	9	1	2	3	4	5	6	7	8	9	1	2	3	5	6	7	8	9	1	2	3	4	5
Aug	3	4	5	6	7	8	9	1	2	3	4	5	6	7	8	9	1	2	3	4	5	6	7	8	9	1	2	3	4	5	6
Sep	4	5	6	7	8	9	1	2	3	4	5	6	7	8	9	1	2	3	4	5	6	7	8	9	1	2	3	4	5	6	
Oct	5	6	7	8	9	1	2	3	4	5	6	7	8	9	1	2	3	4	5	6	7	8	9	1	2	3	4	5	6	7	8
Nov	6	7	8	9	1	2	3	4	5	6	7	8	9	1	2	3	4	5	6	7	8	9	1	2	3	4	5	6	7	8	
Dec	7	8	9	1	2	3	4	5	6	7	8	9	1	2	3	4	5	6	7	8	9	1	2	3	4	5	6	7	8	9	1

JULY 23

	1	2	3	4	5	6	7	8	9	10	11	12	13	14	15	16	17	18	19	20	21	22	23	24	25	26	27	28	29	30	31
Jan	5	6	7	8	9	1	2	3	4	5	6	7	8	9	1	2	3	4	5	6	7	8	9	1	2	3	4	5	6	7	8
Feb	6	7	8	9	1	2	3	4	5	6	7	8	9	1	2	3	4	5	6	7	8	9	1	2	3	4	5	6	7		
Mar	7	8	9	1	2	3	4	5	6	7	8	9	1	2	3	4	5	6	7	8	9	1	2	3	4	5	6	7	8	9	1
Apr	8	9	1	2	3	4	5	6	7	8	9	1	2	3	4	5	6	7	8	9	1	2	3	4	5	6	7	8	9	1	
May	9	1	2	3	4	5	6	7	8	9	1	2	3	4	5	6	7	8	9	1	2	3	4	5	6	7	8	9	1	2	3
Jun	1	2	3	4	5	6	7	8	9	1	2	3	4	5	6	7	8	9	1	2	3	4	5	6	7	8	9	1	2	3	
Jul	2	3	4	5	6	7	8	9	1	2	3	4	5	6	7	8	9	1	2	3	4	5	7	8	9	1	2	3	4	5	6
Aug	4	5	6	7	8	9	1	2	3	4	5	6	7	8	9	1	2	3	4	5	6	7	8	9	1	2	3	4	5	6	7
Sep	5	6	7	8	9	1	2	3	4	5	6	7	8	9	1	2	3	4	5	6	7	8	9	1	2	3	4	5	6	7	
Oct	6	7	8	9	1	2	3	4	5	6	7	8	9	1	2	3	4	5	6	7	8	9	1	2	3	4	5	6	7	8	9
Nov	7	8	9	1	2	3	4	5	6	7	8	9	1	2	3	4	5	6	7	8	9	1	2	3	4	5	6	7	8	9	
Dec	8	9	1	2	3	4	5	6	7	8	9	1	2	3	4	5	6	7	8	9	1	2	3	4	5	6	7	8	9	1	2

JULY 24

	1	2	3	4	5	6	7	8	9	10	11	12	13	14	15	16	17	18	19	20	21	22	23	24	25	26	27	28	29	30	31
Jan	6	7	8	9	1	2	3	4	5	6	7	8	9	1	2	3	4	5	6	7	8	9	1	2	3	4	5	6	7	8	9
Feb	7	8	9	1	2	3	4	5	6	7	8	9	1	2	3	4	5	6	7	8	9	1	2	3	4	5	6	7	8		
Mar	8	9	1	2	3	4	5	6	7	8	9	1	2	3	4	5	6	7	8	9	1	2	3	4	5	6	7	8	9	1	2
Apr	9	1	2	3	4	5	6	7	8	9	1	2	3	4	5	6	7	8	9	1	2	3	4	5	6	7	8	9	1	2	
May	1	2	3	4	5	6	7	8	9	1	2	3	4	5	6	7	8	9	1	2	3	4	5	6	7	8	9	1	2	3	4
Jun	2	3	4	5	6	7	8	9	1	2	3	4	5	6	7	8	9	1	2	3	4	5	6	7	8	9	1	2	3	4	
Jul	3	4	5	6	7	8	9	1	2	3	4	5	6	7	8	9	1	2	3	4	5	6	7	9	1	2	3	4	5	6	7
Aug	5	6	7	8	9	1	2	3	4	5	6	7	8	9	1	2	3	4	5	6	7	8	9	1	2	3	4	5	6	7	8
Sep	6	7	8	9	1	2	3	4	5	6	7	8	9	1	2	3	4	5	6	7	8	9	1	2	3	4	5	6	7	8	
Oct	7	8	9	1	2	3	4	5	6	7	8	9	1	2	3	4	5	6	7	8	9	1	2	3	4	5	6	7	8	9	1
Nov	8	9	1	2	3	4	5	6	7	8	9	1	2	3	4	5	6	7	8	9	1	2	3	4	5	6	7	8	9	1	
Dec	9	1	2	3	4	5	6	7	8	9	1	2	3	4	5	6	7	8	9	1	2	3	4	5	6	7	8	9	1	2	3

JULY 25

	1	2	3	4	5	6	7	8	9	10	11	12	13	14	15	16	17	18	19	20	21	22	23	24	25	26	27	28	29	30	31
Jan	7	8	9	1	2	3	4	5	6	7	8	9	1	2	3	4	5	6	7	8	9	1	2	3	4	5	6	7	8	9	1
Feb	8	9	1	2	3	4	5	6	7	8	9	1	2	3	4	5	6	7	8	9	1	2	3	4	5	6	7	8	9		
Mar	9	1	2	3	4	5	6	7	8	9	1	2	3	4	5	6	7	8	9	1	2	3	4	5	6	7	8	9	1	2	3
Apr	1	2	3	4	5	6	7	8	9	1	2	3	4	5	6	7	8	9	1	2	3	4	5	6	7	8	9	1	2	3	
May	2	3	4	5	6	7	8	9	1	2	3	4	5	6	7	8	9	1	2	3	4	5	6	7	8	9	1	2	3	4	5
Jun	3	4	5	6	7	8	9	1	2	3	4	5	6	7	8	9	1	2	3	4	5	6	7	8	9	1	2	3	4	5	
Jul	4	5	6	7	8	9	1	2	3	4	5	6	7	8	9	1	2	3	4	5	6	7	8	9	2	3	4	5	6	7	8
Aug	6	7	8	9	1	2	3	4	5	6	7	8	9	1	2	3	4	5	6	7	8	9	1	2	3	4	5	6	7	8	9
Sep	7	8	9	1	2	3	4	5	6	7	8	9	1	2	3	4	5	6	7	8	9	1	2	3	4	5	6	7	8	9	
Oct	8	9	1	2	3	4	5	6	7	8	9	1	2	3	4	5	6	7	8	9	1	2	3	4	5	6	7	8	9	1	2
Nov	9	1	2	3	4	5	6	7	8	9	1	2	3	4	5	6	7	8	9	1	2	3	4	5	6	7	8	9	1	2	
Dec	1	2	3	4	5	6	7	8	9	1	2	3	4	5	6	7	8	9	1	2	3	4	5	6	7	8	9	1	2	3	4

JULY 26

	1	2	3	4	5	6	7	8	9	10	11	12	13	14	15	16	17	18	19	20	21	22	23	24	25	26	27	28	29	30	31
Jan	8	9	1	2	3	4	5	6	7	8	9	1	2	3	4	5	6	7	8	9	1	2	3	4	5	6	7	8	9	1	2
Feb	9	1	2	3	4	5	6	7	8	9	1	2	3	4	5	6	7	8	9	1	2	3	4	5	6	7	8	9	1		
Mar	1	2	3	4	5	6	7	8	9	1	2	3	4	5	6	7	8	9	1	2	3	4	5	6	7	8	9	1	2	3	4
Apr	2	3	4	5	6	7	8	9	1	2	3	4	5	6	7	8	9	1	2	3	4	5	6	7	8	9	1	2	3	4	
May	3	4	5	6	7	8	9	1	2	3	4	5	6	7	8	9	1	2	3	4	5	6	7	8	9	1	2	3	4	5	6
Jun	4	5	6	7	8	9	1	2	3	4	5	6	7	8	9	1	2	3	4	5	6	7	8	9	1	2	3	4	5	6	
Jul	5	6	7	8	9	1	2	3	4	5	6	7	8	9	1	2	3	4	5	6	7	8	9	1	2	4	5	6	7	8	9
Aug	7	8	9	1	2	3	4	5	6	7	8	9	1	2	3	4	5	6	7	8	9	1	2	3	4	5	6	7	8	9	1
Sep	8	9	1	2	3	4	5	6	7	8	9	1	2	3	4	5	6	7	8	9	1	2	3	4	5	6	7	8	9	1	
Oct	9	1	2	3	4	5	6	7	8	9	1	2	3	4	5	6	7	8	9	1	2	3	4	5	6	7	8	9	1	2	3
Nov	1	2	3	4	5	6	7	8	9	1	2	3	4	5	6	7	8	9	1	2	3	4	5	6	7	8	9	1	2	3	
Dec	2	3	4	5	6	7	8	9	1	2	3	4	5	6	7	8	9	1	2	3	4	5	6	7	8	9	1	2	3	4	5

JULY 27

	1	2	3	4	5	6	7	8	9	10	11	12	13	14	15	16	17	18	19	20	21	22	23	24	25	26	27	28	29	30	31
Jan	9	1	2	3	4	5	6	7	8	9	1	2	3	4	5	6	7	8	9	1	2	3	4	5	6	7	8	9	1	2	3
Feb	1	2	3	4	5	6	7	8	9	1	2	3	4	5	6	7	8	9	1	2	3	4	5	6	7	8	9	1	2		
Mar	2	3	4	5	6	7	8	9	1	2	3	4	5	6	7	8	9	1	2	3	4	5	6	7	8	9	1	2	3	4	5
Apr	3	4	5	6	7	8	9	1	2	3	4	5	6	7	8	9	1	2	3	4	5	6	7	8	9	1	2	3	4	5	
May	4	5	6	7	8	9	1	2	3	4	5	6	7	8	9	1	2	3	4	5	6	7	8	9	1	2	3	4	5	6	7
Jun	5	6	7	8	9	1	2	3	4	5	6	7	8	9	1	2	3	4	5	6	7	8	9	1	2	3	4	5	6	7	
Jul	6	7	8	9	1	2	3	4	5	6	7	8	9	1	2	3	4	5	6	7	8	9	1	2	3	4	6	7	8	9	1
Aug	8	9	1	2	3	4	5	6	7	8	9	1	2	3	4	5	6	7	8	9	1	2	3	4	5	6	7	8	9	1	2
Sep	9	1	2	3	4	5	6	7	8	9	1	2	3	4	5	6	7	8	9	1	2	3	4	5	6	7	8	9	1	2	
Oct	1	2	3	4	5	6	7	8	9	1	2	3	4	5	6	7	8	9	1	2	3	4	5	6	7	8	9	1	2	3	4
Nov	2	3	4	5	6	7	8	9	1	2	3	4	5	6	7	8	9	1	2	3	4	5	6	7	8	9	1	2	3	4	
Dec	3	4	5	6	7	8	9	1	2	3	4	5	6	7	8	9	1	2	3	4	5	6	7	8	9	1	2	3	4	5	6

JULY 28

	1	2	3	4	5	6	7	8	9	10	11	12	13	14	15	16	17	18	19	20	21	22	23	24	25	26	27	28	29	30	31
Jan	1	2	3	4	5	6	7	8	9	1	2	3	4	5	6	7	8	9	1	2	3	4	5	6	7	8	9	1	2	3	4
Feb	2	3	4	5	6	7	8	9	1	2	3	4	5	6	7	8	9	1	2	3	4	5	6	7	8	9	1	2	3		
Mar	3	4	5	6	7	8	9	1	2	3	4	5	6	7	8	9	1	2	3	4	5	6	7	8	9	1	2	3	4	5	6
Apr	4	5	6	7	8	9	1	2	3	4	5	6	7	8	9	1	2	3	4	5	6	7	8	9	1	2	3	4	5	6	
May	5	6	7	8	9	1	2	3	4	5	6	7	8	9	1	2	3	4	5	6	7	8	9	1	2	3	4	5	6	7	8
Jun	6	7	8	9	1	2	3	4	5	6	7	8	9	1	2	3	4	5	6	7	8	9	1	2	3	4	5	6	7	8	
Jul	7	8	9	1	2	3	4	5	6	7	8	9	1	2	3	4	5	6	7	8	9	1	2	3	4	5	6	8	9	1	2
Aug	9	1	2	3	4	5	6	7	8	9	1	2	3	4	5	6	7	8	9	1	2	3	4	5	6	7	8	9	1	2	3
Sep	1	2	3	4	5	6	7	8	9	1	2	3	4	5	6	7	8	9	1	2	3	4	5	6	7	8	9	1	2	3	
Oct	2	3	4	5	6	7	8	9	1	2	3	4	5	6	7	8	9	1	2	3	4	5	6	7	8	9	1	2	3	4	5
Nov	3	4	5	6	7	8	9	1	2	3	4	5	6	7	8	9	1	2	3	4	5	6	7	8	9	1	2	3	4	5	
Dec	4	5	6	7	8	9	1	2	3	4	5	6	7	8	9	1	2	3	4	5	6	7	8	9	1	2	3	4	5	6	7

JULY 29

	1	2	3	4	5	6	7	8	9	10	11	12	13	14	15	16	17	18	19	20	21	22	23	24	25	26	27	28	29	30	31
Jan	2	3	4	5	6	7	8	9	1	2	3	4	5	6	7	8	9	1	2	3	4	5	6	7	8	9	1	2	3	4	5
Feb	3	4	5	6	7	8	9	1	2	3	4	5	6	7	8	9	1	2	3	4	5	6	7	8	9	1	2	3	4		
Mar	4	5	6	7	8	9	1	2	3	4	5	6	7	8	9	1	2	3	4	5	6	7	8	9	1	2	3	4	5	6	7
Apr	5	6	7	8	9	1	2	3	4	5	6	7	8	9	1	2	3	4	5	6	7	8	9	1	2	3	4	5	6	7	
May	6	7	8	9	1	2	3	4	5	6	7	8	9	1	2	3	4	5	6	7	8	9	1	2	3	4	5	6	7	8	9
Jun	7	8	9	1	2	3	4	5	6	7	8	9	1	2	3	4	5	6	7	8	9	1	2	3	4	5	6	7	8	9	
Jul	8	9	1	2	3	4	5	6	7	8	9	1	2	3	4	5	6	7	8	9	1	2	3	4	5	6	7	8	1	2	3
Aug	1	2	3	4	5	6	7	8	9	1	2	3	4	5	6	7	8	9	1	2	3	4	5	6	7	8	9	1	2	3	4
Sep	2	3	4	5	6	7	8	9	1	2	3	4	5	6	7	8	9	1	2	3	4	5	6	7	8	9	1	2	3	4	
Oct	3	4	5	6	7	8	9	1	2	3	4	5	6	7	8	9	1	2	3	4	5	6	7	8	9	1	2	3	4	5	6
Nov	4	5	6	7	8	9	1	2	3	4	5	6	7	8	9	1	2	3	4	5	6	7	8	9	1	2	3	4	5	6	
Dec	5	6	7	8	9	1	2	3	4	5	6	7	8	9	1	2	3	4	5	6	7	8	9	1	2	3	4	5	6	7	8

JULY 30

	1	2	3	4	5	6	7	8	9	10	11	12	13	14	15	16	17	18	19	20	21	22	23	24	25	26	27	28	29	30	31
Jan	3	4	5	6	7	8	9	1	2	3	4	5	6	7	8	9	1	2	3	4	5	6	7	8	9	1	2	3	4	5	6
Feb	4	5	6	7	8	9	1	2	3	4	5	6	7	8	9	1	2	3	4	5	6	7	8	9	1	2	3	4	5		
Mar	5	6	7	8	9	1	2	3	4	5	6	7	8	9	1	2	3	4	5	6	7	8	9	1	2	3	4	5	6	7	8
Apr	6	7	8	9	1	2	3	4	5	6	7	8	9	1	2	3	4	5	6	7	8	9	1	2	3	4	5	6	7	8	
May	7	8	9	1	2	3	4	5	6	7	8	9	1	2	3	4	5	6	7	8	9	1	2	3	4	5	6	7	8	9	1
Jun	8	9	1	2	3	4	5	6	7	8	9	1	2	3	4	5	6	7	8	9	1	2	3	4	5	6	7	8	9	1	
Jul	9	1	2	3	4	5	6	7	8	9	1	2	3	4	5	6	7	8	9	1	2	3	4	5	6	7	8	9	1	3	4
Aug	2	3	4	5	6	7	8	9	1	2	3	4	5	6	7	8	9	1	2	3	4	5	6	7	8	9	1	2	3	4	5
Sep	3	4	5	6	7	8	9	1	2	3	4	5	6	7	8	9	1	2	3	4	5	6	7	8	9	1	2	3	4	5	
Oct	4	5	6	7	8	9	1	2	3	4	5	6	7	8	9	1	2	3	4	5	6	7	8	9	1	2	3	4	5	6	7
Nov	5	6	7	8	9	1	2	3	4	5	6	7	8	9	1	2	3	4	5	6	7	8	9	1	2	3	4	5	6	7	
Dec	6	7	8	9	1	2	3	4	5	6	7	8	9	1	2	3	4	5	6	7	8	9	1	2	3	4	5	6	7	8	9

JULY 31

	1	2	3	4	5	6	7	8	9	10	11	12	13	14	15	16	17	18	19	20	21	22	23	24	25	26	27	28	29	30	31
Jan	4	5	6	7	8	9	1	2	3	4	5	6	7	8	9	1	2	3	4	5	6	7	8	9	1	2	3	4	5	6	7
Feb	5	6	7	8	9	1	2	3	4	5	6	7	8	9	1	2	3	4	5	6	7	8	9	1	2	3	4	5	6		
Mar	6	7	8	9	1	2	3	4	5	6	7	8	9	1	2	3	4	5	6	7	8	9	1	2	3	4	5	6	7	8	9
Apr	7	8	9	1	2	3	4	5	6	7	8	9	1	2	3	4	5	6	7	8	9	1	2	3	4	5	6	7	8	9	
May	8	9	1	2	3	4	5	6	7	8	9	1	2	3	4	5	6	7	8	9	1	2	3	4	5	6	7	8	9	1	2
Jun	9	1	2	3	4	5	6	7	8	9	1	2	3	4	5	6	7	8	9	1	2	3	4	5	6	7	8	9	1	2	
Jul	1	2	3	4	5	6	7	8	9	1	2	3	4	5	6	7	8	9	1	2	3	4	5	6	7	8	9	1	2	3	5
Aug	3	4	5	6	7	8	9	1	2	3	4	5	6	7	8	9	1	2	3	4	5	6	7	8	9	1	2	3	4	5	6
Sep	4	5	6	7	8	9	1	2	3	4	5	6	7	8	9	1	2	3	4	5	6	7	8	9	1	2	3	4	5	6	
Oct	5	6	7	8	9	1	2	3	4	5	6	7	8	9	1	2	3	4	5	6	7	8	9	1	2	3	4	5	6	7	8
Nov	6	7	8	9	1	2	3	4	5	6	7	8	9	1	2	3	4	5	6	7	8	9	1	2	3	4	5	6	7	8	
Dec	7	8	9	1	2	3	4	5	6	7	8	9	1	2	3	4	5	6	7	8	9	1	2	3	4	5	6	7	8	9	1

AUGUST 1

	1	2	3	4	5	6	7	8	9	10	11	12	13	14	15	16	17	18	19	20	21	22	23	24	25	26	27	28	29	30	31
Jan	2	3	4	5	6	7	8	9	1	2	3	4	5	6	7	8	9	1	2	3	4	5	6	7	8	9	1	2	3	4	5
Feb	3	4	5	6	7	8	9	1	2	3	4	5	6	7	8	9	1	2	3	4	5	6	7	8	9	1	2	3	4		
Mar	4	5	6	7	8	9	1	2	3	4	5	6	7	8	9	1	2	3	4	5	6	7	8	9	1	2	3	4	5	6	7
Apr	5	6	7	8	9	1	2	3	4	5	6	7	8	9	1	2	3	4	5	6	7	8	9	1	2	3	4	5	6	7	
May	6	7	8	9	1	2	3	4	5	6	7	8	9	1	2	3	4	5	6	7	8	9	1	2	3	4	5	6	7	8	9
Jun	7	8	9	1	2	3	4	5	6	7	8	9	1	2	3	4	5	6	7	8	9	1	2	3	4	5	6	7	8	9	
Jul	8	9	1	2	3	4	5	6	7	8	9	1	2	3	4	5	6	7	8	9	1	2	3	4	5	6	7	8	9	1	2
Aug	1	2	3	4	5	6	7	8	9	1	2	3	4	5	6	7	8	9	1	2	3	4	5	6	7	8	9	1	2	3	4
Sep	2	3	4	5	6	7	8	9	1	2	3	4	5	6	7	8	9	1	2	3	4	5	6	7	8	9	1	2	3	4	
Oct	3	4	5	6	7	8	9	1	2	3	4	5	6	7	8	9	1	2	3	4	5	6	7	8	9	1	2	3	4	5	6
Nov	4	5	6	7	8	9	1	2	3	4	5	6	7	8	9	1	2	3	4	5	6	7	8	9	1	2	3	4	5	6	
Dec	5	6	7	8	9	1	2	3	4	5	6	7	8	9	1	2	3	4	5	6	7	8	9	1	2	3	4	5	6	7	8

AUGUST 2

	1	2	3	4	5	6	7	8	9	10	11	12	13	14	15	16	17	18	19	20	21	22	23	24	25	26	27	28	29	30	31
Jan	3	4	5	6	7	8	9	1	2	3	4	5	6	7	8	9	1	2	3	4	5	6	7	8	9	1	2	3	4	5	6
Feb	4	5	6	7	8	9	1	2	3	4	5	6	7	8	9	1	2	3	4	5	6	7	8	9	1	2	3	4	5		
Mar	5	6	7	8	9	1	2	3	4	5	6	7	8	9	1	2	3	4	5	6	7	8	9	1	2	3	4	5	6	7	8
Apr	6	7	8	9	1	2	3	4	5	6	7	8	9	1	2	3	4	5	6	7	8	9	1	2	3	4	5	6	7	8	
May	7	8	9	1	2	3	4	5	6	7	8	9	1	2	3	4	5	6	7	8	9	1	2	3	4	5	6	7	8	9	1
Jun	8	9	1	2	3	4	5	6	7	8	9	1	2	3	4	5	6	7	8	9	1	2	3	4	5	6	7	8	9	1	
Jul	9	1	2	3	4	5	6	7	8	9	1	2	3	4	5	6	7	8	9	1	2	3	4	5	6	7	8	9	1	2	3
Aug	1	3	4	5	6	7	8	9	1	2	3	4	5	6	7	8	9	1	2	3	4	5	6	7	8	9	1	2	3	4	5
Sep	3	4	5	6	7	8	9	1	2	3	4	5	6	7	8	9	1	2	3	4	5	6	7	8	9	1	2	3	4	5	
Oct	4	5	6	7	8	9	1	2	3	4	5	6	7	8	9	1	2	3	4	5	6	7	8	9	1	2	3	4	5	6	7
Nov	5	6	7	8	9	1	2	3	4	5	6	7	8	9	1	2	3	4	5	6	7	8	9	1	2	3	4	5	6	7	
Dec	6	7	8	9	1	2	3	4	5	6	7	8	9	1	2	3	4	5	6	7	8	9	1	2	3	4	5	6	7	8	9

AUGUST 3

	1	2	3	4	5	6	7	8	9	10	11	12	13	14	15	16	17	18	19	20	21	22	23	24	25	26	27	28	29	30	31
Jan	4	5	6	7	8	9	1	2	3	4	5	6	7	8	9	1	2	3	4	5	6	7	8	9	1	2	3	4	5	6	7
Feb	5	6	7	8	9	1	2	3	4	5	6	7	8	9	1	2	3	4	5	6	7	8	9	1	2	3	4	5	6		
Mar	6	7	8	9	1	2	3	4	5	6	7	8	9	1	2	3	4	5	6	7	8	9	1	2	3	4	5	6	7	8	9
Apr	7	8	9	1	2	3	4	5	6	7	8	9	1	2	3	4	5	6	7	8	9	1	2	3	4	5	6	7	8	9	
May	8	9	1	2	3	4	5	6	7	8	9	1	2	3	4	5	6	7	8	9	1	2	3	4	5	6	7	8	9	1	2
Jun	9	1	2	3	4	5	6	7	8	9	1	2	3	4	5	6	7	8	9	1	2	3	4	5	6	7	8	9	1	2	
Jul	1	2	3	4	5	6	7	8	9	1	2	3	4	5	6	7	8	9	1	2	3	4	5	6	7	8	9	1	2	3	4
Aug	2	3	5	6	7	8	9	1	2	3	4	5	6	7	8	9	1	2	3	4	5	6	7	8	9	1	2	3	4	5	6
Sep	4	5	6	7	8	9	1	2	3	4	5	6	7	8	9	1	2	3	4	5	6	7	8	9	1	2	3	4	5	6	
Oct	5	6	7	8	9	1	2	3	4	5	6	7	8	9	1	2	3	4	5	6	7	8	9	1	2	3	4	5	6	7	8
Nov	6	7	8	9	1	2	3	4	5	6	7	8	9	1	2	3	4	5	6	7	8	9	1	2	3	4	5	6	7	8	
Dec	7	8	9	1	2	3	4	5	6	7	8	9	1	2	3	4	5	6	7	8	9	1	2	3	4	5	6	7	8	9	1

AUGUST 4

	1	2	3	4	5	6	7	8	9	10	11	12	13	14	15	16	17	18	19	20	21	22	23	24	25	26	27	28	29	30	31
Jan	5	6	7	8	9	1	2	3	4	5	6	7	8	9	1	2	3	4	5	6	7	8	9	1	2	3	4	5	6	7	8
Feb	6	7	8	9	1	2	3	4	5	6	7	8	9	1	2	3	4	5	6	7	8	9	1	2	3	4	5	6	7		
Mar	7	8	9	1	2	3	4	5	6	7	8	9	1	2	3	4	5	6	7	8	9	1	2	3	4	5	6	7	8	9	1
Apr	8	9	1	2	3	4	5	6	7	8	9	1	2	3	4	5	6	7	8	9	1	2	3	4	5	6	7	8	9	1	
May	9	1	2	3	4	5	6	7	8	9	1	2	3	4	5	6	7	8	9	1	2	3	4	5	6	7	8	9	1	2	3
Jun	1	2	3	4	5	6	7	8	9	1	2	3	4	5	6	7	8	9	1	2	3	4	5	6	7	8	9	1	2	3	
Jul	2	3	4	5	6	7	8	9	1	2	3	4	5	6	7	8	9	1	2	3	4	5	6	7	8	9	1	2	3	4	5
Aug	3	4	5	7	8	9	1	2	3	4	5	6	7	8	9	1	2	3	4	5	6	7	8	9	1	2	3	4	5	6	7
Sep	5	6	7	8	9	1	2	3	4	5	6	7	8	9	1	2	3	4	5	6	7	8	9	1	2	3	4	5	6	7	
Oct	6	7	8	9	1	2	3	4	5	6	7	8	9	1	2	3	4	5	6	7	8	9	1	2	3	4	5	6	7	8	9
Nov	7	8	9	1	2	3	4	5	6	7	8	9	1	2	3	4	5	6	7	8	9	1	2	3	4	5	6	7	8	9	
Dec	8	9	1	2	3	4	5	6	7	8	9	1	2	3	4	5	6	7	8	9	1	2	3	4	5	6	7	8	9	1	2

AUGUST 5

	1	2	3	4	5	6	7	8	9	10	11	12	13	14	15	16	17	18	19	20	21	22	23	24	25	26	27	28	29	30	31
Jan	6	7	8	9	1	2	3	4	5	6	7	8	9	1	2	3	4	5	6	7	8	9	1	2	3	4	5	6	7	8	9
Feb	7	8	9	1	2	3	4	5	6	7	8	9	1	2	3	4	5	6	7	8	9	1	2	3	4	5	6	7	8		
Mar	8	9	1	2	3	4	5	6	7	8	9	1	2	3	4	5	6	7	8	9	1	2	3	4	5	6	7	8	9	1	2
Apr	9	1	2	3	4	5	6	7	8	9	1	2	3	4	5	6	7	8	9	1	2	3	4	5	6	7	8	9	1	2	
May	1	2	3	4	5	6	7	8	9	1	2	3	4	5	6	7	8	9	1	2	3	4	5	6	7	8	9	1	2	3	4
Jun	2	3	4	5	6	7	8	9	1	2	3	4	5	6	7	8	9	1	2	3	4	5	6	7	8	9	1	2	3	4	
Jul	3	4	5	6	7	8	9	1	2	3	4	5	6	7	8	9	1	2	3	4	5	6	7	8	9	1	2	3	4	5	6
Aug	4	5	6	7	9	1	2	3	4	5	6	7	8	9	1	2	3	4	5	6	7	8	9	1	2	3	4	5	6	7	8
Sep	6	7	8	9	1	2	3	4	5	6	7	8	9	1	2	3	4	5	6	7	8	9	1	2	3	4	5	6	7	8	
Oct	7	8	9	1	2	3	4	5	6	7	8	9	1	2	3	4	5	6	7	8	9	1	2	3	4	5	6	7	8	9	1
Nov	8	9	1	2	3	4	5	6	7	8	9	1	2	3	4	5	6	7	8	9	1	2	3	4	5	6	7	8	9	1	
Dec	9	1	2	3	4	5	6	7	8	9	1	2	3	4	5	6	7	8	9	1	2	3	4	5	6	7	8	9	1	2	3

AUGUST 6

	1	2	3	4	5	6	7	8	9	10	11	12	13	14	15	16	17	18	19	20	21	22	23	24	25	26	27	28	29	30	31
Jan	7	8	9	1	2	3	4	5	6	7	8	9	1	2	3	4	5	6	7	8	9	1	2	3	4	5	6	7	8	9	1
Feb	8	9	1	2	3	4	5	6	7	8	9	1	2	3	4	5	6	7	8	9	1	2	3	4	5	6	7	8	9		
Mar	9	1	2	3	4	5	6	7	8	9	1	2	3	4	5	6	7	8	9	1	2	3	4	5	6	7	8	9	1	2	3
Apr	1	2	3	4	5	6	7	8	9	1	2	3	4	5	6	7	8	9	1	2	3	4	5	6	7	8	9	1	2	3	
May	2	3	4	5	6	7	8	9	1	2	3	4	5	6	7	8	9	1	2	3	4	5	6	7	8	9	1	2	3	4	5
Jun	3	4	5	6	7	8	9	1	2	3	4	5	6	7	8	9	1	2	3	4	5	6	7	8	9	1	2	3	4	5	
Jul	4	5	6	7	8	9	1	2	3	4	5	6	7	8	9	1	2	3	4	5	6	7	8	9	1	2	3	4	5	6	7
Aug	5	6	7	8	9	2	3	4	5	6	7	8	9	1	2	3	4	5	6	7	8	9	1	2	3	4	5	6	7	8	9
Sep	7	8	9	1	2	3	4	5	6	7	8	9	1	2	3	4	5	6	7	8	9	1	2	3	4	5	6	7	8	9	
Oct	8	9	1	2	3	4	5	6	7	8	9	1	2	3	4	5	6	7	8	9	1	2	3	4	5	6	7	8	9	1	2
Nov	9	1	2	3	4	5	6	7	8	9	1	2	3	4	5	6	7	8	9	1	2	3	4	5	6	7	8	9	1	2	
Dec	1	2	3	4	5	6	7	8	9	1	2	3	4	5	6	7	8	9	1	2	3	4	5	6	7	8	9	1	2	3	4

AUGUST 7

	1	2	3	4	5	6	7	8	9	10	11	12	13	14	15	16	17	18	19	20	21	22	23	24	25	26	27	28	29	30	31
Jan	8	9	1	2	3	4	5	6	7	8	9	1	2	3	4	5	6	7	8	9	1	2	3	4	5	6	7	8	9	1	2
Feb	9	1	2	3	4	5	6	7	8	9	1	2	3	4	5	6	7	8	9	1	2	3	4	5	6	7	8	9	1		
Mar	1	2	3	4	5	6	7	8	9	1	2	3	4	5	6	7	8	9	1	2	3	4	5	6	7	8	9	1	2	3	4
Apr	2	3	4	5	6	7	8	9	1	2	3	4	5	6	7	8	9	1	2	3	4	5	6	7	8	9	1	2	3	4	
May	3	4	5	6	7	8	9	1	2	3	4	5	6	7	8	9	1	2	3	4	5	6	7	8	9	1	2	3	4	5	6
Jun	4	5	6	7	8	9	1	2	3	4	5	6	7	8	9	1	2	3	4	5	6	7	8	9	1	2	3	4	5	6	
Jul	5	6	7	8	9	1	2	3	4	5	6	7	8	9	1	2	3	4	5	6	7	8	9	1	2	3	4	5	6	7	8
Aug	6	7	8	9	1	2	4	5	6	7	8	9	1	2	3	4	5	6	7	8	9	1	2	3	4	5	6	7	8	9	1
Sep	8	9	1	2	3	4	5	6	7	8	9	1	2	3	4	5	6	7	8	9	1	2	3	4	5	6	7	8	9	1	
Oct	9	1	2	3	4	5	6	7	8	9	1	2	3	4	5	6	7	8	9	1	2	3	4	5	6	7	8	9	1	2	3
Nov	1	2	3	4	5	6	7	8	9	1	2	3	4	5	6	7	8	9	1	2	3	4	5	6	7	8	9	1	2	3	
Dec	2	3	4	5	6	7	8	9	1	2	3	4	5	6	7	8	9	1	2	3	4	5	6	7	8	9	1	2	3	4	5

AUGUST 8

	1	2	3	4	5	6	7	8	9	10	11	12	13	14	15	16	17	18	19	20	21	22	23	24	25	26	27	28	29	30	31
Jan	9	1	2	3	4	5	6	7	8	9	1	2	3	4	5	6	7	8	9	1	2	3	4	5	6	7	8	9	1	2	3
Feb	1	2	3	4	5	6	7	8	9	1	2	3	4	5	6	7	8	9	1	2	3	4	5	6	7	8	9	1	2		
Mar	2	3	4	5	6	7	8	9	1	2	3	4	5	6	7	8	9	1	2	3	4	5	6	7	8	9	1	2	3	4	5
Apr	3	4	5	6	7	8	9	1	2	3	4	5	6	7	8	9	1	2	3	4	5	6	7	8	9	1	2	3	4	5	
May	4	5	6	7	8	9	1	2	3	4	5	6	7	8	9	1	2	3	4	5	6	7	8	9	1	2	3	4	5	6	7
Jun	5	6	7	8	9	1	2	3	4	5	6	7	8	9	1	2	3	4	5	6	7	8	9	1	2	3	4	5	6	7	
Jul	6	7	8	9	1	2	3	4	5	6	7	8	9	1	2	3	4	5	6	7	8	9	1	2	3	4	5	6	7	8	9
Aug	7	8	9	1	2	3	4	6	7	8	9	1	2	3	4	5	6	7	8	9	1	2	3	4	5	6	7	8	9	1	2
Sep	9	1	2	3	4	5	6	7	8	9	1	2	3	4	5	6	7	8	9	1	2	3	4	5	6	7	8	9	1	2	
Oct	1	2	3	4	5	6	7	8	9	1	2	3	4	5	6	7	8	9	1	2	3	4	5	6	7	8	9	1	2	3	4
Nov	2	3	4	5	6	7	8	9	1	2	3	4	5	6	7	8	9	1	2	3	4	5	6	7	8	9	1	2	3	4	
Dec	3	4	5	6	7	8	9	1	2	3	4	5	6	7	8	9	1	2	3	4	5	6	7	8	9	1	2	3	4	5	6

AUGUST 9

	1	2	3	4	5	6	7	8	9	10	11	12	13	14	15	16	17	18	19	20	21	22	23	24	25	26	27	28	29	30	31
Jan	1	2	3	4	5	6	7	8	9	1	2	3	4	5	6	7	8	9	1	2	3	4	5	6	7	8	9	1	2	3	4
Feb	2	3	4	5	6	7	8	9	1	2	3	4	5	6	7	8	9	1	2	3	4	5	6	7	8	9	1	2	3		
Mar	3	4	5	6	7	8	9	1	2	3	4	5	6	7	8	9	1	2	3	4	5	6	7	8	9	1	2	3	4	5	6
Apr	4	5	6	7	8	9	1	2	3	4	5	6	7	8	9	1	2	3	4	5	6	7	8	9	1	2	3	4	5	6	
May	5	6	7	8	9	1	2	3	4	5	6	7	8	9	1	2	3	4	5	6	7	8	9	1	2	3	4	5	6	7	8
Jun	6	7	8	9	1	2	3	4	5	6	7	8	9	1	2	3	4	5	6	7	8	9	1	2	3	4	5	6	7	8	
Jul	7	8	9	1	2	3	4	5	6	7	8	9	1	2	3	4	5	6	7	8	9	1	2	3	4	5	6	7	8	9	1
Aug	8	9	1	2	3	4	5	6	8	9	1	2	3	4	5	6	7	8	9	1	2	3	4	5	6	7	8	9	1	2	3
Sep	1	2	3	4	5	6	7	8	9	1	2	3	4	5	6	7	8	9	1	2	3	4	5	6	7	8	9	1	2	3	
Oct	2	3	4	5	6	7	8	9	1	2	3	4	5	6	7	8	9	1	2	3	4	5	6	7	8	9	1	2	3	4	5
Nov	3	4	5	6	7	8	9	1	2	3	4	5	6	7	8	9	1	2	3	4	5	6	7	8	9	1	2	3	4	5	
Dec	4	5	6	7	8	9	1	2	3	4	5	6	7	8	9	1	2	3	4	5	6	7	8	9	1	2	3	4	5	6	7

AUGUST 10

	1	2	3	4	5	6	7	8	9	10	11	12	13	14	15	16	17	18	19	20	21	22	23	24	25	26	27	28	29	30	31
Jan	2	3	4	5	6	7	8	9	1	2	3	4	5	6	7	8	9	1	2	3	4	5	6	7	8	9	1	2	3	4	5
Feb	3	4	5	6	7	8	9	1	2	3	4	5	6	7	8	9	1	2	3	4	5	6	7	8	9	1	2	3	4		
Mar	4	5	6	7	8	9	1	2	3	4	5	6	7	8	9	1	2	3	4	5	6	7	8	9	1	2	3	4	5	6	7
Apr	5	6	7	8	9	1	2	3	4	5	6	7	8	9	1	2	3	4	5	6	7	8	9	1	2	3	4	5	6	7	
May	6	7	8	9	1	2	3	4	5	6	7	8	9	1	2	3	4	5	6	7	8	9	1	2	3	4	5	6	7	8	9
Jun	7	8	9	1	2	3	4	5	6	7	8	9	1	2	3	4	5	6	7	8	9	1	2	3	4	5	6	7	8	9	
Jul	8	9	1	2	3	4	5	6	7	8	9	1	2	3	4	5	6	7	8	9	1	2	3	4	5	6	7	8	9	1	2
Aug	9	1	2	3	4	5	6	7	8	1	2	3	4	5	6	7	8	9	1	2	3	4	5	6	7	8	9	1	2	3	4
Sep	2	3	4	5	6	7	8	9	1	2	3	4	5	6	7	8	9	1	2	3	4	5	6	7	8	9	1	2	3	4	
Oct	3	4	5	6	7	8	9	1	2	3	4	5	6	7	8	9	1	2	3	4	5	6	7	8	9	1	2	3	4	5	6
Nov	4	5	6	7	8	9	1	2	3	4	5	6	7	8	9	1	2	3	4	5	6	7	8	9	1	2	3	4	5	6	
Dec	5	6	7	8	9	1	2	3	4	5	6	7	8	9	1	2	3	4	5	6	7	8	9	1	2	3	4	5	6	7	8

AUGUST 11

	1	2	3	4	5	6	7	8	9	10	11	12	13	14	15	16	17	18	19	20	21	22	23	24	25	26	27	28	29	30	31
Jan	3	4	5	6	7	8	9	1	2	3	4	5	6	7	8	9	1	2	3	4	5	6	7	8	9	1	2	3	4	5	6
Feb	4	5	6	7	8	9	1	2	3	4	5	6	7	8	9	1	2	3	4	5	6	7	8	9	1	2	3	4	5		
Mar	5	6	7	8	9	1	2	3	4	5	6	7	8	9	1	2	3	4	5	6	7	8	9	1	2	3	4	5	6	7	8
Apr	6	7	8	9	1	2	3	4	5	6	7	8	9	1	2	3	4	5	6	7	8	9	1	2	3	4	5	6	7	8	
May	7	8	9	1	2	3	4	5	6	7	8	9	1	2	3	4	5	6	7	8	9	1	2	3	4	5	6	7	8	9	1
Jun	8	9	1	2	3	4	5	6	7	8	9	1	2	3	4	5	6	7	8	9	1	2	3	4	5	6	7	8	9	1	
Jul	9	1	2	3	4	5	6	7	8	9	1	2	3	4	5	6	7	8	9	1	2	3	4	5	6	7	8	9	1	2	3
Aug	1	2	3	4	5	6	7	8	9	1	3	4	5	6	7	8	9	1	2	3	4	5	6	7	8	9	1	2	3	4	5
Sep	3	4	5	6	7	8	9	1	2	3	4	5	6	7	8	9	1	2	3	4	5	6	7	8	9	1	2	3	4	5	
Oct	4	5	6	7	8	9	1	2	3	4	5	6	7	8	9	1	2	3	4	5	6	7	8	9	1	2	3	4	5	6	7
Nov	5	6	7	8	9	1	2	3	4	5	6	7	8	9	1	2	3	4	5	6	7	8	9	1	2	3	4	5	6	7	
Dec	6	7	8	9	1	2	3	4	5	6	7	8	9	1	2	3	4	5	6	7	8	9	1	2	3	4	5	6	7	8	9

AUGUST 12

	1	2	3	4	5	6	7	8	9	10	11	12	13	14	15	16	17	18	19	20	21	22	23	24	25	26	27	28	29	30	31
Jan	4	5	6	7	8	9	1	2	3	4	5	6	7	8	9	1	2	3	4	5	6	7	8	9	1	2	3	4	5	6	7
Feb	5	6	7	8	9	1	2	3	4	5	6	7	8	9	1	2	3	4	5	6	7	8	9	1	2	3	4	5	6		
Mar	6	7	8	9	1	2	3	4	5	6	7	8	9	1	2	3	4	5	6	7	8	9	1	2	3	4	5	6	7	8	9
Apr	7	8	9	1	2	3	4	5	6	7	8	9	1	2	3	4	5	6	7	8	9	1	2	3	4	5	6	7	8	9	
May	8	9	1	2	3	4	5	6	7	8	9	1	2	3	4	5	6	7	8	9	1	2	3	4	5	6	7	8	9	1	2
Jun	9	1	2	3	4	5	6	7	8	9	1	2	3	4	5	6	7	8	9	1	2	3	4	5	6	7	8	9	1	2	
Jul	1	2	3	4	5	6	7	8	9	1	2	3	4	5	6	7	8	9	1	2	3	4	5	6	7	8	9	1	2	3	4
Aug	2	3	4	5	6	7	8	9	1	2	3	5	6	7	8	9	1	2	3	4	5	6	7	8	9	1	2	3	4	5	6
Sep	4	5	6	7	8	9	1	2	3	4	5	6	7	8	9	1	2	3	4	5	6	7	8	9	1	2	3	4	5	6	
Oct	5	6	7	8	9	1	2	3	4	5	6	7	8	9	1	2	3	4	5	6	7	8	9	1	2	3	4	5	6	7	8
Nov	6	7	8	9	1	2	3	4	5	6	7	8	9	1	2	3	4	5	6	7	8	9	1	2	3	4	5	6	7	8	
Dec	7	8	9	1	2	3	4	5	6	7	8	9	1	2	3	4	5	6	7	8	9	1	2	3	4	5	6	7	8	9	1

AUGUST 13

	1	2	3	4	5	6	7	8	9	10	11	12	13	14	15	16	17	18	19	20	21	22	23	24	25	26	27	28	29	30	31
Jan	5	6	7	8	9	1	2	3	4	5	6	7	8	9	1	2	3	4	5	6	7	8	9	1	2	3	4	5	6	7	8
Feb	6	7	8	9	1	2	3	4	5	6	7	8	9	1	2	3	4	5	6	7	8	9	1	2	3	4	5	6	7		
Mar	7	8	9	1	2	3	4	5	6	7	8	9	1	2	3	4	5	6	7	8	9	1	2	3	4	5	6	7	8	9	1
Apr	8	9	1	2	3	4	5	6	7	8	9	1	2	3	4	5	6	7	8	9	1	2	3	4	5	6	7	8	9	1	
May	9	1	2	3	4	5	6	7	8	9	1	2	3	4	5	6	7	8	9	1	2	3	4	5	6	7	8	9	1	2	3
Jun	1	2	3	4	5	6	7	8	9	1	2	3	4	5	6	7	8	9	1	2	3	4	5	6	7	8	9	1	2	3	
Jul	2	3	4	5	6	7	8	9	1	2	3	4	5	6	7	8	9	1	2	3	4	5	6	7	8	9	1	2	3	4	5
Aug	3	4	5	6	7	8	9	1	2	3	4	5	7	8	9	1	2	3	4	5	6	7	8	9	1	2	3	4	5	6	7
Sep	5	6	7	8	9	1	2	3	4	5	6	7	8	9	1	2	3	4	5	6	7	8	9	1	2	3	4	5	6	7	
Oct	6	7	8	9	1	2	3	4	5	6	7	8	9	1	2	3	4	5	6	7	8	9	1	2	3	4	5	6	7	8	9
Nov	7	8	9	1	2	3	4	5	6	7	8	9	1	2	3	4	5	6	7	8	9	1	2	3	4	5	6	7	8	9	
Dec	8	9	1	2	3	4	5	6	7	8	9	1	2	3	4	5	6	7	8	9	1	2	3	4	5	6	7	8	9	1	2

AUGUST 14

	1	2	3	4	5	6	7	8	9	10	11	12	13	14	15	16	17	18	19	20	21	22	23	24	25	26	27	28	29	30	31
Jan	6	7	8	9	1	2	3	4	5	6	7	8	9	1	2	3	4	5	6	7	8	9	1	2	3	4	5	6	7	8	9
Feb	7	8	9	1	2	3	4	5	6	7	8	9	1	2	3	4	5	6	7	8	9	1	2	3	4	5	6	7	8		
Mar	8	9	1	2	3	4	5	6	7	8	9	1	2	3	4	5	6	7	8	9	1	2	3	4	5	6	7	8	9	1	2
Apr	9	1	2	3	4	5	6	7	8	9	1	2	3	4	5	6	7	8	9	1	2	3	4	5	6	7	8	9	1	2	
May	1	2	3	4	5	6	7	8	9	1	2	3	4	5	6	7	8	9	1	2	3	4	5	6	7	8	9	1	2	3	4
Jun	2	3	4	5	6	7	8	9	1	2	3	4	5	6	7	8	9	1	2	3	4	5	6	7	8	9	1	2	3	4	
Jul	3	4	5	6	7	8	9	1	2	3	4	5	6	7	8	9	1	2	3	4	5	6	7	8	9	1	2	3	4	5	6
Aug	4	5	6	7	8	9	1	2	3	4	5	6	7	9	1	2	3	4	5	6	7	8	9	1	2	3	4	5	6	7	8
Sep	6	7	8	9	1	2	3	4	5	6	7	8	9	1	2	3	4	5	6	7	8	9	1	2	3	4	5	6	7	8	
Oct	7	8	9	1	2	3	4	5	6	7	8	9	1	2	3	4	5	6	7	8	9	1	2	3	4	5	6	7	8	9	1
Nov	8	9	1	2	3	4	5	6	7	8	9	1	2	3	4	5	6	7	8	9	1	2	3	4	5	6	7	8	9	1	
Dec	9	1	2	3	4	5	6	7	8	9	1	2	3	4	5	6	7	8	9	1	2	3	4	5	6	7	8	9	1	2	3

AUGUST 15

	1	2	3	4	5	6	7	8	9	10	11	12	13	14	15	16	17	18	19	20	21	22	23	24	25	26	27	28	29	30	31
Jan	7	8	9	1	2	3	4	5	6	7	8	9	1	2	3	4	5	6	7	8	9	1	2	3	4	5	6	7	8	9	1
Feb	8	9	1	2	3	4	5	6	7	8	9	1	2	3	4	5	6	7	8	9	1	2	3	4	5	6	7	8	9		
Mar	9	1	2	3	4	5	6	7	8	9	1	2	3	4	5	6	7	8	9	1	2	3	4	5	6	7	8	9	1	2	3
Apr	1	2	3	4	5	6	7	8	9	1	2	3	4	5	6	7	8	9	1	2	3	4	5	6	7	8	9	1	2	3	
May	2	3	4	5	6	7	8	9	1	2	3	4	5	6	7	8	9	1	2	3	4	5	6	7	8	9	1	2	3	4	5
Jun	3	4	5	6	7	8	9	1	2	3	4	5	6	7	8	9	1	2	3	4	5	6	7	8	9	1	2	3	4	5	
Jul	4	5	6	7	8	9	1	2	3	4	5	6	7	8	9	1	2	3	4	5	6	7	8	9	1	2	3	4	5	6	7
Aug	5	6	7	8	9	1	2	3	4	5	6	7	8	9	2	3	4	5	6	7	8	9	1	2	3	4	5	6	7	8	9
Sep	7	8	9	1	2	3	4	5	6	7	8	9	1	2	3	4	5	6	7	8	9	1	2	3	4	5	6	7	8	9	
Oct	8	9	1	2	3	4	5	6	7	8	9	1	2	3	4	5	6	7	8	9	1	2	3	4	5	6	7	8	9	1	2
Nov	9	1	2	3	4	5	6	7	8	9	1	2	3	4	5	6	7	8	9	1	2	3	4	5	6	7	8	9	1	2	
Dec	1	2	3	4	5	6	7	8	9	1	2	3	4	5	6	7	8	9	1	2	3	4	5	6	7	8	9	1	2	3	4

AUGUST 16

	1	2	3	4	5	6	7	8	9	10	11	12	13	14	15	16	17	18	19	20	21	22	23	24	25	26	27	28	29	30	31
Jan	8	9	1	2	3	4	5	6	7	8	9	1	2	3	4	5	6	7	8	9	1	2	3	4	5	6	7	8	9	1	2
Feb	9	1	2	3	4	5	6	7	8	9	1	2	3	4	5	6	7	8	9	1	2	3	4	5	6	7	8	9	1		
Mar	1	2	3	4	5	6	7	8	9	1	2	3	4	5	6	7	8	9	1	2	3	4	5	6	7	8	9	1	2	3	4
Apr	2	3	4	5	6	7	8	9	1	2	3	4	5	6	7	8	9	1	2	3	4	5	6	7	8	9	1	2	3	4	
May	3	4	5	6	7	8	9	1	2	3	4	5	6	7	8	9	1	2	3	4	5	6	7	8	9	1	2	3	4	5	6
Jun	4	5	6	7	8	9	1	2	3	4	5	6	7	8	9	1	2	3	4	5	6	7	8	9	1	2	3	4	5	6	
Jul	5	6	7	8	9	1	2	3	4	5	6	7	8	9	1	2	3	4	5	6	7	8	9	1	2	3	4	5	6	7	8
Aug	6	7	8	9	1	2	3	4	5	6	7	8	9	1	2	4	5	6	7	8	9	1	2	3	4	5	6	7	8	9	1
Sep	8	9	1	2	3	4	5	6	7	8	9	1	2	3	4	5	6	7	8	9	1	2	3	4	5	6	7	8	9	1	
Oct	9	1	2	3	4	5	6	7	8	9	1	2	3	4	5	6	7	8	9	1	2	3	4	5	6	7	8	9	1	2	3
Nov	1	2	3	4	5	6	7	8	9	1	2	3	4	5	6	7	8	9	1	2	3	4	5	6	7	8	9	1	2	3	
Dec	2	3	4	5	6	7	8	9	1	2	3	4	5	6	7	8	9	1	2	3	4	5	6	7	8	9	1	2	3	4	5

AUGUST 17

	1	2	3	4	5	6	7	8	9	10	11	12	13	14	15	16	17	18	19	20	21	22	23	24	25	26	27	28	29	30	31
Jan	9	1	2	3	4	5	6	7	8	9	1	2	3	4	5	6	7	8	9	1	2	3	4	5	6	7	8	9	1	2	3
Feb	1	2	3	4	5	6	7	8	9	1	2	3	4	5	6	7	8	9	1	2	3	4	5	6	7	8	9	1	2		
Mar	2	3	4	5	6	7	8	9	1	2	3	4	5	6	7	8	9	1	2	3	4	5	6	7	8	9	1	2	3	4	5
Apr	3	4	5	6	7	8	9	1	2	3	4	5	6	7	8	9	1	2	3	4	5	6	7	8	9	1	2	3	4	5	
May	4	5	6	7	8	9	1	2	3	4	5	6	7	8	9	1	2	3	4	5	6	7	8	9	1	2	3	4	5	6	7
Jun	5	6	7	8	9	1	2	3	4	5	6	7	8	9	1	2	3	4	5	6	7	8	9	1	2	3	4	5	6	7	
Jul	6	7	8	9	1	2	3	4	5	6	7	8	9	1	2	3	4	5	6	7	8	9	1	2	3	4	5	6	7	8	9
Aug	7	8	9	1	2	3	4	5	6	7	8	9	1	2	3	4	6	7	8	9	1	2	3	4	5	6	7	8	9	1	2
Sep	9	1	2	3	4	5	6	7	8	9	1	2	3	4	5	6	7	8	9	1	2	3	4	5	6	7	8	9	1	2	
Oct	1	2	3	4	5	6	7	8	9	1	2	3	4	5	6	7	8	9	1	2	3	4	5	6	7	8	9	1	2	3	4
Nov	2	3	4	5	6	7	8	9	1	2	3	4	5	6	7	8	9	1	2	3	4	5	6	7	8	9	1	2	3	4	
Dec	3	4	5	6	7	8	9	1	2	3	4	5	6	7	8	9	1	2	3	4	5	6	7	8	9	1	2	3	4	5	6

AUGUST 18

	1	2	3	4	5	6	7	8	9	10	11	12	13	14	15	16	17	18	19	20	21	22	23	24	25	26	27	28	29	30	31
Jan	1	2	3	4	5	6	7	8	9	1	2	3	4	5	6	7	8	9	1	2	3	4	5	6	7	8	9	1	2	3	4
Feb	2	3	4	5	6	7	8	9	1	2	3	4	5	6	7	8	9	1	2	3	4	5	6	7	8	9	1	2	3		
Mar	3	4	5	6	7	8	9	1	2	3	4	5	6	7	8	9	1	2	3	4	5	6	7	8	9	1	2	3	4	5	6
Apr	4	5	6	7	8	9	1	2	3	4	5	6	7	8	9	1	2	3	4	5	6	7	8	9	1	2	3	4	5	6	
May	5	6	7	8	9	1	2	3	4	5	6	7	8	9	1	2	3	4	5	6	7	8	9	1	2	3	4	5	6	7	8
Jun	6	7	8	9	1	2	3	4	5	6	7	8	9	1	2	3	4	5	6	7	8	9	1	2	3	4	5	6	7	8	
Jul	7	8	9	1	2	3	4	5	6	7	8	9	1	2	3	4	5	6	7	8	9	1	2	3	4	5	6	7	8	9	1
Aug	8	9	1	2	3	4	5	6	7	8	9	1	2	3	4	5	6	8	9	1	2	3	4	5	6	7	8	9	1	2	3
Sep	1	2	3	4	5	6	7	8	9	1	2	3	4	5	6	7	8	9	1	2	3	4	5	6	7	8	9	1	2	3	
Oct	2	3	4	5	6	7	8	9	1	2	3	4	5	6	7	8	9	1	2	3	4	5	6	7	8	9	1	2	3	4	5
Nov	3	4	5	6	7	8	9	1	2	3	4	5	6	7	8	9	1	2	3	4	5	6	7	8	9	1	2	3	4	5	
Dec	4	5	6	7	8	9	1	2	3	4	5	6	7	8	9	1	2	3	4	5	6	7	8	9	1	2	3	4	5	6	7

AUGUST 19

	1	2	3	4	5	6	7	8	9	10	11	12	13	14	15	16	17	18	19	20	21	22	23	24	25	26	27	28	29	30	31
Jan	2	3	4	5	6	7	8	9	1	2	3	4	5	6	7	8	9	1	2	3	4	5	6	7	8	9	1	2	3	4	5
Feb	3	4	5	6	7	8	9	1	2	3	4	5	6	7	8	9	1	2	3	4	5	6	7	8	9	1	2	3	4		
Mar	4	5	6	7	8	9	1	2	3	4	5	6	7	8	9	1	2	3	4	5	6	7	8	9	1	2	3	4	5	6	7
Apr	5	6	7	8	9	1	2	3	4	5	6	7	8	9	1	2	3	4	5	6	7	8	9	1	2	3	4	5	6	7	
May	6	7	8	9	1	2	3	4	5	6	7	8	9	1	2	3	4	5	6	7	8	9	1	2	3	4	5	6	7	8	9
Jun	7	8	9	1	2	3	4	5	6	7	8	9	1	2	3	4	5	6	7	8	9	1	2	3	4	5	6	7	8	9	
Jul	8	9	1	2	3	4	5	6	7	8	9	1	2	3	4	5	6	7	8	9	1	2	3	4	5	6	7	8	9	1	2
Aug	9	1	2	3	4	5	6	7	8	9	1	2	3	4	5	6	7	8	1	2	3	4	5	6	7	8	9	1	2	3	4
Sep	2	3	4	5	6	7	8	9	1	2	3	4	5	6	7	8	9	1	2	3	4	5	6	7	8	9	1	2	3	4	
Oct	3	4	5	6	7	8	9	1	2	3	4	5	6	7	8	9	1	2	3	4	5	6	7	8	9	1	2	3	4	5	6
Nov	4	5	6	7	8	9	1	2	3	4	5	6	7	8	9	1	2	3	4	5	6	7	8	9	1	2	3	4	5	6	
Dec	5	6	7	8	9	1	2	3	4	5	6	7	8	9	1	2	3	4	5	6	7	8	9	1	2	3	4	5	6	7	8

AUGUST 20

	1	2	3	4	5	6	7	8	9	10	11	12	13	14	15	16	17	18	19	20	21	22	23	24	25	26	27	28	29	30	31
Jan	3	4	5	6	7	8	9	1	2	3	4	5	6	7	8	9	1	2	3	4	5	6	7	8	9	1	2	3	4	5	6
Feb	4	5	6	7	8	9	1	2	3	4	5	6	7	8	9	1	2	3	4	5	6	7	8	9	1	2	3	4	5		
Mar	5	6	7	8	9	1	2	3	4	5	6	7	8	9	1	2	3	4	5	6	7	8	9	1	2	3	4	5	6	7	8
Apr	6	7	8	9	1	2	3	4	5	6	7	8	9	1	2	3	4	5	6	7	8	9	1	2	3	4	5	6	7	8	
May	7	8	9	1	2	3	4	5	6	7	8	9	1	2	3	4	5	6	7	8	9	1	2	3	4	5	6	7	8	9	1
Jun	8	9	1	2	3	4	5	6	7	8	9	1	2	3	4	5	6	7	8	9	1	2	3	4	5	6	7	8	9	1	
Jul	9	1	2	3	4	5	6	7	8	9	1	2	3	4	5	6	7	8	9	1	2	3	4	5	6	7	8	9	1	2	3
Aug	1	2	3	4	5	6	7	8	9	1	2	3	4	5	6	7	8	9	1	3	4	5	6	7	8	9	1	2	3	4	5
Sep	3	4	5	6	7	8	9	1	2	3	4	5	6	7	8	9	1	2	3	4	5	6	7	8	9	1	2	3	4	5	
Oct	4	5	6	7	8	9	1	2	3	4	5	6	7	8	9	1	2	3	4	5	6	7	8	9	1	2	3	4	5	6	7
Nov	5	6	7	8	9	1	2	3	4	5	6	7	8	9	1	2	3	4	5	6	7	8	9	1	2	3	4	5	6	7	
Dec	6	7	8	9	1	2	3	4	5	6	7	8	9	1	2	3	4	5	6	7	8	9	1	2	3	4	5	6	7	8	9

AUGUST 21

	1	2	3	4	5	6	7	8	9	10	11	12	13	14	15	16	17	18	19	20	21	22	23	24	25	26	27	28	29	30	31
Jan	4	5	6	7	8	9	1	2	3	4	5	6	7	8	9	1	2	3	4	5	6	7	8	9	1	2	3	4	5	6	7
Feb	5	6	7	8	9	1	2	3	4	5	6	7	8	9	1	2	3	4	5	6	7	8	9	1	2	3	4	5	6		
Mar	6	7	8	9	1	2	3	4	5	6	7	8	9	1	2	3	4	5	6	7	8	9	1	2	3	4	5	6	7	8	9
Apr	7	8	9	1	2	3	4	5	6	7	8	9	1	2	3	4	5	6	7	8	9	1	2	3	4	5	6	7	8	9	
May	8	9	1	2	3	4	5	6	7	8	9	1	2	3	4	5	6	7	8	9	1	2	3	4	5	6	7	8	9	1	2
Jun	9	1	2	3	4	5	6	7	8	9	1	2	3	4	5	6	7	8	9	1	2	3	4	5	6	7	8	9	1	2	
Jul	1	2	3	4	5	6	7	8	9	1	2	3	4	5	6	7	8	9	1	2	3	4	5	6	7	8	9	1	2	3	4
Aug	2	3	4	5	6	7	8	9	1	2	3	4	5	6	7	8	9	1	2	3	5	6	7	8	9	1	2	3	4	5	6
Sep	4	5	6	7	8	9	1	2	3	4	5	6	7	8	9	1	2	3	4	5	6	7	8	9	1	2	3	4	5	6	
Oct	5	6	7	8	9	1	2	3	4	5	6	7	8	9	1	2	3	4	5	6	7	8	9	1	2	3	4	5	6	7	8
Nov	6	7	8	9	1	2	3	4	5	6	7	8	9	1	2	3	4	5	6	7	8	9	1	2	3	4	5	6	7	8	
Dec	7	8	9	1	2	3	4	5	6	7	8	9	1	2	3	4	5	6	7	8	9	1	2	3	4	5	6	7	8	9	1

AUGUST 22

	1	2	3	4	5	6	7	8	9	10	11	12	13	14	15	16	17	18	19	20	21	22	23	24	25	26	27	28	29	30	31
Jan	5	6	7	8	9	1	2	3	4	5	6	7	8	9	1	2	3	4	5	6	7	8	9	1	2	3	4	5	6	7	8
Feb	6	7	8	9	1	2	3	4	5	6	7	8	9	1	2	3	4	5	6	7	8	9	1	2	3	4	5	6	7		
Mar	7	8	9	1	2	3	4	5	6	7	8	9	1	2	3	4	5	6	7	8	9	1	2	3	4	5	6	7	8	9	1
Apr	8	9	1	2	3	4	5	6	7	8	9	1	2	3	4	5	6	7	8	9	1	2	3	4	5	6	7	8	9	1	
May	9	1	2	3	4	5	6	7	8	9	1	2	3	4	5	6	7	8	9	1	2	3	4	5	6	7	8	9	1	2	3
Jun	1	2	3	4	5	6	7	8	9	1	2	3	4	5	6	7	8	9	1	2	3	4	5	6	7	8	9	1	2	3	
Jul	2	3	4	5	6	7	8	9	1	2	3	4	5	6	7	8	9	1	2	3	4	5	6	7	8	9	1	2	3	4	5
Aug	3	4	5	6	7	8	9	1	2	3	4	5	6	7	8	9	1	2	3	4	5	7	8	9	1	2	3	4	5	6	7
Sep	5	6	7	8	9	1	2	3	4	5	6	7	8	9	1	2	3	4	5	6	7	8	9	1	2	3	4	5	6	7	
Oct	6	7	8	9	1	2	3	4	5	6	7	8	9	1	2	3	4	5	6	7	8	9	1	2	3	4	5	6	7	8	9
Nov	7	8	9	1	2	3	4	5	6	7	8	9	1	2	3	4	5	6	7	8	9	1	2	3	4	5	6	7	8	9	
Dec	8	9	1	2	3	4	5	6	7	8	9	1	2	3	4	5	6	7	8	9	1	2	3	4	5	6	7	8	9	1	2

AUGUST 23

	1	2	3	4	5	6	7	8	9	10	11	12	13	14	15	16	17	18	19	20	21	22	23	24	25	26	27	28	29	30	31
Jan	6	7	8	9	1	2	3	4	5	6	7	8	9	1	2	3	4	5	6	7	8	9	1	2	3	4	5	6	7	8	9
Feb	7	8	9	1	2	3	4	5	6	7	8	9	1	2	3	4	5	6	7	8	9	1	2	3	4	5	6	7	8		
Mar	8	9	1	2	3	4	5	6	7	8	9	1	2	3	4	5	6	7	8	9	1	2	3	4	5	6	7	8	9	1	2
Apr	9	1	2	3	4	5	6	7	8	9	1	2	3	4	5	6	7	8	9	1	2	3	4	5	6	7	8	9	1	2	
May	1	2	3	4	5	6	7	8	9	1	2	3	4	5	6	7	8	9	1	2	3	4	5	6	7	8	9	1	2	3	4
Jun	2	3	4	5	6	7	8	9	1	2	3	4	5	6	7	8	9	1	2	3	4	5	6	7	8	9	1	2	3	4	
Jul	3	4	5	6	7	8	9	1	2	3	4	5	6	7	8	9	1	2	3	4	5	6	7	8	9	1	2	3	4	5	6
Aug	4	5	6	7	8	9	1	2	3	4	5	6	7	8	9	1	2	3	4	5	6	7	9	1	2	3	4	5	6	7	8
Sep	6	7	8	9	1	2	3	4	5	6	7	8	9	1	2	3	4	5	6	7	8	9	1	2	3	4	5	6	7	8	
Oct	7	8	9	1	2	3	4	5	6	7	8	9	1	2	3	4	5	6	7	8	9	1	2	3	4	5	6	7	8	9	1
Nov	8	9	1	2	3	4	5	6	7	8	9	1	2	3	4	5	6	7	8	9	1	2	3	4	5	6	7	8	9	1	
Dec	9	1	2	3	4	5	6	7	8	9	1	2	3	4	5	6	7	8	9	1	2	3	4	5	6	7	8	9	1	2	3

AUGUST 24

	1	2	3	4	5	6	7	8	9	10	11	12	13	14	15	16	17	18	19	20	21	22	23	24	25	26	27	28	29	30	31
Jan	7	8	9	1	2	3	4	5	6	7	8	9	1	2	3	4	5	6	7	8	9	1	2	3	4	5	6	7	8	9	1
Feb	8	9	1	2	3	4	5	6	7	8	9	1	2	3	4	5	6	7	8	9	1	2	3	4	5	6	7	8	9		
Mar	9	1	2	3	4	5	6	7	8	9	1	2	3	4	5	6	7	8	9	1	2	3	4	5	6	7	8	9	1	2	3
Apr	1	2	3	4	5	6	7	8	9	1	2	3	4	5	6	7	8	9	1	2	3	4	5	6	7	8	9	1	2	3	
May	2	3	4	5	6	7	8	9	1	2	3	4	5	6	7	8	9	1	2	3	4	5	6	7	8	9	1	2	3	4	5
Jun	3	4	5	6	7	8	9	1	2	3	4	5	6	7	8	9	1	2	3	4	5	6	7	8	9	1	2	3	4	5	
Jul	4	5	6	7	8	9	1	2	3	4	5	6	7	8	9	1	2	3	4	5	6	7	8	9	1	2	3	4	5	6	7
Aug	5	6	7	8	9	1	2	3	4	5	6	7	8	9	1	2	3	4	5	6	7	8	9	2	3	4	5	6	7	8	9
Sep	7	8	9	1	2	3	4	5	6	7	8	9	1	2	3	4	5	6	7	8	9	1	2	3	4	5	6	7	8	9	
Oct	8	9	1	2	3	4	5	6	7	8	9	1	2	3	4	5	6	7	8	9	1	2	3	4	5	6	7	8	9	1	2
Nov	9	1	2	3	4	5	6	7	8	9	1	2	3	4	5	6	7	8	9	1	2	3	4	5	6	7	8	9	1	2	
Dec	1	2	3	4	5	6	7	8	9	1	2	3	4	5	6	7	8	9	1	2	3	4	5	6	7	8	9	1	2	3	4

AUGUST 25

	1	2	3	4	5	6	7	8	9	10	11	12	13	14	15	16	17	18	19	20	21	22	23	24	25	26	27	28	29	30	31
Jan	8	9	1	2	3	4	5	6	7	8	9	1	2	3	4	5	6	7	8	9	1	2	3	4	5	6	7	8	9	1	2
Feb	9	1	2	3	4	5	6	7	8	9	1	2	3	4	5	6	7	8	9	1	2	3	4	5	6	7	8	9	1		
Mar	1	2	3	4	5	6	7	8	9	1	2	3	4	5	6	7	8	9	1	2	3	4	5	6	7	8	9	1	2	3	4
Apr	2	3	4	5	6	7	8	9	1	2	3	4	5	6	7	8	9	1	2	3	4	5	6	7	8	9	1	2	3	4	
May	3	4	5	6	7	8	9	1	2	3	4	5	6	7	8	9	1	2	3	4	5	6	7	8	9	1	2	3	4	5	6
Jun	4	5	6	7	8	9	1	2	3	4	5	6	7	8	9	1	2	3	4	5	6	7	8	9	1	2	3	4	5	6	
Jul	5	6	7	8	9	1	2	3	4	5	6	7	8	9	1	2	3	4	5	6	7	8	9	1	2	3	4	5	6	7	8
Aug	6	7	8	9	1	2	3	4	5	6	7	8	9	1	2	3	4	5	6	7	8	9	1	2	4	5	6	7	8	9	1
Sep	8	9	1	2	3	4	5	6	7	8	9	1	2	3	4	5	6	7	8	9	1	2	3	4	5	6	7	8	9	1	
Oct	9	1	2	3	4	5	6	7	8	9	1	2	3	4	5	6	7	8	9	1	2	3	4	5	6	7	8	9	1	2	3
Nov	1	2	3	4	5	6	7	8	9	1	2	3	4	5	6	7	8	9	1	2	3	4	5	6	7	8	9	1	2	3	
Dec	2	3	4	5	6	7	8	9	1	2	3	4	5	6	7	8	9	1	2	3	4	5	6	7	8	9	1	2	3	4	5

AUGUST 26

	1	2	3	4	5	6	7	8	9	10	11	12	13	14	15	16	17	18	19	20	21	22	23	24	25	26	27	28	29	30	31
Jan	9	1	2	3	4	5	6	7	8	9	1	2	3	4	5	6	7	8	9	1	2	3	4	5	6	7	8	9	1	2	3
Feb	1	2	3	4	5	6	7	8	9	1	2	3	4	5	6	7	8	9	1	2	3	4	5	6	7	8	9	1	2		
Mar	2	3	4	5	6	7	8	9	1	2	3	4	5	6	7	8	9	1	2	3	4	5	6	7	8	9	1	2	3	4	5
Apr	3	4	5	6	7	8	9	1	2	3	4	5	6	7	8	9	1	2	3	4	5	6	7	8	9	1	2	3	4	5	
May	4	5	6	7	8	9	1	2	3	4	5	6	7	8	9	1	2	3	4	5	6	7	8	9	1	2	3	4	5	6	7
Jun	5	6	7	8	9	1	2	3	4	5	6	7	8	9	1	2	3	4	5	6	7	8	9	1	2	3	4	5	6	7	
Jul	6	7	8	9	1	2	3	4	5	6	7	8	9	1	2	3	4	5	6	7	8	9	1	2	3	4	5	6	7	8	9
Aug	7	8	9	1	2	3	4	5	6	7	8	9	1	2	3	4	5	6	7	8	9	1	2	3	4	6	7	8	9	1	2
Sep	9	1	2	3	4	5	6	7	8	9	1	2	3	4	5	6	7	8	9	1	2	3	4	5	6	7	8	9	1	2	
Oct	1	2	3	4	5	6	7	8	9	1	2	3	4	5	6	7	8	9	1	2	3	4	5	6	7	8	9	1	2	3	4
Nov	2	3	4	5	6	7	8	9	1	2	3	4	5	6	7	8	9	1	2	3	4	5	6	7	8	9	1	2	3	4	
Dec	3	4	5	6	7	8	9	1	2	3	4	5	6	7	8	9	1	2	3	4	5	6	7	8	9	1	2	3	4	5	6

AUGUST 27

	1	2	3	4	5	6	7	8	9	10	11	12	13	14	15	16	17	18	19	20	21	22	23	24	25	26	27	28	29	30	31
Jan	1	2	3	4	5	6	7	8	9	1	2	3	4	5	6	7	8	9	1	2	3	4	5	6	7	8	9	1	2	3	4
Feb	2	3	4	5	6	7	8	9	1	2	3	4	5	6	7	8	9	1	2	3	4	5	6	7	8	9	1	2	3		
Mar	3	4	5	6	7	8	9	1	2	3	4	5	6	7	8	9	1	2	3	4	5	6	7	8	9	1	2	3	4	5	6
Apr	4	5	6	7	8	9	1	2	3	4	5	6	7	8	9	1	2	3	4	5	6	7	8	9	1	2	3	4	5	6	
May	5	6	7	8	9	1	2	3	4	5	6	7	8	9	1	2	3	4	5	6	7	8	9	1	2	3	4	5	6	7	8
Jun	6	7	8	9	1	2	3	4	5	6	7	8	9	1	2	3	4	5	6	7	8	9	1	2	3	4	5	6	7	8	
Jul	7	8	9	1	2	3	4	5	6	7	8	9	1	2	3	4	5	6	7	8	9	1	2	3	4	5	6	7	8	9	1
Aug	8	9	1	2	3	4	5	6	7	8	9	1	2	3	4	5	6	7	8	9	1	2	3	4	5	6	8	9	1	2	3
Sep	1	2	3	4	5	6	7	8	9	1	2	3	4	5	6	7	8	9	1	2	3	4	5	6	7	8	9	1	2	3	
Oct	2	3	4	5	6	7	8	9	1	2	3	4	5	6	7	8	9	1	2	3	4	5	6	7	8	9	1	2	3	4	5
Nov	3	4	5	6	7	8	9	1	2	3	4	5	6	7	8	9	1	2	3	4	5	6	7	8	9	1	2	3	4	5	
Dec	4	5	6	7	8	9	1	2	3	4	5	6	7	8	9	1	2	3	4	5	6	7	8	9	1	2	3	4	5	6	7

AUGUST 28

	1	2	3	4	5	6	7	8	9	10	11	12	13	14	15	16	17	18	19	20	21	22	23	24	25	26	27	28	29	30	31
Jan	2	3	4	5	6	7	8	9	1	2	3	4	5	6	7	8	9	1	2	3	4	5	6	7	8	9	1	2	3	4	5
Feb	3	4	5	6	7	8	9	1	2	3	4	5	6	7	8	9	1	2	3	4	5	6	7	8	9	1	2	3	4		
Mar	4	5	6	7	8	9	1	2	3	4	5	6	7	8	9	1	2	3	4	5	6	7	8	9	1	2	3	4	5	6	7
Apr	5	6	7	8	9	1	2	3	4	5	6	7	8	9	1	2	3	4	5	6	7	8	9	1	2	3	4	5	6	7	
May	6	7	8	9	1	2	3	4	5	6	7	8	9	1	2	3	4	5	6	7	8	9	1	2	3	4	5	6	7	8	9
Jun	7	8	9	1	2	3	4	5	6	7	8	9	1	2	3	4	5	6	7	8	9	1	2	3	4	5	6	7	8	9	
Jul	8	9	1	2	3	4	5	6	7	8	9	1	2	3	4	5	6	7	8	9	1	2	3	4	5	6	7	8	9	1	2
Aug	9	1	2	3	4	5	6	7	8	9	1	2	3	4	5	6	7	8	9	1	2	3	4	5	6	7	8	1	2	3	4
Sep	2	3	4	5	6	7	8	9	1	2	3	4	5	6	7	8	9	1	2	3	4	5	6	7	8	9	1	2	3	4	
Oct	3	4	5	6	7	8	9	1	2	3	4	5	6	7	8	9	1	2	3	4	5	6	7	8	9	1	2	3	4	5	6
Nov	4	5	6	7	8	9	1	2	3	4	5	6	7	8	9	1	2	3	4	5	6	7	8	9	1	2	3	4	5	6	
Dec	5	6	7	8	9	1	2	3	4	5	6	7	8	9	1	2	3	4	5	6	7	8	9	1	2	3	4	5	6	7	8

AUGUST 29

	1	2	3	4	5	6	7	8	9	10	11	12	13	14	15	16	17	18	19	20	21	22	23	24	25	26	27	28	29	30	31
Jan	3	4	5	6	7	8	9	1	2	3	4	5	6	7	8	9	1	2	3	4	5	6	7	8	9	1	2	3	4	5	6
Feb	4	5	6	7	8	9	1	2	3	4	5	6	7	8	9	1	2	3	4	5	6	7	8	9	1	2	3	4	5		
Mar	5	6	7	8	9	1	2	3	4	5	6	7	8	9	1	2	3	4	5	6	7	8	9	1	2	3	4	5	6	7	8
Apr	6	7	8	9	1	2	3	4	5	6	7	8	9	1	2	3	4	5	6	7	8	9	1	2	3	4	5	6	7	8	
May	7	8	9	1	2	3	4	5	6	7	8	9	1	2	3	4	5	6	7	8	9	1	2	3	4	5	6	7	8	9	1
Jun	8	9	1	2	3	4	5	6	7	8	9	1	2	3	4	5	6	7	8	9	1	2	3	4	5	6	7	8	9	1	
Jul	9	1	2	3	4	5	6	7	8	9	1	2	3	4	5	6	7	8	9	1	2	3	4	5	6	7	8	9	1	2	3
Aug	1	2	3	4	5	6	7	8	9	1	2	3	4	5	6	7	8	9	1	2	3	4	5	6	7	8	9	1	3	4	5
Sep	3	4	5	6	7	8	9	1	2	3	4	5	6	7	8	9	1	2	3	4	5	6	7	8	9	1	2	3	4	5	
Oct	4	5	6	7	8	9	1	2	3	4	5	6	7	8	9	1	2	3	4	5	6	7	8	9	1	2	3	4	5	6	7
Nov	5	6	7	8	9	1	2	3	4	5	6	7	8	9	1	2	3	4	5	6	7	8	9	1	2	3	4	5	6	7	
Dec	6	7	8	9	1	2	3	4	5	6	7	8	9	1	2	3	4	5	6	7	8	9	1	2	3	4	5	6	7	8	9

AUGUST 30

	1	2	3	4	5	6	7	8	9	10	11	12	13	14	15	16	17	18	19	20	21	22	23	24	25	26	27	28	29	30	31
Jan	4	5	6	7	8	9	1	2	3	4	5	6	7	8	9	1	2	3	4	5	6	7	8	9	1	2	3	4	5	6	7
Feb	5	6	7	8	9	1	2	3	4	5	6	7	8	9	1	2	3	4	5	6	7	8	9	1	2	3	4	5	6		
Mar	6	7	8	9	1	2	3	4	5	6	7	8	9	1	2	3	4	5	6	7	8	9	1	2	3	4	5	6	7	8	9
Apr	7	8	9	1	2	3	4	5	6	7	8	9	1	2	3	4	5	6	7	8	9	1	2	3	4	5	6	7	8	9	
May	8	9	1	2	3	4	5	6	7	8	9	1	2	3	4	5	6	7	8	9	1	2	3	4	5	6	7	8	9	1	2
Jun	9	1	2	3	4	5	6	7	8	9	1	2	3	4	5	6	7	8	9	1	2	3	4	5	6	7	8	9	1	2	
Jul	1	2	3	4	5	6	7	8	9	1	2	3	4	5	6	7	8	9	1	2	3	4	5	6	7	8	9	1	2	3	4
Aug	2	3	4	5	6	7	8	9	1	2	3	4	5	6	7	8	9	1	2	3	4	5	6	7	8	9	1	2	3	5	6
Sep	4	5	6	7	8	9	1	2	3	4	5	6	7	8	9	1	2	3	4	5	6	7	8	9	1	2	3	4	5	6	
Oct	5	6	7	8	9	1	2	3	4	5	6	7	8	9	1	2	3	4	5	6	7	8	9	1	2	3	4	5	6	7	8
Nov	6	7	8	9	1	2	3	4	5	6	7	8	9	1	2	3	4	5	6	7	8	9	1	2	3	4	5	6	7	8	
Dec	7	8	9	1	2	3	4	5	6	7	8	9	1	2	3	4	5	6	7	8	9	1	2	3	4	5	6	7	8	9	1

AUGUST 31

	1	2	3	4	5	6	7	8	9	10	11	12	13	14	15	16	17	18	19	20	21	22	23	24	25	26	27	28	29	30	31
Jan	5	6	7	8	9	1	2	3	4	5	6	7	8	9	1	2	3	4	5	6	7	8	9	1	2	3	4	5	6	7	8
Feb	6	7	8	9	1	2	3	4	5	6	7	8	9	1	2	3	4	5	6	7	8	9	1	2	3	4	5	6	7		
Mar	7	8	9	1	2	3	4	5	6	7	8	9	1	2	3	4	5	6	7	8	9	1	2	3	4	5	6	7	8	9	1
Apr	8	9	1	2	3	4	5	6	7	8	9	1	2	3	4	5	6	7	8	9	1	2	3	4	5	6	7	8	9	1	
May	9	1	2	3	4	5	6	7	8	9	1	2	3	4	5	6	7	8	9	1	2	3	4	5	6	7	8	9	1	2	3
Jun	1	2	3	4	5	6	7	8	9	1	2	3	4	5	6	7	8	9	1	2	3	4	5	6	7	8	9	1	2	3	
Jul	2	3	4	5	6	7	8	9	1	2	3	4	5	6	7	8	9	1	2	3	4	5	6	7	8	9	1	2	3	4	5
Aug	3	4	5	6	7	8	9	1	2	3	4	5	6	7	8	9	1	2	3	4	5	6	7	8	9	1	2	3	4	5	7
Sep	5	6	7	8	9	1	2	3	4	5	6	7	8	9	1	2	3	4	5	6	7	8	9	1	2	3	4	5	6	7	
Oct	6	7	8	9	1	2	3	4	5	6	7	8	9	1	2	3	4	5	6	7	8	9	1	2	3	4	5	6	7	8	9
Nov	7	8	9	1	2	3	4	5	6	7	8	9	1	2	3	4	5	6	7	8	9	1	2	3	4	5	6	7	8	9	
Dec	8	9	1	2	3	4	5	6	7	8	9	1	2	3	4	5	6	7	8	9	1	2	3	4	5	6	7	8	9	1	2

SEPTEMBER 1

	1	2	3	4	5	6	7	8	9	10	11	12	13	14	15	16	17	18	19	20	21	22	23	24	25	26	27	28	29	30	31
Jan	3	4	5	6	7	8	9	1	2	3	4	5	6	7	8	9	1	2	3	4	5	6	7	8	9	1	2	3	4	5	6
Feb	4	5	6	7	8	9	1	2	3	4	5	6	7	8	9	1	2	3	4	5	6	7	8	9	1	2	3	4	5		
Mar	5	6	7	8	9	1	2	3	4	5	6	7	8	9	1	2	3	4	5	6	7	8	9	1	2	3	4	5	6	7	8
Apr	6	7	8	9	1	2	3	4	5	6	7	8	9	1	2	3	4	5	6	7	8	9	1	2	3	4	5	6	7	8	
May	7	8	9	1	2	3	4	5	6	7	8	9	1	2	3	4	5	6	7	8	9	1	2	3	4	5	6	7	8	9	1
Jun	8	9	1	2	3	4	5	6	7	8	9	1	2	3	4	5	6	7	8	9	1	2	3	4	5	6	7	8	9	1	
Jul	9	1	2	3	4	5	6	7	8	9	1	2	3	4	5	6	7	8	9	1	2	3	4	5	6	7	8	9	1	2	3
Aug	1	2	3	4	5	6	7	8	9	1	2	3	4	5	6	7	8	9	1	2	3	4	5	6	7	8	9	1	2	3	4
Sep	3	4	5	6	7	8	9	1	2	3	4	5	6	7	8	9	1	2	3	4	5	6	7	8	9	1	2	3	4	5	
Oct	4	5	6	7	8	9	1	2	3	4	5	6	7	8	9	1	2	3	4	5	6	7	8	9	1	2	3	4	5	6	7
Nov	5	6	7	8	9	1	2	3	4	5	6	7	8	9	1	2	3	4	5	6	7	8	9	1	2	3	4	5	6	7	
Dec	6	7	8	9	1	2	3	4	5	6	7	8	9	1	2	3	4	5	6	7	8	9	1	2	3	4	5	6	7	8	9

SEPTEMBER 2

	1	2	3	4	5	6	7	8	9	10	11	12	13	14	15	16	17	18	19	20	21	22	23	24	25	26	27	28	29	30	31
Jan	4	5	6	7	8	9	1	2	3	4	5	6	7	8	9	1	2	3	4	5	6	7	8	9	1	2	3	4	5	6	7
Feb	5	6	7	8	9	1	2	3	4	5	6	7	8	9	1	2	3	4	5	6	7	8	9	1	2	3	4	5	6		
Mar	6	7	8	9	1	2	3	4	5	6	7	8	9	1	2	3	4	5	6	7	8	9	1	2	3	4	5	6	7	8	9
Apr	7	8	9	1	2	3	4	5	6	7	8	9	1	2	3	4	5	6	7	8	9	1	2	3	4	5	6	7	8	9	
May	8	9	1	2	3	4	5	6	7	8	9	1	2	3	4	5	6	7	8	9	1	2	3	4	5	6	7	8	9	1	2
Jun	9	1	2	3	4	5	6	7	8	9	1	2	3	4	5	6	7	8	9	1	2	3	4	5	6	7	8	9	1	2	
Jul	1	2	3	4	5	6	7	8	9	1	2	3	4	5	6	7	8	9	1	2	3	4	5	6	7	8	9	1	2	3	4
Aug	2	3	4	5	6	7	8	9	1	2	3	4	5	6	7	8	9	1	2	3	4	5	6	7	8	9	1	2	3	4	5
Sep	3	5	6	7	8	9	1	2	3	4	5	6	7	8	9	1	2	3	4	5	6	7	8	9	1	2	3	4	5	6	
Oct	5	6	7	8	9	1	2	3	4	5	6	7	8	9	1	2	3	4	5	6	7	8	9	1	2	3	4	5	6	7	8
Nov	6	7	8	9	1	2	3	4	5	6	7	8	9	1	2	3	4	5	6	7	8	9	1	2	3	4	5	6	7	8	
Dec	7	8	9	1	2	3	4	5	6	7	8	9	1	2	3	4	5	6	7	8	9	1	2	3	4	5	6	7	8	9	1

SEPTEMBER 3

	1	2	3	4	5	6	7	8	9	10	11	12	13	14	15	16	17	18	19	20	21	22	23	24	25	26	27	28	29	30	31
Jan	5	6	7	8	9	1	2	3	4	5	6	7	8	9	1	2	3	4	5	6	7	8	9	1	2	3	4	5	6	7	8
Feb	6	7	8	9	1	2	3	4	5	6	7	8	9	1	2	3	4	5	6	7	8	9	1	2	3	4	5	6	7		
Mar	7	8	9	1	2	3	4	5	6	7	8	9	1	2	3	4	5	6	7	8	9	1	2	3	4	5	6	7	8	9	1
Apr	8	9	1	2	3	4	5	6	7	8	9	1	2	3	4	5	6	7	8	9	1	2	3	4	5	6	7	8	9	1	
May	9	1	2	3	4	5	6	7	8	9	1	2	3	4	5	6	7	8	9	1	2	3	4	5	6	7	8	9	1	2	3
Jun	1	2	3	4	5	6	7	8	9	1	2	3	4	5	6	7	8	9	1	2	3	4	5	6	7	8	9	1	2	3	
Jul	2	3	4	5	6	7	8	9	1	2	3	4	5	6	7	8	9	1	2	3	4	5	6	7	8	9	1	2	3	4	5
Aug	3	4	5	6	7	8	9	1	2	3	4	5	6	7	8	9	1	2	3	4	5	6	7	8	9	1	2	3	4	5	6
Sep	4	5	7	8	9	1	2	3	4	5	6	7	8	9	1	2	3	4	5	6	7	8	9	1	2	3	4	5	6	7	
Oct	6	7	8	9	1	2	3	4	5	6	7	8	9	1	2	3	4	5	6	7	8	9	1	2	3	4	5	6	7	8	9
Nov	7	8	9	1	2	3	4	5	6	7	8	9	1	2	3	4	5	6	7	8	9	1	2	3	4	5	6	7	8	9	
Dec	8	9	1	2	3	4	5	6	7	8	9	1	2	3	4	5	6	7	8	9	1	2	3	4	5	6	7	8	9	1	2

SEPTEMBER 4

	1	2	3	4	5	6	7	8	9	10	11	12	13	14	15	16	17	18	19	20	21	22	23	24	25	26	27	28	29	30	31
Jan	6	7	8	9	1	2	3	4	5	6	7	8	9	1	2	3	4	5	6	7	8	9	1	2	3	4	5	6	7	8	9
Feb	7	8	9	1	2	3	4	5	6	7	8	9	1	2	3	4	5	6	7	8	9	1	2	3	4	5	6	7	8		
Mar	8	9	1	2	3	4	5	6	7	8	9	1	2	3	4	5	6	7	8	9	1	2	3	4	5	6	7	8	9	1	2
Apr	9	1	2	3	4	5	6	7	8	9	1	2	3	4	5	6	7	8	9	1	2	3	4	5	6	7	8	9	1	2	
May	1	2	3	4	5	6	7	8	9	1	2	3	4	5	6	7	8	9	1	2	3	4	5	6	7	8	9	1	2	3	4
Jun	2	3	4	5	6	7	8	9	1	2	3	4	5	6	7	8	9	1	2	3	4	5	6	7	8	9	1	2	3	4	
Jul	3	4	5	6	7	8	9	1	2	3	4	5	6	7	8	9	1	2	3	4	5	6	7	8	9	1	2	3	4	5	6
Aug	4	5	6	7	8	9	1	2	3	4	5	6	7	8	9	1	2	3	4	5	6	7	8	9	1	2	3	4	5	6	7
Sep	5	6	7	9	1	2	3	4	5	6	7	8	9	1	2	3	4	5	6	7	8	9	1	2	3	4	5	6	7	8	
Oct	7	8	9	1	2	3	4	5	6	7	8	9	1	2	3	4	5	6	7	8	9	1	2	3	4	5	6	7	8	9	1
Nov	8	9	1	2	3	4	5	6	7	8	9	1	2	3	4	5	6	7	8	9	1	2	3	4	5	6	7	8	9	1	
Dec	9	1	2	3	4	5	6	7	8	9	1	2	3	4	5	6	7	8	9	1	2	3	4	5	6	7	8	9	1	2	3

SEPTEMBER 5

	1	2	3	4	5	6	7	8	9	10	11	12	13	14	15	16	17	18	19	20	21	22	23	24	25	26	27	28	29	30	31
Jan	7	8	9	1	2	3	4	5	6	7	8	9	1	2	3	4	5	6	7	8	9	1	2	3	4	5	6	7	8	9	1
Feb	8	9	1	2	3	4	5	6	7	8	9	1	2	3	4	5	6	7	8	9	1	2	3	4	5	6	7	8	9		
Mar	9	1	2	3	4	5	6	7	8	9	1	2	3	4	5	6	7	8	9	1	2	3	4	5	6	7	8	9	1	2	3
Apr	1	2	3	4	5	6	7	8	9	1	2	3	4	5	6	7	8	9	1	2	3	4	5	6	7	8	9	1	2	3	
May	2	3	4	5	6	7	8	9	1	2	3	4	5	6	7	8	9	1	2	3	4	5	6	7	8	9	1	2	3	4	5
Jun	3	4	5	6	7	8	9	1	2	3	4	5	6	7	8	9	1	2	3	4	5	6	7	8	9	1	2	3	4	5	
Jul	4	5	6	7	8	9	1	2	3	4	5	6	7	8	9	1	2	3	4	5	6	7	8	9	1	2	3	4	5	6	7
Aug	5	6	7	8	9	1	2	3	4	5	6	7	8	9	1	2	3	4	5	6	7	8	9	1	2	3	4	5	6	7	8
Sep	6	7	8	9	2	3	4	5	6	7	8	9	1	2	3	4	5	6	7	8	9	1	2	3	4	5	6	7	8	9	
Oct	8	9	1	2	3	4	5	6	7	8	9	1	2	3	4	5	6	7	8	9	1	2	3	4	5	6	7	8	9	1	2
Nov	9	1	2	3	4	5	6	7	8	9	1	2	3	4	5	6	7	8	9	1	2	3	4	5	6	7	8	9	1	2	
Dec	1	2	3	4	5	6	7	8	9	1	2	3	4	5	6	7	8	9	1	2	3	4	5	6	7	8	9	1	2	3	4

SEPTEMBER 6

	1	2	3	4	5	6	7	8	9	10	11	12	13	14	15	16	17	18	19	20	21	22	23	24	25	26	27	28	29	30	31
Jan	8	9	1	2	3	4	5	6	7	8	9	1	2	3	4	5	6	7	8	9	1	2	3	4	5	6	7	8	9	1	2
Feb	9	1	2	3	4	5	6	7	8	9	1	2	3	4	5	6	7	8	9	1	2	3	4	5	6	7	8	9	1		
Mar	1	2	3	4	5	6	7	8	9	1	2	3	4	5	6	7	8	9	1	2	3	4	5	6	7	8	9	1	2	3	4
Apr	2	3	4	5	6	7	8	9	1	2	3	4	5	6	7	8	9	1	2	3	4	5	6	7	8	9	1	2	3	4	
May	3	4	5	6	7	8	9	1	2	3	4	5	6	7	8	9	1	2	3	4	5	6	7	8	9	1	2	3	4	5	6
Jun	4	5	6	7	8	9	1	2	3	4	5	6	7	8	9	1	2	3	4	5	6	7	8	9	1	2	3	4	5	6	
Jul	5	6	7	8	9	1	2	3	4	5	6	7	8	9	1	2	3	4	5	6	7	8	9	1	2	3	4	5	6	7	8
Aug	6	7	8	9	1	2	3	4	5	6	7	8	9	1	2	3	4	5	6	7	8	9	1	2	3	4	5	6	7	8	9
Sep	7	8	9	1	2	4	5	6	7	8	9	1	2	3	4	5	6	7	8	9	1	2	3	4	5	6	7	8	9	1	
Oct	9	1	2	3	4	5	6	7	8	9	1	2	3	4	5	6	7	8	9	1	2	3	4	5	6	7	8	9	1	2	3
Nov	1	2	3	4	5	6	7	8	9	1	2	3	4	5	6	7	8	9	1	2	3	4	5	6	7	8	9	1	2	3	
Dec	2	3	4	5	6	7	8	9	1	2	3	4	5	6	7	8	9	1	2	3	4	5	6	7	8	9	1	2	3	4	5

SEPTEMBER 7

	1	2	3	4	5	6	7	8	9	10	11	12	13	14	15	16	17	18	19	20	21	22	23	24	25	26	27	28	29	30	31
Jan	9	1	2	3	4	5	6	7	8	9	1	2	3	4	5	6	7	8	9	1	2	3	4	5	6	7	8	9	1	2	3
Feb	1	2	3	4	5	6	7	8	9	1	2	3	4	5	6	7	8	9	1	2	3	4	5	6	7	8	9	1	2		
Mar	2	3	4	5	6	7	8	9	1	2	3	4	5	6	7	8	9	1	2	3	4	5	6	7	8	9	1	2	3	4	5
Apr	3	4	5	6	7	8	9	1	2	3	4	5	6	7	8	9	1	2	3	4	5	6	7	8	9	1	2	3	4	5	
May	4	5	6	7	8	9	1	2	3	4	5	6	7	8	9	1	2	3	4	5	6	7	8	9	1	2	3	4	5	6	7
Jun	5	6	7	8	9	1	2	3	4	5	6	7	8	9	1	2	3	4	5	6	7	8	9	1	2	3	4	5	6	7	
Jul	6	7	8	9	1	2	3	4	5	6	7	8	9	1	2	3	4	5	6	7	8	9	1	2	3	4	5	6	7	8	9
Aug	7	8	9	1	2	3	4	5	6	7	8	9	1	2	3	4	5	6	7	8	9	1	2	3	4	5	6	7	8	9	1
Sep	8	9	1	2	3	4	6	7	8	9	1	2	3	4	5	6	7	8	9	1	2	3	4	5	6	7	8	9	1	2	
Oct	1	2	3	4	5	6	7	8	9	1	2	3	4	5	6	7	8	9	1	2	3	4	5	6	7	8	9	1	2	3	4
Nov	2	3	4	5	6	7	8	9	1	2	3	4	5	6	7	8	9	1	2	3	4	5	6	7	8	9	1	2	3	4	
Dec	3	4	5	6	7	8	9	1	2	3	4	5	6	7	8	9	1	2	3	4	5	6	7	8	9	1	2	3	4	5	6

SEPTEMBER 8

	1	2	3	4	5	6	7	8	9	10	11	12	13	14	15	16	17	18	19	20	21	22	23	24	25	26	27	28	29	30	31
Jan	1	2	3	4	5	6	7	8	9	1	2	3	4	5	6	7	8	9	1	2	3	4	5	6	7	8	9	1	2	3	4
Feb	2	3	4	5	6	7	8	9	1	2	3	4	5	6	7	8	9	1	2	3	4	5	6	7	8	9	1	2	3		
Mar	3	4	5	6	7	8	9	1	2	3	4	5	6	7	8	9	1	2	3	4	5	6	7	8	9	1	2	3	4	5	6
Apr	4	5	6	7	8	9	1	2	3	4	5	6	7	8	9	1	2	3	4	5	6	7	8	9	1	2	3	4	5	6	
May	5	6	7	8	9	1	2	3	4	5	6	7	8	9	1	2	3	4	5	6	7	8	9	1	2	3	4	5	6	7	8
Jun	6	7	8	9	1	2	3	4	5	6	7	8	9	1	2	3	4	5	6	7	8	9	1	2	3	4	5	6	7	8	
Jul	7	8	9	1	2	3	4	5	6	7	8	9	1	2	3	4	5	6	7	8	9	1	2	3	4	5	6	7	8	9	1
Aug	8	9	1	2	3	4	5	6	7	8	9	1	2	3	4	5	6	7	8	9	1	2	3	4	5	6	7	8	9	1	2
Sep	9	1	2	3	4	5	6	8	9	1	2	3	4	5	6	7	8	9	1	2	3	4	5	6	7	8	9	1	2	3	
Oct	2	3	4	5	6	7	8	9	1	2	3	4	5	6	7	8	9	1	2	3	4	5	6	7	8	9	1	2	3	4	5
Nov	3	4	5	6	7	8	9	1	2	3	4	5	6	7	8	9	1	2	3	4	5	6	7	8	9	1	2	3	4	5	
Dec	4	5	6	7	8	9	1	2	3	4	5	6	7	8	9	1	2	3	4	5	6	7	8	9	1	2	3	4	5	6	7

SEPTEMBER 9

	1	2	3	4	5	6	7	8	9	10	11	12	13	14	15	16	17	18	19	20	21	22	23	24	25	26	27	28	29	30	31
Jan	2	3	4	5	6	7	8	9	1	2	3	4	5	6	7	8	9	1	2	3	4	5	6	7	8	9	1	2	3	4	5
Feb	3	4	5	6	7	8	9	1	2	3	4	5	6	7	8	9	1	2	3	4	5	6	7	8	9	1	2	3	4		
Mar	4	5	6	7	8	9	1	2	3	4	5	6	7	8	9	1	2	3	4	5	6	7	8	9	1	2	3	4	5	6	7
Apr	5	6	7	8	9	1	2	3	4	5	6	7	8	9	1	2	3	4	5	6	7	8	9	1	2	3	4	5	6	7	
May	6	7	8	9	1	2	3	4	5	6	7	8	9	1	2	3	4	5	6	7	8	9	1	2	3	4	5	6	7	8	9
Jun	7	8	9	1	2	3	4	5	6	7	8	9	1	2	3	4	5	6	7	8	9	1	2	3	4	5	6	7	8	9	
Jul	8	9	1	2	3	4	5	6	7	8	9	1	2	3	4	5	6	7	8	9	1	2	3	4	5	6	7	8	9	1	2
Aug	9	1	2	3	4	5	6	7	8	9	1	2	3	4	5	6	7	8	9	1	2	3	4	5	6	7	8	9	1	2	3
Sep	1	2	3	4	5	6	7	8	1	2	3	4	5	6	7	8	9	1	2	3	4	5	6	7	8	9	1	2	3	4	
Oct	3	4	5	6	7	8	9	1	2	3	4	5	6	7	8	9	1	2	3	4	5	6	7	8	9	1	2	3	4	5	6
Nov	4	5	6	7	8	9	1	2	3	4	5	6	7	8	9	1	2	3	4	5	6	7	8	9	1	2	3	4	5	6	
Dec	5	6	7	8	9	1	2	3	4	5	6	7	8	9	1	2	3	4	5	6	7	8	9	1	2	3	4	5	6	7	8

SEPTEMBER 10

	1	2	3	4	5	6	7	8	9	10	11	12	13	14	15	16	17	18	19	20	21	22	23	24	25	26	27	28	29	30	31
Jan	3	4	5	6	7	8	9	1	2	3	4	5	6	7	8	9	1	2	3	4	5	6	7	8	9	1	2	3	4	5	6
Feb	4	5	6	7	8	9	1	2	3	4	5	6	7	8	9	1	2	3	4	5	6	7	8	9	1	2	3	4	5		
Mar	5	6	7	8	9	1	2	3	4	5	6	7	8	9	1	2	3	4	5	6	7	8	9	1	2	3	4	5	6	7	8
Apr	6	7	8	9	1	2	3	4	5	6	7	8	9	1	2	3	4	5	6	7	8	9	1	2	3	4	5	6	7	8	
May	7	8	9	1	2	3	4	5	6	7	8	9	1	2	3	4	5	6	7	8	9	1	2	3	4	5	6	7	8	9	1
Jun	8	9	1	2	3	4	5	6	7	8	9	1	2	3	4	5	6	7	8	9	1	2	3	4	5	6	7	8	9	1	
Jul	9	1	2	3	4	5	6	7	8	9	1	2	3	4	5	6	7	8	9	1	2	3	4	5	6	7	8	9	1	2	3
Aug	1	2	3	4	5	6	7	8	9	1	2	3	4	5	6	7	8	9	1	2	3	4	5	6	7	8	9	1	2	3	4
Sep	2	3	4	5	6	7	8	9	1	3	4	5	6	7	8	9	1	2	3	4	5	6	7	8	9	1	2	3	4	5	
Oct	4	5	6	7	8	9	1	2	3	4	5	6	7	8	9	1	2	3	4	5	6	7	8	9	1	2	3	4	5	6	7
Nov	5	6	7	8	9	1	2	3	4	5	6	7	8	9	1	2	3	4	5	6	7	8	9	1	2	3	4	5	6	7	
Dec	6	7	8	9	1	2	3	4	5	6	7	8	9	1	2	3	4	5	6	7	8	9	1	2	3	4	5	6	7	8	9

SEPTEMBER 11

	1	2	3	4	5	6	7	8	9	10	11	12	13	14	15	16	17	18	19	20	21	22	23	24	25	26	27	28	29	30	31
Jan	4	5	6	7	8	9	1	2	3	4	5	6	7	8	9	1	2	3	4	5	6	7	8	9	1	2	3	4	5	6	7
Feb	5	6	7	8	9	1	2	3	4	5	6	7	8	9	1	2	3	4	5	6	7	8	9	1	2	3	4	5	6		
Mar	6	7	8	9	1	2	3	4	5	6	7	8	9	1	2	3	4	5	6	7	8	9	1	2	3	4	5	6	7	8	9
Apr	7	8	9	1	2	3	4	5	6	7	8	9	1	2	3	4	5	6	7	8	9	1	2	3	4	5	6	7	8	9	
May	8	9	1	2	3	4	5	6	7	8	9	1	2	3	4	5	6	7	8	9	1	2	3	4	5	6	7	8	9	1	2
Jun	9	1	2	3	4	5	6	7	8	9	1	2	3	4	5	6	7	8	9	1	2	3	4	5	6	7	8	9	1	2	
Jul	1	2	3	4	5	6	7	8	9	1	2	3	4	5	6	7	8	9	1	2	3	4	5	6	7	8	9	1	2	3	4
Aug	2	3	4	5	6	7	8	9	1	2	3	4	5	6	7	8	9	1	2	3	4	5	6	7	8	9	1	2	3	4	5
Sep	3	4	5	6	7	8	9	1	2	3	5	6	7	8	9	1	2	3	4	5	6	7	8	9	1	2	3	4	5	6	
Oct	5	6	7	8	9	1	2	3	4	5	6	7	8	9	1	2	3	4	5	6	7	8	9	1	2	3	4	5	6	7	8
Nov	6	7	8	9	1	2	3	4	5	6	7	8	9	1	2	3	4	5	6	7	8	9	1	2	3	4	5	6	7	8	
Dec	7	8	9	1	2	3	4	5	6	7	8	9	1	2	3	4	5	6	7	8	9	1	2	3	4	5	6	7	8	9	1

SEPTEMBER 12

	1	2	3	4	5	6	7	8	9	10	11	12	13	14	15	16	17	18	19	20	21	22	23	24	25	26	27	28	29	30	31
Jan	5	6	7	8	9	1	2	3	4	5	6	7	8	9	1	2	3	4	5	6	7	8	9	1	2	3	4	5	6	7	8
Feb	6	7	8	9	1	2	3	4	5	6	7	8	9	1	2	3	4	5	6	7	8	9	1	2	3	4	5	6	7		
Mar	7	8	9	1	2	3	4	5	6	7	8	9	1	2	3	4	5	6	7	8	9	1	2	3	4	5	6	7	8	9	1
Apr	8	9	1	2	3	4	5	6	7	8	9	1	2	3	4	5	6	7	8	9	1	2	3	4	5	6	7	8	9	1	
May	9	1	2	3	4	5	6	7	8	9	1	2	3	4	5	6	7	8	9	1	2	3	4	5	6	7	8	9	1	2	3
Jun	1	2	3	4	5	6	7	8	9	1	2	3	4	5	6	7	8	9	1	2	3	4	5	6	7	8	9	1	2	3	
Jul	2	3	4	5	6	7	8	9	1	2	3	4	5	6	7	8	9	1	2	3	4	5	6	7	8	9	1	2	3	4	5
Aug	3	4	5	6	7	8	9	1	2	3	4	5	6	7	8	9	1	2	3	4	5	6	7	8	9	1	2	3	4	5	6
Sep	4	5	6	7	8	9	1	2	3	4	5	7	8	9	1	2	3	4	5	6	7	8	9	1	2	3	4	5	6	7	
Oct	6	7	8	9	1	2	3	4	5	6	7	8	9	1	2	3	4	5	6	7	8	9	1	2	3	4	5	6	7	8	9
Nov	7	8	9	1	2	3	4	5	6	7	8	9	1	2	3	4	5	6	7	8	9	1	2	3	4	5	6	7	8	9	
Dec	8	9	1	2	3	4	5	6	7	8	9	1	2	3	4	5	6	7	8	9	1	2	3	4	5	6	7	8	9	1	2

SEPTEMBER 13

	1	2	3	4	5	6	7	8	9	10	11	12	13	14	15	16	17	18	19	20	21	22	23	24	25	26	27	28	29	30	31
Jan	6	7	8	9	1	2	3	4	5	6	7	8	9	1	2	3	4	5	6	7	8	9	1	2	3	4	5	6	7	8	9
Feb	7	8	9	1	2	3	4	5	6	7	8	9	1	2	3	4	5	6	7	8	9	1	2	3	4	5	6	7	8		
Mar	8	9	1	2	3	4	5	6	7	8	9	1	2	3	4	5	6	7	8	9	1	2	3	4	5	6	7	8	9	1	2
Apr	9	1	2	3	4	5	6	7	8	9	1	2	3	4	5	6	7	8	9	1	2	3	4	5	6	7	8	9	1	2	
May	1	2	3	4	5	6	7	8	9	1	2	3	4	5	6	7	8	9	1	2	3	4	5	6	7	8	9	1	2	3	4
Jun	2	3	4	5	6	7	8	9	1	2	3	4	5	6	7	8	9	1	2	3	4	5	6	7	8	9	1	2	3	4	
Jul	3	4	5	6	7	8	9	1	2	3	4	5	6	7	8	9	1	2	3	4	5	6	7	8	9	1	2	3	4	5	6
Aug	4	5	6	7	8	9	1	2	3	4	5	6	7	8	9	1	2	3	4	5	6	7	8	9	1	2	3	4	5	6	7
Sep	5	6	7	8	9	1	2	3	4	5	6	7	9	1	2	3	4	5	6	7	8	9	1	2	3	4	5	6	7	8	
Oct	7	8	9	1	2	3	4	5	6	7	8	9	1	2	3	4	5	6	7	8	9	1	2	3	4	5	6	7	8	9	1
Nov	8	9	1	2	3	4	5	6	7	8	9	1	2	3	4	5	6	7	8	9	1	2	3	4	5	6	7	8	9	1	
Dec	9	1	2	3	4	5	6	7	8	9	1	2	3	4	5	6	7	8	9	1	2	3	4	5	6	7	8	9	1	2	3

SEPTEMBER 14

	1	2	3	4	5	6	7	8	9	10	11	12	13	14	15	16	17	18	19	20	21	22	23	24	25	26	27	28	29	30	31
Jan	7	8	9	1	2	3	4	5	6	7	8	9	1	2	3	4	5	6	7	8	9	1	2	3	4	5	6	7	8	9	1
Feb	8	9	1	2	3	4	5	6	7	8	9	1	2	3	4	5	6	7	8	9	1	2	3	4	5	6	7	8	9		
Mar	9	1	2	3	4	5	6	7	8	9	1	2	3	4	5	6	7	8	9	1	2	3	4	5	6	7	8	9	1	2	3
Apr	1	2	3	4	5	6	7	8	9	1	2	3	4	5	6	7	8	9	1	2	3	4	5	6	7	8	9	1	2	3	
May	2	3	4	5	6	7	8	9	1	2	3	4	5	6	7	8	9	1	2	3	4	5	6	7	8	9	1	2	3	4	5
Jun	3	4	5	6	7	8	9	1	2	3	4	5	6	7	8	9	1	2	3	4	5	6	7	8	9	1	2	3	4	5	
Jul	4	5	6	7	8	9	1	2	3	4	5	6	7	8	9	1	2	3	4	5	6	7	8	9	1	2	3	4	5	6	7
Aug	5	6	7	8	9	1	2	3	4	5	6	7	8	9	1	2	3	4	5	6	7	8	9	1	2	3	4	5	6	7	8
Sep	6	7	8	9	1	2	3	4	5	6	7	8	9	2	3	4	5	6	7	8	9	1	2	3	4	5	6	7	8	9	
Oct	8	9	1	2	3	4	5	6	7	8	9	1	2	3	4	5	6	7	8	9	1	2	3	4	5	6	7	8	9	1	2
Nov	9	1	2	3	4	5	6	7	8	9	1	2	3	4	5	6	7	8	9	1	2	3	4	5	6	7	8	9	1	2	
Dec	1	2	3	4	5	6	7	8	9	1	2	3	4	5	6	7	8	9	1	2	3	4	5	6	7	8	9	1	2	3	4

SEPTEMBER 15

	1	2	3	4	5	6	7	8	9	10	11	12	13	14	15	16	17	18	19	20	21	22	23	24	25	26	27	28	29	30	31
Jan	8	9	1	2	3	4	5	6	7	8	9	1	2	3	4	5	6	7	8	9	1	2	3	4	5	6	7	8	9	1	2
Feb	9	1	2	3	4	5	6	7	8	9	1	2	3	4	5	6	7	8	9	1	2	3	4	5	6	7	8	9	1		
Mar	1	2	3	4	5	6	7	8	9	1	2	3	4	5	6	7	8	9	1	2	3	4	5	6	7	8	9	1	2	3	4
Apr	2	3	4	5	6	7	8	9	1	2	3	4	5	6	7	8	9	1	2	3	4	5	6	7	8	9	1	2	3	4	
May	3	4	5	6	7	8	9	1	2	3	4	5	6	7	8	9	1	2	3	4	5	6	7	8	9	1	2	3	4	5	6
Jun	4	5	6	7	8	9	1	2	3	4	5	6	7	8	9	1	2	3	4	5	6	7	8	9	1	2	3	4	5	6	
Jul	5	6	7	8	9	1	2	3	4	5	6	7	8	9	1	2	3	4	5	6	7	8	9	1	2	3	4	5	6	7	8
Aug	6	7	8	9	1	2	3	4	5	6	7	8	9	1	2	3	4	5	6	7	8	9	1	2	3	4	5	6	7	8	9
Sep	7	8	9	1	2	3	4	5	6	7	8	9	1	2	4	5	6	7	8	9	1	2	3	4	5	6	7	8	9	1	
Oct	9	1	2	3	4	5	6	7	8	9	1	2	3	4	5	6	7	8	9	1	2	3	4	5	6	7	8	9	1	2	3
Nov	1	2	3	4	5	6	7	8	9	1	2	3	4	5	6	7	8	9	1	2	3	4	5	6	7	8	9	1	2	3	
Dec	2	3	4	5	6	7	8	9	1	2	3	4	5	6	7	8	9	1	2	3	4	5	6	7	8	9	1	2	3	4	5

SEPTEMBER 16

	1	2	3	4	5	6	7	8	9	10	11	12	13	14	15	16	17	18	19	20	21	22	23	24	25	26	27	28	29	30	31
Jan	9	1	2	3	4	5	6	7	8	9	1	2	3	4	5	6	7	8	9	1	2	3	4	5	6	7	8	9	1	2	3
Feb	1	2	3	4	5	6	7	8	9	1	2	3	4	5	6	7	8	9	1	2	3	4	5	6	7	8	9	1	2		
Mar	2	3	4	5	6	7	8	9	1	2	3	4	5	6	7	8	9	1	2	3	4	5	6	7	8	9	1	2	3	4	5
Apr	3	4	5	6	7	8	9	1	2	3	4	5	6	7	8	9	1	2	3	4	5	6	7	8	9	1	2	3	4	5	
May	4	5	6	7	8	9	1	2	3	4	5	6	7	8	9	1	2	3	4	5	6	7	8	9	1	2	3	4	5	6	7
Jun	5	6	7	8	9	1	2	3	4	5	6	7	8	9	1	2	3	4	5	6	7	8	9	1	2	3	4	5	6	7	
Jul	6	7	8	9	1	2	3	4	5	6	7	8	9	1	2	3	4	5	6	7	8	9	1	2	3	4	5	6	7	8	9
Aug	7	8	9	1	2	3	4	5	6	7	8	9	1	2	3	4	5	6	7	8	9	1	2	3	4	5	6	7	8	9	1
Sep	8	9	1	2	3	4	5	6	7	8	9	1	2	3	4	6	7	8	9	1	2	3	4	5	6	7	8	9	1	2	
Oct	1	2	3	4	5	6	7	8	9	1	2	3	4	5	6	7	8	9	1	2	3	4	5	6	7	8	9	1	2	3	4
Nov	2	3	4	5	6	7	8	9	1	2	3	4	5	6	7	8	9	1	2	3	4	5	6	7	8	9	1	2	3	4	
Dec	3	4	5	6	7	8	9	1	2	3	4	5	6	7	8	9	1	2	3	4	5	6	7	8	9	1	2	3	4	5	6

SEPTEMBER 17

	1	2	3	4	5	6	7	8	9	10	11	12	13	14	15	16	17	18	19	20	21	22	23	24	25	26	27	28	29	30	31
Jan	1	2	3	4	5	6	7	8	9	1	2	3	4	5	6	7	8	9	1	2	3	4	5	6	7	8	9	1	2	3	4
Feb	2	3	4	5	6	7	8	9	1	2	3	4	5	6	7	8	9	1	2	3	4	5	6	7	8	9	1	2	3		
Mar	3	4	5	6	7	8	9	1	2	3	4	5	6	7	8	9	1	2	3	4	5	6	7	8	9	1	2	3	4	5	6
Apr	4	5	6	7	8	9	1	2	3	4	5	6	7	8	9	1	2	3	4	5	6	7	8	9	1	2	3	4	5	6	
May	5	6	7	8	9	1	2	3	4	5	6	7	8	9	1	2	3	4	5	6	7	8	9	1	2	3	4	5	6	7	8
Jun	6	7	8	9	1	2	3	4	5	6	7	8	9	1	2	3	4	5	6	7	8	9	1	2	3	4	5	6	7	8	
Jul	7	8	9	1	2	3	4	5	6	7	8	9	1	2	3	4	5	6	7	8	9	1	2	3	4	5	6	7	8	9	1
Aug	8	9	1	2	3	4	5	6	7	8	9	1	2	3	4	5	6	7	8	9	1	2	3	4	5	6	7	8	9	1	2
Sep	9	1	2	3	4	5	6	7	8	9	1	2	3	4	5	6	8	9	1	2	3	4	5	6	7	8	9	1	2	3	
Oct	2	3	4	5	6	7	8	9	1	2	3	4	5	6	7	8	9	1	2	3	4	5	6	7	8	9	1	2	3	4	5
Nov	3	4	5	6	7	8	9	1	2	3	4	5	6	7	8	9	1	2	3	4	5	6	7	8	9	1	2	3	4	5	
Dec	4	5	6	7	8	9	1	2	3	4	5	6	7	8	9	1	2	3	4	5	6	7	8	9	1	2	3	4	5	6	7

SEPTEMBER 18

	1	2	3	4	5	6	7	8	9	10	11	12	13	14	15	16	17	18	19	20	21	22	23	24	25	26	27	28	29	30	31
Jan	2	3	4	5	6	7	8	9	1	2	3	4	5	6	7	8	9	1	2	3	4	5	6	7	8	9	1	2	3	4	5
Feb	3	4	5	6	7	8	9	1	2	3	4	5	6	7	8	9	1	2	3	4	5	6	7	8	9	1	2	3	4		
Mar	4	5	6	7	8	9	1	2	3	4	5	6	7	8	9	1	2	3	4	5	6	7	8	9	1	2	3	4	5	6	7
Apr	5	6	7	8	9	1	2	3	4	5	6	7	8	9	1	2	3	4	5	6	7	8	9	1	2	3	4	5	6	7	
May	6	7	8	9	1	2	3	4	5	6	7	8	9	1	2	3	4	5	6	7	8	9	1	2	3	4	5	6	7	8	9
Jun	7	8	9	1	2	3	4	5	6	7	8	9	1	2	3	4	5	6	7	8	9	1	2	3	4	5	6	7	8	9	
Jul	8	9	1	2	3	4	5	6	7	8	9	1	2	3	4	5	6	7	8	9	1	2	3	4	5	6	7	8	9	1	2
Aug	9	1	2	3	4	5	6	7	8	9	1	2	3	4	5	6	7	8	9	1	2	3	4	5	6	7	8	9	1	2	3
Sep	1	2	3	4	5	6	7	8	9	1	2	3	4	5	6	7	8	1	2	3	4	5	6	7	8	9	1	2	3	4	
Oct	3	4	5	6	7	8	9	1	2	3	4	5	6	7	8	9	1	2	3	4	5	6	7	8	9	1	2	3	4	5	6
Nov	4	5	6	7	8	9	1	2	3	4	5	6	7	8	9	1	2	3	4	5	6	7	8	9	1	2	3	4	5	6	
Dec	5	6	7	8	9	1	2	3	4	5	6	7	8	9	1	2	3	4	5	6	7	8	9	1	2	3	4	5	6	7	8

SEPTEMBER 19

	1	2	3	4	5	6	7	8	9	10	11	12	13	14	15	16	17	18	19	20	21	22	23	24	25	26	27	28	29	30	31
Jan	3	4	5	6	7	8	9	1	2	3	4	5	6	7	8	9	1	2	3	4	5	6	7	8	9	1	2	3	4	5	6
Feb	4	5	6	7	8	9	1	2	3	4	5	6	7	8	9	1	2	3	4	5	6	7	8	9	1	2	3	4	5		
Mar	5	6	7	8	9	1	2	3	4	5	6	7	8	9	1	2	3	4	5	6	7	8	9	1	2	3	4	5	6	7	8
Apr	6	7	8	9	1	2	3	4	5	6	7	8	9	1	2	3	4	5	6	7	8	9	1	2	3	4	5	6	7	8	
May	7	8	9	1	2	3	4	5	6	7	8	9	1	2	3	4	5	6	7	8	9	1	2	3	4	5	6	7	8	9	1
Jun	8	9	1	2	3	4	5	6	7	8	9	1	2	3	4	5	6	7	8	9	1	2	3	4	5	6	7	8	9	1	
Jul	9	1	2	3	4	5	6	7	8	9	1	2	3	4	5	6	7	8	9	1	2	3	4	5	6	7	8	9	1	2	3
Aug	1	2	3	4	5	6	7	8	9	1	2	3	4	5	6	7	8	9	1	2	3	4	5	6	7	8	9	1	2	3	4
Sep	2	3	4	5	6	7	8	9	1	2	3	4	5	6	7	8	9	1	3	4	5	6	7	8	9	1	2	3	4	5	
Oct	4	5	6	7	8	9	1	2	3	4	5	6	7	8	9	1	2	3	4	5	6	7	8	9	1	2	3	4	5	6	7
Nov	5	6	7	8	9	1	2	3	4	5	6	7	8	9	1	2	3	4	5	6	7	8	9	1	2	3	4	5	6	7	
Dec	6	7	8	9	1	2	3	4	5	6	7	8	9	1	2	3	4	5	6	7	8	9	1	2	3	4	5	6	7	8	9

SEPTEMBER 20

	1	2	3	4	5	6	7	8	9	10	11	12	13	14	15	16	17	18	19	20	21	22	23	24	25	26	27	28	29	30	31
Jan	4	5	6	7	8	9	1	2	3	4	5	6	7	8	9	1	2	3	4	5	6	7	8	9	1	2	3	4	5	6	7
Feb	5	6	7	8	9	1	2	3	4	5	6	7	8	9	1	2	3	4	5	6	7	8	9	1	2	3	4	5	6		
Mar	6	7	8	9	1	2	3	4	5	6	7	8	9	1	2	3	4	5	6	7	8	9	1	2	3	4	5	6	7	8	9
Apr	7	8	9	1	2	3	4	5	6	7	8	9	1	2	3	4	5	6	7	8	9	1	2	3	4	5	6	7	8	9	
May	8	9	1	2	3	4	5	6	7	8	9	1	2	3	4	5	6	7	8	9	1	2	3	4	5	6	7	8	9	1	2
Jun	9	1	2	3	4	5	6	7	8	9	1	2	3	4	5	6	7	8	9	1	2	3	4	5	6	7	8	9	1	2	
Jul	1	2	3	4	5	6	7	8	9	1	2	3	4	5	6	7	8	9	1	2	3	4	5	6	7	8	9	1	2	3	4
Aug	2	3	4	5	6	7	8	9	1	2	3	4	5	6	7	8	9	1	2	3	4	5	6	7	8	9	1	2	3	4	5
Sep	3	4	5	6	7	8	9	1	2	3	4	5	6	7	8	9	1	2	3	5	6	7	8	9	1	2	3	4	5	6	
Oct	5	6	7	8	9	1	2	3	4	5	6	7	8	9	1	2	3	4	5	6	7	8	9	1	2	3	4	5	6	7	8
Nov	6	7	8	9	1	2	3	4	5	6	7	8	9	1	2	3	4	5	6	7	8	9	1	2	3	4	5	6	7	8	
Dec	7	8	9	1	2	3	4	5	6	7	8	9	1	2	3	4	5	6	7	8	9	1	2	3	4	5	6	7	8	9	1

SEPTEMBER 21

	1	2	3	4	5	6	7	8	9	10	11	12	13	14	15	16	17	18	19	20	21	22	23	24	25	26	27	28	29	30	31
Jan	5	6	7	8	9	1	2	3	4	5	6	7	8	9	1	2	3	4	5	6	7	8	9	1	2	3	4	5	6	7	8
Feb	6	7	8	9	1	2	3	4	5	6	7	8	9	1	2	3	4	5	6	7	8	9	1	2	3	4	5	6	7		
Mar	7	8	9	1	2	3	4	5	6	7	8	9	1	2	3	4	5	6	7	8	9	1	2	3	4	5	6	7	8	9	1
Apr	8	9	1	2	3	4	5	6	7	8	9	1	2	3	4	5	6	7	8	9	1	2	3	4	5	6	7	8	9	1	
May	9	1	2	3	4	5	6	7	8	9	1	2	3	4	5	6	7	8	9	1	2	3	4	5	6	7	8	9	1	2	3
Jun	1	2	3	4	5	6	7	8	9	1	2	3	4	5	6	7	8	9	1	2	3	4	5	6	7	8	9	1	2	3	
Jul	2	3	4	5	6	7	8	9	1	2	3	4	5	6	7	8	9	1	2	3	4	5	6	7	8	9	1	2	3	4	5
Aug	3	4	5	6	7	8	9	1	2	3	4	5	6	7	8	9	1	2	3	4	5	6	7	8	9	1	2	3	4	5	6
Sep	4	5	6	7	8	9	1	2	3	4	5	6	7	8	9	1	2	3	4	5	7	8	9	1	2	3	4	5	6	7	
Oct	6	7	8	9	1	2	3	4	5	6	7	8	9	1	2	3	4	5	6	7	8	9	1	2	3	4	5	6	7	8	9
Nov	7	8	9	1	2	3	4	5	6	7	8	9	1	2	3	4	5	6	7	8	9	1	2	3	4	5	6	7	8	9	
Dec	8	9	1	2	3	4	5	6	7	8	9	1	2	3	4	5	6	7	8	9	1	2	3	4	5	6	7	8	9	1	2

SEPTEMBER 22

	1	2	3	4	5	6	7	8	9	10	11	12	13	14	15	16	17	18	19	20	21	22	23	24	25	26	27	28	29	30	31
Jan	6	7	8	9	1	2	3	4	5	6	7	8	9	1	2	3	4	5	6	7	8	9	1	2	3	4	5	6	7	8	9
Feb	7	8	9	1	2	3	4	5	6	7	8	9	1	2	3	4	5	6	7	8	9	1	2	3	4	5	6	7	8		
Mar	8	9	1	2	3	4	5	6	7	8	9	1	2	3	4	5	6	7	8	9	1	2	3	4	5	6	7	8	9	1	2
Apr	9	1	2	3	4	5	6	7	8	9	1	2	3	4	5	6	7	8	9	1	2	3	4	5	6	7	8	9	1	2	
May	1	2	3	4	5	6	7	8	9	1	2	3	4	5	6	7	8	9	1	2	3	4	5	6	7	8	9	1	2	3	4
Jun	2	3	4	5	6	7	8	9	1	2	3	4	5	6	7	8	9	1	2	3	4	5	6	7	8	9	1	2	3	4	
Jul	3	4	5	6	7	8	9	1	2	3	4	5	6	7	8	9	1	2	3	4	5	6	7	8	9	1	2	3	4	5	6
Aug	4	5	6	7	8	9	1	2	3	4	5	6	7	8	9	1	2	3	4	5	6	7	8	9	1	2	3	4	5	6	7
Sep	5	6	7	8	9	1	2	3	4	5	6	7	8	9	1	2	3	4	5	6	7	9	1	2	3	4	5	6	7	8	
Oct	7	8	9	1	2	3	4	5	6	7	8	9	1	2	3	4	5	6	7	8	9	1	2	3	4	5	6	7	8	9	1
Nov	8	9	1	2	3	4	5	6	7	8	9	1	2	3	4	5	6	7	8	9	1	2	3	4	5	6	7	8	9	1	
Dec	9	1	2	3	4	5	6	7	8	9	1	2	3	4	5	6	7	8	9	1	2	3	4	5	6	7	8	9	1	2	3

SEPTEMBER 23

	1	2	3	4	5	6	7	8	9	10	11	12	13	14	15	16	17	18	19	20	21	22	23	24	25	26	27	28	29	30	31
Jan	7	8	9	1	2	3	4	5	6	7	8	9	1	2	3	4	5	6	7	8	9	1	2	3	4	5	6	7	8	9	1
Feb	8	9	1	2	3	4	5	6	7	8	9	1	2	3	4	5	6	7	8	9	1	2	3	4	5	6	7	8	9		
Mar	9	1	2	3	4	5	6	7	8	9	1	2	3	4	5	6	7	8	9	1	2	3	4	5	6	7	8	9	1	2	3
Apr	1	2	3	4	5	6	7	8	9	1	2	3	4	5	6	7	8	9	1	2	3	4	5	6	7	8	9	1	2	3	
May	2	3	4	5	6	7	8	9	1	2	3	4	5	6	7	8	9	1	2	3	4	5	6	7	8	9	1	2	3	4	5
Jun	3	4	5	6	7	8	9	1	2	3	4	5	6	7	8	9	1	2	3	4	5	6	7	8	9	1	2	3	4	5	
Jul	4	5	6	7	8	9	1	2	3	4	5	6	7	8	9	1	2	3	4	5	6	7	8	9	1	2	3	4	5	6	7
Aug	5	6	7	8	9	1	2	3	4	5	6	7	8	9	1	2	3	4	5	6	7	8	9	1	2	3	4	5	6	7	8
Sep	6	7	8	9	1	2	3	4	5	6	7	8	9	1	2	3	4	5	6	7	8	9	2	3	4	5	6	7	8	9	
Oct	8	9	1	2	3	4	5	6	7	8	9	1	2	3	4	5	6	7	8	9	1	2	3	4	5	6	7	8	9	1	2
Nov	9	1	2	3	4	5	6	7	8	9	1	2	3	4	5	6	7	8	9	1	2	3	4	5	6	7	8	9	1	2	
Dec	1	2	3	4	5	6	7	8	9	1	2	3	4	5	6	7	8	9	1	2	3	4	5	6	7	8	9	1	2	3	4

SEPTEMBER 24

	1	2	3	4	5	6	7	8	9	10	11	12	13	14	15	16	17	18	19	20	21	22	23	24	25	26	27	28	29	30	31
Jan	8	9	1	2	3	4	5	6	7	8	9	1	2	3	4	5	6	7	8	9	1	2	3	4	5	6	7	8	9	1	2
Feb	9	1	2	3	4	5	6	7	8	9	1	2	3	4	5	6	7	8	9	1	2	3	4	5	6	7	8	9	1		
Mar	1	2	3	4	5	6	7	8	9	1	2	3	4	5	6	7	8	9	1	2	3	4	5	6	7	8	9	1	2	3	4
Apr	2	3	4	5	6	7	8	9	1	2	3	4	5	6	7	8	9	1	2	3	4	5	6	7	8	9	1	2	3	4	
May	3	4	5	6	7	8	9	1	2	3	4	5	6	7	8	9	1	2	3	4	5	6	7	8	9	1	2	3	4	5	6
Jun	4	5	6	7	8	9	1	2	3	4	5	6	7	8	9	1	2	3	4	5	6	7	8	9	1	2	3	4	5	6	
Jul	5	6	7	8	9	1	2	3	4	5	6	7	8	9	1	2	3	4	5	6	7	8	9	1	2	3	4	5	6	7	8
Aug	6	7	8	9	1	2	3	4	5	6	7	8	9	1	2	3	4	5	6	7	8	9	1	2	3	4	5	6	7	8	9
Sep	7	8	9	1	2	3	4	5	6	7	8	9	1	2	3	4	5	6	7	8	9	1	2	4	5	6	7	8	9	1	
Oct	9	1	2	3	4	5	6	7	8	9	1	2	3	4	5	6	7	8	9	1	2	3	4	5	6	7	8	9	1	2	3
Nov	1	2	3	4	5	6	7	8	9	1	2	3	4	5	6	7	8	9	1	2	3	4	5	6	7	8	9	1	2	3	
Dec	2	3	4	5	6	7	8	9	1	2	3	4	5	6	7	8	9	1	2	3	4	5	6	7	8	9	1	2	3	4	5

SEPTEMBER 25

	1	2	3	4	5	6	7	8	9	10	11	12	13	14	15	16	17	18	19	20	21	22	23	24	25	26	27	28	29	30	31
Jan	9	1	2	3	4	5	6	7	8	9	1	2	3	4	5	6	7	8	9	1	2	3	4	5	6	7	8	9	1	2	3
Feb	1	2	3	4	5	6	7	8	9	1	2	3	4	5	6	7	8	9	1	2	3	4	5	6	7	8	9	1	2		
Mar	2	3	4	5	6	7	8	9	1	2	3	4	5	6	7	8	9	1	2	3	4	5	6	7	8	9	1	2	3	4	5
Apr	3	4	5	6	7	8	9	1	2	3	4	5	6	7	8	9	1	2	3	4	5	6	7	8	9	1	2	3	4	5	
May	4	5	6	7	8	9	1	2	3	4	5	6	7	8	9	1	2	3	4	5	6	7	8	9	1	2	3	4	5	6	7
Jun	5	6	7	8	9	1	2	3	4	5	6	7	8	9	1	2	3	4	5	6	7	8	9	1	2	3	4	5	6	7	
Jul	6	7	8	9	1	2	3	4	5	6	7	8	9	1	2	3	4	5	6	7	8	9	1	2	3	4	5	6	7	8	9
Aug	7	8	9	1	2	3	4	5	6	7	8	9	1	2	3	4	5	6	7	8	9	1	2	3	4	5	6	7	8	9	1
Sep	8	9	1	2	3	4	5	6	7	8	9	1	2	3	4	5	6	7	8	9	1	2	3	4	6	7	8	9	1	2	
Oct	1	2	3	4	5	6	7	8	9	1	2	3	4	5	6	7	8	9	1	2	3	4	5	6	7	8	9	1	2	3	4
Nov	2	3	4	5	6	7	8	9	1	2	3	4	5	6	7	8	9	1	2	3	4	5	6	7	8	9	1	2	3	4	
Dec	3	4	5	6	7	8	9	1	2	3	4	5	6	7	8	9	1	2	3	4	5	6	7	8	9	1	2	3	4	5	6

SEPTEMBER 26

	1	2	3	4	5	6	7	8	9	10	11	12	13	14	15	16	17	18	19	20	21	22	23	24	25	26	27	28	29	30	31
Jan	1	2	3	4	5	6	7	8	9	1	2	3	4	5	6	7	8	9	1	2	3	4	5	6	7	8	9	1	2	3	4
Feb	2	3	4	5	6	7	8	9	1	2	3	4	5	6	7	8	9	1	2	3	4	5	6	7	8	9	1	2	3		
Mar	3	4	5	6	7	8	9	1	2	3	4	5	6	7	8	9	1	2	3	4	5	6	7	8	9	1	2	3	4	5	6
Apr	4	5	6	7	8	9	1	2	3	4	5	6	7	8	9	1	2	3	4	5	6	7	8	9	1	2	3	4	5	6	
May	5	6	7	8	9	1	2	3	4	5	6	7	8	9	1	2	3	4	5	6	7	8	9	1	2	3	4	5	6	7	8
Jun	6	7	8	9	1	2	3	4	5	6	7	8	9	1	2	3	4	5	6	7	8	9	1	2	3	4	5	6	7	8	
Jul	7	8	9	1	2	3	4	5	6	7	8	9	1	2	3	4	5	6	7	8	9	1	2	3	4	5	6	7	8	9	1
Aug	8	9	1	2	3	4	5	6	7	8	9	1	2	3	4	5	6	7	8	9	1	2	3	4	5	6	7	8	9	1	2
Sep	9	1	2	3	4	5	6	7	8	9	1	2	3	4	5	6	7	8	9	1	2	3	4	5	6	8	9	1	2	3	
Oct	2	3	4	5	6	7	8	9	1	2	3	4	5	6	7	8	9	1	2	3	4	5	6	7	8	9	1	2	3	4	5
Nov	3	4	5	6	7	8	9	1	2	3	4	5	6	7	8	9	1	2	3	4	5	6	7	8	9	1	2	3	4	5	
Dec	4	5	6	7	8	9	1	2	3	4	5	6	7	8	9	1	2	3	4	5	6	7	8	9	1	2	3	4	5	6	7

SEPTEMBER 27

	1	2	3	4	5	6	7	8	9	10	11	12	13	14	15	16	17	18	19	20	21	22	23	24	25	26	27	28	29	30	31
Jan	2	3	4	5	6	7	8	9	1	2	3	4	5	6	7	8	9	1	2	3	4	5	6	7	8	9	1	2	3	4	5
Feb	3	4	5	6	7	8	9	1	2	3	4	5	6	7	8	9	1	2	3	4	5	6	7	8	9	1	2	3	4		
Mar	4	5	6	7	8	9	1	2	3	4	5	6	7	8	9	1	2	3	4	5	6	7	8	9	1	2	3	4	5	6	7
Apr	5	6	7	8	9	1	2	3	4	5	6	7	8	9	1	2	3	4	5	6	7	8	9	1	2	3	4	5	6	7	
May	6	7	8	9	1	2	3	4	5	6	7	8	9	1	2	3	4	5	6	7	8	9	1	2	3	4	5	6	7	8	9
Jun	7	8	9	1	2	3	4	5	6	7	8	9	1	2	3	4	5	6	7	8	9	1	2	3	4	5	6	7	8	9	
Jul	8	9	1	2	3	4	5	6	7	8	9	1	2	3	4	5	6	7	8	9	1	2	3	4	5	6	7	8	9	1	2
Aug	9	1	2	3	4	5	6	7	8	9	1	2	3	4	5	6	7	8	9	1	2	3	4	5	6	7	8	9	1	2	3
Sep	1	2	3	4	5	6	7	8	9	1	2	3	4	5	6	7	8	9	1	2	3	4	5	6	7	8	1	2	3	4	
Oct	3	4	5	6	7	8	9	1	2	3	4	5	6	7	8	9	1	2	3	4	5	6	7	8	9	1	2	3	4	5	6
Nov	4	5	6	7	8	9	1	2	3	4	5	6	7	8	9	1	2	3	4	5	6	7	8	9	1	2	3	4	5	6	
Dec	5	6	7	8	9	1	2	3	4	5	6	7	8	9	1	2	3	4	5	6	7	8	9	1	2	3	4	5	6	7	8

SEPTEMBER 28

	1	2	3	4	5	6	7	8	9	10	11	12	13	14	15	16	17	18	19	20	21	22	23	24	25	26	27	28	29	30	31
Jan	3	4	5	6	7	8	9	1	2	3	4	5	6	7	8	9	1	2	3	4	5	6	7	8	9	1	2	3	4	5	6
Feb	4	5	6	7	8	9	1	2	3	4	5	6	7	8	9	1	2	3	4	5	6	7	8	9	1	2	3	4	5		
Mar	5	6	7	8	9	1	2	3	4	5	6	7	8	9	1	2	3	4	5	6	7	8	9	1	2	3	4	5	6	7	8
Apr	6	7	8	9	1	2	3	4	5	6	7	8	9	1	2	3	4	5	6	7	8	9	1	2	3	4	5	6	7	8	
May	7	8	9	1	2	3	4	5	6	7	8	9	1	2	3	4	5	6	7	8	9	1	2	3	4	5	6	7	8	9	1
Jun	8	9	1	2	3	4	5	6	7	8	9	1	2	3	4	5	6	7	8	9	1	2	3	4	5	6	7	8	9	1	
Jul	9	1	2	3	4	5	6	7	8	9	1	2	3	4	5	6	7	8	9	1	2	3	4	5	6	7	8	9	1	2	3
Aug	1	2	3	4	5	6	7	8	9	1	2	3	4	5	6	7	8	9	1	2	3	4	5	6	7	8	9	1	2	3	4
Sep	2	3	4	5	6	7	8	9	1	2	3	4	5	6	7	8	9	1	2	3	4	5	6	7	8	9	1	3	4	5	
Oct	4	5	6	7	8	9	1	2	3	4	5	6	7	8	9	1	2	3	4	5	6	7	8	9	1	2	3	4	5	6	7
Nov	5	6	7	8	9	1	2	3	4	5	6	7	8	9	1	2	3	4	5	6	7	8	9	1	2	3	4	5	6	7	
Dec	6	7	8	9	1	2	3	4	5	6	7	8	9	1	2	3	4	5	6	7	8	9	1	2	3	4	5	6	7	8	9

SEPTEMBER 29

	1	2	3	4	5	6	7	8	9	10	11	12	13	14	15	16	17	18	19	20	21	22	23	24	25	26	27	28	29	30	31
Jan	4	5	6	7	8	9	1	2	3	4	5	6	7	8	9	1	2	3	4	5	6	7	8	9	1	2	3	4	5	6	7
Feb	5	6	7	8	9	1	2	3	4	5	6	7	8	9	1	2	3	4	5	6	7	8	9	1	2	3	4	5	6		
Mar	6	7	8	9	1	2	3	4	5	6	7	8	9	1	2	3	4	5	6	7	8	9	1	2	3	4	5	6	7	8	9
Apr	7	8	9	1	2	3	4	5	6	7	8	9	1	2	3	4	5	6	7	8	9	1	2	3	4	5	6	7	8	9	
May	8	9	1	2	3	4	5	6	7	8	9	1	2	3	4	5	6	7	8	9	1	2	3	4	5	6	7	8	9	1	2
Jun	9	1	2	3	4	5	6	7	8	9	1	2	3	4	5	6	7	8	9	1	2	3	4	5	6	7	8	9	1	2	
Jul	1	2	3	4	5	6	7	8	9	1	2	3	4	5	6	7	8	9	1	2	3	4	5	6	7	8	9	1	2	3	4
Aug	2	3	4	5	6	7	8	9	1	2	3	4	5	6	7	8	9	1	2	3	4	5	6	7	8	9	1	2	3	4	5
Sep	3	4	5	6	7	8	9	1	2	3	4	5	6	7	8	9	1	2	3	4	5	6	7	8	9	1	2	3	5	6	
Oct	5	6	7	8	9	1	2	3	4	5	6	7	8	9	1	2	3	4	5	6	7	8	9	1	2	3	4	5	6	7	8
Nov	6	7	8	9	1	2	3	4	5	6	7	8	9	1	2	3	4	5	6	7	8	9	1	2	3	4	5	6	7	8	
Dec	7	8	9	1	2	3	4	5	6	7	8	9	1	2	3	4	5	6	7	8	9	1	2	3	4	5	6	7	8	9	1

SEPTEMBER 30

	1	2	3	4	5	6	7	8	9	10	11	12	13	14	15	16	17	18	19	20	21	22	23	24	25	26	27	28	29	30	31
Jan	5	6	7	8	9	1	2	3	4	5	6	7	8	9	1	2	3	4	5	6	7	8	9	1	2	3	4	5	6	7	8
Feb	6	7	8	9	1	2	3	4	5	6	7	8	9	1	2	3	4	5	6	7	8	9	1	2	3	4	5	6	7		
Mar	7	8	9	1	2	3	4	5	6	7	8	9	1	2	3	4	5	6	7	8	9	1	2	3	4	5	6	7	8	9	1
Apr	8	9	1	2	3	4	5	6	7	8	9	1	2	3	4	5	6	7	8	9	1	2	3	4	5	6	7	8	9	1	
May	9	1	2	3	4	5	6	7	8	9	1	2	3	4	5	6	7	8	9	1	2	3	4	5	6	7	8	9	1	2	3
Jun	1	2	3	4	5	6	7	8	9	1	2	3	4	5	6	7	8	9	1	2	3	4	5	6	7	8	9	1	2	3	
Jul	2	3	4	5	6	7	8	9	1	2	3	4	5	6	7	8	9	1	2	3	4	5	6	7	8	9	1	2	3	4	5
Aug	3	4	5	6	7	8	9	1	2	3	4	5	6	7	8	9	1	2	3	4	5	6	7	8	9	1	2	3	4	5	6
Sep	4	5	6	7	8	9	1	2	3	4	5	6	7	8	9	1	2	3	4	5	6	7	8	9	1	2	3	4	5	7	
Oct	6	7	8	9	1	2	3	4	5	6	7	8	9	1	2	3	4	5	6	7	8	9	1	2	3	4	5	6	7	8	9
Nov	7	8	9	1	2	3	4	5	6	7	8	9	1	2	3	4	5	6	7	8	9	1	2	3	4	5	6	7	8	9	
Dec	8	9	1	2	3	4	5	6	7	8	9	1	2	3	4	5	6	7	8	9	1	2	3	4	5	6	7	8	9	1	2

OCTOBER 1

	1	2	3	4	5	6	7	8	9	10	11	12	13	14	15	16	17	18	19	20	21	22	23	24	25	26	27	28	29	30	31
Jan	4	5	6	7	8	9	1	2	3	4	5	6	7	8	9	1	2	3	4	5	6	7	8	9	1	2	3	4	5	6	7
Feb	5	6	7	8	9	1	2	3	4	5	6	7	8	9	1	2	3	4	5	6	7	8	9	1	2	3	4	5	6		
Mar	6	7	8	9	1	2	3	4	5	6	7	8	9	1	2	3	4	5	6	7	8	9	1	2	3	4	5	6	7	8	9
Apr	7	8	9	1	2	3	4	5	6	7	8	9	1	2	3	4	5	6	7	8	9	1	2	3	4	5	6	7	8	9	
May	8	9	1	2	3	4	5	6	7	8	9	1	2	3	4	5	6	7	8	9	1	2	3	4	5	6	7	8	9	1	2
Jun	9	1	2	3	4	5	6	7	8	9	1	2	3	4	5	6	7	8	9	1	2	3	4	5	6	7	8	9	1	2	
Jul	1	2	3	4	5	6	7	8	9	1	2	3	4	5	6	7	8	9	1	2	3	4	5	6	7	8	9	1	2	3	4
Aug	2	3	4	5	6	7	8	9	1	2	3	4	5	6	7	8	9	1	2	3	4	5	6	7	8	9	1	2	3	4	5
Sep	3	4	5	6	7	8	9	1	2	3	4	5	6	7	8	9	1	2	3	4	5	6	7	8	9	1	2	3	4	5	
Oct	5	6	7	8	9	1	2	3	4	5	6	7	8	9	1	2	3	4	5	6	7	8	9	1	2	3	4	5	6	7	8
Nov	6	7	8	9	1	2	3	4	5	6	7	8	9	1	2	3	4	5	6	7	8	9	1	2	3	4	5	6	7	8	
Dec	7	8	9	1	2	3	4	5	6	7	8	9	1	2	3	4	5	6	7	8	9	1	2	3	4	5	6	7	8	9	1

OCTOBER 2

	1	2	3	4	5	6	7	8	9	10	11	12	13	14	15	16	17	18	19	20	21	22	23	24	25	26	27	28	29	30	31
Jan	5	6	7	8	9	1	2	3	4	5	6	7	8	9	1	2	3	4	5	6	7	8	9	1	2	3	4	5	6	7	8
Feb	6	7	8	9	1	2	3	4	5	6	7	8	9	1	2	3	4	5	6	7	8	9	1	2	3	4	5	6	7		
Mar	7	8	9	1	2	3	4	5	6	7	8	9	1	2	3	4	5	6	7	8	9	1	2	3	4	5	6	7	8	9	1
Apr	8	9	1	2	3	4	5	6	7	8	9	1	2	3	4	5	6	7	8	9	1	2	3	4	5	6	7	8	9	1	
May	9	1	2	3	4	5	6	7	8	9	1	2	3	4	5	6	7	8	9	1	2	3	4	5	6	7	8	9	1	2	3
Jun	1	2	3	4	5	6	7	8	9	1	2	3	4	5	6	7	8	9	1	2	3	4	5	6	7	8	9	1	2	3	
Jul	2	3	4	5	6	7	8	9	1	2	3	4	5	6	7	8	9	1	2	3	4	5	6	7	8	9	1	2	3	4	5
Aug	3	4	5	6	7	8	9	1	2	3	4	5	6	7	8	9	1	2	3	4	5	6	7	8	9	1	2	3	4	5	6
Sep	4	5	6	7	8	9	1	2	3	4	5	6	7	8	9	1	2	3	4	5	6	7	8	9	1	2	3	4	5	6	
Oct	5	7	8	9	1	2	3	4	5	6	7	8	9	1	2	3	4	5	6	7	8	9	1	2	3	4	5	6	7	8	9
Nov	7	8	9	1	2	3	4	5	6	7	8	9	1	2	3	4	5	6	7	8	9	1	2	3	4	5	6	7	8	9	
Dec	8	9	1	2	3	4	5	6	7	8	9	1	2	3	4	5	6	7	8	9	1	2	3	4	5	6	7	8	9	1	2

OCTOBER 3

	1	2	3	4	5	6	7	8	9	10	11	12	13	14	15	16	17	18	19	20	21	22	23	24	25	26	27	28	29	30	31
Jan	6	7	8	9	1	2	3	4	5	6	7	8	9	1	2	3	4	5	6	7	8	9	1	2	3	4	5	6	7	8	9
Feb	7	8	9	1	2	3	4	5	6	7	8	9	1	2	3	4	5	6	7	8	9	1	2	3	4	5	6	7	8		
Mar	8	9	1	2	3	4	5	6	7	8	9	1	2	3	4	5	6	7	8	9	1	2	3	4	5	6	7	8	9	1	2
Apr	9	1	2	3	4	5	6	7	8	9	1	2	3	4	5	6	7	8	9	1	2	3	4	5	6	7	8	9	1	2	
May	1	2	3	4	5	6	7	8	9	1	2	3	4	5	6	7	8	9	1	2	3	4	5	6	7	8	9	1	2	3	4
Jun	2	3	4	5	6	7	8	9	1	2	3	4	5	6	7	8	9	1	2	3	4	5	6	7	8	9	1	2	3	4	
Jul	3	4	5	6	7	8	9	1	2	3	4	5	6	7	8	9	1	2	3	4	5	6	7	8	9	1	2	3	4	5	6
Aug	4	5	6	7	8	9	1	2	3	4	5	6	7	8	9	1	2	3	4	5	6	7	8	9	1	2	3	4	5	6	7
Sep	5	6	7	8	9	1	2	3	4	5	6	7	8	9	1	2	3	4	5	6	7	8	9	1	2	3	4	5	6	7	
Oct	6	7	9	1	2	3	4	5	6	7	8	9	1	2	3	4	5	6	7	8	9	1	2	3	4	5	6	7	8	9	1
Nov	8	9	1	2	3	4	5	6	7	8	9	1	2	3	4	5	6	7	8	9	1	2	3	4	5	6	7	8	9	1	
Dec	9	1	2	3	4	5	6	7	8	9	1	2	3	4	5	6	7	8	9	1	2	3	4	5	6	7	8	9	1	2	3

OCTOBER 4

	1	2	3	4	5	6	7	8	9	10	11	12	13	14	15	16	17	18	19	20	21	22	23	24	25	26	27	28	29	30	31
Jan	7	8	9	1	2	3	4	5	6	7	8	9	1	2	3	4	5	6	7	8	9	1	2	3	4	5	6	7	8	9	1
Feb	8	9	1	2	3	4	5	6	7	8	9	1	2	3	4	5	6	7	8	9	1	2	3	4	5	6	7	8	9		
Mar	9	1	2	3	4	5	6	7	8	9	1	2	3	4	5	6	7	8	9	1	2	3	4	5	6	7	8	9	1	2	3
Apr	1	2	3	4	5	6	7	8	9	1	2	3	4	5	6	7	8	9	1	2	3	4	5	6	7	8	9	1	2	3	
May	2	3	4	5	6	7	8	9	1	2	3	4	5	6	7	8	9	1	2	3	4	5	6	7	8	9	1	2	3	4	5
Jun	3	4	5	6	7	8	9	1	2	3	4	5	6	7	8	9	1	2	3	4	5	6	7	8	9	1	2	3	4	5	
Jul	4	5	6	7	8	9	1	2	3	4	5	6	7	8	9	1	2	3	4	5	6	7	8	9	1	2	3	4	5	6	7
Aug	5	6	7	8	9	1	2	3	4	5	6	7	8	9	1	2	3	4	5	6	7	8	9	1	2	3	4	5	6	7	8
Sep	6	7	8	9	1	2	3	4	5	6	7	8	9	1	2	3	4	5	6	7	8	9	1	2	3	4	5	6	7	8	
Oct	7	8	9	2	3	4	5	6	7	8	9	1	2	3	4	5	6	7	8	9	1	2	3	4	5	6	7	8	9	1	2
Nov	9	1	2	3	4	5	6	7	8	9	1	2	3	4	5	6	7	8	9	1	2	3	4	5	6	7	8	9	1	2	
Dec	1	2	3	4	5	6	7	8	9	1	2	3	4	5	6	7	8	9	1	2	3	4	5	6	7	8	9	1	2	3	4

OCTOBER 5

	1	2	3	4	5	6	7	8	9	10	11	12	13	14	15	16	17	18	19	20	21	22	23	24	25	26	27	28	29	30	31
Jan	8	9	1	2	3	4	5	6	7	8	9	1	2	3	4	5	6	7	8	9	1	2	3	4	5	6	7	8	9	1	2
Feb	9	1	2	3	4	5	6	7	8	9	1	2	3	4	5	6	7	8	9	1	2	3	4	5	6	7	8	9	1		
Mar	1	2	3	4	5	6	7	8	9	1	2	3	4	5	6	7	8	9	1	2	3	4	5	6	7	8	9	1	2	3	4
Apr	2	3	4	5	6	7	8	9	1	2	3	4	5	6	7	8	9	1	2	3	4	5	6	7	8	9	1	2	3	4	
May	3	4	5	6	7	8	9	1	2	3	4	5	6	7	8	9	1	2	3	4	5	6	7	8	9	1	2	3	4	5	6
Jun	4	5	6	7	8	9	1	2	3	4	5	6	7	8	9	1	2	3	4	5	6	7	8	9	1	2	3	4	5	6	
Jul	5	6	7	8	9	1	2	3	4	5	6	7	8	9	1	2	3	4	5	6	7	8	9	1	2	3	4	5	6	7	8
Aug	6	7	8	9	1	2	3	4	5	6	7	8	9	1	2	3	4	5	6	7	8	9	1	2	3	4	5	6	7	8	9
Sep	7	8	9	1	2	3	4	5	6	7	8	9	1	2	3	4	5	6	7	8	9	1	2	3	4	5	6	7	8	9	
Oct	8	9	1	2	4	5	6	7	8	9	1	2	3	4	5	6	7	8	9	1	2	3	4	5	6	7	8	9	1	2	3
Nov	1	2	3	4	5	6	7	8	9	1	2	3	4	5	6	7	8	9	1	2	3	4	5	6	7	8	9	1	2	3	
Dec	2	3	4	5	6	7	8	9	1	2	3	4	5	6	7	8	9	1	2	3	4	5	6	7	8	9	1	2	3	4	5

OCTOBER 6

	1	2	3	4	5	6	7	8	9	10	11	12	13	14	15	16	17	18	19	20	21	22	23	24	25	26	27	28	29	30	31
Jan	9	1	2	3	4	5	6	7	8	9	1	2	3	4	5	6	7	8	9	1	2	3	4	5	6	7	8	9	1	2	3
Feb	1	2	3	4	5	6	7	8	9	1	2	3	4	5	6	7	8	9	1	2	3	4	5	6	7	8	9	1	2		
Mar	2	3	4	5	6	7	8	9	1	2	3	4	5	6	7	8	9	1	2	3	4	5	6	7	8	9	1	2	3	4	5
Apr	3	4	5	6	7	8	9	1	2	3	4	5	6	7	8	9	1	2	3	4	5	6	7	8	9	1	2	3	4	5	
May	4	5	6	7	8	9	1	2	3	4	5	6	7	8	9	1	2	3	4	5	6	7	8	9	1	2	3	4	5	6	7
Jun	5	6	7	8	9	1	2	3	4	5	6	7	8	9	1	2	3	4	5	6	7	8	9	1	2	3	4	5	6	7	
Jul	6	7	8	9	1	2	3	4	5	6	7	8	9	1	2	3	4	5	6	7	8	9	1	2	3	4	5	6	7	8	9
Aug	7	8	9	1	2	3	4	5	6	7	8	9	1	2	3	4	5	6	7	8	9	1	2	3	4	5	6	7	8	9	1
Sep	8	9	1	2	3	4	5	6	7	8	9	1	2	3	4	5	6	7	8	9	1	2	3	4	5	6	7	8	9	1	
Oct	9	1	2	3	4	6	7	8	9	1	2	3	4	5	6	7	8	9	1	2	3	4	5	6	7	8	9	1	2	3	4
Nov	2	3	4	5	6	7	8	9	1	2	3	4	5	6	7	8	9	1	2	3	4	5	6	7	8	9	1	2	3	4	
Dec	3	4	5	6	7	8	9	1	2	3	4	5	6	7	8	9	1	2	3	4	5	6	7	8	9	1	2	3	4	5	6

OCTOBER 7

	1	2	3	4	5	6	7	8	9	10	11	12	13	14	15	16	17	18	19	20	21	22	23	24	25	26	27	28	29	30	31
Jan	1	2	3	4	5	6	7	8	9	1	2	3	4	5	6	7	8	9	1	2	3	4	5	6	7	8	9	1	2	3	4
Feb	2	3	4	5	6	7	8	9	1	2	3	4	5	6	7	8	9	1	2	3	4	5	6	7	8	9	1	2	3		
Mar	3	4	5	6	7	8	9	1	2	3	4	5	6	7	8	9	1	2	3	4	5	6	7	8	9	1	2	3	4	5	6
Apr	4	5	6	7	8	9	1	2	3	4	5	6	7	8	9	1	2	3	4	5	6	7	8	9	1	2	3	4	5	6	
May	5	6	7	8	9	1	2	3	4	5	6	7	8	9	1	2	3	4	5	6	7	8	9	1	2	3	4	5	6	7	8
Jun	6	7	8	9	1	2	3	4	5	6	7	8	9	1	2	3	4	5	6	7	8	9	1	2	3	4	5	6	7	8	
Jul	7	8	9	1	2	3	4	5	6	7	8	9	1	2	3	4	5	6	7	8	9	1	2	3	4	5	6	7	8	9	1
Aug	8	9	1	2	3	4	5	6	7	8	9	1	2	3	4	5	6	7	8	9	1	2	3	4	5	6	7	8	9	1	2
Sep	9	1	2	3	4	5	6	7	8	9	1	2	3	4	5	6	7	8	9	1	2	3	4	5	6	7	8	9	1	2	
Oct	1	2	3	4	5	6	8	9	1	2	3	4	5	6	7	8	9	1	2	3	4	5	6	7	8	9	1	2	3	4	5
Nov	3	4	5	6	7	8	9	1	2	3	4	5	6	7	8	9	1	2	3	4	5	6	7	8	9	1	2	3	4	5	
Dec	4	5	6	7	8	9	1	2	3	4	5	6	7	8	9	1	2	3	4	5	6	7	8	9	1	2	3	4	5	6	7

OCTOBER 8

	1	2	3	4	5	6	7	8	9	10	11	12	13	14	15	16	17	18	19	20	21	22	23	24	25	26	27	28	29	30	31
Jan	2	3	4	5	6	7	8	9	1	2	3	4	5	6	7	8	9	1	2	3	4	5	6	7	8	9	1	2	3	4	5
Feb	3	4	5	6	7	8	9	1	2	3	4	5	6	7	8	9	1	2	3	4	5	6	7	8	9	1	2	3	4		
Mar	4	5	6	7	8	9	1	2	3	4	5	6	7	8	9	1	2	3	4	5	6	7	8	9	1	2	3	4	5	6	7
Apr	5	6	7	8	9	1	2	3	4	5	6	7	8	9	1	2	3	4	5	6	7	8	9	1	2	3	4	5	6	7	
May	6	7	8	9	1	2	3	4	5	6	7	8	9	1	2	3	4	5	6	7	8	9	1	2	3	4	5	6	7	8	9
Jun	7	8	9	1	2	3	4	5	6	7	8	9	1	2	3	4	5	6	7	8	9	1	2	3	4	5	6	7	8	9	
Jul	8	9	1	2	3	4	5	6	7	8	9	1	2	3	4	5	6	7	8	9	1	2	3	4	5	6	7	8	9	1	2
Aug	9	1	2	3	4	5	6	7	8	9	1	2	3	4	5	6	7	8	9	1	2	3	4	5	6	7	8	9	1	2	3
Sep	1	2	3	4	5	6	7	8	9	1	2	3	4	5	6	7	8	9	1	2	3	4	5	6	7	8	9	1	2	3	
Oct	2	3	4	5	6	7	8	1	2	3	4	5	6	7	8	9	1	2	3	4	5	6	7	8	9	1	2	3	4	5	6
Nov	4	5	6	7	8	9	1	2	3	4	5	6	7	8	9	1	2	3	4	5	6	7	8	9	1	2	3	4	5	6	
Dec	5	6	7	8	9	1	2	3	4	5	6	7	8	9	1	2	3	4	5	6	7	8	9	1	2	3	4	5	6	7	8

OCTOBER 9

	1	2	3	4	5	6	7	8	9	10	11	12	13	14	15	16	17	18	19	20	21	22	23	24	25	26	27	28	29	30	31
Jan	3	4	5	6	7	8	9	1	2	3	4	5	6	7	8	9	1	2	3	4	5	6	7	8	9	1	2	3	4	5	6
Feb	4	5	6	7	8	9	1	2	3	4	5	6	7	8	9	1	2	3	4	5	6	7	8	9	1	2	3	4	5		
Mar	5	6	7	8	9	1	2	3	4	5	6	7	8	9	1	2	3	4	5	6	7	8	9	1	2	3	4	5	6	7	8
Apr	6	7	8	9	1	2	3	4	5	6	7	8	9	1	2	3	4	5	6	7	8	9	1	2	3	4	5	6	7	8	
May	7	8	9	1	2	3	4	5	6	7	8	9	1	2	3	4	5	6	7	8	9	1	2	3	4	5	6	7	8	9	1
Jun	8	9	1	2	3	4	5	6	7	8	9	1	2	3	4	5	6	7	8	9	1	2	3	4	5	6	7	8	9	1	
Jul	9	1	2	3	4	5	6	7	8	9	1	2	3	4	5	6	7	8	9	1	2	3	4	5	6	7	8	9	1	2	3
Aug	1	2	3	4	5	6	7	8	9	1	2	3	4	5	6	7	8	9	1	2	3	4	5	6	7	8	9	1	2	3	4
Sep	2	3	4	5	6	7	8	9	1	2	3	4	5	6	7	8	9	1	2	3	4	5	6	7	8	9	1	2	3	4	
Oct	3	4	5	6	7	8	9	1	3	4	5	6	7	8	9	1	2	3	4	5	6	7	8	9	1	2	3	4	5	6	7
Nov	5	6	7	8	9	1	2	3	4	5	6	7	8	9	1	2	3	4	5	6	7	8	9	1	2	3	4	5	6	7	
Dec	6	7	8	9	1	2	3	4	5	6	7	8	9	1	2	3	4	5	6	7	8	9	1	2	3	4	5	6	7	8	9

OCTOBER 10

	1	2	3	4	5	6	7	8	9	10	11	12	13	14	15	16	17	18	19	20	21	22	23	24	25	26	27	28	29	30	31
Jan	4	5	6	7	8	9	1	2	3	4	5	6	7	8	9	1	2	3	4	5	6	7	8	9	1	2	3	4	5	6	7
Feb	5	6	7	8	9	1	2	3	4	5	6	7	8	9	1	2	3	4	5	6	7	8	9	1	2	3	4	5	6		
Mar	6	7	8	9	1	2	3	4	5	6	7	8	9	1	2	3	4	5	6	7	8	9	1	2	3	4	5	6	7	8	9
Apr	7	8	9	1	2	3	4	5	6	7	8	9	1	2	3	4	5	6	7	8	9	1	2	3	4	5	6	7	8	9	
May	8	9	1	2	3	4	5	6	7	8	9	1	2	3	4	5	6	7	8	9	1	2	3	4	5	6	7	8	9	1	2
Jun	9	1	2	3	4	5	6	7	8	9	1	2	3	4	5	6	7	8	9	1	2	3	4	5	6	7	8	9	1	2	
Jul	1	2	3	4	5	6	7	8	9	1	2	3	4	5	6	7	8	9	1	2	3	4	5	6	7	8	9	1	2	3	4
Aug	2	3	4	5	6	7	8	9	1	2	3	4	5	6	7	8	9	1	2	3	4	5	6	7	8	9	1	2	3	4	5
Sep	3	4	5	6	7	8	9	1	2	3	4	5	6	7	8	9	1	2	3	4	5	6	7	8	9	1	2	3	4	5	
Oct	4	5	6	7	8	9	1	2	3	5	6	7	8	9	1	2	3	4	5	6	7	8	9	1	2	3	4	5	6	7	8
Nov	6	7	8	9	1	2	3	4	5	6	7	8	9	1	2	3	4	5	6	7	8	9	1	2	3	4	5	6	7	8	
Dec	7	8	9	1	2	3	4	5	6	7	8	9	1	2	3	4	5	6	7	8	9	1	2	3	4	5	6	7	8	9	1

OCTOBER 11

	1	2	3	4	5	6	7	8	9	10	11	12	13	14	15	16	17	18	19	20	21	22	23	24	25	26	27	28	29	30	31
Jan	5	6	7	8	9	1	2	3	4	5	6	7	8	9	1	2	3	4	5	6	7	8	9	1	2	3	4	5	6	7	8
Feb	6	7	8	9	1	2	3	4	5	6	7	8	9	1	2	3	4	5	6	7	8	9	1	2	3	4	5	6	7		
Mar	7	8	9	1	2	3	4	5	6	7	8	9	1	2	3	4	5	6	7	8	9	1	2	3	4	5	6	7	8	9	1
Apr	8	9	1	2	3	4	5	6	7	8	9	1	2	3	4	5	6	7	8	9	1	2	3	4	5	6	7	8	9	1	
May	9	1	2	3	4	5	6	7	8	9	1	2	3	4	5	6	7	8	9	1	2	3	4	5	6	7	8	9	1	2	3
Jun	1	2	3	4	5	6	7	8	9	1	2	3	4	5	6	7	8	9	1	2	3	4	5	6	7	8	9	1	2	3	
Jul	2	3	4	5	6	7	8	9	1	2	3	4	5	6	7	8	9	1	2	3	4	5	6	7	8	9	1	2	3	4	5
Aug	3	4	5	6	7	8	9	1	2	3	4	5	6	7	8	9	1	2	3	4	5	6	7	8	9	1	2	3	4	5	6
Sep	4	5	6	7	8	9	1	2	3	4	5	6	7	8	9	1	2	3	4	5	6	7	8	9	1	2	3	4	5	6	
Oct	5	6	7	8	9	1	2	3	4	5	7	8	9	1	2	3	4	5	6	7	8	9	1	2	3	4	5	6	7	8	9
Nov	7	8	9	1	2	3	4	5	6	7	8	9	1	2	3	4	5	6	7	8	9	1	2	3	4	5	6	7	8	9	
Dec	8	9	1	2	3	4	5	6	7	8	9	1	2	3	4	5	6	7	8	9	1	2	3	4	5	6	7	8	9	1	2

OCTOBER 12

	1	2	3	4	5	6	7	8	9	10	11	12	13	14	15	16	17	18	19	20	21	22	23	24	25	26	27	28	29	30	31
Jan	6	7	8	9	1	2	3	4	5	6	7	8	9	1	2	3	4	5	6	7	8	9	1	2	3	4	5	6	7	8	9
Feb	7	8	9	1	2	3	4	5	6	7	8	9	1	2	3	4	5	6	7	8	9	1	2	3	4	5	6	7	8		
Mar	8	9	1	2	3	4	5	6	7	8	9	1	2	3	4	5	6	7	8	9	1	2	3	4	5	6	7	8	9	1	2
Apr	9	1	2	3	4	5	6	7	8	9	1	2	3	4	5	6	7	8	9	1	2	3	4	5	6	7	8	9	1	2	
May	1	2	3	4	5	6	7	8	9	1	2	3	4	5	6	7	8	9	1	2	3	4	5	6	7	8	9	1	2	3	4
Jun	2	3	4	5	6	7	8	9	1	2	3	4	5	6	7	8	9	1	2	3	4	5	6	7	8	9	1	2	3	4	
Jul	3	4	5	6	7	8	9	1	2	3	4	5	6	7	8	9	1	2	3	4	5	6	7	8	9	1	2	3	4	5	6
Aug	4	5	6	7	8	9	1	2	3	4	5	6	7	8	9	1	2	3	4	5	6	7	8	9	1	2	3	4	5	6	7
Sep	5	6	7	8	9	1	2	3	4	5	6	7	8	9	1	2	3	4	5	6	7	8	9	1	2	3	4	5	6	7	
Oct	6	7	8	9	1	2	3	4	5	6	7	9	1	2	3	4	5	6	7	8	9	1	2	3	4	5	6	7	8	9	1
Nov	8	9	1	2	3	4	5	6	7	8	9	1	2	3	4	5	6	7	8	9	1	2	3	4	5	6	7	8	9	1	
Dec	9	1	2	3	4	5	6	7	8	9	1	2	3	4	5	6	7	8	9	1	2	3	4	5	6	7	8	9	1	2	3

OCTOBER 13

	1	2	3	4	5	6	7	8	9	10	11	12	13	14	15	16	17	18	19	20	21	22	23	24	25	26	27	28	29	30	31
Jan	7	8	9	1	2	3	4	5	6	7	8	9	1	2	3	4	5	6	7	8	9	1	2	3	4	5	6	7	8	9	1
Feb	8	9	1	2	3	4	5	6	7	8	9	1	2	3	4	5	6	7	8	9	1	2	3	4	5	6	7	8	9		
Mar	9	1	2	3	4	5	6	7	8	9	1	2	3	4	5	6	7	8	9	1	2	3	4	5	6	7	8	9	1	2	3
Apr	1	2	3	4	5	6	7	8	9	1	2	3	4	5	6	7	8	9	1	2	3	4	5	6	7	8	9	1	2	3	
May	2	3	4	5	6	7	8	9	1	2	3	4	5	6	7	8	9	1	2	3	4	5	6	7	8	9	1	2	3	4	5
Jun	3	4	5	6	7	8	9	1	2	3	4	5	6	7	8	9	1	2	3	4	5	6	7	8	9	1	2	3	4	5	
Jul	4	5	6	7	8	9	1	2	3	4	5	6	7	8	9	1	2	3	4	5	6	7	8	9	1	2	3	4	5	6	7
Aug	5	6	7	8	9	1	2	3	4	5	6	7	8	9	1	2	3	4	5	6	7	8	9	1	2	3	4	5	6	7	8
Sep	6	7	8	9	1	2	3	4	5	6	7	8	9	1	2	3	4	5	6	7	8	9	1	2	3	4	5	6	7	8	
Oct	7	8	9	1	2	3	4	5	6	7	8	9	2	3	4	5	6	7	8	9	1	2	3	4	5	6	7	8	9	1	2
Nov	9	1	2	3	4	5	6	7	8	9	1	2	3	4	5	6	7	8	9	1	2	3	4	5	6	7	8	9	1	2	
Dec	1	2	3	4	5	6	7	8	9	1	2	3	4	5	6	7	8	9	1	2	3	4	5	6	7	8	9	1	2	3	4

OCTOBER 14

	1	2	3	4	5	6	7	8	9	10	11	12	13	14	15	16	17	18	19	20	21	22	23	24	25	26	27	28	29	30	31
Jan	8	9	1	2	3	4	5	6	7	8	9	1	2	3	4	5	6	7	8	9	1	2	3	4	5	6	7	8	9	1	2
Feb	9	1	2	3	4	5	6	7	8	9	1	2	3	4	5	6	7	8	9	1	2	3	4	5	6	7	8	9	1		
Mar	1	2	3	4	5	6	7	8	9	1	2	3	4	5	6	7	8	9	1	2	3	4	5	6	7	8	9	1	2	3	4
Apr	2	3	4	5	6	7	8	9	1	2	3	4	5	6	7	8	9	1	2	3	4	5	6	7	8	9	1	2	3	4	
May	3	4	5	6	7	8	9	1	2	3	4	5	6	7	8	9	1	2	3	4	5	6	7	8	9	1	2	3	4	5	6
Jun	4	5	6	7	8	9	1	2	3	4	5	6	7	8	9	1	2	3	4	5	6	7	8	9	1	2	3	4	5	6	
Jul	5	6	7	8	9	1	2	3	4	5	6	7	8	9	1	2	3	4	5	6	7	8	9	1	2	3	4	5	6	7	8
Aug	6	7	8	9	1	2	3	4	5	6	7	8	9	1	2	3	4	5	6	7	8	9	1	2	3	4	5	6	7	8	9
Sep	7	8	9	1	2	3	4	5	6	7	8	9	1	2	3	4	5	6	7	8	9	1	2	3	4	5	6	7	8	9	
Oct	8	9	1	2	3	4	5	6	7	8	9	1	2	4	5	6	7	8	9	1	2	3	4	5	6	7	8	9	1	2	3
Nov	1	2	3	4	5	6	7	8	9	1	2	3	4	5	6	7	8	9	1	2	3	4	5	6	7	8	9	1	2	3	
Dec	2	3	4	5	6	7	8	9	1	2	3	4	5	6	7	8	9	1	2	3	4	5	6	7	8	9	1	2	3	4	5

OCTOBER 15

	1	2	3	4	5	6	7	8	9	10	11	12	13	14	15	16	17	18	19	20	21	22	23	24	25	26	27	28	29	30	31
Jan	9	1	2	3	4	5	6	7	8	9	1	2	3	4	5	6	7	8	9	1	2	3	4	5	6	7	8	9	1	2	3
Feb	1	2	3	4	5	6	7	8	9	1	2	3	4	5	6	7	8	9	1	2	3	4	5	6	7	8	9	1	2		
Mar	2	3	4	5	6	7	8	9	1	2	3	4	5	6	7	8	9	1	2	3	4	5	6	7	8	9	1	2	3	4	5
Apr	3	4	5	6	7	8	9	1	2	3	4	5	6	7	8	9	1	2	3	4	5	6	7	8	9	1	2	3	4	5	
May	4	5	6	7	8	9	1	2	3	4	5	6	7	8	9	1	2	3	4	5	6	7	8	9	1	2	3	4	5	6	7
Jun	5	6	7	8	9	1	2	3	4	5	6	7	8	9	1	2	3	4	5	6	7	8	9	1	2	3	4	5	6	7	
Jul	6	7	8	9	1	2	3	4	5	6	7	8	9	1	2	3	4	5	6	7	8	9	1	2	3	4	5	6	7	8	9
Aug	7	8	9	1	2	3	4	5	6	7	8	9	1	2	3	4	5	6	7	8	9	1	2	3	4	5	6	7	8	9	1
Sep	8	9	1	2	3	4	5	6	7	8	9	1	2	3	4	5	6	7	8	9	1	2	3	4	5	6	7	8	9	1	
Oct	9	1	2	3	4	5	6	7	8	9	1	2	3	4	6	7	8	9	1	2	3	4	5	6	7	8	9	1	2	3	4
Nov	2	3	4	5	6	7	8	9	1	2	3	4	5	6	7	8	9	1	2	3	4	5	6	7	8	9	1	2	3	4	
Dec	3	4	5	6	7	8	9	1	2	3	4	5	6	7	8	9	1	2	3	4	5	6	7	8	9	1	2	3	4	5	6

OCTOBER 16

	1	2	3	4	5	6	7	8	9	10	11	12	13	14	15	16	17	18	19	20	21	22	23	24	25	26	27	28	29	30	31
Jan	1	2	3	4	5	6	7	8	9	1	2	3	4	5	6	7	8	9	1	2	3	4	5	6	7	8	9	1	2	3	4
Feb	2	3	4	5	6	7	8	9	1	2	3	4	5	6	7	8	9	1	2	3	4	5	6	7	8	9	1	2	3		
Mar	3	4	5	6	7	8	9	1	2	3	4	5	6	7	8	9	1	2	3	4	5	6	7	8	9	1	2	3	4	5	6
Apr	4	5	6	7	8	9	1	2	3	4	5	6	7	8	9	1	2	3	4	5	6	7	8	9	1	2	3	4	5	6	
May	5	6	7	8	9	1	2	3	4	5	6	7	8	9	1	2	3	4	5	6	7	8	9	1	2	3	4	5	6	7	8
Jun	6	7	8	9	1	2	3	4	5	6	7	8	9	1	2	3	4	5	6	7	8	9	1	2	3	4	5	6	7	8	
Jul	7	8	9	1	2	3	4	5	6	7	8	9	1	2	3	4	5	6	7	8	9	1	2	3	4	5	6	7	8	9	1
Aug	8	9	1	2	3	4	5	6	7	8	9	1	2	3	4	5	6	7	8	9	1	2	3	4	5	6	7	8	9	1	2
Sep	9	1	2	3	4	5	6	7	8	9	1	2	3	4	5	6	7	8	9	1	2	3	4	5	6	7	8	9	1	2	
Oct	1	2	3	4	5	6	7	8	9	1	2	3	4	5	6	8	9	1	2	3	4	5	6	7	8	9	1	2	3	4	5
Nov	3	4	5	6	7	8	9	1	2	3	4	5	6	7	8	9	1	2	3	4	5	6	7	8	9	1	2	3	4	5	
Dec	4	5	6	7	8	9	1	2	3	4	5	6	7	8	9	1	2	3	4	5	6	7	8	9	1	2	3	4	5	6	7

OCTOBER 17

	1	2	3	4	5	6	7	8	9	10	11	12	13	14	15	16	17	18	19	20	21	22	23	24	25	26	27	28	29	30	31
Jan	2	3	4	5	6	7	8	9	1	2	3	4	5	6	7	8	9	1	2	3	4	5	6	7	8	9	1	2	3	4	5
Feb	3	4	5	6	7	8	9	1	2	3	4	5	6	7	8	9	1	2	3	4	5	6	7	8	9	1	2	3	4		
Mar	4	5	6	7	8	9	1	2	3	4	5	6	7	8	9	1	2	3	4	5	6	7	8	9	1	2	3	4	5	6	7
Apr	5	6	7	8	9	1	2	3	4	5	6	7	8	9	1	2	3	4	5	6	7	8	9	1	2	3	4	5	6	7	
May	6	7	8	9	1	2	3	4	5	6	7	8	9	1	2	3	4	5	6	7	8	9	1	2	3	4	5	6	7	8	9
Jun	7	8	9	1	2	3	4	5	6	7	8	9	1	2	3	4	5	6	7	8	9	1	2	3	4	5	6	7	8	9	
Jul	8	9	1	2	3	4	5	6	7	8	9	1	2	3	4	5	6	7	8	9	1	2	3	4	5	6	7	8	9	1	2
Aug	9	1	2	3	4	5	6	7	8	9	1	2	3	4	5	6	7	8	9	1	2	3	4	5	6	7	8	9	1	2	3
Sep	1	2	3	4	5	6	7	8	9	1	2	3	4	5	6	7	8	9	1	2	3	4	5	6	7	8	9	1	2	3	
Oct	2	3	4	5	6	7	8	9	1	2	3	4	5	6	7	8	1	2	3	4	5	6	7	8	9	1	2	3	4	5	6
Nov	4	5	6	7	8	9	1	2	3	4	5	6	7	8	9	1	2	3	4	5	6	7	8	9	1	2	3	4	5	6	
Dec	5	6	7	8	9	1	2	3	4	5	6	7	8	9	1	2	3	4	5	6	7	8	9	1	2	3	4	5	6	7	8

OCTOBER 18

	1	2	3	4	5	6	7	8	9	10	11	12	13	14	15	16	17	18	19	20	21	22	23	24	25	26	27	28	29	30	31
Jan	3	4	5	6	7	8	9	1	2	3	4	5	6	7	8	9	1	2	3	4	5	6	7	8	9	1	2	3	4	5	6
Feb	4	5	6	7	8	9	1	2	3	4	5	6	7	8	9	1	2	3	4	5	6	7	8	9	1	2	3	4	5		
Mar	5	6	7	8	9	1	2	3	4	5	6	7	8	9	1	2	3	4	5	6	7	8	9	1	2	3	4	5	6	7	8
Apr	6	7	8	9	1	2	3	4	5	6	7	8	9	1	2	3	4	5	6	7	8	9	1	2	3	4	5	6	7	8	
May	7	8	9	1	2	3	4	5	6	7	8	9	1	2	3	4	5	6	7	8	9	1	2	3	4	5	6	7	8	9	1
Jun	8	9	1	2	3	4	5	6	7	8	9	1	2	3	4	5	6	7	8	9	1	2	3	4	5	6	7	8	9	1	
Jul	9	1	2	3	4	5	6	7	8	9	1	2	3	4	5	6	7	8	9	1	2	3	4	5	6	7	8	9	1	2	3
Aug	1	2	3	4	5	6	7	8	9	1	2	3	4	5	6	7	8	9	1	2	3	4	5	6	7	8	9	1	2	3	4
Sep	2	3	4	5	6	7	8	9	1	2	3	4	5	6	7	8	9	1	2	3	4	5	6	7	8	9	1	2	3	4	
Oct	3	4	5	6	7	8	9	1	2	3	4	5	6	7	8	9	1	3	4	5	6	7	8	9	1	2	3	4	5	6	7
Nov	5	6	7	8	9	1	2	3	4	5	6	7	8	9	1	2	3	4	5	6	7	8	9	1	2	3	4	5	6	7	
Dec	6	7	8	9	1	2	3	4	5	6	7	8	9	1	2	3	4	5	6	7	8	9	1	2	3	4	5	6	7	8	9

OCTOBER 19

	1	2	3	4	5	6	7	8	9	10	11	12	13	14	15	16	17	18	19	20	21	22	23	24	25	26	27	28	29	30	31
Jan	4	5	6	7	8	9	1	2	3	4	5	6	7	8	9	1	2	3	4	5	6	7	8	9	1	2	3	4	5	6	7
Feb	5	6	7	8	9	1	2	3	4	5	6	7	8	9	1	2	3	4	5	6	7	8	9	1	2	3	4	5	6		
Mar	6	7	8	9	1	2	3	4	5	6	7	8	9	1	2	3	4	5	6	7	8	9	1	2	3	4	5	6	7	8	9
Apr	7	8	9	1	2	3	4	5	6	7	8	9	1	2	3	4	5	6	7	8	9	1	2	3	4	5	6	7	8	9	
May	8	9	1	2	3	4	5	6	7	8	9	1	2	3	4	5	6	7	8	9	1	2	3	4	5	6	7	8	9	1	2
Jun	9	1	2	3	4	5	6	7	8	9	1	2	3	4	5	6	7	8	9	1	2	3	4	5	6	7	8	9	1	2	
Jul	1	2	3	4	5	6	7	8	9	1	2	3	4	5	6	7	8	9	1	2	3	4	5	6	7	8	9	1	2	3	4
Aug	2	3	4	5	6	7	8	9	1	2	3	4	5	6	7	8	9	1	2	3	4	5	6	7	8	9	1	2	3	4	5
Sep	3	4	5	6	7	8	9	1	2	3	4	5	6	7	8	9	1	2	3	4	5	6	7	8	9	1	2	3	4	5	
Oct	4	5	6	7	8	9	1	2	3	4	5	6	7	8	9	1	2	3	5	6	7	8	9	1	2	3	4	5	6	7	8
Nov	6	7	8	9	1	2	3	4	5	6	7	8	9	1	2	3	4	5	6	7	8	9	1	2	3	4	5	6	7	8	
Dec	7	8	9	1	2	3	4	5	6	7	8	9	1	2	3	4	5	6	7	8	9	1	2	3	4	5	6	7	8	9	1

OCTOBER 20

	1	2	3	4	5	6	7	8	9	10	11	12	13	14	15	16	17	18	19	20	21	22	23	24	25	26	27	28	29	30	31
Jan	5	6	7	8	9	1	2	3	4	5	6	7	8	9	1	2	3	4	5	6	7	8	9	1	2	3	4	5	6	7	8
Feb	6	7	8	9	1	2	3	4	5	6	7	8	9	1	2	3	4	5	6	7	8	9	1	2	3	4	5	6	7		
Mar	7	8	9	1	2	3	4	5	6	7	8	9	1	2	3	4	5	6	7	8	9	1	2	3	4	5	6	7	8	9	1
Apr	8	9	1	2	3	4	5	6	7	8	9	1	2	3	4	5	6	7	8	9	1	2	3	4	5	6	7	8	9	1	
May	9	1	2	3	4	5	6	7	8	9	1	2	3	4	5	6	7	8	9	1	2	3	4	5	6	7	8	9	1	2	3
Jun	1	2	3	4	5	6	7	8	9	1	2	3	4	5	6	7	8	9	1	2	3	4	5	6	7	8	9	1	2	3	
Jul	2	3	4	5	6	7	8	9	1	2	3	4	5	6	7	8	9	1	2	3	4	5	6	7	8	9	1	2	3	4	5
Aug	3	4	5	6	7	8	9	1	2	3	4	5	6	7	8	9	1	2	3	4	5	6	7	8	9	1	2	3	4	5	6
Sep	4	5	6	7	8	9	1	2	3	4	5	6	7	8	9	1	2	3	4	5	6	7	8	9	1	2	3	4	5	6	
Oct	5	6	7	8	9	1	2	3	4	5	6	7	8	9	1	2	3	4	5	7	8	9	1	2	3	4	5	6	7	8	9
Nov	7	8	9	1	2	3	4	5	6	7	8	9	1	2	3	4	5	6	7	8	9	1	2	3	4	5	6	7	8	9	
Dec	8	9	1	2	3	4	5	6	7	8	9	1	2	3	4	5	6	7	8	9	1	2	3	4	5	6	7	8	9	1	2

OCTOBER 21

	1	2	3	4	5	6	7	8	9	10	11	12	13	14	15	16	17	18	19	20	21	22	23	24	25	26	27	28	29	30	31
Jan	6	7	8	9	1	2	3	4	5	6	7	8	9	1	2	3	4	5	6	7	8	9	1	2	3	4	5	6	7	8	9
Feb	7	8	9	1	2	3	4	5	6	7	8	9	1	2	3	4	5	6	7	8	9	1	2	3	4	5	6	7	8		
Mar	8	9	1	2	3	4	5	6	7	8	9	1	2	3	4	5	6	7	8	9	1	2	3	4	5	6	7	8	9	1	2
Apr	9	1	2	3	4	5	6	7	8	9	1	2	3	4	5	6	7	8	9	1	2	3	4	5	6	7	8	9	1	2	
May	1	2	3	4	5	6	7	8	9	1	2	3	4	5	6	7	8	9	1	2	3	4	5	6	7	8	9	1	2	3	4
Jun	2	3	4	5	6	7	8	9	1	2	3	4	5	6	7	8	9	1	2	3	4	5	6	7	8	9	1	2	3	4	
Jul	3	4	5	6	7	8	9	1	2	3	4	5	6	7	8	9	1	2	3	4	5	6	7	8	9	1	2	3	4	5	6
Aug	4	5	6	7	8	9	1	2	3	4	5	6	7	8	9	1	2	3	4	5	6	7	8	9	1	2	3	4	5	6	7
Sep	5	6	7	8	9	1	2	3	4	5	6	7	8	9	1	2	3	4	5	6	7	8	9	1	2	3	4	5	6	7	
Oct	6	7	8	9	1	2	3	4	5	6	7	8	9	1	2	3	4	5	6	7	9	1	2	3	4	5	6	7	8	9	1
Nov	8	9	1	2	3	4	5	6	7	8	9	1	2	3	4	5	6	7	8	9	1	2	3	4	5	6	7	8	9	1	
Dec	9	1	2	3	4	5	6	7	8	9	1	2	3	4	5	6	7	8	9	1	2	3	4	5	6	7	8	9	1	2	3

OCTOBER 22

	1	2	3	4	5	6	7	8	9	10	11	12	13	14	15	16	17	18	19	20	21	22	23	24	25	26	27	28	29	30	31
Jan	7	8	9	1	2	3	4	5	6	7	8	9	1	2	3	4	5	6	7	8	9	1	2	3	4	5	6	7	8	9	1
Feb	8	9	1	2	3	4	5	6	7	8	9	1	2	3	4	5	6	7	8	9	1	2	3	4	5	6	7	8	9		
Mar	9	1	2	3	4	5	6	7	8	9	1	2	3	4	5	6	7	8	9	1	2	3	4	5	6	7	8	9	1	2	3
Apr	1	2	3	4	5	6	7	8	9	1	2	3	4	5	6	7	8	9	1	2	3	4	5	6	7	8	9	1	2	3	
May	2	3	4	5	6	7	8	9	1	2	3	4	5	6	7	8	9	1	2	3	4	5	6	7	8	9	1	2	3	4	5
Jun	3	4	5	6	7	8	9	1	2	3	4	5	6	7	8	9	1	2	3	4	5	6	7	8	9	1	2	3	4	5	
Jul	4	5	6	7	8	9	1	2	3	4	5	6	7	8	9	1	2	3	4	5	6	7	8	9	1	2	3	4	5	6	7
Aug	5	6	7	8	9	1	2	3	4	5	6	7	8	9	1	2	3	4	5	6	7	8	9	1	2	3	4	5	6	7	8
Sep	6	7	8	9	1	2	3	4	5	6	7	8	9	1	2	3	4	5	6	7	8	9	1	2	3	4	5	6	7	8	
Oct	7	8	9	1	2	3	4	5	6	7	8	9	1	2	3	4	5	6	7	8	9	2	3	4	5	6	7	8	9	1	2
Nov	9	1	2	3	4	5	6	7	8	9	1	2	3	4	5	6	7	8	9	1	2	3	4	5	6	7	8	9	1	2	
Dec	1	2	3	4	5	6	7	8	9	1	2	3	4	5	6	7	8	9	1	2	3	4	5	6	7	8	9	1	2	3	4

OCTOBER 23

	1	2	3	4	5	6	7	8	9	10	11	12	13	14	15	16	17	18	19	20	21	22	23	24	25	26	27	28	29	30	31
Jan	8	9	1	2	3	4	5	6	7	8	9	1	2	3	4	5	6	7	8	9	1	2	3	4	5	6	7	8	9	1	2
Feb	9	1	2	3	4	5	6	7	8	9	1	2	3	4	5	6	7	8	9	1	2	3	4	5	6	7	8	9	1		
Mar	1	2	3	4	5	6	7	8	9	1	2	3	4	5	6	7	8	9	1	2	3	4	5	6	7	8	9	1	2	3	4
Apr	2	3	4	5	6	7	8	9	1	2	3	4	5	6	7	8	9	1	2	3	4	5	6	7	8	9	1	2	3	4	
May	3	4	5	6	7	8	9	1	2	3	4	5	6	7	8	9	1	2	3	4	5	6	7	8	9	1	2	3	4	5	6
Jun	4	5	6	7	8	9	1	2	3	4	5	6	7	8	9	1	2	3	4	5	6	7	8	9	1	2	3	4	5	6	
Jul	5	6	7	8	9	1	2	3	4	5	6	7	8	9	1	2	3	4	5	6	7	8	9	1	2	3	4	5	6	7	8
Aug	6	7	8	9	1	2	3	4	5	6	7	8	9	1	2	3	4	5	6	7	8	9	1	2	3	4	5	6	7	8	9
Sep	7	8	9	1	2	3	4	5	6	7	8	9	1	2	3	4	5	6	7	8	9	1	2	3	4	5	6	7	8	9	
Oct	8	9	1	2	3	4	5	6	7	8	9	1	2	3	4	5	6	7	8	9	1	2	4	5	6	7	8	9	1	2	3
Nov	1	2	3	4	5	6	7	8	9	1	2	3	4	5	6	7	8	9	1	2	3	4	5	6	7	8	9	1	2	3	
Dec	2	3	4	5	6	7	8	9	1	2	3	4	5	6	7	8	9	1	2	3	4	5	6	7	8	9	1	2	3	4	5

OCTOBER 24

	1	2	3	4	5	6	7	8	9	10	11	12	13	14	15	16	17	18	19	20	21	22	23	24	25	26	27	28	29	30	31
Jan	9	1	2	3	4	5	6	7	8	9	1	2	3	4	5	6	7	8	9	1	2	3	4	5	6	7	8	9	1	2	3
Feb	1	2	3	4	5	6	7	8	9	1	2	3	4	5	6	7	8	9	1	2	3	4	5	6	7	8	9	1	2		
Mar	2	3	4	5	6	7	8	9	1	2	3	4	5	6	7	8	9	1	2	3	4	5	6	7	8	9	1	2	3	4	5
Apr	3	4	5	6	7	8	9	1	2	3	4	5	6	7	8	9	1	2	3	4	5	6	7	8	9	1	2	3	4	5	
May	4	5	6	7	8	9	1	2	3	4	5	6	7	8	9	1	2	3	4	5	6	7	8	9	1	2	3	4	5	6	7
Jun	5	6	7	8	9	1	2	3	4	5	6	7	8	9	1	2	3	4	5	6	7	8	9	1	2	3	4	5	6	7	
Jul	6	7	8	9	1	2	3	4	5	6	7	8	9	1	2	3	4	5	6	7	8	9	1	2	3	4	5	6	7	8	9
Aug	7	8	9	1	2	3	4	5	6	7	8	9	1	2	3	4	5	6	7	8	9	1	2	3	4	5	6	7	8	9	1
Sep	8	9	1	2	3	4	5	6	7	8	9	1	2	3	4	5	6	7	8	9	1	2	3	4	5	6	7	8	9	1	
Oct	9	1	2	3	4	5	6	7	8	9	1	2	3	4	5	6	7	8	9	1	2	3	4	6	7	8	9	1	2	3	4
Nov	2	3	4	5	6	7	8	9	1	2	3	4	5	6	7	8	9	1	2	3	4	5	6	7	8	9	1	2	3	4	
Dec	3	4	5	6	7	8	9	1	2	3	4	5	6	7	8	9	1	2	3	4	5	6	7	8	9	1	2	3	4	5	6

OCTOBER 25

	1	2	3	4	5	6	7	8	9	10	11	12	13	14	15	16	17	18	19	20	21	22	23	24	25	26	27	28	29	30	31
Jan	1	2	3	4	5	6	7	8	9	1	2	3	4	5	6	7	8	9	1	2	3	4	5	6	7	8	9	1	2	3	4
Feb	2	3	4	5	6	7	8	9	1	2	3	4	5	6	7	8	9	1	2	3	4	5	6	7	8	9	1	2	3		
Mar	3	4	5	6	7	8	9	1	2	3	4	5	6	7	8	9	1	2	3	4	5	6	7	8	9	1	2	3	4	5	6
Apr	4	5	6	7	8	9	1	2	3	4	5	6	7	8	9	1	2	3	4	5	6	7	8	9	1	2	3	4	5	6	
May	5	6	7	8	9	1	2	3	4	5	6	7	8	9	1	2	3	4	5	6	7	8	9	1	2	3	4	5	6	7	8
Jun	6	7	8	9	1	2	3	4	5	6	7	8	9	1	2	3	4	5	6	7	8	9	1	2	3	4	5	6	7	8	
Jul	7	8	9	1	2	3	4	5	6	7	8	9	1	2	3	4	5	6	7	8	9	1	2	3	4	5	6	7	8	9	1
Aug	8	9	1	2	3	4	5	6	7	8	9	1	2	3	4	5	6	7	8	9	1	2	3	4	5	6	7	8	9	1	2
Sep	9	1	2	3	4	5	6	7	8	9	1	2	3	4	5	6	7	8	9	1	2	3	4	5	6	7	8	9	1	2	
Oct	1	2	3	4	5	6	7	8	9	1	2	3	4	5	6	7	8	9	1	2	3	4	5	6	8	9	1	2	3	4	5
Nov	3	4	5	6	7	8	9	1	2	3	4	5	6	7	8	9	1	2	3	4	5	6	7	8	9	1	2	3	4	5	
Dec	4	5	6	7	8	9	1	2	3	4	5	6	7	8	9	1	2	3	4	5	6	7	8	9	1	2	3	4	5	6	7

OCTOBER 26

	1	2	3	4	5	6	7	8	9	10	11	12	13	14	15	16	17	18	19	20	21	22	23	24	25	26	27	28	29	30	31
Jan	2	3	4	5	6	7	8	9	1	2	3	4	5	6	7	8	9	1	2	3	4	5	6	7	8	9	1	2	3	4	5
Feb	3	4	5	6	7	8	9	1	2	3	4	5	6	7	8	9	1	2	3	4	5	6	7	8	9	1	2	3	4		
Mar	4	5	6	7	8	9	1	2	3	4	5	6	7	8	9	1	2	3	4	5	6	7	8	9	1	2	3	4	5	6	7
Apr	5	6	7	8	9	1	2	3	4	5	6	7	8	9	1	2	3	4	5	6	7	8	9	1	2	3	4	5	6	7	
May	6	7	8	9	1	2	3	4	5	6	7	8	9	1	2	3	4	5	6	7	8	9	1	2	3	4	5	6	7	8	9
Jun	7	8	9	1	2	3	4	5	6	7	8	9	1	2	3	4	5	6	7	8	9	1	2	3	4	5	6	7	8	9	
Jul	8	9	1	2	3	4	5	6	7	8	9	1	2	3	4	5	6	7	8	9	1	2	3	4	5	6	7	8	9	1	2
Aug	9	1	2	3	4	5	6	7	8	9	1	2	3	4	5	6	7	8	9	1	2	3	4	5	6	7	8	9	1	2	3
Sep	1	2	3	4	5	6	7	8	9	1	2	3	4	5	6	7	8	9	1	2	3	4	5	6	7	8	9	1	2	3	
Oct	2	3	4	5	6	7	8	9	1	2	3	4	5	6	7	8	9	1	2	3	4	5	6	7	8	1	2	3	4	5	6
Nov	4	5	6	7	8	9	1	2	3	4	5	6	7	8	9	1	2	3	4	5	6	7	8	9	1	2	3	4	5	6	
Dec	5	6	7	8	9	1	2	3	4	5	6	7	8	9	1	2	3	4	5	6	7	8	9	1	2	3	4	5	6	7	8

OCTOBER 27

	1	2	3	4	5	6	7	8	9	10	11	12	13	14	15	16	17	18	19	20	21	22	23	24	25	26	27	28	29	30	31
Jan	3	4	5	6	7	8	9	1	2	3	4	5	6	7	8	9	1	2	3	4	5	6	7	8	9	1	2	3	4	5	6
Feb	4	5	6	7	8	9	1	2	3	4	5	6	7	8	9	1	2	3	4	5	6	7	8	9	1	2	3	4	5		
Mar	5	6	7	8	9	1	2	3	4	5	6	7	8	9	1	2	3	4	5	6	7	8	9	1	2	3	4	5	6	7	8
Apr	6	7	8	9	1	2	3	4	5	6	7	8	9	1	2	3	4	5	6	7	8	9	1	2	3	4	5	6	7	8	
May	7	8	9	1	2	3	4	5	6	7	8	9	1	2	3	4	5	6	7	8	9	1	2	3	4	5	6	7	8	9	1
Jun	8	9	1	2	3	4	5	6	7	8	9	1	2	3	4	5	6	7	8	9	1	2	3	4	5	6	7	8	9	1	
Jul	9	1	2	3	4	5	6	7	8	9	1	2	3	4	5	6	7	8	9	1	2	3	4	5	6	7	8	9	1	2	3
Aug	1	2	3	4	5	6	7	8	9	1	2	3	4	5	6	7	8	9	1	2	3	4	5	6	7	8	9	1	2	3	4
Sep	2	3	4	5	6	7	8	9	1	2	3	4	5	6	7	8	9	1	2	3	4	5	6	7	8	9	1	2	3	4	
Oct	3	4	5	6	7	8	9	1	2	3	4	5	6	7	8	9	1	2	3	4	5	6	7	8	9	1	3	4	5	6	7
Nov	5	6	7	8	9	1	2	3	4	5	6	7	8	9	1	2	3	4	5	6	7	8	9	1	2	3	4	5	6	7	
Dec	6	7	8	9	1	2	3	4	5	6	7	8	9	1	2	3	4	5	6	7	8	9	1	2	3	4	5	6	7	8	9

OCTOBER 28

	1	2	3	4	5	6	7	8	9	10	11	12	13	14	15	16	17	18	19	20	21	22	23	24	25	26	27	28	29	30	31
Jan	4	5	6	7	8	9	1	2	3	4	5	6	7	8	9	1	2	3	4	5	6	7	8	9	1	2	3	4	5	6	7
Feb	5	6	7	8	9	1	2	3	4	5	6	7	8	9	1	2	3	4	5	6	7	8	9	1	2	3	4	5	6		
Mar	6	7	8	9	1	2	3	4	5	6	7	8	9	1	2	3	4	5	6	7	8	9	1	2	3	4	5	6	7	8	9
Apr	7	8	9	1	2	3	4	5	6	7	8	9	1	2	3	4	5	6	7	8	9	1	2	3	4	5	6	7	8	9	
May	8	9	1	2	3	4	5	6	7	8	9	1	2	3	4	5	6	7	8	9	1	2	3	4	5	6	7	8	9	1	2
Jun	9	1	2	3	4	5	6	7	8	9	1	2	3	4	5	6	7	8	9	1	2	3	4	5	6	7	8	9	1	2	
Jul	1	2	3	4	5	6	7	8	9	1	2	3	4	5	6	7	8	9	1	2	3	4	5	6	7	8	9	1	2	3	4
Aug	2	3	4	5	6	7	8	9	1	2	3	4	5	6	7	8	9	1	2	3	4	5	6	7	8	9	1	2	3	4	5
Sep	3	4	5	6	7	8	9	1	2	3	4	5	6	7	8	9	1	2	3	4	5	6	7	8	9	1	2	3	4	5	
Oct	4	5	6	7	8	9	1	2	3	4	5	6	7	8	9	1	2	3	4	5	6	7	8	9	1	2	3	5	6	7	8
Nov	6	7	8	9	1	2	3	4	5	6	7	8	9	1	2	3	4	5	6	7	8	9	1	2	3	4	5	6	7	8	
Dec	7	8	9	1	2	3	4	5	6	7	8	9	1	2	3	4	5	6	7	8	9	1	2	3	4	5	6	7	8	9	1

OCTOBER 29

	1	2	3	4	5	6	7	8	9	10	11	12	13	14	15	16	17	18	19	20	21	22	23	24	25	26	27	28	29	30	31
Jan	5	6	7	8	9	1	2	3	4	5	6	7	8	9	1	2	3	4	5	6	7	8	9	1	2	3	4	5	6	7	8
Feb	6	7	8	9	1	2	3	4	5	6	7	8	9	1	2	3	4	5	6	7	8	9	1	2	3	4	5	6	7		
Mar	7	8	9	1	2	3	4	5	6	7	8	9	1	2	3	4	5	6	7	8	9	1	2	3	4	5	6	7	8	9	1
Apr	8	9	1	2	3	4	5	6	7	8	9	1	2	3	4	5	6	7	8	9	1	2	3	4	5	6	7	8	9	1	
May	9	1	2	3	4	5	6	7	8	9	1	2	3	4	5	6	7	8	9	1	2	3	4	5	6	7	8	9	1	2	3
Jun	1	2	3	4	5	6	7	8	9	1	2	3	4	5	6	7	8	9	1	2	3	4	5	6	7	8	9	1	2	3	
Jul	2	3	4	5	6	7	8	9	1	2	3	4	5	6	7	8	9	1	2	3	4	5	6	7	8	9	1	2	3	4	5
Aug	3	4	5	6	7	8	9	1	2	3	4	5	6	7	8	9	1	2	3	4	5	6	7	8	9	1	2	3	4	5	6
Sep	4	5	6	7	8	9	1	2	3	4	5	6	7	8	9	1	2	3	4	5	6	7	8	9	1	2	3	4	5	6	
Oct	5	6	7	8	9	1	2	3	4	5	6	7	8	9	1	2	3	4	5	6	7	8	9	1	2	3	4	5	7	8	9
Nov	7	8	9	1	2	3	4	5	6	7	8	9	1	2	3	4	5	6	7	8	9	1	2	3	4	5	6	7	8	9	
Dec	8	9	1	2	3	4	5	6	7	8	9	1	2	3	4	5	6	7	8	9	1	2	3	4	5	6	7	8	9	1	2

OCTOBER 30

	1	2	3	4	5	6	7	8	9	10	11	12	13	14	15	16	17	18	19	20	21	22	23	24	25	26	27	28	29	30	31
Jan	6	7	8	9	1	2	3	4	5	6	7	8	9	1	2	3	4	5	6	7	8	9	1	2	3	4	5	6	7	8	9
Feb	7	8	9	1	2	3	4	5	6	7	8	9	1	2	3	4	5	6	7	8	9	1	2	3	4	5	6	7	8		
Mar	8	9	1	2	3	4	5	6	7	8	9	1	2	3	4	5	6	7	8	9	1	2	3	4	5	6	7	8	9	1	2
Apr	9	1	2	3	4	5	6	7	8	9	1	2	3	4	5	6	7	8	9	1	2	3	4	5	6	7	8	9	1	2	
May	1	2	3	4	5	6	7	8	9	1	2	3	4	5	6	7	8	9	1	2	3	4	5	6	7	8	9	1	2	3	4
Jun	2	3	4	5	6	7	8	9	1	2	3	4	5	6	7	8	9	1	2	3	4	5	6	7	8	9	1	2	3	4	
Jul	3	4	5	6	7	8	9	1	2	3	4	5	6	7	8	9	1	2	3	4	5	6	7	8	9	1	2	3	4	5	6
Aug	4	5	6	7	8	9	1	2	3	4	5	6	7	8	9	1	2	3	4	5	6	7	8	9	1	2	3	4	5	6	7
Sep	5	6	7	8	9	1	2	3	4	5	6	7	8	9	1	2	3	4	5	6	7	8	9	1	2	3	4	5	6	7	
Oct	6	7	8	9	1	2	3	4	5	6	7	8	9	1	2	3	4	5	6	7	8	9	1	2	3	4	5	6	7	9	1
Nov	8	9	1	2	3	4	5	6	7	8	9	1	2	3	4	5	6	7	8	9	1	2	3	4	5	6	7	8	9	1	
Dec	9	1	2	3	4	5	6	7	8	9	1	2	3	4	5	6	7	8	9	1	2	3	4	5	6	7	8	9	1	2	3

OCTOBER 31

	1	2	3	4	5	6	7	8	9	10	11	12	13	14	15	16	17	18	19	20	21	22	23	24	25	26	27	28	29	30	31
Jan	7	8	9	1	2	3	4	5	6	7	8	9	1	2	3	4	5	6	7	8	9	1	2	3	4	5	6	7	8	9	1
Feb	8	9	1	2	3	4	5	6	7	8	9	1	2	3	4	5	6	7	8	9	1	2	3	4	5	6	7	8	9		
Mar	9	1	2	3	4	5	6	7	8	9	1	2	3	4	5	6	7	8	9	1	2	3	4	5	6	7	8	9	1	2	3
Apr	1	2	3	4	5	6	7	8	9	1	2	3	4	5	6	7	8	9	1	2	3	4	5	6	7	8	9	1	2	3	
May	2	3	4	5	6	7	8	9	1	2	3	4	5	6	7	8	9	1	2	3	4	5	6	7	8	9	1	2	3	4	5
Jun	3	4	5	6	7	8	9	1	2	3	4	5	6	7	8	9	1	2	3	4	5	6	7	8	9	1	2	3	4	5	
Jul	4	5	6	7	8	9	1	2	3	4	5	6	7	8	9	1	2	3	4	5	6	7	8	9	1	2	3	4	5	6	7
Aug	5	6	7	8	9	1	2	3	4	5	6	7	8	9	1	2	3	4	5	6	7	8	9	1	2	3	4	5	6	7	8
Sep	6	7	8	9	1	2	3	4	5	6	7	8	9	1	2	3	4	5	6	7	8	9	1	2	3	4	5	6	7	8	
Oct	7	8	9	1	2	3	4	5	6	7	8	9	1	2	3	4	5	6	7	8	9	1	2	3	4	5	6	7	8	9	2
Nov	9	1	2	3	4	5	6	7	8	9	1	2	3	4	5	6	7	8	9	1	2	3	4	5	6	7	8	9	1	2	
Dec	1	2	3	4	5	6	7	8	9	1	2	3	4	5	6	7	8	9	1	2	3	4	5	6	7	8	9	1	2	3	4

NOVEMBER 1

	1	2	3	4	5	6	7	8	9	10	11	12	13	14	15	16	17	18	19	20	21	22	23	24	25	26	27	28	29	30	31
Jan	5	6	7	8	9	1	2	3	4	5	6	7	8	9	1	2	3	4	5	6	7	8	9	1	2	3	4	5	6	7	8
Feb	6	7	8	9	1	2	3	4	5	6	7	8	9	1	2	3	4	5	6	7	8	9	1	2	3	4	5	6	7		
Mar	7	8	9	1	2	3	4	5	6	7	8	9	1	2	3	4	5	6	7	8	9	1	2	3	4	5	6	7	8	9	1
Apr	8	9	1	2	3	4	5	6	7	8	9	1	2	3	4	5	6	7	8	9	1	2	3	4	5	6	7	8	9	1	
May	9	1	2	3	4	5	6	7	8	9	1	2	3	4	5	6	7	8	9	1	2	3	4	5	6	7	8	9	1	2	3
Jun	1	2	3	4	5	6	7	8	9	1	2	3	4	5	6	7	8	9	1	2	3	4	5	6	7	8	9	1	2	3	
Jul	2	3	4	5	6	7	8	9	1	2	3	4	5	6	7	8	9	1	2	3	4	5	6	7	8	9	1	2	3	4	5
Aug	3	4	5	6	7	8	9	1	2	3	4	5	6	7	8	9	1	2	3	4	5	6	7	8	9	1	2	3	4	5	6
Sep	4	5	6	7	8	9	1	2	3	4	5	6	7	8	9	1	2	3	4	5	6	7	8	9	1	2	3	4	5	6	
Oct	5	6	7	8	9	1	2	3	4	5	6	7	8	9	1	2	3	4	5	6	7	8	9	1	2	3	4	5	6	7	8
Nov	7	8	9	1	2	3	4	5	6	7	8	9	1	2	3	4	5	6	7	8	9	1	2	3	4	5	6	7	8	9	
Dec	8	9	1	2	3	4	5	6	7	8	9	1	2	3	4	5	6	7	8	9	1	2	3	4	5	6	7	8	9	1	2

NOVEMBER 2

	1	2	3	4	5	6	7	8	9	10	11	12	13	14	15	16	17	18	19	20	21	22	23	24	25	26	27	28	29	30	31
Jan	6	7	8	9	1	2	3	4	5	6	7	8	9	1	2	3	4	5	6	7	8	9	1	2	3	4	5	6	7	8	9
Feb	7	8	9	1	2	3	4	5	6	7	8	9	1	2	3	4	5	6	7	8	9	1	2	3	4	5	6	7	8		
Mar	8	9	1	2	3	4	5	6	7	8	9	1	2	3	4	5	6	7	8	9	1	2	3	4	5	6	7	8	9	1	2
Apr	9	1	2	3	4	5	6	7	8	9	1	2	3	4	5	6	7	8	9	1	2	3	4	5	6	7	8	9	1	2	
May	1	2	3	4	5	6	7	8	9	1	2	3	4	5	6	7	8	9	1	2	3	4	5	6	7	8	9	1	2	3	4
Jun	2	3	4	5	6	7	8	9	1	2	3	4	5	6	7	8	9	1	2	3	4	5	6	7	8	9	1	2	3	4	
Jul	3	4	5	6	7	8	9	1	2	3	4	5	6	7	8	9	1	2	3	4	5	6	7	8	9	1	2	3	4	5	6
Aug	4	5	6	7	8	9	1	2	3	4	5	6	7	8	9	1	2	3	4	5	6	7	8	9	1	2	3	4	5	6	7
Sep	5	6	7	8	9	1	2	3	4	5	6	7	8	9	1	2	3	4	5	6	7	8	9	1	2	3	4	5	6	7	
Oct	6	7	8	9	1	2	3	4	5	6	7	8	9	1	2	3	4	5	6	7	8	9	1	2	3	4	5	6	7	8	9
Nov	7	9	1	2	3	4	5	6	7	8	9	1	2	3	4	5	6	7	8	9	1	2	3	4	5	6	7	8	9	1	
Dec	9	1	2	3	4	5	6	7	8	9	1	2	3	4	5	6	7	8	9	1	2	3	4	5	6	7	8	9	1	2	3

NOVEMBER 3

	1	2	3	4	5	6	7	8	9	10	11	12	13	14	15	16	17	18	19	20	21	22	23	24	25	26	27	28	29	30	31
Jan	7	8	9	1	2	3	4	5	6	7	8	9	1	2	3	4	5	6	7	8	9	1	2	3	4	5	6	7	8	9	1
Feb	8	9	1	2	3	4	5	6	7	8	9	1	2	3	4	5	6	7	8	9	1	2	3	4	5	6	7	8	9		
Mar	9	1	2	3	4	5	6	7	8	9	1	2	3	4	5	6	7	8	9	1	2	3	4	5	6	7	8	9	1	2	3
Apr	1	2	3	4	5	6	7	8	9	1	2	3	4	5	6	7	8	9	1	2	3	4	5	6	7	8	9	1	2	3	
May	2	3	4	5	6	7	8	9	1	2	3	4	5	6	7	8	9	1	2	3	4	5	6	7	8	9	1	2	3	4	5
Jun	3	4	5	6	7	8	9	1	2	3	4	5	6	7	8	9	1	2	3	4	5	6	7	8	9	1	2	3	4	5	
Jul	4	5	6	7	8	9	1	2	3	4	5	6	7	8	9	1	2	3	4	5	6	7	8	9	1	2	3	4	5	6	7
Aug	5	6	7	8	9	1	2	3	4	5	6	7	8	9	1	2	3	4	5	6	7	8	9	1	2	3	4	5	6	7	8
Sep	6	7	8	9	1	2	3	4	5	6	7	8	9	1	2	3	4	5	6	7	8	9	1	2	3	4	5	6	7	8	
Oct	7	8	9	1	2	3	4	5	6	7	8	9	1	2	3	4	5	6	7	8	9	1	2	3	4	5	6	7	8	9	1
Nov	8	9	2	3	4	5	6	7	8	9	1	2	3	4	5	6	7	8	9	1	2	3	4	5	6	7	8	9	1	2	
Dec	1	2	3	4	5	6	7	8	9	1	2	3	4	5	6	7	8	9	1	2	3	4	5	6	7	8	9	1	2	3	4

NOVEMBER 4

	1	2	3	4	5	6	7	8	9	10	11	12	13	14	15	16	17	18	19	20	21	22	23	24	25	26	27	28	29	30	31
Jan	8	9	1	2	3	4	5	6	7	8	9	1	2	3	4	5	6	7	8	9	1	2	3	4	5	6	7	8	9	1	2
Feb	9	1	2	3	4	5	6	7	8	9	1	2	3	4	5	6	7	8	9	1	2	3	4	5	6	7	8	9	1		
Mar	1	2	3	4	5	6	7	8	9	1	2	3	4	5	6	7	8	9	1	2	3	4	5	6	7	8	9	1	2	3	4
Apr	2	3	4	5	6	7	8	9	1	2	3	4	5	6	7	8	9	1	2	3	4	5	6	7	8	9	1	2	3	4	
May	3	4	5	6	7	8	9	1	2	3	4	5	6	7	8	9	1	2	3	4	5	6	7	8	9	1	2	3	4	5	6
Jun	4	5	6	7	8	9	1	2	3	4	5	6	7	8	9	1	2	3	4	5	6	7	8	9	1	2	3	4	5	6	
Jul	5	6	7	8	9	1	2	3	4	5	6	7	8	9	1	2	3	4	5	6	7	8	9	1	2	3	4	5	6	7	8
Aug	6	7	8	9	1	2	3	4	5	6	7	8	9	1	2	3	4	5	6	7	8	9	1	2	3	4	5	6	7	8	9
Sep	7	8	9	1	2	3	4	5	6	7	8	9	1	2	3	4	5	6	7	8	9	1	2	3	4	5	6	7	8	9	
Oct	8	9	1	2	3	4	5	6	7	8	9	1	2	3	4	5	6	7	8	9	1	2	3	4	5	6	7	8	9	1	2
Nov	9	1	2	4	5	6	7	8	9	1	2	3	4	5	6	7	8	9	1	2	3	4	5	6	7	8	9	1	2	3	
Dec	2	3	4	5	6	7	8	9	1	2	3	4	5	6	7	8	9	1	2	3	4	5	6	7	8	9	1	2	3	4	5

NOVEMBER 5

	1	2	3	4	5	6	7	8	9	10	11	12	13	14	15	16	17	18	19	20	21	22	23	24	25	26	27	28	29	30	31
Jan	9	1	2	3	4	5	6	7	8	9	1	2	3	4	5	6	7	8	9	1	2	3	4	5	6	7	8	9	1	2	3
Feb	1	2	3	4	5	6	7	8	9	1	2	3	4	5	6	7	8	9	1	2	3	4	5	6	7	8	9	1	2		
Mar	2	3	4	5	6	7	8	9	1	2	3	4	5	6	7	8	9	1	2	3	4	5	6	7	8	9	1	2	3	4	5
Apr	3	4	5	6	7	8	9	1	2	3	4	5	6	7	8	9	1	2	3	4	5	6	7	8	9	1	2	3	4	5	
May	4	5	6	7	8	9	1	2	3	4	5	6	7	8	9	1	2	3	4	5	6	7	8	9	1	2	3	4	5	6	7
Jun	5	6	7	8	9	1	2	3	4	5	6	7	8	9	1	2	3	4	5	6	7	8	9	1	2	3	4	5	6	7	
Jul	6	7	8	9	1	2	3	4	5	6	7	8	9	1	2	3	4	5	6	7	8	9	1	2	3	4	5	6	7	8	9
Aug	7	8	9	1	2	3	4	5	6	7	8	9	1	2	3	4	5	6	7	8	9	1	2	3	4	5	6	7	8	9	1
Sep	8	9	1	2	3	4	5	6	7	8	9	1	2	3	4	5	6	7	8	9	1	2	3	4	5	6	7	8	9	1	
Oct	9	1	2	3	4	5	6	7	8	9	1	2	3	4	5	6	7	8	9	1	2	3	4	5	6	7	8	9	1	2	3
Nov	1	2	3	4	6	7	8	9	1	2	3	4	5	6	7	8	9	1	2	3	4	5	6	7	8	9	1	2	3	4	
Dec	3	4	5	6	7	8	9	1	2	3	4	5	6	7	8	9	1	2	3	4	5	6	7	8	9	1	2	3	4	5	6

NOVEMBER 6

	1	2	3	4	5	6	7	8	9	10	11	12	13	14	15	16	17	18	19	20	21	22	23	24	25	26	27	28	29	30	31
Jan	1	2	3	4	5	6	7	8	9	1	2	3	4	5	6	7	8	9	1	2	3	4	5	6	7	8	9	1	2	3	4
Feb	2	3	4	5	6	7	8	9	1	2	3	4	5	6	7	8	9	1	2	3	4	5	6	7	8	9	1	2	3		
Mar	3	4	5	6	7	8	9	1	2	3	4	5	6	7	8	9	1	2	3	4	5	6	7	8	9	1	2	3	4	5	6
Apr	4	5	6	7	8	9	1	2	3	4	5	6	7	8	9	1	2	3	4	5	6	7	8	9	1	2	3	4	5	6	
May	5	6	7	8	9	1	2	3	4	5	6	7	8	9	1	2	3	4	5	6	7	8	9	1	2	3	4	5	6	7	8
Jun	6	7	8	9	1	2	3	4	5	6	7	8	9	1	2	3	4	5	6	7	8	9	1	2	3	4	5	6	7	8	
Jul	7	8	9	1	2	3	4	5	6	7	8	9	1	2	3	4	5	6	7	8	9	1	2	3	4	5	6	7	8	9	1
Aug	8	9	1	2	3	4	5	6	7	8	9	1	2	3	4	5	6	7	8	9	1	2	3	4	5	6	7	8	9	1	2
Sep	9	1	2	3	4	5	6	7	8	9	1	2	3	4	5	6	7	8	9	1	2	3	4	5	6	7	8	9	1	2	
Oct	1	2	3	4	5	6	7	8	9	1	2	3	4	5	6	7	8	9	1	2	3	4	5	6	7	8	9	1	2	3	4
Nov	2	3	4	5	6	8	9	1	2	3	4	5	6	7	8	9	1	2	3	4	5	6	7	8	9	1	2	3	4	5	
Dec	4	5	6	7	8	9	1	2	3	4	5	6	7	8	9	1	2	3	4	5	6	7	8	9	1	2	3	4	5	6	7

NOVEMBER 7

	1	2	3	4	5	6	7	8	9	10	11	12	13	14	15	16	17	18	19	20	21	22	23	24	25	26	27	28	29	30	31
Jan	2	3	4	5	6	7	8	9	1	2	3	4	5	6	7	8	9	1	2	3	4	5	6	7	8	9	1	2	3	4	5
Feb	3	4	5	6	7	8	9	1	2	3	4	5	6	7	8	9	1	2	3	4	5	6	7	8	9	1	2	3	4		
Mar	4	5	6	7	8	9	1	2	3	4	5	6	7	8	9	1	2	3	4	5	6	7	8	9	1	2	3	4	5	6	7
Apr	5	6	7	8	9	1	2	3	4	5	6	7	8	9	1	2	3	4	5	6	7	8	9	1	2	3	4	5	6	7	
May	6	7	8	9	1	2	3	4	5	6	7	8	9	1	2	3	4	5	6	7	8	9	1	2	3	4	5	6	7	8	9
Jun	7	8	9	1	2	3	4	5	6	7	8	9	1	2	3	4	5	6	7	8	9	1	2	3	4	5	6	7	8	9	
Jul	8	9	1	2	3	4	5	6	7	8	9	1	2	3	4	5	6	7	8	9	1	2	3	4	5	6	7	8	9	1	2
Aug	9	1	2	3	4	5	6	7	8	9	1	2	3	4	5	6	7	8	9	1	2	3	4	5	6	7	8	9	1	2	3
Sep	1	2	3	4	5	6	7	8	9	1	2	3	4	5	6	7	8	9	1	2	3	4	5	6	7	8	9	1	2	3	
Oct	2	3	4	5	6	7	8	9	1	2	3	4	5	6	7	8	9	1	2	3	4	5	6	7	8	9	1	2	3	4	5
Nov	3	4	5	6	7	8	1	2	3	4	5	6	7	8	9	1	2	3	4	5	6	7	8	9	1	2	3	4	5	6	
Dec	5	6	7	8	9	1	2	3	4	5	6	7	8	9	1	2	3	4	5	6	7	8	9	1	2	3	4	5	6	7	8

NOVEMBER 8

	1	2	3	4	5	6	7	8	9	10	11	12	13	14	15	16	17	18	19	20	21	22	23	24	25	26	27	28	29	30	31
Jan	3	4	5	6	7	8	9	1	2	3	4	5	6	7	8	9	1	2	3	4	5	6	7	8	9	1	2	3	4	5	6
Feb	4	5	6	7	8	9	1	2	3	4	5	6	7	8	9	1	2	3	4	5	6	7	8	9	1	2	3	4	5		
Mar	5	6	7	8	9	1	2	3	4	5	6	7	8	9	1	2	3	4	5	6	7	8	9	1	2	3	4	5	6	7	8
Apr	6	7	8	9	1	2	3	4	5	6	7	8	9	1	2	3	4	5	6	7	8	9	1	2	3	4	5	6	7	8	
May	7	8	9	1	2	3	4	5	6	7	8	9	1	2	3	4	5	6	7	8	9	1	2	3	4	5	6	7	8	9	1
Jun	8	9	1	2	3	4	5	6	7	8	9	1	2	3	4	5	6	7	8	9	1	2	3	4	5	6	7	8	9	1	
Jul	9	1	2	3	4	5	6	7	8	9	1	2	3	4	5	6	7	8	9	1	2	3	4	5	6	7	8	9	1	2	3
Aug	1	2	3	4	5	6	7	8	9	1	2	3	4	5	6	7	8	9	1	2	3	4	5	6	7	8	9	1	2	3	4
Sep	2	3	4	5	6	7	8	9	1	2	3	4	5	6	7	8	9	1	2	3	4	5	6	7	8	9	1	2	3	4	
Oct	3	4	5	6	7	8	9	1	2	3	4	5	6	7	8	9	1	2	3	4	5	6	7	8	9	1	2	3	4	5	6
Nov	4	5	6	7	8	9	1	3	4	5	6	7	8	9	1	2	3	4	5	6	7	8	9	1	2	3	4	5	6	7	
Dec	6	7	8	9	1	2	3	4	5	6	7	8	9	1	2	3	4	5	6	7	8	9	1	2	3	4	5	6	7	8	9

NOVEMBER 9

	1	2	3	4	5	6	7	8	9	10	11	12	13	14	15	16	17	18	19	20	21	22	23	24	25	26	27	28	29	30	31
Jan	4	5	6	7	8	9	1	2	3	4	5	6	7	8	9	1	2	3	4	5	6	7	8	9	1	2	3	4	5	6	7
Feb	5	6	7	8	9	1	2	3	4	5	6	7	8	9	1	2	3	4	5	6	7	8	9	1	2	3	4	5	6		
Mar	6	7	8	9	1	2	3	4	5	6	7	8	9	1	2	3	4	5	6	7	8	9	1	2	3	4	5	6	7	8	9
Apr	7	8	9	1	2	3	4	5	6	7	8	9	1	2	3	4	5	6	7	8	9	1	2	3	4	5	6	7	8	9	
May	8	9	1	2	3	4	5	6	7	8	9	1	2	3	4	5	6	7	8	9	1	2	3	4	5	6	7	8	9	1	2
Jun	9	1	2	3	4	5	6	7	8	9	1	2	3	4	5	6	7	8	9	1	2	3	4	5	6	7	8	9	1	2	
Jul	1	2	3	4	5	6	7	8	9	1	2	3	4	5	6	7	8	9	1	2	3	4	5	6	7	8	9	1	2	3	4
Aug	2	3	4	5	6	7	8	9	1	2	3	4	5	6	7	8	9	1	2	3	4	5	6	7	8	9	1	2	3	4	5
Sep	3	4	5	6	7	8	9	1	2	3	4	5	6	7	8	9	1	2	3	4	5	6	7	8	9	1	2	3	4	5	
Oct	4	5	6	7	8	9	1	2	3	4	5	6	7	8	9	1	2	3	4	5	6	7	8	9	1	2	3	4	5	6	7
Nov	5	6	7	8	9	1	2	3	5	6	7	8	9	1	2	3	4	5	6	7	8	9	1	2	3	4	5	6	7	8	
Dec	7	8	9	1	2	3	4	5	6	7	8	9	1	2	3	4	5	6	7	8	9	1	2	3	4	5	6	7	8	9	1

NOVEMBER 10

	1	2	3	4	5	6	7	8	9	10	11	12	13	14	15	16	17	18	19	20	21	22	23	24	25	26	27	28	29	30	31
Jan	5	6	7	8	9	1	2	3	4	5	6	7	8	9	1	2	3	4	5	6	7	8	9	1	2	3	4	5	6	7	8
Feb	6	7	8	9	1	2	3	4	5	6	7	8	9	1	2	3	4	5	6	7	8	9	1	2	3	4	5	6	7		
Mar	7	8	9	1	2	3	4	5	6	7	8	9	1	2	3	4	5	6	7	8	9	1	2	3	4	5	6	7	8	9	1
Apr	8	9	1	2	3	4	5	6	7	8	9	1	2	3	4	5	6	7	8	9	1	2	3	4	5	6	7	8	9	1	
May	9	1	2	3	4	5	6	7	8	9	1	2	3	4	5	6	7	8	9	1	2	3	4	5	6	7	8	9	1	2	3
Jun	1	2	3	4	5	6	7	8	9	1	2	3	4	5	6	7	8	9	1	2	3	4	5	6	7	8	9	1	2	3	
Jul	2	3	4	5	6	7	8	9	1	2	3	4	5	6	7	8	9	1	2	3	4	5	6	7	8	9	1	2	3	4	5
Aug	3	4	5	6	7	8	9	1	2	3	4	5	6	7	8	9	1	2	3	4	5	6	7	8	9	1	2	3	4	5	6
Sep	4	5	6	7	8	9	1	2	3	4	5	6	7	8	9	1	2	3	4	5	6	7	8	9	1	2	3	4	5	6	
Oct	5	6	7	8	9	1	2	3	4	5	6	7	8	9	1	2	3	4	5	6	7	8	9	1	2	3	4	5	6	7	8
Nov	6	7	8	9	1	2	3	4	5	7	8	9	1	2	3	4	5	6	7	8	9	1	2	3	4	5	6	7	8	9	
Dec	8	9	1	2	3	4	5	6	7	8	9	1	2	3	4	5	6	7	8	9	1	2	3	4	5	6	7	8	9	1	2

NOVEMBER 11

	1	2	3	4	5	6	7	8	9	10	11	12	13	14	15	16	17	18	19	20	21	22	23	24	25	26	27	28	29	30	31
Jan	6	7	8	9	1	2	3	4	5	6	7	8	9	1	2	3	4	5	6	7	8	9	1	2	3	4	5	6	7	8	9
Feb	7	8	9	1	2	3	4	5	6	7	8	9	1	2	3	4	5	6	7	8	9	1	2	3	4	5	6	7	8		
Mar	8	9	1	2	3	4	5	6	7	8	9	1	2	3	4	5	6	7	8	9	1	2	3	4	5	6	7	8	9	1	2
Apr	9	1	2	3	4	5	6	7	8	9	1	2	3	4	5	6	7	8	9	1	2	3	4	5	6	7	8	9	1	2	
May	1	2	3	4	5	6	7	8	9	1	2	3	4	5	6	7	8	9	1	2	3	4	5	6	7	8	9	1	2	3	4
Jun	2	3	4	5	6	7	8	9	1	2	3	4	5	6	7	8	9	1	2	3	4	5	6	7	8	9	1	2	3	4	
Jul	3	4	5	6	7	8	9	1	2	3	4	5	6	7	8	9	1	2	3	4	5	6	7	8	9	1	2	3	4	5	6
Aug	4	5	6	7	8	9	1	2	3	4	5	6	7	8	9	1	2	3	4	5	6	7	8	9	1	2	3	4	5	6	7
Sep	5	6	7	8	9	1	2	3	4	5	6	7	8	9	1	2	3	4	5	6	7	8	9	1	2	3	4	5	6	7	
Oct	6	7	8	9	1	2	3	4	5	6	7	8	9	1	2	3	4	5	6	7	8	9	1	2	3	4	5	6	7	8	9
Nov	7	8	9	1	2	3	4	5	6	7	9	1	2	3	4	5	6	7	8	9	1	2	3	4	5	6	7	8	9	1	
Dec	9	1	2	3	4	5	6	7	8	9	1	2	3	4	5	6	7	8	9	1	2	3	4	5	6	7	8	9	1	2	3

NOVEMBER 12

	1	2	3	4	5	6	7	8	9	10	11	12	13	14	15	16	17	18	19	20	21	22	23	24	25	26	27	28	29	30	31
Jan	7	8	9	1	2	3	4	5	6	7	8	9	1	2	3	4	5	6	7	8	9	1	2	3	4	5	6	7	8	9	1
Feb	8	9	1	2	3	4	5	6	7	8	9	1	2	3	4	5	6	7	8	9	1	2	3	4	5	6	7	8	9		
Mar	9	1	2	3	4	5	6	7	8	9	1	2	3	4	5	6	7	8	9	1	2	3	4	5	6	7	8	9	1	2	3
Apr	1	2	3	4	5	6	7	8	9	1	2	3	4	5	6	7	8	9	1	2	3	4	5	6	7	8	9	1	2	3	
May	2	3	4	5	6	7	8	9	1	2	3	4	5	6	7	8	9	1	2	3	4	5	6	7	8	9	1	2	3	4	5
Jun	3	4	5	6	7	8	9	1	2	3	4	5	6	7	8	9	1	2	3	4	5	6	7	8	9	1	2	3	4	5	
Jul	4	5	6	7	8	9	1	2	3	4	5	6	7	8	9	1	2	3	4	5	6	7	8	9	1	2	3	4	5	6	7
Aug	5	6	7	8	9	1	2	3	4	5	6	7	8	9	1	2	3	4	5	6	7	8	9	1	2	3	4	5	6	7	8
Sep	6	7	8	9	1	2	3	4	5	6	7	8	9	1	2	3	4	5	6	7	8	9	1	2	3	4	5	6	7	8	
Oct	7	8	9	1	2	3	4	5	6	7	8	9	1	2	3	4	5	6	7	8	9	1	2	3	4	5	6	7	8	9	1
Nov	8	9	1	2	3	4	5	6	7	8	9	2	3	4	5	6	7	8	9	1	2	3	4	5	6	7	8	9	1	2	
Dec	1	2	3	4	5	6	7	8	9	1	2	3	4	5	6	7	8	9	1	2	3	4	5	6	7	8	9	1	2	3	4

NOVEMBER 13

	1	2	3	4	5	6	7	8	9	10	11	12	13	14	15	16	17	18	19	20	21	22	23	24	25	26	27	28	29	30	31
Jan	8	9	1	2	3	4	5	6	7	8	9	1	2	3	4	5	6	7	8	9	1	2	3	4	5	6	7	8	9	1	2
Feb	9	1	2	3	4	5	6	7	8	9	1	2	3	4	5	6	7	8	9	1	2	3	4	5	6	7	8	9	1		
Mar	1	2	3	4	5	6	7	8	9	1	2	3	4	5	6	7	8	9	1	2	3	4	5	6	7	8	9	1	2	3	4
Apr	2	3	4	5	6	7	8	9	1	2	3	4	5	6	7	8	9	1	2	3	4	5	6	7	8	9	1	2	3	4	
May	3	4	5	6	7	8	9	1	2	3	4	5	6	7	8	9	1	2	3	4	5	6	7	8	9	1	2	3	4	5	6
Jun	4	5	6	7	8	9	1	2	3	4	5	6	7	8	9	1	2	3	4	5	6	7	8	9	1	2	3	4	5	6	
Jul	5	6	7	8	9	1	2	3	4	5	6	7	8	9	1	2	3	4	5	6	7	8	9	1	2	3	4	5	6	7	8
Aug	6	7	8	9	1	2	3	4	5	6	7	8	9	1	2	3	4	5	6	7	8	9	1	2	3	4	5	6	7	8	9
Sep	7	8	9	1	2	3	4	5	6	7	8	9	1	2	3	4	5	6	7	8	9	1	2	3	4	5	6	7	8	9	
Oct	8	9	1	2	3	4	5	6	7	8	9	1	2	3	4	5	6	7	8	9	1	2	3	4	5	6	7	8	9	1	2
Nov	9	1	2	3	4	5	6	7	8	9	1	2	4	5	6	7	8	9	1	2	3	4	5	6	7	8	9	1	2	3	
Dec	2	3	4	5	6	7	8	9	1	2	3	4	5	6	7	8	9	1	2	3	4	5	6	7	8	9	1	2	3	4	5

NOVEMBER 14

	1	2	3	4	5	6	7	8	9	10	11	12	13	14	15	16	17	18	19	20	21	22	23	24	25	26	27	28	29	30	31
Jan	9	1	2	3	4	5	6	7	8	9	1	2	3	4	5	6	7	8	9	1	2	3	4	5	6	7	8	9	1	2	3
Feb	1	2	3	4	5	6	7	8	9	1	2	3	4	5	6	7	8	9	1	2	3	4	5	6	7	8	9	1	2		
Mar	2	3	4	5	6	7	8	9	1	2	3	4	5	6	7	8	9	1	2	3	4	5	6	7	8	9	1	2	3	4	5
Apr	3	4	5	6	7	8	9	1	2	3	4	5	6	7	8	9	1	2	3	4	5	6	7	8	9	1	2	3	4	5	
May	4	5	6	7	8	9	1	2	3	4	5	6	7	8	9	1	2	3	4	5	6	7	8	9	1	2	3	4	5	6	7
Jun	5	6	7	8	9	1	2	3	4	5	6	7	8	9	1	2	3	4	5	6	7	8	9	1	2	3	4	5	6	7	
Jul	6	7	8	9	1	2	3	4	5	6	7	8	9	1	2	3	4	5	6	7	8	9	1	2	3	4	5	6	7	8	9
Aug	7	8	9	1	2	3	4	5	6	7	8	9	1	2	3	4	5	6	7	8	9	1	2	3	4	5	6	7	8	9	1
Sep	8	9	1	2	3	4	5	6	7	8	9	1	2	3	4	5	6	7	8	9	1	2	3	4	5	6	7	8	9	1	
Oct	9	1	2	3	4	5	6	7	8	9	1	2	3	4	5	6	7	8	9	1	2	3	4	5	6	7	8	9	1	2	3
Nov	1	2	3	4	5	6	7	8	9	1	2	3	4	6	7	8	9	1	2	3	4	5	6	7	8	9	1	2	3	4	
Dec	3	4	5	6	7	8	9	1	2	3	4	5	6	7	8	9	1	2	3	4	5	6	7	8	9	1	2	3	4	5	6

NOVEMBER 15

	1	2	3	4	5	6	7	8	9	10	11	12	13	14	15	16	17	18	19	20	21	22	23	24	25	26	27	28	29	30	31
Jan	1	2	3	4	5	6	7	8	9	1	2	3	4	5	6	7	8	9	1	2	3	4	5	6	7	8	9	1	2	3	4
Feb	2	3	4	5	6	7	8	9	1	2	3	4	5	6	7	8	9	1	2	3	4	5	6	7	8	9	1	2	3		
Mar	3	4	5	6	7	8	9	1	2	3	4	5	6	7	8	9	1	2	3	4	5	6	7	8	9	1	2	3	4	5	6
Apr	4	5	6	7	8	9	1	2	3	4	5	6	7	8	9	1	2	3	4	5	6	7	8	9	1	2	3	4	5	6	
May	5	6	7	8	9	1	2	3	4	5	6	7	8	9	1	2	3	4	5	6	7	8	9	1	2	3	4	5	6	7	8
Jun	6	7	8	9	1	2	3	4	5	6	7	8	9	1	2	3	4	5	6	7	8	9	1	2	3	4	5	6	7	8	
Jul	7	8	9	1	2	3	4	5	6	7	8	9	1	2	3	4	5	6	7	8	9	1	2	3	4	5	6	7	8	9	1
Aug	8	9	1	2	3	4	5	6	7	8	9	1	2	3	4	5	6	7	8	9	1	2	3	4	5	6	7	8	9	1	2
Sep	9	1	2	3	4	5	6	7	8	9	1	2	3	4	5	6	7	8	9	1	2	3	4	5	6	7	8	9	1	2	
Oct	1	2	3	4	5	6	7	8	9	1	2	3	4	5	6	7	8	9	1	2	3	4	5	6	7	8	9	1	2	3	4
Nov	2	3	4	5	6	7	8	9	1	2	3	4	5	6	8	9	1	2	3	4	5	6	7	8	9	1	2	3	4	5	
Dec	4	5	6	7	8	9	1	2	3	4	5	6	7	8	9	1	2	3	4	5	6	7	8	9	1	2	3	4	5	6	7

NOVEMBER 16

	1	2	3	4	5	6	7	8	9	10	11	12	13	14	15	16	17	18	19	20	21	22	23	24	25	26	27	28	29	30	31
Jan	2	3	4	5	6	7	8	9	1	2	3	4	5	6	7	8	9	1	2	3	4	5	6	7	8	9	1	2	3	4	5
Feb	3	4	5	6	7	8	9	1	2	3	4	5	6	7	8	9	1	2	3	4	5	6	7	8	9	1	2	3	4		
Mar	4	5	6	7	8	9	1	2	3	4	5	6	7	8	9	1	2	3	4	5	6	7	8	9	1	2	3	4	5	6	7
Apr	5	6	7	8	9	1	2	3	4	5	6	7	8	9	1	2	3	4	5	6	7	8	9	1	2	3	4	5	6	7	
May	6	7	8	9	1	2	3	4	5	6	7	8	9	1	2	3	4	5	6	7	8	9	1	2	3	4	5	6	7	8	9
Jun	7	8	9	1	2	3	4	5	6	7	8	9	1	2	3	4	5	6	7	8	9	1	2	3	4	5	6	7	8	9	
Jul	8	9	1	2	3	4	5	6	7	8	9	1	2	3	4	5	6	7	8	9	1	2	3	4	5	6	7	8	9	1	2
Aug	9	1	2	3	4	5	6	7	8	9	1	2	3	4	5	6	7	8	9	1	2	3	4	5	6	7	8	9	1	2	3
Sep	1	2	3	4	5	6	7	8	9	1	2	3	4	5	6	7	8	9	1	2	3	4	5	6	7	8	9	1	2	3	
Oct	2	3	4	5	6	7	8	9	1	2	3	4	5	6	7	8	9	1	2	3	4	5	6	7	8	9	1	2	3	4	5
Nov	3	4	5	6	7	8	9	1	2	3	4	5	6	7	8	1	2	3	4	5	6	7	8	9	1	2	3	4	5	6	
Dec	5	6	7	8	9	1	2	3	4	5	6	7	8	9	1	2	3	4	5	6	7	8	9	1	2	3	4	5	6	7	8

NOVEMBER 17

	1	2	3	4	5	6	7	8	9	10	11	12	13	14	15	16	17	18	19	20	21	22	23	24	25	26	27	28	29	30	31
Jan	3	4	5	6	7	8	9	1	2	3	4	5	6	7	8	9	1	2	3	4	5	6	7	8	9	1	2	3	4	5	6
Feb	4	5	6	7	8	9	1	2	3	4	5	6	7	8	9	1	2	3	4	5	6	7	8	9	1	2	3	4	5		
Mar	5	6	7	8	9	1	2	3	4	5	6	7	8	9	1	2	3	4	5	6	7	8	9	1	2	3	4	5	6	7	8
Apr	6	7	8	9	1	2	3	4	5	6	7	8	9	1	2	3	4	5	6	7	8	9	1	2	3	4	5	6	7	8	
May	7	8	9	1	2	3	4	5	6	7	8	9	1	2	3	4	5	6	7	8	9	1	2	3	4	5	6	7	8	9	1
Jun	8	9	1	2	3	4	5	6	7	8	9	1	2	3	4	5	6	7	8	9	1	2	3	4	5	6	7	8	9	1	
Jul	9	1	2	3	4	5	6	7	8	9	1	2	3	4	5	6	7	8	9	1	2	3	4	5	6	7	8	9	1	2	3
Aug	1	2	3	4	5	6	7	8	9	1	2	3	4	5	6	7	8	9	1	2	3	4	5	6	7	8	9	1	2	3	4
Sep	2	3	4	5	6	7	8	9	1	2	3	4	5	6	7	8	9	1	2	3	4	5	6	7	8	9	1	2	3	4	
Oct	3	4	5	6	7	8	9	1	2	3	4	5	6	7	8	9	1	2	3	4	5	6	7	8	9	1	2	3	4	5	6
Nov	4	5	6	7	8	9	1	2	3	4	5	6	7	8	9	1	3	4	5	6	7	8	9	1	2	3	4	5	6	7	
Dec	6	7	8	9	1	2	3	4	5	6	7	8	9	1	2	3	4	5	6	7	8	9	1	2	3	4	5	6	7	8	9

NOVEMBER 18

	1	2	3	4	5	6	7	8	9	10	11	12	13	14	15	16	17	18	19	20	21	22	23	24	25	26	27	28	29	30	31
Jan	4	5	6	7	8	9	1	2	3	4	5	6	7	8	9	1	2	3	4	5	6	7	8	9	1	2	3	4	5	6	7
Feb	5	6	7	8	9	1	2	3	4	5	6	7	8	9	1	2	3	4	5	6	7	8	9	1	2	3	4	5	6		
Mar	6	7	8	9	1	2	3	4	5	6	7	8	9	1	2	3	4	5	6	7	8	9	1	2	3	4	5	6	7	8	9
Apr	7	8	9	1	2	3	4	5	6	7	8	9	1	2	3	4	5	6	7	8	9	1	2	3	4	5	6	7	8	9	
May	8	9	1	2	3	4	5	6	7	8	9	1	2	3	4	5	6	7	8	9	1	2	3	4	5	6	7	8	9	1	2
Jun	9	1	2	3	4	5	6	7	8	9	1	2	3	4	5	6	7	8	9	1	2	3	4	5	6	7	8	9	1	2	
Jul	1	2	3	4	5	6	7	8	9	1	2	3	4	5	6	7	8	9	1	2	3	4	5	6	7	8	9	1	2	3	4
Aug	2	3	4	5	6	7	8	9	1	2	3	4	5	6	7	8	9	1	2	3	4	5	6	7	8	9	1	2	3	4	5
Sep	3	4	5	6	7	8	9	1	2	3	4	5	6	7	8	9	1	2	3	4	5	6	7	8	9	1	2	3	4	5	
Oct	4	5	6	7	8	9	1	2	3	4	5	6	7	8	9	1	2	3	4	5	6	7	8	9	1	2	3	4	5	6	7
Nov	5	6	7	8	9	1	2	3	4	5	6	7	8	9	1	2	3	5	6	7	8	9	1	2	3	4	5	6	7	8	
Dec	7	8	9	1	2	3	4	5	6	7	8	9	1	2	3	4	5	6	7	8	9	1	2	3	4	5	6	7	8	9	1

NOVEMBER 19

	1	2	3	4	5	6	7	8	9	10	11	12	13	14	15	16	17	18	19	20	21	22	23	24	25	26	27	28	29	30	31
Jan	5	6	7	8	9	1	2	3	4	5	6	7	8	9	1	2	3	4	5	6	7	8	9	1	2	3	4	5	6	7	8
Feb	6	7	8	9	1	2	3	4	5	6	7	8	9	1	2	3	4	5	6	7	8	9	1	2	3	4	5	6	7		
Mar	7	8	9	1	2	3	4	5	6	7	8	9	1	2	3	4	5	6	7	8	9	1	2	3	4	5	6	7	8	9	1
Apr	8	9	1	2	3	4	5	6	7	8	9	1	2	3	4	5	6	7	8	9	1	2	3	4	5	6	7	8	9	1	
May	9	1	2	3	4	5	6	7	8	9	1	2	3	4	5	6	7	8	9	1	2	3	4	5	6	7	8	9	1	2	3
Jun	1	2	3	4	5	6	7	8	9	1	2	3	4	5	6	7	8	9	1	2	3	4	5	6	7	8	9	1	2	3	
Jul	2	3	4	5	6	7	8	9	1	2	3	4	5	6	7	8	9	1	2	3	4	5	6	7	8	9	1	2	3	4	5
Aug	3	4	5	6	7	8	9	1	2	3	4	5	6	7	8	9	1	2	3	4	5	6	7	8	9	1	2	3	4	5	6
Sep	4	5	6	7	8	9	1	2	3	4	5	6	7	8	9	1	2	3	4	5	6	7	8	9	1	2	3	4	5	6	
Oct	5	6	7	8	9	1	2	3	4	5	6	7	8	9	1	2	3	4	5	6	7	8	9	1	2	3	4	5	6	7	8
Nov	6	7	8	9	1	2	3	4	5	6	7	8	9	1	2	3	4	5	7	8	9	1	2	3	4	5	6	7	8	9	
Dec	8	9	1	2	3	4	5	6	7	8	9	1	2	3	4	5	6	7	8	9	1	2	3	4	5	6	7	8	9	1	2

NOVEMBER 20

	1	2	3	4	5	6	7	8	9	10	11	12	13	14	15	16	17	18	19	20	21	22	23	24	25	26	27	28	29	30	31
Jan	6	7	8	9	1	2	3	4	5	6	7	8	9	1	2	3	4	5	6	7	8	9	1	2	3	4	5	6	7	8	9
Feb	7	8	9	1	2	3	4	5	6	7	8	9	1	2	3	4	5	6	7	8	9	1	2	3	4	5	6	7	8		
Mar	8	9	1	2	3	4	5	6	7	8	9	1	2	3	4	5	6	7	8	9	1	2	3	4	5	6	7	8	9	1	2
Apr	9	1	2	3	4	5	6	7	8	9	1	2	3	4	5	6	7	8	9	1	2	3	4	5	6	7	8	9	1	2	
May	1	2	3	4	5	6	7	8	9	1	2	3	4	5	6	7	8	9	1	2	3	4	5	6	7	8	9	1	2	3	4
Jun	2	3	4	5	6	7	8	9	1	2	3	4	5	6	7	8	9	1	2	3	4	5	6	7	8	9	1	2	3	4	
Jul	3	4	5	6	7	8	9	1	2	3	4	5	6	7	8	9	1	2	3	4	5	6	7	8	9	1	2	3	4	5	6
Aug	4	5	6	7	8	9	1	2	3	4	5	6	7	8	9	1	2	3	4	5	6	7	8	9	1	2	3	4	5	6	7
Sep	5	6	7	8	9	1	2	3	4	5	6	7	8	9	1	2	3	4	5	6	7	8	9	1	2	3	4	5	6	7	
Oct	6	7	8	9	1	2	3	4	5	6	7	8	9	1	2	3	4	5	6	7	8	9	1	2	3	4	5	6	7	8	9
Nov	7	8	9	1	2	3	4	5	6	7	8	9	1	2	3	4	5	6	7	9	1	2	3	4	5	6	7	8	9	1	
Dec	9	1	2	3	4	5	6	7	8	9	1	2	3	4	5	6	7	8	9	1	2	3	4	5	6	7	8	9	1	2	3

NOVEMBER 21

	1	2	3	4	5	6	7	8	9	10	11	12	13	14	15	16	17	18	19	20	21	22	23	24	25	26	27	28	29	30	31
Jan	7	8	9	1	2	3	4	5	6	7	8	9	1	2	3	4	5	6	7	8	9	1	2	3	4	5	6	7	8	9	1
Feb	8	9	1	2	3	4	5	6	7	8	9	1	2	3	4	5	6	7	8	9	1	2	3	4	5	6	7	8	9		
Mar	9	1	2	3	4	5	6	7	8	9	1	2	3	4	5	6	7	8	9	1	2	3	4	5	6	7	8	9	1	2	3
Apr	1	2	3	4	5	6	7	8	9	1	2	3	4	5	6	7	8	9	1	2	3	4	5	6	7	8	9	1	2	3	
May	2	3	4	5	6	7	8	9	1	2	3	4	5	6	7	8	9	1	2	3	4	5	6	7	8	9	1	2	3	4	5
Jun	3	4	5	6	7	8	9	1	2	3	4	5	6	7	8	9	1	2	3	4	5	6	7	8	9	1	2	3	4	5	
Jul	4	5	6	7	8	9	1	2	3	4	5	6	7	8	9	1	2	3	4	5	6	7	8	9	1	2	3	4	5	6	7
Aug	5	6	7	8	9	1	2	3	4	5	6	7	8	9	1	2	3	4	5	6	7	8	9	1	2	3	4	5	6	7	8
Sep	6	7	8	9	1	2	3	4	5	6	7	8	9	1	2	3	4	5	6	7	8	9	1	2	3	4	5	6	7	8	
Oct	7	8	9	1	2	3	4	5	6	7	8	9	1	2	3	4	5	6	7	8	9	1	2	3	4	5	6	7	8	9	1
Nov	8	9	1	2	3	4	5	6	7	8	9	1	2	3	4	5	6	7	8	9	2	3	4	5	6	7	8	9	1	2	
Dec	1	2	3	4	5	6	7	8	9	1	2	3	4	5	6	7	8	9	1	2	3	4	5	6	7	8	9	1	2	3	4

NOVEMBER 22

	1	2	3	4	5	6	7	8	9	10	11	12	13	14	15	16	17	18	19	20	21	22	23	24	25	26	27	28	29	30	31
Jan	8	9	1	2	3	4	5	6	7	8	9	1	2	3	4	5	6	7	8	9	1	2	3	4	5	6	7	8	9	1	2
Feb	9	1	2	3	4	5	6	7	8	9	1	2	3	4	5	6	7	8	9	1	2	3	4	5	6	7	8	9	1		
Mar	1	2	3	4	5	6	7	8	9	1	2	3	4	5	6	7	8	9	1	2	3	4	5	6	7	8	9	1	2	3	4
Apr	2	3	4	5	6	7	8	9	1	2	3	4	5	6	7	8	9	1	2	3	4	5	6	7	8	9	1	2	3	4	
May	3	4	5	6	7	8	9	1	2	3	4	5	6	7	8	9	1	2	3	4	5	6	7	8	9	1	2	3	4	5	6
Jun	4	5	6	7	8	9	1	2	3	4	5	6	7	8	9	1	2	3	4	5	6	7	8	9	1	2	3	4	5	6	
Jul	5	6	7	8	9	1	2	3	4	5	6	7	8	9	1	2	3	4	5	6	7	8	9	1	2	3	4	5	6	7	8
Aug	6	7	8	9	1	2	3	4	5	6	7	8	9	1	2	3	4	5	6	7	8	9	1	2	3	4	5	6	7	8	9
Sep	7	8	9	1	2	3	4	5	6	7	8	9	1	2	3	4	5	6	7	8	9	1	2	3	4	5	6	7	8	9	
Oct	8	9	1	2	3	4	5	6	7	8	9	1	2	3	4	5	6	7	8	9	1	2	3	4	5	6	7	8	9	1	2
Nov	9	1	2	3	4	5	6	7	8	9	1	2	3	4	5	6	7	8	9	1	2	4	5	6	7	8	9	1	2	3	
Dec	2	3	4	5	6	7	8	9	1	2	3	4	5	6	7	8	9	1	2	3	4	5	6	7	8	9	1	2	3	4	5

NOVEMBER 23

	1	2	3	4	5	6	7	8	9	10	11	12	13	14	15	16	17	18	19	20	21	22	23	24	25	26	27	28	29	30	31
Jan	9	1	2	3	4	5	6	7	8	9	1	2	3	4	5	6	7	8	9	1	2	3	4	5	6	7	8	9	1	2	3
Feb	1	2	3	4	5	6	7	8	9	1	2	3	4	5	6	7	8	9	1	2	3	4	5	6	7	8	9	1	2		
Mar	2	3	4	5	6	7	8	9	1	2	3	4	5	6	7	8	9	1	2	3	4	5	6	7	8	9	1	2	3	4	5
Apr	3	4	5	6	7	8	9	1	2	3	4	5	6	7	8	9	1	2	3	4	5	6	7	8	9	1	2	3	4	5	
May	4	5	6	7	8	9	1	2	3	4	5	6	7	8	9	1	2	3	4	5	6	7	8	9	1	2	3	4	5	6	7
Jun	5	6	7	8	9	1	2	3	4	5	6	7	8	9	1	2	3	4	5	6	7	8	9	1	2	3	4	5	6	7	
Jul	6	7	8	9	1	2	3	4	5	6	7	8	9	1	2	3	4	5	6	7	8	9	1	2	3	4	5	6	7	8	9
Aug	7	8	9	1	2	3	4	5	6	7	8	9	1	2	3	4	5	6	7	8	9	1	2	3	4	5	6	7	8	9	1
Sep	8	9	1	2	3	4	5	6	7	8	9	1	2	3	4	5	6	7	8	9	1	2	3	4	5	6	7	8	9	1	
Oct	9	1	2	3	4	5	6	7	8	9	1	2	3	4	5	6	7	8	9	1	2	3	4	5	6	7	8	9	1	2	3
Nov	1	2	3	4	5	6	7	8	9	1	2	3	4	5	6	7	8	9	1	2	3	4	6	7	8	9	1	2	3	4	
Dec	3	4	5	6	7	8	9	1	2	3	4	5	6	7	8	9	1	2	3	4	5	6	7	8	9	1	2	3	4	5	6

NOVEMBER 24

	1	2	3	4	5	6	7	8	9	10	11	12	13	14	15	16	17	18	19	20	21	22	23	24	25	26	27	28	29	30	31
Jan	1	2	3	4	5	6	7	8	9	1	2	3	4	5	6	7	8	9	1	2	3	4	5	6	7	8	9	1	2	3	4
Feb	2	3	4	5	6	7	8	9	1	2	3	4	5	6	7	8	9	1	2	3	4	5	6	7	8	9	1	2	3		
Mar	3	4	5	6	7	8	9	1	2	3	4	5	6	7	8	9	1	2	3	4	5	6	7	8	9	1	2	3	4	5	6
Apr	4	5	6	7	8	9	1	2	3	4	5	6	7	8	9	1	2	3	4	5	6	7	8	9	1	2	3	4	5	6	
May	5	6	7	8	9	1	2	3	4	5	6	7	8	9	1	2	3	4	5	6	7	8	9	1	2	3	4	5	6	7	8
Jun	6	7	8	9	1	2	3	4	5	6	7	8	9	1	2	3	4	5	6	7	8	9	1	2	3	4	5	6	7	8	
Jul	7	8	9	1	2	3	4	5	6	7	8	9	1	2	3	4	5	6	7	8	9	1	2	3	4	5	6	7	8	9	1
Aug	8	9	1	2	3	4	5	6	7	8	9	1	2	3	4	5	6	7	8	9	1	2	3	4	5	6	7	8	9	1	2
Sep	9	1	2	3	4	5	6	7	8	9	1	2	3	4	5	6	7	8	9	1	2	3	4	5	6	7	8	9	1	2	
Oct	1	2	3	4	5	6	7	8	9	1	2	3	4	5	6	7	8	9	1	2	3	4	5	6	7	8	9	1	2	3	4
Nov	2	3	4	5	6	7	8	9	1	2	3	4	5	6	7	8	9	1	2	3	4	5	6	8	9	1	2	3	4	5	
Dec	4	5	6	7	8	9	1	2	3	4	5	6	7	8	9	1	2	3	4	5	6	7	8	9	1	2	3	4	5	6	7

NOVEMBER 25

	1	2	3	4	5	6	7	8	9	10	11	12	13	14	15	16	17	18	19	20	21	22	23	24	25	26	27	28	29	30	31
Jan	2	3	4	5	6	7	8	9	1	2	3	4	5	6	7	8	9	1	2	3	4	5	6	7	8	9	1	2	3	4	5
Feb	3	4	5	6	7	8	9	1	2	3	4	5	6	7	8	9	1	2	3	4	5	6	7	8	9	1	2	3	4		
Mar	4	5	6	7	8	9	1	2	3	4	5	6	7	8	9	1	2	3	4	5	6	7	8	9	1	2	3	4	5	6	7
Apr	5	6	7	8	9	1	2	3	4	5	6	7	8	9	1	2	3	4	5	6	7	8	9	1	2	3	4	5	6	7	
May	6	7	8	9	1	2	3	4	5	6	7	8	9	1	2	3	4	5	6	7	8	9	1	2	3	4	5	6	7	8	9
Jun	7	8	9	1	2	3	4	5	6	7	8	9	1	2	3	4	5	6	7	8	9	1	2	3	4	5	6	7	8	9	
Jul	8	9	1	2	3	4	5	6	7	8	9	1	2	3	4	5	6	7	8	9	1	2	3	4	5	6	7	8	9	1	2
Aug	9	1	2	3	4	5	6	7	8	9	1	2	3	4	5	6	7	8	9	1	2	3	4	5	6	7	8	9	1	2	3
Sep	1	2	3	4	5	6	7	8	9	1	2	3	4	5	6	7	8	9	1	2	3	4	5	6	7	8	9	1	2	3	
Oct	2	3	4	5	6	7	8	9	1	2	3	4	5	6	7	8	9	1	2	3	4	5	6	7	8	9	1	2	3	4	5
Nov	3	4	5	6	7	8	9	1	2	3	4	5	6	7	8	9	1	2	3	4	5	6	7	8	1	2	3	4	5	6	
Dec	5	6	7	8	9	1	2	3	4	5	6	7	8	9	1	2	3	4	5	6	7	8	9	1	2	3	4	5	6	7	8

NOVEMBER 26

	1	2	3	4	5	6	7	8	9	10	11	12	13	14	15	16	17	18	19	20	21	22	23	24	25	26	27	28	29	30	31
Jan	3	4	5	6	7	8	9	1	2	3	4	5	6	7	8	9	1	2	3	4	5	6	7	8	9	1	2	3	4	5	6
Feb	4	5	6	7	8	9	1	2	3	4	5	6	7	8	9	1	2	3	4	5	6	7	8	9	1	2	3	4	5		
Mar	5	6	7	8	9	1	2	3	4	5	6	7	8	9	1	2	3	4	5	6	7	8	9	1	2	3	4	5	6	7	8
Apr	6	7	8	9	1	2	3	4	5	6	7	8	9	1	2	3	4	5	6	7	8	9	1	2	3	4	5	6	7	8	
May	7	8	9	1	2	3	4	5	6	7	8	9	1	2	3	4	5	6	7	8	9	1	2	3	4	5	6	7	8	9	1
Jun	8	9	1	2	3	4	5	6	7	8	9	1	2	3	4	5	6	7	8	9	1	2	3	4	5	6	7	8	9	1	
Jul	9	1	2	3	4	5	6	7	8	9	1	2	3	4	5	6	7	8	9	1	2	3	4	5	6	7	8	9	1	2	3
Aug	1	2	3	4	5	6	7	8	9	1	2	3	4	5	6	7	8	9	1	2	3	4	5	6	7	8	9	1	2	3	4
Sep	2	3	4	5	6	7	8	9	1	2	3	4	5	6	7	8	9	1	2	3	4	5	6	7	8	9	1	2	3	4	
Oct	3	4	5	6	7	8	9	1	2	3	4	5	6	7	8	9	1	2	3	4	5	6	7	8	9	1	2	3	4	5	6
Nov	4	5	6	7	8	9	1	2	3	4	5	6	7	8	9	1	2	3	4	5	6	7	8	9	1	3	4	5	6	7	
Dec	6	7	8	9	1	2	3	4	5	6	7	8	9	1	2	3	4	5	6	7	8	9	1	2	3	4	5	6	7	8	9

NOVEMBER 27

	1	2	3	4	5	6	7	8	9	10	11	12	13	14	15	16	17	18	19	20	21	22	23	24	25	26	27	28	29	30	31
Jan	4	5	6	7	8	9	1	2	3	4	5	6	7	8	9	1	2	3	4	5	6	7	8	9	1	2	3	4	5	6	7
Feb	5	6	7	8	9	1	2	3	4	5	6	7	8	9	1	2	3	4	5	6	7	8	9	1	2	3	4	5	6		
Mar	6	7	8	9	1	2	3	4	5	6	7	8	9	1	2	3	4	5	6	7	8	9	1	2	3	4	5	6	7	8	9
Apr	7	8	9	1	2	3	4	5	6	7	8	9	1	2	3	4	5	6	7	8	9	1	2	3	4	5	6	7	8	9	
May	8	9	1	2	3	4	5	6	7	8	9	1	2	3	4	5	6	7	8	9	1	2	3	4	5	6	7	8	9	1	2
Jun	9	1	2	3	4	5	6	7	8	9	1	2	3	4	5	6	7	8	9	1	2	3	4	5	6	7	8	9	1	2	
Jul	1	2	3	4	5	6	7	8	9	1	2	3	4	5	6	7	8	9	1	2	3	4	5	6	7	8	9	1	2	3	4
Aug	2	3	4	5	6	7	8	9	1	2	3	4	5	6	7	8	9	1	2	3	4	5	6	7	8	9	1	2	3	4	5
Sep	3	4	5	6	7	8	9	1	2	3	4	5	6	7	8	9	1	2	3	4	5	6	7	8	9	1	2	3	4	5	
Oct	4	5	6	7	8	9	1	2	3	4	5	6	7	8	9	1	2	3	4	5	6	7	8	9	1	2	3	4	5	6	7
Nov	5	6	7	8	9	1	2	3	4	5	6	7	8	9	1	2	3	4	5	6	7	8	9	1	2	3	5	6	7	8	
Dec	7	8	9	1	2	3	4	5	6	7	8	9	1	2	3	4	5	6	7	8	9	1	2	3	4	5	6	7	8	9	1

NOVEMBER 28

	1	2	3	4	5	6	7	8	9	10	11	12	13	14	15	16	17	18	19	20	21	22	23	24	25	26	27	28	29	30	31
Jan	5	6	7	8	9	1	2	3	4	5	6	7	8	9	1	2	3	4	5	6	7	8	9	1	2	3	4	5	6	7	8
Feb	6	7	8	9	1	2	3	4	5	6	7	8	9	1	2	3	4	5	6	7	8	9	1	2	3	4	5	6	7		
Mar	7	8	9	1	2	3	4	5	6	7	8	9	1	2	3	4	5	6	7	8	9	1	2	3	4	5	6	7	8	9	1
Apr	8	9	1	2	3	4	5	6	7	8	9	1	2	3	4	5	6	7	8	9	1	2	3	4	5	6	7	8	9	1	
May	9	1	2	3	4	5	6	7	8	9	1	2	3	4	5	6	7	8	9	1	2	3	4	5	6	7	8	9	1	2	3
Jun	1	2	3	4	5	6	7	8	9	1	2	3	4	5	6	7	8	9	1	2	3	4	5	6	7	8	9	1	2	3	
Jul	2	3	4	5	6	7	8	9	1	2	3	4	5	6	7	8	9	1	2	3	4	5	6	7	8	9	1	2	3	4	5
Aug	3	4	5	6	7	8	9	1	2	3	4	5	6	7	8	9	1	2	3	4	5	6	7	8	9	1	2	3	4	5	6
Sep	4	5	6	7	8	9	1	2	3	4	5	6	7	8	9	1	2	3	4	5	6	7	8	9	1	2	3	4	5	6	
Oct	5	6	7	8	9	1	2	3	4	5	6	7	8	9	1	2	3	4	5	6	7	8	9	1	2	3	4	5	6	7	8
Nov	6	7	8	9	1	2	3	4	5	6	7	8	9	1	2	3	4	5	6	7	8	9	1	2	3	4	5	7	8	9	
Dec	8	9	1	2	3	4	5	6	7	8	9	1	2	3	4	5	6	7	8	9	1	2	3	4	5	6	7	8	9	1	2

NOVEMBER 29

	1	2	3	4	5	6	7	8	9	10	11	12	13	14	15	16	17	18	19	20	21	22	23	24	25	26	27	28	29	30	31
Jan	6	7	8	9	1	2	3	4	5	6	7	8	9	1	2	3	4	5	6	7	8	9	1	2	3	4	5	6	7	8	9
Feb	7	8	9	1	2	3	4	5	6	7	8	9	1	2	3	4	5	6	7	8	9	1	2	3	4	5	6	7	8		
Mar	8	9	1	2	3	4	5	6	7	8	9	1	2	3	4	5	6	7	8	9	1	2	3	4	5	6	7	8	9	1	2
Apr	9	1	2	3	4	5	6	7	8	9	1	2	3	4	5	6	7	8	9	1	2	3	4	5	6	7	8	9	1	2	
May	1	2	3	4	5	6	7	8	9	1	2	3	4	5	6	7	8	9	1	2	3	4	5	6	7	8	9	1	2	3	4
Jun	2	3	4	5	6	7	8	9	1	2	3	4	5	6	7	8	9	1	2	3	4	5	6	7	8	9	1	2	3	4	
Jul	3	4	5	6	7	8	9	1	2	3	4	5	6	7	8	9	1	2	3	4	5	6	7	8	9	1	2	3	4	5	6
Aug	4	5	6	7	8	9	1	2	3	4	5	6	7	8	9	1	2	3	4	5	6	7	8	9	1	2	3	4	5	6	7
Sep	5	6	7	8	9	1	2	3	4	5	6	7	8	9	1	2	3	4	5	6	7	8	9	1	2	3	4	5	6	7	
Oct	6	7	8	9	1	2	3	4	5	6	7	8	9	1	2	3	4	5	6	7	8	9	1	2	3	4	5	6	7	8	9
Nov	7	8	9	1	2	3	4	5	6	7	8	9	1	2	3	4	5	6	7	8	9	1	2	3	4	5	6	7	9	1	
Dec	9	1	2	3	4	5	6	7	8	9	1	2	3	4	5	6	7	8	9	1	2	3	4	5	6	7	8	9	1	2	3

NOVEMBER 30

	1	2	3	4	5	6	7	8	9	10	11	12	13	14	15	16	17	18	19	20	21	22	23	24	25	26	27	28	29	30	31
Jan	7	8	9	1	2	3	4	5	6	7	8	9	1	2	3	4	5	6	7	8	9	1	2	3	4	5	6	7	8	9	1
Feb	8	9	1	2	3	4	5	6	7	8	9	1	2	3	4	5	6	7	8	9	1	2	3	4	5	6	7	8	9		
Mar	9	1	2	3	4	5	6	7	8	9	1	2	3	4	5	6	7	8	9	1	2	3	4	5	6	7	8	9	1	2	3
Apr	1	2	3	4	5	6	7	8	9	1	2	3	4	5	6	7	8	9	1	2	3	4	5	6	7	8	9	1	2	3	
May	2	3	4	5	6	7	8	9	1	2	3	4	5	6	7	8	9	1	2	3	4	5	6	7	8	9	1	2	3	4	5
Jun	3	4	5	6	7	8	9	1	2	3	4	5	6	7	8	9	1	2	3	4	5	6	7	8	9	1	2	3	4	5	
Jul	4	5	6	7	8	9	1	2	3	4	5	6	7	8	9	1	2	3	4	5	6	7	8	9	1	2	3	4	5	6	7
Aug	5	6	7	8	9	1	2	3	4	5	6	7	8	9	1	2	3	4	5	6	7	8	9	1	2	3	4	5	6	7	8
Sep	6	7	8	9	1	2	3	4	5	6	7	8	9	1	2	3	4	5	6	7	8	9	1	2	3	4	5	6	7	8	
Oct	7	8	9	1	2	3	4	5	6	7	8	9	1	2	3	4	5	6	7	8	9	1	2	3	4	5	6	7	8	9	1
Nov	8	9	1	2	3	4	5	6	7	8	9	1	2	3	4	5	6	7	8	9	1	2	3	4	5	6	7	8	9	2	
Dec	1	2	3	4	5	6	7	8	9	1	2	3	4	5	6	7	8	9	1	2	3	4	5	6	7	8	9	1	2	3	4

DECEMBER 1

	1	2	3	4	5	6	7	8	9	10	11	12	13	14	15	16	17	18	19	20	21	22	23	24	25	26	27	28	29	30	31
Jan	6	7	8	9	1	2	3	4	5	6	7	8	9	1	2	3	4	5	6	7	8	9	1	2	3	4	5	6	7	8	9
Feb	7	8	9	1	2	3	4	5	6	7	8	9	1	2	3	4	5	6	7	8	9	1	2	3	4	5	6	7	8		
Mar	8	9	1	2	3	4	5	6	7	8	9	1	2	3	4	5	6	7	8	9	1	2	3	4	5	6	7	8	9	1	2
Apr	9	1	2	3	4	5	6	7	8	9	1	2	3	4	5	6	7	8	9	1	2	3	4	5	6	7	8	9	1	2	
May	1	2	3	4	5	6	7	8	9	1	2	3	4	5	6	7	8	9	1	2	3	4	5	6	7	8	9	1	2	3	4
Jun	2	3	4	5	6	7	8	9	1	2	3	4	5	6	7	8	9	1	2	3	4	5	6	7	8	9	1	2	3	4	
Jul	3	4	5	6	7	8	9	1	2	3	4	5	6	7	8	9	1	2	3	4	5	6	7	8	9	1	2	3	4	5	6
Aug	4	5	6	7	8	9	1	2	3	4	5	6	7	8	9	1	2	3	4	5	6	7	8	9	1	2	3	4	5	6	7
Sep	5	6	7	8	9	1	2	3	4	5	6	7	8	9	1	2	3	4	5	6	7	8	9	1	2	3	4	5	6	7	
Oct	6	7	8	9	1	2	3	4	5	6	7	8	9	1	2	3	4	5	6	7	8	9	1	2	3	4	5	6	7	8	9
Nov	7	8	9	1	2	3	4	5	6	7	8	9	1	2	3	4	5	6	7	8	9	1	2	3	4	5	6	7	8	9	
Dec	9	1	2	3	4	5	6	7	8	9	1	2	3	4	5	6	7	8	9	1	2	3	4	5	6	7	8	9	1	2	3

DECEMBER 2

	1	2	3	4	5	6	7	8	9	10	11	12	13	14	15	16	17	18	19	20	21	22	23	24	25	26	27	28	29	30	31
Jan	7	8	9	1	2	3	4	5	6	7	8	9	1	2	3	4	5	6	7	8	9	1	2	3	4	5	6	7	8	9	1
Feb	8	9	1	2	3	4	5	6	7	8	9	1	2	3	4	5	6	7	8	9	1	2	3	4	5	6	7	8	9		
Mar	9	1	2	3	4	5	6	7	8	9	1	2	3	4	5	6	7	8	9	1	2	3	4	5	6	7	8	9	1	2	3
Apr	1	2	3	4	5	6	7	8	9	1	2	3	4	5	6	7	8	9	1	2	3	4	5	6	7	8	9	1	2	3	
May	2	3	4	5	6	7	8	9	1	2	3	4	5	6	7	8	9	1	2	3	4	5	6	7	8	9	1	2	3	4	5
Jun	3	4	5	6	7	8	9	1	2	3	4	5	6	7	8	9	1	2	3	4	5	6	7	8	9	1	2	3	4	5	
Jul	4	5	6	7	8	9	1	2	3	4	5	6	7	8	9	1	2	3	4	5	6	7	8	9	1	2	3	4	5	6	7
Aug	5	6	7	8	9	1	2	3	4	5	6	7	8	9	1	2	3	4	5	6	7	8	9	1	2	3	4	5	6	7	8
Sep	6	7	8	9	1	2	3	4	5	6	7	8	9	1	2	3	4	5	6	7	8	9	1	2	3	4	5	6	7	8	
Oct	7	8	9	1	2	3	4	5	6	7	8	9	1	2	3	4	5	6	7	8	9	1	2	3	4	5	6	7	8	9	1
Nov	8	9	1	2	3	4	5	6	7	8	9	1	2	3	4	5	6	7	8	9	1	2	3	4	5	6	7	8	9	1	
Dec	9	2	3	4	5	6	7	8	9	1	2	3	4	5	6	7	8	9	1	2	3	4	5	6	7	8	9	1	2	3	4

DECEMBER 3

	1	2	3	4	5	6	7	8	9	10	11	12	13	14	15	16	17	18	19	20	21	22	23	24	25	26	27	28	29	30	31
Jan	8	9	1	2	3	4	5	6	7	8	9	1	2	3	4	5	6	7	8	9	1	2	3	4	5	6	7	8	9	1	2
Feb	9	1	2	3	4	5	6	7	8	9	1	2	3	4	5	6	7	8	9	1	2	3	4	5	6	7	8	9	1		
Mar	1	2	3	4	5	6	7	8	9	1	2	3	4	5	6	7	8	9	1	2	3	4	5	6	7	8	9	1	2	3	4
Apr	2	3	4	5	6	7	8	9	1	2	3	4	5	6	7	8	9	1	2	3	4	5	6	7	8	9	1	2	3	4	
May	3	4	5	6	7	8	9	1	2	3	4	5	6	7	8	9	1	2	3	4	5	6	7	8	9	1	2	3	4	5	6
Jun	4	5	6	7	8	9	1	2	3	4	5	6	7	8	9	1	2	3	4	5	6	7	8	9	1	2	3	4	5	6	
Jul	5	6	7	8	9	1	2	3	4	5	6	7	8	9	1	2	3	4	5	6	7	8	9	1	2	3	4	5	6	7	8
Aug	6	7	8	9	1	2	3	4	5	6	7	8	9	1	2	3	4	5	6	7	8	9	1	2	3	4	5	6	7	8	9
Sep	7	8	9	1	2	3	4	5	6	7	8	9	1	2	3	4	5	6	7	8	9	1	2	3	4	5	6	7	8	9	
Oct	8	9	1	2	3	4	5	6	7	8	9	1	2	3	4	5	6	7	8	9	1	2	3	4	5	6	7	8	9	1	2
Nov	9	1	2	3	4	5	6	7	8	9	1	2	3	4	5	6	7	8	9	1	2	3	4	5	6	7	8	9	1	2	
Dec	1	2	4	5	6	7	8	9	1	2	3	4	5	6	7	8	9	1	2	3	4	5	6	7	8	9	1	2	3	4	5

DECEMBER 4

	1	2	3	4	5	6	7	8	9	10	11	12	13	14	15	16	17	18	19	20	21	22	23	24	25	26	27	28	29	30	31
Jan	9	1	2	3	4	5	6	7	8	9	1	2	3	4	5	6	7	8	9	1	2	3	4	5	6	7	8	9	1	2	3
Feb	1	2	3	4	5	6	7	8	9	1	2	3	4	5	6	7	8	9	1	2	3	4	5	6	7	8	9	1	2		
Mar	2	3	4	5	6	7	8	9	1	2	3	4	5	6	7	8	9	1	2	3	4	5	6	7	8	9	1	2	3	4	5
Apr	3	4	5	6	7	8	9	1	2	3	4	5	6	7	8	9	1	2	3	4	5	6	7	8	9	1	2	3	4	5	
May	4	5	6	7	8	9	1	2	3	4	5	6	7	8	9	1	2	3	4	5	6	7	8	9	1	2	3	4	5	6	7
Jun	5	6	7	8	9	1	2	3	4	5	6	7	8	9	1	2	3	4	5	6	7	8	9	1	2	3	4	5	6	7	
Jul	6	7	8	9	1	2	3	4	5	6	7	8	9	1	2	3	4	5	6	7	8	9	1	2	3	4	5	6	7	8	9
Aug	7	8	9	1	2	3	4	5	6	7	8	9	1	2	3	4	5	6	7	8	9	1	2	3	4	5	6	7	8	9	1
Sep	8	9	1	2	3	4	5	6	7	8	9	1	2	3	4	5	6	7	8	9	1	2	3	4	5	6	7	8	9	1	
Oct	9	1	2	3	4	5	6	7	8	9	1	2	3	4	5	6	7	8	9	1	2	3	4	5	6	7	8	9	1	2	3
Nov	1	2	3	4	5	6	7	8	9	1	2	3	4	5	6	7	8	9	1	2	3	4	5	6	7	8	9	1	2	3	
Dec	2	3	4	6	7	8	9	1	2	3	4	5	6	7	8	9	1	2	3	4	5	6	7	8	9	1	2	3	4	5	6

DECEMBER 5

	1	2	3	4	5	6	7	8	9	10	11	12	13	14	15	16	17	18	19	20	21	22	23	24	25	26	27	28	29	30	31
Jan	1	2	3	4	5	6	7	8	9	1	2	3	4	5	6	7	8	9	1	2	3	4	5	6	7	8	9	1	2	3	4
Feb	2	3	4	5	6	7	8	9	1	2	3	4	5	6	7	8	9	1	2	3	4	5	6	7	8	9	1	2	3		
Mar	3	4	5	6	7	8	9	1	2	3	4	5	6	7	8	9	1	2	3	4	5	6	7	8	9	1	2	3	4	5	6
Apr	4	5	6	7	8	9	1	2	3	4	5	6	7	8	9	1	2	3	4	5	6	7	8	9	1	2	3	4	5	6	
May	5	6	7	8	9	1	2	3	4	5	6	7	8	9	1	2	3	4	5	6	7	8	9	1	2	3	4	5	6	7	8
Jun	6	7	8	9	1	2	3	4	5	6	7	8	9	1	2	3	4	5	6	7	8	9	1	2	3	4	5	6	7	8	
Jul	7	8	9	1	2	3	4	5	6	7	8	9	1	2	3	4	5	6	7	8	9	1	2	3	4	5	6	7	8	9	1
Aug	8	9	1	2	3	4	5	6	7	8	9	1	2	3	4	5	6	7	8	9	1	2	3	4	5	6	7	8	9	1	2
Sep	9	1	2	3	4	5	6	7	8	9	1	2	3	4	5	6	7	8	9	1	2	3	4	5	6	7	8	9	1	2	
Oct	1	2	3	4	5	6	7	8	9	1	2	3	4	5	6	7	8	9	1	2	3	4	5	6	7	8	9	1	2	3	4
Nov	2	3	4	5	6	7	8	9	1	2	3	4	5	6	7	8	9	1	2	3	4	5	6	7	8	9	1	2	3	4	
Dec	3	4	5	6	8	9	1	2	3	4	5	6	7	8	9	1	2	3	4	5	6	7	8	9	1	2	3	4	5	6	7

DECEMBER 6

	1	2	3	4	5	6	7	8	9	10	11	12	13	14	15	16	17	18	19	20	21	22	23	24	25	26	27	28	29	30	31
Jan	2	3	4	5	6	7	8	9	1	2	3	4	5	6	7	8	9	1	2	3	4	5	6	7	8	9	1	2	3	4	5
Feb	3	4	5	6	7	8	9	1	2	3	4	5	6	7	8	9	1	2	3	4	5	6	7	8	9	1	2	3	4		
Mar	4	5	6	7	8	9	1	2	3	4	5	6	7	8	9	1	2	3	4	5	6	7	8	9	1	2	3	4	5	6	7
Apr	5	6	7	8	9	1	2	3	4	5	6	7	8	9	1	2	3	4	5	6	7	8	9	1	2	3	4	5	6	7	
May	6	7	8	9	1	2	3	4	5	6	7	8	9	1	2	3	4	5	6	7	8	9	1	2	3	4	5	6	7	8	9
Jun	7	8	9	1	2	3	4	5	6	7	8	9	1	2	3	4	5	6	7	8	9	1	2	3	4	5	6	7	8	9	
Jul	8	9	1	2	3	4	5	6	7	8	9	1	2	3	4	5	6	7	8	9	1	2	3	4	5	6	7	8	9	1	2
Aug	9	1	2	3	4	5	6	7	8	9	1	2	3	4	5	6	7	8	9	1	2	3	4	5	6	7	8	9	1	2	3
Sep	1	2	3	4	5	6	7	8	9	1	2	3	4	5	6	7	8	9	1	2	3	4	5	6	7	8	9	1	2	3	
Oct	2	3	4	5	6	7	8	9	1	2	3	4	5	6	7	8	9	1	2	3	4	5	6	7	8	9	1	2	3	4	5
Nov	3	4	5	6	7	8	9	1	2	3	4	5	6	7	8	9	1	2	3	4	5	6	7	8	9	1	2	3	4	5	
Dec	4	5	6	7	8	1	2	3	4	5	6	7	8	9	1	2	3	4	5	6	7	8	9	1	2	3	4	5	6	7	8

DECEMBER 7

	1	2	3	4	5	6	7	8	9	10	11	12	13	14	15	16	17	18	19	20	21	22	23	24	25	26	27	28	29	30	31
Jan	3	4	5	6	7	8	9	1	2	3	4	5	6	7	8	9	1	2	3	4	5	6	7	8	9	1	2	3	4	5	6
Feb	4	5	6	7	8	9	1	2	3	4	5	6	7	8	9	1	2	3	4	5	6	7	8	9	1	2	3	4	5		
Mar	5	6	7	8	9	1	2	3	4	5	6	7	8	9	1	2	3	4	5	6	7	8	9	1	2	3	4	5	6	7	8
Apr	6	7	8	9	1	2	3	4	5	6	7	8	9	1	2	3	4	5	6	7	8	9	1	2	3	4	5	6	7	8	
May	7	8	9	1	2	3	4	5	6	7	8	9	1	2	3	4	5	6	7	8	9	1	2	3	4	5	6	7	8	9	1
Jun	8	9	1	2	3	4	5	6	7	8	9	1	2	3	4	5	6	7	8	9	1	2	3	4	5	6	7	8	9	1	
Jul	9	1	2	3	4	5	6	7	8	9	1	2	3	4	5	6	7	8	9	1	2	3	4	5	6	7	8	9	1	2	3
Aug	1	2	3	4	5	6	7	8	9	1	2	3	4	5	6	7	8	9	1	2	3	4	5	6	7	8	9	1	2	3	4
Sep	2	3	4	5	6	7	8	9	1	2	3	4	5	6	7	8	9	1	2	3	4	5	6	7	8	9	1	2	3	4	
Oct	3	4	5	6	7	8	9	1	2	3	4	5	6	7	8	9	1	2	3	4	5	6	7	8	9	1	2	3	4	5	6
Nov	4	5	6	7	8	9	1	2	3	4	5	6	7	8	9	1	2	3	4	5	6	7	8	9	1	2	3	4	5	6	
Dec	5	6	7	8	9	1	3	4	5	6	7	8	9	1	2	3	4	5	6	7	8	9	1	2	3	4	5	6	7	8	9

DECEMBER 8

	1	2	3	4	5	6	7	8	9	10	11	12	13	14	15	16	17	18	19	20	21	22	23	24	25	26	27	28	29	30	31
Jan	4	5	6	7	8	9	1	2	3	4	5	6	7	8	9	1	2	3	4	5	6	7	8	9	1	2	3	4	5	6	7
Feb	5	6	7	8	9	1	2	3	4	5	6	7	8	9	1	2	3	4	5	6	7	8	9	1	2	3	4	5	6		
Mar	6	7	8	9	1	2	3	4	5	6	7	8	9	1	2	3	4	5	6	7	8	9	1	2	3	4	5	6	7	8	9
Apr	7	8	9	1	2	3	4	5	6	7	8	9	1	2	3	4	5	6	7	8	9	1	2	3	4	5	6	7	8	9	
May	8	9	1	2	3	4	5	6	7	8	9	1	2	3	4	5	6	7	8	9	1	2	3	4	5	6	7	8	9	1	2
Jun	9	1	2	3	4	5	6	7	8	9	1	2	3	4	5	6	7	8	9	1	2	3	4	5	6	7	8	9	1	2	
Jul	1	2	3	4	5	6	7	8	9	1	2	3	4	5	6	7	8	9	1	2	3	4	5	6	7	8	9	1	2	3	4
Aug	2	3	4	5	6	7	8	9	1	2	3	4	5	6	7	8	9	1	2	3	4	5	6	7	8	9	1	2	3	4	5
Sep	3	4	5	6	7	8	9	1	2	3	4	5	6	7	8	9	1	2	3	4	5	6	7	8	9	1	2	3	4	5	
Oct	4	5	6	7	8	9	1	2	3	4	5	6	7	8	9	1	2	3	4	5	6	7	8	9	1	2	3	4	5	6	7
Nov	5	6	7	8	9	1	2	3	4	5	6	7	8	9	1	2	3	4	5	6	7	8	9	1	2	3	4	5	6	7	
Dec	6	7	8	9	1	2	3	5	6	7	8	9	1	2	3	4	5	6	7	8	9	1	2	3	4	5	6	7	8	9	1

DECEMBER 9

	1	2	3	4	5	6	7	8	9	10	11	12	13	14	15	16	17	18	19	20	21	22	23	24	25	26	27	28	29	30	31
Jan	5	6	7	8	9	1	2	3	4	5	6	7	8	9	1	2	3	4	5	6	7	8	9	1	2	3	4	5	6	7	8
Feb	6	7	8	9	1	2	3	4	5	6	7	8	9	1	2	3	4	5	6	7	8	9	1	2	3	4	5	6	7		
Mar	7	8	9	1	2	3	4	5	6	7	8	9	1	2	3	4	5	6	7	8	9	1	2	3	4	5	6	7	8	9	1
Apr	8	9	1	2	3	4	5	6	7	8	9	1	2	3	4	5	6	7	8	9	1	2	3	4	5	6	7	8	9	1	
May	9	1	2	3	4	5	6	7	8	9	1	2	3	4	5	6	7	8	9	1	2	3	4	5	6	7	8	9	1	2	3
Jun	1	2	3	4	5	6	7	8	9	1	2	3	4	5	6	7	8	9	1	2	3	4	5	6	7	8	9	1	2	3	
Jul	2	3	4	5	6	7	8	9	1	2	3	4	5	6	7	8	9	1	2	3	4	5	6	7	8	9	1	2	3	4	5
Aug	3	4	5	6	7	8	9	1	2	3	4	5	6	7	8	9	1	2	3	4	5	6	7	8	9	1	2	3	4	5	6
Sep	4	5	6	7	8	9	1	2	3	4	5	6	7	8	9	1	2	3	4	5	6	7	8	9	1	2	3	4	5	6	
Oct	5	6	7	8	9	1	2	3	4	5	6	7	8	9	1	2	3	4	5	6	7	8	9	1	2	3	4	5	6	7	8
Nov	6	7	8	9	1	2	3	4	5	6	7	8	9	1	2	3	4	5	6	7	8	9	1	2	3	4	5	6	7	8	
Dec	7	8	9	1	2	3	4	5	7	8	9	1	2	3	4	5	6	7	8	9	1	2	3	4	5	6	7	8	9	1	2

DECEMBER 10

	1	2	3	4	5	6	7	8	9	10	11	12	13	14	15	16	17	18	19	20	21	22	23	24	25	26	27	28	29	30	31
Jan	6	7	8	9	1	2	3	4	5	6	7	8	9	1	2	3	4	5	6	7	8	9	1	2	3	4	5	6	7	8	9
Feb	7	8	9	1	2	3	4	5	6	7	8	9	1	2	3	4	5	6	7	8	9	1	2	3	4	5	6	7	8		
Mar	8	9	1	2	3	4	5	6	7	8	9	1	2	3	4	5	6	7	8	9	1	2	3	4	5	6	7	8	9	1	2
Apr	9	1	2	3	4	5	6	7	8	9	1	2	3	4	5	6	7	8	9	1	2	3	4	5	6	7	8	9	1	2	
May	1	2	3	4	5	6	7	8	9	1	2	3	4	5	6	7	8	9	1	2	3	4	5	6	7	8	9	1	2	3	4
Jun	2	3	4	5	6	7	8	9	1	2	3	4	5	6	7	8	9	1	2	3	4	5	6	7	8	9	1	2	3	4	
Jul	3	4	5	6	7	8	9	1	2	3	4	5	6	7	8	9	1	2	3	4	5	6	7	8	9	1	2	3	4	5	6
Aug	4	5	6	7	8	9	1	2	3	4	5	6	7	8	9	1	2	3	4	5	6	7	8	9	1	2	3	4	5	6	7
Sep	5	6	7	8	9	1	2	3	4	5	6	7	8	9	1	2	3	4	5	6	7	8	9	1	2	3	4	5	6	7	
Oct	6	7	8	9	1	2	3	4	5	6	7	8	9	1	2	3	4	5	6	7	8	9	1	2	3	4	5	6	7	8	9
Nov	7	8	9	1	2	3	4	5	6	7	8	9	1	2	3	4	5	6	7	8	9	1	2	3	4	5	6	7	8	9	
Dec	8	9	1	2	3	4	5	6	7	9	1	2	3	4	5	6	7	8	9	1	2	3	4	5	6	7	8	9	1	2	3

DECEMBER 11

	1	2	3	4	5	6	7	8	9	10	11	12	13	14	15	16	17	18	19	20	21	22	23	24	25	26	27	28	29	30	31
Jan	7	8	9	1	2	3	4	5	6	7	8	9	1	2	3	4	5	6	7	8	9	1	2	3	4	5	6	7	8	9	1
Feb	8	9	1	2	3	4	5	6	7	8	9	1	2	3	4	5	6	7	8	9	1	2	3	4	5	6	7	8	9		
Mar	9	1	2	3	4	5	6	7	8	9	1	2	3	4	5	6	7	8	9	1	2	3	4	5	6	7	8	9	1	2	3
Apr	1	2	3	4	5	6	7	8	9	1	2	3	4	5	6	7	8	9	1	2	3	4	5	6	7	8	9	1	2	3	
May	2	3	4	5	6	7	8	9	1	2	3	4	5	6	7	8	9	1	2	3	4	5	6	7	8	9	1	2	3	4	5
Jun	3	4	5	6	7	8	9	1	2	3	4	5	6	7	8	9	1	2	3	4	5	6	7	8	9	1	2	3	4	5	
Jul	4	5	6	7	8	9	1	2	3	4	5	6	7	8	9	1	2	3	4	5	6	7	8	9	1	2	3	4	5	6	7
Aug	5	6	7	8	9	1	2	3	4	5	6	7	8	9	1	2	3	4	5	6	7	8	9	1	2	3	4	5	6	7	8
Sep	6	7	8	9	1	2	3	4	5	6	7	8	9	1	2	3	4	5	6	7	8	9	1	2	3	4	5	6	7	8	
Oct	7	8	9	1	2	3	4	5	6	7	8	9	1	2	3	4	5	6	7	8	9	1	2	3	4	5	6	7	8	9	1
Nov	8	9	1	2	3	4	5	6	7	8	9	1	2	3	4	5	6	7	8	9	1	2	3	4	5	6	7	8	9	1	
Dec	9	1	2	3	4	5	6	7	8	9	2	3	4	5	6	7	8	9	1	2	3	4	5	6	7	8	9	1	2	3	4

DECEMBER 12

	1	2	3	4	5	6	7	8	9	10	11	12	13	14	15	16	17	18	19	20	21	22	23	24	25	26	27	28	29	30	31
Jan	8	9	1	2	3	4	5	6	7	8	9	1	2	3	4	5	6	7	8	9	1	2	3	4	5	6	7	8	9	1	2
Feb	9	1	2	3	4	5	6	7	8	9	1	2	3	4	5	6	7	8	9	1	2	3	4	5	6	7	8	9	1		
Mar	1	2	3	4	5	6	7	8	9	1	2	3	4	5	6	7	8	9	1	2	3	4	5	6	7	8	9	1	2	3	4
Apr	2	3	4	5	6	7	8	9	1	2	3	4	5	6	7	8	9	1	2	3	4	5	6	7	8	9	1	2	3	4	
May	3	4	5	6	7	8	9	1	2	3	4	5	6	7	8	9	1	2	3	4	5	6	7	8	9	1	2	3	4	5	6
Jun	4	5	6	7	8	9	1	2	3	4	5	6	7	8	9	1	2	3	4	5	6	7	8	9	1	2	3	4	5	6	
Jul	5	6	7	8	9	1	2	3	4	5	6	7	8	9	1	2	3	4	5	6	7	8	9	1	2	3	4	5	6	7	8
Aug	6	7	8	9	1	2	3	4	5	6	7	8	9	1	2	3	4	5	6	7	8	9	1	2	3	4	5	6	7	8	9
Sep	7	8	9	1	2	3	4	5	6	7	8	9	1	2	3	4	5	6	7	8	9	1	2	3	4	5	6	7	8	9	
Oct	8	9	1	2	3	4	5	6	7	8	9	1	2	3	4	5	6	7	8	9	1	2	3	4	5	6	7	8	9	1	2
Nov	9	1	2	3	4	5	6	7	8	9	1	2	3	4	5	6	7	8	9	1	2	3	4	5	6	7	8	9	1	2	
Dec	1	2	3	4	5	6	7	8	9	1	2	4	5	6	7	8	9	1	2	3	4	5	6	7	8	9	1	2	3	4	5

DECEMBER 13

	1	2	3	4	5	6	7	8	9	10	11	12	13	14	15	16	17	18	19	20	21	22	23	24	25	26	27	28	29	30	31
Jan	9	1	2	3	4	5	6	7	8	9	1	2	3	4	5	6	7	8	9	1	2	3	4	5	6	7	8	9	1	2	3
Feb	1	2	3	4	5	6	7	8	9	1	2	3	4	5	6	7	8	9	1	2	3	4	5	6	7	8	9	1	2		
Mar	2	3	4	5	6	7	8	9	1	2	3	4	5	6	7	8	9	1	2	3	4	5	6	7	8	9	1	2	3	4	5
Apr	3	4	5	6	7	8	9	1	2	3	4	5	6	7	8	9	1	2	3	4	5	6	7	8	9	1	2	3	4	5	
May	4	5	6	7	8	9	1	2	3	4	5	6	7	8	9	1	2	3	4	5	6	7	8	9	1	2	3	4	5	6	7
Jun	5	6	7	8	9	1	2	3	4	5	6	7	8	9	1	2	3	4	5	6	7	8	9	1	2	3	4	5	6	7	
Jul	6	7	8	9	1	2	3	4	5	6	7	8	9	1	2	3	4	5	6	7	8	9	1	2	3	4	5	6	7	8	9
Aug	7	8	9	1	2	3	4	5	6	7	8	9	1	2	3	4	5	6	7	8	9	1	2	3	4	5	6	7	8	9	1
Sep	8	9	1	2	3	4	5	6	7	8	9	1	2	3	4	5	6	7	8	9	1	2	3	4	5	6	7	8	9	1	
Oct	9	1	2	3	4	5	6	7	8	9	1	2	3	4	5	6	7	8	9	1	2	3	4	5	6	7	8	9	1	2	3
Nov	1	2	3	4	5	6	7	8	9	1	2	3	4	5	6	7	8	9	1	2	3	4	5	6	7	8	9	1	2	3	
Dec	2	3	4	5	6	7	8	9	1	2	3	4	6	7	8	9	1	2	3	4	5	6	7	8	9	1	2	3	4	5	6

DECEMBER 14

	1	2	3	4	5	6	7	8	9	10	11	12	13	14	15	16	17	18	19	20	21	22	23	24	25	26	27	28	29	30	31
Jan	1	2	3	4	5	6	7	8	9	1	2	3	4	5	6	7	8	9	1	2	3	4	5	6	7	8	9	1	2	3	4
Feb	2	3	4	5	6	7	8	9	1	2	3	4	5	6	7	8	9	1	2	3	4	5	6	7	8	9	1	2	3		
Mar	3	4	5	6	7	8	9	1	2	3	4	5	6	7	8	9	1	2	3	4	5	6	7	8	9	1	2	3	4	5	6
Apr	4	5	6	7	8	9	1	2	3	4	5	6	7	8	9	1	2	3	4	5	6	7	8	9	1	2	3	4	5	6	
May	5	6	7	8	9	1	2	3	4	5	6	7	8	9	1	2	3	4	5	6	7	8	9	1	2	3	4	5	6	7	8
Jun	6	7	8	9	1	2	3	4	5	6	7	8	9	1	2	3	4	5	6	7	8	9	1	2	3	4	5	6	7	8	
Jul	7	8	9	1	2	3	4	5	6	7	8	9	1	2	3	4	5	6	7	8	9	1	2	3	4	5	6	7	8	9	1
Aug	8	9	1	2	3	4	5	6	7	8	9	1	2	3	4	5	6	7	8	9	1	2	3	4	5	6	7	8	9	1	2
Sep	9	1	2	3	4	5	6	7	8	9	1	2	3	4	5	6	7	8	9	1	2	3	4	5	6	7	8	9	1	2	
Oct	1	2	3	4	5	6	7	8	9	1	2	3	4	5	6	7	8	9	1	2	3	4	5	6	7	8	9	1	2	3	4
Nov	2	3	4	5	6	7	8	9	1	2	3	4	5	6	7	8	9	1	2	3	4	5	6	7	8	9	1	2	3	4	
Dec	3	4	5	6	7	8	9	1	2	3	4	5	6	8	9	1	2	3	4	5	6	7	8	9	1	2	3	4	5	6	7

DECEMBER 15

	1	2	3	4	5	6	7	8	9	10	11	12	13	14	15	16	17	18	19	20	21	22	23	24	25	26	27	28	29	30	31
Jan	2	3	4	5	6	7	8	9	1	2	3	4	5	6	7	8	9	1	2	3	4	5	6	7	8	9	1	2	3	4	5
Feb	3	4	5	6	7	8	9	1	2	3	4	5	6	7	8	9	1	2	3	4	5	6	7	8	9	1	2	3	4		
Mar	4	5	6	7	8	9	1	2	3	4	5	6	7	8	9	1	2	3	4	5	6	7	8	9	1	2	3	4	5	6	7
Apr	5	6	7	8	9	1	2	3	4	5	6	7	8	9	1	2	3	4	5	6	7	8	9	1	2	3	4	5	6	7	
May	6	7	8	9	1	2	3	4	5	6	7	8	9	1	2	3	4	5	6	7	8	9	1	2	3	4	5	6	7	8	9
Jun	7	8	9	1	2	3	4	5	6	7	8	9	1	2	3	4	5	6	7	8	9	1	2	3	4	5	6	7	8	9	
Jul	8	9	1	2	3	4	5	6	7	8	9	1	2	3	4	5	6	7	8	9	1	2	3	4	5	6	7	8	9	1	2
Aug	9	1	2	3	4	5	6	7	8	9	1	2	3	4	5	6	7	8	9	1	2	3	4	5	6	7	8	9	1	2	3
Sep	1	2	3	4	5	6	7	8	9	1	2	3	4	5	6	7	8	9	1	2	3	4	5	6	7	8	9	1	2	3	
Oct	2	3	4	5	6	7	8	9	1	2	3	4	5	6	7	8	9	1	2	3	4	5	6	7	8	9	1	2	3	4	5
Nov	3	4	5	6	7	8	9	1	2	3	4	5	6	7	8	9	1	2	3	4	5	6	7	8	9	1	2	3	4	5	
Dec	4	5	6	7	8	9	1	2	3	4	5	6	7	8	1	2	3	4	5	6	7	8	9	1	2	3	4	5	6	7	8

DECEMBER 16

	1	2	3	4	5	6	7	8	9	10	11	12	13	14	15	16	17	18	19	20	21	22	23	24	25	26	27	28	29	30	31
Jan	3	4	5	6	7	8	9	1	2	3	4	5	6	7	8	9	1	2	3	4	5	6	7	8	9	1	2	3	4	5	6
Feb	4	5	6	7	8	9	1	2	3	4	5	6	7	8	9	1	2	3	4	5	6	7	8	9	1	2	3	4	5		
Mar	5	6	7	8	9	1	2	3	4	5	6	7	8	9	1	2	3	4	5	6	7	8	9	1	2	3	4	5	6	7	8
Apr	6	7	8	9	1	2	3	4	5	6	7	8	9	1	2	3	4	5	6	7	8	9	1	2	3	4	5	6	7	8	
May	7	8	9	1	2	3	4	5	6	7	8	9	1	2	3	4	5	6	7	8	9	1	2	3	4	5	6	7	8	9	1
Jun	8	9	1	2	3	4	5	6	7	8	9	1	2	3	4	5	6	7	8	9	1	2	3	4	5	6	7	8	9	1	
Jul	9	1	2	3	4	5	6	7	8	9	1	2	3	4	5	6	7	8	9	1	2	3	4	5	6	7	8	9	1	2	3
Aug	1	2	3	4	5	6	7	8	9	1	2	3	4	5	6	7	8	9	1	2	3	4	5	6	7	8	9	1	2	3	4
Sep	2	3	4	5	6	7	8	9	1	2	3	4	5	6	7	8	9	1	2	3	4	5	6	7	8	9	1	2	3	4	
Oct	3	4	5	6	7	8	9	1	2	3	4	5	6	7	8	9	1	2	3	4	5	6	7	8	9	1	2	3	4	5	6
Nov	4	5	6	7	8	9	1	2	3	4	5	6	7	8	9	1	2	3	4	5	6	7	8	9	1	2	3	4	5	6	
Dec	5	6	7	8	9	1	2	3	4	5	6	7	8	9	1	3	4	5	6	7	8	9	1	2	3	4	5	6	7	8	9

DECEMBER 17

	1	2	3	4	5	6	7	8	9	10	11	12	13	14	15	16	17	18	19	20	21	22	23	24	25	26	27	28	29	30	31
Jan	4	5	6	7	8	9	1	2	3	4	5	6	7	8	9	1	2	3	4	5	6	7	8	9	1	2	3	4	5	6	7
Feb	5	6	7	8	9	1	2	3	4	5	6	7	8	9	1	2	3	4	5	6	7	8	9	1	2	3	4	5	6		
Mar	6	7	8	9	1	2	3	4	5	6	7	8	9	1	2	3	4	5	6	7	8	9	1	2	3	4	5	6	7	8	9
Apr	7	8	9	1	2	3	4	5	6	7	8	9	1	2	3	4	5	6	7	8	9	1	2	3	4	5	6	7	8	9	
May	8	9	1	2	3	4	5	6	7	8	9	1	2	3	4	5	6	7	8	9	1	2	3	4	5	6	7	8	9	1	2
Jun	9	1	2	3	4	5	6	7	8	9	1	2	3	4	5	6	7	8	9	1	2	3	4	5	6	7	8	9	1	2	
Jul	1	2	3	4	5	6	7	8	9	1	2	3	4	5	6	7	8	9	1	2	3	4	5	6	7	8	9	1	2	3	4
Aug	2	3	4	5	6	7	8	9	1	2	3	4	5	6	7	8	9	1	2	3	4	5	6	7	8	9	1	2	3	4	5
Sep	3	4	5	6	7	8	9	1	2	3	4	5	6	7	8	9	1	2	3	4	5	6	7	8	9	1	2	3	4	5	
Oct	4	5	6	7	8	9	1	2	3	4	5	6	7	8	9	1	2	3	4	5	6	7	8	9	1	2	3	4	5	6	7
Nov	5	6	7	8	9	1	2	3	4	5	6	7	8	9	1	2	3	4	5	6	7	8	9	1	2	3	4	5	6	7	
Dec	6	7	8	9	1	2	3	4	5	6	7	8	9	1	2	3	5	6	7	8	9	1	2	3	4	5	6	7	8	9	1

DECEMBER 18

	1	2	3	4	5	6	7	8	9	10	11	12	13	14	15	16	17	18	19	20	21	22	23	24	25	26	27	28	29	30	31
Jan	5	6	7	8	9	1	2	3	4	5	6	7	8	9	1	2	3	4	5	6	7	8	9	1	2	3	4	5	6	7	8
Feb	6	7	8	9	1	2	3	4	5	6	7	8	9	1	2	3	4	5	6	7	8	9	1	2	3	4	5	6	7		
Mar	7	8	9	1	2	3	4	5	6	7	8	9	1	2	3	4	5	6	7	8	9	1	2	3	4	5	6	7	8	9	1
Apr	8	9	1	2	3	4	5	6	7	8	9	1	2	3	4	5	6	7	8	9	1	2	3	4	5	6	7	8	9	1	
May	9	1	2	3	4	5	6	7	8	9	1	2	3	4	5	6	7	8	9	1	2	3	4	5	6	7	8	9	1	2	3
Jun	1	2	3	4	5	6	7	8	9	1	2	3	4	5	6	7	8	9	1	2	3	4	5	6	7	8	9	1	2	3	
Jul	2	3	4	5	6	7	8	9	1	2	3	4	5	6	7	8	9	1	2	3	4	5	6	7	8	9	1	2	3	4	5
Aug	3	4	5	6	7	8	9	1	2	3	4	5	6	7	8	9	1	2	3	4	5	6	7	8	9	1	2	3	4	5	6
Sep	4	5	6	7	8	9	1	2	3	4	5	6	7	8	9	1	2	3	4	5	6	7	8	9	1	2	3	4	5	6	
Oct	5	6	7	8	9	1	2	3	4	5	6	7	8	9	1	2	3	4	5	6	7	8	9	1	2	3	4	5	6	7	8
Nov	6	7	8	9	1	2	3	4	5	6	7	8	9	1	2	3	4	5	6	7	8	9	1	2	3	4	5	6	7	8	
Dec	7	8	9	1	2	3	4	5	6	7	8	9	1	2	3	4	5	7	8	9	1	2	3	4	5	6	7	8	9	1	2

DECEMBER 19

	1	2	3	4	5	6	7	8	9	10	11	12	13	14	15	16	17	18	19	20	21	22	23	24	25	26	27	28	29	30	31
Jan	6	7	8	9	1	2	3	4	5	6	7	8	9	1	2	3	4	5	6	7	8	9	1	2	3	4	5	6	7	8	9
Feb	7	8	9	1	2	3	4	5	6	7	8	9	1	2	3	4	5	6	7	8	9	1	2	3	4	5	6	7	8		
Mar	8	9	1	2	3	4	5	6	7	8	9	1	2	3	4	5	6	7	8	9	1	2	3	4	5	6	7	8	9	1	2
Apr	9	1	2	3	4	5	6	7	8	9	1	2	3	4	5	6	7	8	9	1	2	3	4	5	6	7	8	9	1	2	
May	1	2	3	4	5	6	7	8	9	1	2	3	4	5	6	7	8	9	1	2	3	4	5	6	7	8	9	1	2	3	4
Jun	2	3	4	5	6	7	8	9	1	2	3	4	5	6	7	8	9	1	2	3	4	5	6	7	8	9	1	2	3	4	
Jul	3	4	5	6	7	8	9	1	2	3	4	5	6	7	8	9	1	2	3	4	5	6	7	8	9	1	2	3	4	5	6
Aug	4	5	6	7	8	9	1	2	3	4	5	6	7	8	9	1	2	3	4	5	6	7	8	9	1	2	3	4	5	6	7
Sep	5	6	7	8	9	1	2	3	4	5	6	7	8	9	1	2	3	4	5	6	7	8	9	1	2	3	4	5	6	7	
Oct	6	7	8	9	1	2	3	4	5	6	7	8	9	1	2	3	4	5	6	7	8	9	1	2	3	4	5	6	7	8	9
Nov	7	8	9	1	2	3	4	5	6	7	8	9	1	2	3	4	5	6	7	8	9	1	2	3	4	5	6	7	8	9	
Dec	8	9	1	2	3	4	5	6	7	8	9	1	2	3	4	5	6	7	9	1	2	3	4	5	6	7	8	9	1	2	3

DECEMBER 20

	1	2	3	4	5	6	7	8	9	10	11	12	13	14	15	16	17	18	19	20	21	22	23	24	25	26	27	28	29	30	31
Jan	7	8	9	1	2	3	4	5	6	7	8	9	1	2	3	4	5	6	7	8	9	1	2	3	4	5	6	7	8	9	1
Feb	8	9	1	2	3	4	5	6	7	8	9	1	2	3	4	5	6	7	8	9	1	2	3	4	5	6	7	8	9		
Mar	9	1	2	3	4	5	6	7	8	9	1	2	3	4	5	6	7	8	9	1	2	3	4	5	6	7	8	9	1	2	3
Apr	1	2	3	4	5	6	7	8	9	1	2	3	4	5	6	7	8	9	1	2	3	4	5	6	7	8	9	1	2	3	
May	2	3	4	5	6	7	8	9	1	2	3	4	5	6	7	8	9	1	2	3	4	5	6	7	8	9	1	2	3	4	5
Jun	3	4	5	6	7	8	9	1	2	3	4	5	6	7	8	9	1	2	3	4	5	6	7	8	9	1	2	3	4	5	
Jul	4	5	6	7	8	9	1	2	3	4	5	6	7	8	9	1	2	3	4	5	6	7	8	9	1	2	3	4	5	6	7
Aug	5	6	7	8	9	1	2	3	4	5	6	7	8	9	1	2	3	4	5	6	7	8	9	1	2	3	4	5	6	7	8
Sep	6	7	8	9	1	2	3	4	5	6	7	8	9	1	2	3	4	5	6	7	8	9	1	2	3	4	5	6	7	8	
Oct	7	8	9	1	2	3	4	5	6	7	8	9	1	2	3	4	5	6	7	8	9	1	2	3	4	5	6	7	8	9	1
Nov	8	9	1	2	3	4	5	6	7	8	9	1	2	3	4	5	6	7	8	9	1	2	3	4	5	6	7	8	9	1	
Dec	9	1	2	3	4	5	6	7	8	9	1	2	3	4	5	6	7	8	9	2	3	4	5	6	7	8	9	1	2	3	4

DECEMBER 21

	1	2	3	4	5	6	7	8	9	10	11	12	13	14	15	16	17	18	19	20	21	22	23	24	25	26	27	28	29	30	31
Jan	8	9	1	2	3	4	5	6	7	8	9	1	2	3	4	5	6	7	8	9	1	2	3	4	5	6	7	8	9	1	2
Feb	9	1	2	3	4	5	6	7	8	9	1	2	3	4	5	6	7	8	9	1	2	3	4	5	6	7	8	9	1		
Mar	1	2	3	4	5	6	7	8	9	1	2	3	4	5	6	7	8	9	1	2	3	4	5	6	7	8	9	1	2	3	4
Apr	2	3	4	5	6	7	8	9	1	2	3	4	5	6	7	8	9	1	2	3	4	5	6	7	8	9	1	2	3	4	
May	3	4	5	6	7	8	9	1	2	3	4	5	6	7	8	9	1	2	3	4	5	6	7	8	9	1	2	3	4	5	6
Jun	4	5	6	7	8	9	1	2	3	4	5	6	7	8	9	1	2	3	4	5	6	7	8	9	1	2	3	4	5	6	
Jul	5	6	7	8	9	1	2	3	4	5	6	7	8	9	1	2	3	4	5	6	7	8	9	1	2	3	4	5	6	7	8
Aug	6	7	8	9	1	2	3	4	5	6	7	8	9	1	2	3	4	5	6	7	8	9	1	2	3	4	5	6	7	8	9
Sep	7	8	9	1	2	3	4	5	6	7	8	9	1	2	3	4	5	6	7	8	9	1	2	3	4	5	6	7	8	9	
Oct	8	9	1	2	3	4	5	6	7	8	9	1	2	3	4	5	6	7	8	9	1	2	3	4	5	6	7	8	9	1	2
Nov	9	1	2	3	4	5	6	7	8	9	1	2	3	4	5	6	7	8	9	1	2	3	4	5	6	7	8	9	1	2	
Dec	1	2	3	4	5	6	7	8	9	1	2	3	4	5	6	7	8	9	1	2	4	5	6	7	8	9	1	2	3	4	5

DECEMBER 22

	1	2	3	4	5	6	7	8	9	10	11	12	13	14	15	16	17	18	19	20	21	22	23	24	25	26	27	28	29	30	31
Jan	9	1	2	3	4	5	6	7	8	9	1	2	3	4	5	6	7	8	9	1	2	3	4	5	6	7	8	9	1	2	3
Feb	1	2	3	4	5	6	7	8	9	1	2	3	4	5	6	7	8	9	1	2	3	4	5	6	7	8	9	1	2		
Mar	2	3	4	5	6	7	8	9	1	2	3	4	5	6	7	8	9	1	2	3	4	5	6	7	8	9	1	2	3	4	5
Apr	3	4	5	6	7	8	9	1	2	3	4	5	6	7	8	9	1	2	3	4	5	6	7	8	9	1	2	3	4	5	
May	4	5	6	7	8	9	1	2	3	4	5	6	7	8	9	1	2	3	4	5	6	7	8	9	1	2	3	4	5	6	7
Jun	5	6	7	8	9	1	2	3	4	5	6	7	8	9	1	2	3	4	5	6	7	8	9	1	2	3	4	5	6	7	
Jul	6	7	8	9	1	2	3	4	5	6	7	8	9	1	2	3	4	5	6	7	8	9	1	2	3	4	5	6	7	8	9
Aug	7	8	9	1	2	3	4	5	6	7	8	9	1	2	3	4	5	6	7	8	9	1	2	3	4	5	6	7	8	9	1
Sep	8	9	1	2	3	4	5	6	7	8	9	1	2	3	4	5	6	7	8	9	1	2	3	4	5	6	7	8	9	1	
Oct	9	1	2	3	4	5	6	7	8	9	1	2	3	4	5	6	7	8	9	1	2	3	4	5	6	7	8	9	1	2	3
Nov	1	2	3	4	5	6	7	8	9	1	2	3	4	5	6	7	8	9	1	2	3	4	5	6	7	8	9	1	2	3	
Dec	2	3	4	5	6	7	8	9	1	2	3	4	5	6	7	8	9	1	2	3	4	6	7	8	9	1	2	3	4	5	6

DECEMBER 23

	1	2	3	4	5	6	7	8	9	10	11	12	13	14	15	16	17	18	19	20	21	22	23	24	25	26	27	28	29	30	31
Jan	1	2	3	4	5	6	7	8	9	1	2	3	4	5	6	7	8	9	1	2	3	4	5	6	7	8	9	1	2	3	4
Feb	2	3	4	5	6	7	8	9	1	2	3	4	5	6	7	8	9	1	2	3	4	5	6	7	8	9	1	2	3		
Mar	3	4	5	6	7	8	9	1	2	3	4	5	6	7	8	9	1	2	3	4	5	6	7	8	9	1	2	3	4	5	6
Apr	4	5	6	7	8	9	1	2	3	4	5	6	7	8	9	1	2	3	4	5	6	7	8	9	1	2	3	4	5	6	
May	5	6	7	8	9	1	2	3	4	5	6	7	8	9	1	2	3	4	5	6	7	8	9	1	2	3	4	5	6	7	8
Jun	6	7	8	9	1	2	3	4	5	6	7	8	9	1	2	3	4	5	6	7	8	9	1	2	3	4	5	6	7	8	
Jul	7	8	9	1	2	3	4	5	6	7	8	9	1	2	3	4	5	6	7	8	9	1	2	3	4	5	6	7	8	9	1
Aug	8	9	1	2	3	4	5	6	7	8	9	1	2	3	4	5	6	7	8	9	1	2	3	4	5	6	7	8	9	1	2
Sep	9	1	2	3	4	5	6	7	8	9	1	2	3	4	5	6	7	8	9	1	2	3	4	5	6	7	8	9	1	2	
Oct	1	2	3	4	5	6	7	8	9	1	2	3	4	5	6	7	8	9	1	2	3	4	5	6	7	8	9	1	2	3	4
Nov	2	3	4	5	6	7	8	9	1	2	3	4	5	6	7	8	9	1	2	3	4	5	6	7	8	9	1	2	3	4	
Dec	3	4	5	6	7	8	9	1	2	3	4	5	6	7	8	9	1	2	3	4	5	6	8	9	1	2	3	4	5	6	7

DECEMBER 24

	1	2	3	4	5	6	7	8	9	10	11	12	13	14	15	16	17	18	19	20	21	22	23	24	25	26	27	28	29	30	31
Jan	2	3	4	5	6	7	8	9	1	2	3	4	5	6	7	8	9	1	2	3	4	5	6	7	8	9	1	2	3	4	5
Feb	3	4	5	6	7	8	9	1	2	3	4	5	6	7	8	9	1	2	3	4	5	6	7	8	9	1	2	3	4		
Mar	4	5	6	7	8	9	1	2	3	4	5	6	7	8	9	1	2	3	4	5	6	7	8	9	1	2	3	4	5	6	7
Apr	5	6	7	8	9	1	2	3	4	5	6	7	8	9	1	2	3	4	5	6	7	8	9	1	2	3	4	5	6	7	
May	6	7	8	9	1	2	3	4	5	6	7	8	9	1	2	3	4	5	6	7	8	9	1	2	3	4	5	6	7	8	9
Jun	7	8	9	1	2	3	4	5	6	7	8	9	1	2	3	4	5	6	7	8	9	1	2	3	4	5	6	7	8	9	
Jul	8	9	1	2	3	4	5	6	7	8	9	1	2	3	4	5	6	7	8	9	1	2	3	4	5	6	7	8	9	1	2
Aug	9	1	2	3	4	5	6	7	8	9	1	2	3	4	5	6	7	8	9	1	2	3	4	5	6	7	8	9	1	2	3
Sep	1	2	3	4	5	6	7	8	9	1	2	3	4	5	6	7	8	9	1	2	3	4	5	6	7	8	9	1	2	3	
Oct	2	3	4	5	6	7	8	9	1	2	3	4	5	6	7	8	9	1	2	3	4	5	6	7	8	9	1	2	3	4	5
Nov	3	4	5	6	7	8	9	1	2	3	4	5	6	7	8	9	1	2	3	4	5	6	7	8	9	1	2	3	4	5	
Dec	4	5	6	7	8	9	1	2	3	4	5	6	7	8	9	1	2	3	4	5	6	7	8	1	2	3	4	5	6	7	8

DECEMBER 25

	1	2	3	4	5	6	7	8	9	10	11	12	13	14	15	16	17	18	19	20	21	22	23	24	25	26	27	28	29	30	31
Jan	3	4	5	6	7	8	9	1	2	3	4	5	6	7	8	9	1	2	3	4	5	6	7	8	9	1	2	3	4	5	6
Feb	4	5	6	7	8	9	1	2	3	4	5	6	7	8	9	1	2	3	4	5	6	7	8	9	1	2	3	4	5		
Mar	5	6	7	8	9	1	2	3	4	5	6	7	8	9	1	2	3	4	5	6	7	8	9	1	2	3	4	5	6	7	8
Apr	6	7	8	9	1	2	3	4	5	6	7	8	9	1	2	3	4	5	6	7	8	9	1	2	3	4	5	6	7	8	
May	7	8	9	1	2	3	4	5	6	7	8	9	1	2	3	4	5	6	7	8	9	1	2	3	4	5	6	7	8	9	1
Jun	8	9	1	2	3	4	5	6	7	8	9	1	2	3	4	5	6	7	8	9	1	2	3	4	5	6	7	8	9	1	
Jul	9	1	2	3	4	5	6	7	8	9	1	2	3	4	5	6	7	8	9	1	2	3	4	5	6	7	8	9	1	2	3
Aug	1	2	3	4	5	6	7	8	9	1	2	3	4	5	6	7	8	9	1	2	3	4	5	6	7	8	9	1	2	3	4
Sep	2	3	4	5	6	7	8	9	1	2	3	4	5	6	7	8	9	1	2	3	4	5	6	7	8	9	1	2	3	4	
Oct	3	4	5	6	7	8	9	1	2	3	4	5	6	7	8	9	1	2	3	4	5	6	7	8	9	1	2	3	4	5	6
Nov	4	5	6	7	8	9	1	2	3	4	5	6	7	8	9	1	2	3	4	5	6	7	8	9	1	2	3	4	5	6	
Dec	5	6	7	8	9	1	2	3	4	5	6	7	8	9	1	2	3	4	5	6	7	8	9	1	3	4	5	6	7	8	9

DECEMBER 26

	1	2	3	4	5	6	7	8	9	10	11	12	13	14	15	16	17	18	19	20	21	22	23	24	25	26	27	28	29	30	31
Jan	4	5	6	7	8	9	1	2	3	4	5	6	7	8	9	1	2	3	4	5	6	7	8	9	1	2	3	4	5	6	7
Feb	5	6	7	8	9	1	2	3	4	5	6	7	8	9	1	2	3	4	5	6	7	8	9	1	2	3	4	5	6		
Mar	6	7	8	9	1	2	3	4	5	6	7	8	9	1	2	3	4	5	6	7	8	9	1	2	3	4	5	6	7	8	9
Apr	7	8	9	1	2	3	4	5	6	7	8	9	1	2	3	4	5	6	7	8	9	1	2	3	4	5	6	7	8	9	
May	8	9	1	2	3	4	5	6	7	8	9	1	2	3	4	5	6	7	8	9	1	2	3	4	5	6	7	8	9	1	2
Jun	9	1	2	3	4	5	6	7	8	9	1	2	3	4	5	6	7	8	9	1	2	3	4	5	6	7	8	9	1	2	
Jul	1	2	3	4	5	6	7	8	9	1	2	3	4	5	6	7	8	9	1	2	3	4	5	6	7	8	9	1	2	3	4
Aug	2	3	4	5	6	7	8	9	1	2	3	4	5	6	7	8	9	1	2	3	4	5	6	7	8	9	1	2	3	4	5
Sep	3	4	5	6	7	8	9	1	2	3	4	5	6	7	8	9	1	2	3	4	5	6	7	8	9	1	2	3	4	5	
Oct	4	5	6	7	8	9	1	2	3	4	5	6	7	8	9	1	2	3	4	5	6	7	8	9	1	2	3	4	5	6	7
Nov	5	6	7	8	9	1	2	3	4	5	6	7	8	9	1	2	3	4	5	6	7	8	9	1	2	3	4	5	6	7	
Dec	6	7	8	9	1	2	3	4	5	6	7	8	9	1	2	3	4	5	6	7	8	9	1	2	3	5	6	7	8	9	1

DECEMBER 27

	1	2	3	4	5	6	7	8	9	10	11	12	13	14	15	16	17	18	19	20	21	22	23	24	25	26	27	28	29	30	31
Jan	5	6	7	8	9	1	2	3	4	5	6	7	8	9	1	2	3	4	5	6	7	8	9	1	2	3	4	5	6	7	8
Feb	6	7	8	9	1	2	3	4	5	6	7	8	9	1	2	3	4	5	6	7	8	9	1	2	3	4	5	6	7		
Mar	7	8	9	1	2	3	4	5	6	7	8	9	1	2	3	4	5	6	7	8	9	1	2	3	4	5	6	7	8	9	1
Apr	8	9	1	2	3	4	5	6	7	8	9	1	2	3	4	5	6	7	8	9	1	2	3	4	5	6	7	8	9	1	
May	9	1	2	3	4	5	6	7	8	9	1	2	3	4	5	6	7	8	9	1	2	3	4	5	6	7	8	9	1	2	3
Jun	1	2	3	4	5	6	7	8	9	1	2	3	4	5	6	7	8	9	1	2	3	4	5	6	7	8	9	1	2	3	
Jul	2	3	4	5	6	7	8	9	1	2	3	4	5	6	7	8	9	1	2	3	4	5	6	7	8	9	1	2	3	4	5
Aug	3	4	5	6	7	8	9	1	2	3	4	5	6	7	8	9	1	2	3	4	5	6	7	8	9	1	2	3	4	5	6
Sep	4	5	6	7	8	9	1	2	3	4	5	6	7	8	9	1	2	3	4	5	6	7	8	9	1	2	3	4	5	6	
Oct	5	6	7	8	9	1	2	3	4	5	6	7	8	9	1	2	3	4	5	6	7	8	9	1	2	3	4	5	6	7	8
Nov	6	7	8	9	1	2	3	4	5	6	7	8	9	1	2	3	4	5	6	7	8	9	1	2	3	4	5	6	7	8	
Dec	7	8	9	1	2	3	4	5	6	7	8	9	1	2	3	4	5	6	7	8	9	1	2	3	4	5	7	8	9	1	2

DECEMBER 28

	1	2	3	4	5	6	7	8	9	10	11	12	13	14	15	16	17	18	19	20	21	22	23	24	25	26	27	28	29	30	31
Jan	6	7	8	9	1	2	3	4	5	6	7	8	9	1	2	3	4	5	6	7	8	9	1	2	3	4	5	6	7	8	9
Feb	7	8	9	1	2	3	4	5	6	7	8	9	1	2	3	4	5	6	7	8	9	1	2	3	4	5	6	7	8		
Mar	8	9	1	2	3	4	5	6	7	8	9	1	2	3	4	5	6	7	8	9	1	2	3	4	5	6	7	8	9	1	2
Apr	9	1	2	3	4	5	6	7	8	9	1	2	3	4	5	6	7	8	9	1	2	3	4	5	6	7	8	9	1	2	
May	1	2	3	4	5	6	7	8	9	1	2	3	4	5	6	7	8	9	1	2	3	4	5	6	7	8	9	1	2	3	4
Jun	2	3	4	5	6	7	8	9	1	2	3	4	5	6	7	8	9	1	2	3	4	5	6	7	8	9	1	2	3	4	
Jul	3	4	5	6	7	8	9	1	2	3	4	5	6	7	8	9	1	2	3	4	5	6	7	8	9	1	2	3	4	5	6
Aug	4	5	6	7	8	9	1	2	3	4	5	6	7	8	9	1	2	3	4	5	6	7	8	9	1	2	3	4	5	6	7
Sep	5	6	7	8	9	1	2	3	4	5	6	7	8	9	1	2	3	4	5	6	7	8	9	1	2	3	4	5	6	7	
Oct	6	7	8	9	1	2	3	4	5	6	7	8	9	1	2	3	4	5	6	7	8	9	1	2	3	4	5	6	7	8	9
Nov	7	8	9	1	2	3	4	5	6	7	8	9	1	2	3	4	5	6	7	8	9	1	2	3	4	5	6	7	8	9	
Dec	8	9	1	2	3	4	5	6	7	8	9	1	2	3	4	5	6	7	8	9	1	2	3	4	5	6	7	9	1	2	3

DECEMBER 29

	1	2	3	4	5	6	7	8	9	10	11	12	13	14	15	16	17	18	19	20	21	22	23	24	25	26	27	28	29	30	31
Jan	7	8	9	1	2	3	4	5	6	7	8	9	1	2	3	4	5	6	7	8	9	1	2	3	4	5	6	7	8	9	1
Feb	8	9	1	2	3	4	5	6	7	8	9	1	2	3	4	5	6	7	8	9	1	2	3	4	5	6	7	8	9		
Mar	9	1	2	3	4	5	6	7	8	9	1	2	3	4	5	6	7	8	9	1	2	3	4	5	6	7	8	9	1	2	3
Apr	1	2	3	4	5	6	7	8	9	1	2	3	4	5	6	7	8	9	1	2	3	4	5	6	7	8	9	1	2	3	
May	2	3	4	5	6	7	8	9	1	2	3	4	5	6	7	8	9	1	2	3	4	5	6	7	8	9	1	2	3	4	5
Jun	3	4	5	6	7	8	9	1	2	3	4	5	6	7	8	9	1	2	3	4	5	6	7	8	9	1	2	3	4	5	
Jul	4	5	6	7	8	9	1	2	3	4	5	6	7	8	9	1	2	3	4	5	6	7	8	9	1	2	3	4	5	6	7
Aug	5	6	7	8	9	1	2	3	4	5	6	7	8	9	1	2	3	4	5	6	7	8	9	1	2	3	4	5	6	7	8
Sep	6	7	8	9	1	2	3	4	5	6	7	8	9	1	2	3	4	5	6	7	8	9	1	2	3	4	5	6	7	8	
Oct	7	8	9	1	2	3	4	5	6	7	8	9	1	2	3	4	5	6	7	8	9	1	2	3	4	5	6	7	8	9	1
Nov	8	9	1	2	3	4	5	6	7	8	9	1	2	3	4	5	6	7	8	9	1	2	3	4	5	6	7	8	9	1	
Dec	9	1	2	3	4	5	6	7	8	9	1	2	3	4	5	6	7	8	9	1	2	3	4	5	6	7	8	9	2	3	4

DECEMBER 30

	1	2	3	4	5	6	7	8	9	10	11	12	13	14	15	16	17	18	19	20	21	22	23	24	25	26	27	28	29	30	31
Jan	8	9	1	2	3	4	5	6	7	8	9	1	2	3	4	5	6	7	8	9	1	2	3	4	5	6	7	8	9	1	2
Feb	9	1	2	3	4	5	6	7	8	9	1	2	3	4	5	6	7	8	9	1	2	3	4	5	6	7	8	9	1		
Mar	1	2	3	4	5	6	7	8	9	1	2	3	4	5	6	7	8	9	1	2	3	4	5	6	7	8	9	1	2	3	4
Apr	2	3	4	5	6	7	8	9	1	2	3	4	5	6	7	8	9	1	2	3	4	5	6	7	8	9	1	2	3	4	
May	3	4	5	6	7	8	9	1	2	3	4	5	6	7	8	9	1	2	3	4	5	6	7	8	9	1	2	3	4	5	6
Jun	4	5	6	7	8	9	1	2	3	4	5	6	7	8	9	1	2	3	4	5	6	7	8	9	1	2	3	4	5	6	
Jul	5	6	7	8	9	1	2	3	4	5	6	7	8	9	1	2	3	4	5	6	7	8	9	1	2	3	4	5	6	7	8
Aug	6	7	8	9	1	2	3	4	5	6	7	8	9	1	2	3	4	5	6	7	8	9	1	2	3	4	5	6	7	8	9
Sep	7	8	9	1	2	3	4	5	6	7	8	9	1	2	3	4	5	6	7	8	9	1	2	3	4	5	6	7	8	9	
Oct	8	9	1	2	3	4	5	6	7	8	9	1	2	3	4	5	6	7	8	9	1	2	3	4	5	6	7	8	9	1	2
Nov	9	1	2	3	4	5	6	7	8	9	1	2	3	4	5	6	7	8	9	1	2	3	4	5	6	7	8	9	1	2	
Dec	1	2	3	4	5	6	7	8	9	1	2	3	4	5	6	7	8	9	1	2	3	4	5	6	7	8	9	1	2	4	5

DECEMBER 31

	1	2	3	4	5	6	7	8	9	10	11	12	13	14	15	16	17	18	19	20	21	22	23	24	25	26	27	28	29	30	31
Jan	9	1	2	3	4	5	6	7	8	9	1	2	3	4	5	6	7	8	9	1	2	3	4	5	6	7	8	9	1	2	3
Feb	1	2	3	4	5	6	7	8	9	1	2	3	4	5	6	7	8	9	1	2	3	4	5	6	7	8	9	1	2		
Mar	2	3	4	5	6	7	8	9	1	2	3	4	5	6	7	8	9	1	2	3	4	5	6	7	8	9	1	2	3	4	5
Apr	3	4	5	6	7	8	9	1	2	3	4	5	6	7	8	9	1	2	3	4	5	6	7	8	9	1	2	3	4	5	
May	4	5	6	7	8	9	1	2	3	4	5	6	7	8	9	1	2	3	4	5	6	7	8	9	1	2	3	4	5	6	7
Jun	5	6	7	8	9	1	2	3	4	5	6	7	8	9	1	2	3	4	5	6	7	8	9	1	2	3	4	5	6	7	
Jul	6	7	8	9	1	2	3	4	5	6	7	8	9	1	2	3	4	5	6	7	8	9	1	2	3	4	5	6	7	8	9
Aug	7	8	9	1	2	3	4	5	6	7	8	9	1	2	3	4	5	6	7	8	9	1	2	3	4	5	6	7	8	9	1
Sep	8	9	1	2	3	4	5	6	7	8	9	1	2	3	4	5	6	7	8	9	1	2	3	4	5	6	7	8	9	1	
Oct	9	1	2	3	4	5	6	7	8	9	1	2	3	4	5	6	7	8	9	1	2	3	4	5	6	7	8	9	1	2	3
Nov	1	2	3	4	5	6	7	8	9	1	2	3	4	5	6	7	8	9	1	2	3	4	5	6	7	8	9	1	2	3	
Dec	2	3	4	5	6	7	8	9	1	2	3	4	5	6	7	8	9	1	2	3	4	5	6	7	8	9	1	2	3	4	6

ACKNOWLEDGMENTS

Gregg Hackethal has loved me through thick and thin and has moved heaven and earth to help me get where I am today.

Touradje and Said Torab, of Teletel, Inc., recognized my potential and helped my voice reach America with call-in phone lines.

Gerri French, M.S., R.D., nutritional consultant for this book, made sure the menus were healthy and balanced.

Stela Fejtek saved the day by shopping, slicing, dicing, and stirring up a storm to help me taste-test and perfect the Numbers Diet recipes.

Jacquie Eastlund Sibson cared enough to be honest. Her encouraging words have kept me going.

Dr. Frank Richelieu, my mentor, stayed with me in thought every step of the way.

Arnie Horwitz, Ph.D., kept me in touch with reality, taught me to trust my abilities, and reminded me to stay focused.

Julius Griffin, M.D.—his words of wisdom have always given me food for thought that has helped me validate my own parking ticket in life.

Frank Moran, my personal trainer, taught me how to walk away my weight problem and how to tone my muscles after forty-six years of non-use.

INDEX